Your fully reengineered Microsoft Study Guide.

The all-new learning format of your Microsoft study guide delivers in-depth preparation for the exam—including full objective-by-objective review—along with great new study tools to help prepare you for the job. Features include:

- Relevant exam objectives highlighted at the start of each chapter

- "Why This Chapter Matters" and "Real World" sidebars on how you can apply learning concepts to the job

- Practice and lab exercises where you work through multi-step, real-world solutions

---

3-14   Chapter 3   User Accounts

Lesson 2: Creating Multiple User Objects

There occasionally situations that require you to create multiple user objects quickly, such as a new class of incoming students at a school, or a group of new hires at an organization. In these situations you need to know how to effectively facilitate or automate user object creation so that you are not approaching the task on an account-by-account basis. In Lesson 1, you learned how to create and manage user objects with Active Directory Users and Computers. This lesson will extend those concepts, skills and tools to include user object creation through template objects, imported objects, and command line scripting of objects.

After this lesson, you will be able to
- Create and utilize user object templates
- Import user objects from comma-delimited files
- Leverage new command-line tools to create and manage user objects

Estimated lesson time: 15 minutes

Creating and Using User Templates

It is common for objects to share similar properties. For example, all sales representatives may belong to the same security groups, are allowed to log on to the network during the same hours, and have home folders and roaming profiles on the same server. In such cases, it is helpful when creating a user object for that object to be prepopulated with common properties. This can be accomplished by creating a generic user object—often called a *template*—and then copying that object to create new users.

To generate a user template, create a user and populate its properties. Put the user into appropriate groups.

 Security Alert   Be certain to disable the user, since it is just a template, to ensure that the account is not used for access to network resources.

To create a new user based on the template, select the template and choose Copy from the Action menu. You will be prompted for properties similar to those when you create a new user: first and last name, initials, logon names, password, and account options. When the object is created, you will find that properties are copied from the template based on the following property-page based description:

- **General**   No properties copied.
- **Address**   All properties except Street address are copied.

- "Off the Record" sidebars bridge the gap between how things *should* work and how they *do* work

- Security Alerts and Planning Tips you can apply in the real world

- Numerous side-by-side code examples for both Visual Basic .NET and Visual C# .NET

- Exam highlights—key points and terms you should know

- Exam tips written by an industry insider

---

2   Using Secure Coding Best Practices

Why This Chapter Matters

Although defense-in-depth is a complex subject, you can prevent many security vulnerabilities by simply using secure coding best practices. Most importantly, applications must thoroughly validate all user input. This chapter provides general guidelines for validating many different types of input, as well as detailed specifications for preventing common types of attacks. It is time-consuming to write and maintain the additional code required to validate input, but the level of protection this provides against attacks cannot be duplicated by firewalls, intrusion detection systems, or other security mechanisms.

Security is an ongoing process. After you write the application, systems administrators are responsible for maintaining it. Administrators must be able to both troubleshoot problems and detect potential attacks. Providing administrators with the detailed information they need can be challenging, especially when you consider the importance of *not* sharing information about the application's inner workings with potential attackers. This chapter also gives guidelines for reporting errors without introducing additional vulnerabilities.

Exam Objectives in this Chapter:

- Validate external input at every boundary level to prevent security problems.
  - ❏ Write code to test strings by using regular expressions.
  - ❏ Write code to test the size of data.
  - ❏ Write code to prevent SQL injection and cross-site scripting.
- Write code to prevent canonicalization problems.
  - ❏ Create canonical references for resources.
  - ❏ Validate that a reference is canonical.
- Write code that addresses failures in a manner than does not compromise security.
  - ❏ Create error messages that do not compromise security.

2-1

Lesson 3   Managing User Profiles   3-29

 Note   Be sure to configure share permissions allowing Everyone Full Control. The Windows Server 2003 default share permissions allow Read, which is not sufficient for a roaming profile share.

On the Profile tab of the user's Properties dialog box, type the Profile Path in the format: \\<**server**>\<**share**>*%username%*. The *%username%* variable will automatically be replaced with the user's logon name.

It's that simple. The next time the user logs on to their system, the system will identify the roaming profile location.

 Exam Tip   Roaming user profiles are nothing more than a shared folder and a path to the user's profile folder, within that share, entered into the user object's profile path property. Roaming profiles are not, in any way, a property of a computer object.

When the user logs off of their system, it will upload the profile to the profile server. The user can now log on to their system, or any other system in the domain, and the documents and settings that are part of the RUP will be applied.

 Note   Windows Server 2003 introduces a new policy: Only allow local user profiles. This policy, linked to an OU containing computer accounts, will prevent roaming profiles from being used on those computers. Users will, instead, maintain local profiles.

When a user with an RUP logs on to a new system for the first time, the system does not copy its Default User profile. Instead, it downloads the RUP from the network location. When a user logs off, or when a user logs on to a system on which they've worked before, the system copies only files that have changed.

 Real World   **Roaming Profile Synchronization**

Unlike previous versions of Microsoft Windows, Windows 2000, Windows XP, and Windows Server 2003 do not upload and download the entire user profile at logoff and logon. Instead, the user profile is *synchronized*. Only files that have changed are transferred between the local system and the network RUP folder. This means that logon and logoff with RUPs are significantly faster than with earlier Windows systems. Organizations that have not implemented RUPs for fear of their impact on logon and network traffic should reevaluate their configuration in this light.

MCAD/MCSD Self-Paced Training Kit: Implementing Security for Applications with Microsoft Visual Basic .NET and Microsoft Visual C# .NET

Objective	Pages
Developing Applications by Using Security Best Practices	
Develop code under a least privilege account within the development environment.	4-30 to 4-40
■ Configure the Microsoft .NET development environment and operating system.	4-32 to 4-40
■ Select the appropriate privileges.	4-30 to 4-31
Develop code that runs under a least-privilege account at run time.	1-37 to 1-52
■ Develop code to run under a least-privilege account that does not have administrator privileges.	1-36 to 1-45
■ Use least privilege for access to resources such as the file system, registry entries, and databases.	1-36 to 1-45
Analyze security implications of calling unknown code. Third-party components include .NET components, legacy COM components, ActiveX controls, Win32 DLLs, and Web services.	10-3 to 10-25
■ Write code to verify that the identity of a COM component matches the identity expected.	10-5 to 10-8
■ Validate that data to and from third-party components conforms to the expected size, format, and type.	10-5, 2-3 to 2-18
■ Test for integrity of data after transmission.	10-16 to 10-19, 8-34 to 8-48
■ Evaluate unmanaged code.	10-3 to 10-5
Write code that addresses failures in a manner that does not compromise security.	2-46 to 2-51
■ Write code that defaults to a permission set that is more secure than the permission set that existed before the errors or issues occurred.	6-53 to 6-55
■ Create error messages that do not compromise security.	2-48 to 2-50
Develop code that includes security measures in each tier of the solution, also known as defense in depth.	1-17 to 1-33
Implement application functionality to apply defaults that minimize security threats.	1-25 to 1-28
Write code to prevent canonicalization problems.	2-20 to 2-25
■ Create canonical references for resources.	2-20 to 2-25
■ Validate that a reference is canonical.	2-20 to 2-25
Validate external input at every boundary level to prevent security problems.	2-3 to 2-18
■ Write code to test strings by using regular expressions.	2-5 to 2-12
■ Write code to test the size of data.	2-13
■ Write code to prevent SQL injection and cross-site scripting.	2-26 to 2-35
Developing .NET Applications That Include Security Enhancements	
Implement security by using application domains.	6-68 to 6-76
Implement authentication.	5-31 to 5-45
■ Implement a custom authentication mechanism in a Windows Forms application.	5-41 to 5-45
■ Implement an appropriate Web application or Web service authentication mechanism to accommodate specific application security requirements.	9-3 to 9-16
■ Implement functionality by consuming authenticated user information such as the IPrincipal, Membership, and Identity components of the .NET base class library.	5-31 to 5-41
Write authorization code.	5-8 to 5-15, 5-18 to 5-27
■ Programmatically control access to functionality and data by using user information such as user identity, group membership, and other custom user information.	5-8 to 5-15, 5-18 to 5-27
■ Control access to Web applications by using URL authorization.	9-21 to 9-23
■ Programmatically control access to functionality and data by using identities or criteria that are independent of user identity.	9-27 to 9-29
Sign data by using certificates.	8-42 to 8-48
Implement data protection.	4-3 to 4-17, 8-3 to 8-39
■ Use .NET cryptographic techniques.	8-3 to 8-39
❑ Encrypt and decrypt data by using symmetric and asymmetric cryptographic functions.	8-3 to 8-19, 8-22 to 8-30
❑ Compute hashes by using cryptographic functions.	8-34 to 8-39
❑ Write code to create cryptographically random numbers for cryptographic functions.	8-10 to 8-11
■ Protect data in files and folders by creating, modifying, and deleting discretionary access control list (DACL) or security access control list (SACL) entries.	4-8 to 4-17
■ Encrypt and decrypt data by using the Data Protection API (DPAPI).	8-18 to 8-19

Objective	Pages
Implement security for an application or shared library by using .NET code access security.	6-33 to 6-41, 6-44 to 6-60, 6-68 to 6-79
■ Demand a code access permission such as FileIOPermission.	6-33 to 6-41, 6-41 to 6-52
■ Group code access permissions into a permission set.	6-59 to 6-60
■ Override code access security checks.	6-47 to 6-49, 6-55 to 6-59
■ Protect a resource in a library.	6-41 to 6-52
■ Specify the permission requests of an application.	6-33 to 6-41
■ Customize code access security.	6-68 to 6-79
Access remote functionality in a manner that minimizes security risks.	10-11 to 10-35
■ Use Web Services Enhancements for Microsoft .NET (WSE), such as WS-Security and WS-Interoperability.	10-11 to 10-25
■ Configure .NET remoting for security.	10-27 to 10-35
Configuring Application Security by Using the Microsoft .NET Framework and Operating System Tools	
Work with .NET Security policies. Tools include the .NET Framework Configuration tool and the Code Access Security Policy tool.	6-17 to 6-29
Analyze the code access permissions of an assembly by using the Permissions View tool.	3-18 to 3-19, 6-40
Configure security by using IIS and ASP.NET.	9-19 to 9-45
■ Understand the security implications of impersonation.	9-25 to 9-27
■ Configure ASP.NET impersonation.	9-25 to 9-27
■ Configure Web folder permissions.	9-19 to 9-23
■ Set appropriate permissions on Web application files.	9-23 to 9-25
■ Configure a Web page or Web service to use SSL/TLS.	9-37 to 9-45
Stabilizing and Releasing Applications in a Manner That Minimizes Security Risks	
Perform unit testing on applications and components to identify security vulnerabilities.	3-2 to 3-8
Release applications in a manner that minimizes security risks.	7-4 to 7-28
■ Evaluate when to sign an assembly.	7-4 to 7-5
■ Implement delayed signing.	7-12 to 7-14
■ Create a strong named assembly.	7-5 to 7-11
■ Configure security settings by using the .NET Framework Configuration tool and the Code Access Security Policy tool at deployment.	7-25 to 7-28

Note Exam objectives are subject to change at anytime without prior notice and at Microsoft's sole discretion. Please visit Microsoft's Training & Certification Web site (*www.microsoft.com/traincert*) for the most current listing of exam objectives.

Microsoft

MCAD/MCSD Self-Paced Training Kit: Implementing Security for Applications with Microsoft® Visual Basic® .NET and Microsoft Visual C#® .NET

Tony Northrup

PUBLISHED BY
Microsoft Press
A Division of Microsoft Corporation
One Microsoft Way
Redmond, Washington 98052-6399

Library of Congress Cataloging-in-Publication Data
Northrup, Anthony.
    MCAD/MCSD Self-Paced Training Kit: Implementing Security for Applications with
    Microsft Visual Basic .NET and Microsoft Visual C# .NET / Tony Northrup.
        p. cm.
    Includes index.
    ISBN 0-7356-2121-7
        1. Electronic data processing personnel--Certification.   2. Microsoft
    software--Examinations--Study guides.   3. Microsoft Visual BASIC.   4. Microsoft .NET.   5.
    Microsoft Visual C# .NET.   I. Title.

    QA76.3.N63   2004
    005.8--dc22   2004054652

Printed and bound in the United States of America.

2 3 4 5 6 7 8 9   QWT   9 8 7 6 5 4

Distributed in Canada by H.B. Fenn and Company Ltd.

A CIP catalogue record for this book is available from the British Library.

Microsoft Press books are available through booksellers and distributors worldwide. For further information about international editions, contact your local Microsoft Corporation office or contact Microsoft Press International directly at fax (425) 936-7329. Visit our Web site at www.microsoft.com/learning/. Send comments to *tkinput@microsoft.com*.

Product Planner: Chris Boar   **Content Development Manager:** Lori Kane
Technologist: Bill Rebozo   **Project Manager:** Paul Blount
Copyeditor: Victoria Thulman   **Indexer:** Julie Bess

Body Part No. X10-79125

To Shashoon on her 100th birthday.

Tony Northrup

In the mid 1980s, Tony Northrup, CISPP, MCSE, and MVP, learned to program in BASIC on a ZX-81 personal computer built from a kit. Later, he mastered 68000 assembly and ANSI C on the Motorola VERSAdos operating system before beginning to write code for MS-DOS. After a brief time with the NEXTSTEP operating system, Tony returned to a Microsoft platform because he was impressed by the beta version of Microsoft Windows NT 3.1. Although he has dabbled in other operating systems, he has since focused on Windows development in Microsoft Visual C++, ASP 3.0 with Microsoft Visual Basic, C#, and Perl (for automation projects).

Tony was first exposed to the importance of application security in the early 1990s while working for a software development company that created an application for use by law enforcement. Because of the nature of the data being accessed by the application, the potential customers were extremely concerned about the confidentiality of that data. Since that time, Tony has been fascinated by application and network security. He continued to hone his application security skills while working for several years at a healthcare firm, where he developed a database application with Microsoft Visual C++. This application provided employees with access to the private healthcare records of thousands of patients, so data confidentiality was vital.

In the mid 1990s, he took a job at Bolt, Beranek, and Newman (BBN), one of the founders of the Internet. This gave him the opportunity to learn network security from some of the very individuals who had overseen the Internet's growth during the previous decades. Tony spent the next eight years working closely with hundreds of customers to design and deploy some of the first financial, government, and retail Web applications. During this time, he developed the broad range of skills necessary to protect these applications from the onslaught of constantly evolving network attacks. Tony eventually earned the title of Principal Engineer, the highest engineering title at BBN, held by only a handful of the staff.

Tony started writing in 1997 and has since published seven technology books on the topics of security, development, and networking. In addition, he has written some of the most important security-related papers on the Microsoft.com Web site, covering topics ranging from securing ASP.NET applications to designing firewalls to protect networks and computers. Tony spends his spare time hiking through the woods near his Woburn, Massachusetts home. He's rarely without his camera, and in the past six years has created what might be the largest and most popular publicly accessible database of nature and wildlife photographs on the Internet. Tony lives with his wife Erica and his cat (also his favorite photographic subject) Sammy.

Contents at a Glance

Practices

Tables

Labs

Contents

What do you think of this book? **We want to hear from you!**	Microsoft is interested in hearing your feedback about this publication so we can continually improve our books and learning resources for you. To participate in a brief online survey, please visit: *www.microsoft.com/learning/booksurvey/*

Section 2   Using the .NET Security Framework

4   Taking Advantage of Platform Security   4-1

5   Implementing Role-Based Security   5-1

Section 3 Protecting Data and Networked Applications

8 Protecting Data by Using Cryptography   8-1

What do you think of this book?
We want to hear from you!

Microsoft is interested in hearing your feedback about this publication so we can continually improve our books and learning resources for you. To participate in a brief online survey, please visit: *www.microsoft.com/learning/booksurvey/*

Acknowledgments

The author's name appears on the cover of a book, but the author is only one member of a large team. This particular book started with a call from Neil Salkind of Studio B— a respected author himself, with far more credits to his name than I have. Neil, and a team at Studio B that included Jackie Coder, David Rogelberg, and Stacey Barone, worked closely with the folks at Microsoft Press to put together the team that would create this book.

The team at Microsoft was fantastic. I worked most closely with Lori Kane, the content development manager. Thanks, Lori, for patiently teaching me a new style of writing. Victoria Thulman, the copyeditor, made the book much more readable than it would have been otherwise. Bill Rebozo, the technologist, caught those several important errors in my code. I didn't get to work with everyone at Microsoft directly, but I definitely appreciate the work of the rest of the Microsoft team:

- Julie Bess, Indexer
- Chris Boar, Product Planner
- Charlotte Bowden, Tester
- Paul Blount, Project Manager
- Elizabeth Hansford, Senior Desktop Publisher
- Joel Panchot, Senior Graphic Designer
- Sandi Resnick, Proofreader
- Bill Teel, Media Specialist

Many other people helped with this book, albeit a bit more indirectly. My friends, especially Tara Banks; Kristin Casciato and the twins, Kurt Dillard de Northrup and Beatriz Brites de Dillard; Eric and Alyssa Faulkner; Chris and Diane Geggis; Bob Hogan and Khristina Jones; Samuel Jackson; Tom Keegan; Eric John Parucki; Reality TV; and Nick Warhead helped me enjoy my time away from the keyboard. I have to thank my wife Erica more than anyone for being so patient during many long days of writing.

It makes a huge difference when you consider the people you work with to be friends. Having a great team not only improves the quality of the book, but it makes writing it a more enjoyable experience. Writing this book was my most enjoyable project yet, and I hope I get the chance in the future to work with everyone who was involved.

About This Book

Welcome to *MCAD/MCSD Self-Paced Training Kit: Implementing Security for Applications with Microsoft Visual Basic .NET and Microsoft Visual C# .NET*.

Developers have learned an important lesson in the last few years: they cannot rely on networks and operating systems to protect applications from attack. Any application, including both Web applications and Microsoft Windows Forms applications, is susceptible to several different types of attacks that might reveal a user's private information or allow an attacker to gain elevated privileges. If you create an application that has a security vulnerability, your users will almost certainly hold you responsible. Reducing the risk of an attacker exploiting your application requires specialized skills—the skills that are taught in this book. Developing these skills will not only help you secure your system, but will also help prepare you to take Microsoft Certified Professional (MCP) exam 70-330, "Implementing Security for Applications with Microsoft Visual Basic .NET," and exam 70-340, "Implementing Security for Applications with Microsoft Visual C# .NET."

Each chapter addresses an important aspect of development security and a range of exam objectives. The goal of both the objectives and the chapter orientation is to provide a complete guide to Visual C# .NET and Visual Basic .NET development security. The book focuses primarily on the skills necessary to implement security when developing applications and only briefly covers concepts related to network security design and implementing security infrastructure.

Note   For more information about becoming a Microsoft Certified Professional, see the section titled "The Microsoft Certified Professional Program" later in this introduction.

Intended Audience

This book was created for developers who design, develop, and implement software solutions for Microsoft Windows–based environments using Microsoft tools and technologies. It was also created for developers who plan to take the related MCP exam 70-330, "Implementing Security for Applications with Microsoft Visual Basic .NET," and exam 70-340, "Implementing Security for Applications with Microsoft Visual C# .NET."

Note   Exam skills are subject to change without prior notice and at the sole discretion of Microsoft.

Prerequisites

This training kit requires that students meet the following prerequisites:

- Must be full-time application developers with 1 year minimum experience using Visual Studio .NET.

- Must be developers creating the following types of applications:
  - ❑ Web applications
  - ❑ Windows Forms applications
  - ❑ Server components
  - ❑ XML Web services

- Must understand security across Tiers and Lifecycle phases.

- Must understand best security practices for accessing and modifying data stored in databases using ADO.NET.

About the CD-ROM

For your use, this book includes a companion CD-ROM that contains a variety of informational aids to complement the book content:

- The Microsoft Press Readiness Review Suite Powered by MeasureUp. This suite of practice tests and objective reviews contains questions of varying degrees of complexity and offers multiple testing modes. You can assess your understanding of the concepts presented in this book and use the results to develop a learning plan that meets your needs.

- An electronic version of this book (eBook). For information about using the eBook, see the "The eBook" section later in this introduction.

- C# and Visual Basic .NET projects for use with certain practices.

A second CD-ROM contains a 180-day evaluation edition of Microsoft Windows Server 2003, Standard Edition, and a DVD includes a 60-day evaluation edition of Microsoft Visual Studio .NET 2003, Professional Edition, which includes the Microsoft SQL Server Desktop Engine (MSDE).

> **Caution**   The evaluation software provided with this training kit is not the full retail product and is provided only for the purposes of training and evaluation. Microsoft Technical Support does not support this evaluation edition.

For additional support information regarding this book and the CD-ROM (including answers to commonly asked questions about installation and use), visit the Microsoft Learning Technical Support Web site at *http://www.microsoft.com/learning/support/*. You can also e-mail tkinput@microsoft.com or send a letter to Microsoft Learning, Attention: Microsoft Learning Technical Support, One Microsoft Way, Redmond, WA 98052-6399.

Features of This Book

Each chapter in this book identifies the exam objectives that are covered within the chapter, provides an overview of why the topics matter by identifying how the information is applied in the real world, and lists any prerequisites that must be met to complete the lessons presented in the chapter.

The chapters are divided into lessons. Lessons contain practices that include hands-on exercises. These exercises give you an opportunity to use the skills being presented or explore the part of the application being described. Most of the practices include fictitious scenarios that require you to apply what you learned in the lesson to a realistic work situation—responding to the needs and requirements of various organizations, bosses, stakeholders, and co-workers.

After the lessons, you are given an opportunity to apply what you've learned in a chapter-ending lab. In this lab, you work through a multi-step solution for a realistic case scenario—this time applying what you learned in all the lessons in the chapter to the scenario.

Each chapter ends with a short summary of key concepts and a short section listing key terms and summarizing topics you need to know before taking the exam, with a focus on demonstrating that knowledge on the exam.

Real World   Helpful Information
You will find sidebars like this one that contain related information you might find helpful. "Real World" sidebars contain specific information gained through the experience of the author and other developers on the job.

Informational Notes

Several types of reader aids appear throughout the training kit.

- **Tip**   Contains methods of performing a task more quickly or in a not-so-obvious way.

- **Important**   Contains information that is essential to completing a task.

- **Note**   Contains supplemental information.

- **Caution**   Contains valuable information about possible loss of data; be sure to read this information carefully.

- **Warning**   Contains critical information about possible physical injury; be sure to read this information carefully.

- **See also**   Contains references to other sources of information.

- **Design**   Reminds the reader that something needs to be considered during design, not during implementation.

- **On the CD**   Points you to supplementary information or files you need that are on the companion CD.

- **Security Alert**   Highlights information you need to know to maximize security in your work environment.

- **Exam Tip**   Flags information you should know before taking the certification exam.

- **Off the Record**   Contains practical advice about the real-world implications of information presented in the lesson.

Notational Conventions

The following conventions are used throughout this book:

- Characters or commands that you type appear in **bold** type.

- The names of screen elements appear in Title caps, regardless of how they appear on the screen.

- *Italic* in syntax statements indicates placeholders for variable information. Italic is also used for book titles, for new terms when they are being defined, and for URLs.

- Names of files and folders appear in Title caps. Unless otherwise indicated, you can use all lowercase letters when you type a filename in a dialog box or at a command prompt.

- Filename extensions appear in all lowercase letters and are preceded by a period (.)—for example, .exe.

- Acronyms appear in all uppercase.

- Monospace type represents code samples, or entries that you might type at a command prompt or in initialization files.

- Square brackets [ ] are used in syntax statements to enclose optional items. For example, [*filename*] in command syntax indicates that you can choose to type a filename with the command. Type only the information within the brackets, not the brackets themselves.

- Braces { } are used in syntax statements to enclose required items. Type only the information within the braces, not the braces themselves.

Keyboard Conventions

- A plus sign (+) between two key names means that you must press those keys at the same time. For example, "Press ALT+TAB" means that you hold down ALT while you press TAB.

- A comma (,) between two or more key names means that you must press each of the keys consecutively, not together. For example, "Press ALT, F, X" means that you press and release each key in sequence. "Press ALT+W, L" means that you first press ALT and W at the same time, and then release them and press L.

Getting Started

This training kit contains hands-on practices and labs to help you learn about implementing application security. Use this section to prepare your self-paced training environment.

Hardware Requirements

Each computer must have the following minimum configuration. All hardware should be on the Microsoft Windows Server 2003 Hardware Compatibility List.

- Minimum CPU speed of 450 MHz

- 160 MB RAM

- 6 GB free disk space

- CD-ROM drive or DVD drive for installing software

- Super VGA (1024 x 768) or higher-resolution display with 256 colors

- Microsoft Mouse or compatible pointing device

- Some Internet functionality might require Internet access, a Microsoft Passport account, and payment of a separate fee to a service provider. Local and/or long-distance telephone toll charges might apply. A high-speed modem or broadband Internet connection is recommended.

- For networking, you must have a network adapter appropriate for the type of local-area, wide-area, wireless, or home network to which you want to connect and access to an appropriate network infrastructure. Access to third-party networks might require additional charges.

Software Requirements

The following software is required to complete the procedures in this training kit. (A 180-day evaluation edition of Windows Server 2003, Standard Edition is included on a CD-ROM included with this book. A 60-day evaluation version of Microsoft Visual Studio .NET 2003, which includes the SQL Server Desktop Engine [MSDE], is included on a DVD included with this book.)

- Windows Server 2003, Standard Edition, or Windows Server 2003, Enterprise Edition

- Microsoft Visual Studio .NET 2003

- Microsoft SQL Server 2000

> **Caution** The evaluation software provided with this training is not the full retail product and is provided only for the purposes of training and evaluation. Microsoft Technical Support does not support these evaluation editions. For additional support information regarding this book and the CD-ROMs and DVD (including answers to commonly asked questions about installation and use), visit the Microsoft Press Technical Support Web site at *http://mspress.microsoft.com/mspress/support/*. You can also e-mail tkinput@microsoft.com or send a letter to Microsoft Press, Attn: Microsoft Press Technical Support, One Microsoft Way, Redmond, WA 98502-6399.

Setup Instructions

To complete the practices and labs in this chapter, you must have one computer running Microsoft Windows Server 2003. Set up your computer according to the manufacturer's instructions.

During the course of performing the practices and labs in this chapter, the computer's security can be reduced. Therefore, the computer should not be a production computer and should not be connected to any network, especially the Internet, even if a firewall is present. Install Microsoft Visual Studio .NET 2003 by using the default settings. In particular, install Visual Studio .NET so that it is accessible to all users on the computer.

The Readiness Review Suite

The companion CD-ROM includes two practice tests with a total of 600 sample exam questions (300 C#-related questions and 300 Visual Basic–related questions). Use these tools to reinforce your learning and to identify any areas in which you need to gain more experience before taking the exam.

▶ **To install the practice tests**

1. Insert the companion CD-ROM into your CD-ROM drive.

> **Note**   If AutoRun is disabled on your machine, refer to the Readme.txt file on the CD-ROM.

2. Click Readiness Review Suite 70-330 or Readiness Review Suite 70-340 on the user interface menu.

The eBook

The companion CD-ROM includes an electronic version of the training kit. The eBook is in portable document format (PDF) and can be viewed using Adobe Acrobat Reader.

▶ **To use the eBook**

1. Insert the companion CD-ROM into your CD-ROM drive.

> **Note**   If AutoRun is disabled on your machine, refer to the Readme.txt file on the CD-ROM.

2. Click Training Kit eBook on the user interface menu.

The Microsoft Certified Professional Program

The Microsoft Certified Professional (MCP) program provides the best method to prove your command of current Microsoft products and technologies. The exams and corresponding certifications are developed to validate your mastery of critical competencies as you design and develop, or implement and support, solutions with Microsoft products and technologies. Computer professionals who become Microsoft certified are recognized as experts and are sought after industry-wide. Certification brings a variety of benefits to the individual and to employers and organizations.

> **See Also**   For a detailed list of available training, certification, and reference resources, see *http://www.microsoft.com/learning/developer/default.asp*.

Certifications

The Microsoft Certified Professional program offers multiple certifications, based on specific areas of technical expertise:

- *Microsoft Certified Professional (MCP)*. Demonstrated in-depth knowledge of at least one Microsoft Windows operating system or architecturally significant platform. An MCP is qualified to implement a Microsoft product or technology as part of a business solution for an organization.

- *Microsoft Certified Solution Developer (MCSD)*. Professional developers qualified to analyze, design, and develop enterprise business solutions with Microsoft development tools and technologies including the Microsoft .NET Framework.

- *Microsoft Certified Application Developer (MCAD)*. Professional developers qualified to develop, test, deploy, and maintain powerful applications using Microsoft tools and technologies including Microsoft Visual Studio .NET and XML Web services.

- *Microsoft Certified Systems Engineer (MCSE)*. Qualified to effectively analyze the business requirements and design and implement the infrastructure for business solutions based on the Microsoft Windows and Microsoft Windows Server 2003 operating systems.

- *Microsoft Certified Systems Administrator (MCSA)*. Individuals with the skills to manage and troubleshoot existing network and system environments based on the Microsoft Windows and Microsoft Server 2003 operating systems.

- *Microsoft Certified Desktop Support Technician (MCDST)*. Individuals who support end users and troubleshoot desktop environments running on the Windows operating system.

- *Microsoft Certified Database Administrator (MCDBA)*. Individuals who design, implement, and administer Microsoft SQL Server databases.

- *Microsoft Certified Trainer (MCT)*. Instructionally and technically qualified to deliver Microsoft Official Curriculum through a Certified Partner for Learning Solutions (CPLS).

Requirements for Becoming a Microsoft Certified Professional

The certification requirements differ for each certification and are specific to the products and job functions addressed by the certification.

To become a Microsoft Certified Professional, you must pass rigorous certification exams that provide a valid and reliable measure of technical proficiency and expertise. These exams are designed to test your expertise and ability to perform a role or task with a product and are developed with the input of professionals in the industry. Questions in the exams reflect how Microsoft products are used in actual organizations, giving them "real-world" relevance. Requirements for certifications are as follows:

- Microsoft Certified Product (MCP) candidates are required to pass one current Microsoft certification exam. Candidates can pass additional Microsoft certification exams to further qualify their skills with other Microsoft products, development tools, or desktop applications.

- Microsoft Certified Solution Developers (MCSDs) are required to pass three core exams and one elective exam. (MCSD for Microsoft .NET candidates are required to pass four core exams and one elective.)

- Microsoft Certified Application Developers (MCADs) are required to pass two core exams and one elective exam in an area of specialization.

- Microsoft Certified Systems Engineers (MCSEs) are required to pass five core exams and two elective exams.

- Microsoft Certified Systems Administrators (MCSAs) are required to pass three core exams and one elective exam that provide a valid and reliable measure of technical proficiency and expertise.

- Microsoft Certified Database Administrators (MCDBAs) are required to pass three core exams and one elective exam that provide a valid and reliable measure of technical proficiency and expertise.

- Microsoft Certified Trainers (MCTs) are required to meet instructional and technical requirements specific to each Microsoft Official Curriculum course they are certified to deliver. The MCT program requires on-going training to meet the requirements for the annual renewal of certification. For more information about becoming a Microsoft Certified Trainer, visit *http://www.microsoft.com/learning/mcp/mct/* or contact a regional service center near you.

Technical Support

Every effort has been made to ensure the accuracy of this book and the contents of the companion disc. If you have comments, questions, or ideas regarding this book or the companion disc, please send them to Microsoft Press using either of the following methods:

E-mail: tkinput@microsoft.com

Postal mail: Microsoft Press
                  Attn: *MCAD/MCSD Self-Paced Training Kit (Exams 70-330/70-340):*
                  Implementing Security for Applications with Microsoft Visual Basic .NET
                  and Microsoft Visual C# .NET Editor
                  One Microsoft Way
                  Redmond, WA 98052-6399

For additional support information regarding this book and the CD-ROMs and DVD (including answers to commonly asked questions about installation and use), visit the Microsoft Learning Technical Support Web site at *http://www.microsoft.com/learning /support/*. To connect directly to the Microsoft Press Knowledge Base and enter a query, visit *http://www.microsoft.com/mspress/support/search.asp*. For support information regarding Microsoft software, please visit *http://support.microsoft.com/*.

Evaluation Edition Software Support

The 180-day evaluation edition of Microsoft Windows Server 2003 and the 60-day evaluation edition of Microsoft Visual Studio .NET 2003 (and Microsoft SQL Server 2000) that are provided with this training kit are not the full retail products and are provided only for the purposes of training and evaluation. Microsoft and Microsoft Technical Support do not support these evaluation editions.

Caution   The evaluation editions of the software included with this book should not be used on a primary work computer. The evaluation editions are unsupported. For online support information relating to the full version of these products that *might* also apply to the evaluation editions, please visit *http://support.microsoft.com/*.

Information about any issues relating to the use of these evaluation editions with this training kit is posted to the Support section of the Microsoft Learning Web site (*http://www.microsoft.com/learning/support/*). For information about ordering the full version of any Microsoft software, please call Microsoft Sales at (800) 426-9400 or visit *http://www.microsoft.com*.

Section 1
Application Security Fundamentals

Section 1 of this book teaches the fundamentals of application security. These first three chapters form a foundation of knowledge that is common to application development in any environment—whether you are programming for the .NET Framework, Microsoft Win32, or Java:

- Chapter 1, "Implementing Security at Design Time," teaches how applications are compromised and helps you get inside the head of the attacker. You must understand how, and why, attacks take place to defend against them. After you understand the enemy, you can begin to design security into your application. Your coding won't be perfect, but you can protect mistakes from being exploited by using a security principle called defense-in-depth.

- Chapter 2, "Using Secure Coding Best Practices," teaches how to develop defensively to protect your applications against the most common attacks. Any user input might be malicious, and your application must carefully examine all input and accept only valid requests. Attackers *will* intentionally submit invalid input, and when they do, you must take care to be fail-safe— by providing friendly error messages to end users (and potential attackers) while not giving away any information about the internal structure of your application or the

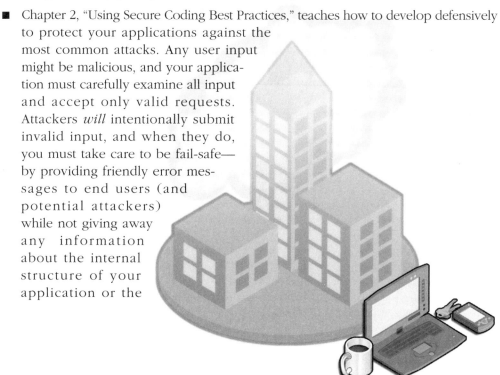

server. This doesn't mean you shouldn't record detailed information about errors. In fact, you must record information that can be used to track, and potentially prosecute, attackers. However, you need to store the error information in a place where only administrators can access it.

- Chapter 3, "Testing Applications for Vulnerabilities," teaches the final application security fundamental: testing. Smart developers create vulnerable applications. Although you can't hope to write perfect code, you can reduce human errors by thoroughly testing your application. Not only should you look for potential buffer overflows and parsing errors, you should test your application for resistance to denial-of-service attacks by simulating heavy loads of unauthenticated requests. Testing won't prove your application invulnerable, but it will demonstrate that you've done your due diligence, and testing greatly improves your chances of finding vulnerabilities before your application goes into production.

1 Implementing Security at Design Time

Why This Chapter Matters

Applications are constantly under attack by buffer overflows, cross-site scripting (CSS), denial-of-service (DoS) attacks, and man-in-the-middle (MITM) attacks, just to name a few. Although any application can be updated to prevent such simple attacks, these attacks continue to be successful because of one inescapable factor: human error. Defense-in-depth is the only way to prevent human errors and vulnerabilities from being exploited, and it must be part of the application's design, before the first line of code is written.

Lesson 1 in this chapter provides a sense of the hostile nature of today's networks by describing the most common types of application attacks. Lesson 2 teaches how to design your application to be resilient against attacks, even when a legitimate vulnerability exists. Lesson 3 introduces the security tenet of least privilege, and walks you through the process of debugging an application to be run by a standard user.

Exam Objectives in this Chapter:

- Develop code that includes security measures in each tier of the solution, also known as *defense-in-depth*.
- Implement application functionality to apply defaults that minimize security threats.
- Develop code that runs under a least privilege account at run time.
- Develop code to run under a least privilege account that does not have administrator privileges.
    - ❑ Use least privilege for access to resources such as the file system, registry entries, and databases.

Lessons in this Chapter:

Before You Begin

To complete the practices and lab exercises in this chapter, you must have one computer running Microsoft Windows Server 2003 or Windows XP Professional. During the course of performing the exercises in this chapter, the computer's security can be reduced. Therefore, the computer that you use should not be a production computer and should not be connected to any network—especially the Internet—even if a firewall is present. Install Microsoft Visual Studio .NET 2003 on the computer.

Lesson 1: Evaluating Security Threats

Modern applications must be designed to withstand many different types of attacks. Before you can defend against those attacks, you must understand how to perform them yourself. Put on your black hat for the remainder of this lesson, read about how vulnerable applications are attacked, and think about applications you have worked with or written that might be vulnerable.

Exam Tip   Make this the first and last chapter you read in this book. The first time you read it, you will get an overview of the best practices and technologies that the rest of the book explores in detail. After you read the entire book, this chapter will tie everything together, and bring important information from throughout the book to the top of your mind so that you will be ready for the exam.

The purpose of this lesson is not to teach you how to attack other developers' applications. Instead, its intent is to demonstrate that security threats are real and tangible, and that even skilled programmers can write code that contains vulnerabilities.

After this lesson, you will be able to
- Explain the reasons developers write vulnerable applications.
- Describe each major type of application attack.
- List the types of attacks to which a specific application is vulnerable.

Estimated lesson time: 45 minutes

Why Developers Write Vulnerable Applications

Reading the technology news, you could get the impression that only the least intelligent application developers create code with security vulnerabilities. The real reasons are much more complex, however. The three main reasons programmers write vulnerable applications are:

- **Many applications were simply not designed to withstand a hostile environment**   Although network-based attacks have existed for decades, most of the attention has been focused on vulnerabilities found in the operating system. Security wasn't a priority for most application developers, who instead focused their energy on adding features and improving reliability.

- **Most application developers haven't been formally trained to write secure code**   Keeping up with the latest operating systems and development environments is difficult enough for most developers. Studying network security, and keeping up with the latest types of attacks and how to prevent them, can be a full-time job (and it is, for many people).

- **Application developers are human, and humans make mistakes**   Even developers who make application security a priority are capable of forgetting to carefully parse user input, or of storing secret information in a location where the data can be compromised. There's no shame in making this type of mistake, because it will happen to every developer at some point in his or her career.

Types of Application Attacks

Developers create vulnerable code for many reasons, and application vulnerabilities can never be completely eliminated. It's not the vulnerabilities that cause problems, though—it's the exploits. *Exploits* take advantage of an application's vulnerability to perform some malicious task, such as crashing the application, corrupting data, compromising secrets, and spreading malicious code. The sections that follow describe the most common types of exploits and how they happen.

> **Tip**   The term *vulnerability* refers to a security weakness in an application. The term *attack* is used to describe an attempt at exploiting an application. Attacks can be successful or unsuccessful, because attackers often use attacks just to determine whether an application is vulnerable. The term *exploit* describes a successful attack against a known vulnerability.

What Is a Buffer Overflow Attack?

A *buffer overflow* (also known as a buffer overrun) occurs when an application attempts to store too much data in a buffer, and memory not allocated to the buffer is overwritten. When the data is user input, an attacker might be able to intentionally induce a buffer overflow by entering more data than the application expects. A particularly crafty attacker can even enter data that instructs the operating system to run the attacker's malicious code with the application's privileges.

One of the most common types of buffer overflows is the *stack overflow*. To understand how this attack is used, you must first understand how applications normally store variables and other information on the stack. Figure 1-1 shows a simplified example of how a C console application might store the contents of a variable on the stack. In this example, the string *"Hello"* is passed to the application and is stored in the variable *argv[1]*.

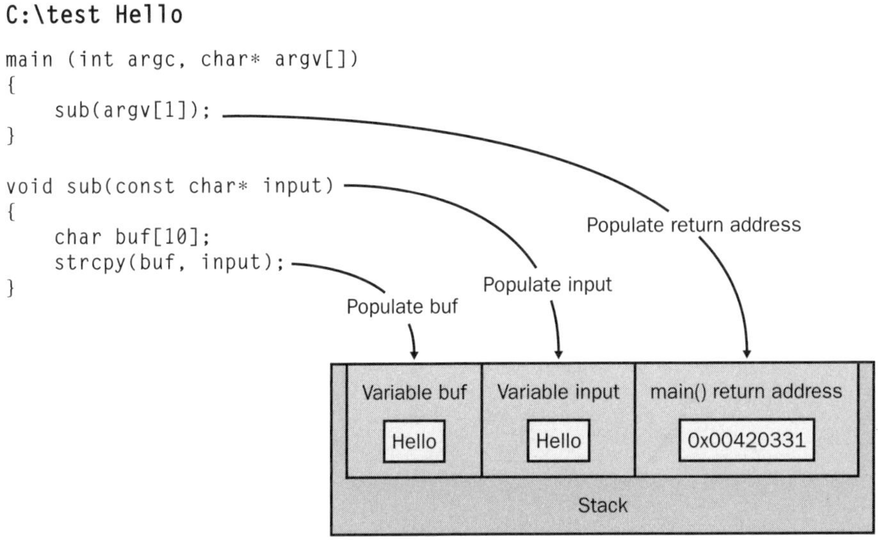

```
C:\test Hello
main (int argc, char* argv[])
{
    sub(argv[1]);
}

void sub(const char* input)
{
    char buf[10];
    strcpy(buf, input);
}
```

Populate return address

Populate input

Populate buf

Variable buf	Variable input	main() return address
Hello	Hello	0x00420331

Stack

Figure 1-1 A simple illustration of normal stack operations

Notice that the first command-line parameter passed to the application is ultimately copied into the *buf* 10-character array. While the program runs, it stores information temporarily on the stack, including the return address where processing should continue after the subroutine has completed and the variable is passed to the subroutine. The application works fine when fewer than 10 characters are passed to it. However, passing more than 10 characters will result in a buffer overflow.

Figure 1-2 shows that same application being deliberately attacked by providing input longer than 10 characters. When the line *strcpy(buf, input);* is run, the application attempts to store the string *"hello-aaaaaaaa0066ACB1"* into the 10-character array named *buf*. Because the input is too long, the input overwrites the contents of other information on the stack, including the stored address that the program will use to return control to *main()*. After the subroutine finishes running, the processor returns to the address stored in the stack. Because it has been modified, execution begins at memory address 0x0066ACB1, where, presumably, the attacker has stored malicious code. This code will run with the same privilege as the original application. After all, the operating system thinks the application called the code.

```
C:\test hello-aaaaaaaa0066ACB1
```

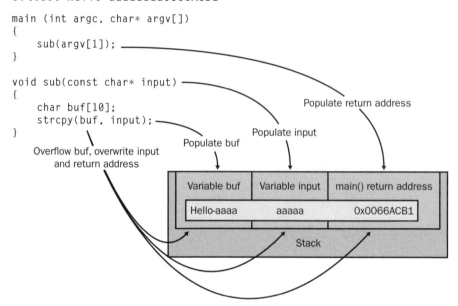

```
main (int argc, char* argv[])
{
    sub(argv[1]);
}

void sub(const char* input)
{
    char buf[10];
    strcpy(buf, input);
}
```

Overflow buf, overwrite input and return address

Populate buf

Populate input

Populate return address

Variable buf	Variable input	main() return address
Hello-aaaa	aaaaa	0x0066ACB1

Stack

Figure 1-2 A buffer overflow attack that redirects execution

This simplified example passes the destination memory address in ASCII characters just to make it clear how the memory is overwritten. In reality, the attacker would need to pass the 4 bytes that describe the actual memory address where processing should continue to interrupt normal processing. Although you can't type these characters with a keyboard, you can use tools that pass memory addresses to command-line applications. Additionally, the simplified example assumes the attacker has already stored malicious code in memory and just needs to run the code. Storing the code in memory would be very difficult. Usually, the malicious instructions would be passed as input to the application, where it would be stored on the stack.

Real World   The CodeRed Worm

Perhaps the most well-known buffer overflow exploit in recent memory is the CodeRed worm, which exploited a vulnerability in an Index Server Internet Server Application Programming Interface (ISAPI) application shipped as part of Microsoft Internet Information Server (IIS). Ironically, the vulnerable code did actually check the length of the user input to ensure it did not contain more characters than the maximum number of bytes allocated for the buffer—the recommended best practice for preventing buffer overruns. However, the developer who wrote the code verified the width of the buffer by checking the number of bytes instead of checking the number of characters. The buffer was allocated using the double-byte WCHAR type (using the command, *"WCHAR wcsAt-tribute[200];"* in the example that follows). Therefore, although the buffer could hold only 200 characters, it was 400 bytes long.

The programmer wrote code to throw an exception if the *cchAttribute* variable, which held the character count of the user input, was greater than or equal to the length of the *wcsAttribute*, which contained the number of bytes allocated to the buffer:

```
if ( cchAttribute >= sizeof wcsAttribute)
    THROW( CException( DB_E_ERRORSINCOMMAND ) );
```

Because the input was single-byte Unicode, the programmer's *if* statement would not throw an exception when the CodeRed worm passed more than 200 single-byte characters. As long as the total byte length was still less than the 400-byte length of the buffer, the *if* statement evaluated as true. The CodeRed worm used this discrepancy to overflow the buffer and run malicious code.

The following is the original, vulnerable Index Server ISAPI code:

```
WCHAR wcsAttribute[200];
if ( cchAttribute >= sizeof wcsAttribute)
    THROW( CException( DB_E_ERRORSINCOMMAND ) );
DecodeURLEscapes( (BYTE *) pszAttribute, cchAttribute,  wcsAttribute,web-
Server.CodePage());
```

After the vulnerability was discovered, Microsoft fixed it by dividing the size of the *wcsAttribute* variable by the size of the *WCHAR* type. This is the fixed code:

```
WCHAR wcsAttribute[200];
if ( cchAttribute >= sizeof wcsAttribute / sizeof WCHAR)
    THROW( CException( DB_E_ERRORSINCOMMAND ) );
DecodeURLEscapes( (BYTE *) pszAttribute, cchAttribute, wcsAttribute,web-
Server.CodePage());
```

The change was very simple; eliminating the vulnerability required adding only a single calculation. However, fixing the bug in the source code did not remove the vulnerability from the thousands of computers that were currently running the code. Customers using the application needed to retrieve and install an update issued by Microsoft before the vulnerability could be eliminated. The delay in deploying the patch gave the CodeRed worm sufficient time to infect thousands upon thousands of computers.

See Also   For information about validating external input, see Chapter 2, "Using Secure Coding Best Practices."

> **Important**   This book does not provide a detailed description of the various types of buffer overflows, because the exams are focused on Microsoft Visual Basic .NET and C#. The .NET framework dramatically reduces the opportunity for buffer overflows by automatically checking that data being placed into a buffer will fit. If you program in earlier languages such as C or C++ that do not use the .NET Framework, read Chapter 5 of *Writing Secure Code* by Michael Howard and David LeBlanc (Microsoft Press, 2002).

Although applications built on top of the .NET Framework automatically take advantage of the platform's buffer overflow capabilities, it is still possible for buffer overflow vulnerabilities to be discovered in the .NET Framework itself. Of course, Microsoft will release updates to fix vulnerabilities as they are discovered.

What Is a Parsing Error?

As discussed in the topic about buffer overflows, any user input has the potential to be malicious. Buffer overflows are one of the most sophisticated ways an attacker can exploit an application, and using them to do more than generate an error requires very sophisticated skills. However, one particular set of common exploits is much easier for an attacker to take advantage of: parsing errors. *Parsing errors*, including canonicalization errors, CSS vulnerabilities, and SQL injection vulnerabilities, occur when an application fails to adequately check user input for potentially malicious content.

What Is a Canonicalization Error?   A *canonicalization error* is an application vulnerability that occurs when an application parses a filename before the operating system has canonicalized it. Operating systems *canonicalize* filenames when processing a file to identify the absolute, physical path of a file given a virtual or relative path. Understanding canonicalization errors requires knowing that files and folders can have multiple names. If an application parses input looking for files that should not be accessed, the attacker might be able to defeat the parsing by using a synonymous name. For example, each of these names can identify the same file:

- DoNotTouch.txt
- DoNotT~1.txt
- DoNotTouch.txt.
- DoNotTouch.txt::$DATA

As you can see, an application developer who attempted to prevent users from referencing files with a .txt extension would need to do more than examine the last three characters of the filename if the operating system allowed "::$DATA" to be appended to the end of a filename.

> **See Also** For information about validating external input, see Chapter 2.

Attackers can exploit canonicalization error vulnerabilities to bypass the security checks an application makes to restrict access to files. The most common canonicalization error exploit is a canonicalization attack against a Web server, in which an attacker requests a specially formed filename to a Web server, causing the Web server to process and display a file that would not normally be accessible.

Example: Canonicalization Error

A typical request from a Web server would resemble this, *"GET /docs/index.htm"*. An attacker could perform a canonicalization attack by submitting a request such as, *"GET /../../autoexec.bat"*. This type of attack worked against many early Web servers, because the Web server passed the requested filename to the operating system without removing the *"/../.."* portion of the request. The operating system interpreted this to mean that it should retrieve the file from a folder not being used to store Web content.

Besides forcing Web servers to return files outside of the folders designated to contain Web content, canonicalization has been used by attackers to specify a path to an executable file. With a properly formed request, an attacker could run commands on the server using the Web server service's own authority. Known, documented attacks include an attacker adding user accounts that allow the attacker to connect directly to the Web server as an administrator.

Although modern Web servers have been tested to ensure they are free of obvious canonicalization vulnerabilities, parsing errors can exist anywhere a user provides a filename to your application. Most parsing error exploits are targeted against Web servers, but any application that has access to files the user isn't authorized to read or execute, and that accepts input from users as filenames, has the potential to contain a canonicalization vulnerability.

What Is Cross-Site Scripting? *Cross-site scripting (CSS)* attacks exploit Web server applications to cause them to display malicious content to end users. Web applications that accept input from a user and include that input on Web pages viewed by other users might be vulnerable to cross-site scripting attacks. These applications include Web forum applications, guestbooks, and any others intended to display comments. A CSS attack is another form of a parsing error.

Example: Cross-Site Scripting

A simple guestbook application might accept and display comments from users. Most users enter a comment using standard characters, and the guestbook functions as intended. However, a malicious attacker that controlled a server with the host name attacker.contoso.com could enter a comment that contains HTML code such as the following:

```
Hi, great page!<img src="attacker.contoso.com/counter.aspx" width=1 height=1/>
```

When this comment is displayed to other users, the users' browsers submit a request for the file /user-counter.aspx from the server named attacker.contoso.com. Although this attack would not compromise files on the client or server computers nor give the attacker elevated privileges, it would compromise the privacy of users visiting the guestbook. The attacker could examine the log files generated from the requests submitted to the attacker.contoso.com server and use these log files to identify the IP addresses of visitors to the site, the types of browsers they are using, and the users' operating systems.

More sophisticated CSS attacks include client-side scripts. After injecting the script into a page, the Web browsers of future visitors will run the client-side script. Although the capabilities of client-side scripts vary, as do the permissions granted to client-side scripts, the scripts have the potential to compromise the user's privacy, infect the user's computer with a virus, and even grant an attacker elevated privileges to the computer.

Security Alert   Be especially concerned about CSS attacks if users are granted a higher-than-normal level of trust to your Web application. In particular, Internet Explorer might grant scripts that are downloaded from a server on an intranet higher privileges than those downloaded from a Web server on the Internet. Remember—attacks come from within the company's network, too.

What Is SQL Injection?   *SQL injection* attacks insert database commands into user input to modify commands sent from an application to a back-end database. Applications that employ user input in SQL queries can be vulnerable to SQL injection attacks.

Consider the following simplified C# source code, intended to determine whether an order number (stored in the variable *Id* and provided by the user) has shipped:

```csharp
sql.Open();
sqlstring="SELECT HasShipped FROM orders WHERE ID='" + Id + "'";
SqlCommand cmd = new SqlCommand(sqlstring,sql);
if ((int)cmd.ExecuteScalar() != 0) {
    Status = "Yes";
} else {
    Status = "No";
}
```

```vbnet
sql.Open()
sqlstring="SELECT HasShipped FROM orders WHERE ID='" + Id + "'"
Dim cmd As SqlCommand =  New SqlCommand(sqlstring,sql)
If CType(cmd.ExecuteScalar() <> 0,Integer) Then
    Status = "Yes"
Else
    Status = "No"
End If
```

Legitimate users will submit an order ID such as, "**1234**", and the code sets the Status variable to "*Yes*" if the *HasShipped* value in the row with that ID number is true. However, a malicious attacker could submit a value such as, "**1234' drop table customers – **". The preceding C# code would then construct the following SQL query:

```sql
SELECT HasShipped FROM orders WHERE ID='1234' drop table customers --
```

Note   The exact structure of SQL commands varies between database servers. Some database servers, for example, require each command to be separated by a semicolon. Microsoft SQL Server does not have this requirement, however.

Assuming a table named customers existed, and the application had the right to drop the table, the table would be lost. Depending on the application and the database configuration, such maliciously malformed queries can also be used to retrieve data from the database and run operating system commands.

What Are Denial-Of-Service Attacks?

A *denial-of-service (DoS)* attack prevents legitimate users from accessing a network service. A DoS attack does not give the attacker a higher level of access; instead, it denies legitimate users from accessing the application. Although the most dangerous attacks allow an attacker to gain elevated privilege on the target computer, DoS attacks can be very costly to victims. Generally, the loss of private information is much more devastating than the damage done by a denial-of-service attack, and as a developer, you should focus more of your energy on preventing potential vulnerabilities that an attacker could exploit to reveal information.

> **Important**   Denial-of-service attacks often target bugs that you would not otherwise classify as security vulnerabilities. For example, fixing the vulnerability for a client-server application that prompts the user to provide her first name but crashes when she provides a name longer than 200 characters might seem like a low priority. After all, reproducing the error requires conditions that would never occur under normal circumstances. However, if an attacker discovers that your application crashes under this circumstance, the attacker can cause your application to repeatedly fail by intentionally providing an extremely long first name.

Not all denial-of-service attacks cause an application to fail outright. The potential for a denial-of-service attack exists any time a server uses more resources to process a request than the client uses to submit the request. For example, if you are creating a client-server application that allocates 10 MB of memory for each authenticated user, you could use the following process:

1. Receive request from user.

2. Allocate memory for user.

3. Request and receive authentication from user.

However, this application would be extremely vulnerable to a denial-of-service attack because it allocates memory before authenticating the user. Allocating the memory after authenticating the user would make the application much more resistant to denial-of-service attacks, because the attacker would be required to provide credentials before the server allocated resources. Therefore, the following application flow would be more secure:

1. Receive request from user.

2. Request and receive authentication from user.

3. Allocate memory for user.

What Is Cryptography Cracking?

Cryptography cracking is the process of capturing encrypted content and deriving the original, unencrypted data without a key. Cryptography cracking is a complex and costly process, and attackers generally rely on it only when other, simpler attacks against an application fail. If the attacker can successfully crack the encryption, the attacker can gain access to the unencrypted communications.

> ## How Communications Are Compromised
>
> Communications between a client and a server occur across a network. If an attacker can gain control of that network hardware, the attacker might be able to capture the communications. This capture will, at a minimum, reveal important information about how the application works. Additionally, it can reveal private information, such as user names and passwords, that the attacker can use to gain elevated privileges.

Only the most sophisticated attackers are capable of cracking encrypted cyphertext. Even with the proper skills and tools, it can take an attacker years (or even thousands of years) to identify the unencrypted data given in an encrypted message. However, many cryptographic techniques have flaws that allow the attacker to crack the cryptography much faster. Additionally, a developer who does not follow best practices for implementing encryption might introduce weaknesses into an otherwise strong encryption method. For example, an application that uses a strong encryption method but stores the private key in a location that is publicly accessible to an attacker might allow an attacker to gain access to private, encrypted communications.

See Also   For more information about cryptography, see Chapter 8, "Protecting Data by Using Cryptography."

What Are Man-In-The-Middle Attacks?

A *man-in-the-middle (MITM)* attack is a sophisticated attack in which an attacker impersonates a server to intercept requests from a legitimate client. Then, the attacker impersonates the user to the destination server, as shown in Figure 1-3. At that point the attacker can examine and potentially modify the communications between the client and server.

Figure 1-3   Man-in-the-middle attack

Any application that does not require both encryption and authentication is susceptible to man-in-the-middle attacks. Man-in-the-middle attacks are usually prevented by implementing authentication and encryption at the level of the operating system, rather than at the application level. IP Security (IPSec) is commonly used to prevent man-in-the-middle attacks between two hosts without requiring individual applications to implement server authentication and encryption.

> **See Also**   For more information about IPSec and cryptography, see Chapter 8.

What Is Password Cracking?

Password cracking is an attack that tries to guess a user's password by attempting hundreds, thousands, or millions of passwords. Any application that authenticates a user by using static credentials is susceptible to password cracking. In other words, if you prompt a user for a user name and password, an attacker can guess passwords until he finds a valid combination. Normally, the attacker does not manually type user names and passwords at a keyboard, but instead automates the password-guessing process using a script.

There are two approaches to guessing passwords: brute force and dictionary. Whereas a true brute force attack uses a methodical approach to guessing passwords ("a", "b" … "aaa", "aab to zzzzzzz"), password-cracking attacks usually use a password dictionary to increase the chances of finding a valid password quickly. *Password dictionaries* contain lists of commonly used passwords. Password cracking using a dictionary is very effective, because most users choose easy-to-remember words and names as passwords. Lesson 2 in this chapter discusses techniques for limiting the effectiveness of this type of attack by using error reporting.

Types of Attacks That Specific Applications Are Vulnerable To

Table 1-1 shows which types of applications are vulnerable to each of the major types of attacks.

Table 1-1   Application Vulnerability Matrix

	ASP.NET Web Application	x.NET Framework Windows Forms Application
Buffer overflow attack	O	O
Canonicalization error attack	X	X
Cross-site scripting	X	O
SQL injection	X	X
Denial-of-service attack	X	X
Man-in-the-middle attack	X	X
Password cracking	X	X
Cryptography cracking	X	X

O = generally not vulnerable, X = potentially vulnerable

Practice: Evaluating Security Threats

In this practice, you will answer questions that require you to explain how to exploit vulnerable applications. If you are unable to answer a question, review the lesson materials and try the question again. You can find answers to the questions in the "Questions and Answers" section at the end of this chapter.

1. An application on the Internet that does not require authentication would potentially be vulnerable to which of the following types of attacks? (Choose all that apply.)

   a. Buffer overflows

   b. Parsing errors

   c. Denial-of-service attacks

   d. Man-in-the-middle attacks

   e. Compromising communications

   f. Password cracking

2. You created a Windows forms application that runs on a kiosk in a shopping mall to gather the name, address, and other demographic information from shoppers. The information is stored within a SQL Server database on the same computer. Your application is potentially vulnerable to which of the following types of attacks? (Choose all that apply.)

   a. Buffer overflows

   b. Parsing errors

   c. Denial-of-service attacks

   d. Man-in-the-middle attacks

   e. Compromising communications

   f. Password cracking

3. Which of the following types of attacks can lead to private information being compromised? (Choose the best answer.)

   a. Buffer overflows

   b. Parsing errors

   c. Denial-of-service attacks

   d. Man-in-the-middle attacks

   e. Compromising communications

   f. Password cracking

4. Think back to the last application you developed. Theoretically, which types of attacks could that application have been vulnerable to? Of those potential vulnerabilities, which do you feel you were sufficiently protected against? Did you use defense-in-depth, secure coding practices, or other techniques to limit your risk?

Lesson Summary

- Any developer's application can have a security vulnerability, because anyone can make a mistake, and new security attacks are discovered constantly.

- Although specific attacks change regularly, most attacks fall into one of several different categories:

  - ❏ Attackers use buffer overflow attacks by providing input longer than the application was designed to process. The attack will corrupt memory and can be used to run malicious code.

  - ❏ Parsing errors, including canonicalization errors, CSS, and SQL injection, exploit applications that fail to successfully remove invalid characters from user input. A malicious attacker can exploit this type of vulnerability by generating input that includes special characters and commands that will be interpreted by the operating system, Web server, or database, rather than by the application.

  - ❏ Denial-of-service attacks take systems offline, preventing legitimate users from accessing the resource.

  - ❏ Even though cryptography is the best way to reduce the risk of private communications being compromised, it is vulnerable to being cracked by a skilled attacker.

  - ❏ Man-in-the-middle attacks give an attacker access to network communications, but are difficult to implement because they require the attacker to impersonate both the client and the server.

  - ❏ Password-cracking attacks attempt to compromise credentials by repeatedly guessing passwords until authentication is successful.

- Different applications are more likely to be vulnerable to different types of attacks, depending on the development platform and whether the application uses a Web or a Windows Forms front end.

Lesson 2: Implementing Best Practices to Design Secure Applications

Before you write the first line of code for an application, you must think about how the application's design will limit the potential for vulnerabilities. Having a design that takes security into account will limit the damage done by any mistakes you make, ease the burden of releasing security updates, and reduce the likelihood of your application being successfully exploited by an attacker.

The goal of Lesson 1 was to demonstrate that applications must be able to survive hostile environments because attacks are varied and numerous. To grasp the need for defense-in-depth, you must acknowledge that software is written by people, and that people make mistakes. The attacks described in Lesson 1 exploit those mistakes. You cannot hope to make your applications invulnerable by eliminating every mistake. Instead, strive to create the fewest number of mistakes possible, and use defense-in-depth to reduce the likelihood that your remaining mistakes will be exploited.

See Also   This lesson provides an introduction to the concepts of secure application design. For a thorough discussion on the complete secure development process, threat modeling, and risk management, read *Writing Secure Code* by Michael Howard and David LeBlanc (Microsoft Press, 2002).

After this lesson, you will be able to

- Describe the purpose of defense-in-depth.
- Describe the SD^3 strategy that Microsoft developers use to implement defense-in-depth.
- Design security features into your application, and use a secure design process.
- Design applications to be secure by default.
- Design applications to maintain security during and after deployment.

Estimated lesson time: 45 minutes

What Is Defense-In-Depth?

Defense-in-depth is a proven technique for reducing the exposure of vulnerabilities. Network engineers use defense-in-depth to protect computers on a network by providing multiple layers of protection from potential attackers. For example, an engineer might design a network (such as the one shown in Figure 1-4) with three layers of packet filtering: a packet-filtering router, a hardware firewall, and software firewalls on each of the hosts (such as Internet Connection Firewall). If an attacker manages to bypass one or two of the layers of protection, the hosts will still be protected from communications that have not specifically been allowed.

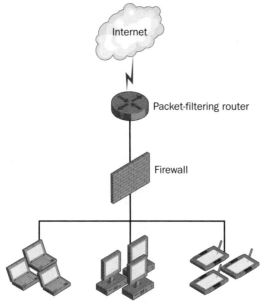

Figure 1-4   Defense-in-depth used to protect a network

Networks should be designed with defense-in-depth in mind, but the concept must be extended deep into the code that makes up the applications themselves. As a developer, you cannot rely on customers providing network-level protection. First, many customers will be unable or unwilling to properly secure their networks. Second, configuring your application to work in different environments might require your customers to allow specific requests through their firewalls. If nothing else, the network must be configured to allow communications between the client and server components of a network application.

What Is the SD³ Strategy?

To guide application developers to follow defense-in-depth principles, Microsoft uses a strategy nicknamed SD³, which stands for secure by design, secure by default, secure in deployment. The tenets of this strategy include:

- **Secure by design**   Developers follow secure coding principles and implement security features to offset potential vulnerabilities.

- **Secure by default**   Applications that are secure by default assume that most end users install the application without changing the default settings, and therefore require these users to specifically select features that might not be used or that might reduce security.

- **Secure in deployment**   The application can be kept secure after installation by updating it with security patches, monitoring it for attacks, and auditing it for abuse.

No single human error will allow an application that uses defense-in-depth to be exploited. For example, consider an internal client-server accounting application that allows members of the accounting team to view and edit financial data. If the programmer of the client-side front-end application forgot to parse user input, an attacker could input SQL commands and perform a SQL injection attack against the server. However, one of the secure by design principles states that input should be parsed in every function that receives the input. As a result, the server would detect invalid input from the client and reject the query.

The secure in deployment tenet states that the application must include monitoring and auditing features so that the organization's application-monitoring software can detect the attack. Being able to detect the attack would enable support staff to track down the user who attempted to initiate the attack and contact human resources to help prevent that user from attacking the system in the future. Additionally, the support staff would be able to identify that the client application contained a security vulnerability, notify the developer of the bug, and then release an update to all clients. In this example, defense-in-depth did more than protect critical data from being exploited. It allowed the vulnerability, the attack, and the attacker to be identified, improving the security of the application in the long term.

Best Practices for Implementing the Secure by Design Tenet

Secure by design is the most complex of the SD^3 tenets. It consists of using security features, such as cryptography, authentication, authorization, and firewalls, to reduce the risks of several types of attacks. Secure by design also dictates least privilege, separation of privilege, and reducing the attack surface of the application. Effectively implementing the many secure coding best practices, described throughout this book, requires the use of a security-oriented design process. This section presents the best practices for implementing the secure by design tenet.

When Your Application Stores or Transmits Data That Attackers Want, Use Cryptography

Often, attackers won't directly attack your application, but they will attempt to compromise data located in memory, stored on the hard disk, or being transferred across the network. Today, the best way to protect this data is by using cryptography. Cryptography encrypts information in such a way that it can be deciphered only by users with a valid key. If your application stores or transmits data that would be potentially useful to an attacker, especially personal information about people, financial information, or authentication credentials, encrypt this data. You can implement this encryption your-self, or require your end users to use platform encryption features such as Encrypting File System (EFS), Secure Sockets Layer (SSL), and IP Security (IPSec).

> **See Also**   For more information about cryptography, see Chapter 8. Isolated storage, described in Chapter 4, "Taking Advantage of Platform Security," is an excellent way to use cryptography.

Use Authentication Mechanisms Built into the .NET Framework

Authentication is the process of proving a user's identity and is most often done by requiring a user to provide a user name and password. When designing your applica-tion, consider how you will authenticate users. Authentication mechanisms are fre-quently attacked by attackers using brute force or dictionary password-cracking tools, or by attackers who can capture authentication data from the network. Fortunately, designing an authentication method is fairly simple, because you can and should lever-age the authentication mechanisms built into the .NET framework.

> **See Also**   For more information about authentication, see Chapter 5, "Implementing Role-Based Security."

Use .NET Framework APIs for Authorization

After a user is authenticated, your application must determine whether the user has suf-ficient rights to perform the action she has requested—this is known as *authorization*. Although authorization often can be controlled by configuring access control lists (ACLs) for files, databases, and other objects used by your application, you might have to examine a user's authorization within your application. The .NET Framework pro-vides Application Programming Interfaces (APIs) for examining a user's properties, including group memberships.

> **See Also**   For more information about authorization, see Chapter 5.

Use Standard Network Protocols for Network Communications When Possible

Firewalls analyze network traffic and drop all packets that are not specifically allowed. Even though designing an application for security does not require you to implement your own firewall functionality, you must plan on firewalls being present on the net-works where your application is deployed. To improve compatibility with firewalls, leverage standard network protocols for network communications whenever possible.

For example, use .NET remoting or Web services to communicate between two computers rather than design a network protocol from scratch. Administrators implementing your application will probably know how to allow standardized protocols through firewalls, which reduces the likelihood that they will configure the firewall to be too permissive.

Real World   Top Mistakes Developers Make When Choosing a Network Protocol

Here's a list of the top mistakes I've seen developers make when using network protocols:

- **Developers did not document the port numbers they used**   This requires the system administrator to use a protocol analyzer to identify each of the port numbers so that the administrator can properly configure firewalls. This can lead to a lengthy process of trial and error, and if the administrator misses a port number, it can lead to difficult-to-troubleshoot application errors (and support calls to you!).

- **Developers used port numbers seemingly pulled out of thin air (or, perhaps, based on their birth dates)**   Sometimes, these port numbers conflict with existing applications, which means the two applications cannot be run on a single computer.

- **Developers did not allow port numbers to be redefined**   Administrators often change port numbers to eliminate application conflicts and to reduce the likelihood of the service being identified with a port scan.

- **Developers used multiple port numbers**   Some applications require five or six ports to be opened on a firewall, which is difficult to manage.

- **Developers used UDP**   User Datagram Protocol (UDP) is sessionless, which makes it very difficult for the firewall to filter packets being sent to the clients. After all, without a session, the firewall can't determine whether the packet is part of an expected response or a malicious attack.

- **Developers initiated connections from the server to the client**   Most firewalls block all incoming connections by default, making this type of protocol particularly difficult to configure. When designing the network protocol, assume that you can establish a Transmission Control Protocol (TCP) session to the server but cannot establish a TCP session to a client.

Implement the Principle of Least Privilege

Design and implement your applications so that they use the least privileges necessary to carry out any action. Doing so reduces the damage that can be done if your application is successfully misused by an attacker. For example, if you need to read the contents of a file, open that file for read access only. Least privilege is more than using the minimal level of file lock, however. During the design phase, plan to allow your application to run without Administrator or System privileges. Further, document specifically what privileges are necessary to allow end users to configure accounts to run your application with minimal permissions.

For example, if your application needs to update a registry value in the HKEY_LOCAL_MACHINE hive, document that requirement because standard user accounts lack that permission. If your application only reads the Customers table in a database but must both read and write the Orders table, specify that those permissions be granted or restricted during the setup process. Whenever possible, plan to provide setup procedures that handle the configuration of ACLs automatically.

> **Tip**   Remember these two rules:
>
> 1. Interactive applications, such as the graphical front-end of an application, should run with standard User privileges, not Administrator privileges.
> 2. Non-interactive applications such as services should run in the context of a restricted user account created specifically for the service. Services should not run as System.

Use a Security-Oriented Design Process

Even the process that you use to design your application should consider security. Here is an example of a security-oriented design process:

1. The organization assigns a single person to be ultimately responsible for security issues. This person can be a developer, manager, or the Chief Security Officer.

2. All developers receive security training.

3. All developers follow the code review processes and coding guidelines that the organization has in place to ensure all developers adhere to secure design practices.

4. Engineers with security experience analyze all code for security vulnerabilities before releasing it to customers. Requiring your application to withstand a *tiger team* analysis from an objective outside organization can identify vulnerabilities before the application is deployed in production environments.

Implement the Separation of Privilege Principle

Design your application so that day-to-day functions run in a separate process and separate security context from management functions. Figure 1-5 shows a simplified design of an e-commerce application without separation of privilege. In this example, the entire application is run in the context of the ASP.NET user account. This requires that the ASP.NET user account have privileges to perform management tasks, such as deleting rows from the Orders table. Additionally, application management functionality such as the *Management.ShipOrder()* and *Management.AddInventory()* functions could be called by an attacker who would be able to compromise the application.

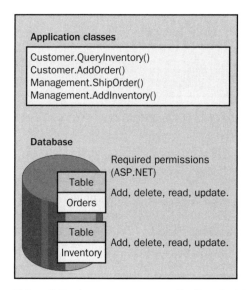

Figure 1-5   An e-commerce application designed without separation of privilege

Figure 1-6 shows the same simplified e-commerce application designed using separation of privilege. This example implements separate applications for use by customers and internal management. The Customer application uses the ASP.NET account to access resources, whereas the Management application uses impersonation so that it runs in the context of an authenticated user. In the event an attacker successfully exploits the Customer application, this design will limit the damage the attacker can do because the ASP.NET user account's permissions are restricted to only those permissions required for end users. Specifically, in this design, the ASP.NET user account does not need permission to update, add, or delete rows of the Inventory table. Therefore, an attacker would not be able to insert or change records of inventory. However, since internal users will have these permissions, the Management application will be able to update the inventory when required.

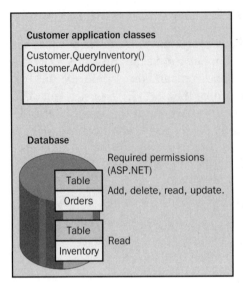
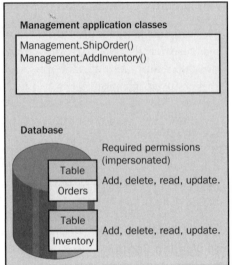

Figure 1-6   An e-commerce application designed with separation of privilege

See Also   For more information about impersonation, see Chapter 5.

Follow Known Techniques for Reducing the Attack Surface

Your application should minimize the attack surface by offering the simplest possible user interface and exposing the fewest number of ways for users (including other applications) to submit requests. Reducing the attack surface gives attackers fewer targets, which reduces the likelihood of an exploit. Use the following techniques to reduce attack surface:

- Listen for inbound connections on the fewest possible number of ports.

- Minimize the number of services running.

- Minimize the number of pages in an ASP.NET application.

- Minimize the number of accounts authorized to use your application, while still following the principles of least privilege and separation of privilege.

- Minimize the number of authentication methods available to users, while still providing flexibility.

- Minimize the number of methods that accept input from users.

- Minimize the number of application components installed by default.

Best Practices for Implementing the Secure by Default Tenet

Experience shows that most users accept every default setting when installing an application. After all, many users install the application before reading the accompanying documentation. As a result, your application's default settings will almost always be the settings used in production environments.

You cannot burden your users by instructing them to change default settings or uninstall unnecessary components to improve security. After the application is up and running, there's an excellent chance the user will never again reconfigure it. Instead, you must make your application's default settings as secure as possible. If those default settings don't provide functionality that your users need, they're better off manually adding the functionality later.

Ensure That the Setup Routine's Default Settings Install Only Necessary Application Components

Many applications, particularly those written for Windows systems, are designed to provide maximum functionality after a default installation. Developers choose to enable as many features as possible by default to make the application easier for administrators to configure. Although these developers' intentions are noble, experience has shown that modern applications must be able to survive in a hostile environment. Each feature that is enabled in an application is another potential security vulnerability.

To reduce the likelihood of end users being affected by a vulnerability in an optional component, your setup routine's default settings should install only necessary application components. Users should be prompted to select optional components during the setup procedure and have the option to add those components later by re-running setup.

> **Real World   The Importance of Minimizing Components Installed by Default**
>
> IIS, a Windows component, provides an excellent example of the importance of minimizing the components installed by default. IIS 5.0 was included with Microsoft Windows 2000 Server. Not only was IIS installed by default, but many nonessential subcomponents were also installed. In 2001, a vulnerability was discovered in the Index Server ISAPI extension, one of the nonessential IIS subcomponents installed by default. Soon thereafter, the CodeRed worm began exploiting this vulnerability. CodeRed propagated quickly, and infected thousands of computers. Very few of those computers were actually using the Index

Server ISAPI extension, however. If IIS 4.0 had followed the secure by default principle, the Index Server ISAPI extension would not have been installed on the vast majority of those systems, and the costs associated with the CodeRed worm would have been minimal.

You can learn from the mistakes made with IIS 4.0, or you can follow the example set by IIS 6.0 (included with Windows Server 2003). First, Windows Server 2003 does not install IIS 6.0 by default. If an administrator does choose to install IIS, she is prompted to enable optional functionality such as the FrontPage Server Extensions and ASP.NET, as shown in Figure 1-7. Both of these features are commonly used, but neither is selected by default. Administrators must explicitly choose to enable these features. That requirement alone will not prevent vulnerabilities in IIS from being exploited, but it will reduce the number of compromised computers.

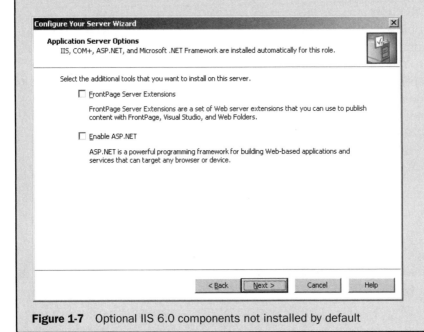

Figure 1-7   Optional IIS 6.0 components not installed by default

Configure the Most Restrictive Permissions Possible During Configuration

In addition to minimizing the number of installed components, take care to configure the most restrictive permissions possible during configuration. To use Windows as an example once again, earlier versions of Windows granted the Everyone group Full Control over most files, folders, and registry settings. Since the release of those earlier versions of Windows, Microsoft learned many important secure development lessons.

As a result, Windows Server 2003 provides much more restrictive permissions, dramatically reducing the potential for vulnerabilities to be exploited in systems with the default configuration settings. End users still have the opportunity to modify security settings to make them less restrictive, but they must consciously select those security settings.

Implement Application Diversity

The most wide-spread worms, including the CodeRed and SQLSlammer worms, propagate by connecting to random IP addresses using a well-known port number. For example, SQLSlammer always sends packets with a destination port of 1434/udp, the port Microsoft SQL Server listens on by default. The port number a SQL Server listens on is configurable, but because SQL Server uses 1434/udp by default, the vast majority of installations listen on the default port number.

One of the ways to avoid being infected with the SQLSlammer worm is to simply change the port number to something other than the default. If the SQL Server installation routine had provided a randomized default port number, a worm such as the SQLSlammer would not have been able to propagate as quickly. Rather than sending attacks to random IP addresses with static port numbers, the worm would have needed to send packets to both random IP addresses and random port numbers, which would have dramatically decreased the possibility of finding vulnerable computers. Since there are 65,535 possible port numbers, the use of random port numbers would have slowed the spread of the SQLSlammer worm to a crawl. In fact, with sufficient application diversity, you would never have heard of SQLSlammer.

> **Note**   Now is a good time to think back to the definition of defense-in-depth. Remember, the goal is not necessarily to eliminate every vulnerability in your code, but to reduce the possibility of vulnerabilities being exploited. Application diversity would not have prevented the vulnerability that the SQLSlammer worm exploited, but it would have stopped the worm's rapid spreading.

Application diversity does have a drawback—it complicates configuration and management. In particular, if the port number a database server uses is randomized, the administrator must configure clients with both the database's IP address and port number. Additionally, firewalls and management tools will need to be individually configured with the custom port number. This requires little additional work on internal networks, where administrators already track this type of configuration information. However, changing the port number on public services can be confusing to end users. For example, end users connecting to an e-commerce application can be expected to type the URL **http://www.contoso.com/**. However, they cannot be expected to remember *http://www.contoso.com:5293/*.

Randomizing server port numbers is the most obvious way to take advantage of application diversity to provide an additional layer of protection against application exploits, because most modern worms only attempt to contact an application's well-known port number. However, you can also provide diversity for folder names, file names, file extensions, and other application settings. For example, some versions of IIS installed sample content that an administrator could use to verify that the Web server was running correctly. Later, vulnerabilities were discovered in this content, and worms exploited these vulnerabilities to quickly propagate. Using random folder names to store this sample content would not have prevented the vulnerability, but it would have prevented a worm from exploiting it in an automated fashion, because the worm would need to first discover the path to the sample content, which would be different on every server.

Best Practices for Implementing the Secure in Deployment Tenet

The third tenet of Microsoft's secure development strategy is secure in deployment. The development process isn't finished when the application is released; you must keep the application secure as your customers run it. The following list describes the three best practices.

■ You must have a process for identifying newly discovered security vulnerabilities and issuing updates that remove those vulnerabilities. This is perhaps the most important best practice.

■ You must have a system in place to allow customers to monitor events that take place while your application is running; customers must be able to detect whether your application is actively being attacked.

■ Your application must handle failures and errors in a secure fashion, revealing minimal information to end users, while allowing administrators to identify and resolve the problem.

These are discussed in more detail in the next few sections.

Have a Process for Identifying Newly Discovered Security Vulnerabilities and Issuing Updates

Microsoft itself provides an interesting example of how to handle security updates, because they have an extremely large installed base of customers, and new vulnerabilities are discovered in Microsoft software on a regular basis. The security update process begins when a new vulnerability is reported to the Microsoft Security Responses Center (MSRC) by a customer, a security organization, or an internal Microsoft employee. After the MSRC verifies that the vulnerability is genuine, they determine the severity of the vulnerability. The severity takes into account the potential damage an exploit could cause, the number of customers affected, and whether an exploit already exists.

Based on the severity, Microsoft will release an update to customers using the Windows Update Web site. Additionally, updates can be distributed directly to individual computers using the Automatic Updates feature available for Windows 2000 and later operating systems, or distributed throughout entire organizations by using Microsoft Software Update Services (SUS). Many individuals and organizations choose to use these tools to automatically deploy security updates; IT professionals have the option of subscribing to an e-mail service to be notified when new vulnerabilities are discovered and patches or workarounds are announced.

See Also   For more information about the MSRC, see "A Tour of the Microsoft Security Response Center" on the TechNet page of the Microsoft Web site at *http:// www.microsoft.com/technet/archive/community/columns/security/essays/sectour.mspx.*

Most software does not require an infrastructure as robust as the MSRC to manage security vulnerabilities. However, Microsoft provides an interesting model for discovering vulnerabilities, issuing updates, and notifying customers. Figure 1-8 shows a typical process that every application developer should provide to customers. Communication is critical: you must provide a way for customers to notify you about potential security vulnerabilities, and for you to notify customers about verified vulnerabilities, patches, and workarounds.

Design   Patching takes time. Make sure management allocates development time to creating and releasing security updates.

The simpler it is for your customers to discover and deploy patches, the more secure your application will be in deployment, so provide security updates immediately as vulnerabilities are discovered. Because the process of installing the updates requires critical systems to be taken offline for several hours, your customers will be less likely to install your patches within the first few days. In fact, when faced with updates that consume hours of labor or cause extended downtime, many customers choose to simply ignore the patch. When designing your application, you must plan for updates to be installed with minimal downtime and administrative overhead.

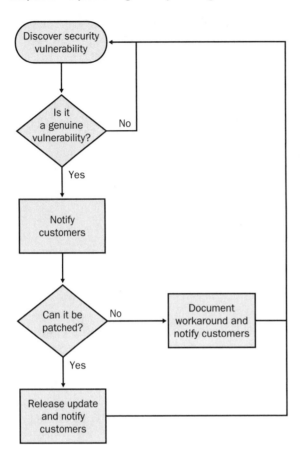

Figure 1-8   A typical security vulnerability discovery and patch release process

Real World   Why People Might Resist Deploying Updates

We've seen it over and over again: a vulnerability is discovered, and the software developer releases a patch within a few weeks. Then, months later, a worm or virus is released that exploits the vulnerability. The malicious software shouldn't spread at all, right? After all, the developer released a patch for it.

Some application developers have a bit of an attitude when it comes to customers delaying the deployment of their patches. You have to remember: your customers *rely* on your application. They have to allocate time (often, weeks of time) to testing the update to verify that it will not break their critical services. To install your patch, they need to schedule staff to stay after hours to install the update, and then make sure that your application still works as expected. They also need to schedule time for your application to be offline while the patch is being applied.

In organizations that run 24 hours a day, even a few minutes of downtime must be scheduled weeks in advance.

Many organizations might choose to not deploy your updates at all. This is understandable, because the cost of deploying updates is huge. Sometimes, deploying an update causes more problems than it fixes, which further increases the cost. All security updates fix security vulnerabilities, but most of those updates would never have been successfully exploited. In other words, it *usually* doesn't cause a problem to skip an update, and the labor and downtime saved has an immediate benefit.

Yes, systems administrators should make an effort to promptly deploy security updates. But if they don't, be sympathetic to their reasons.

Have a System That Allows Customers to Monitor Events That Occur While Your Application Runs

Has your application ever been attacked or exploited? How would you know?

Systems administrators monitor applications to identify problems that are causing downtime, as well as to detect potential problems before they have an impact on end users. The simplest form of monitoring checks is to determine whether a particular application is responding to requests. If the application fails to respond, the monitoring system notifies an administrator.

In the security world, intrusion detection systems (IDS) use application monitoring to determine when an attack is currently under way, and whether an attacker has successfully compromised an application. IDS use complex algorithms to detect signs of an attack. For example, a series of 20 unsuccessful authentication attempts could signal that an attacker is actively using a password-cracking technique to identify a user's credentials. If an administrator is able to respond while the attack is under way, the administrator might be able to collect evidence that can be used to prosecute the attacker, identify the vulnerability that the attacker is attempting to exploit, or simply block traffic from the attacker's network.

Your application does not need to include IDS capabilities, but it should provide information that can be used to monitor your application for signs that an attack is under way, and it should be capable of recording detailed information that can give administrators clues about an attacker's actions. If you use the platform's authentication and authorization systems, you can take advantage of the operating system's auditing capabilities. For example, if your application authenticates users with its Windows user account, an event can be automatically added to the event log every time a user attempts to authenticate—without requiring you to write a single line of code.

Provide similar auditing capabilities to monitor custom authentication mechanisms for signs of password-cracking attacks, and to record malformed requests for signs of attacks targeting parsing error vulnerabilities. Adding events to the Application or Security event log is simple, and most monitoring systems can analyze custom application events for problems. Additionally, allow customers to configure auditing for other events that might be significant, such as updating the application's configuration, adding users, and changing privileges. Enabling customers to control the level of auditing will give them the ability to carefully analyze application usage while preventing event logs from becoming filled unnecessarily.

When recording events, record the type of request and as much information about the user's identity as possible. For example, you could add the following information from a Web request to the event log:

- Type of request
- User name (if authenticated)
- Client IP address
- Client agent (for example, the Web browser name and version)
- Client computer name
- Client operating system

When generating an event about a client request, always record as much information as possible about the client. However, it's important to understand that you cannot trust information provided by the client. For example, an attacker could create a tool to submit requests to a Web application, and have that tool incorrectly identify itself as Microsoft Internet Explorer. Similarly, it is theoretically possible for an attacker to spoof another's IP address, or to send requests through another computer, effectively hiding the original IP address. Although this client information cannot be trusted, always record it, because it might be useful in understanding and tracking down the attacker. The event log will automatically record the date and time of day the event occurred.

The term *monitoring* is used to indicate continuous analysis of an application's status to enable real-time administrator notification and response. *Auditing* is very similar to monitoring, except that auditing requires events to be archived over a long period of time. Monitoring can notify administrators that an attack is currently taking place. If administrators discover that an attack took place several weeks or months in the past, they might perform auditing to identify how the attack took place and what damage was done. From an application developer's perspective, you can provide for both monitoring and auditing by writing important events to the event log, because administrators will be able to archive those logs.

Ensure That Applications Can Handle Failures and Errors Securely

Developers create descriptive error messages to help administrators troubleshoot problems. Unfortunately, attackers can use these descriptive error messages to discover details about an application's design.

For example, a well-written application will use exception handling to detect problems accessing a database. If that application then displays the contents of the database connection string, the *Exception.Message* string, and the database query to the end user, it can compromise the application's security by revealing too much information to a potential attacker. Instead, the application should write the details of the exception to the event log and display a friendly, but ambiguous, message to the end user.

See Also   For more information about reporting errors, see Chapter 2.

Practice: Implementing Best Practices to Design Secure Applications

In this practice, you will answer questions to show that you can implement best practices to design secure applications. If you are unable to answer a question, review the lesson materials and try the question again. You can find answers to the questions in the "Questions and Answers" section at the end of this chapter.

1. Which of the following best describes the concept of defense-in-depth? (Choose the best answer.)

   a. Using multiple layers of firewalls to protect an application

   b. Dividing an application into separate tiers for the front end, application, and database

   c. Providing a path for escalating problems relating to known security vulnerabilities by first notifying a security engineer, and then notifying a higher level of management until executive management is asked to address the vulnerability

   d. Using various security techniques to protect against a single potential vulnerability

2. How is each of the SD^3 principles implemented in the original release of the Windows XP Professional operating system? In your opinion, which of the SD^3 principles was implemented least successfully?

3. Which of the following techniques could be a component of a defense-in-depth approach to protect against the possibility of a buffer overflow in an optional component of an application? (Choose all that apply.)

   a. Not installing the optional component by default

   b. Building the application using the .NET Framework

   c. Using peer code reviews to identify unchecked buffers in code before the software is released to customers

   d. Implementing a process for efficiently creating, releasing, and deploying patches to vulnerable systems after a vulnerability is discovered

   e. Training developers in proper coding techniques to reduce the possibility of buffer overflows

   f. Providing error messages to end users that include detailed descriptions of failures

4. In retrospect, how would you have designed the last application you developed differently if you were using defense-in-depth?

Lesson Summary

- Defense-in-depth protects against vulnerabilities caused by human error by providing multiple layers of protection.

- Microsoft developers use the SD^3 strategy to implement defense-in-depth: secure by design, secure by default, and secure in deployment.

- The secure by design security tenet dictates the use of security features, secure coding techniques, and secure application design concepts to prevent vulnerabilities.

- The secure by default security tenet reduces the risk of vulnerabilities by installing an application in its most secure configuration by default.

- Applications that are secure in deployment provide methods for administrators to monitor the application for attacks and patch against known security vulnerabilities. Additionally, the application should handle failures without revealing unnecessary information to potential attackers.

Lesson 3: Accessing Resources with Least Privilege

When I visit my bank, I am allowed to enter the lobby and talk to a teller. However, I am not allowed to walk behind the counter. In fact, a locked door prevents customers from entering the area where the bank tellers work.

It's OK that my access is restricted, because I don't need to go behind the counter. The bank tellers do, though, so they are given a key to enter that area. Even the bank tellers don't have unrestricted access to the bank, however. The bank's vault is accessible only to a manager. This restriction is for the tellers' safety, because a thief won't bother to ask them to enter the vault. They simply don't have access.

Banks use the principle of least privilege to reduce the risk of theft. Each role— customer, teller, and manager—has the minimum privileges necessary to carry out their tasks. If customers were allowed directly into the bank vault, there's a good chance that a thief would steal something valuable. If tellers had access to the vault, thieves would use their access to steal the vault's contents. Similarly, if users are allowed unrestricted access to an operating system and application, it's very likely that an attacker will abuse that privilege.

Applications that are designed for least privilege do not require administrator rights to run. This allows users to run your application by using a standard user account. This increases your application's defense-in-depth, because if your application is exploited, the damage that can be done is minimized by the user's limited privileges.

After this lesson, you will be able to

- Explain why application developers should implement the principle of least privilege.
- Describe best practices for writing code to use the least privilege principle.
- Determine appropriate levels of privilege for accessing resources.
- Isolate privileges that your applications require, but that a standard user account lacks.

Estimated lesson time: 60 minutes

Why You Should Use Least Privilege

Many security-conscious users willingly restrict their own privileges to make an attacker less likely to abuse their access level by corrupting system components. The simplest way to restrict your privileges is to log on to the operating system using a user account that is not a member of the Administrators group. You've no doubt seen this practice recommended before, but if you tried it, you probably discovered that it is not as simple as it sounds.

Many applications attempt to perform functions that require administrator privileges. When you attempt to use these applications while logged on as a standard user, the application fails. As a result, users need to run the application using administrator privileges. If the application is compromised while it has administrator privileges, it can do far more damage than if it were restricted to standard user privileges. For example, an administrator could replace key system files with files containing a virus, whereas a standard user would not be allowed to overwrite those files.

Guidelines for Writing Code to Use the Least Privilege Principle

You can provide an additional layer of protection for your application by designing Windows Forms applications to run using only standard user privileges, and by encouraging users to not run the application as an administrator. If a vulnerability is discovered in your application, the potential damage an exploit can do is limited to the restricted rights the user has to the system. If you are creating an ASP.NET application or a Windows service, design your application to run in the context of a standard user with customized privileges rather than in the context of the System account.

Off the Record   You can't blame developers for writing applications that can't be run by a standard user. After all, it's only in the last few years that logging on to Windows computers with standard user accounts has become common practice. If every single one of your customers was logging on as an Administrator, and nobody complained about not being able to run your application as a user, wouldn't adding features be a better way to spend your time than using least privilege? Today, however, there's no excuse for not using least privilege, because everyone *should* be logging on as a standard user.

Follow these two rules to use the principle of least privilege:

1. Do not request more access to resources than necessary.

2. Create new files and registry values in locations that standard users have rights to edit.

If you are going to read a file, request only read access. If you are going to read a registry value, there is no need to request access to update the registry. This is less of a problem when using the .NET Framework than it was with different development environments, because the .NET Framework provides specialized classes for reading resources, and it is less tempting to simply request maximum permissions every time you access a resource.

Any time you need to create registry values, files, or other resources, store these resources in locations that are available to all users. Specifically, create registry values in the HKEY_CURRENT_USER hive, and not the HKEY_LOCAL_MACHINE hive. Files should be created within the user's My Documents folder, or stored under C:\Program Files\. However, files should not be created in the Windows or Systems folders, because those resources do not allow files to be edited by members of the Users group.

See Also   Isolated storage is the preferred location for storing files that will be accessed only by your application. For more information about isolated storage, see Chapter 4, "Taking Advantage of Platform Security."

If you develop and debug new applications using a standard user account, it will be obvious when you fail to use these guidelines because the .NET Framework will throw a security exception. If you cannot change your application to require fewer permissions, you do have the option of changing permissions on the computer on which the application will be deployed. As you debug the permission problems, document the changes that are required for privileges and ACLs so that you can either make the necessary changes during the setup procedure or inform end users of the changes required.

Even if you are the original developer, identifying every privilege and resource required by an existing application can be very challenging. For example, the application might require access to Dynamic Link Libraries (DLLs) located in the system directory, or the application might call an external resource that attempts to write temporary files to the system folder. The more lines of code in the application, the more time required to identify the privilege changes necessary to a standard user account.

Guidelines for Determining Appropriate Levels of Privilege

Even if your application requires permissions that members of the Users group lack, do not instruct users to run the application as an administrator. Members of the Administrators group have several additional privileges and greater rights to files, registry values, and other resources. However, these permissions can be granted to any group or any user account. Any application can be run by a non-Administrator once you understand the permissions required and have granted those permissions to a user account.

To understand how to assign permissions to a user account at a granular level, you must understand the various types of permissions that can be granted to a user. Permissions to access resources, such as files, registry values, and printers, are controlled by using an ACL. The ACL lists users and groups and the permissions each has to the resource.

For example, Figure 1-9 shows that the Power Users group appears in the ACL for the Boot.ini file and has Read and Read & Execute permissions. Because Power Users lack the Modify permission, members of that group cannot edit the Boot.ini file. The Users group does not appear at all, which prevents standard Users from either viewing or editing the file—a good thing, since malicious software could edit the file to take control of the computer the next time it starts. Both Administrators and SYSTEM have Full Control over the file, which enables Administrators to change the computer's startup configuration.

Figure 1-9   Using Explorer to view the Boot.ini file's ACL

ACLs control a user's access to system resources, and privileges control a user's access to important system APIs. For example, only users with the *SeShutdownPrivilege* are allowed to turn the computer off. If your application turns the computer off, the user running the application must have that privilege or the .NET Framework throws an exception. Members of the Administrators group do have this privilege by default, but Users on computers running Windows Server 2003 lack this privilege. However, this does not mean that users must be members of the Administrators group to run an application that shuts down the computer—it means that users must be granted *SeShutdownPrivilege* to run the application. Understanding the distinction is important: group memberships can be used to grant privileges, but privileges can also be granted directly to users and groups without changing group memberships.

Controlling user privileges is a task best left to the system administrator responsible for managing your application. However, it is the developer's responsibility to inform system administrators what privileges and ACLs must be modified to allow a standard user to run an application. You can examine and edit privileges on the local computer by following this process:

1. Log on to your computer as an administrator.

2. Click Start, click Administrative Tools, and then click Local Security Policy.

3. Expand Local Policies, and then click User Rights Assignment.

   The Local Security Settings console

   displays a list of all user rights assignments in the right pane, as shown in Figure 1-10.

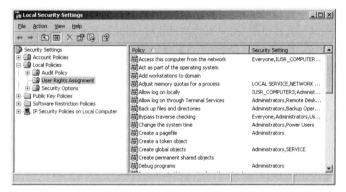

Figure 1-10   The Local Security Settings console displaying user rights assignments

4. In the right pane, double-click any policy to examine or edit the memberships.

> **See Also**   For information about programmatically controlling ACLs, see Chapter 4. For information about programmatically examining user privileges, see Chapter 5.

An alternative to adjusting ACLs and privileges is to prompt the user for administrators' credentials when additional privileges are required, and use impersonation to temporarily gain elevated rights while running code that requires higher privileges than a standard user has. Although providing administrator credentials would be too cumbersome for tasks that users performed constantly, impersonation is useful when building rarely used management functions.

For example, consider a human resources application that is typically used by standard users but that requires elevated privileges when new user accounts are added. When a new employee is added, your application should prompt the user for credentials that show permission to add users immediately before creating the user account. If an attacker accesses the application while it is running as a standard user, the attacker will be prevented from creating a new user account—often one of the first tasks an attacker will attempt.

> **See Also** For more information about impersonating users, see Chapter 9, "Hardening ASP .NET Applications."

The Process of Isolating Missing Privileges

Fortunately, Windows 2000, Windows XP, and Windows Server 2003 each include auditing capabilities that add an event to the Security event log each time a resource is accessed with insufficient permissions. Identifying the source of authorization problems using auditing is complex, but auditing will identify insufficient privileges that would be nearly impossible to find debugging code line by line. The flow chart in Figure 1-11 shows the authorization troubleshooting process that occurs when you use auditing.

> **Off the Record** Most people think of auditing as solely an intrusion detection mechanism. In reality, its usefulness for intrusion detection is limited because it tends to generate far too many events to successfully parse. However, it is immensely useful when troubleshooting authorization problems.

Most of the troubleshooting process is self-explanatory, but enabling system auditing, enabling resource auditing, and analyzing events by using Event Viewer deserve further explanation.

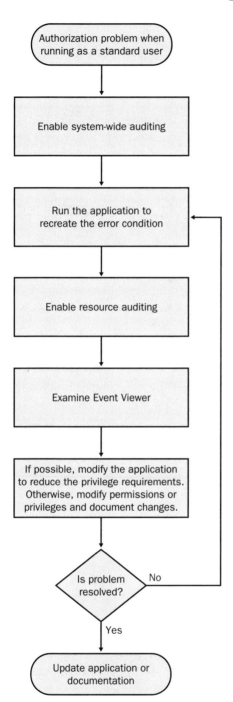

Figure 1-11   Using auditing to identify authorization problems

How to Enable System Auditing

The first step in identifying resources with insufficient privileges is to enable auditing on a system-wide basis:

1. Log on to your computer using an administrator account.

2. Click Start, and then click Administrative Tools. If this is a domain member or a stand-alone computer, click Local Security Policy. If this is a domain controller, click Domain Controller Security Policy.

3. Expand Local Policies, and then click Audit Policy.

4. If you are troubleshooting access to Active Directory objects, double-click Audit Directory Service Access. If you are troubleshooting access to any other type of object, double-click Audit Object Access.

5. Make note of the current setting. You will return this setting to its original state after you complete the troubleshooting process.

6. Select Define These Policy Settings, and then select Failure, as shown in Figure 1-12. Click OK.

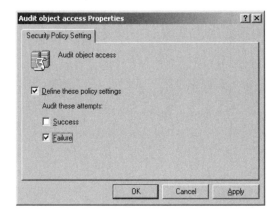

Figure 1-12   Enabling auditing

How to Enable Resource Auditing

After enabling failure auditing for the Audit Object Access or Audit Directory Services Access policies, you must enable auditing for the individual resources that are being accessed. The exact process varies depending on the type of object you want to audit. The following process applies to enabling auditing for folders or files, the most common source of authorization problems. The process for auditing other types of objects is very similar, although you will use a different tool for each object.

1. Click Start, point to All Programs, point to Accessories, and then click Windows Explorer.

2. Navigate to the file or folder you want to audit. If you are not sure which object is being accessed, you can enable auditing for entire disks.

3. Right-click the file or folder, and then click Properties.

> **Tip** If you were auditing the registry, you would open the Registry Editor, right-click the registry key, and then select Permissions.

4. On the Security tab, click the Advanced button.

5. In the Advanced Security Settings dialog box, click the Auditing tab. Make note of the current settings, and then click Add.

6. In the Select User Or Group dialog box, type the name of the user account you are using to debug the application, and then click OK. The Auditing Entry dialog box appears.

7. Select the Failed check box for the Full Control entry, as shown in Figure 1-13. All Failed check boxes will be automatically selected.

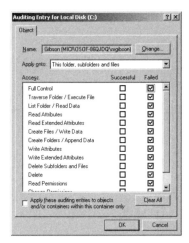

Figure 1-13 Enabling resource failure auditing

8. Click OK twice. Windows will apply the auditing setting to the folder, subfolder, and files automatically. If you are applying access to a large number of files, such as the entire C drive, this can take a moment.

9. Click OK to close the properties dialog box and return to Windows Explorer.

Now that failure auditing is enabled for those resources, every time the specified user is denied access to the resource, Windows will add an event to the security event log.

How to Analyze Events in Event Viewer

After you enable auditing and re-create the problem condition, Windows adds events to the Security event log that describe which resource could not be accessed and the type of operation that was attempted. To view failure audit events by using Event Viewer:

1. Log on to your computer using an administrator account.

2. Click Start, click Administrative Tools, and then click Event Viewer.

3. In the left pane, click Security. The Security event log will be displayed.

4. On the View menu, click Filter. The Security Properties dialog box appears.

5. Clear the Information, Warning, Error, and Success Audit check boxes. Only the Failure Audit check box should remain selected. Click OK.

6. Event Viewer will now display only failure audits in the right pane. Double-click the most recent failure audit to examine the contents of the event. The Event Properties dialog box appears, as shown in Figure 1-14.

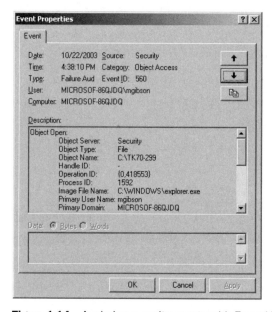

Figure 1-14   Analyzing security events with Event Viewer

7. Examine the Description box. This box shows the type of object, the object name, the process ID and image filename of the application used to access the object, and the type of operation that was performed on the object. For example, the following are the contents of the Description box for a user, mgibson, who was denied access to the C:\TK70-330 folder when she attempted to access the folder using Windows Explorer.

```
Object Open:
 Object Server:Security
 Object Type:File
 Object Name:C:\TK70-330
 Handle ID:-
 Operation ID:{0,419122}
 Process ID:1592
 Image File Name:C:\WINDOWS\explorer.exe
 Primary User Name:mgibson
 Primary Domain:MICROSOF-86QJDQ
 Primary Logon ID:(0x0,0x60641)
 Client User Name:-
 Client Domain:-
 Client Logon ID:-
 Accesses:SYNCHRONIZE
ReadData (or ListDirectory)
Privileges:-
 Restricted Sid Count:0
 Access Mask:0x100001
```

Notice that the *Accesses* line lists *Synchronize* and *ReadData*. This indicates that the application was attempting to gain read access to the C:\TK70-330 directory. To resolve this problem, you would either modify the application so that it no longer requires the right to read the directory, or you would document the fact that system administrators deploying your application need to make one of the following changes:

❑ Modify the folder's ACL to grant the user (or a group to which the user belongs) read access to that folder.

❑ Add the user to a group that already has read access to the folder.

8. Browse through other failure audit events to determine other resources to which the user might require access.

After identifying the resources the user requires access to and assigning new permissions, repeat the troubleshooting process by re-creating the problem.

Practice: Updating an Application to Use Least Privilege

In this practice, you will test a simple application as both an administrator and a standard user account. You will then debug any problems accessing resources as a standard user. Complete Exercises 1 through 3 and then answer the questions in Exercise 4.

Exercise 1: Running Code as an Administrator

In this exercise, you will test a simple application to determine whether it is capable of running using the Administrator account.

1. Use the Administrator user account to log on to your test computer.

2. Use Windows Explorer to copy the MostPrivileges folder and its contents to the C:\Program Files\MostPrivileges\ folder on your test computer.

3. In Windows Explorer, select the C:\Program Files\MostPrivileges\ folder, and then double-click MostPrivileges.csproj.

   Visual Studio .NET 2003 will open the project.

4. On the Standard toolbar, verify that the Release configuration is selected. Click the Debug menu, and then click Start Without Debugging.

   Visual Studio will compile and launch the application, which will display the contents of your Hosts file, as shown in Figure 1-15.

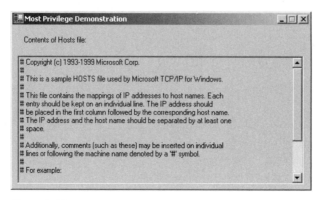

Figure 1-15   MostPrivileges running successfully

5. Close MostPrivileges, and then close Visual Studio. Remain logged on as Administrator.

Exercise 2: Running Code as a User

In this exercise, you will test a simple application to determine whether it is capable of running using a standard user account.

1. While logged on as Administrator, click Start, click Administrative Tools, and then click Computer Management.

2. Expand Local Users And Groups, and then click Users.

3. Right-click Users, and then click New User.

4. In the User Name box, type **Regular User**.

5. In the Password and Confirm Password boxes, type a complex password.

6. Clear the User Must Change Password At Next Logon check box, and then click Create.

7. Click Close, and then close the Computer Management console.

8. Log off Windows.

9. Log on to your test computer with the Regular User account you created.

10. Use Windows Explorer to navigate to the folder C:\Program Files\MostPrivileges\bin\Release. Double-click MostPrivileges.exe.

The MostPrivileges application launches and shows an error message, as shown in Figure 1-16.

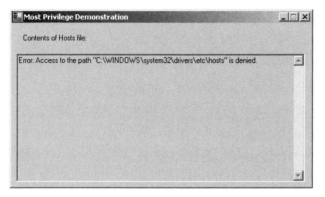

Figure 1-16   MostPrivileges without sufficient permissions

11. Use Windows Explorer to navigate to the folder   C:\Windows\System32\Drivers\Etc.

12. Right-click Hosts, and then click Properties.

13. Click the Security tab.

As shown in Figure 1-17, the Users group has only Read and Read & Execute permissions to the Hosts file. This should be enough for the MostPrivileges application to run correctly, however, because the application displays only the contents of the file.

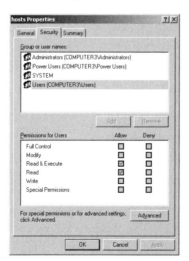

Figure 1-17   Default permissions assigned to the Hosts file

14. Click OK, and then log off Windows.

Exercise 3: Updating the Application to Use Least Privilege

In this exercise, you will update the sample application so that it uses least privilege and will run while logged on as a standard user. Then, you will test it to verify that it runs correctly.

1. Use the Administrator user account to log on to your test computer.

2. In Windows Explorer, select the C:\Program Files\MostPrivileges\ folder, and then double-click MostPrivileges.csproj.

   Visual Studio .NET 2003 will open the project.

3. Modify line 36 so that the file is opened with only the Read file access method.

   Before modification, the line reads:

   ```
   FileStream hostsFile=File.Open(hostsPath,FileMode.Open,FileAccess.ReadWrite);
   ```

   Using *FileAccess.ReadWrite* allows the application to both read and write to the file as needed. This permission might occasionally be required. However, since this application only displays the contents of the Hosts file, it is unnecessary to request both read and write access. Modify the line so that it requests only read access. After modification, the line should read:

   ```
   FileStream hostsFile = File.Open(hostsPath, FileMode.Open, FileAccess.Read);
   ```

> **Design**   As you probably noticed, this application does not use the most efficient method for reading a text file. In fact, I had to go to great lengths to request excess access for this demonstration. The structure of the .NET Framework encourages developers to use least privilege.

4. Click the Build menu, and then click Build Solution.

5. Log off Windows.

6. Log on to your test computer with the Regular User account you created.

7. Use Windows Explorer to navigate to the folder C:\Program Files\MostPrivileges\bin\Release. Double-click MostPrivileges.exe.

   The MostPrivileges application launches and shows the contents of the Hosts file. This version of the application runs correctly because the application requests read access to the Hosts file, and members of the Users group have the Read permission. The previous version did not work because the application requested both read and write access. Even though the application did not attempt to write to the file, the .NET Framework generated an exception when the application requested access.

Security Alert   The fact that administrators have access to edit the Hosts file is an excellent reason to not log on as an administrator. If you were to unknowingly run a virus or Trojan horse while logged on as an administrator, the malicious software could modify your Hosts file without your knowledge. Modifications to the Hosts file override DNS lookups by any application. Therefore, the malicious software can perform a man-in-the-middle attack by adding an entry to your Hosts file with the host name of a legitimate server and the IP address of a malicious server. The next time you attempted to initiate a connection to your server, your traffic would be sent to the malicious IP address. For example, adding the following line to your Hosts file would redirect all traffic destined for *www.microsoft.com* to *192.168.1.100*:

```
192.168.1.100 www.microsoft.com
```

Exercise 4: Reflecting on Updating an Application to Use Least Privilege

Answer the following questions. If you are unable to answer a question, review the lesson materials and try the question again. You can find answers to the questions in the "Questions and Answers" section at the end of this chapter.

1. In Exercises 1 through 3, you explored an application that did not work correctly when the user was logged on as an administrator. Besides modifying the application, how else could you have resolved the problem? What drawbacks would that approach have?

2. Least privilege provides which of the following benefits? (Choose the best answer.)

   a. Enables standard users to debug your application line by line

   b. Grants standard users access to the Security event log

   c. Allows your application to run with minimal privileges

   d. Provides standard users access to the .NET Framework

Lesson Summary

- Develop applications using a standard user account to identify resources and privileges your application requires that standard users lack access to.

- If your application requires more privileges than provided by the standard user account, you can either provide system administrators deploying your application with instructions to modify ACLs and grant additional privileges, or give administrators the option of automatically performing those changes during the setup process.

- Use auditing and the Event Viewer to identify required privileges that a user lacks.

Lab: Implementing Best Practices for Designing Secure Applications

Read the following scenario and then complete the exercise that follows. If you are unable to answer a question, review the lessons and try the question again. You can find answers to the questions in the "Questions and Answers" section at the end of this chapter.

Scenario

You have spent the last five years employed as an internal application developer in the information technology department of an enterprise health care company. Employees throughout your organization use the application you developed to manage subscriber benefit information. Although it was not originally designed with security in mind, your application is a portal for extremely sensitive information, including medical details about your subscribers.

You've had quiet times and busy weeks in the last five years, but management has never made security a priority—until last week, when a temporary employee in the West coast office discovered that he could use your application to view any subscriber's personal information. Fortunately for you, he bragged about his hacking skills to another temp, who reported his acts to management. Your company's human resources team questioned him at length, and he revealed that he used a SQL injection attack that he read about on the Internet to allow normally restricted database queries to return records for all subscribers. Instead of typing in a social security number into a box, the temp typed a value such as ' **OR TRUE** --. Your application then provided a list of every single subscriber record.

Your Chief Information Officer asks you to provide guidance regarding preventing security vulnerabilities in the applications you develop. You decide to examine your code, perform some interviews, and review legal and technical requirements before you meet with him again.

Results of the Code Examination

After examining your code, you realized that the vulnerability existed because you placed user input directly into a SQL query. The temp simply had to type his own *WHERE* clause into the social security number box to gain unrestricted access to subscriber records.

Interviews

Following is a list of company personnel interviewed and their statements:

- **Public relations** "Wow. If news of this gets out, we'd have subscribers dropping left and right. Our stock would drop like a rock. It would take years to win back the trust of our subscribers."

- **Legal** "Government regulations require us to carefully control access to subscriber information. This is a direct violation of those regulations. We are liable for hundreds of thousands of dollars."

- **IT Manager** "You told us you were a good programmer when we hired you. Why would you do this? I really need you to try harder, or be smarter, or something. We can never again have a security vulnerability."

- **Chief Information Officer** "This is unacceptable, but it's not entirely your fault. Your manager should have put you through security training and implemented code review processes. We'll keep you around, but this better not happen again."

Legal Requirements

These are the legal requirements:

- Your organization must make reasonable efforts, in accordance with commonly accepted business practices, to protect subscriber information.

- To control liability, your code and application must be reviewed by an outside organization.

Technical Requirements

These are the technical requirements:

- Development of new features is on hold indefinitely.

- One hundred percent of your time will be dedicated to improving the security of your application.

- Existing application functionality must be retained, but users can tolerate some additional inconvenience for improved security.

Exercise

Questions

Answer the following questions.

1. The discovery of the security vulnerability has shaken your manager's confidence in you. What changes to your current development process can you suggest to prevent vulnerabilities from appearing in the future?

2. How can you guarantee that no security vulnerability will occur in the future?

3. Which of the following infrastructure components could prevent similar SQL injection attacks in the future? (Choose the best answer.)

   a. A firewall in front of the database server

   b. IPSec encryption enabled between all clients and the database server

   c. IDS monitoring authentication attempts for password-cracking attacks

   d. None of the above

4. How can you use least privilege to reduce the likelihood of a similar exploit happening in the future?

5. Which of the following secure in deployment principles would limit damage from similar SQL injection attacks in the future? (Choose all that apply.)

   a. An efficient process for deploying updates

   b. An effective monitoring system that detects attempted break-ins

   c. Error messages that reveal no private information to potential attackers

   d. None of the above

Chapter Summary

- Attackers can use a wide variety of attacks to compromise a vulnerable application, including buffer overflows, parsing errors, capturing network communications, cryptography hacking, denial-of-service attacks, man-in-the-middle attacks, and password cracking.

- Defense-in-depth protects against vulnerabilities caused by human error by providing multiple layers of protection. There are three defense-in-depth security tenets that Microsoft recommends for application developers:

  - The secure by design security tenet, which dictates the use of security features, secure coding techniques, and secure application design concepts to prevent vulnerabilities.

❑ The secure by default security tenet, which reduces the risk of vulnerabilities by installing an application in its most secure configuration by default.

❑ The secure in deployment security tenet, which provides methods for administrators to monitor the application for attacks and patch against known security vulnerabilities. Additionally, the application should handle failures without revealing unnecessary information to potential attackers.

■ Develop applications using a standard user account to identify resources and privileges your application requires that standard users lack access to. If your application requires more privileges than provided by the standard user account, you can either provide system administrators deploying your application with instructions to modify ACLs and grant additional privileges, or give administrators the option of automatically performing those changes during the setup process.

Exam Highlights

Before taking the exam, review the key points and terms that are presented in this chapter. You need to know this information.

Key Points

■ The reasons applications have security vulnerabilities

■ The need for defense-in-depth, and why it is effective

■ Security features that can limit the risk of vulnerabilities

■ The benefits of using least privilege

■ How to troubleshoot problems implementing least privilege

Key Terms

buffer overflow   An attack in which the attacker submits user input that is longer than the application was designed to process

canonicalization attack   An attack that takes advantage of special characters that the operating system uses to identify filenames

defense-in-depth   A technique for reducing the risk associated with potential vulnerabilities by providing multiple, redundant layers of protection

exploits   A successful attack that uses a vulnerability to expose private information, gain elevated privileges, or deny legitimate users of a service

vulnerability   A security weakness in an application that can be exploited by an attacker

Questions and Answers

Page
1-15

Practice: Evaluating Security Threats

1. An application on the Internet that does not require authentication would potentially be vulnerable to which of the following types of attacks? (Choose all that apply.)

   a. Buffer overflows

   b. Parsing errors

   c. Denial-of-service attacks

   d. Man-in-the-middle attacks

   e. Compromising communications

   f. Password cracking

   The answers are a, b, c, d, and e. The Web application would be vulnerable to every type of attack discussed in this lesson except for password cracking. Because the application does not offer the opportunity for an attacker to attempt to authenticate, password cracking cannot be attempted. Note, however, that default virtual directories requiring authentication might have been configured when IIS was installed. An attacker could submit requests to one of these default directories to perform a brute force or dictionary attack and determine valid passwords.

2. You created a Windows forms application that runs on a kiosk in a shopping mall to gather the name, address, and other demographic information from shoppers. The information is stored within a SQL Server database on the same computer. Your application is potentially vulnerable to which of the following types of attacks? (Choose all that apply.)

   a. Buffer overflows

   b. Parsing errors

   c. Denial-of-service attacks

   d. Man-in-the-middle attacks

   e. Compromising communications

   f. Password cracking

   The answers are a, b, and c. Your application accepts user input, which makes it potentially vulnerable to buffer overflows, parsing errors, and denial-of-service attacks. Because your application does not communicate over a network, it is not vulnerable to man-in-the-middle attacks or compromised communications. In addition to the potential vulnerabilities introduced by your application, the computer hardware and operating system might be vulnerable to other types of attacks, such as theft and vandalism.

3. Which of the following types of attacks can lead to private information being compromised? (Choose the best answer.)

    a. Buffer overflows

    b. Parsing errors

    c. Denial-of-service attacks

    d. Man-in-the-middle attacks

    e. Compromising communications

    f. Password cracking

The answers are a, b, d, e, and f. With the exception of denial-of-service attacks, any of the attacks discussed in this lesson can be used to compromise private information.

4. Think back to the last application you developed. Theoretically, which types of attacks could that application have been vulnerable to? Of those potential vulnerabilities, which do you feel you were sufficiently protected against? Did you use defense-in-depth, secure coding practices, or other techniques to limit your risk?

Answers will vary.

Page 1-33

Practice: Implementing Best Practices to Design Secure Applications

1. Which of the following best describes the concept of defense-in-depth? (Choose the best answer.)

    a. Using multiple layers of firewalls to protect an application

    b. Dividing an application into separate tiers for the front end, application, and database

    c. Providing a path for escalating problems relating to known security vulnerabilities by first notifying a security engineer, and then notifying a higher level of management until executive management is asked to address the vulnerability

    d. Using various security techniques to protect against a single potential vulnerability

The answer is d. Defense-in-depth is a multi-layered, "belt-and-suspenders" approach to protecting against vulnerabilities that relies on multiple levels of protection for a single potential vulnerability.

2. How is each of the SD^3 principles implemented in the original release of the Windows XP Professional operating system? In your opinion, which of the SD^3 principles was implemented least successfully?

Windows XP Professional does an excellent job of implementing secure by design, with key features such as the ability to use least privilege, the Internet Connection Firewall, and the Encrypting File System. The automatic updates feature in Windows XP is a good example of the secure in deployment tenet. However, none of these features are enabled by default. Therefore, the secure by default principle could have been followed more closely. It's worth noting that implementing secure by default would have made Windows XP a less user-friendly operating system, because many key features would not have been immediately available to users when they first started their computers.

3. Which of the following techniques could be a component of a defense-in-depth approach to protect against the possibility of a buffer overflow in an optional component of an application? (Choose all that apply.)

   a. Not installing the optional component by default

   b. Building the application using the .NET Framework

   c. Using peer code reviews to identify unchecked buffers in code before the software is released to customers

   d. Implementing a process for efficiently creating, releasing, and deploying patches to vulnerable systems after a vulnerability is discovered

   e. Training developers in proper coding techniques to reduce the possibility of buffer overflows

   f. Providing error messages to end users that include detailed descriptions of failures

   The answers are a, b, c, d, and e. Each of these techniques is a valid way to implement defense-in-depth except for providing detailed error messages to end users. Recording detailed information about errors is important, but the details of the error should be treated as confidential, and stored where only administrators have access to it.

4. In retrospect, how would you have designed the last application you developed differently if you were using defense-in-depth?

   Answers will vary.

Practice: Updating an Application to Use Least Privilege

Page
1-50

Exercise 4: Reflecting on Updating an Application to Use Least Privilege

1. In Exercises 1 through 3, you explored an application that did not work correctly when the user was logged on as an administrator. Besides modifying the application, how else could you have resolved the problem? What drawbacks would that approach have?

One alternative approach would be to modify the ACL on the Hosts file. This could be done directly, during the setup procedure for the application, or manually by the systems administrator installing your application. This approach would allow the application to run correctly, but it permanently reduces the security of the computer. After modifying the ACL, any application (including a virus or Trojan horse) could modify the Hosts file.

A second approach is to create a shortcut to your application, and instruct the user to select the Run With Different Credentials check box on the shortcut's properties. When the user runs the application, he is prompted to provide an alternative set of user credentials. The user can then provide administrator credentials, or can authenticate as a user specifically created to have the necessary privileges required to run your application. This approach does not follow the application development principle of least privilege, however, because the application still requires elevated privileges.

Another approach would be to make the user running the application a member of the Administrators group. However, this approach does not follow the security principle of least privilege. Indeed, any application the user ran would have almost unlimited access to system resources.

2. Least privilege provides which of the following benefits? (Choose the best answer.)

a. Enables standard users to debug your application line by line

b. Grants standard users access to the Security event log

c. Allows your application to run with minimal privileges

d. Provides standard users access to the .NET Framework

The answer is c. Least privilege reduces the damage an attacker can do after compromising your application by minimizing the rights required by your application.

Lab: Implementing Best Practices for Designing Secure Applications

Page
1-52

Exercise

1. The discovery of the security vulnerability has shaken your manager's confidence in you. What changes to your current development process can you suggest to prevent vulnerabilities from appearing in the future?

First, assure your manager that you will take extra time to use secure coding best practices. Additionally, you should suggest that your organization begin to use defense-in-depth. The multi-layered approach to security will help prevent vulnerabilities from being exploited, even if you do make a mistake.

All development projects should have time for code review. Additionally, database permissions should be restricted carefully. Employees should have permission to access only those parts of the database actually required to do their job.

2. How can you guarantee that no security vulnerability will occur in the future?

Unfortunately, you can't guarantee this. Instead, you must manage the risk. Managers must acknowledge that some risk always exists because developers are human and make mistakes.

3. Which of the following infrastructure components could prevent similar SQL injection attacks in the future? (Choose the best answer.)

   a. A firewall in front of the database server

   b. IPSec encryption enabled between all clients and the database server

   c. IDS monitoring authentication attempts for password-cracking attacks

   d. None of the above

The answer is d. None of these infrastructure components can prevent a SQL injection attack. The attack manipulates otherwise legitimate user queries, and as a result, cannot be filtered by a firewall.

4. How can you use least privilege to reduce the likelihood of a similar exploit happening in the future?

You can carefully analyze and document the privilege requirements for different types of users, and then restrict database permission to not allow users access to more than they need.

5. Which of the following secure in deployment principles would limit damage from similar SQL injection attacks in the future? (Choose all that apply.)

   a. An efficient process for deploying updates

   b. An effective monitoring system that detects attempted break-ins

   c. Error messages that reveal no private information to potential attackers

   d. None of the above

The answers are a and b. The attacker probably tried several different queries before succeeding. An effective monitoring system could have detected these attempted attacks and notified system administrators before the attacker succeeded. Even if the administrators could not respond until after the attack was successful, they could have acted quickly to control damage. After the vulnerability was discovered, an efficient update process would allow you to patch and fix the application quickly.

2 Using Secure Coding Best Practices

Why This Chapter Matters

Although defense-in-depth is a complex subject, you can prevent many security vulnerabilities by simply using secure coding best practices. Most importantly, applications must thoroughly validate all user input. This chapter provides general guidelines for validating many different types of input, as well as detailed specifications for preventing common types of attacks. It is time-consuming to write and maintain the additional code required to validate input, but the level of protection this provides against attacks cannot be duplicated by firewalls, intrusion detection systems, or other security mechanisms.

Security is an ongoing process. After you write the application, systems administrators are responsible for maintaining it. Administrators must be able to both troubleshoot problems and detect potential attacks. Providing administrators with the detailed information they need can be challenging, especially when you consider the importance of *not* sharing information about the application's inner workings with potential attackers. This chapter also gives guidelines for reporting errors without introducing additional vulnerabilities.

Exam Objectives in this Chapter:

- Validate external input at every boundary level to prevent security problems.
    - ❏ Write code to test strings by using regular expressions.
    - ❏ Write code to test the size of data.
    - ❏ Write code to prevent SQL injection and cross-site scripting.
- Write code to prevent canonicalization problems.
    - ❏ Create canonical references for resources.
    - ❏ Validate that a reference is canonical.
- Write code that addresses failures in a manner than does not compromise security.
    - ❏ Create error messages that do not compromise security.

Lessons in this Chapter:

Before You Begin

To complete the practices and lab exercises in this chapter, you must have one computer running Microsoft Windows Server 2003. During the course of performing the exercises in this chapter, the computer's security can be reduced. Therefore, the computer should not be a production computer and should not be connected to any network, especially the Internet, even if a firewall is present. Use the Manage Your Server tool to add the Application Server role, and enable both FrontPage Server Extensions and ASP.NET. Then, install Visual Studio .NET 2003 using the default settings. Finally, install Microsoft SQL Server 2000 configured to use the System account, Windows authentication, and processor licensing.

Lesson 1: Validating Input

Treat all input as hostile. All input, whether received directly from a user or from another application, must go through a three-step validation process before being considered safe by your application. This lesson describes techniques for implementing each of these three phases in your application:

1. **Constrain**   Reject input unless it meets your expectations for type, length, format, and range.

2. **Reject**   Reject input that meets the constraining requirements and contains known malicious values and phrases.

3. **Sanitize**   Filter out characters nested within input that might have a special meaning when processed by your application or end users.

Figure 2-1 shows the input validation process.

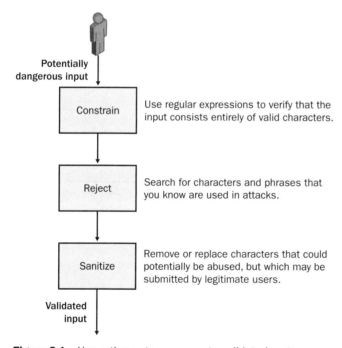

Figure 2-1   Use a three-step process to validate input.

After this lesson, you will be able to

- Constrain most invalid input by allowing only valid formats, types, lengths, and ranges.
- Reject malicious input by examining input for specific characters and phrases.
- Sanitize valid input that contains characters that have the potential to interrupt normal application processing.

Estimated lesson time: 35 minutes

Guidelines for Constraining Input

Start the input validation process by constraining input and checking for known good data by validating for type, length, format, and range. There are several different techniques for validating data, including using regular expressions, strong types, ASP.NET validator controls, typed data expressions, and the *String.Length* property. Use regular expressions to constrain string input, or use the *String.Length* property when you are only checking the length. Use strong types to constrain input other than strings, such as numbers and dates, and use typed data comparisons to limit their range. When creating a Web application, use regular expressions to validate input without writing code by using ASP.NET validator controls.

Options for Constraining Data

Table 2-1 summarizes the options that are available for constraining and sanitizing data.

Table 2-1   Options for Constraining Data

Data Checks	Validation Technique
Type checks	■ Strong types ■ Regular expressions ■ ASP.NET validator controls
Length checks	■ Regular expressions ■ *String.Length* property
Format checks	■ Strong types ■ Regular expressions
Range checks	■ ASP.NET validator controls ■ Typed data comparisons

Use Regular Expressions to Constrain String Input

When building security into your application, regular expressions are the most efficient way to validate user input. If you build an application that accepts a five-digit number from a user, you can use a regular expression to ensure that the input is exactly five characters long and that each character is a number between 0 and 9, inclusive. Similarly, when prompting a user for her first and last name, you can check her input with a regular expression and throw an exception when the input contains numbers, delimiters, or any other non-alphabetic character.

> **Tip** A *regular expression* is a set of characters that can be compared with a string to determine whether the string meets specified format requirements. For example, you can create regular expressions that match strings consisting entirely of integers, strings that contain only lowercase letters, or strings that match hexadecimal input. Regular expressions have been used for decades in tools like the Unix console tool grep, and the scripting language Perl. The .NET Framework also supports regular expressions.

The .NET Framework classes that perform the parsing of regular expressions are contained within the *System.Text.RegularExpressions* assembly. To demonstrate how regular expressions can be used, create a console application named TestRegExp that accepts two strings as input and determines whether the first string (a regular expression) matches the second string. The following console application performs this check, and throws an exception when the input is invalid.

```csharp
using System;
using System.Text.RegularExpressions;

namespace TestRegExp
{
    class Class1
    {
        [STAThread]
        static void Main(string[] args)
        {
            if (Regex.IsMatch(args[1], args[0]))
            {
                Console.WriteLine("Input matches regular expression.");
            }
            else
            {
                Console.WriteLine("Input DOES NOT match regular expression.");
            }
        }
    }
}
```

```vb
Imports System
Imports System.Text.RegularExpressions

Namespace TestRegExp
    Class Class1
        <STAThread> _
        Shared  Sub Main(ByVal args() As String)
            If Regex.IsMatch(args(1),args(0)) Then
                Console.WriteLine("Input matches regular expression.")
            Else
                Console.WriteLine("Input DOES NOT match regular expression.")
            End If
        End Sub
    End Class
End Namespace
```

Next, test the application by determining whether the regular expression "^\d{5}$" matches the string "12345" or "1234". Your output should resemble the following:

```
C:\>TestRegExp ^\d{5}$ 1234
Input DOES NOT match regular expression.

C:\>TestRegExp ^\d{5}$ 12345
Input matches regular expression.
```

The simple TestRegExp application uses regular expressions without declaring any additional variables. However, the *System.Text.RegularExpressions* namespace provides a robust and flexible set of classes.

See Also   For more information about the classes, search for the namespace within MSDN at *http://msdn.microsoft.com/*.

Understanding the syntax is the most complex part of using regular expressions. Table 2-2 contains the complete list of regular expression metacharacters and a detailed description of each. As you read the description of each of the metacharacters, use the TextRegExp application to experiment with how metacharacters can be used to match various types of input.

Characters Used in Regular Expressions

Table 2-2 describes the characters used in regular expressions.

Table 2-2   Characters Used in Regular Expressions

Character	Description
\	Marks the next character as either a special character, a literal, a back reference, or an octal escape. For example, "n" matches the character "n". The sequence "\n" matches a newline character. The sequence "\\" matches "\", and "\(" matches "(".
^	Matches the position at the beginning of the input string. If the *RegExp* object's *Multiline* property is set, "^" also matches the position following "\n" or "\r".
$	Matches the position at the end of the input string. If the *RegExp* object's *Multiline* property is set, "$" also matches the position preceding "\n" or "\r".
*	Matches the preceding character or subexpression, zero or more times. For example, "zo*" matches "z" and "zoo". The "*" character is equivalent to "{0,}".
+	Matches the preceding character or subexpression, one or more times. For example, "zo+" matches "zo" and "zoo", but not "z". The "+" character is equivalent to "{1,}".
?	Matches the preceding character or subexpression, zero or one time. For example, "do(es)?" matches the "do" in "do" or "does". The ? character is equivalent to "{0,1}".
{n}	The n is a non-negative integer. Matches exactly n times. For example, "o{2}" does not match the "o" in "Bob", but does match the two "o"s in "food".
{n,}	The n is a non-negative integer. Matches at least n times. For example, "o{2,}" does not match the "o" in "Bob" but does match all the "o"s in "foooood". The sequence "o{1,}" is equivalent to "o+". The sequence "o{0,}" is equivalent to "o*".
{n,m}	The m and n are non-negative integers, where "n <= m". Matches at least n and at most m times. For example, "o{1,3}" matches the first three "o"s in "fooooood". "o{0,1}" is equivalent to "o?". Note that you cannot put a space between the comma and the numbers.
?	When this character immediately follows any of the other quantifiers (*, +, ?, {n}, {n,}, {n,m}), the matching pattern is non-greedy. A non-greedy pattern matches as little of the searched string as possible, whereas the default greedy pattern matches as much of the searched string as possible. For example, in the string "oooo", "o+?" matches a single "o", whereas "o+" matches all "o"s.
.	Matches any single character except "\n". To match any character including the "\n", use a pattern such as "[\s\S]".

Table 2-2   Characters Used in Regular Expressions

Character	Description
(pattern)	Matches pattern and captures the match. The captured match can be retrieved from the resulting Matches collection, using the SubMatches collection in Microsoft Visual Basic Script (VBScript) or the $0…$9 properties in JScript. To match parentheses characters ( ), use "\(" or "\)".
(?:pattern)	Matches pattern but does not capture the match, that is, it is a non-capturing match that is not stored for possible later use. This is useful for combining parts of a pattern with the "or" character ("|"). For example, "industr(?:y|ies)" is a more economical expression than "industry|industries".
(?=pattern)	Positive lookahead search pattern that matches the search string at any point where a string matching pattern begins. This is a non-capturing match, that is, the match is not captured for possible later use. For example, "Windows (?=95|98|NT|2000)" matches "Windows" in "Windows 2000" but not "Windows" in "Windows 3.1". Lookaheads do not consume characters, that is, after a match occurs, the search for the next match begins immediately following the last match, not after the characters that make up the lookahead.
(?!pattern)	Negative lookahead that matches the search string at any point where a string not-matching pattern begins. This is a non-capturing match, that is, the match is not captured for possible later use. For example, "Windows (?!95|98|NT|2000)" matches "Windows" in "Windows 3.1" but does not match "Windows" in "Windows 2000". Lookaheads do not consume characters, that is, after a match occurs, the search for the next match begins immediately following the last match, not after the characters that make up the lookahead.
x|y	Matches either x or y. For example, "z|food" matches "z" or "food". "(z|f)ood" matches "zood" or "food".
[xyz]	A character set. Matches any one of the enclosed characters. For example, "[abc]" matches the "a" in "plain".
[^xyz]	A negative character set. Matches any character not enclosed. For example, "[^abc]" matches the "p" in "plain".
[a-z]	A range of characters. Matches any character in the specified range. For example, "[a-z]" matches any lowercase alphabetic character in the range "a" through "z".
[^a-z]	A negative range of characters. Matches any character not in the specified range. For example, "[^a-z]" matches any character not in the range "a" through "z".
\b	Matches a word boundary, that is, the position between a word and a space. For example, "er\b" matches the "er" in "never" but not the "er" in "verb".
\B	Matches a nonword boundary. For example, "er\B" matches the "er" in "verb" but not the "er" in "never".

Table 2-2 Characters Used in Regular Expressions

Character	Description
\cx	Matches the control character indicated by *x*. For example, "\cM" matches Control+M, or a carriage return character. The value of x must be in the range of A–Z or a–z. If not, c is assumed to be a literal "c" character.
\d	Matches a digit character. Equivalent to "[0-9]".
\D	Matches a nondigit character. Equivalent to "[^0-9]".
\f	Matches a form-feed character. Equivalent to "\x0c" and "\cL".
\n	Matches a newline character. Equivalent to "\x0a" and "\cJ".
\r	Matches a carriage return character. Equivalent to "\x0d" and "\cM".
\s	Matches any whitespace character including SPACE, TAB, and form-feed. Equivalent to "[\f\n\r\t\v]".
\S	Matches any non-whitespace character. Equivalent to "[^ \f\n\r\t\v]".
\t	Matches a TAB character. Equivalent to "\x09" and "\cI".
\v	Matches a vertical TAB character. Equivalent to "\x0b" and "\cK".
\w	Matches any word character including underscore. Equivalent to "[A-Za-z0-9_]".
\W	Matches any nonword character. Equivalent to "[^A-Za-z0-9_]".
\xn	Matches n, where n is a hexadecimal escape value. Hexadecimal escape values must be exactly two digits long. For example, "\x41" matches "A"; and "\x041" is equivalent to "A1". Allows ASCII codes to be used in regular expressions.
\num	Matches num, where num is a positive integer. A reference back to captured matches. For example, "(.)\1" matches two consecutive identical characters.
\n	Identifies either an octal escape value or a backreference. If "\n" is preceded by at least n captured subexpressions, n is a backreference. Otherwise, n is an octal escape value if n is an octal digit (0–7).
\nm	Identifies either an octal escape value or a backreference. If "\nm" is preceded by at least nm captured subexpressions, nm is a backreference. If "\nm" is preceded by at least n captures, n is a backreference followed by literal m. If neither of the preceding conditions exists, "\nm" matches octal escape value nm when n and m are octal digits (0–7).
\nml	Matches octal escape value nml when n is an octal digit (0–3), and m and l are octal digits (0–7).
\un	Matches n, where n is a Unicode character expressed as four hexadecimal digits. For example, "\u00A9" matches the copyright symbol (©).

Compare each of the metacharacters used in the example code's regular expression, "^\d{5}$", with the metacharacters in Table 2-2. The first character, ^, matches the beginning of the input string. This character is critical. If you remove it, the regular expression "\d{5}$" will still match valid five-digit numbers, such as "12345". However, it will also match the input string "abcd12345" or "' drop table customers -- 12345". In fact, the modified regular expression will match any input string that ends in any five-digit number.

> **Important**   When building an application, forgetting that leading carat can expose a security vulnerability! Use peer code reviews to limit the risk of human error.

The second and third characters, "\d", match numeric characters from 0 through 9. As Table 2-2 points out, the "\d" syntax has exactly the same meaning as "[0-9]". Therefore, you could also write the regular expression "^[0-9]{5}$" to validate that input is a five-digit number.

The fourth, fifth, and sixth characters in the regular expression "{5}" mean the *preceding* symbol must be repeated five times. To match a seven-digit number, you could replace this with "{7}". This can also match a range of repeated values. For example, to verify that input is a three-, four-, or five-digit number, you would use the regular expression "^\d{3,5}$". This would match the values "123" and "1455", but would not match "12" or "12a3".

The last character in the regular expression, "$", matches the end of the input string. If this character is omitted, any characters can follow the matched input. If you remove this character, the regular expression "^\d{5}" will still match valid five-digit numbers, such as "12345". However, it will also match the input string "12345abcd" or "12345' drop table customers --". In fact, the modified regular expression will match any input string that begins in a five-digit number. Figure 2-2 summarizes the analysis of this simple regular expression.

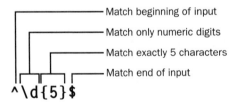

Figure 2-2   Analysis of a regular expression

Security Alert   When validating input, always begin regular expressions with a "^" character and end them with "$". This ensures that input exactly matches the specified regular expression, and does not merely *contain* matching input.

Regular expressions can be used to match complex input patterns, too. The following regular expression matches e-mail addresses:

```
^([\w-\.]+)@((\[[0-9]{1,3}\.[0-9]{1,3}\.[0-9]{1,3}\.)|(([\w-]+\.)+))([a-zA-Z]{2,4}|[0-9]{1,3})(\]?)$
```

Regular expressions are an extremely efficient way to check user input; however, using regular expressions has a downside:

- **Regular expressions are difficult to create unless you are extremely familiar with the format**   If you have years of Perl programming experience, you won't have any problem using regular expressions in C# code. However, if you have a background in Visual Basic scripting, the cryptic format of regular expressions will seem completely illogical.

- **Creating regular expressions *can* be confusing, but reading regular expressions definitely is**   There is a good chance that other programmers will overlook errors in regular expressions when performing a peer code review. The more complex the regular expression, the greater the chance that the structure of the expression contains an error that will be overlooked.

Unfortunately, not all input is as easy to describe as numbers and e-mail addresses. Names and street addresses are particularly difficult to validate because they can contain a wide variety of characters from international alphabets unfamiliar to you. For example, O'Dell, Varkey Chudukatil, Skjønaa, Crciun, and McAskill-White are all legitimate last names of real people. Programmatically filtering these examples of valid input from malicious input such as "1' DROP TABLE PRODUCTS --" (a SQL injection attack) is difficult.

One common approach is to instruct users to replace characters in their own names. For example, users who normally enter an apostrophe or a hyphen in their names could omit those characters. Users with letters that are not part of the standard Roman alphabet could replace letters with the closest similar Roman character. Although this allows you to more rigorously validate input, it requires users to sacrifice the accurate spelling of their names—something many people take very personally.

As an alternative, perform as much filtering as possible on the input, and then clean the input of any potentially malicious content. Most input validation should be pessimistic and allow only input that consists entirely of approved characters, but input validation of real names might need to be optimistic and cause an error only when specifically denied characters exist. For example, you could reject a user's name if it contained one of the following characters: !, @, #, $, %, ^, *, (,), <, >. All these characters are unlikely to appear in a name but likely to be used in an attack. Microsoft Visual Studio .NET provides the following regular expression to match valid names: "[a-zA-Z'`-Ã,Â^\s]{1,40}".

Use Strong Types and Typed Data Comparisons for Non-String Data

User input is generally received in the form of a string. For example, input from an ASP.NET form is received by retrieving the "System.Web.UI.WebControls.TextBox.Text" string, and input from a Windows Form application is available within the "System.Windows.Forms.TextBox.Text" string.

If the user is not typing text, your application should immediately convert the user input into a stronger type. For example, if you use a *TextBox* control to allow the user to enter a number from 1 through 100, the following code would convert that input and then validate the range:

```csharp
int myNumber = Int16.Parse(TextBox1.Text);
if ( !((myNumber >= 1) && (myNumber <= 100)) )
    throw new Exception("Invalid input: Number out of bounds.");
```

```vb
Dim myNumber As Integer =  Int16.Parse(TextBox1.Text)
If Not ((myNumber >= 1) && (myNumber <= 100)) Then
    Throw New Exception("Invalid input: Number out of bounds.")
End If
```

This technique is extremely effective for filtering invalid input, because the .NET Framework throws a format exception when any part of the input string cannot be interpreted as an integer. If the user enters alphabetic characters, a decimal number, or anything other than the characters 0–9 (inclusive), the .NET Framework throws a *FormatException* with the message "Input string was not in a correct format". If the input can be successfully converted but falls outside the inclusive range of 1–100, the example code manually throws an exception.

Use similar techniques for validating decimal numbers, currency, dates, and any other input type for which the .NET Framework has a specialized class. The following code verifies that the content of *TextBox1* is a valid date, and catches the format exception if the conversion fails:

```csharp
try
{
    DateTime dt = DateTime.Parse(TextBox1.Text).Date;
}
catch(FormatException ex)
{
    // Return invalid date message to caller
}
```

```
Try
    Dim dt As DateTime =  DateTime.Parse(TextBox1.Text).Date
Catch ex As FormatException
    ' Return invalid date message to caller
End Try
```

Validate Strings Based on Their Length

Most strings that users type, including names, have a practical (if not theoretical) length limit. Therefore, validating strings based on their length can be extremely useful for .NET Framework applications. However, it is more than *useful* to other development environments—it is *critical*. Accepting input that is longer than the application was designed to handle leads to buffer overflow attacks. Fortunately, applications built on the .NET Framework are naturally resistant to buffer overflows, because the .NET Framework automatically verifies that the buffer can hold the contents you are writing into it.

There are times when you should check length, however. If there is a reasonable limit to how long a particular piece of user input should be, use a regular expression to verify that the input is of an expected length. As an alternative to using regular expressions, use strings that include the *Length* property. To throw an exception if the length of a string named *input* is greater than 20 characters, use the following line of code:

```
if (input.Length > 20) throw new Exception("Input too long.");
```

```
If input.Length > 20 Then
    Throw New Exception("Input too long.")
End If
```

> **Tip**   If the string is going to be stored in a database or used to query a database value, verify that the string is not longer than the space allocated to the column in the database.

Validate Input in Your ASP.NET Controls

Any application that accepts user input can be attacked, but Web applications are the most likely to be attacked for the following reasons:

- Web applications are often accessible from the public Internet, where anyone can submit requests.

- Web applications typically use HTML forms to request user input. Attackers can easily analyze HTML forms to understand exactly what types of input the application accepts.

- For attackers with the skills to manually submit malicious input, techniques for attacking Web applications are well documented on the public Internet.

- For attackers who lack the skill to manually submit malicious input to a Web application, tools are available to simplify and automate the process.

For these reasons, validating input in your ASP.NET applications is especially critical. You can use any technique supported by the .NET Framework, including regular expressions. ASP.NET also provides additional functionality in the form of five validator Web controls in the *System.Web.UI.WebControls* namespace:

- **RequiredFieldValidator**   Verifies that a box contains at least one character.

- **CompareValidator**   Verifies that input in one box exactly matches another. Primarily used to verify that a user completes Password and Confirm Password text boxes with identical characters.

- **RangeValidator**   Validates that input falls within a defined upper and lower range. You can validate numbers, dates, and characters.

- **RegularExpressionValidator**   Matches input against a defined regular expression.

- **CustomValidator**   Allows you to write a custom method to validate user input.

Of these five controls, *RangeValidator*, *RegularExpressionValidator*, and *CustomValidator* are the most useful for filtering potentially malicious user input. Follow these steps to use a validator Web control:

1. Add Web controls, such as *TextBox*, to an ASP.NET Web form.

2. Add a validator Web control to the Web form.

3. Define the *ErrorMessage* property of the validator Web control. This message will be displayed when the user has entered invalid input.

4. Define the *ControlToValidate* property of the validator Web control as the name of the input Web control created in step 1 (Figure 2-3).

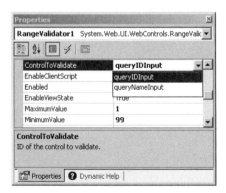

Figure 2-3   Defining a property of a validator control to reduce the risk of accepting malicious input

5. Specify additional settings specific to each type of validator Web control:

❑ *RangeValidator*   Define the *MaximumValue* and *MinimumValue* properties, and then set the *Type* property to String, Integer, Double, Date, or Currency.

❑ *RegularExpressionValidator*   Define the *ValidationExpression* property with a regular expression that the input must match. As shown in Figure 2-4, Visual Studio .NET includes the Regular Expression Editor to simplify generating regular expressions.

❑ *CustomValidator*   Create a custom method to validate the input, and then set the *ServerValidate* property to the name of the server-side method that will validate the input. Optionally, you can set the *ClientValidationFunction* property to the name of a client script that the browser will run.

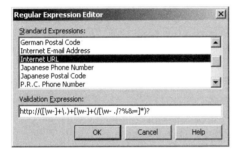

Figure 2-4   Regular Expression Editor simplifying validation of complex input in ASP.NET forms

6. Add code to check the status of the validator controls. For example, the following code checks the status of a validator Web control, and throws an exception if the input is invalid:

```csharp
if (RangeValidator1.IsValid == true)
{
    // Parse validated input
}
else
{
    throw new Exception("Invalid input");
}
```

```vb
If myValidator.IsValid = True Then
    ' Parse validated input
Else
    Throw New Exception("Invalid input")
End If
```

Each of these validators includes both a client-side and server-side component. The client-side component runs on the user's browser in the form of a JavaScript. Using the client-side script *does not improve the security of your application*. Client-side validation gives immediate feedback to legitimate users who accidentally enter invalid input into a box. However, malicious attackers will simply bypass the client-side scripts.

Tip   You can disable the generation of client-side scripts by setting the *EnableClientScript* property of the control to False. You might choose to do this to keep attackers from learning the details of your validation method. Knowing those details *could* help an attacker identify a vulnerability, but it wouldn't help that much, so it's probably not worth the trouble.

The server-side component of the validator Web controls does improve security, however. When a validator Web control is configured to validate input, ASP.NET examines the user input before passing control back to your code. ASP.NET will *not* stop the processing of the input if the validator's conditions are not met, however. You must manually check the state of the Boolean *IsValid* property of the validator control. If this property is true, the input was successfully validated. If it's false, don't trust the input.

Note   Everyone knows Web applications will be attacked with malicious input, but many Windows Forms developers wrongly think GUI applications are immune. Windows Forms applications can be attacked, but it doesn't happen as frequently. That's probably why the .NET Framework includes an excellent set of validator controls in the *System.Web.UI.WebControls* namespace, but doesn't include any validator controls in *System.Windows.Forms*. You can, and should, make your own GUI validator controls, however. For information about creating your own validator controls, read *http://msdn.microsoft.com/library/en-us/dnadvnet/html /vbnet04082003.asp*.

Guidelines for Rejecting Malicious Input

The best way to validate input is to force it to constrain to a specific type, format, length, and range. However, not all potentially malicious input can be identified using this technique. Sometimes, you must constrain the input, and then specifically seek out potentially malicious input. For example, the following regular expression could be used to identify a script block within HTML input:

```
<\s*script\s*>
```

Rejecting input that matched that regular expression would make it more difficult for an attacker to perform a cross-site scripting (CSS) attack that used a browser script, but it would not make the attack impossible. The attacker would merely need to find a way to format the script that did not match the regular expression you specified. For example, the sample regular expression would catch *<script>*, *< script >*, and *<script language="JavaScript">*, but it would not catch *<SCRIPT>*. A persistent attacker would quickly discover that your filtering algorithm was case-sensitive, and use that weakness to exploit your application.

In summary, rejecting input that contains known, dangerous content can reduce the risk of your application being exploited. However, this technique is error-prone. You should use this technique only after input has been tightly constrained.

Guidelines for Sanitizing Input

Sometimes, valid characters can be used with malicious intent by attackers. For example, an attacker can use apostrophes during SQL injection attacks because they are the most common delimiter in SQL commands. However, when trying to protect against this, you might not be able to reject all input containing an apostrophe because the character can appear in names, locations, and sentences.

In these circumstances, you must sanitize the input. You can use special characters to replace characters that might be legitimate but might also be part of an attack. For example, SQL handles two apostrophes together as a single, non-delimiting apostrophe. Therefore, replacing a single apostrophe with two apostrophes allows a name to be inserted into a dynamically generated SQL query without allowing the apostrophe to act as a delimiter. The following command performs this replacement:

```csharp
output = input.Replace("'", "''");
```

```vb
output = input.Replace("'", "''")
```

You can also use regular expressions to remove or replace invalid characters. For example, the following command removes all non-alphanumeric characters except for "@", "-", and ".":

```csharp
Regex.Replace(input, "[^\w\.@-]", "");
```

```vb
Regex.Replace(input, "[^\w\.@-]", "")
```

Similarly, the following commands replace the characters "<" and ">" with "&lt" and "&gt". Browsers interpret the "<" and ">" characters as delimiters for HTML codes or client-side scripts, and so they do not normally display them to the user. However, browsers will display "&lt" and "&gt" as less-than and greater-than signs. As a result, running these two commands on user input that is displayed on a Web page can help reduce the likelihood of CSS attacks while still allowing legitimate users to use those characters:

```
comment = comment.Replace("<", "&lt");
comment = comment.Replace(">", "&gt");
```

```
comment = comment.Replace("<", "&lt")
comment = comment.Replace(">", "&gt")
```

> **Tip** Simply stripping out "<" and ">" from user input will ruin everyone's emoticons. :-<

Practice: Validating Input

In this practice, you create an ASP.NET application that rigorously validates input. Read the scenario and then complete the exercise that follows. If you are unable to answer a question, review the lesson materials and try the question again. You can find answers to the questions in the "Questions and Answers" section at the end of this chapter.

Scenario

Your organization, Northwind Traders, is creating a Web-based application to allow customers to enter their own contact information into your database. As a new employee, you are assigned a simple task: create the front-end interface and prepare the user input to be stored in a database. You begin by interviewing several company personnel and reviewing the technical requirements.

Interviews Following is a list of company personnel interviewed and their statements:

- **IT Manager** "This is your first assignment, so I'm starting you out easy. Slap together a Web page that takes user input. That should take you, what, five minutes?"

- **Database Developer** "Just drop the input into strings named 'companyName', 'contactName', and 'phoneNumber'. It's going into a SQL back-end database, but I'll write that code after you're done. Oh, the 'companyName' can't be longer than 40 characters, 'contactName' is limited to 30 characters, and 'phoneNumber' is limited to 24 characters."

- **Chief Security Officer** "This is not as easy an assignment as it seems. This page is going to be available to the unwashed public on the Internet, and there are lots of black hats out there. We've gotten some negative attention in the press recently for our international trade practices. Specifically, we've irritated a couple of groups with close ties to hacker organizations. Just do your best to clean up the input, because you're going to see some malicious junk thrown at you."

Technical Requirements   Create an ASP.NET application that accepts the following pieces of information from users, and validate them rigorously:

- Company name
- Contact name
- Phone number

Exercise

Answer the following questions to show that you can implement best practices for validating potentially malicious user input:

1. How can you constrain the input before you write any code?
2. How can you further constrain the input by writing code?

Lesson Summary

- Your primary defense against malicious input is to reject all input that does not meet exacting requirements for format, length, type, and range.
- Your secondary defense against malicious input is to examine it for known malicious content.
- Your final defense against malicious input is to sanitize it to remove potentially dangerous characters.

Lesson 2: Minimizing Canonicalization Problems

Attacks exploiting canonicalization problems in Web applications have been, and will continue to be, one of the biggest challenges to Web developers. Canonicalization problems are not unique to Web applications, however. The same problems can be exploited in Windows Forms applications, because local filenames can be represented in multiple, and often confusing, ways. This lesson provides best practices for reducing your vulnerability to canonicalization problems by using features built into the .NET Framework.

After this lesson, you will be able to

■ Avoid canonicalization problems in Windows Forms applications.

■ Avoid canonicalization problems in ASP.NET applications.

Estimated lesson time: 15 minutes

Best Practices for Avoiding Canonicalization Problems in Windows Forms Applications

If you validate a filename before the operating system canonicalizes it, an attacker can pass a filename that you won't detect as invalid. You can reduce your vulnerability to canonicalization attacks by manually canonicalizing a path before validating it. Additionally, rather than optimistically attempting to match invalid input, you should validate that the path contains only allowed characters.

Tip   *Canonicalization* is the process of simplifying a path to its most simple, absolute form. Any file can be identified by multiple names, such as C:\boot.ini, ..\..\..\BOOT.INI, and C:/ boot%2eini, so the operating system must canonicalize the name before processing the file. Applications don't always canonicalize the name, which can introduce a vulnerability. For more information about canonicalization, see Chapter 1, "Implementing Security at Design Time."

Consider a Windows Forms application, designed to run on a kiosk in the lobby of a business, that allows the user to view text files containing public information about the company. The following method accomplishes this simple task by displaying the contents of the file in the *outputBox TextBox*. If an error occurs, the method displays an error message.

```csharp
private void showFile(string fileName)
{
    try
    {
        System.IO.StreamReader sr = new System.IO.StreamReader(fileName);
        outputBox.Text = sr.ReadToEnd();
        sr.Close();
    }
```

```
    catch (Exception ex)
    {
        outputBox.Text = "ERROR: " + ex.Message;
    }
}
```

```
Private  Sub showFile(ByVal fileName As String)
    Try
        System.IO.StreamReader sr = New System.IO.StreamReader(fileName)
        outputBox.Text = sr.ReadToEnd()
        sr.Close()
    Catch ex As Exception
        outputBox.Text = "ERROR: " + ex.Message
    End Try
End Sub
```

> **Note**   For the sake of simplicity, please suspend disbelief for a moment—I know this example is a bit silly!

There's a problem, though. An attacker could use the program to view the contents of the C:\boot.ini file, which would give her information that could be used to compromise the computer. Adding the following condition to the method *should* eliminate that possibility:

```
if (fileName == @"C:\boot.ini")
{
    throw new Exception ("No, that's a system file!");
}
```

```
If fileName = "C:\boot.ini" Then
    Throw New Exception ("No, that's a system file!")
End If
```

This condition will catch the attacker if she browses to select the C:\boot.ini file, or if she manually types C:\boot.ini. However, because the check is so specific, the attacker can type any of the following filenames to view the file:

- C:\boot.ini.
- ..\..\..\..\..\..\..\..\..\..\..\..\boot.ini
- \boot.ini

There are two ways you can fix this problem:

- **Use regular expressions to search for the phrase "boot.ini" in the filename**   This will work, but it is risky because the attacker can find another way to identify the file. For example, a Web application might interpret "%2e" as a period, which will allow the name "C:\boot%2eini" to be used to identify the file.

■ **Canonicalize the filename, and then compare it**   This is the more secure option, because the .NET Framework will provide the application with the absolute name of the file in a consistent format that you can reliably compare against.

Ultimately, evaluating the canonicalized filename is the most reliable way to ensure the C:\boot.ini file is never selected. To do this, the method can use the *System.IO.Path.GetFullPath* method, as demonstrated here:

```csharp
try
{
    fileName = Path.GetFullPath(fileName);
    if (fileName == @"C:\boot.ini")
    {
        throw new Exception ("No, that's a system file!");
    }
    System.IO.StreamReader sr = new System.IO.StreamReader(fileName);
    outputBox.Text = sr.ReadToEnd();
    sr.Close();
}
catch (Exception ex)
{
    outputBox.Text = "ERROR: " + ex.Message;
}
```

```vb
Try
    fileName = Path.GetFullPath(fileName)
    If fileName = "C:\boot.ini" Then
        Throw New Exception ("No, that's a system file!")
    End If
    System.IO.StreamReader sr = New System.IO.StreamReader(fileName)
    outputBox.Text = sr.ReadToEnd()
    sr.Close()
Catch ex As Exception
    outputBox.Text = "ERROR: " + ex.Message
End Try
```

As you can see, this code calls the *System.IO.Path.GetFullPath* method to return the absolute, canonicalized path to the file. This code will detect any variation on the name boot.ini, including the three examples cited earlier. For an attacker to defeat this check and open the boot.ini file, she would need to discover a vulnerability in the .NET Framework itself. Although discovering such a vulnerability is not impossible, the .NET Framework is much less likely to be exploited than any single application.

Caution   There's still at least one way to trick the application into opening the boot.ini file—can you find it? If you pass the filename "\\localhost\c$\boot.ini", *Path.GetFullPath* won't translate the network share into the local C drive. This vulnerability would exist only if the user could connect to the default \\localhost\c$ share, which is limited to Administrators.

The *System.IO.Path* class includes several other methods that are useful for avoiding canonicalization errors, including the following:

- **Combine**   Combines two path strings, enabling you to manually construct the path to a file while minimizing the potential for canonicalization vulnerabilities.

- **GetDirectoryName**   Returns the absolute path to the file's folder, without the filename or extension.

- **GetExtension**   Returns only the file's extension, such as .txt.

- **GetFileName**   Returns the file's name and extension, with all folder information removed.

- **GetFileNameWithoutExtension**   Returns the file's name without the extension.

- **IsPathRooted**   Allows you to reliably determine whether a path is absolute or relative. Accepts a path string as an argument, and returns true if the path is absolute, or false if the path is relative.

> **Note**   It's worth mentioning that the .NET Framework inherently eliminates several well-known canonicalization problems. For example, the Win32 API would have accepted the name "C:\boot.ini::$DATA" as a valid path, but the .NET Framework throws an exception with the message "The given path's format is not supported."

Best Practices for Avoiding Canonicalization Problems in ASP.NET Applications

To avoid canonicalization problems in ASP.NET applications, use the *Request.MapPath* method to canonicalize input that specifies the path to a file. To understand how the *Request.MapPath* method works, you must know that Web requests are submitted to a *virtual path* that maps to a *physical path* on the server. For example, if an HTTP request for the virtual path "/index.htm" is submitted to the default Web site, the Web server canonicalizes the virtual path into the physical path C:\Inetpub\Wwwroot\Index.htm. Many paths are not as straightforward, however.

Microsoft Internet Information Server (IIS) allows for a great deal of flexibility when creating virtual paths. Any given path, such as /images/, can map to the default location under C:\Inetpub\, a location elsewhere on the local hard disk, or a shared folder on another networked computer. Therefore, canonicalizing a virtual path to a physical path requires analyzing the IIS virtual path structure.

Additionally, virtual paths can appear in both relative and absolute formats. Relative virtual paths, such as "logo.gif" or "../../images/logo.gif", state the location of an object in relation to another object. Absolute virtual paths must include the root of a given Web site.

Another factor that must be accommodated when deriving physical paths from virtual paths is character translation. Web browsers cannot transmit a space as part of a filename. Therefore, they encode the space using the sequence "%20", which represents the space in hexadecimal ASCII notation. Other characters can be similarly encoded: a period can become "%2e", a forward slash can become "%2f", and the letter e can be rendered as "%65".

The complexity of calculating physical paths from virtual paths, and the multiple ways Web servers and Web browsers can represent characters, makes analyzing the locations of Web files and folders extremely error prone. Fortunately, you can reduce canonicalization problems in ASP.NET applications by following the same guideline you use for Windows Forms applications: allow the .NET Framework to do the work for you. The *Request.MapPath* method, shown in the following code, accepts a relative or absolute virtual path, and returns the corresponding physical path. This not only saves you the labor of writing code to manually parse virtual paths, it also reduces the possibility that human error will lead to a vulnerability.

```
string mappedPath = Request.MapPath(inputPath.Text);
```

```
Dim mappedPath As String =  Request.MapPath(inputPath.Text)
```

After the *Request.MapPath* method translates the virtual path, you can use standard techniques to verify the path of the request without worrying about intentionally malicious characters in the path. As an additional layer of protection, you can use the overloaded *Request.MapPath* method to verify that the path is within your application's virtual folder. When this mode is used to prevent cross-application mapping, *Request.MapPath* throws an *HttpException* if the requested path is outside of your application's directory, virtually eliminating the possibility that an attacker will exploit a canonicalization problem to force your application to process a file outside of its directory. To prevent cross-application mapping, pass *Request.MapPath* three parameters: the virtual path, the root path of your application, and the Boolean false value.

```
try
{
    string mappedPath = Request.MapPath(inputPath.Text,↵
Request.ApplicationPath, false);
}
catch (HttpException ex)
{
    // Cross-application mapping attempted
}
```

```
Try
Dim mappedPath As String =  Request.MapPath(inputPath.Text,→
Request.ApplicationPath,False)
Catch ex As HttpException
    ' Cross-application mapping attempted
End Try
```

Lesson Summary

- Use the *System.IO.Path.GetFullPath* method to reduce the vulnerability of canonicalization problems in Windows Forms applications.

- Use the *Request.MapPath* method to manually canonicalize virtual paths, reducing the likelihood of a canonicalization exploit in ASP.NET applications.

Lesson 3: Minimizing SQL Injection Attacks

Although not as common as canonicalization problems or CSS attacks, SQL injection attacks might be the most harmful common server attack. By submitting malicious characters and commands to a database application that processes user input, a SQL injection attack can expose private data and modify (or even destroy) information stored in a database. This lesson provides guidelines for creating database applications that are resistant to SQL injection attacks, and provides detailed instructions for using features built into the .NET Framework to help prevent a database server from interpreting commands issued by attackers.

> **Note**   The Structured Query Language (SQL) command examples in this book were created for Microsoft SQL Server 2000. SQL commands for other back-end databases might require slight changes.

After this lesson, you will be able to

- Structure your application to simplify the maintenance of your database access code.
- Describe how to best use SQL permissions to limit damage done by successful SQL injection attacks.
- Describe what stored procedures are and how they can be used to limit the possibility of a successful SQL injection exploit.
- Explain what parameterized SQL commands are and how you can use them to reduce the risk of a back-end database running malicious commands.
- Protect pattern matching statements.

Estimated lesson time: 45 minutes

Guidelines for Structuring Your Application to Simplify Maintenance of Database Access Code

Even skilled developers can make mistakes that lead to SQL injection vulnerabilities. You can greatly reduce the likelihood of making mistakes, and simplify the process of identifying and fixing mistakes, by creating separate classes for interacting with your database.

Real World   When Security Isn't a Priority

The reason I say that it's possible for skilled developers to write code with vulnerabilities is that every developer I know, thousands of developers I don't know, and I have done this. Everyone has been in the situation in which a deadline is looming and you're making shortcuts in your code. Unfortunately, there are lots of shortcuts you can use when communicating with a database. Most of those shortcuts, like building dynamic SQL queries and not validating user input, lead to SQL injection vulnerabilities.

After all, when you have a deadline looming, all you want is the application to *work*. Applications don't have to be secure to work, because most employers only test basic functionality—not how an application responds to invalid input.

This code sample shows the wrong way to issue a database request:

```csharp
private void Button1_Click(object sender, System.EventArgs e)
{
    string selectString = "SELECT * FROM table WHERE id = " + input.text;
    SqlDataAdapter myData = new SqlDataAdapter(selectString, myConnection);
    DataSet myDS = new DataSet();
    myData.Fill(myDS, "DataSet");
}
```

```vb
Private  Sub Button1_Click(ByVal sender As Object, ByVal e As System.EventArgs)
    Dim selectString As String="SELECT * FROM table WHERE id = " + input.text
    Dim myData As SqlDataAdapter=New SqlDataAdapter(selectString,myConnection)
    Dim myDS As DataSet =  New DataSet()
    myData.Fill(myDS, "DataSet")
End Sub
```

And this code sample shows a much better technique:

```csharp
private void Button1_Click(object sender, System.EventArgs e)
{
    DataSet myDataSet = new DataSet();
    myDataSet = GetDSFromID(input.txt);
}

private DataSet GetDSFromID(string ID)
{
    string selectString = "SELECT * FROM table WHERE id = " + input.text;
    SqlDataAdapter myData = new SqlDataAdapter(selectString, myConnection);
    DataSet myDS = new DataSet();
    myData.Fill(myDS, "DataSet");
    return myDS;
}
```

```
Private  Sub Button1_Click(ByVal sender As Object, ByVal e As System.EventArgs)
    Dim myDataSet As DataSet =  New DataSet()
    myDataSet = GetDSFromID(input.txt)
End Sub

Private Function GetDSFromID(ByVal ID As String) As DataSet
    Dim selectString As String="SELECT * FROM table WHERE id = " + input.text
    Dim myData As SqlDataAdapter=New SqlDataAdapter(selectString,myConnection)
    Dim myDS As DataSet =  New DataSet()
    myData.Fill(myDS, "DataSet")
    Return myDS
End Function
```

Both of these code samples contain SQL injection vulnerabilities. However, the second code sample is easier to fix, because code that is accessing the database is located in a separate method. Ideally, database access methods are centralized in a single class in your application. To make your code easier to maintain and fix, never open a database connection directly from methods that perform non-database functions.

Best Practices for Configuring SQL Permissions

When starting the development of a database application, you must not only plan the structure of the tables, views, and indices, you must also plan and assign the database privileges. Each role in your application, including guests, authenticated users, and administrators who manage the application, should have a separate role in the database. Each of these roles should be granted the minimal privileges required to access the tables, views, and stored procedures in the database.

Microsoft SQL Server, and most other client-server databases, include robust authentication and authorization features. In the case of Microsoft SQL Server, these features are tightly integrated with the operating system, allowing a database administrator (DBA) to grant privileges to Windows users and groups. For example, a DBA could grant the Administrators group access to manage all functions of a database, whereas members of the Users group have permissions to only read data from specific tables within the database.

Microsoft SQL Server, when run in Mixed Mode, also supports creating user accounts solely for the purpose of authenticating to the database. A DBA can create a user account within the database and assign permissions to this user. An application can then authenticate to the database using the user's credentials without requiring a Windows user account.

By default, only members of the Administrators group have access to a freshly installed SQL Server. Members of the Users group and Web applications have absolutely no access to the SQL Server and its databases. This is a good example of the secure-by-default principle.

However, many application vulnerabilities have been caused by developers overreacting to this lack of default privileges. After all, the quickest way to debug database

errors caused by missing privileges is to connect to the database as the System Administrator (sa) user. As a developer, you can place the sa user name and password in your
connection string, and never worry about not having sufficient access to your database.
However, this causes two types of problems:

■ Every request your application submits to the database is run without checking
privileges. Though this alone is not a vulnerability that an attacker could exploit,
if you fail to correctly parse user input and expose a SQL injection vulnerability, an
attacker will have unrestricted access to your database.

■ An attacker who gains access to your connection string (which might be stored in
your source code but should be stored elsewhere) can authenticate directly to
your database server.

Design   Invite the database administrators to examine the structure of your application during the design phase—they'll have interesting feedback about how you can improve the security of their data.

As shown in Figure 2-5, you can restrict what types of queries each user and role can
run against each object in the database. Allowing SELECT queries enables the user to
retrieve any information from the table. UPDATE enables making changes to existing
rows, whereas INSERT allows the user to add new rows. Roles with DELETE permissions can remove rows from the database—a very dangerous permission to grant.

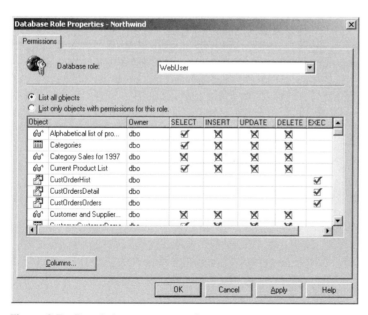

Figure 2-5   Restricting query types for users and roles

The more granular you assign permissions, the better. If tables contain a combination of information that should be available to a given role and information that should be kept private, you should assign permissions to individual columns. For example, if you are creating an employee directory application that pulls data from a human resources database containing personal information about employees, grant users access to only the rows your application will display, as shown in Figure 2-6. Restricting access to individual columns isn't sufficiently secure, because you are trusting that an attacker will not modify your SQL queries and will not bypass your application by connecting directly to the database.

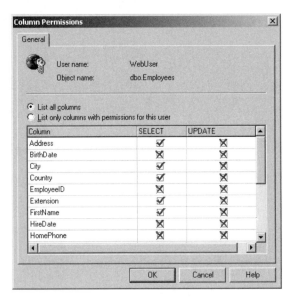

Figure 2-6   Assigning permissions to individual columns in a table containing confidential information

See Also   Databases are an important part of most business applications, and you must be familiar with database security concepts. However, detailed coverage of SQL Server security configuration is outside the scope of this book. For more information, see "Security Resources" on the Windows Server System page of the Microsoft Web site at *http://www.microsoft.com/sql/techinfo/administration/2000/security/*.

What Are Stored Procedures?

Whenever possible, use stored procedures, rather than dynamically generated SQL, to communicate with the database. *Stored procedures* are SQL commands that are stored on the database. Calling a stored procedure is as easy as issuing a database query, but stored procedures are more difficult to abuse with a SQL injection attack. You should use parameterized stored procedures for data access whenever possible. The security benefits include:

- Being able to restrict user privileges so that users have access only to run stored procedures. There is no need to grant a user direct table access if the data in the table is returned through a stored procedure.

- Being able to add additional data validation to the stored procedure itself.

- Developers who call the stored procedure are required to use SQL parameters, which minimizes the risk of SQL injection attacks. (SQL parameters are described in more detail in the next section.)

Note   Stored procedures also run a bit quicker than dynamically generated SQL, but this doesn't improve security at all.

Important   Using limited user accounts, permissions, and stored procedures cannot prevent SQL injection attacks. Only correctly parsing input prevents SQL injection attacks. These other techniques reduce the damage of successful SQL injection attacks, which is an important part of implementing defense-in-depth.

What Are Parameterized SQL Commands?

You *can* dynamically generate SQL queries based on user input while minimizing the risk of being vulnerable to a SQL injection attack. It is never the most secure method for querying a database, however. The most secure way to query a database is to build SQL statements using parameterized SQL commands. *Parameterized SQL commands* are SQL commands that use typed parameters and parameter placeholders to ensure that input data is checked for length and type.

SQL parameters are placeholders in SQL commands that the database substitutes with values you provide separately. Because the values are provided separately from the SQL query, there is no opportunity for a value to include SQL commands. Additionally, you do not need to include delimiters in your SQL query.

> **Exam Tip**   In order from least secure to most secure: dynamically generated SQL, parameterized SQL commands, and parameterized stored procedures.

Examples: Parameterized SQL Commands

Consider the following method, which retrieves the first row of the Products table based on the *productID* argument:

```csharp
private static DataRow GetRowFromID(string productID)
{
    // Construct a parameterized SQL query to retrieve the first row from
    // the Products table with the supplied ProductID
    // Note that no value is specified in the constructed query.
    // Instead, @ProductID, a parameter, is specified.
    SqlDataAdapter productAdapter=new SqlDataAdapter("SELECT ProductID,↵
ProductName FROM Products WHERE ProductID='" + productID + "'",↵
ConfigurationSettings.AppSettings["appDSN"]);
    DataSet productDataSet = new DataSet();

    // Run the query, fill the dataset, and return the first row
    productAdapter.Fill(productDataSet, "DataSet");
    DataTable productsTable = productDataSet.Tables[0];
    return productsTable.Rows[0];
}
```

```vb
Private Shared Function GetRowFromID(ByVal productID As String) As DataRow
    ' Construct a parameterized SQL query to retrieve the first row from
    ' the Products table with the supplied ProductID
    ' Note that no value is specified in the constructed query.
    ' Instead, @ProductID, a parameter, is specified.
    Dim productAdapter As SqlDataAdapter =  New SqlDataAdapter↵
("SELECT ProductID, ProductName FROM Products WHERE ProductID='" +↵
productID +"'",ConfigurationSettings.AppSettings("appDSN"))
    Dim productDataSet As DataSet =  New DataSet()

    ' Run the query, fill the dataset, and return the first row
    productAdapter.Fill(productDataSet, "DataSet")
    Dim productsTable As DataTable =  productDataSet.Tables(0)
    Return productsTable.Rows(0)
End Function
```

Next, consider the same method, implemented using SQL parameters:

```csharp
private static DataRow GetRowFromID(int productID)
{
    // Construct a parameterized SQL query to retrieve the first row from
    // the Products table with the supplied ProductID
    // Note that no value is specified in the constructed query.
    // Instead, @ProductID, a parameter, is specified.
    SqlDataAdapter productAdapter=new SqlDataAdapter("SELECT ProductID,↵
ProductName FROM Products WHERE ProductID=@ProductID",↵
ConfigurationSettings.AppSettings["appDSN"]);
    DataSet productDataSet = new DataSet();
```

```
    // Add a parameter to the SqlDataAdapter, and specify its value
    SqlParameter parm = ⤶
productAdapter.SelectCommand.Parameters.Add("@ProductID", SqlDbType.Int);
    parm.Value = productID;

    // Run the query, fill the dataset, and return the first row
    productAdapter.Fill(productDataSet, "DataSet");
    DataTable productsTable = productDataSet.Tables[0];
    return productsTable.Rows[0];
}
```

```
Private Shared Function GetRowFromID(ByVal productID As Integer) As DataRow
    ' Construct a parameterized SQL query to retrieve the first row from
    ' the Products table with the supplied ProductID
    ' Note that no value is specified in the constructed query.
    ' Instead, @ProductID, a parameter, is specified.
    Dim productAdapter As SqlDataAdapter = New SqlDataAdapter(⤶
"SELECT ProductID, ProductName FROM Products WHERE ⤶
ProductID=@ProductID",ConfigurationSettings.AppSettings("appDSN"))
    Dim productDataSet As DataSet = New DataSet()

    ' Add a parameter to the SqlDataAdapter, and specify its value
    Dim parm As SqlParameter =   ⤶
productAdapter.SelectCommand.Parameters.Add("@ProductID",SqlDbType.Int)
    parm.Value = productID

    ' Run the query, fill the dataset, and return the first row
    productAdapter.Fill(productDataSet, "DataSet")
    Dim productsTable As DataTable = productDataSet.Tables(0)
    Return productsTable.Rows(0)
End Function
```

Why the Second Example Is More Secure Than the First Example

If you compare the two methods without considering security, the first is clearly superior. It is several lines shorter, and shorter code is almost always better. Also, it accepts the *productID* parameter in the native string format that it will have when entered by the user—saving the need to convert it from a string to an integer, and then back to a string.

The second method is dramatically more secure, however. The first method *is* more efficient, but it won't seem so efficient when it is exploited by a SQL injection attack. The second method is essentially impossible to exploit with a traditional SQL injection attack. First, it accepts the *productID* parameter as an integer. The code that calls the method will be forced to convert the user's input from a string to the integer format, using a command such as Int32.Parse(productIDString.Text). However, the process of converting the string to an integer ensures that no SQL injection commands are present in the input.

Even if the value being queried were a string, the second method would be more secure because the query value is passed by using a SQL parameter. The SQL Profiler tool reveals the SQL query generated by the .NET Framework. First, consider how a dynamically generated SQL query looks when a SQL injection vulnerability is successfully exploited when a user types the phrase ' **drop table deleteme --** in a text box prompting for a product name:

```
exec sp_executesql N'SELECT * FROM Products WHERE ProductName='' →
drop table deleteme --'
```

Next, examine the parameterized SQL query when the same input is provided as a value in a parameterized SQL query:

```
exec sp_executesql N'SELECT * FROM Products WHERE ProductName=@ProductName', →
N'@ProductName nvarchar(40)', @ProductName = N''' drop table deleteme --'
```

The parameterized SQL query is functionally identical, except for a single character—an extra apostrophe. The .NET Framework sanitized the value provided for the *@ProductName* parameter by automatically replacing the single apostrophe (a SQL delimiter) with two apostrophes, which the SQL engine will interpret as a single, non-delimiter apostrophe. Yes, you could make this replacement manually in your code, but if you forget to sanitize the input for any box, your application will be vulnerable to SQL injection attacks. Using parameterized SQL queries lets the .NET Framework do the work for you.

Off the Record   The .NET Framework provides separate classes for submitting database queries that SELECT data, and for submitting queries that UPDATE data. These classes don't protect your application from SQL injection attacks, however. The sample application in the practice at the end of this lesson demonstrates a SQL injection attack that drops a table using the .NET Framework *DataSet* class. You should use the *SqlCommand* class to perform updates in your application, but an attacker can still abuse other classes.

Note   Remember, defense-in-depth isn't about being a perfect programmer. It's about providing multiple layers of defense to prevent the inevitable mistakes from being exploited. Using parameterized SQL queries is an excellent way to reduce the possibility for human error to be exploited.

Best Practices for Protecting Pattern Matching Statements

The SQL injection attacks discussed so far in this chapter take advantage of the fact that dynamically generated SQL queries use an apostrophe as a delimiter. The apostrophe is not the only special character that can be exploited, however. Queries that use the *LIKE* clause assign special meanings to the %, [, and _ characters. For example, the following SQL command would return all rows in which the *ProductName* column starts with an A:

```
SELECT * FROM Products WHERE ProductName LIKE 'a%'
```

Passing wildcards into SQL parameters is acceptable, so you cannot rely on the .NET Framework to sanitize the input. Instead, create a method that sanitizes the input by enclosing the special characters in brackets. The following method performs this function:

```csharp
private string SafeSqlLikeClauseLiteral(string inputSQL)
{
    // Make the following replacements:
    // [   becomes   [[]
    // %   becomes   [%]
    // _   becomes   [_]

    string s = inputSQL.Replace("[", "[[]");
    s = s.Replace("%", "[%]");
    s = s.Replace("_", "[_]");
    return s;
}
```

```vbnet
Private Function SafeSqlLikeClauseLiteral(ByVal inputSQL As String) As String
    ' Make the following replacements:
    ' [   becomes   [[]
    ' %   becomes   [%]
    ' _   becomes   [_]

    Dim s As String =  inputSQL.Replace("[","[[]")
    s = s.Replace("%", "[%]")
    s = s.Replace("_", "[_]")
    Return s
End Function
```

Notice that these methods do not replace a single apostrophe with a double apostrophe. If you are using SQL parameters, you should not replace single apostrophes, because the .NET Framework will do that for you. In fact, manually replacing the apostrophe in a SQL parameter would result in a single apostrophe being interpreted as two apostrophes by the SQL engine. As a result, the sentence "I won't place user input into SQL queries" would be stored as "I won''t place user input into SQL queries." If you are not using SQL parameters, also add the command `Replace("'", "''")`.

Practice: Preventing SQL Injection Attacks

In this practice, you will configure a SQL Server database to allow queries from an ASP.NET application. Then, you will improve the application to reduce the vulnerability to SQL injection exploits. Complete the procedures in Exercises 1 and 2, and then complete the task and answer the questions in Exercise 3. If you are unable to answer a question, review the lesson materials and try the question again. You can find answers to the questions in the "Questions and Answers" section at the end of this chapter.

Exercise 1: Creating a Vulnerable Application

In this exercise, you compile and run an ASP.NET application that is vulnerable to SQL injection attacks. Then, you will perform a SQL injection attack to drop a table in the database.

1. Launch SQL Enterprise Manager by clicking Start, All Programs, Microsoft SQL Server, and then Enterprise Manager.

2. In the left pane, expand Microsoft SQL Servers, SQL Server Group, local, and Security. Click Logins.

3. Right-click Logins, and then click New Login.

4. In the Name box, type **NT AUTHORITY\NETWORK SERVICE**. Click OK.

5. Under local, expand Databases and Northwind. Click Users.

6. Right-click Users, and then click New Database User.

7. Click the Login Name list, and then click NT AUTHORITY\NETWORK SERVICE.

8. In the Permit In Database Role list, select the public and db_owner check boxes, as shown in Figure 2-7.

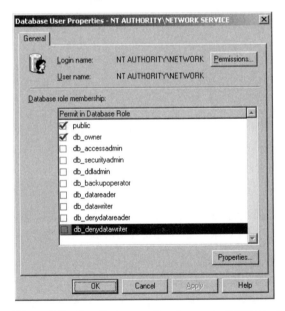

Figure 2-7   Granting users the db_owner Database role to give almost unrestricted access to the database

Security Alert   Assigning a user the db_owner role is a very bad thing to do because it gives that user a great many rights to your database. However, it is a very common mistake for developers to make, because selecting the db_owner check box immediately resolves all database authorization-related problems.

9. Click OK.

10. Use Windows Explorer to copy the Northwind folder and its contents from the companion CD to the C:\Inetpub\Wwwroot\ folder.

11. From the Administrative Tools group, launch the Internet Information Services (IIS) Manager.

12. Expand your computer node, expand Web Sites, and then expand Default Web Site. Right-click Northwind, and then click Properties.

    The Northwind Properties dialog box appears.

13. On the Directory tab, click the Create button. Click OK, and then close the Internet Information Services (IIS) Manager.

14. In Windows Explorer, select the C:\Inetpub\Wwwroot\Northwind\ folder, and then double-click Northwind.csproj.

    Microsoft Visual Studio .NET 2003 opens the Northwind project.

15. On the Standard toolbar, verify that the Release configuration is selected. Click the Debug menu, and then click Start Without Debugging.

16. When prompted, save the solution file.

    Visual Studio compiles and launches the application from within Internet Explorer.

17. In the Query by name box, type **Chocolade**. Click Search.

    The Northwind application shows the ID and name of the product, as shown in Figure 2-8. This verifies that the sample application is configured correctly. Leave SQL Enterprise Manager and Internet Explorer open for the next exercise.

Figure 2-8   Querying for a product to verify that the sample application is correctly configured

Exercise 2: Exploiting a Vulnerable Application

In this exercise, you perform a SQL injection attack to exploit the vulnerability in the Northwind application.

1. In Internet Explorer, click the Create DeleteMe Table button.

   The Northwind application displays the message Table Created. Later, you will drop this table by using a SQL injection attack. Creating a table specifically for this purpose prevents doing permanent damage to the database.

2. In Enterprise Manager, expand Databases and Northwind, and then click Tables. Press F5. In the right pane, notice that the DeleteMe table exists.

3. In the Query by name box, type **' drop table DeleteMe --**. Click Search.

   The Northwind application shows an exception error message, as shown in Figure 2-9. The error message indicates that it couldn't find any rows matching your input. However, it did submit the query to the database.

Figure 2-9   Error message indicating that no matching rows were found

4. In Enterprise Manager, select the Tables node in the left pane, and then press F5 to refresh the display. The DeleteMe table disappears, indicating that the table was successfully deleted.

Exercise 3: Fixing a Vulnerable Application

In this exercise, you fix the vulnerable application, and then answer questions about the techniques you used to repair the vulnerabilities. First, modify the application to remove all obvious SQL injection exploits. Then, answer the following questions:

1. What techniques did you use to limit your exposure to SQL injection vulnerabilities entered into the *queryIDInput TextBox?*

2. What techniques do you use to limit your exposure to SQL injection vulnerabilities entered into the *queryNameInput TextBox?*

3. Besides changing the code in the application, what techniques could be used to reduce the likelihood of a SQL injection exploit?

Lesson Summary

- Create separate methods and classes for database access code to make managing the code more efficient.

- Use SQL permissions as an additional defense-in-depth layer to reduce the damage done by successful SQL injection attacks.

- Stored procedures reduce the likelihood of a SQL injection attack being successful.

- Parameterized dynamic SQL commands are not as secure as stored procedures, but are dramatically more resistant to SQL injection attacks when compared with standard dynamic SQL commands.

- If you use the *LIKE* clause in a SQL command, you must sanitize user input to remove characters that can be used as wildcards.

Lesson 4: Minimizing Cross-Site Scripting

SQL injection attacks and attacks that exploit canonicalization problems both directly attack the server. Cross-site scripting attacks are different, because they use the server to attack end users. An attacker exploiting a CSS vulnerability places HTML or client-side script code into user input that the server then displays to other users. CSS attacks can cause your server to send dangerous and possibly objectionable content to innocent end users, which can hurt the Web site's reputation. Applications that might be vulnerable to CSS attacks are online forums, comment pages, and guest books.

Off the Record   I'm guilty of writing code vulnerable to a CSS attack. Lucky for me, the attacker was relatively kind and exploited only the vulnerability that causes visitors to the Web site to perform a denial-of-service attack against the site. The attacker inserted HTML code into a comment label that was displayed to all visitors. The HTML code caused the browsers to constantly refresh the page. The large number of requests brought the site down, but also made me aware of the vulnerability.

CSS attacks exploit one of two types of applications:

- Online forums, guest books, and comment pages in which user input is displayed to other users

- Dynamically generated pages that display request parameters

This lesson teaches you how to reduce the likelihood that both types of CSS vulnerabilities will be exploited by an attacker.

After this lesson, you will be able to
- Sanitize user comments that will be displayed to other users.
- Sanitize request parameters that will be rendered in the user's own browser.

Estimated lesson time: 10 minutes

Guidelines for Sanitizing User Comments

See Also   For information about how CSS vulnerabilities are exploited, see Chapter 1.

To prevent CSS attacks, rigorously validate any user input that will be displayed to other users. In particular, be wary of HTML and client-side scripts contained in < > brackets. If you do not plan to allow users to create HTML, you can use the following code to sanitize input:

```
string sanitizedInput = HttpUtility.HtmlEncode(dirtyInput);
```

```
Dim sanitizedInput As String =  HttpUtility.HtmlEncode(dirtyInput)
```

If you do want to allow users to enter HTML input, it is much more difficult to validate input. The best approach to allowing use of limited HTML tags is to sanitize the entire input using the *HtmlEncode* method, and then convert specific tags back to native HTML. The following code sanitizes input while allowing HTML tags for bold and italic fonts:

```
StringBuilder sanitizedInput = new StringBuilder(HttpUtility.HtmlEncode(dirtyInput));
sanitizedInput.Replace("&lt;b&gt;", "<b>");
sanitizedInput.Replace("&lt;/b&gt;", "</b>");
sanitizedInput.Replace("&lt;i&gt;", "<i>");
sanitizedInput.Replace("&lt;/i&gt;", "</i>");
```

```
Dim sanitizedInput As StringBuilder =  New StringBuilder(HttpUtility.HtmlEncode(dirtyI
nput))
sanitizedInput.Replace("&lt;b&gt;", "<b>")
sanitizedInput.Replace("&lt;/b&gt;", "</b>")
sanitizedInput.Replace("&lt;i&gt;", "<i>")
sanitizedInput.Replace("&lt;/i&gt;", "</i>")
```

If you want to provide users with more robust HTML capabilities, it will be almost impossible to prevent CSS exploits. Unfortunately, even the most mundane HTML tags can be used to launch client-side scripts on some browsers. For example, each of the following tags can cause a browser (but not necessarily all browsers, or even any modern browser) to run client-side code:

- <img dynsrc="javascript:*[code]*">
- <a href=http://www.contoso.com onmouseover="*[code]*">*Hyperlink text*</a>
- <img src="*foo*"onmouseover="*[code]*">

All modern browsers should ignore these attempted CSS exploits. However, not everyone uses a modern browser, and developers usually don't have the option of limiting the browsers that request pages from a Web application. Additionally, you never know when a vulnerability will be discovered in a modern browser. Learn from the mistakes of the past, and avoid echoing input containing any type of HTML content to end users.

Guidelines for Sanitizing Request Parameters

The second form of a CSS attack involves an attacker enticing a victim to click a hyperlink to a vulnerable application. The hyperlink is specially formed to contain codes that will cause the application to generate a Web page that launches a client-side script on the user's browser or causes the browser to send a request to a malicious server. Consider the Web page shown in Figure 2-10, which displays the contents of the *name* request parameter.

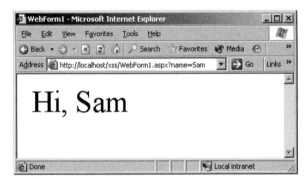

Figure 2-10   Web page that could be used to trick a user

An attacker could abuse the Web page shown in Figure 2-10 by tricking an unsuspecting user into clicking a hyperlink that passed HTML code to the page, such as *http://localhost/xss/WebForm1.aspx?name=<a%20href="javascript:alert(1);">Click%20here</a>*.

Many Web platforms would then pass the HTML unfiltered to the user. Fortunately, ASP.NET 1.1 enables the *validateRequest* attribute by default to make this type of vulnerability more difficult to exploit. Figure 2-11 shows the page that results when malicious HTML code is passed to an ASP.NET page. ASP.NET will throw this same exception any time HTML code is received as part of a request parameter, even if you do not attempt to display the contents of the request parameter.

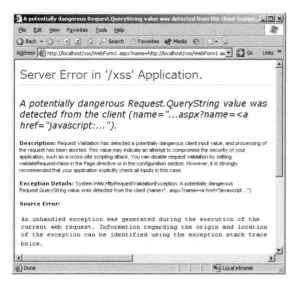

Figure 2-11   Error resulting from malicious HTML code being passed to an ASP.NET page

You cannot rely on ASP.NET to prevent CSS attacks, however. You must constrain, reject, and sanitize user input received in ASP.NET request parameters just as you would any other input. If you decide that you'd rather not use ASP.NET's protection, you can disable the *validateRequest* attribute on a page-by-page basis by adding <%@ Page validateRequest="false" %> to the *Page* attribute. Alternatively, you can disable the feature for your entire application by adding the following element to the application's Web.Config file:

```
<configuration>
  <system.web>
    <pages validateRequest="false" />
  </system.web>
</configuration>
```

See Also   For more information about the *validateRequest* attribute, including details about how to enable similar functionality for ASP.NET 1.0 application, read "Adding Cross-Site Scripting Protection to ASP.NET 1.0" on the MSDN page of the Microsoft Web site at http: //msdn.microsoft.com/library/en-us/dnaspp/html/scriptingprotection.asp.

Practice: Preventing Cross-Site Scripting

In this practice, you will discuss techniques for preventing canonicalization problems from being exploited. Read the scenario and then complete the exercise that follows. If you are unable to answer the question, review the lesson materials and try the question again. You can find the answer to the question in the "Questions and Answers" section at the end of this chapter.

Scenario

Your organization, Northwind Traders, is using a Perl script on its public Web site to allow potential customers to submit questions to your Sales team. This Perl script accepts several different request parameters, and then displays them to the user to request confirmation before storing the request to the database. Unfortunately, one of the systems administrators discovered that this Perl script was being exploited using a CSS attack. The attacker tricks users into clicking on a www.northwindtraders.com link (which users trust because your company has an excellent reputation) that passes HTML-encoded parameters to the Perl script. The Perl script then sends the parameters back to the user, as if the malicious input needed to be confirmed. The malicious input includes a client-side browser script that redirects the user's browser to an unfavorable site that Northwind Traders would definitely not want to be associated with.

Your boss, the IT manager, asks you to interview key personnel and then to recommend how this problem should be fixed.

Interviews   Following is a list of company personnel interviewed and their statements:

- **IT Manager**   "A few years back we hired a consultant to write that Perl script. It seemed to be working fine, so we just never worried about it. I'm pretty irritated that it was being abused though. We really need to make sure this doesn't happen again, and then check the rest of our scripts to make sure they don't have the same vulnerability."

- **Database Administrator**   "Look, you can't just remove the confirmation page from the script. If you do that, you'll have users loading all sorts of stupid data into my database. They'll forget to type their names, or they'll put in the wrong phone numbers, whatever. Just make sure people still have a chance to double-check their input before it's saved."

- **Chief Security Officer**   "This problem is more serious than a bad contract programmer. Clearly Perl isn't a secure enough application environment, so we'd better find something less prone to vulnerabilities. Also, why did this go undiscovered for so long? What do I have to do to get your boss to perform a code review once in a while?"

Exercise

Answer the following question to show that you can implement best practices for validating potentially malicious request parameters and echoing them back to the user's browser.

1. How would you recommend creating a form that meets everyone's requirements?

Lesson Summary

- Sanitize user comments that are displayed to other users by removing all HTML encoding. When necessary, you can allow a limited number of very specific HTML codes.

- Always sanitize request parameters by removing HTML codes. ASP.NET 1.1 provides this functionality automatically.

Lesson 5: Reporting Errors and Handling Failures

If you follow the guidance in this book, your application will generate errors when attacked. Generating an error is certainly much better than being exploited by an attacker, but the process of reporting errors can also become a vulnerability. To maintain security after an unexpected exception or other failure occurs, you must reduce the user's privileges (if necessary), record information about the error in a private location, and provide as little information to the end user as possible.

After this lesson, you will be able to

■ Describe the importance of ambiguous error messages and why you should allow only administrators to view detailed error messages.

■ Write code that stores error message information in the event log.

■ Write code that shows detailed error messages to privileged users.

■ Reduce vulnerabilities to denial-of-service attacks by closing database connections when an unhandled exception occurs.

■ Write code that defaults to a more secure mode.

Estimated lesson time: 25 minutes

Why You Should Allow Only Administrators to View Detailed Error Messages

Any details about the inner workings of your application that an attacker gains access to can potentially be used to identify a vulnerability. For this reason, attackers commonly use port scanning and system profiling to gain information about a target computer. Often, one of the most detailed sources of information for attackers is error messages.

Everyone has been frustrated by ambiguous error messages at some point. For example, consider this error message found in the author's application event log: "Faulting application , version , faulting module , version 0.0.0.0, fault address 0x00000000". This message doesn't provide any information that would be useful for troubleshooting the problem. To avoid this frustration and to facilitate troubleshooting, good developers provide very detailed error messages. Although this is a very user-friendly practice, it can also weaken the security of your application. You should not provide detailed error messages to end users, but you should allow administrators and developers to view error messages.

ASP.NET provides an excellent example of how to handle reporting errors. Figure 2-12 shows a detailed error message about an unhandled exception in an ASP.NET application. As you can see, this message includes highly confidential source code, the full physical path to the file, and a stack trace—all information an attacker could abuse.

Figure 2-12   Details of an ASP.NET error

ASP.NET limits the risk of providing detailed error messages by displaying them only to users logged on to the local computer. Generally, attackers won't be visiting a Web page from the console of the Web server, and as a result will not be able to view the detailed error message. However, developers and administrators still have the option of connecting to the server's console to reproduce the error. Figure 2-13 shows the error message that ASP.NET returns to users requesting the same page across the network.

Figure 2-13   Ambiguous error message sent to end users connecting across a network

How to Store Error Messages in the Event Log

Obviously, unhandled exceptions are not a concern because the .NET Framework will not reveal detailed information to end users. However, your application *should* catch the majority of exceptions, making you responsible for handling error reporting for those exceptions that really do indicate error conditions. Fortunately, recording detailed error messages without giving away your secrets to an attacker is easy.

First, if your application is not running as an administrator, you must register an event source on the application server. To manually add the event source:

1. Log on as an administrator to the application server.

2. Launch the Registry Editor by clicking Start, clicking Run, typing **regedit**, and then clicking OK.

3. Locate the following registry subkey:

    HKEY_LOCAL_MACHINE\SYSTEM\CurrentControlSet\Services\Eventlog\Application

4. Right-click the Application subkey, click New, and then click Key.

5. Type the name of your event source for the key name (for example, **My Application**).

6. Close the Registry Editor.

> **See Also**   For information about registering event sources programmatically, see Microsoft Knowledge Base article 329291, "PRB: 'Requested Registry Access Is Not Allowed' Error Message When ASP.NET Application Tries to Write New EventSource in the EventLog" on the Support page of the Microsoft Web site at *http://support.microsoft.com/?kbid=329291*.

Next, create a method (and possibly a class or an assembly) to handle error logging. Depending on your needs, this can be a simple method that accepts a string error message, or an *Exception* object, or a more complex class that accepts multiple application-specific parameters. After you centralize error handling for your application, create code to add an event to the event log with the relevant information. The following method does this:

> **Tip**   You must use the *System.Diagnostics* namespace to gain access to the *EventLog* classes.

```csharp
private void Report_Error(Exception ex, EventLogEntryType type, int eventID, →
short category)
{
    EventLog myLog = new EventLog("Application");
    myLog.Source = "My Application";
    myLog.WriteEntry("An exception occurred: "+ ex.Message, type,→
eventID, category);
}
```

```vbnet
Private  Sub Report_Error(ByVal ex As Exception, ByVal type As EventLogEnTryType, →
ByVal eventID As Integer, ByVal category As Short)
    Dim myLog As EventLog =  New EventLog("Application")
    myLog.Source = "My Application"
    myLog.WriteEnTry("An exception occurred: " + ex.Message, type,→
eventID, category)
End Sub
```

> **Tip**   Create overloaded error reporting methods to give yourself more flexibility for reporting errors. For example, create a method that accepts an exception, another method that accepts a string, and a third method that accepts a combination of both.

Finally, write code to call the method whenever something worthy of an administrator's attention occurs within your application. The following code segment would catch exceptions and pass them on to the *Report_Error* method:

```csharp
try
{
    // Code that might throw an exception
}
catch (Exception ex)
{
    Report_Error(ex, EventLogEntryType.Error, 100, 200);
}
```

```vbnet
Try
    ' Code that might throw an exception
Catch ex As Exception
    Report_Error(ex, EventLogEnTryType.Error, 100, 200)
End Try
```

How to Control Error Messages Based on User Properties

Storing information in the server's Application event log represents an ideal way to report errors, because only the systems administrators will have access to read the event log. Additionally, systems administrators have a wide variety of tools available to analyze and aggregate event logs, simplifying management of the information. However, examining the event log is a tedious process during debugging. For that reason, you might choose to display detailed error messages to users connected directly to the application server, users who are members of the Administrators group, or users who are on the server's local subnet.

For Web requests, you can determine whether the user is connecting from the local computer by comparing the user's IP address with the value "127.0.0.1", a special value used only by the local computer:

```csharp
if (Request.UserHostAddress == "127.0.0.1")
{
    // User is connecting from the local computer
}
```

```vb
If Request.UserHostAddress = "127.0.0.1" Then
    ' User is connecting from the local computer
End If
```

See Also   For more information about examining user group memberships, see Chapter 5, "Implementing Role-Based Security."

Guidelines for Closing Open Connections

To reduce the risk of denial-of-service attacks, you should close all open connections when an unhandled exception occurs. Otherwise, an attacker can repeatedly generate an error and intentionally consume the entire pool of available connections. The most common example of a limited connection pool is connecting to a database. The following code shows how to use `finally` to close an open connection after an exception occurs:

```csharp
SqlConnection conn = new SqlConnection(connectString);
// Enclose all data access code within a try block
try
{
    conn.Open();
    // Perform database functions
}
catch (SqlException sqlex)
{
    // Handle exception and report the error
    Report_Error(sqlex, EventLogEnTryType.Error, 100, 200);
}
finally
{
    conn.Close(); // Ensures connection is closed
}
```

```
Dim conn As SqlConnection =  New SqlConnection(connectString)
' Enclose all data access code within a try block
Try
    conn.Open()
    ' Perform database functions
Catch sqlex As SqlException
    ' Handle exception and report the error
    Report_Error(sqlex, EventLogEnTryType.Error, 100, 200)
Finally
    conn.Close() ' Ensures connection is closed
End Try
```

Considerations for Failing to a More Secure Mode

Although most exceptions and failures have benign causes, such as an unavailable network resource, you should always assume that a failure has been intentionally induced by an attacker. Specifically, after you understand code access security, you should write code that defaults to a permission set that is more secure than the permission set that existed before the errors or issues occurred.

> **See Also**   For more information about code access security and failing to a more secure mode, see Chapter 6, "Implementing Code Access Security."

Lesson Summary

- Hide detailed error messages from end users, but store the information where administrators can access it.

- Use the event log to store error messages so that systems administrators can easily analyze your application's output.

- When you must display detailed error messages to end users, provide detailed information only to those users who are authenticated and highly privileged, or who are connecting from the local computer.

- Reduce the application's vulnerability to denial-of-service attacks by closing open database connections when a failure occurs.

- Reduce privileges when a failure occurs to reduce the opportunity for an attacker to exploit a weakness in your error-handling code.

Lab: Using Secure Coding Best Practices

Read the scenario and then complete the exercise that follows. If you are unable to answer a question, review the lessons in the chapter and try the question again. You can find answers to the questions in the "Questions and Answers" section at the end of this chapter.

Scenario

You have been hired by Trey Research to perform a code security review of an internal Windows Forms application used by the Human Resources team to control payroll. The application is used by both permanent employees and contractors, and the IT department is concerned that a contractor will gain access to employees' personal information or, even worse, modify the data. Your boss asks you to interview a few of the organization's personnel and then make recommendations to reduce the application's vulnerabilities.

Interviews

Following is a list of company personnel interviewed and their statements:

- **IT Manager**   "I trust our employees not to mess around with the payroll database, but some of our contractors seem a little shady. Just make sure they can't see what I—er, the employees—earn."

- **Systems Administrator**   "As far as I know, nobody has ever abused our payroll application. The problem is, I have no way of knowing. For all I know, that temp with the mustache is changing my salary right now. I really need to be able to monitor that application. If I could use our existing event management system to detect problems, that would be awesome."

- **Chief Security Officer**   "I am more concerned about internal employees abusing this application than I am about the contractors. Internal employees are more likely to be motivated to examine others' salaries. Certainly, the motivation for changing their salaries is there."

Exercise

Answer the following questions for your boss:

1. What types of exploits is the application potentially vulnerable to?

2. How can an attacker exploit a Windows Forms application?

3. During your code review, what problems would you look for?

4. What recommendation can you make to address the systems administrator's concern?

Chapter Summary

- Follow a three-step process to validate user input: constrain, reject, and sanitize.

- Prevent canonicalization problems by using the .NET Framework to manually canonicalize paths before processing them.

- Reduce the likelihood of being exploited by a SQL injection attack by rigorously validating user input that will be included in a database query, using parameterized SQL commands instead of dynamic SQL queries, and using stored procedures.

- Remove HTML encoding from user input to reduce your application's vulnerabilities to CSS.

- Detailed error messages are a potentially useful source of information to an attacker. Therefore, you should display detailed error messages only to users who have been authenticated. To prevent failures from causing additional problems, close all open connections, and fail to a more secure mode.

Exam Highlights

Before taking the exam, review the key points and terms that are presented in this chapter. You need to know this information.

Key Points

- The reasons user input must be carefully validated

- The most secure methods for validating user input

- The most important methods for reducing the likelihood of canonicalization problems

- Input-sanitizing techniques for reducing exposure to SQL injection attacks

- The multiple layers of defense against database attacks

- The two types of CSS attacks, and the single method that can be used to prevent them

- The risks associated with detailed error messages, and the proper place to store information about potential attacks

Key Terms

canonicalization   The process of simplifying a path to its most simple, absolute form

parameterized SQL commands   SQL commands that use typed parameters and parameter placeholders to ensure that input data is checked for length and type

physical path   The location of a folder or file on a local hard drive, such as C:\Inetpub \Wwwroot\Docs\Index.htm

regular expression   A set of characters that can be compared with a string to determine whether the string meets specified format requirements

stored procedures   A series of SQL commands that is stored within the database and called like an application, rather than submitted like a query

virtual path   The location from which Web content is requested, such as /docs/ index.htm

Questions and Answers

Practice: Validating Input

Page
2-19

Exercise

1. How can you constrain the input before you write any code?

   You can use separate ASP.NET *RegularExpressionValidator* controls to restrict the input for each of the three boxes. For the company name validator, set the *ValidationExpression* property to "[a-zA-Z'`-Ã,Â´\s]{1,40}". For the contact name validator, you can use the regular expression "[a-zA-Z'`-Ã,Â´\s]{1,30}". Finally, for the phone number validator, you can use ASP.NET's built-in regular expression "((\(\d{3}\) ?)|(\d{3}-))?\d{3}-\d{4}".

2. How can you further constrain the input by writing code?

   You can write code to further constrain, reject, and sanitize the input. In particular, if the database developer provides further restrictions such as not allowing apostrophes or percent symbols, you can remove those symbols from the input by using the *String.Replace()* method.

Practice: Preventing SQL Injection Attacks

Page
2-39

Exercise 3: Fixing a Vulnerable Application

1. What techniques did you use to limit your exposure to SQL injection vulnerabilities entered into the *queryIDInput TextBox?*

   Although there is no single correct answer to this question, there are several best practices that you can use. You should add a *RangeValidator* control, and specify a range of integers. By examining the data in the Products table, you can determine that the lowest valid value is 1, and the highest value is 77. You wouldn't want your application to break if additional products were added, but you could set the *MaximumValue* property of the *RangeValidator* control to a large number such as 10,000.

   As an additional layer of protection, you should replace the *GetRowFromQuery* method with a method that accepts an integer instead of a string. This will force the developer to convert the product ID value being queried to an integer, which could not possibly contain SQL injection commands. Using parameterized SQL commands and, optionally, a stored procedure instead of a SQL query would further improve security. The following method would work:

```csharp
private static DataRow GetRowFromID(int productID)
{
    // Construct a parameterized SQL query to retrieve the first row from
    // the Products table with the supplied ProductID
    // Note that no value is specified in the constructed query.
    // Instead, @ProductID, a parameter, is specified.
    SqlDataAdapter productAdapter=new SqlDataAdapter("SELECT ProductID,
ProductName FROM Products WHERE ProductID=@ProductID",
ConfigurationSettings.AppSettings["appDSN"]);
    DataSet productDataSet = new DataSet();
```

```
        // Add a parameter to the SqlDataAdapter, and specify its value
        SqlParameter parm = ↵
    productAdapter.SelectCommand.Parameters.Add("@ProductID", SqlDbType.Int);
        parm.Value = productID;

        // Run the query, fill the dataset, and return the first row
        productAdapter.Fill(productDataSet, "DataSet");
        DataTable productsTable = productDataSet.Tables[0];
        return productsTable.Rows[0];
    }
```

```
Private Shared Function GetRowFromID(ByVal productID As Integer) As DataRow
        ' Construct a parameterized SQL query to retrieve the first row from
        ' the Products table with the supplied ProductID
        ' Note that no value is specified in the constructed query.
        ' Instead, @ProductID, a parameter, is specified.
        Dim productAdapter As SqlDataAdapter = New SqlDataAdapter(↵
    "SELECT ProductID, ProductName FROM Products WHERE ↵
    ProductID=@ProductID",ConfigurationSettings.AppSettings("appDSN"))
        Dim productDataSet As DataSet = New DataSet()

        ' Add a parameter to the SqlDataAdapter, and specify its value
        Dim parm As SqlParameter = ↵
    productAdapter.SelectCommand.Parameters.Add("@ProductID",SqlDbType.Int)
        parm.Value = productID

        ' Run the query, fill the dataset, and return the first row
        productAdapter.Fill(productDataSet, "DataSet")
        Dim productsTable As DataTable = productDataSet.Tables(0)
        Return productsTable.Rows(0)
End Function
```

2. What techniques do you use to limit your exposure to SQL injection vulnerabilities entered into the *queryNameInput TextBox?*

    You should add a *RegularExpressionValidator* control, bind it to the *queryNameInput TextBox*, and then specify a regular expression that constrains input to only those characters that can appear in the *ProductName* column in the database. Additionally, you should use the regular expression to restrict the length of the input to 40 characters. Forty characters is the maximum length of the field in the database, which you can determine by using SQL Enterprise Manager to examine the Product table's design.

    Also, you should replace the *GetRowFromQuery* method with a method that uses a parameterized SQL command. SQL parameters will automatically neutralize any delimiters, such as a single apostrophe, which will dramatically reduce the opportunity to exploit a SQL injection vulnerability. The following method would suffice:

```
private static DataRow GetRowFromName(string productName)
{
    // Construct a parameterized SQL query to retrieve the first row from
    // the Products table with the supplied ProductName
    // Note that no value is specified in the constructed query.
    // Instead, @ProductName, a parameter, is specified.
    SqlDataAdapter productAdapter = new SqlDataAdapter("SELECT ProductID,↵
ProductName FROM Products WHERE ProductName=@ProductName",↵
ConfigurationSettings.AppSettings["appDSN"]);
    DataSet productDataSet = new DataSet();
```

```
    // Add a parameter to the SqlDataAdapter, and specify its value
    SqlParameter parm = productAdapter.SelectCommand.Parameters.Add(
"@ProductName", SqlDbType.NVarChar, 40);
    parm.Value = productName;

    // Run the query, fill the dataset, and return the first row
    productAdapter.Fill(productDataSet, "DataSet");
    DataTable productsTable = productDataSet.Tables[0];
    return productsTable.Rows[0];
}
```

```
Private Shared Function GetRowFromName(ByVal productName As String) As DataRow
If productName.Length > 40 Then
 Throw New Exception("Input too long.")
End If
    ' Construct a parameterized SQL query to retrieve the first row from
    ' the Products table with the supplied ProductName
    ' Note that no value is specified in the constructed query.
    ' Instead, @ProductName, a parameter, is specified.
    Dim productAdapter As SqlDataAdapter =  New SqlDataAdapter(
"SELECT ProductID, ProductName FROM Products WHERE
ProductName=@ProductName",ConfigurationSettings.AppSettings("appDSN"))
    Dim productDataSet As DataSet =  New DataSet()

    ' Add a parameter to the SqlDataAdapter, and specify its value
    Dim parm As SqlParameter = productAdapter.SelectCommand.Parameters.Add(
"@ProductName",SqlDbType.NVarChar,40)
    parm.Value = productName

    ' Run the query, fill the dataset, and return the first row
    productAdapter.Fill(productDataSet, "DataSet")
    Dim productsTable As DataTable =  productDataSet.Tables(0)
    Return productsTable.Rows(0)
End Function
```

3. Besides changing the code in the application, what techniques could be used to reduce the likelihood of a SQL injection exploit?

Most significantly, the database permissions should be restricted. The ASP.NET application should not be running with privileges to drop a table. Instead, the application should run in an extremely limited security context that has access only to issue *SELECT* queries that retrieve the *ProductID* and *ProductName* rows from the Products table.

Practice: Preventing Cross-Site Scripting

Page
2-45

Exercise

1. How would you recommend creating a form that meets everyone's requirements?

Recreating the form using ASP.NET is a natural choice. ASP.NET's default configuration will prevent the exploit you've been experiencing, because it blocks request parameters that are HTML-encoded. You can, and should, further validate the input in the request parameters by constraining it for size and format, rejecting it if potentially malicious characters appear, and sanitizing it by removing or replacing characters with special meaning to your application and the underlying database.

Lab: Using Secure Coding Best Practices

Page
2-52

Exercise

Answer the following questions for your boss:

1. **What types of exploits is the application potentially vulnerable to?**

   Primarily SQL injection attacks. There's no mention of retrieving files, so there's no reason to think canonicalization might be a problem. CSS attacks target only Web applications.

2. **How can an attacker exploit a Windows Forms application?**

   An attacker can perform a SQL injection attack by typing a delimiter and SQL commands directly into a text box. If the application inserts that input directly into a dynamically generated SQL query, the attack will be successful. Depending on the permissions assigned to the user account used to connect to the database, the attacker might be able to add a highly privileged user account, view detailed information about the database structure, gain direct access to the contents of the database, and modify values in the database.

3. **During your code review, what problems would you look for?**

   You should look for user input that is not properly validated. In particular, user input that is inserted directly into a database query would enable an attacker to successfully exploit a SQL injection attack. Every piece of information provided by a user should be constrained to the data's type, format, and length. Then, the input should be parsed for malicious content. Finally, the input should be sanitized to remove or replace potentially malicious characters.

4. **What recommendation can you make to address the systems administrator's concern?**

   The application should add events to the event log—preferably on the server itself. The systems administrator can then use standardized tools to parse the events and identify patterns that could signal an attack has taken place or is currently under way.

3 Testing Applications for Vulnerabilities

Why This Chapter Matters

A chapter on testing in a book for developers might seem out of place, because developers usually have a dedicated testing and quality assurance (QA) team. However, unit testing is becoming a common technique for improving the quality of code submitted to QA by reducing the number of bugs ahead of time. Unit testing is an automated testing technique that developers can use to catch problems before passing code to QA—effectively reducing the number of testing cycles. Lesson 1 in this chapter focuses on using unit testing for resistance to security vulnerabilities.

The security level of complete assemblies can be tested with minimal effort, too, thanks to a handful of specialized tools. Lesson 2 in this chapter describes these tools and provides best practices for testing your assemblies for security vulnerabilities.

Exam Objectives in this Chapter:

- Perform unit testing on applications and components to identify security vulnerabilities.

Lessons in this Chapter:

Before You Begin

To complete the practices, examples, and lab exercises in this chapter, you must have one computer running Microsoft Windows Server 2003. During the course of performing the exercises in this chapter, the computer's security can be reduced. Therefore, the computer should not be a production computer and should not be connected to any network, especially the Internet, even if a firewall is present. Install Microsoft Visual Studio .NET 2003 using the default settings. Then, install Microsoft SQL Server 2000 configured to use the System account, Windows authentication, and processor licensing.

Lesson 1: Building Automated Unit Tests

If you've ever introduced a bug or security vulnerability into previously functional code, you will appreciate the techniques described in this chapter, because they will improve the security and reliability of your code. Employing these techniques will make your QA team's job a bit more challenging, though, because your code will never again have any obvious bugs.

After this lesson, you will be able to

- Describe unit testing and its benefits.
- Describe the purpose of a test-first development methodology.
- Explain the test-first development process.
- Implement unit testing with the NUnit tool.

Estimated lesson time: 40 minutes

What Is Unit Testing?

Unit testing is a technique that developers use to automatically test an application's components after making updates. The fact that *developers* perform unit testing is key, because it means that the testing occurs before the application is handed off to a QA team. Unit testing makes the development process more streamlined, enabling developers to find bugs and security vulnerabilities in their own code without having to add a QA cycle.

Unit tests are modules that exercise other modules. A unit test makes a call to a module that should produce a predictable result. The unit test then analyzes the result, and if the output is invalid, the unit test fails. For example, a unit test might call a method named *AddIntegers* with the values 2 and 3. If *AddIntegers* returns a result other than 5, it fails the test.

Unit tests can also be used to verify that a method fails correctly, which is particularly useful for testing resistance to security vulnerabilities. A unit test for a method that processes a file can verify that the method throws an exception when asked to process a system file. Using this technique, the unit test can request the file by using several different names and detect a possible canonicalization error.

 See Also For more information about canonicalization errors, see Chapter 1, "Implementing Security at Design Time," and Chapter 2, "Using Secure Coding Best Practices."

What Is Test-First Development?

Test-first development is a methodology that developers follow that involves creating unit tests before the units themselves. It's an odd concept to many developers—you first write code to exercise a class that you haven't yet written, and then you write the methods so that they pass your unit tests.

Although it might seem unconventional, the technique has merit. First, if you create unit tests for each major feature of your application, you can't possibly forget to implement a feature because your unit tests will fail until you have completed your work. Second, unit tests highlight security features and countermeasures that you haven't yet implemented, making the dropping of security features because of changing priorities and tight deadlines painfully obvious.

Test-first development has an upfront cost: writing the tests to exercise your methods can take 25 percent to 50 percent as much time as writing the methods themselves. However, this investment pays off in the long run. The unit tests can be used throughout the lifetime of your application and can immediately detect when bugs are introduced by updates and new features. In the context of preventing security vulnerabilities, security-focused unit tests can detect updates to your code that inadvertently disable security features. For example, if you comment out a line of code that sanitizes user input, a properly formed unit test will immediately detect the change and serve as a reminder that important security functionality is missing.

See Also   For more information about using test-first development and unit tests together, read Eric Gunnerson's article "Unit Testing and Test-First Development" on MSDN: *http://msdn.microsoft.com/library/en-us/dncscol/html/csharp03202003.asp*.

The Process of Performing Test-First Unit Testing

As mentioned earlier, although the test-first development process might seem counterintuitive at first, it is actually straightforward:

1. Create methods to test the security aspects of each piece of functionality in your application, including the following:

   ❑ Methods return correct responses when valid data is passed.

   ❑ Methods return failures when invalid data is passed.

   ❑ Methods report errors correctly.

   ❑ Methods fail when called by users with insufficient privileges.

2. Create or extend your application's methods.

3. Test to verify that the methods pass the security tests. Make updates if necessary.

The sections that follow show you how to perform steps 1 and 3 by using a tool called NUnit. Writing the application is up to you, though.

How to Implement Unit Testing Using the NUnit Tool

You can choose to implement the concepts of unit testing and test-first development using your own custom tools and techniques; however, a powerful framework for unit testing is freely available: NUnit. NUnit provides classes useful for quickly creating unit tests. NUnit also offers both command-line and graphical interfaces for running tests and examining the results. Perhaps best of all, NUnit was written specifically for the .NET Framework.

NUnit has several useful extensions. NUnitAsp, available from *http://nunitasp.sourceforge .net/*, facilitates testing ASP.NET code. TestRunner, available from *http://www.mailframe .net/Products/TestRunner.htm*, integrates NUnit directly into the Visual Studio .NET interface. Similarly, the NUnit Addin for Visual Studio .NET, available for download at *http: //sourceforge.net/projects/nunitaddin/*, allows you to use NUnit's functionality without leaving your development environment.

> **Exam Tip**   For the exam, understand unit testing. You don't need to know details about the tools described here, though. The exam won't test you on non-Microsoft software.

The sections that follow describe how to add a reference to NUnit in your application, and then provide code samples showing different types of unit test methods.

How to Use NUnit in an Application

To use NUnit in an application, you must download and install the tools, and then add a reference to your application. Follow these steps:

1. Download and install the latest version of NUnit from *http://www.nunit.org/*.

2. Use Visual Studio .NET 2003 to open or create the project that will use unit testing.

3. Click the Project menu, and then click Add Reference.

   The Add Reference dialog box appears.

4. On the .NET tab, click the nunit.framework component. Click Select, and then click OK.

5. Create a new class to contain the unit testing methods. First, click the Project menu, and then click Add Class. Click Class, and then type a descriptive name to the class such as **UnitTests**. Click Open.

6. In the new class, add the *[TestFixture]*attribute. NUnit looks for this attribute to determine which classes contain test methods.

7. Add test methods to granularly test your application's existing or planned functionality. Add the *[Test]* attribute to each test method. NUnit looks for this attribute to determine which methods should be run as tests. Use the *Assertion* class, as described in the sections that follow, to exercise the methods being tested.

The following code sample shows a class and test method created for NUnit that tests a method named *Database.GetInventoryFromProductName*:

```csharp
using System;
using NUnit.Framework;

namespace NorthwindUnitTesting
{
    [TestFixture]
    public class DatabaseClassTest
    {
        [Test]
        public void CheckInventoryByName()
        {
            // ProductName "Chai" should exist & inventory should be < 10,000
            int testInteger = Database.GetInventoryFromProductName("Chai");
            Assertion.Assert((testInteger >= 0) && (testInteger < 10000));
        }
    }
}
```

```vb
Imports System
Imports NUnit.Framework
Namespace NorthwindUnitTesting

    <TestFixture()> _
    Public Class DatabaseClassTest

        <Test()> _
        Public Sub CheckInventoryByName()
            'ProductName "Chai" should exist & inventory should be < 10,000
            Dim testInteger As Integer
            testInteger = Database.GetInventoryFromProductName("Chai")
            Assertion.Assert((testInteger>=0) AndAlso (testInteger<10000))
        End Sub
    End Class
End Namespace
```

How to Test for Success Conditions

Unit testing that does not focus on security generally checks for success conditions: if *x* is passed to method *y*, the value *z* should be returned. This type of testing is important for detecting functionality problems in your application. The following code demonstrates how to use the NUnit tool to verify that the *CheckInventoryByID* method returns a valid value for a known product ID:

Important   Because most attackers submit invalid input, testing for success conditions is rarely the proper way to detect vulnerabilities.

```csharp
[Test]
public void CheckInventoryByID()
{
    // ProductID 1 should exist, and inventory should be between 0 and 10,000
    int testInteger;
    testInteger = Database.GetInventoryFromProductID(1);
    Assertion.Assert((testInteger >= 0) && (testInteger < 10000));
}
```

```vbnet
<Test()> _
Public  Sub CheckInventoryByID()
    ' ProductID 1 should exist, and inventory should be between 0 and 10,000
    Dim testInteger As Integer
    testInteger = DataMyBase.GetInventoryFromProductID(1)
    Assertion.Assert((testInteger > =  0) AndAlso (testInteger < 10000))
End Sub
```

Note   The examples in this section are using the *NUnit.Framework* namespace, which is not part of the .NET Framework. As mentioned earlier, NUnit is a no-cost tool used for unit testing and can be downloaded from *http://www.nunit.org/*.

How to test for exceptions

To test for security vulnerabilities, you must test how methods respond to potentially malicious input. Well-written methods usually reject the input by throwing an exception. Therefore, most security-focused unit testing methods submit malicious input, and then pass the test only when an exception is thrown.

When you test methods that accept an integer within a specific range, submit an integer outside of that range and then verify that the application throws an *ArgumentOutOfRangeException*. Similarly, when you test methods that accept as input a string of limited length, submit a string that is too long or does not meet other requirements to be valid. If, during planning, you determine that your application should reject any input containing HTML, test the method by submitting HTML, and fail the test unless the correct exception is detected.

The following code demonstrates two methods that use the NUnit tool to verify that the *GetInventoryFromProductName* method throws an *ArgumentOutOfRangeException* when it receives invalid input:

```csharp
[Test]
[ExpectedException(typeof(ArgumentOutOfRangeException))]
public void FilterProductNameTooLong()
{
    // Method should throw an exception if ProductName is longer
    // than 40 characters
    int testInteger;
    testInteger = Database.GetInventoryFromProductName ⟶
("Thisisaverylongproductnamethatislongerthanfortycharacters");
}

[Test]
[ExpectedException(typeof(ArgumentOutOfRangeException))]
public void FilterProductNameTooShort()
{
    // Method should throw an exception if ProductName has no characters
    int testInteger = Database.GetInventoryFromProductName("");
}
```

```vbnet
<Test> _
<ExpectedException(Type.GetType(ArgumentOutOfRangeException))> _
Public  Sub FilterProductNameTooLong()
    ' Method should throw an exception if ProductName is longer
    ' than 40 characters
    Dim testInteger As Integer
    testInteger = DataMyBase.GetInventoryFromProductName ⟶
("Thisisaverylongproductnamethatislongerthanfortycharacters")
End Sub

<Test> _
<ExpectedException(Type.GetType(ArgumentOutOfRangeException))> _
Public  Sub FilterProductNameTooShort()
    ' Method should throw an exception if ProductName has no characters
    Dim testInteger As Integer
    testInteger = DataMyBase.GetInventoryFromProductName("")
End Sub
```

> **Important** Naturally, the exception that you test for must be the same type of exception that your application throws.

How to Test for Specific Countermeasures

Some methods sanitize input rather than reject it outright. For example, methods that accept Web input need to encode HTML characters, and methods that submit string input to a SQL database need to parse SQL delimiters. Methods that sanitize potentially malicious input are much more difficult to test, because they don't simply throw an exception or otherwise return an easily testable condition. In these circumstances, generate a test that checks both the input and the output to verify that the input was successfully sanitized.

If you are testing a method that inserts string input into a SQL command, you can use test input that includes a single apostrophe. If the method is handling the input using a technique that is susceptible to SQL injection attacks, the SQL query returns an error. For example, the following method queries for a product named "Sir Rodney's Scones." This value exists in the database being queried, but the name contains an apostrophe. Therefore, the tested method will return a valid result if it handles the apostrophe correctly, but will fail if it does not parse the apostrophe.

```csharp
[Test]
public void SQLInjectionFiltering()
{
    // Method should throw an argument if ProductName has no characters
    int testInteger;
    testInteger = Database.GetInventoryFromProductName("Sir Rodney's Scones");
    Assertion.Assert((testInteger >= 0) && (testInteger < 10000));
}
```

```vb
<Test> _
Public  Sub SQLInjectionFiltering()
    ' Method should throw an argument if ProductName has no characters
    Dim testInteger As Integer
    testInteger=DataMyBase.GetInventoryFromProductName("Sir Rodney's Scones")
    Assertion.Assert((testInteger > =  0) AndAlso (testInteger < 10000))
End Sub
```

To test a Web application for vulnerability to cross-site scripting (CSS) attacks, your test method should perform the following steps:

1. Submit HTML-encoded input (such as "<test />") to the method that processes user input.

2. Call the method that generates user output, and check for the presence of the HTML-encoded input. Fail the test if the input was not sanitized.

See Also   For more information about techniques for sanitizing input, see Chapter 2.

Practice: Building Automated Unit Tests

In this practice, you use NUnit to perform unit testing on a sample application. Then you add unit tests, and update the application so that it passes these unit tests. Complete the procedure in Exercise 1, and then answer the questions and complete the tasks in Exercises 2 and 3. If you are unable to answer a question, review the lesson materials and try the question again. You can find answers to the questions in the "Questions and Answers" section at the end of this chapter.

Exercise 1: Running a Unit Test Against a Sample Application

In this exercise, you install NUnit and then run unit tests built into a sample application.

1. Download and install the latest version of NUnit from *http://www.nunit.org/*.

2. Use Microsoft Windows Explorer to copy the NorthwindUnitTesting folder from the companion CD to your My Documents\Visual Studio Projects\ folder.

3. In Windows Explorer, select the My Documents\Visual Studio Projects\ folder, and then double-click NorthwindUnitTesting.csproj.

   Visual Studio .NET 2003 will open the Northwind project.

4. In Visual Studio .NET, verify that the nunit.framework reference exists. If it does not, click the Project menu, and then click Add Reference. On the .NET tab, click the nunit.framework component. Click Select, and then click OK.

5. Click the Build menu, and then click Build Solution.

   Visual Studio .NET 2003 compiles the application.

6. Launch the NUnit graphical tool named Nunit Gui.

7. Click the File menu, and then click Open. In the Open Project dialog box, select the My Documents\Visual Studio Projects\NorthwindUnitTesting\bin\Debug \NorthwindUnitTesting.exe file. Click Open.

8. Click the Run button.

As shown in Figure 3-1, NUnit runs each of the test methods and reports the results. There were two failures, which indicates that you have some work to do to protect against vulnerabilities. Also, you should add several unit tests.

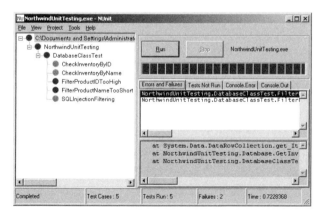

Figure 3-1   NUnit detects two failed tests in the assembly.

Exercise 2: Adding Unit Tests

In this exercise, you identify additional tests that should be added to the sample application, and then create the tests. Read the scenario and answer the questions that follow.

Scenario   Currently, the *DatabaseClassTest* class contains five tests:

- **CheckInventoryByID**   Verifies that the application can successfully return a valid inventory value given a known product ID

- **CheckInventoryByName**   Verifies that the application can successfully return a valid inventory value given a known product name

- **FilterProductIDTooHigh**   Verifies that the application throws an *ArgumentOutOfRangeException* given an invalid product ID that is too high

- **FilterProductNameTooShort**   Verifies that the application throws an *ArgumentOutOfRangeException* given an invalid product name that is zero characters

- **SQLInjectionFiltering**   Verifies that the application can successfully query for a product name containing a SQL delimiter (an apostrophe)

However, your manager does not think that these tests are sufficient.

Questions and Tasks

1. What other tests should you add?

2. Add the extra test methods, and rerun the tests.

3. How long did step 2 take?

4. Why should you bother to do this? Is it worth it?

5. What additional test methods did you create? Show your work.

Exercise 3: Adding Bounds Checking to the Application

In this exercise, you update the sample application so that it passes the existing unit tests.

1. The FilterProductNameTooShort test is currently failing because the *Database.GetInventoryFromProductName* method is not throwing an exception when an empty string is passed. How can you fix the method?

2. The FilterProductIDTooHigh test is currently failing because the *Database.GetInventoryFromProductID* method is not throwing an exception when a high value is passed. How can you fix the method?

3. How will you fix the application so that it passes the tests you added?

Lesson Summary

- Unit testing enables developers to find bugs and security vulnerabilities in their code before releasing it to QA.

- Test-first development starts with the creation of a testing infrastructure that exercises every planned feature and method in your application and ends only when all tests are passed.

- To perform unit testing, first create test unit methods. Then, implement your application's methods and test the application using the test unit methods.

- The free NUnit tool provides a framework for developing test unit methods and evaluating the tests.

Lesson 2: Testing Assemblies for Vulnerabilities

Unit testing has its limits for vulnerability testing. Specifically, unit testing cannot detect poor coding practices, such as not declaring permission requirements. Unit testing also cannot detect confidential data being transmitted through unencrypted communications channels, nor vulnerability to denial-of-service (DoS) attacks. As a developer, it is worthwhile for you to perform these fundamental types of tests against your own assemblies.

After this lesson, you will be able to

■ List key steps in the developer's pre-release security testing process.

■ Improve the effectiveness of vulnerability testing.

■ List no-cost tools for testing your applications for security vulnerabilities.

Estimated lesson time: 30 minutes

The Developer's Pre-Release Security Testing Process

Formal security testing involves using one of several different well-known processes. This book won't attempt to describe these formalized processes, because this book is about development, not testing. However, before handing off an application you develop to QA, you should consider the following steps when examining it for potential security vulnerabilities:

1. **Assess the attack surface**   Identify all potential points of direct entry to your application, including ASP.NET pages that accept input, Web services, and all public methods. Each potential point of entry should be examined for vulnerabilities.

2. **Identify likely targets, and also potential attackers who would be attracted to those targets**   For example, a Web application with forum capabilities is likely to be targeted with CSS attacks by forum users against other forum users. An e-commerce application is more likely to be targeted by financially motivated attackers seeking credit card numbers. Assume an application is vulnerable to all major types of attack, unless it has a specific resistance. For example, Windows Forms applications are generally not targeted by CSS attacks, and applications built on the .NET Framework are very resistant to buffer overflow attacks.

3. **Assess communication security**   Can an attacker with access to the network equipment capture traffic and derive confidential information?

4. **Verify that your application's default configuration is the most secure**   If your application requires tuning after installation to improve the security, it is not following the secure by default tenet.

5. **Verify that the least privilege principle is followed**   Specifically, test that databases have restricted permissions and client-side applications that can be run by a standard user account.

> **See Also**   For more information about the secure-by-default and least privilege principles, see Chapter 2.

6. **Test the server component's resistance to DoS attacks**   Generally, tools that test scalability reveal DoS susceptibility.

> **See Also**   For more information about formal security testing methodologies, read the *Open Source Security Testing Methodology Manual*, available at *http://www.isecom.org/projects /osstmm.shtml.*

Best Practices for Vulnerability Testing

Thoroughly covering vulnerability testing would require an entire book, so this section provides best practices. Developers who are performing preliminary vulnerability testing on their own applications prior to handoff to QA should apply as many of these best practices as they can:

- **Monitor attack trends**   Stay up to date on the latest types of attacks, because new types of exploits appear regularly.

> **See Also**   For information about exploiting vulnerable applications, see Chapter 1.

- **Simulate attacks and examine events**   Determine whether administrators can detect and analyze a particular attack based on the monitoring information provided by the application. Do log files provide enough information to identify the attacker and understand the attack technique?

- **Test beyond the application**   If your application trusts DNS when contacting a server because it doesn't use any server authentication, that might be okay—but it's important to disclose this to your customers.

- **Filter test requests from usage logs**   If you are testing a Web application that is already in a production environment, configure your usage-reporting software to ignore requests from the test computer or computers.

- **Test Windows Forms applications as a regular user**   By not using an administrator account, you will identify any problems your application has complying with the principle of least privilege.

Available Security Testing Tools

As a developer, you probably do not have a significant amount of time allocated to testing your own applications. To allow you to perform some pre-QA security testing as efficiently as possible, this section describes no-cost tools that automate and simplify the process of identifying vulnerabilities in your application.

FxCop

FxCop compares assemblies to a list of rules based on the Microsoft .NET Framework Design Guidelines. FxCop reveals a large number of both common and uncommon coding mistakes, many of which are security related. For example, making *IntPtr* and *UIntPtr* pointers public fields exposes a potential security vulnerability, because another assembly might be able to read or modify the pointers. Most rules do not have a direct impact on the vulnerability level of the application. However, following the .NET Framework Design Guidelines will make the code more consistent and easier to review, which in turn improves security.

See Also   Read the .NET Framework Design Guidelines at *http://msdn.microsoft.com /library/en-us/cpgenref/html/cpconnetframeworkdesignguidelines.asp.*

See Also   The practice at the end of this lesson walks you through the process of using FxCop.

Figure 3-2 shows FxCop discovering a number of weaknesses in an assembly, including uncaught exceptions.

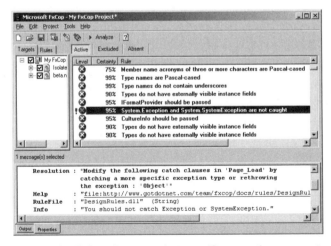

Figure 3-2 FxCop discovers that specific exceptions are not caught.

Network Monitor

Network Monitor is a protocol analyzer (more commonly known as a *sniffer*) that is included free with Microsoft server operating systems. Network Monitor captures and analyzes raw network communications. After it captures traffic, you can examine the communications to determine whether encryption is used and whether any confidential information is being transmitted across the network without being encrypted or obscured.

To install Network Monitor on Windows Server 2003:

1. From Control Panel, launch the Add or Remove Programs applet.

2. Click Add/Remove Windows Components.

3. In the Windows Components Wizard, click Management And Monitoring Tools, and then click Details.

4. Select the Network Monitor Tools check box, and then click OK.

5. Click Next. Respond to any prompts that appear. Finally, click Finish.

After installation, you can run Network Monitor from the Administrative Tools group. You can run Network Monitor on either the client or the server; however, the version of Network Monitor included free with Microsoft server operating systems is capable of capturing only traffic sent to or from the computer on which it is running. Figure 3-3 shows captured Web communications—evidently unencrypted, because the details of the request are visible.

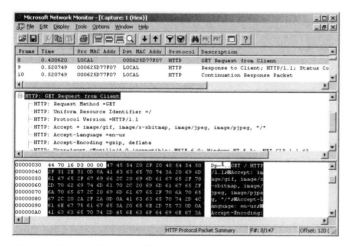

Figure 3-3   Use Network Monitor to verify that Network Communications cannot be easily analyzed.

See Also   To use Network Monitor effectively, you must have a detailed understanding of network protocols. For more information about using Network Monitor, see Windows Server 2003 Help And Support Center.

Real World   Detecting Communications Vulnerabilities

If your application is sending user names and passwords in clear text across the network, Network Monitor will make that weakness painfully obvious. Several no-cost tools are available that perform the same type of protocol analysis, so attackers won't have any problem re-creating your test and using the information against you. Network Monitor makes it obvious that your application exposes private information only when you use the clear text format. For example, anyone can manually decode ROT13 (which rotates characters 13 letters through the alphabet), but Network Monitor won't help you out.

Early in my career I spent some time studying Request For Comments (RFCs), especially those relating to Web communications. The RFCs taught me that basic user authentication between a browser and a Web server uses Base64 encoding, but every other piece of documentation I read said that the password was transmitted in "clear text." To reconcile this, I pulled up Network Monitor and captured an authentication attempt. I quickly found where the password was in the packet, but it was definitely not in clear text—it appeared to be gibberish. I knew that Base64 encoding could be decoded without a password or key, but not simply. Eventually, I wrote a Perl script to do the conversion and verified that it was, indeed, easy to identify the raw password.

To the untrained eye, the weakest of encryption techniques, or even reversible encoding, appears to be encrypted. In short, you can use Network Monitor to detect only obvious, glaring communications vulnerabilities. However, you not *seeing* any problems doesn't mean a sophisticated attacker can't find a weakness.

Application Center Test

Application Center Test, a tool included with Visual Studio .NET, is primarily designed to test the performance of ASP.NET applications. However, it should not be overlooked as a tool for testing resistance to DoS attacks. DoS attacks against applications are effective because the applications do not scale efficiently. Testing an ASP.NET application under heavy load simulates one type of a DoS attack against your application, and Application Center Test will reveal how your application responds to heavy load, and which pages in your application fail.

Figure 3-4 shows a Web application being tested. As shown in the figure, the Web application is responding to between 0 and 40 requests per second—a relatively low rate that is not likely to withstand even an unsophisticated DoS attack. However, the application is not producing HTTP errors, which is a good sign.

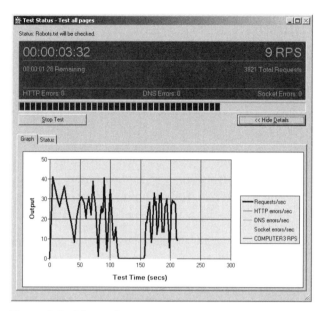

Figure 3-4   Microsoft Application Center Test is a good way to test resistance to DoS attacks.

Application Center Test produced the following summary output from a live Web server that handled about 250 requests per second. In the Response Codes section, notice that 100 percent of the response codes were 200—the HTTP success response code. An application that was less resistant to DoS attacks would have begun returning other HTTP response codes, such as 500.

Errors Counts

- HTTP: 0

- DNS: 0

- Socket: 0

Additional Network Statistics

- Average bandwidth (bytes/sec): 1,120,257.96

- Number of bytes sent (bytes): 18,957,590

- Number of bytes received (bytes): 317,119,798

- Average rate of sent bytes (bytes/sec): 63,191.97

- Average rate of received bytes (bytes/sec): 1,057,065.99

- Number of connection errors: 0

- Number of send errors: 0

- Number of receive errors: 0

- Number of timeout errors: 0

Response Codes

- Response Code: 200 - The request completed successfully.

- Count: 48,719

- Percent (%): 100.00

If the application does not scale well, you can view the Requests report to determine which pages are the sources of the bottleneck. Application Center Test records the average time to first byte and time to last byte for each page in your test.

> **Tip** You should focus your development time on increasing the efficiency of the pages that had the highest response times; they are the most likely to be targeted during a DoS attack.

When creating tests, remember that attackers might not use standard, well-formed HTTP requests. They might submit invalid information to your application specifically to induce a processor-intensive error-handling routine. Fortunately, Application Center Test provides a great deal of flexibility and can simulate a potentially malicious request during a test.

> **Off the Record** Unfortunately, no amount of testing or scalability can make your application entirely resistant to DoS attacks. Well-formed distributed DoS attacks will almost always cause an application, computer, or the underlying network to become inaccessible. Yes, with proper tuning, you can enable your application to resist an attacker with a single computer. However, if your application gets targeted by an attacker who controls thousands of *zombie computers* (compromised computers that an attacker controls), you're going offline.

Permissions View Tool

The Permissions View tool (Permview.exe) is a command-line tool that developers and testers can use to view the permission sets requested by an assembly or to view all declarative security used by an assembly. For example, you can use Permview.exe to verify that a developer has specifically requested permissions in the assembly, and that the permissions are not excessive. The following output shows Permview analyzing an assembly that contains a minimum permission set request of Unrestricted, which would be considered excessive in most circumstances:

```
Microsoft (R) .NET Framework Permission Request Viewer.  Version 1.1.4322.573 Copyright
(C) Microsoft Corp. 1998-2000

minimal permission set:
<PermissionSet class="System.Security.PermissionSet" version ="1">
   <Unrestricted/>
</PermissionSet>

optional permission set:
   Not specified

refused permission set:
   Not specified
```

Permview is included with the .NET Framework software development kit. It is probably not in your path by default, but if you installed Visual Studio .NET 2003, you can find it in the C:\Program Files\Microsoft Visual Studio .NET 2003\SDK\v1.1\Bin\ folder.

PEVerify Tool

The PEVerify (PEVerify.exe) tool helps developers who generate Microsoft intermediate language (MSIL)—such as compiler writers and script engine developers—determine whether their MSIL code and associated metadata meet type safety requirements. Some compilers generate verifiably type-safe code only if you avoid using certain language constructs. If, as a developer, you are using such a compiler, you might want to verify that you have not compromised the type safety of your code. In this situation, you can run the PEVerify tool on your files to check the MSIL and metadata.

PEVerify is included with the .NET Framework software development kit. It is probably not in your path by default, but if you installed Visual Studio .NET 2003, you can find it in the C:\Program Files\Microsoft Visual Studio .NET 2003\SDK\v1.1\Bin\ folder.

Practice: Testing Assemblies for Vulnerabilities

In this practice, you use FxCop to analyze a sample assembly. Then, you analyze one of your own assemblies, and answer questions about the results. Complete the procedure in Exercise 1, and then answer the questions and complete the tasks in Exercise 2. If you are unable to answer a question, review the lesson materials and try the question again. You can find answers to the questions in the "Questions and Answers" section at the end of this chapter

Exercise 1: Using FxCop to Test an Assembly for Security Weaknesses

In this exercise, you use FxCop to analyze a sample assembly to identify potential security weaknesses.

1. Download and install the latest version of FxCop from *http://www.gotdotnet.com /team/fxcop/*.

2. If you did not complete the Practice associated with Lesson 1, complete the following steps:

    a. Use Windows Explorer to copy the NorthwindUnitTesting folder from the companion CD to your My Documents\Visual Studio Projects\ folder.

    b. In Windows Explorer, select the My Documents\Visual Studio Projects\ folder, and then double-click NorthwindUnitTesting.csproj.

    Visual Studio .NET 2003 will open the Northwind project.

    c. Remove the contents of the *DatabaseClassTest* class.

3. In Visual Studio .NET 2003, with the NorthwindUnitTesting project open, click the Build menu, and then click Build Solution.

    Visual Studio .NET 2003 compiles the application.

4. Launch the FxCop tool.

5. Click the File menu, and then click New Project.

6. Click the Project menu, and then click Add Targets. In the Open dialog box, select the My Documents\Visual Studio Projects\NorthwindUnitTesting\bin\Debug \NorthwindUnitTesting.exe file. Click Open.

7. Click the Project menu, and then click Analyze.

8. In the Analysis Summary dialog box, click OK.

    FxCop displays a list of rules that have been violated, as shown in Figure 3-5.

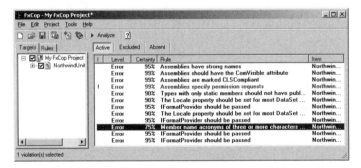

Figure 3-5   FxCop displays an analysis of the sample application.

9. Double-click the Assemblies Specify Permission Requests rule.

10. In the Active Message Details dialog box, click the Rule Details tab, shown in Figure 3-6.

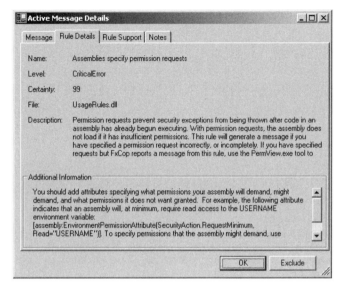

Figure 3-6 FxCop provides detailed information about broken rules.

11. Read the description and additional information. (Chapter 6, "Implementing Code Access Security," provides more information about permission requests.)

12. Click the Rule Support tab. Note that a URL is provided that contains additional information about the rule and about how to write code that uses permissions requests.

13. Click OK to return to FxCop, examine each of the other rules, and think about which of the rules could have an impact on security.

Exercise 2: Analyzing FxCop Results

In this exercise, you answer questions about FxCop's analysis of an application you have written. First, use FxCop to analyze the assembly you most recently compiled.

1. Which of the rules highlight weaknesses in your code that should be addressed?

2. Which of the rules can be safely ignored?

3. What potential security vulnerabilities are not discovered by FxCop? Is using FxCop sufficient to limit your risk from vulnerabilities?

Lesson Summary

- An effective security testing process starts with a thorough analysis of points of entry, potential vulnerabilities, and attack targets. Then, it examines the application's communications security, compliance to the secure by default and least privilege principles, and resistance to DoS attacks.

- To effectively write and test code for resistance to attacks, you must stay on top of new attack trends, exercise your code by simulating attacks, examine the security of the network infrastructure, and test applications as a standard user.

- There are several tools you can use to aid the vulnerability testing process:

  - **FxCop**   A tool for analyzing your code against the .NET Framework Design Guidelines.

  - **Network Monitor**   A protocol analyzer that can examine raw network communications for confidential information that should be encrypted.

  - **Application Center Test**   A Web site scalability testing tool useful for identifying DoS vulnerabilities.

  - **Permissions View Tool**   A command-line tool to display the permission sets requested by an assembly.

  - **PEVerify Tool**   A tool for compiler writers and script engine developers to use to determine whether their MSIL code and associated metadata meet type safety requirements.

Lab: Testing Applications for Vulnerabilities

In this lab, you recommend changes to your development environment to improve the efficiency of the development process for a fictitious organization. Read the following scenario and then complete the exercise that follows. If you are unable to answer a question, review the lessons and try the question again. You can find answers to the questions in the "Questions and Answers" section at the end of this chapter.

Scenario

You are a member of a development team for Woodgrove Bank. Your team develops and maintains an internal Windows Forms application that provides tellers with access to bank account data. Your team has also created an ASP.NET Web site to provide your customers with direct access to their financial information over the Web.

Your company safeguards a great deal of personal financial information for your clients. Recently, in an effort to demonstrate your company's commitment to security and privacy, Woodgrove Bank created and staffed a Chief Security Officer (CSO) position. One of the CSO's first acts was to hire a consulting firm to audit your team's development process. The consulting firm reported that although your team was well educated about secure development methodologies, vulnerabilities still slipped into your applications.

The CSO decided to remedy the situation by increasing the staffing of the QA team that tests your applications before they are released. Specifically, the new members of the QA team are dedicated to finding vulnerabilities and ensuring they are remedied before allowing the application to be released. They're very good at their jobs, and they have discovered quite a few potential vulnerabilities.

Unfortunately, their thoroughness has a downside. Each time they find a vulnerability, they reject your team's code. Your team then has to fix the vulnerability and resubmit the code to the QA team for additional testing. Because of scheduling difficulties, this cycle takes at least a week each time. Sometimes, this cycle happens several times for a given release, because fixing one problem introduces a new vulnerability. This delay has kept your team from releasing any new updates, and the low productivity has reflected poorly on you. Your manager is looking for ways to streamline the process.

You talk to your manager and a few other key people so that you can formulate the best responses to your boss' inevitable questions.

Interviews

Following is a list of company personnel interviewed and their statements:

- **Your manager** "These new QA procedures are ponderous. Who cares if you forgot to validate input for one function? Well, the new CSO has something to prove, and he's not going to back down, so we had better just figure out a way to adapt. We need to start writing code that can slip through the QA team's checks. They seem to focus on verifying that all functions validate and sanitize input, whether the input is directly from users or from a front-end interface like the Windows Forms client or the ASP.NET pages."

- **QA Manager** "Don't take the rejections personally; we're just doing our jobs. We have to test each of your methods to verify that it correctly responds to invalid input by throwing an exception. We also need to make sure that input is properly sanitized so that an attacker can't do something like sneak a SQL injection attack in."

- **Chief Security Officer** "I anticipated the temporary delay while you adjusted your development process to better enforce input validation requirements. It's not a problem—just make whatever changes to your development cycle necessary to ensure your code meets the security requirements that the QA team enforces."

Exercise

Your manager shows up in your office before her big meeting with the CSO and asks you the following questions.

1. "I guess I'm going to have to accept that you guys can't write perfect code. How do you suggest we go about reducing the number of QA cycles?"

2. "Why should my developers waste their time doing testing? That's why we have the QA group."

3. "What tools can we use to keep the time we spend testing to a minimum?"

Chapter Summary

- When using unit testing with a test-first methodology, you start the development process by creating code that exercises the methods and functionality you plan to implement. Then, during the development process, you continually use the unit tests to validate that functionality and resistance to vulnerability remain stable.

- After an assembly is completed, perform additional testing to check for compliance to coding guidelines, communications security, and resistance to DoS attacks.

Exam Highlights

Before taking the exam, review the key points and terms that are presented in this chapter. You need to know this information.

Key Points

- The reasons unit testing improves application security
- The costs and benefits of test-first development
- Methods for identifying vulnerabilities in assemblies

Key Terms

test-first development   A methodology that developers follow that involves creating unit tests before the units themselves

unit tests   Modules that exercise other modules

unit testing   A technique that developers use to automatically test an application's components after making updates

Questions and Answers

Practice: Building Automated Unit Tests

Page
3-10

Exercise 2: Adding Unit Tests

1. What other tests should you add?

   Examine the units in the application, and test that each method handles valid and invalid input correctly. At a minimum, additional tests should:

   - Verify that the *Database.GetInventoryByProductID* method throws an *ArgumentOutOfRangeException* when input that is too low is passed
   - Verify that the *Database.GetInventoryByProductName* method throws an *ArgumentOutOfRangeException* when input that is too long is passed

2. Add the extra test methods, and rerun the tests.

3. How long did step 2 take?

   It should have taken only a few minutes.

4. Why should you bother to do this? Is it worth it?

   It is worth it, because preventing a security compromise could save millions of dollars. Answers will vary, but spending these extra few minutes seems well worth the effort.

5. What additional test methods did you create? Show your work.

   Answers will vary. Although you can create additional test methods in many different ways, you can create the two suggested tests by using the following methods:

```
[Test]
[ExpectedException(typeof(ArgumentOutOfRangeException))]
public void FilterProductNameTooLong()
{
    // Method should throw an exception if ProductName is
    // longer than 40 characters
    int testInteger = Database.GetInventoryFromProductName(→
"Thisisaverylongproductnamethatislongerthanfortycharacters");
}

[Test]
[ExpectedException(typeof(ArgumentOutOfRangeException))]
public void FilterProductIDTooLow()
{
    // Method should throw an argument if ProductID is less than 1
    int testInteger = Database.GetInventoryFromProductID(-1);
}
```

```
<Test()> _
<ExpectedException(Type.GetType(ArgumentOutOfRangeException))> _
Public  Sub FilterProductNameTooLong()
    ' Method should throw an exception if ProductName is
    ' longer than 40 characters
    Dim testInteger As Integer = DataMyBase.GetInventoryFromProductName(→
"Thisisaverylongproductnamethatislongerthanfortycharacters")
End Sub


<Test()> _
<ExpectedException(Type.GetType(ArgumentOutOfRangeException))> _
Public  Sub FilterProductIDTooLow()
    ' Method should throw an argument if ProductID is less than 1
    Dim testInteger As Integer =  DataMyBase.GetInventoryFromProductID(-1)
End Sub
```

Page
3-10

Exercise 3: Adding Bounds Checking to the Application

1. The FilterProductNameTooShort test is currently failing because the *Database.Get-InventoryFromProductName* method is not throwing an exception when an empty string is passed. How can you fix the method?

Answers will vary, but the following command would test input for both minimum and maximum length:

```
if (!((productName.Length > 0) && (productName.Length <= 40))) →
throw new ArgumentOutOfRangeException("productName", productName, →
"Input too long or short.");

If Not ((productName.Length > 0) AndAlso (productName.Length <= 40)) Then
      Throw New ArgumentOutOfRangeException("productName", productName, →
"Input too long or short.")
End If
```

Note that the first line of the *Database.GetInventoryFromProductName* method is a comment from another developer, reminding himself to uncomment the command that checks the input length.

2. The FilterProductIDTooHigh test is currently failing because the *Database.Get-InventoryFromProductID* method is not throwing an exception when a high value is passed. How can you fix the method?

This answer is similar to that of the previous question: you simply need to add an if statement that checks for acceptable range and throws an exception if the input is invalid.

3. How will you fix the application so that it passes the tests you added?

Answers will vary. However, simple bounds checking can be implemented by using an if statement at the beginning of a method and throwing an exception if the input is not within a valid range.

Practice: Testing Assemblies for Vulnerabilities

Page
3-21
Exercise 2: Analyzing FxCop Results

1. Which of the rules highlight weaknesses in your code that should be addressed?

   The specific rules that FxCop identifies as errors in your application will vary. However, the rules displayed with an exclamation point are the most critical.

2. Which of the rules can be safely ignored?

   FxCop also checks for design, performance, and naming rules that do not have a direct impact on an application's security vulnerabilities, but that can reduce the readability and testability of an assembly. The rules that can be ignored will vary according to how strictly style and design rules are enforced in your organization, and whether your internal rules match those built into FxCop. FxCop does allow you to selectively exclude rules you consider unimportant.

3. What potential security vulnerabilities are not discovered by FxCop? Is using FxCop sufficient to limit your risk from vulnerabilities?

   FxCop cannot discover canonicalization errors, SQL injection vulnerabilities, CSS vulnerabilities, and many other weaknesses to specific attacks. Therefore, you cannot rely solely on FxCop to test the security of your code.

Lab: Testing Applications for Vulnerabilities

Page
3-24
Exercise

1. "I guess I'm going to have to accept that you guys can't write perfect code. How do you suggest we go about reducing the number of QA cycles?"

   Unit testing is an effective way to reduce the number of QA cycles, particularly when combined with a test-first methodology. This allows developers to find bugs (security-related or otherwise) in code before sending the code off to another group for testing.

2. "Why should my developers waste their time doing testing? That's why we have the QA group."

   Unit testing does take time, especially at the beginning of the project. However, real-life experience has proven that it makes the development team more efficient in the long run. When used to check for security vulnerabilities, testing can effectively improve the security of an application.

3. "What tools can we use to keep the time we spend testing to a minimum?"

   NUnit is a free tool that provides a framework for creating unit tests. There are several other no-cost tools that can be used to test different security aspects of an application. FxCop analyzes an assembly's compliance to the Microsoft .NET Framework Design Guidelines. Network Monitor captures and displays raw communications between the client side and server side of an application, which can reveal unencrypted traffic. Application Center Test is useful for testing the performance and scalability of a Web application, which is a good way of determining how resilient an application is to DoS attacks.

Section 2
Using the .NET Security Framework

Section 2 of this book teaches how to use the security features inherent in the .NET Framework. These four chapters provide instruction for configuring your application, the common language runtime, and the underlying operating system to allow your application to run in the most secure environment possible.

■ Chapter 4, "Taking Advantage of Platform Security," teaches the fundamentals of access control lists—the basic building blocks that operating systems use to control access to files and folders. Then you learn how to use isolated storage, a private file-system-within-a-file system provided by the .NET Framework, to reduce the privileges required for using persistent storage. Finally, you learn how to configure your development environment to enable you to create new applications without using an administrator account.

■ Chapter 5, "Implementing Role-Based Security," explains how you can use authorization and authentication in your application. This chapter teaches how to take advantage of the mechanisms built into the platform, as well as how to create your own custom techniques.

■ Chapter 6, "Implementing Code Access Security," teaches you about relatively new security techniques introduced with the .NET Framework. You learn how

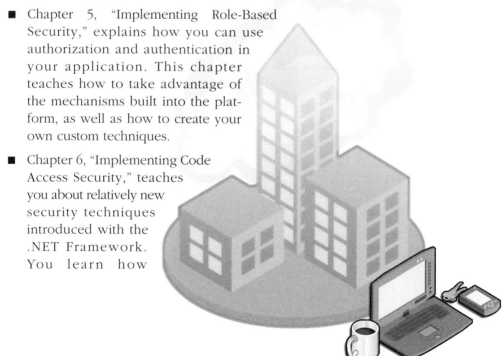

assemblies are granted or denied permissions based on aspects of the code rather than on the more conventional user name and password credentials.

- Chapter 7, "Maximizing Security During Deployment," provides instruction for ensuring your application is deployed in the most secure environment possible. You learn how, and when, to sign your assemblies, and when to implement delayed signing. Additionally, hands-on exercises teach how to configure destination run-time environments by using tools included with the .NET Framework.

4 Taking Advantage of Platform Security

Why This Chapter Matters

File permissions and user rights are not solely the domain of the system administrators. Developers must understand these concepts, too, to develop applications that take advantage of these platform security features.

Most importantly, you must understand how access control lists (ACLs) work, how to configure them manually, and how to automatically set them during your application's setup procedure. ACLs are an excellent way to limit access to files, but conventional files are often not the best way to protect information. Isolated storage, a feature of the .NET Framework, provides additional privacy and protection for files with minimal additional programming effort. Finally, you must understand how to configure your operating system's security so that you can do your job without administrator rights.

Exam Objectives in this Chapter:

- Implement data protection.

  - Protect data in files and folders by creating, modifying, and deleting discretionary access control list (DACL) or security access control list (SACL) entries.

- Develop code under a least privilege account within the development environment.

  - Configure the Microsoft .NET development environment and operating system.

  - Select the appropriate privileges.

Lessons in this Chapter:

Before You Begin

To complete the practices and lab exercises in this chapter, you must have one computer running Microsoft Windows Server 2003. During the course of performing the exercises in this chapter, the computer's security can be reduced. Therefore, the computer should not be a production computer and should not be connected to any network, especially the Internet, even if a firewall is present. Install Microsoft Visual Studio .NET 2003 using the default settings.

Lesson 1: Protecting Files Using Access Control Lists

ACLs are the most common technique for restricting access to files, folders, printers, services, registry values, and just about every object that exists within an operating system. As a developer, you must understand ACLs for two important reasons:

- You can configure them to restrict access to sensitive files, folders, and other objects used by your application.

- You can configure them to allow users to access files and other objects that they are not typically allowed to access, but that the application needs to access.

This lesson teaches the fundamentals of ACLs, how to manually configure them, and how you can configure them using automated tools or from within your application.

After this lesson, you will be able to

- Explain the purpose of a discretionary access control list.
- Explain the purpose of a security access control list.
- Describe standard and special file and folder permissions.
- Calculate effective permissions.
- Configure ACLs using graphical tools or command-line tools, or from within an assembly.

Estimated lesson time: 45 minutes

What Is a Discretionary Access Control List?

A *discretionary access control list* (DACL) is an authorization restriction mechanism that identifies the users and groups that are assigned or denied access permissions on an object. Windows Server 2003, like all recent members of the Microsoft Windows family, keeps track of the privileges users have for accessing resources by using a DACL. If a DACL does not explicitly identify a user, or any groups that a user is a member of, the user is denied access to that object. By default, a DACL is controlled by the owner of an object or the person who created the object, and it contains access control entries (ACEs) that determine user access to the object. An *ACE* is an entry in an object's DACL that grants permissions to a user or group.

What Is a Security Access Control List?

A *security access control list* (SACL) is a usage event logging mechanism that determines how file or folder access is audited. Unlike a DACL, an SACL cannot restrict access to a file or folder. However, an SACL can cause an event to be recorded in the security event log when a user accesses a file or folder. This auditing can be used to troubleshoot access problems or identify intrusions.

To a security professional, an SACL is a critical tool for intrusion detection. A systems administrator is more likely to use SACLs to identify permissions that need to be granted to a user to allow an application to run correctly. A developer uses SACLs to track resources that her application is denied access to, so that she can customize the application to allow it to run, without problems, under a less privileged account.

Off the Record   It's important to understand the difference between SACLs and DACLs for the exam. The difference between the two is also a common question in technical interviews. Fortunately, it's simple: DACLs restrict access, whereas SACLs audit access. Realistically, though, you're not going to spend much time thinking about SACLs when you write an application. You might, however, dedicate many hours to troubleshooting problems relating to DACLs. For that reason, this book will use the term ACL to refer to DACLs.

See Also   For detailed information about using SACLs and auditing, see Lesson 3 of Chapter 1, "Implementing Security at Design Time."

Standard and Special File and Folder Permissions

File and folder permissions enable users to restrict access to content stored on NTFS volumes. You can grant access to open, edit, or delete files and folders. Files and folders also have the concept of *ownership*: the user who creates a file or folder is the owner of that object and by default has the ability to specify the level of access that other users have.

The following are the standard permissions that can be applied to files and folders:

- **Full Control**   Users can perform any action on the file or folder, including creating and deleting it, and modifying its permissions.
- **Modify**   Users can read, edit, and delete files and folders.
- **Read & Execute**   Users can view files and run applications.
- **List Folder Contents**   Users can browse a folder.
- **Read**   Users can view a file or the contents of a folder. If an executable file has Read but not Read & Execute permission, the user will not be able to start the executable.
- **Write**   Users can create files in a directory but not necessarily read them. This permission is useful for creating a folder in which multiple users can deliver files but not access each other's files or even see what other files exist.

- **Special Permissions**   There are more than a dozen special permissions that can be assigned to a user or group. This permission shows as selected if the set of selected special permissions does not match a standard permission.

Standard and Special Permissions Compared

Access control lists for the file system, registry, printers, services, and Active Directory can all be configured using both standard and special permissions. Special permissions are very granular, and enable minute control over a user's access to an object. Standard permissions exist to make special permissions easier to manage. When you select a standard permission, Windows Server 2003 selects a set of special permissions that have been assigned to that standard permission.

The permissions available when you view the Security tab of a file or folder's properties dialog box are standard permissions. These include the Full Control, Modify, Read & Execute, Read, and Write standard permissions. If you grant Read & Execute standard permission, Windows Server 2003 automatically grants the List Folder/Read Data, Read Attributes, Read Extended Attributes, and Read Permissions special permissions. Similarly, if you deny the Read & Execute standard permission, the same special permissions are denied. You could choose to select those special permissions manually, but selecting the standard permission is more efficient.

When any of these standard permissions are selected, Windows Server 2003 automatically selects one or more of the following special permissions:

- **Traverse Folder/Execute File**   Traverse Folder, which applies only to folders, allows moving through folders to reach other files or folders, even when the user has no permissions for the traversed folders. Traverse folder takes effect only when the group or user is not granted the Bypass traverse checking user right, which the Everyone group has by default. Execute File, which applies only to files, allows running program files. Setting the Traverse Folder permission on a folder does not automatically set the Execute File permission on all files within that folder.

> **Tip**   Some special permissions, such as Traverse Folder/Execute File and List Folder/Read Data, have a different effect depending on the object type to which the permission is applied.

- **List Folder/Read Data**   List Folder, which applies only to folders, allows viewing filenames and subfolder names within the folder. Read Data, which applies only to files, allows viewing the contents of a file.

- **Read Attributes**   Allows viewing the attributes of a file or folder, such as read-only and hidden.

- **Read Extended Attributes**   Allows viewing the extended attributes of a file or folder. Extended attributes are defined by programs and can vary by program.

- **Create Files/Write Data**   Create Files, which applies only to folders, allows creating files within the folder. Write Data, which applies only to files, allows or denies making changes to the file and overwriting existing content.

- **Create Folders/Append Data**   Create Folders, which applies only to folders, allows or denies creating folders within the folder. Append Data, which applies only to files, allows or denies making changes to the end of the file but not changing, deleting, or overwriting existing data.

- **Write Attributes**   Allows changing the attributes of a file or folder, such as read-only or hidden.

- **Write Extended Attributes**   Allows changing the extended attributes of a file or folder.

- **Delete Subfolders and Files**   Allows deleting subfolders and files, even when the Delete permission has not been granted on the subfolder or file.

- **Delete**   Allows deleting the file or folder. If you don't have Delete permission on a file or folder, you can still delete it if you have been granted the Delete Subfolders and Files permission on the parent folder.

- **Read Permissions**   Allows reading permissions of the file or folder, such as Full Control, Read, and Write.

- **Change Permissions**   Allows changing permissions of the file or folder, such as Full Control, Read, and Write.

- **Take Ownership**   Allows taking ownership of the file or folder. The owner of a file or folder can always change permissions on it, regardless of any existing permissions that protect the file or folder.

Exam Tip   Neither standard nor special permissions map directly to ACEs. However, for the exam, it's sufficient to understand that standard permissions are used to simplify management of special permissions. Don't bother memorizing all the special permissions.

When you are editing file and folder permissions and you specify the Full Control standard permission, every possible special permission is added to the ACE for the user or group. When you specify the Modify standard permission, every special permission is assigned except the Change Permissions and Take Ownership special permissions.

Selecting the Read & Execute standard permission adds ACEs for Traverse Folder/Execute File, List Folder/Read Data, Read Attributes, Read Extended Attributes, and Read Permissions special permissions. The standard Read permission is identical to Read & Execute, except that it lacks the Traverse Folder/Execute File special permission. Finally, the friendly Write standard permission grants Create Files/Write Data, Create Folders/Append Data, Write Attributes, and Write Extended Attributes special permissions.

Security Alert   In the real world, you rarely have to deal with special permissions. In fact, you should avoid it whenever possible because managing special permissions is more difficult than managing standard permissions. Standard permissions are granular enough to meet all but the tightest security requirements.

Exam Tip   Most operating system objects use ACLs, including shared folders, printers, registry values, Active Directory objects, and services. However, the 70-330 and 70-340 exam objectives mention using ACLs only in the context of protecting files and folders. Therefore, file and folder permissions are the focus of this chapter and should be the focus of your preparation for the exam.

How Windows Calculates Effective Permissions

Calculating a user's effective permissions requires more than simply looking up that user's name in the ACL. ACEs can assign rights directly to the user, or they can assign rights to a security group or a special group. Additionally, users can be members of multiple groups, and groups can be nested within each other. Therefore, a single user can have several different ACEs in a single ACL. To understand what a user's effective permissions will be, you must understand how permissions are calculated when multiple ACEs apply to the user.

Permissions that are granted to a user, or the groups to which the user belongs, are cumulative. If Mary is a member of both the Accounting group and the Managers group, and the ACL for a file grants Mary's user account Read privileges, the Accounting group Modify privileges, and the Managers group Full Control privileges, Mary will have Full Control privileges. There's a catch, though. ACEs that deny access always override ACEs that grant access. Therefore, if the Accounting group is explicitly denied access to the file, Mary will not be able to open the file. Even though Mary is a member of the Managers group, and the Managers group has Full Control privileges, the Deny ACE means that all members of the Managers group are denied access to the file.

If no ACEs in an ACL apply to a user, that user is denied access to the object. In other words, not explicitly having privileges to an object is exactly the same as being explicitly denied access.

Explicit and Inherited Permissions

When you assign permissions directly to an object, you create an *explicit permission*. Assigning explicit permissions to every individual folder, file, registry value, and Active Directory object would be a ponderous task. In fact, managing the massive number of ACLs that would be required would have a significant impact on the performance of Windows Server 2003.

To make managing permissions more efficient, Windows Server 2003 includes the concept of inheritance. When Windows Server 2003 is initially installed, most objects have only *inherited permissions*. Inherited permissions propagate to an object from its parent object.

For example, the file system uses inherited permissions. Therefore, each new folder you create in the root C:\ folder inherits the exact permissions assigned to the C:\ folder. Similarly, each subkey you create in the HKEY_LOCAL_MACHINE\Software\ key inherits the exact permissions assigned to the parent key.

How to Configure ACLs

There are three different ways to configure ACLs:

- **Graphically, by using Windows Explorer**   This is the most common, and convenient, way to manually modify ACLs.

- **At a command line, by using Cacls or XCacls**   Two command-line tools exist for modifying ACLs: Cacls and XCacls. You can use either manually, but they are more commonly used within a batch file. You can call such a batch file from your application's setup routine.

- **From within an assembly**   The .NET Framework includes no native way to control ACLs. However, you can configure ACLs from your application by calling command-line tools or by referencing Microsoft Win32 security application programming interfaces (APIs).

The sections that follow describe each of these different techniques.

How to Configure ACLs Using Windows Explorer

To set, view, change, or remove permissions for files and folders by using Windows Explorer, follow these steps:

1. Open Windows Explorer, and then locate the file or folder for which you want to set special permissions.

2. Right-click the file or folder, click Properties, and then click the Security tab, as shown in Figure 4-1.

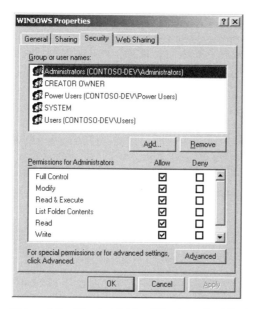

Figure 4-1   Viewing folder ACLs by using Windows Explorer

3. In the Group Or User Name list, click a group or user. The Permissions list will display that security principle's ACLs.

4. You can now perform the following actions:

    ❑ To modify a group or user's ACLs, select or clear the appropriate check boxes in the Permissions list.

    ❑ To add users or groups, click the Add button. In the Enter The Object Names To Select box, type the name of the user or group using the format ***domainname \name***. When you are finished, click OK.

    ❑ To remove an existing user's ACL, click the group or user, and then click Remove.

5. To modify special permissions, click Advanced, and then do one of the following:

❑ To set special permissions for a new group or user, click Add. In the Name box, type the name of the user or group using the format ***domainname \name***. When you are finished, click OK to automatically open the Permission Entry dialog box.

❑ To view or change special permissions for an existing group or user, click the name of the group or user and then click Edit.

❑ To remove a group or user and its special permissions, click the name of the group or user and then click Remove. If the Remove button is unavailable, clear the Allow Inheritable Permissions check box. The file or folder will no longer inherit permissions.

This book does not describe individual special permissions for other types of objects, nor how to edit them. However, the user interface for editing special permissions for other objects is similar to that for files and folders.

How to Override Inheritance for a New Permission   After you set permissions on a parent object, new child objects automatically inherit these permissions. You can override this default behavior when adding a new permission, however. Using the file system as an example, if you do not want child folders to inherit a new permission, follow these steps:

1. Use Windows Explorer to view the folder's properties.

2. Click the Security tab, and then click the Advanced button.

3. In the Advanced Security Settings dialog box, click the Add button.

4. In the Select User Or Group dialog box, specify the user or group that the ACE will apply to, and then click OK.

5. In the Permission Entry dialog box, select This Folder Only in the Apply Onto list when you specify permissions for the parent folder, as shown in Figure 4-2. To specify permissions that do not apply to the parent folder, but exist only to be inherited, select Subfolders And Files Only, Subfolders Only, or Files Only. Other objects, such as the registry, provide similar functionality.

Tip   If the Apply Onto list is dimmed, the permission was inherited from the parent. You can change inheritance only for explicit permissions.

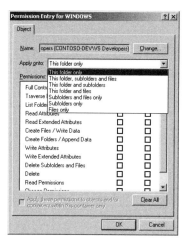

Figure 4-2 New permissions are inherited by default, but this behavior can be manually overridden.

How to Override Inheritance from a Child Object   You can also control inheritance from the child objects. If you do not want a child object to inherit the parent's permissions, follow these steps:

1. Use Windows Explorer to view the folder's properties.

2. Click the Security tab and then click the Advanced button.

3. Clear the Allow Inheritable Permissions From The Parent To Propagate To This Object And All Child Objects check box, as shown in Figure 4-3.

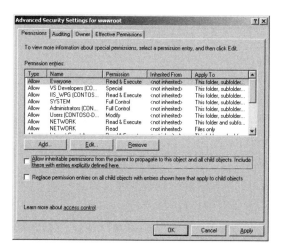

Figure 4-3 Disabling inheritance requires simply clearing a check box.

4. Click Copy to copy the inherited permissions to explicit permissions, or click Remove to simply discard the inherited permissions. If you choose not to copy the permissions, you will need to immediately assign explicit permissions so that users can access the object.

5. Click OK. When prompted to verify your change, click Yes.

How to Re-enable Inheritance from a Parent Object   If you do disable inheritance on a child object and later want to re-enable inheritance, you can do so by following these steps:

1. Use Windows Explorer to view the folder's properties.

2. Click the Security tab and then click the Advanced button.

3. In the Advanced Security Settings dialog box, select the Replace Permission Entries On All Child Objects check box.

   Windows Server 2003 will remove all explicit permissions on all child objects and replace them with inherited permissions. This is an excellent way to recover files, folders, or registry values that users have made inaccessible by removing inherited permissions.

4. Click OK.

How to Configure ACLs from the Command Line

As mentioned earlier in the chapter, you can specify ACLs from the command line by using two tools: the Change Access Control List tool (Cacls.exe) and the Extended Change Access Control List tool (XCacls.exe).

> **Tip**   The easiest way to configure ACLs at setup time is by defining a custom action on your Visual Studio .NET setup project to call Cacls.

How to Use Cacls   Cacls is a command-line tool that performs functions similar to the Security tab of the Windows Explorer file and folders Properties dialog box. With Cacls, you can do the following tasks from a command prompt or batch file:

- Modify or completely replace a file's or folder's ACL.

- Modify ACLs for a folder and all subfolders.

- Completely remove a user's or group's privileges to a file or folder.

- Grant users and groups Read, Write, Change, or Full Control privileges on a file or folder.

Cacls uses the following syntax:

```
cacls filename [/T] [/E] [/C] [/G user:perm;spec] [/R user [...]]
[/P user:perm;spec [...]] [/D user [...]]
```

The parameters have the following purposes:

- **/T** Recursively walks through the current folder and all its subfolders, applying the chosen access rights to the matching files or folders.

- **/E** Edits the ACL instead of replacing it. For example, only the administrator will have access to the Test.dat file if you run the `XCacls test.dat /G Administra-tor:F` command. All ACEs applied earlier are lost.

- **/C** Causes Cacls.exe to continue if an "access denied" error message occurs. If /C is not specified, Cacls.exe stops on this error.

- **/G user:perm** Grants a user access to the matching file or folder. The *perm* (permission) variable applies the specified access right to files and represents the special file-access-right mask for folders. The *perm* variable accepts the following values:

    ❑ **R** Read

    ❑ **W** Write

    ❑ **C** Change

    ❑ **F** Full Control

- **/R user** Revokes all access rights for the specified user.

- **/P user:perm** Replaces access rights for the user. The rules for specifying the *perm* and *spec* (special access) variables are the same as for the /G option, with the addition of the N value, which denies all access.

- **/D user** Denies the user access to the file or directory.

For example, to grant the Users group Read access to the C:\test.txt file, you would run the following command:

```
cacls C:\test.txt /E /G Users:R
```

> **Important** Using Cacls to grant a user Read access actually grants the user both Read and Read & Execute permissions. To grant the user only Read access, use XCacls and specify E for the *perm* variable.

To grant the Users group Change access, and the Administrators group Full Control to the C:\Inetpub\ folder and all subfolders, you would run this command:

```
cacls C:\Inetpub /T /E /G Users:C Administrators:F
```

How to Use XCacls   XCacls provides all the functionality of Cacls and adds more granular control over ACLs as well as completely automated functionality. (Cacls will, at times, require the user to press Y to continue.) For these reasons, choose XCacls to specify ACLs at the command line when you need to specify special access permissions such as Execute or Delete.

> **Tip**   XCacls can be downloaded from the Microsoft Windows 2000 page of the Microsoft Web site at *http://www.microsoft.com/windows2000/techinfo/reskit/tools/existing /xcacls-o.asp.*

XCacls uses the following syntax:

```
xcacls filename [/T] [/E] [/C] [/G user:perm;spec] [/R user] [/
P user:perm;spec [...]] [/D user [...]] [/Y]
```

The parameters have the following purposes:

- **/T**   Recursively walks through the current folder and all its subfolders, applying the chosen access rights to the matching files or folders.

- **/E**   Edits the ACL instead of replacing it. For example, only the administrator has access to the Test.dat file when you run the XCacls test.dat /G Administrator:F command. All ACEs applied earlier are lost.

- **/C**   Causes Xcacls.exe to continue when an "access denied" error message occurs. If /C is not specified, Xcacls.exe stops on this error.

- **/G user:perm;spec**   Grants a user access to the matching file or folder.

  The *perm* (permission) variable applies the specified access right to files and represents the special file-access-right mask for folders. The perm variable accepts the following values:

  - ❏ **R**   Read
  - ❏ **C**   Change
  - ❏ **F**   Full Control
  - ❏ **P**   Change Permissions (special access)
  - ❏ **O**   Take Ownership (special access)

❑ **X**   EXecute (special access)

❑ **E**   REad (Special access)

❑ **W**   Write (Special access)

❑ **D**   Delete (Special access)

The *spec* (special access) variable applies only to folders and accepts the same values as *perm*, with the addition of the T special value. The T value sets an ACE for the directory without specifying an ACE that is applied to new files created in that directory. At least one access right has to follow. Entries between a semicolon (;) and T are ignored.

- **/R user**   Revokes all access rights for the specified user.

- **/P user:perm;spec**   Replaces access rights for the user. The rules for specifying *perm* and *spec* are the same as for the */G* option.

- **/D user**   Denies the user access to the file or directory.

- **/Y**   Disables confirmation when replacing user access rights. By default, Cacls asks for confirmation. Because of this feature, when Cacls is used in a batch routine, the routine stops responding until the right answer is entered. The */Y* option was introduced to avoid this confirmation, so that Xcacls.exe can be used in batch mode.

You can use XCacls with almost exactly the same syntax as Cacls. For example, to grant the Users group access to delete but not read the C:\test.txt file, you would run the following command:

```
xcacls C:\test.txt /E /G Users:D
```

To grant the Users group the Read special access permission (which provides Read but not Read & Execute), and to grant the Administrators group Full Control to the C:\Inetpub\ folder and all subfolders, you would run this command:

```
xcacls C:\Inetpub /T /E /G Users:E Administrators:F
```

How to Configure ACLs from Within an Assembly

The .NET Framework includes thousands of methods for handling almost every programming task imaginable, from processing requests from a Web browser, to drawing three-dimensional images. However, the .NET Framework completely lacks APIs for modifying file and folder ACLs.

Manipulating ACLs from within .NET Framework applications is a common need, however. There are two ways you can accomplish this: calling command-line tools from your application, or building a .NET Framework wrapper around Win32 API calls.

How to Call Cacls from Your Application

The simplest way to configure ACLs from within a .NET Framework application is to call the Cacls or XCacls command-line tools directly. You do this by using the *Process* class in the *System.Diagnostics* namespace. Although it is not an elegant approach, it is effective.

The following code sample from a Windows Forms application grants the Users group Read access to the C:\boot.ini file, and then displays a message box showing the Cacls output:

```csharp
using System.Diagnostics;
using System.IO;

...

// Create a new Process object
Process newProcess = new Process();

// Specify the filename and arguments of the application
newProcess.StartInfo.FileName = "cacls";
newProcess.StartInfo.Arguments = @"C:\boot.ini /E /G Users:R";

// Configure the new process to not open a visible window
newProcess.StartInfo.UseShellExecute = false;
newProcess.StartInfo.CreateNoWindow = true;

// Allow the output to be redirected so that it can be analyzed
newProcess.StartInfo.RedirectStandardOutput = true;

// Launch the new process
newProcess.Start();

// Capture the Cacls output to the variable named output
StreamReader outputStream = newProcess.StandardOutput;
string output = outputStream.ReadToEnd();

// Stop processing until Cacls has completed its task
newProcess.WaitForExit();
outputStream.Close();

// Display the Cacls output in a message box
MessageBox.Show("output: " + output);
```

```vb
Imports System.Diagnostics
Imports System.IO

...

' Create a new Process object
Dim NewProcess As Process =  New Process()

' Specify the filename and arguments of the application
NewProcess.StartInfo.FileName = "cacls"
NewProcess.StartInfo.Arguments = "C:\boot.ini /E /G Users:R"
```

```
' Configure the new process to not open a visible window
NewProcess.StartInfo.UseShellExecute = False
NewProcess.StartInfo.CreateNoWindow = True

' Allow the output to be redirected so that it can be analyzed
NewProcess.StartInfo.RedirectStandardOutput = True

' Launch the new process
NewProcess.Start()

' Capture the Cacls output to the variable named output
Dim outputStream As StreamReader =  NewProcess.StandardOutput
Dim output As String =  outputStream.ReadToEnd()

' Stop processing until Cacls has completed its task
NewProcess.WaitForExit()
outputStream.Close()

' Display the Cacls output in a message box
MessageBox.Show("output: " + output)
```

This sample code can be used to modify the ACL of any file or folder, simply by cus-tomizing the *Process.StartInfo.Arguments* string. Because Cacls is in the user's default path, you do not need to specify the full path to the Cacls.exe executable.

How to Call Win32 Security APIs from Your Application   The most elegant way to modify an ACL from within your application is to write a .NET Framework wrapper class around the Win32 security functions. An excellent example of how to do this is provided by the GotDotNet user sample named ACLs in .NET, available from the *http://www.gotdotnet.com* Web site at *http://www.gotdotnet.com/Community/UserSamples/Details.aspx?SampleGuid=e6098575-dda0-48b8-9abf-e0705af065d9*. The details of writing such a wrapper are complex, however, and are outside the scope of this book.

Practice: Protecting Files Using Access Control Lists

In this practice, you will modify an ACL using a technique that can be easily used dur-ing your application's setup routine, or from within an application. Read the scenario and then complete the two exercises that follow. If you are unable to answer a ques-tion, review the lesson materials and try the question again. You can find answers to the questions in the "Questions and Answers" section at the end of this chapter.

Scenario

You have written an application that reads the Boot.ini file to determine the location of installed operating systems on the local computer. Your application runs fine when launched by a member of the local Administrators group. However, it fails when run by a standard user because users have no permissions to access the Boot.ini file.

To follow the principle of least privilege, you must allow users to run the application when logged on as standard users. Your users would prefer not to use the Run As operating system feature to run your application, so you decide that the most efficient method is to grant standard users Read access to the Boot.ini file during the setup procedure. It is acceptable to have users run the setup procedure as an administrator.

Exercise 1: Creating a Batch File to Modify an ACL

In this exercise, you create a batch file to modify the permissions of the C:\Boot.ini file so that standard users can read the file.

1. Log on to your computer as Administrator.

2. Launch Windows Explorer and navigate to C:\.

3. Open the Tools menu, and then click Folder options.

4. Click the View tab. Clear the Hide Protected Operating System Files check box. When prompted, click Yes. Click OK to return to Windows Explorer.

5. In the right pane, right-click the Boot.ini file, and then click Properties.

6. Click the Security tab. As shown in Figure 4-4, Administrators have Full Control permissions. Also note that Power Users have Read access, and the standard Users group is not listed in the ACL.

Figure 4-4   Standard users lack access to the Boot.ini file.

7. Click OK to return to Windows Explorer.

Next, you create a batch file to modify the permissions on the Boot.ini file. Later, you can call this batch file (or the command in the batch file) to modify permissions as required by your application.

1. Click Start, and then click Run. In the Open box, type **Notepad**, and then click OK.

2. In Notepad, type **cacls C:\boot.ini /E /G Users:R**.

3. Click the File menu, and then click Save As.

4. In the File Name box, type **C:\set-acl.bat**. Click Save. Close Notepad.

5. Open a command prompt. At the command prompt, type **C:\set-acl.bat**, and then press ENTER.

   The batch file runs the Cacls command. Cacls will display the following output:

   ```
   processed file: C:\boot.ini
   ```

6. Return to Windows Explorer and navigate to C:\. In the right pane, right-click the Boot.ini file, and then click Properties.

7. Click the Security tab. Note that Administrators have Full Control, Power Users have Read access, and the standard Users group now also has Read access, as shown in Figure 4-5.

Figure 4-5   Standard users now have Read access to the Boot.ini file.

8. Click OK to return to Windows Explorer.

Exercise 2: Explaining How to Modify ACLs During Setup

Answer the following questions:

1. In Exercise 1, you created a batch file consisting of a single command that sets the ACL on the Boot.ini file. How could you call this command during the setup procedure for your application?

2. How could you modify the ACL from within a .NET Framework assembly without calling a command-line tool?

3. What tools could you have used to manually change the ACL?

Lesson Summary

- DACLs are used to restrict access to files, folders, and other operating system objects.

- SACLs determine the conditions under which object access is audited.

- You can use two types of permissions to create an ACL: standard and special. Standard permissions consist of one or more special permissions, and are used to simplify the management of ACEs.

- File and folder permissions determine whether a user will have access to a file based on the type of access requested, ACEs, group memberships, and inherited permissions.

- ACLs can be configured using Windows Explorer, Cacls, XCacls, or from an assembly.

Lesson 2: Protecting Files Using Isolated Storage

Traditionally, applications store persistent data to the hard disk by interacting directly with the file system. However, the code access security mechanisms built into the .NET Framework will prevent your assembly from writing directly to the file system if you lack sufficient permissions. For example, assemblies running in the Internet security zone won't have this permission by default. Alternatively, the user might lack access to the part of the file system that you're attempting to write to. If you're storing files in the System directory and the user is not logged on as an administrator, the user probably won't have the access needed.

> **See Also**   For more information about code access security, see Chapter 6, "Implementing Code Access Security."

Even if you do have permission to write files to the disk, you must worry about how the data can be misused. It's difficult for a programmer to judge which information requires security. For example, developers who wrote the first several generations of Web browsers did not protect the browser's Web cache nor the history of Web sites the user visited. At first glance, this information might not seem to require protection, because an attacker cannot use it to gain elevated permissions to the computer. However, the attacker can use the information to determine what actions a user has taken on the computer, which violates the user's privacy.

Fortunately, isolated storage can be used to protect the privacy of the files you store without requiring you to interact directly with the file system. The .NET Framework provides assemblies access to assembly-specific or user-specific storage, and automatically encrypts this storage to protect it from uninvited access. Isolated storage can be accessed almost as easily as any file.

> **Exam Tip**   Understanding isolated storage is important for improving the security of applications. However, isolated storage is not specifically mentioned in the 70-330 and 70-340 exam objectives. As a result, you might not see it on the test.

After this lesson, you will be able to
- Describe the purpose of isolated storage.
- Explain where stores are located on the file system and the significance of those locations.
- List the .NET Framework classes used to access isolated storage.
- Access isolated storage.
- Use the Storeadm command-line tool to manage isolated storage stores.

Estimated lesson time: 45 minutes

What Is Isolated Storage?

Isolated storage is a private file system managed by the .NET Framework. Like the standard file system, you can use familiar techniques (such as *StreamReader* and *StreamWriter*) to read and write files. However, isolated storage requires your code to use fewer privileges, making it useful for implementing least privilege. Additionally, isolated storage is private, and isolated by user, domain, and assembly. The following sections describe when to use isolated storage and the types of isolated storage.

When to Use Isolated Storage

Isolated storage is not always the best solution for storing persistent data. Isolated storage should not be used to store configuration and deployment settings, which administrators control. It is a good way to store user preferences, however—because administrators do not control them, they are not considered to be configuration settings.

If you require high encryption for your data, you can use isolated storage, but don't rely on its built-in security. Encrypt the data before writing it to isolated storage. Isolated storage should not be used to store high-value secrets, such as unencrypted keys or passwords, because isolated storage is not protected from highly trusted code, unmanaged code, or trusted users of the computer.

Types of Isolated Storage

Access to isolated storage is always restricted to the user who created it. In addition to isolation by user, access to isolated storage is generally restricted to a specific assembly. In other words, AssemblyB cannot access files located in an isolated store created by AssemblyA.

In addition to isolating storage by user and assembly, you can isolate assemblies in one additional, optional way: by the application domain. If a store is isolated by application domain, the same assembly running in different application domains cannot access a single store. Figure 4-6 compares isolation by assembly and isolation by application domain.

> **Important**   Always isolate storage by application domain unless you specifically need to share data between instances of the application. For example, if you create a shared assembly that will be called from multiple external assemblies, and you plan to use isolated storage to allow the external assemblies to share data, you must not isolate storage by application domain.

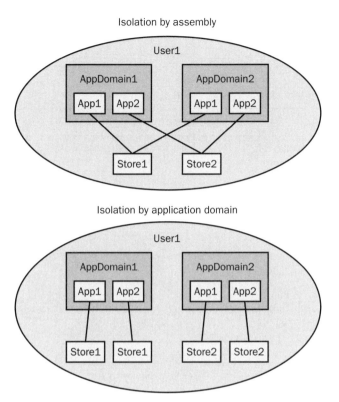

Figure 4-6   Isolated storage is separated by user and either assembly or domain.

Where Stores Are Located on the File System

When using isolated storage, applications save data to a unique *isolated storage store* (or simply *store*). You use *isolated storage files* to write data within a store.

For you as a developer, the location of the store is transparent. Physically, though, the isolated storage store is implemented as a file on the file system. Generally, the store exists on the client's file system, but a server application could create server-side isolated stores for individual users by impersonating the user when creating the store. Isolated storage can also store information on a server with a user's roaming profile so that the information travels with the roaming user.

Different versions of Windows create isolated storage stores in different places on the file system. Table 4-1 shows the root locations where isolated storage is created when roaming is enabled, and Table 4-2 shows the root locations when roaming is not enabled. The stores are located in Microsoft\IsolatedStorage folders under each root location.

Tip   To see isolated storage in the file system, you must change folder settings to show hidden files and folders.

Table 4-1   Roaming-Enabled Isolated Storage Store Locations

Operating System	Location
Microsoft Windows 98 and Windows ME without user profiles	*<systemroot>*\Application Data
Windows 98 and Windows ME with user profiles	*<systemroot>*\Profiles*<user>*\Application Data
Microsoft Windows NT 4.0 (any Service Pack)	*<systemroot>*\Profiles*<user>*\Application Data
Windows 2000, Windows XP and Windows Server 2003 when upgraded from Windows NT 4.0	*<systemroot>*\Profiles*<user>*\Application Data
Windows 2000, when upgraded from Windows 98 and Windows NT 3.51, or when not upgraded	*<systemroot>*\Documents and Settings *<user>*\Application Data
Windows XP and Windows Server 2003, when upgraded from Windows 2000 and Windows 98, or when not upgraded	*<systemroot>*\Documents and Settings *<user>*\Application Data

Table 4-2   Non-Roaming-Enabled Isolated Storage Store Locations

Operating System	Location
Windows 98 and Windows ME	*<systemdrive>*\Windows\Local Settings \Application Data
Windows NT 4.0 before Service Pack 4	*<systemroot>*\Profiles*<user>*\Application Data
Windows NT 4.0 with Service Pack 4	*<systemroot>*\Profiles*<user>*\Local Settings \Application Data
Windows 2000, Windows XP and Windows Server 2003 when upgraded from Windows NT 4.0	*<systemroot>*\Profiles*<user>*\Local Settings \Application Data
Windows 2000, when upgraded from Windows 98 or Windows NT 3.51, or when not upgraded	*<systemdrive>*\Documents and Settings*<user>* \Local Settings\Application Data
Windows XP and Windows Server 2003 when upgraded from Windows 2000 or Windows 98, or when not upgraded	*<systemdrive>*\Documents and Settings*<user>* \Local Settings\Application Data

Exam Tip   Don't memorize the file locations for the exam. Instead, know that isolated storage resides in the user's profile.

Classes for Working with Isolated Storage

The *System.IO.IsolatedStorage* namespace has three classes that are useful for interacting with isolated storage:

- **IsolatedStorageException**   A class for exceptions relating to isolated storage.

- **IsolatedStorageFile**   Provides management of isolated storage stores. Individual stores are separate isolated storage systems that are implemented as a single file in the file system.

- **IsolatedStorageFileStream**   Provides access to read and write isolated storage files within stores. Isolated storage files behave exactly like conventional files stored directly on a file system, however, they exist within an isolated storage store.

Understanding the difference between *IsolatedStrorageFile* and *IsolatedStorage-FileStream* is important. *IsolatedStorageFile* is used to access the individual stores, whereas *IsolatedStorageFileStream* manages individual files within a store. Figure 4-7 shows the relationship between these two classes and the file system.

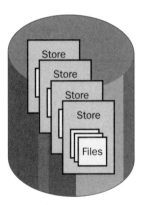

Figure 4-7   Files are contained within stores, which are in turn contained in the file system.

How to Access Isolated Storage

Working with isolated storage is very similar to working with standard files. The primary differences are that you must:

- Use or import the *System.IO.IsolatedStorage* namespace, in addition to the *System.IO* namespace.

- Optionally, declare an *IsolatedStorageFile* object to specify the type of isolation.

- Construct file system objects, *StreamWriters*, *StreamReaders*, and other *System.IO* objects by using objects in the *System.IO.IsolatedStorage* namespace.

The following code gets a user store isolated by assembly, creates a file named Myfile.txt, creates a new *StreamWriter* object using the isolated storage file, writes a line of text to the file, and then closes the isolated storage file:

```csharp
// Get the store isolated by the assembly
IsolatedStorageFile isoStore =  IsolatedStorageFile.GetUserStoreForAssembly();

// Create the isolated storage file in the assembly we just grabbed
IsolatedStorageFileStream isoFile = new IsolatedStorageFileStream("myfile.txt", ⤸
FileMode.Create, isoStore);

// Create a StreamWriter using the isolated storage file
StreamWriter sw = new StreamWriter(isoFile);

// Write a line of text to the file
sw.WriteLine("This text is written to a isolated storage file.");

// Close the file
sw.Close();
```

```vb
' Get the store isolated by the assembly
Dim isoStore As IsolatedStorageFile = ⤸
IsolatedStorageFile.GetUserStoreForAssembly()

' Create the isolated storage file in the assembly we just grabbed
Dim isoFile As IsolatedStorageFileStream =  New ⤸
IsolatedStorageFileStream("myfile.txt",FileMode.Create,isoStore)

' Create a StreamWriter using the isolated storage file
Dim sw As StreamWriter =  New StreamWriter(isoFile)

' Write a line of text to the file
sw.WriteLine("This text is written to a isolated storage file.")

' Close the file
sw.Close()
```

To use the store isolated by the application domain, simply change the *IsolatedStorageFile.GetUserStoreForAssembly()* method call to *IsolatedStorageFile.GetUserStoreForDomain()*. Similarly, the following code would read the contents of the same isolated storage file:

```csharp
// Get the store isolated by the assembly
IsolatedStorageFile isoStore = IsolatedStorageFile.GetUserStoreForAssembly();

// Open the isolated storage file in the assembly we just grabbed
IsolatedStorageFileStream isoFile = new IsolatedStorageFileStream
("myfile.txt", FileMode.Open, isoStore);

// Create a StreamReader using the isolated storage file
StreamReader sr = new StreamReader(isoFile);

// Read a line of text from the file
string fileContents = sr.ReadLine();

// Close the file
sr.Close();
```

```vb
' Get the store isolated by the assembly
Dim isoStore As IsolatedStorageFile =
IsolatedStorageFile.GetUserStoreForAssembly()

' Open the isolated storage file in the assembly we just grabbed
Dim isoFile As IsolatedStorageFileStream = New
IsolatedStorageFileStream("myfile.txt",FileMode.Open,isoStore)

' Create a StreamReader using the isolated storage file
Dim sr As StreamReader = New StreamReader(isoFile)

' Read a line of text from the file
Dim fileContents As String = sr.ReadLine()

' Close the file
sr.Close()
```

If the *IsolatedStorageFile.GetUserStoreForAssembly* and *IsolatedStorageFile.GetUser-StoreForDomain* are not granular enough to specify the specific store you need to access, you can use the *IsolatedStorageFile.GetStore* method instead. To create or access isolated storage, code must be granted *IsolatedStorageFilePermission*.

> **See Also** For more information about *IsolatedStorageFile.GetStore*, refer to MSDN. This topic is available online at *http://msdn.microsoft.com/library/en-us/cpref/html /frlrfSystemIOIsolatedStorageIsolatedStorageFileClassGetStoreTopic.asp*.

How to Use the Storeadm Tool

Storeadm is a command-line tool that you can use to list or remove isolated storage stores for the current user. To use it, open a command prompt and run the command `storeadm [/list][/remove][/roaming][/quiet]`. Running the tool without the /roaming option applies all actions to the local store. Running the tool with the /roaming option applies all actions to the store that is able to roam.

Storeadm is included with the .NET Framework SDK. After installing Visual Studio .NET 2003, you can find it in the C:\Program Files\Microsoft Visual Studio .NET 2003\SDK\v1.1\Bin\ directory. However, it is not included in the default path. Therefore, you will need to either specify the complete path to the tool from the standard command prompt, or you will need to open the Visual Studio .NET 2003 Command Prompt from within the Visual Studio .NET Tools group.

The following listing is Storeadm's output for a user with a single isolated storage store created by the C:\Program Files\MyApp\MyApp.exe assembly. Note that Storeadm lists the same store twice, because this store exists in both the Domain and Assembly scopes.

```
C:\>storeadm /list
Microsoft (R) .NET Framework Store Admin 1.1.4322.573
Copyright (C) Microsoft Corporation 1998-2002. All rights reserved.

Record #1
[Domain]
<System.Security.Policy.Url version="1">
   <Url>file://C:/Program Files/MyApp/MyApp.exe</Url>
</System.Security.Policy.Url>

[Assembly]
<System.Security.Policy.Url version="1">
   <Url>file://C:/Program Files/MyApp/MyApp.exe</Url>
</System.Security.Policy.Url>

        Size : 2048
```

In the preceding output, the store's total size is 2k, or 2048 bytes. Each file in an isolated store consumes a minimum of 1024 bytes.

Storeadm can also be used to remove a user's isolated storage by executing the command `storeadm /remove`. Do this only when you are sure the data contained in the stores is no longer required.

Practice: Updating Existing Code to Use Isolated Storage

In this practice, you write code that uses isolated storage to comply with the principle of least privilege and improve the privacy of data. Read the following scenario and then complete the exercise that follows. If you are unable to answer the question, review the lesson materials and try the question again. You can find the answer to the question in the "Questions and Answers" section at the end of this chapter.

Scenario

Recently, your IT department decided to allow remote users to access your application from the company's Web site. However, this failed because code access security restricted your assembly from accessing the file system when it was running in the Internet zone. After some research, you noticed that the assembly was writing a temporary file directly to the file system rather than using isolated storage. Your manager felt that you should update the application so that it would not access the file system directly, both to reduce the likelihood that other applications and users could access the content that you wrote to disk and to allow the assembly to run from the Internet zone.

Exercise

1. How could you rewrite the following piece of code to store the information in isolated storage, isolated by user, domain, and assembly?

```
using System;
using System.IO;

...
StreamWriter sw = File.CreateText("mytemp.txt");
sw.WriteLine("Hello, world!");
sw.Close();
```

```
Imports System.IO

...
Dim sw As StreamWriter = File.CreateText("mytemp.txt")
sw.WriteLine("Hello, world!")
sw.Close()
```

Lesson Summary

- Isolated storage is a private, persistent storage mechanism implemented by the .NET Framework. Your assemblies can use isolated storage in the same ways that they use the file system, but with increased privacy and reduced privilege requirements.

- The .NET Framework creates the files to contain isolated storage within a user's profile, which ensures the content will be protected from other users.

- You use three classes to access isolated storage: *IsolatedStorageException*, *IsolatedStorageFile*, and *IsolatedStorageFileStream*.

- To access isolated storage, first import the *System.IO.IsolatedStorage* namespace. Then, declare an *IsolatedStorageFile* object to specify the type of isolation. Finally, use the objects in the *System.IO.IsolatedStorage* namespace when creating file system objects.

- The Storeadm tool is a command-line tool for listing and deleting isolated storage stores. Use the command `storeadm /list` to view stores, and the command `storeadm /remove` to delete stores.

Lesson 3: Configuring Your Development Environment

The principle of least privilege applies not only to the code you write but also to how you write the code. To help ensure that your applications function correctly when run by a standard user, develop them using a standard user account. Unfortunately, standard user accounts, by default, do not have sufficient rights to create and debug applications. For that reason, you must understand exactly how to configure your development environment to allow you to effectively develop applications while not logged on as an administrator.

After this lesson, you will be able to

- List the group memberships required to allow a standard user to perform development tasks.
- Configure a user account to use Visual Studio to create .NET Framework applications without being a member of the Power Users or Administrators groups.
- Manually create Web applications on remote computers when your development user account lacks sufficient privileges.
- Configure Web applications to allow debugging without Administrators group membership.
- Register components without administrator access.
- Configure your system to enable the rapid isolation of problems related to insufficient privileges.

Estimated lesson time: 45 minutes

Group Memberships Required to Allow a Standard User to Perform Development Tasks

Developing with least privilege requires using an account that is not a member of the Administrators group or the Power Users group. However, you will definitely require rights that are not granted to the standard Users group. Fortunately, several groups are designed to grant the additional rights you need, without granting excessive privileges. Table 4-3 lists these groups and the rights that each group grants.

Table 4-3   Groups Used for Granting Development Privileges

Group	Permissions Granted	Notes
Debugger Users	Debug processes	Naturally, membership in this group is critical for developers, but the rights granted can be abused by a user or by malicious software to gain elevated privileges.
IIS_WPG	Run a Web application	Membership in this group is required only when you will be using your user account to run a Web application, which is required for debugging a Web application when not an administrator.
VS Developers	Create new Web applications	Membership in this group is required only when creating Web applications.

How to Configure an Account for Development with Least Privileges

Creating a non-Administrator user account to be used for development requires adding that user account to one or more groups, and assigning additional user rights to that account. The exact steps you follow vary depending on whether you are using Windows Server 2003 or Windows XP as your development platform.

Real World   Why Logging On as a Standard User Will Save You Time

In the real world, everyone knows they shouldn't log on as administrators, but everyone does it anyway. Even security people like myself, who preach about the importance of using lesser privileged accounts, can be caught logged on as an administrator. The fact is, using a standard user account requires extra time while you discover applications that must be run with higher privileges, and configure those applications to use different credentials. The steps you must follow just to *configure* a standard account to use Visual Studio .NET effectively is evidence of that.

However, as a developer, you can hope to recoup that time. Developing as a standard user will help you discover resources that your application is using that standard users don't have access to. Finding these problems before your end users do will save you time, because avoiding a bug is easier than patching it later. Additionally, you might save one of your users from having a vulnerability in your application exploited by an attacker.

How to Configure an Account for Least Development Privileges on Windows Server 2003

To configure an account to perform development tasks with least privilege on a computer running Windows Server 2003, first create the user account, and then assign it the Log On As A Batch Job user right. The following steps create a new user account:

1. Log on to your computer as an Administrator.

2. Click Start, Administrative Tools, and then click Computer Management.

3. Expand System Tools, expand Local Users And Groups, and then click Users.

4. Right-click Users, and then click New User.

5. In the New User dialog box, complete the fields for a new user account that you will use for development and other day-to-day tasks on your computer and that do not require administrator access. Click Create.

6. After creating the user, click Close to return to the Computer Management console.

7. In the right pane, double-click the new user account. Click the Member Of tab.

   Note that the account is a member of the Users group, but not a member of Power Users or Administrators.

8. Click the Add button. The Select Groups dialog box appears.

9. In the Enter The Object Names To Select box, type **Debugger Users; IIS_WPG; VS Developers**, as shown in Figure 4-8, and then click OK.

> **Note**   If you do not plan to develop Web applications, you should not add the IIS_WPG or VS Developers group memberships.

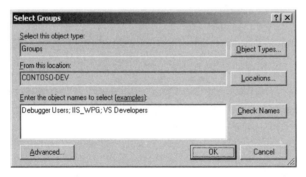

Figure 4-8   Add a user to the Debugger Users group to enable common development tasks.

10. Click OK again, and then close Computer Management.

In the following steps, you grant the user account the Log On As A Batch Job user right. If you chose to add your user to the IIS_WPG group, you can skip the remaining steps, because by default the IIS_WPG group has the Log On As A Batch Job user right.

1. Click Start, All Programs, and Administrative Tools, and then click Local Security Policy.

2. Expand Local Policies, and then click User Rights Assignment.

3. In the right pane, double-click Log On As A Batch Job.

   The Log On As A Batch Job Properties dialog box appears, as shown in Figure 4-9.

Figure 4-9   The Log On As A Batch Job user right is required for some development tasks.

4. Click the Add User Or Group button. The Select Users Or Groups dialog box appears. In the Enter The Object Names To Select box, type the name of your new user account, and then click OK.

5. Click OK again, and then close the Local Security Settings console.

How to Configure an Account for Least Development Privileges on Windows XP

To configure an account to perform development tasks with least privilege on a computer running Windows XP, first create the user account, and then assign it the Log On As A Batch Job user right. The following steps create a new user account:

1. Log on to your computer as an Administrator.

2. Click Start, All Programs, Administrative Tools, and then click Computer Management.

3. Expand System Tools, expand Local Users And Groups, and then click Users.

4. Right-click Users, and then click New User.

5. In the New User dialog box, complete the fields for a new user account that you will use for development and other day-to-day tasks on your computer and that do not require administrator access. Click Create.

6. After creating the user, click Close to return to the Computer Management console.

7. In the right pane, double-click the new user account. Click the Member Of tab.

   Note that the account is a member of the Users group, but not a member of Power Users or Administrators.

8. Click the Add button.

9. The Select Groups dialog box appears. In the Enter The Object Names To Select box, type **Debugger Users; VS Developers**, and then click OK.

10. Click OK again, and then close Computer Management.

In the following steps, you grant the user account the Log On As A Batch Job user right.

1. Click Start, All Programs, Administrative Tools, and then click Local Security Policy.

2. Expand Local Policies, and then click User Rights Assignment.

3. In the right pane, double-click Log On As A Batch Job.

   The Log On As A Batch Job Properties dialog box appears.

4. Click the Add User Or Group button. The Select Users Or Groups dialog box appears. In the Enter The Object Names To Select box, type the name of your new user account, and then click OK.

5. Click OK again, and then close the Local Security Settings console.

How to Create Web Applications on Computers That Do Not Have Visual Studio .NET Installed

Creating a new Web application requires privileges that standard user accounts lack. Specifically, you must create a subdirectory of the Web site's root directly, configure a Web application, and then specify file permissions to protect the assembly's files from unauthorized access. By default, standard users lack rights to perform any of these actions. As a result, you will see an error message such as the one shown in Figure 4-10 when you attempt to create a new Web application with Visual Studio .NET.

Figure 4-10   Standard user accounts lack permission to create Web applications.

The simplest way to allow a standard user to create a Web application is to add the user to the VS Developers group. This group provides member user accounts with the necessary permissions for creating Web applications. This is the perfect way to allow your account to create Web applications when an instance of Microsoft Internet Information Services (IIS) is running on your development computer. However, this group will exist only when Visual Studio .NET is installed on the Web server.

Therefore, when creating applications on a remote Web server that does not have Visual Studio .NET installed, you must use an administrator account to create the Web application and then grant the standard developer user account Full Control permissions over the directory. As an alternative, you can place the standard developer user in the Administrators group on the remote Web server long enough for the application to be created.

How to Debug Web Applications

Debugging Web applications on a remote computer is particularly challenging as a standard user, because by default it requires the user performing the debugging to be a member of the Administrators group. There is only one way to work around this: the user performing the debugging must be the same user account the Web application is using. Given these conditions, you can debug a Web application on a remote server in two ways:

- Add your user account to the Administrators group on the remote computer.

- Configure the Web application to run in the context of the user account you use for debugging.

If you choose to add your account to the Administrators group, no other changes are necessary. If you prefer to follow the principle of least privilege, you must do two things:

■ Configure file permissions to grant your account access to folders necessary for debugging.

■ Enable the ASP.NET Web application to run in the context of your user account.

Required File Permissions

If you choose to perform debugging on a remote Web server by using the same account that the Web server runs as, you must have the file permissions shown in Table 4-4 on the remote Web server.

> **Note** If you authenticate as an administrator, you automatically have these permissions.

Table 4-4 Permissions Required for Debugging

Directory	Permissions Needed in the Directory and All Its Children
%windir%\Temp	Read and Write
%windir%\Microsoft.NET\Framework*version*	Read
%windir%\Microsoft.NET\Framework*version*\Temporary ASP.NET Files	Read and Write

How to Enable ASP.NET to Run as Another User on Windows XP Professional and Windows 2000 Server

On Windows XP Professional and Windows 2000 Server, you configure the account that the Web server uses by editing either the Machine.Config or Web.Config files. The Machine.Config file, located in %windir%\Microsoft.NET\Framework*version*\Config\, controls the default settings for all Web applications. The Web.Config file (which does not exist unless you specifically create it) is located in the root of each Web application and controls the setting for the Web application folder it resides in.

> **Note** The steps in this section assume that if you are using Windows XP, you installed only Service Pack 1. Additional configuration might be required if you are using Windows XP with Service Pack 2.

Whether you choose to modify the settings for the entire server or for an individual Web application, you must modify the processModel tag by specifying the user name and password of the account you will use for debugging. This is the primary disadvantage of this technique, and you must carefully weigh the security benefits. Adding your user account and password in clear text is dangerous, because anyone with Read access to the file can steal your user credentials. Additionally, each time you change your password, you need to update the password stored in the Machine.Config or Web.Config file.

Off the Record   You need to understand the various approaches to debugging Web applications because these might appear on the test. However, I think the drawbacks to storing your user name and password in clear text in the Web application's config file are greater than the drawbacks associated with adding yourself to the Administrators group on the remote Web server.

As an Administrator, edit the attributes of the Machine.Config or Web.Config file on the processModel tag, as shown:

```
<processModel
    enable="true"
    userName="DOMAIN\username"
    password="password"
    ...
/
```

How to enable ASP.NET to Run as Another User on Windows Server 2003

Fortunately, configuring Windows Server 2003 and IIS 6 Web applications to run with your user credentials is slightly less risky than it is on Windows 2000 or Windows XP, because your password is not stored in clear text. However, you still need to manually update the password each time it is changed.

You configure the Web application's user account by using an application pool. Each pool can be configured to run as a different user (which must be a member of the IIS_WPG group). Virtual roots can be added to an application pool, which the debugger can then attach to when the pool is running as the same user who launched the debugger. This mechanism provides an easy way to set up an alternate execution environment, safely protect user credentials, and set up additional virtual roots.

To specify the user account used for an application pool, follow these steps:

1. Click Start, click Administrative Tools, and then click Internet Information Services (IIS) Manager.

2. Expand Application Pools.

3. Right-click the Application Pools node, click New, and then click Application Pool.

4. Type the name for the application pool and click OK.

5. Right-click the new application pool and click Properties.

6. Click the Identity tab, and then click the Configurable option button.

7. As shown in Figure 4-11, specify your user name and password. Click OK.

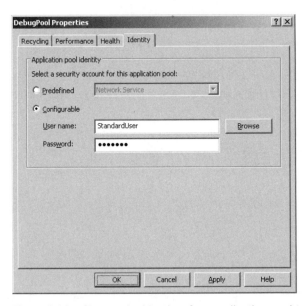

Figure 4-11   Change the identity of an application pool to allow debugging.

8. When prompted, re-enter your password, and then click OK again.

Next, you must configure the Web application to use the application pool by following these steps:

1. In the Internet Information Services (IIS) Manager, expand Web Sites, and locate the application you want to configure.

2. Right-click the Web application, and then click Properties.

3. Click the Application Pool list and select the newly created application pool, as illustrated in Figure 4-12.

Figure 4-12   Specify the custom pool to enable an application for remote debugging.

4. Click OK.

How to Register Components

If your application is currently performing registration steps that require write access to secured portions of the registry, you might discover that you do not have sufficient access to register the component when logged on as a standard user. Specifically, standard users lack access to the HKEY_LOCAL_MACHINE\Software\Classes key. However, you can work around this limitation by using HKEY_CURRENT_USER\Software\Classes. This key is writeable by any user, and shows up in HKEY_CLASSES_ROOT just as well, but the scope is limited to individual users.

Unfortunately, many of the tools and operating system APIs allow registration only to HKEY_LOCAL_MACHINE\Software\Classes; type library registration is a prime example of this. In these cases, the most feasible method for registering the class is to use Run As to open a command prompt with administrative privileges, change the directory to the output directory, and then run the registration steps by hand.

Table 4-5 shows common post-build registration tasks and their registration. Perform the registration the first time you run your assembly, and you should be able to build and run as normal thereafter. You might need to repeat the registration when you switch between Debug and Release configurations, and when you make changes to your application that have an impact on the items being registered.

Table 4-5 Registration Actions for Various Registration Types

Post-Build Registration Type	Registration Action
Component Object Model (COM) Executable registration	`output.exe /RegServer`
COM dynamic link library (DLL) registration	`regsvr32 output.dll`
Assembly registration for COM interoperability	`regasm output.dll`
Installation of an assembly into the global assembly cache	`gacutil /if output.dll`
.NET Services installation registration	`regsvcs output.dll`

How to Configure Your System for Simplified Troubleshooting

After you configure your development environment to use a standard user account, you might have to perform troubleshooting to identify resources your application is attempting to access but cannot because it lacks permissions. There are two ways to do this, and you can choose either or both:

■ Enable failure security auditing on your system, files, and registry.

> **See Also**   For information about configuring security auditing, see Lesson 3 in Chapter 1.

■ Install tools to monitor file and registry usage. Two such tools, FileMon and Reg-Mon, are available from *http://www.sysinternals.com*.

Whichever technique you choose, you will find it helpful to configure your environment before you begin developing your application.

Practice: Configuring Your Development Environment

In this practice, you configure your development environment to enable you to create applications while logged on as a standard user. Read the following scenario and then complete Exercises 1 and 2.

Scenario

Your organization has decided to begin following the security principle of least privilege for all application development. As part of that approach, you must do your development using a user account that is a standard user. Specifically, this account must not be a member of the Administrators and Power Users groups. It can, however, have other non-standard permissions and group membership as required for development tasks.

You need to create a new account to use for development, and then verify that the account can debug a Web application.

Exercise 1: Configuring Your Computer for Least Privilege Development

In this exercise, you configure your computer to allow development by a new user account that is not a member of the Administrators or Power Users group.

1. Log on to your computer as Administrator.

2. Click Start, All Programs, and Administrative Tools, and then click Computer Management.

3. Expand System Tools, expand Local Users And Groups, and then click Users.

4. Right-click Users, and then click New User.

5. In the New User dialog box, type **StandardUser** in the User Name field. Provide a complex password. Clear the User Must Change Password At Next Logon check box, as shown in Figure 4-13.

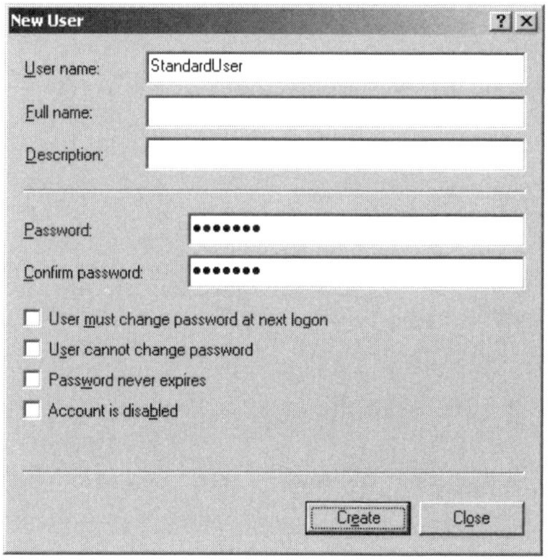

Figure 4-13   Create a standard user account for development.

6. Click OK, and then click Close to return to the Computer Management console.

7. In the right pane, double-click StandardUser. Click the Member Of tab.

8. Click the Add button. The Select Groups dialog box appears.

9. In the Enter The Object Names To Select box, type **Debugger Users; IIS_WPG; VS Developers**, and then click OK. The StandardUser Properties dialog box shows the group memberships, as shown in Figure 4-14.

Figure 4-14   Add group memberships to enable a user to perform administrative tasks.

10. Click OK again, and then close Computer Management.

Exercise 2: Creating and Debugging a Web Application

In this exercise, you create a Web application using your new StandardUser account, and then configure the application to allow you to debug it.

1. Log on to your computer as StandardUser.

2. Launch Visual Studio .NET 2003.

3. Click the File menu, click New, and then click Project.

4. Click either Visual Basic Projects or Visual C# Projects, depending on your language preference.

5. In the right pane, click ASP.NET Web Application.

6. In the Location box, type **http://localhost/WebDebugging** and then click OK.

Visual Studio .NET creates a new Web application. It succeeds, because the user is a member of the VS Developers group.

7. Use the Toolbox to add a button to the Webform1.aspx page, as shown in Figure 4-15.

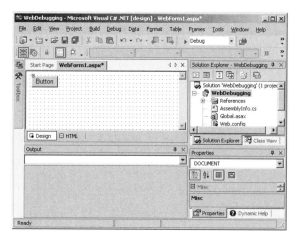

Figure 4-15   Create a simple form to test debugging ability.

8. Double-click Button1.

Visual Studio .NET creates a *Button1_Click* method.

9. Add the following code to the *Button1_Click* method:

```
string newText = "Hello, World!";
Button1.Text = newText;
```

```
Dim NewText As String =  "Hello, World!"
Button1.Text = NewText
```

10. Set a debugging breakpoint on the line that declares the *newText* variable by clicking in the left margin. Your development environment should resemble Figure 4-16 (shown with C#).

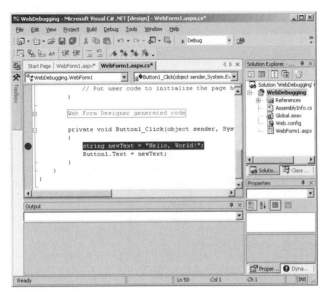

Figure 4-16 This breakpoint will demonstrate that debugging works properly.

11. Click the Debug menu, and then click Start.

Visual Studio .NET compiles the application, and then displays the error message shown in Figure 4-17. This indicates that you lack sufficient permissions to debug the Web application.

Figure 4-17 Standard users lack permissions to debug Web applications.

12. Click OK.

In the next process, you configure the Web application to run in the context of the StandardUser account.

1. Click Start, and then click Run.

2. In the Open box, type **runas /user:administrator "mmc %System-Root%\system32\inetsrv\iis.msc"**. Click OK.

3. When prompted, type the Administrator password and press ENTER.

The Internet Information Services (IIS) Manager appears, running with administrative privileges.

4. Expand the Web server node. Right-click the Application Pools node, click New, and then click Application Pool.

5. Type **DebugPool** in the Application Pool ID field, as shown in Figure 4-18, and click OK.

Figure 4-18 Creating a new application pool is the first step to changing a Web application's identity.

6. Right-click DebugPool, and click Properties.

7. Click the Identity tab, and then click the Configurable option button.

8. In the User name field, type **StandardUser**. Type your password, and then click OK.

9. When prompted, re-enter your password, and then click OK again.

Next, you must configure the Web application to use the application pool by following these steps:

1. In the Internet Information Services (IIS) Manager, expand Web Sites and then expand Default Web Site.

2. Right-click WebDebugging and then click Properties.

3. Click the Application Pool list and then click DebugPool.

4. Click OK.

5. Close Internet Information Services (IIS) Manager.

Finally, you can attempt to debug your Web application again.

1. Return to Visual Studio .NET.

2. Click Debug, and then click Start.

3. If prompted by Internet Explorer, click OK.

   The simple Web application appears, with a single button.

4. Click the button.

   Visual Studio .NET appears, as shown in Figure 4-19, because it is executing the code in the *Button1_Click* method, and it has reached the breakpoint you set earlier in this exercise.

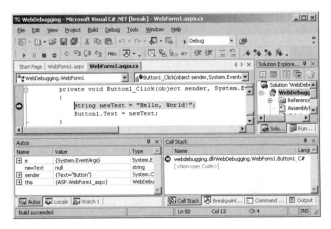

Figure 4-19 Debugging the Web application succeeds.

Debugging is successful because the Web application is running using the same credentials as the current user. Earlier in the exercise, debugging failed because the Web application was running in the default security context, and your user account was not a member of the Administrators group.

Lesson Summary

- Membership in the Debugger Users group enables application debugging. The IIS_WPG and VS Developers groups provide the permissions necessary to configure a Web application for remote debugging without administrator privileges.

- To configure a non-administrator account for development, add it to the Debugger Users group, and assign it the Logon As A Batch Job right. If you plan to debug Web applications, also add the user to the IIS_WPG and VS Developers groups.

- To create Web applications on remote computers, authenticate as an administrator, manually create the Web application, and then assign to the development account the file permissions required for development and debugging.

- To debug Web applications, you must configure the Web application to use the same account you use for debugging. On Windows Server 2003, you do this by configuring the identity of the Application pool. On Windows XP and Windows 2000 Server, you do this by specifying your credentials in a .Config file.

- Whenever possible, register components in HKEY_CURRENT_USER\Software\Classes to avoid requiring administrator rights.

- Before beginning development with a non-administrator account, prepare your development environment to troubleshoot access problems by enabling auditing and installing file and registry monitoring tools.

Lab: Taking Advantage of Platform Security

In this lab, you make recommendations to change an application's design to make it use platform security more efficiently. Read the following scenario and then complete the exercise that follows. If you are unable to answer a question, review the lessons and try the question again. You can find answers to the questions in the "Questions and Answers" section at the end of this chapter.

Scenario

You are a consultant who was recently hired by the IT department of Fabrikam, Inc. Fabrikam is a firm that does outsourcing of data analysis and customer support tasks for businesses in the health care industry. Specifically, you were hired by the internal software development team to solve a problem that, from their point of view, the desktop management team caused. You gather information about the problem by talking to staff members and reviewing the technical requirements that your manager gives you.

Interviews

Following is a list of company personnel interviewed and their statements:

- **IT Software Development Team Manager**   "Welcome to the team. You really shouldn't be working for me; you should be working for the IT desktop management team, because they are the ones who caused this problem. Anyway, it's up to me—us—to fix it. We develop software for the internal employees to use to do their jobs. Some of this software is Web-based, and is still working fine. However, one of the applications is this nifty C# Windows Forms application. The front end is installed on each user's Windows XP Professional computer, and it communicates with a back-end SQL Server 2000 database. Well, it's broken now, because the desktop management team decided employees aren't allowed to log on to their desktops as an administrator anymore…. You'd think they'd know that logging on as standard users doesn't work, because they are the desktop management team, after all. Anyway, I suggested we fix the problem by letting users log on as administrators again, but my boss wasn't too keen on the idea. I told him that none of my developers has time to work on solving this problem, so they told me to hire a consultant, which brings me back to you. What I need you to do is examine our application, and either fix it so that it can run as a standard user, or tell us that it's impossible and give me the ammunition I need to tell my boss that users simply must log on as an administrator."

- **IT Software Development Team member**   "I've been using FileMon and RegMon to monitor the front-end app's behavior. I think one of the problems is that standard users don't have write access to the HKEY_LOCAL_MACHINE\Software \Fabrikam\ registry key that we create. We use that key to store user preferences, and things like the last position of the window. Also, standard users can't update or add files to the C:\Windows\ directory, which our app needs access to because it stores some temporary information in a file. Well, I'll leave it to you to recommend how to fix it."

■ **IT Desktop Management Team Manager**   "I think you understand the cause of the problem by now: the software development team's front-end application writes to some areas of the registry and file system that are reserved for administrators. We were actually aware that the problem existed before we started requiring users to log on using a standard user account, but we needed to stick to our schedule. I had asked the software development team manager to test his application in that environment about six months ago, but that's neither here nor there. Well, in the meantime, we've been installing the application as an administrator and we've been using Run As to allow users to launch the application...but we really do need it fixed."

■ **End user**   "What's the point of logging on with a standard user account if I keep having to type an Administrator password to run my app?"

Technical Requirements

Your recommendation must allow users to run the front-end application as a standard user without using Run As.

Exercise

Answer the following questions for your manager:

1. What approaches can you take to resolve the problem of writing to an inaccessible location in the registry? Which approach would you recommend?

2. What approaches can you take to resolve the problem of writing to the inaccessible location on the file system? Which approach would you recommend?

Chapter Summary

■ Access to files and folders is restricted by using DACLs, and audited by using SACLs. A user's effective permissions are determined by the operating system, which compares the user's group memberships with the ACLs of the file or folder being accessed, and any folders from which permissions are inherited. You can configure ACLs with graphical tools or command-line tools, or from within an assembly.

■ Store files in isolated storage instead of the file system to improve privacy and reduce the privileges required by your code. The .NET Framework provides classes for using isolated storage that minimize the number of changes required when updating an existing application that interacts directly with the file system.

■ To reduce problems that end users experience when running your application using a standard user account, configure your development environment to work with a non-administrator account. Although you cannot debug applications using an unmodified standard user account, you can configure a standard user account with additional group memberships and user rights to fully enable development and debugging tasks. When working with a Web server, you will need to configure the Web application to use your development user account.

Exam Highlights

Before taking the exam, review the key points and terms that are presented in this chapter. You need to know this information.

Key Points

■ How you can control the ACLs that restrict access to files and folders

■ The benefits of using isolated storage

■ The changes required to allow a standard user to create and debug .NET Framework assemblies

Key Terms

access control list (ACL)   A term most commonly used to refer to a DACL

discretionary access control list (DACL)   An authorization restriction mechanism that identifies the users and groups that are assigned or denied access permissions on an object

inherited permission   Permissions that propagate to an object from its parent object

isolated storage   A private file system managed by the .NET Framework

isolated storage files   Files that provide access to read and write isolated storage files (or simply files) within stores. Isolated storage files behave exactly like conventional files that are stored directly on a file system, but they exist within an isolated storage store

isolated storage stores   Separate isolated storage systems that are implemented as a single file in the file system

security access control list (SACL)   A usage event logging mechanism that determines how file or folder access is audited

Questions and Answers

Practice: Protecting Files Using Access Control Lists

Page
4-20

Exercise 2: Explaining How to Modify ACLs During Setup

1. In Exercise 1, you created a batch file consisting of a single command that sets the ACL on the Boot.ini file. How could you call this command during the setup procedure for your application?

You could define a custom action for your Visual Studio .NET setup project to call the batch file, or to run the command directly.

2. How could you modify the ACL from within a .NET Framework assembly without calling a command-line tool?

The .NET Framework lacks APIs to directly manipulate ACLs. You could call the Cacls command directly from your application by using the *System.Diagnostics.Process* class. Alternatively, you could write a wrapper class around the existing Win32 security APIs. Such wrapper classes are freely available for download.

3. What tools could you have used to manually change the ACL?

Windows Explorer, Cacls, or the XCacls tools can be used to set the ACL. Additionally, Domain Admins can use Group Policy to specify file permissions for computers in a domain.

Practice: Updating Existing Code to Use Isolated Storage

Page
4-29

Exercise

1. How could you rewrite the following piece of code to store the information in isolated storage, isolated by user, domain, and assembly

```
using System;
using System.IO;
…
StreamWriter sw = File.CreateText("mytemp.txt");
sw.WriteLine("Hello, world!");
sw.Close();
```

```
Imports System.IO
…
Dim sw As StreamWriter = File.CreateText("mytemp.txt")
sw.WriteLine("Hello, world!")
sw.Close()
```

There are several ways to write the code. However, the following code would work:

```csharp
using System;
using System.IO;
using System.IO.IsolatedStorage;
…
StreamWriter sw = new StreamWriter(new →
IsolatedStorageFileStream("mytemp.txt", FileMode.CreateNew));
sw.WriteLine("Hello, world!");
sw.Close();
```

```vb
Imports System.IO
Imports System.IO.IsolatedStorage
…
Dim sw As StreamWriter =  New StreamWriter(New →
IsolatedStorageFileStream("mytemp.txt",FileMode.CreateNew))
sw.WriteLine("Hello, world!")
sw.Close()
```

Although the exact code you create might vary from this answer, the key difference between the original code and the code you create must be that the *StreamWriter* construction uses the overloaded method that accepts an *IsolatedStorageFileStream* object.

Lab: Taking Advantage of Platform Security

Page
4-48

Exercise

1. What approaches can you take to resolve the problem of writing to an inaccessible location in the registry? Which approach would you recommend?

    There are several different approaches:

    ■ Modify the setup procedure to grant the Users group the right to update the HKEY_LOCAL_MACHINE\Software\Fabrikam\ registry key. The setup procedure will need to be run by a member of the Administrators group.

    ■ Change the application to use the HKEY_CURRENT_USER\Software\Fabrikam key. Members of the Users group can update this key by default.

    ■ Store information in a location other than the registry, such as the file system, or in the database itself.

    In this case, the best solution is to store the information in the HKEY_CURRENT_USER\Software\Fabrikam key. This requires only a minimal change to the application. The most significant drawback to this approach is that the application must create the key for every user who logs on to the computer.

2. What approaches can you take to resolve the problem of writing to the inaccessible location on the file system? Which approach would you recommend?

There are three approaches:

- Modify the setup procedure to grant the Users group the right to add and update new files in the C:\Windows\ directory. The setup procedure will need to be run by a member of the Administrators group.

- Change the application to use a directory that members of the Users group can add files to, such as C:\Windows\Temp\.

- Store files in the .NET Framework's isolated storage mechanism.

The first option is clearly wrong, because granting additional rights would reduce the security of the computer. The second option would work and be very easy to implement, because it would require only changing the path in the application. The third option would also work, and would provide additional security by isolating the data stored in the temporary files. However, the third option also would require additional programming to cause the application to use isolated storage rather than access the file system directly. Therefore either the second or third options are valid answers.

5 Implementing Role-Based Security

Why This Chapter Matters

Everyone is familiar with the concept of role-based security (or RBS, and also known as role access security), although you might not know the term. *Role-based security* is the process of authenticating users and then authorizing them based on the permissions assigned to their user accounts and group memberships. In Chapter 4, "Taking Advantage of Platform Security," you learned how to restrict access to files and folders based on a user's account and group memberships. This approach is perfect for systems administrators who are restricting access to data. However, developers need to be able to use RBS to restrict access to parts of an application.

This chapter focuses on implementing RBS by using the .NET Framework. First, you explore how authentication and authorization are related. Next, you learn to examine a user's credentials to restrict access to parts of your application based on that user's group memberships. Then, you learn how to create custom authentication methods to allow you to authenticate users against a database or any other mechanism.

Exam Objectives in this Chapter:

- Write authorization code.

  - Programmatically control access to functionality and data by using user information such as user identity, group membership, and other custom user information.

- Implement authentication.

  - Implement a custom authentication mechanism in a Microsoft Windows Forms application.

  - Implement functionality by consuming authenticated user information such as the *IPrincipal*, *Membership*, and *Identity* components of the .NET base class library.

Lessons in this Chapter:

Before You Begin

To complete the practices, examples, and lab exercises in this chapter, you must have one computer running Microsoft Windows Server 2003. During the course of performing the exercises in this chapter, the computer's security can be reduced. Therefore, the computer should not be a production computer and should not be connected to any network, especially the Internet, even if a firewall is present. Install Microsoft Visual Studio .NET 2003 using the default settings.

Lesson 1: Introduction to Authenticating and Authorizing Users

In this lesson, you will learn the meaning of the term authentication and how it differs from authorization. The lesson explains how network authentication is similar in function to the common methods of authenticating people in the physical world. You will also learn about the various credentials that can be used to verify a user's identity and the variety of protocols that can be used to transmit credentials across a network.

After this lesson, you will be able to

- Explain the purpose of authentication.
- Describe how authentication occurs on computer networks.
- Explain the purpose of multifactor authentication.
- Explain how authorization relates to authentication.

Estimated lesson time: 20 minutes

What Is Authentication?

Authentication is the process of identifying a user and is the most visible and fundamental concept in security. From personal identification numbers (PINs), to driver's licenses, to user names and passwords, authentication is a part of everyone's daily life. Without authentication, restricting access to resources based on a person's identity would be impossible. Figure 5-1 shows an example of authentication.

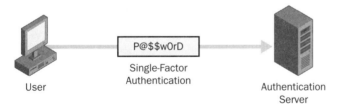

Figure 5-1   Using a password to provide authentication

Authentication, like every aspect of security, is a compromise between convenience and resistance to attack. If an authentication strategy is too weak, uninvited guests such as worms and Trojans could easily gain access to your network by impersonating legitimate users. Password guessing, password cracking, and man-in-the-middle attacks all attempt to exploit weaknesses in an organization's authentication strategy.

If an authentication strategy is too restrictive, attackers are more likely to be kept out, but legitimate users might not be able to do their jobs. Requiring extremely complex passwords makes it more difficult for attackers to impersonate legitimate users. However, if those users cannot remember their passwords, they will be denied access to network resources, which decreases their productivity.

How Authentication Occurs on Computer Networks

Traditionally, a password is used to prove a user's identity on a network. A password is a form of a shared secret. The user knows his or her password, and the server authenticating the user either has the password stored, or has some information that can be used to validate the password.

Passwords prove your identity because they are *something you know*. Presumably, only you know the password, and that knowledge proves who you are. Other ways to prove your identity are with *something you have* or *something you are*. Many modern computer systems authenticate users by reading information from a smart card—something you have. Other computer systems are satisfied that you are who you claim to be only when you prove it with something you are. *Biometrics* is a form of authentication in which a unique part of your body is scanned, such as your fingerprint, your retina, or your facial features.

Something you are is the most secure and reliable authentication method, because you cannot lose or forget it. However, it's also the least commonly used. Reliable biometric readers are too expensive to buy and maintain. Additionally, many users dislike biometric readers because they feel these readers violate their privacy.

What Is Multifactor Authentication?

Multifactor authentication is the process of combining two or more authentication methods for the purpose of significantly reducing the likelihood that an attacker will be able to impersonate a user during the authentication process. The most common example of multifactor authentication is combining a smart card with a password. Typically, the password is required to retrieve a key stored on the smart card. Before you can authenticate to such a system, you must provide a password (something you know) and a smart card (something you have). Figure 5-2 shows an example of multifactor authentication.

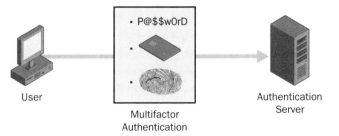

Figure 5-2   Using a password, a smart card, and a fingerprint to provide authentication

> **Note**   The examples in this book rely on using passwords alone for authentication. Although this is one of the less secure ways to authenticate users, you probably don't have smart cards or fingerprint readers connected to your computer. You almost certainly have a keyboard, though.

If you've used a credit card at a retail store, you've used multifactor authentication. The cashier runs the credit card through a machine to read the number—this is *something you have*. Then, the cashier compares your signature to the signature on the card—this is *something you are*. Similarly, when you use an automated teller machine (ATM), you produce a card (something you have) and a PIN (something you know). E-commerce sites typically require only single-factor authentication to use a credit card, which is one reason credit card thieves are more likely to use a stolen credit card to purchase something on a Web site than to go to a physical store location to purchase something.

As with most techniques for improving security, there is a trade-off. Users don't like multifactor authentication because it takes more time. It costs more to manage because there are two types of authentication for users to forget or misplace. Despite these drawbacks, multifactor authentication is the single best way to reduce the risk of an attacker impersonating a legitimate user.

How Authorization Relates to Authentication

Authorization is the process of verifying that a user is allowed to access a requested resource. Authorization generally happens only after authentication. After all, how can you determine whether someone is allowed to do something if you don't yet know who that person is? Figure 5-3 shows how authentication and authorization together provide a user's identity and validate the user's permissions.

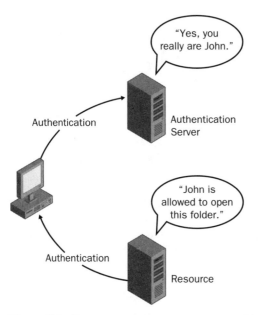

Figure 5-3   To access a resource, a user must be authenticated and then authorized.

Whether you're withdrawing money from a bank, entering a restricted building, or boarding an airplane, gaining access to a restricted resource requires both authentication and authorization. The two processes are closely related and often confused. To understand the difference between authentication and authorization, consider an example in the physical world that most people are familiar with: boarding an airplane. Before you can board a plane, you must present both your identification and your ticket. Your identification, typically a driver's license or a passport, enables the airport staff to determine who you are. Validating your identity is the *authentication* part of the boarding process. The airport staff also checks your ticket to make sure that the flight you are boarding is the correct one. Verifying that you are allowed to board the plane is the *authorization* process.

On networks, authentication is often performed during the process of providing a user name and password. The user name identifies you, and the password offers the computer system some assurance that you really are who you claim to be. After you are authenticated, the computer agrees that you are who you claim to be. However, it doesn't yet know whether you are allowed to access the resource you are requesting. For example, help desk support staff should have the right to reset a user's password, but members of the accounting department should be able to change their only own passwords. To authorize the user, the computer system typically checks an access control list (ACL). The ACL lists users, and groups of users, who are permitted to access a resource.

Practice: Thinking About Authenticating and Authorizing Users

In this practice, you will study the effectiveness of various authentication mechanisms by thinking about authentication in the physical world. If you are unable to answer a question, review the lesson materials and try the question again. You can find answers to the questions in the "Questions and Answers" section at the end of this chapter.

1. List every time you have been authenticated in the past week. How many of those authentications required something you have? Something you are? Something you know? How many of them required two-factor authentication?

2. List every time you have been authorized in the past week. Which of these authorizations were separate from authentication? Which did not require any authentication?

3. Biometrics are not often used for authentication. Why do you think that is the case?

Lesson Summary

- Authentication, such as checking your photo identification, verifies your identity by requiring you to provide unique credentials that are not easily impersonated.

- Networks typically use passwords for authentication, which is known as *something you know*. More advanced networks use smart cards, known as *something you have*, or biometrics, known as *something you are*.

- Multifactor authentication combines two or more authentication techniques to make impersonating legitimate users more difficult.

- Authorization, such as checking your plane ticket, verifies that you have permission to perform the action you are attempting. Authentication, which is determining who you are, must happen before authorization, which determines whether you are allowed to access a resource.

Lesson 2: Authorizing Users with Windows Security

ACLs control access to resources, such as individual files and folders, based on a user's Windows identity. Operating system objects aren't the only resources that need protection, however. Often, you need to protect the very logic contained within your application. To provide that type of authorization within your application, you can use the *WindowsIdentity* and *WindowsPrincipal* classes of the .NET Framework, which restricts specific features based on a user's name or group memberships.

After this lesson, you will be able to

- Describe the purpose of the *WindowsIdentity* class.
- Examine a user's name and authentication type to make decisions within your application.
- Explain the purpose of the *WindowsPrincipal* class.
- Examine group memberships to make choices within your application.

Estimated lesson time: 40 minutes

What Is the *WindowsIdentity* Class?

The *System.Security.Principal.WindowsIdentity* class represents a Windows user account. This class provides access to the current user's name, authentication type, and account token. It does not allow you to authenticate a user; Windows has already taken care of the authentication. *WindowsIdentity* simply stores the results of the authentication, including the user's name and authentication token.

Generally, when you create an instance of the *WindowsIdentity* class, you call one of three methods to create the object:

- **GetAnonymous**   Returns a *WindowsIdentity* object that represents an anonymous, unauthenticated Windows user. You can use this method to impersonate an anonymous user to ensure your code operates without credentials.

- **GetCurrent**   Returns a *WindowsIdentity* object that represents the current Windows user. You can use this method to examine the current user's user name and group memberships.

- **Impersonate**   Returns a *WindowsImpersonationContext* object that represents a specified user on the system. You can use this method to impersonate a particular user account when your application has access to the user's credentials.

See Also   Impersonation is most commonly used in Web applications. For more information about impersonation, see Chapter 9, "Hardening ASP.NET Applications."

For example, the following code creates a *WindowsIdentity* object named *currentIdentity* that represents the current user:

```csharp
using System.Security.Principal;
...
// Create a WindowsIdentity object representing the current user
WindowsIdentity currentIdentity = WindowsIdentity.GetCurrent();
```

```vb
Imports System.Security.Principal
...
' Create a WindowsIdentity object representing the current user
Dim currentIdentity As WindowsIdentity = WindowsIdentity.GetCurrent()
```

After the variable is assigned, you can access several useful properties that provide information about the user:

- **AuthenticationType**   A string representing the authentication method. This is usually "NTLM".

- **IsAnonymous**   A Boolean value set to true if the user is anonymous.

- **IsAuthenticated**   A Boolean value set to true if the user is authenticated.

- **IsGuest**   A Boolean value set to true if the user is a guest.

- **IsSystem**   A Boolean value set to true if the user is part of the system.

- **Name**   A string representing the authentication domain and user name of the user, separated by a backslash in the format, "DOMAIN\Username". If the user's account is in the local user database, the domain is the machine name. Otherwise, domain represents the name of the Active Directory domain.

- **Token**   An integer representing the user's authentication token, assigned by the computer that authenticated the user.

How to Examine the Current User's Name and Authentication Type to Make Decisions in Your Application

Use the *WindowsIdentity* class to examine the current user's name and authentication type to determine whether the user is authorized to run privileged portions of your code. Examining objects of this class is useful if, for example, a section of your code displays information that should be available only to authenticated users.

The following simple console application demonstrates the use of the *WindowsIdentity* class by displaying information about the current user:

```csharp
using System;

// WindowsIdentity requires the System.Security.Principal namespace
using System.Security.Principal;

namespace ExerciseWindowsIdentity
{
    /// <summary>
    /// Writes information about the current user to the console.
    /// </summary>
    class Class1
    {
        [STAThread]
        static void Main(string[] args)
        {
            // Grab the current user
            WindowsIdentity currentIdentity = WindowsIdentity.GetCurrent();

            // Display the name, token, and authentication type
            // for the current user
            Console.WriteLine("Name: " + currentIdentity.Name);
            Console.WriteLine("Token: " + currentIdentity.Token.ToString());
            Console.WriteLine("Authentication Type: "
+ currentIdentity.AuthenticationType);

            // Display information based on Boolean properties of
            // the current user
            if (currentIdentity.IsAnonymous)
                Console.WriteLine("Is an anonymous user");
            if (currentIdentity.IsAuthenticated)
                Console.WriteLine("Is an authenticated user");
            if (currentIdentity.IsGuest)
                Console.WriteLine("Is a guest");
            if (currentIdentity.IsSystem)
                Console.WriteLine("Is part of the system");
        }
    }
}
```

```vbnet
' WindowsIdentity requires the System.Security.Principal namespace
Imports System.Security.Principal

Module Module1

    Sub Main()
        ' Grab the current user
        Dim currentIdentity As WindowsIdentity = WindowsIdentity.GetCurrent()

        ' Display the name, token, and authentication type
        ' for the current user
        Console.WriteLine("Name: " + currentIdentity.Name)
```

```
        Console.WriteLine("Token: " + currentIdentity.Token.ToString())
        Console.WriteLine("Authentication Type: "↴
+ currentIdentity.AuthenticationType)

        ' Display information based on Boolean properties of the current user
        If currentIdentity.IsAnonymous = True Then
            Console.WriteLine("Is an anonymous user")
        End If
        If currentIdentity.IsAuthenticated = True Then
            Console.WriteLine("Is an authenticated user")
        End If
        If currentIdentity.IsSystem = True Then
            Console.WriteLine("Is part of the system")
        End If
        If currentIdentity.IsGuest = True Then
            Console.WriteLine("Is a guest")
        End If
    End Sub
End Module
```

What Is the *WindowsPrincipal* Class?

The *System.Security.Principal.WindowsPrincipal* class provides access to a user's group memberships. This class must be created by using an instance of the *Windows-Identity* class. For example, the following code creates a *WindowsIdentity* object named *currentIdentity* that represents the current user, and then creates a *WindowsPrincipal* object named *currentPrincipal* that represents the current user by creating the object using an existing *WindowsIdentity* object:

```
using System.Security.Principal;
…
// Create a WindowsIdentity object representing the current user
WindowsIdentity currentIdentity = WindowsIdentity.GetCurrent();

// Create a WindowsPrincipal object representing the current user
WindowsPrincipal currentPrincipal = new WindowsPrincipal(currentIdentity);
```

```
Imports System.Security.Principal
…
' Create a WindowsIdentity object representing the current user
Dim currentIdentity As WindowsIdentity = WindowsIdentity.GetCurrent()

' Create a WindowsPrincipal object representing the current user
Dim currentPrincipal As WindowsPrincipal=New WindowsPrincipal(currentIdentity)
```

As an alternative to creating a *WindowsIdentity* object using the *WindowsIdentity.Get-Current* method, you can extract the current *WindowsPrincipal* object by querying the current thread directly. To do this, first set the current principal policy to use Windows security, and then create a new *WindowsPrincipal* object by casting *System.Threading.Thread.CurrentPrincipal* as a *WindowsPrincipal* object. The following code demonstrates this:

```csharp
using System.Security.Principal;
using System.Threading;
…
// Specify that WindowsPrincipal should be used
AppDomain.CurrentDomain.SetPrincipalPolicy(PrincipalPolicy.WindowsPrincipal);

// Cast the current principal as a WindowsPrincipal object
WindowsPrincipal currentPrincipal = (WindowsPrincipal)Thread.CurrentPrincipal;
```

```vb
Imports System.Security.Principal
Imports System.Threading
…
' Specify that WindowsPrincipal should be used
AppDomain.CurrentDomain.SetPrincipalPolicy(PrincipalPolicy.WindowsPrincipal)

' Cast the current principal as a WindowsPrincipal object
Dim currentPrincipal As WindowsPrincipal = _
CType(Thread.CurrentPrincipal, WindowsPrincipal)
```

What Is Principal Policy?

Principal policy is the scheme that the .NET Framework uses to determine which default principal will be returned when the current principal is queried by an application. The *System.Security.Principal.PrincipalPolicy* enumeration defines three policy schemes:

- *NoPrincipal*   A scheme with no built-in functionality

- *UnauthenticatedPrincipal*   The default policy scheme, which assumes all principals are unauthenticated

- *WindowsPrincipal*   The policy scheme required for working with Windows security

Because *WindowsPrincipal* is not the default, you must set it as the active policy before working with Windows security principals by using the following code:

```csharp
using System.Security.Principal;
…
AppDomain.CurrentDomain.SetPrincipalPolicy(PrincipalPolicy.WindowsPrincipal);
```

```vb
Imports System.Security.Principal
…
AppDomain.CurrentDomain.SetPrincipalPolicy(PrincipalPolicy.WindowsPrincipal)
```

The *WindowsPrincipal* class contains a single useful method: *IsInRole*. Use the *WindowsPrincipal.IsInRole* method to determine whether the user is a member of a particular group. Note that you cannot use this class to simply enumerate all group memberships. Instead, you must query for a specific user membership by passing this method one of three parameters:

- Group's *WindowsBuiltInRole* object

- Authentication domain and group name (as a string)

- Role identity (as an integer)

How to Examine Group Memberships to Make Choices in Your Application

You can use the *WindowsPrincipal* class to determine which groups a user is a member of. To query for built-in groups, pass to the *WindowsPrincipal.IsInRole* method a member of the *System.Security.Principal.WindowsBuiltInRole* class. Each member of the *WindowsBuiltInRole* class represents a built-in group that exists either within the computer's local user database, or within an Active Directory domain. Some of the roles won't exist at all, depending on the type of computer your assembly is running on. For example, the following code fragment always throws a *System.ArgumentException* when run on a Windows Server 2003 domain controller, because the Power Users group does not exist:

```
if (currentPrincipal.IsInRole(WindowsBuiltInRole.PowerUser))
```

```
If currentPrincipal.IsInRole(WindowsBuiltInRole.Administrator)
```

Similarly, attempting to call *WindowsPrincipal.IsInRole(WindowsBuiltInRole.AccountOperator)* or *WindowsPrincipal.IsInRole(WindowsBuiltInRole.SystemOperator)* on a Windows Server 2003 computer that does not have Active Directory installed will cause the runtime to throw an exception. The presence of built-in groups on Microsoft Windows 2000 and Windows XP computers will vary as well, so always be prepared to catch an exception.

Table 5-1 lists the members of the *WindowsBuiltInRole* class, the built-in groups that each corresponds to, and whether the group is a local or domain group.

Table 5-1   *WindowsBuiltInRole* Members for Local Users

Member	Group	Scope
AccountOperator	Account Operators	Domain
Administrator	Administrators	Local
BackupOperator	Backup Operators	Local
Guest	Guests	Local
PowerUser	Power Users	Local
PrintOperator	Print Operators	Local
Replicator	Replicator	Local
SystemOperator	Server Operators	Domain
User	Users	Local

For example, the following portion of a console application checks three separate members of the *WindowsBuiltInRole* class and displays whether the current local user is a member:

```csharp
using System.Security.Principal;
…

// Create a WindowsIdentity object representing the current user
WindowsIdentity currentIdentity = WindowsIdentity.GetCurrent();

// Create a WindowsPrincipal object representing the current user
WindowsPrincipal currentPrincipal = new WindowsPrincipal(currentIdentity);

Console.WriteLine("The current user is a member of the following roles: ");

// Check for three common group memberships
if (currentPrincipal.IsInRole(WindowsBuiltInRole.Administrator))
{
    Console.WriteLine(WindowsBuiltInRole.Administrator.ToString());
    }
if (currentPrincipal.IsInRole(WindowsBuiltInRole.PowerUser))
{
    Console.WriteLine(WindowsBuiltInRole.PowerUser.ToString());
}
if (currentPrincipal.IsInRole(WindowsBuiltInRole.User))
{
    Console.WriteLine(WindowsBuiltInRole.User.ToString());
}
```

```
Imports System.Security.Principal
...
' Create a WindowsIdentity object representing the current user
Dim currentIdentity As WindowsIdentity = WindowsIdentity.GetCurrent()

' Create a WindowsPrincipal object representing the current user
Dim currentPrincipal As WindowsPrincipal = New WindowsPrincipal(currentIdentity)

Console.WriteLine("The current user is a member of the following roles: ")

' Check for three common group memberships
If currentPrincipal.IsInRole(WindowsBuiltInRole.Administrator) Then
    Console.WriteLine(WindowsBuiltInRole.Administrator.ToString())
End If
If currentPrincipal.IsInRole(WindowsBuiltInRole.PowerUser) Then
    Console.WriteLine(WindowsBuiltInRole.PowerUser.ToString())
End If
If currentPrincipal.IsInRole(WindowsBuiltInRole.User) Then
    Console.WriteLine(WindowsBuiltInRole.User.ToString())
End If
```

To query for custom groups or groups in a domain rather than for the local user database, pass a string value to the overloaded *IsInRole* method in the format "***DOMAIN\Group Name***". For example, if you have code that should execute only if the user is a member of the CONTOSO\Accountants group, you could use the following `if` statement:

```
if (currentPrincipal.IsInRole(@"CONTOSO\Accounting"))
{
    Console.WriteLine("User is in Accounting");
}
```

```
If currentPrincipal.IsInRole("CONTOSO\Accounting") Then
    Console.WriteLine("User is in Accounting")
End If
```

> **Exam Tip**   For the exam, know how to use the *IsInRole* method with both *WindowsBuiltIn-Role* and strings. In particular, remember how to concatenate domain and group names.

In most circumstances, however, you will not know the computer name or domain name ahead of time to insert it into the string you pass the *IsInRole* method. Instead, construct it using the *System.Environment.MachineName* string property or the *System.Environment.UserDomainName* string property. *System.Environment.Machine-Name* can be used to specify group names only on the local computer. Use *System.Environment.UserDomainName* to specify group names that exist on the local computer or in the Active Directory domain, depending on how the user logged on.

Practice: Authorizing Users with Windows Security

In this practice, you will use your knowledge of Windows security authorization to write a console application that determines whether the user has appropriate group memberships for least privilege development. You will be demonstrating your mastery of the *WindowsIdentity* and *WindowsPrincipal* classes. Read the following scenario and then complete the exercise that follows. If you are unable to answer the question, review the lessons and try the question again. You can find an answer to the question in the "Questions and Answers" section at the end of this chapter.

Scenario

You are an application developer working for Humongous Insurance. Recently, the IT group changed the standard desktop configuration so that all users log onto their computers as members of the Users group, but not as members of the Administrators group. You and the other developers on your team need to use least privilege development to ensure the applications you create will run correctly when run by standard users, but many of your teammates forget this policy and log on to their computers as administrators.

Your boss tells you the following: "Apparently IT has decided it's better to make us bend over backward than to teach people not to run every executable they get in the mail. Changing our whole development process is easier than telling people not to double-click or adding a virus scanner to our mail server, apparently. Anyway, do me a favor and write a simple console app that tells the team whether they're logged on with appropriate permissions."

You decide to talk to a few people and review the technical requirements before you begin developing the application.

Interviews   Following is a list of company personnel interviewed and their statements:

- **IT Manager, Carol Philips**   "After that last virus hit, we decided to make everyone log on as a standard user. Developers are no exception. Besides, if you guys are writing our apps as administrators, how do you know that everyone who logs on as a standard user like they're supposed to will even be able to run those apps?"

- **Developer, Deborah Poe**   "How are you going to write this app, anyway? Don't you have to query Active Directory or something? Seems like a lot of trouble. It's not like I'm going to get a virus."

Technical Requirements   Developers are currently using an account that is a member of the local Administrators or Power Users groups. Instead, they should be using an account that is a member of the Users, Debugger Users, and VS Developers groups. Write a console application in either C# or Microsoft Visual Basic .NET that checks the current user's group memberships and warns the user if he is logged on with inappropriate group memberships.

Exercise

Complete the following task for your boss:

1. Write an application that meets the technical requirements, and show your work.

Lesson Summary

- The *WindowsIdentity* class provides .NET Framework applications access to a Windows user's account properties.

- You can examine the current user's user name and authentication type by creating a new *WindowsIdentity* object by using the *WindowsIdentity.GetCurrent* method.

- The *WindowsPrincipal* class enables assemblies to query the Windows security database to determine whether a user is a member of a particular group.

- To examine the current user's group memberships, create a *WindowsPrincipal* object by using the current user's identity, and then call the *WindowsPrincipal.IsInRole* method.

Lesson 3: Demanding Role-Based Security

In Lesson 2, you learned how to build RBS authorization into your applications by using the *WindowsIdentity* and *WindowsPrincipal* classes to examine the current user's properties and group memberships. This is a useful technique when you need to make simple decisions; however, it is somewhat prone to errors that can lead to security vulnerabilities.

A more secure, robust way to restrict access is by using imperative and declarative RBS demands. When you use declarative demands, you can require that users meet certain criteria before the runtime will run a method. If the user lacks the necessary permissions, the runtime throws an exception—ensuring the code is never run. Imperative demands function similarly but provide more flexibility.

After this lesson, you will be able to

■ Describe the purpose of the *PrincipalPermission* class.

■ Describe what declarative RBS demands are used for.

■ Use declarative RBS demands to restrict access to methods.

■ Explain the purpose of imperative RBS demands.

■ Use imperative RBS demands to create applications that restrict access to portions of your application's logic.

■ Decide when to use different RBS techniques.

Estimated lesson time: 45 minutes

What Is the *PrincipalPermission* Class?

The *System.Security.Permissions.PrincipalPermission* class and the related *Principal-PermissionAttribute* class enable you to check the active principal for both declarative and imperative security actions. They (collectively referred to as *PrincipalPermission*) are typically used to declaratively demand that users running your code have been authenticated or belong to a specified role. By passing identity information (user name and/or role) to the constructor, *PrincipalPermission* can be used to demand that the identity of the active principal match this information.

You can set any combination of three properties for *PrincipalPermission*:

■ **Authenticated** A Boolean value. If set to true, the permission requires the user to be authenticated.

■ **Name** A string that must match the identity's user name.

■ **Role** A string that must match one of the principal's roles.

Exam Tip   Memorize these three properties. Remember, *PrincipalPermission* doesn't expose any other properties—not a user's full name, phone number, password, or any other attribute.

PrincipalPermission has several methods, however, only the *PrincipalPermission.Demand* method is used with the RBS techniques described in this chapter. The *Demand* method verifies that the active principal meets the requirements specified in the *Authenticated, Name,* and *Role* properties. If the principal does not match any properties that are not null, the principal throws an exception.

See Also   The *PrincipalPermission* class is hard to understand but easy to use. Refer to "How to Use Declarative Role-Based Security Demands to Restrict Access to Methods" and "How to Use Imperative Role-Based Security Demands to Create Applications that Restrict Access to Portions of Their Logic" in this lesson for examples.

What Are Declarative Role-Based Security Demands?

Declarative RBS demands instruct the runtime to perform an RBS check before running a method. This is the most secure way to use RBS to restrict access to code, because security is enforced by the runtime before it runs your code. There are two primary disadvantages to declarative RBS demands:

- They can be used only to restrict access to entire methods.
- They might result in the runtime throwing an exception. If the method was called by a Windows event, Windows catches the exception, and your application might stop running.

How to Use Declarative Role-Based Security Demands to Restrict Access to Methods

To use declarative RBS demands, you must have three elements in your code:

- The *System.AppDomain.CurrentDomain.SetPrincipalPolicy* method to specify the principal security policy
- A *try/catch* block to catch underprivileged access attempts and to report the error appropriately
- A *PrincipalPermission* attribute to declare the method's access requirements

First, specify the principal policy for the thread from within your application using the *System.AppDomain.CurrentDomain.SetPrincipalPolicy* method. Generally, you call this method when your assembly is initialized. If you are using Windows security (in other words, if you haven't created a custom security policy), you can add the following line of code:

```
System.AppDomain.CurrentDomain.SetPrincipalPolicy(PrincipalPolicy.WindowsPrincipal);
```

```
System.AppDomain.CurrentDomain.SetPrincipalPolicy(PrincipalPolicy.WindowsPrincipal)
```

Next, create a *try/catch* block to catch the *System.Security.SecurityException* exceptions that the runtime will throw when it attempts to run the method but lacks the permission demanded. It's important to catch this type of exception and provide a useful error message to the user, because without the error message, the user could quickly become frustrated and might spend a significant amount of time attempting to troubleshoot the access problem. Additionally, log failed access attempts so that administrators can analyze the events to detect potential compromises.

For example, the following code calls a method named *AdministratorsOnlyMethod* that is protected with a declarative RBS demand and displays a message box if the user lacks the necessary permission:

```
try
{
    AdministratorsOnlyMethod();
}
catch (System.Security.SecurityException ex)
{
    MessageBox.Show("Your account lacks permission to that function.");
}
```

```
Try
    AdministratorsOnlyMethod()
Catch ex As System.Security.SecurityException
    MessageBox.Show("Your account lacks permission to that function.")
End Try
```

Reporting Errors

Remember Lesson 5 of Chapter 2, "Using Secure Coding Best Practices":

- Don't give too much information to the user. For example, telling the user that she must be a member of the Administrators group to perform a function reveals to an attacker exactly what the next step is, and allows the attacker to work toward bypassing your security mechanism.

- Log the event to the event log to allow Administrators to detect and analyze attacks.

The examples shown are simplified to focus on the lessons taught in this chapter.

Finally, add declarative permission statements using the *PrincipalPermission* class before each method you need to restrict access to. You must define two things for *PrincipalPermission*:

1. The action *PrincipalPermission* will take using the *System.Security.Permissions.SecurityAction* enumeration. Typically, you use *SecurityAction.Demand* for declarative RBS.

2. One or more *PrincipalPermission* properties. Use *Authenticated* to restrict access to authenticated users, *Role* to restrict access by group memberships, and *User* to restrict access to a specific user name.

For example, the following code causes the runtime to throw a *System.Security.SecurityException* exception when the user is not a member of the local Administrators group:

```
[PrincipalPermission(SecurityAction.Demand, Role = @"BUILTIN\Administrators")]
private void AdministratorsOnlyMethod()
{
    // Code that can only be run by Administrators
}
```

```
<PrincipalPermission(SecurityAction.Demand, Role:="BUILTIN\Administrators")> _ Private
 Sub AdministratorsOnlyMethod ()
    ' Code that can only be run by Administrators
End Sub
```

Similarly, the following code causes the runtime to throw an exception when the user is not authenticated using the user name CONTOSO\Administrator:

```
[PrincipalPermission(SecurityAction.Demand, Name = @"CONTOSO\Administrator")]
private void AdministratorsOnlyMethod()
{
    // Code that can only be run by CONTOSO\Administrator
}
```

```
<PrincipalPermission(SecurityAction.Demand, Name:="CONTOSO\Administrator")> _
Private Sub AdministratorsOnlyMethod ()
    ' Code that can only be run by CONTOSO\Administrator
End Sub
```

You can also use multiple declarative demands to allows users who meet any of the demands to execute the code. The following code allows any of the following to run the method:

- Members of the local Administrators group

- A user named CONTOSO\User1 who is also a member of the CONTOSO\Managers group

- Any user who is authenticated

```csharp
[PrincipalPermission(SecurityAction.Demand, Name = @"CONTOSO\Administrator")]
[PrincipalPermission(SecurityAction.Demand, Name = @"CONTOSO\User1", →
Role = @"CONTOSO\Managers")]
[PrincipalPermission(SecurityAction.Demand, Authenticated = true)]
private void AdministratorsOnlyMethod()
{
    // Code that can only be run by CONTOSO\Administrator
}
```

```vbnet
<PrincipalPermission(SecurityAction.Demand, Name:="CONTOSO\Administrator")> _
<PrincipalPermission(SecurityAction.Demand, Name:="CONTOSO\User1", →
Role:="CONTOSO\Managers")> _
<PrincipalPermission(SecurityAction.Demand, Authenticated:=True)> _
Private Sub AdministratorsOnlyMethod ()
    ' Code that can only be run by CONTOSO\Administrator
End Sub
```

What Are Imperative Role-Based Security Demands?

Imperative RBS demands are declared within your code and can be used to restrict access to portions of code on a more granular basis than declarative RBS demands. In other words, imperative RBS demands allow you to restrict portions of a method, whereas declarative RBS demands require you to restrict entire methods.

How to Use Imperative Role-Based Security Demands to Create Applications that Restrict Access to Portions of Their Logic

To use imperative RBS demands, you must have four elements in your code:

- The *System.AppDomain.CurrentDomain.SetPrincipalPolicy* method to specify the principal security policy

- A *try/catch* block to catch underprivileged access attempts and report the error appropriately

- A *PrincipalPermission* object, with properties set according to the restrictions you want to impose

- A call to the *PrincipalPermission.Demand* method to declare the method's access requirements

The first two elements are exactly the same as those required by declarative RBS demands, and should be implemented in exactly the same way. The use of the *PrincipalPermission* class is very different, however. First, you must create a new *PrincipalPermission* object. *PrincipalPermission* has three overloaded constructors:

- ***PrincipalPermission(PermissionState)***   Allows you to specify the *Principal-Permisson* object's properties by using a *System.Security.Permissions.Permission-State* object.

- *PrincipalPermission(Name, Role)*   Specifies values for the new object's *Name* and *Role* properties. If you want to specify only a user name or a role, simply specify null for the other value.

- *PrincipalPermission(Name, Role, Authenticated)*   Specifies values for the new object's *Name*, *Role*, and *Authenticated* properties. Specify null for any properties that you do not want to use to restrict access.

The following two lines of code throw an exception when the user is not a member of the local Administrators group. Note that the first argument to the *PrincipalPermission* constructor is null, which indicates that no particular user name is required. The last argument, set to true, requires that the user be authenticated (which is redundant and could effectively be left out, because no unauthenticated user would be a member of the Administrators group).

```
PrincipalPermission myPerm = new →
PrincipalPermission(null, @"BUILTIN\Administrators", true);
administratorPermission.Demand();
```

```
Dim myPerm As PrincipalPermission=→
New PrincipalPermission (Nothing, "BUILTIN\Administrators", True)
administratorPermission.Demand
```

The following code throws an exception unless the current user is using the Administrator account in a domain named Contoso. Notice that this code is using the overloaded constructor that does not define the Boolean *Authentication* property.

```
PrincipalPermission myPerm = new →
PrincipalPermission(@"CONTOSO\Administrator", null);
administratorPermission.Demand();
```

```
Dim myPerm As PrincipalPermission=→
New PrincipalPermission ("CONTOSO\Administrator", Nothing)
administratorPermission.Demand
```

To tie the imperative use of the *PrincipalPermission* object into a larger application, consider the following console application. This application displays "Access allowed." if the current user is a member of the local VS Developers group. Otherwise, it catches the exception thrown by the *PrincipalPermission.Demand* method and displays "Access denied."

```
using System;

// Include namespaces required for RBS demands
using System.Security.Permissions;
using System.Security.Principal;
```

```
namespace ConsoleImperativeRBS
{
    class Class1
    {
        [STAThread]
        static void Main(string[] args)
        {
            // Define the security policy in use as Windows security
            System.AppDomain.CurrentDomain.SetPrincipalPolicy→
(PrincipalPolicy.WindowsPrincipal);

            // Concatenate the group name as "MachineName\VS Developers"
            string requiredRole = System.Environment.MachineName + →
@"\VS Developers";

            // Catch any security denied exceptions so that they can be logged
            try
            {
                // Create and demand the PrincipalPermission object
                PrincipalPermission administratorPermission = →
new PrincipalPermission(null, requiredRole, true);
                administratorPermission.Demand();

                Console.WriteLine("Access allowed.");
                // TODO: Main application
            }
            catch(System.Security.SecurityException ex)
            {
                Console.WriteLine("Access denied.");
                // TODO: Log error
            }
        }
    }
}
```

```
Imports System

' Include namespaces required for RBS demands
Imports System.Security.Permissions
Imports System.Security.Principal
Namespace ConsoleImperativeRBS

    Class Class1

        <STAThread()> _
        Shared Sub Main(ByVal args As String())
            ' Define the security policy in use as Windows security
            System.AppDomain.CurrentDomain.SetPrincipalPolicy→
(PrincipalPolicy.WindowsPrincipal)

            ' Concatenate the group name as "MachineName\VS Developers"
            Dim requiredRole As String = →
System.Environment.MachineName + "\VS Developers"
```

```
                    'Catch any security denied exceptions so that they
                    'can be logged
                Try
                    ' Create and demand the PrincipalPermission object
                        Dim administratorPermission As PrincipalPermission=→
New PrincipalPermission (Nothing, requiredRole, True)
                    administratorPermission.Demand
                    Console.WriteLine("Access allowed.")
                        ' TODO: Main application
                Catch ex As System.Security.SecurityException
                    Console.WriteLine("Access denied.")
                        ' TODO: Log error
                End Try
            End Sub
        End Class
End Namespace
```

Guidelines for Deciding When to Use Different RBS Techniques

In this chapter, you explored three different techniques for validating a user's group memberships:

- Using the *WindowsPrincipal.IsInRole* method

- Using declarative RBS demands

- Using imperative RBS demands

Each of the techniques accomplishes the same goal—changing the program execution flow based on a user's memberships. However, use each in different circumstances. Table 5-2 lists the conditions in which each RBS technique should be used.

Table 5-2   RBS Techniques

Condition	Preferred Technique for Validating Group Membership
Restrict access to an entire method when the conditions are statically defined.	Declarative RBS demands
Restrict access to all or a portion of a method when conditions are statically or dynamically defined.	Imperative RBS demands
Branch processing based on a user's group memberships	*WindowsPrincipal.IsInRole*

If your development scenario is flexible enough to allow you to use more than one of the RBS validation techniques, use declarative RBS demands first, imperative RBS demands second, and the *WindowsPrincipal.IsInRole* method only when absolutely necessary. The reason for this is that exceptions are the most reliable way to prevent underprivileged users from executing a method.

Consider the following scenario: You create a method that must be run only by members of the local Administrators group. Several years from now, a new developer must expand the functionality in the method by adding additional code to the end of your existing code. If you use declarative RBS demands, the new code will definitely be protected by your restriction, as demonstrated by the following pseudo-code:

```
[PrincipalPermission(SecurityAction.Demand, Role = @"BUILTIN\Administrators")]
private void secureMethod()
{
    // Old code here
    // New code would go here, where it would be restricted.

}
```

However, if you use imperative RBS demands, the new developer *might* make the mistake of adding the code outside the *try* block. In this circumstance, an underprivileged user would be able to successfully run the code, as demonstrated by the following pseudo-code:

```
private void secureMethod()
{
    try
    {
        PrincipalPermission administratorPermission = ↴
new PrincipalPermission(null, @"BUILTIN\Administrator", true);
        administratorPermission.Demand();
        // Old code here
        // New code might go here, where it would be restricted...
    }
    catch
    {
        // Old code here
    }
    // Or new code might go here, where it would be unrestricted.
}
```

Developers are accustomed to seeing *try/catch* blocks used to surround the main part of a method, however, and a new developer would be likely to add the code within the *try* block, where it would be protected. However, the *WindowsPrincipal.IsInRole* method is typically used with conditional statements, and the new developer is likely to miss the purpose of the conditional and add the code at the end of the method, where it would be exempt from the security checks. The following pseudo-code demonstrates this:

```
private void secureMethod()
{
    if (user.IsInRole(WindowsBuiltInRole.Administrator))
    {
        // Old code here
        // New code might go here, where it would be restricted...
    }
    else
```

```
    {
        // Old code here
    }
    // Or new code might go here, where it would be unrestricted.
}
```

Each of the three techniques can be used to similar effect. However, declarative RBS demands are slightly more secure because they are less likely to suffer from security vulnerabilities introduced because of updates added after the initial development.

Practice: Selecting and Implementing RBS

In this practice, you will validate your understanding of the different techniques for implementing RBS, as well as your ability to restrict access to application functionality based on a user's identity and group memberships. Complete the following two exercises. If you are unable to answer a question, review the lesson materials and try the question again. You can find answers to the questions in the "Questions and Answers" section at the end of this chapter.

Exercise 1: Identifying the Proper RBS Technique

Answer the following questions:

1. You must restrict access to a method based on a user's group memberships. You want to use the most secure method possible. Which technique will you use? Choose the correct answer.

    a. *WindowsPrincipal.IsInRole*

    b. Imperative RBS demands

    c. Declarative RBS demands

2. You must restrict access to a method that is called by a Windows event based on a user's group memberships. If the user lacks sufficient access, you want to log an event and display a message to the user. You want to use the most secure method possible. Which technique will you use? Choose the correct answer.

    a. *WindowsPrincipal.IsInRole*

    b. Imperative RBS demands

    c. Declarative RBS demands

3. You are writing a method for a console application that lists options available to a user based on his group memberships. Which technique should you use? Choose the correct answer.

    a. *WindowsPrincipal.IsInRole*

    b. Imperative RBS demands

    c. Declarative RBS demands

Exercise 2: Using RBS Demands

Read the following scenario and then answer the questions that follow.

Scenario   You are an independent consultant who has been hired by Proseware, Inc., a software development company that develops software for law enforcement agencies. The software identifies crimes that might have been committed by the same individual, enabling law enforcement officials to combine evidence collected in the crimes to more accurately identify a suspect. Proseware's Development Manager, Christina Philp, has asked you to add security features to an internal application. She gives you the following application, which was developed by Proseware, Inc.'s chief scientist, Jose Luis Auricchio, to perform complex calculations.

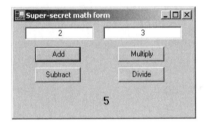

She asks you to interview key personnel, review technical requirements, and then bring her a solution.

Interviews   Following is a list of company personnel interviewed and their statements:

- **IT Manager**   "Our chief scientist, Jose, has developed four highly complex, confidential algorithms that take two integers, perform some heavy-duty calculations, and then produce a result. One of these algorithms, named *addition*, can be run by anyone in the local Users group. The algorithms named *subtraction* and *multiplication* should be run only by members of the local Administrators group. The *division* algorithm is extremely confidential, and should be run only by me. My user name is CPhilp, and I have a local account on the computer. If that *division* algorithm falls into the wrong hands...well, let's just make sure that doesn't happen. Oh, I don't even want people to see the buttons that they aren't allowed to use, so hide the buttons if people don't have permission to access them. Double-check their permissions before running the algorithms, though, and display a friendly message if they are denied access."

■ **Chief Scientist** "I'm a mathematician, not a programmer. The IT Manager is all concerned about who runs my algorithms, but I don't know anything about security. Frankly, I'd rather share the algorithms with the public so that everyone could benefit. Anyway, let me tell you a little about the application. It's a simple Windows Forms application with two text boxes, one label, and four buttons. The user enters integers into the two text boxes, and then clicks a button. The button click causes the application to run some calculations on the two integers, and then it displays the output using the label. Well, you'll figure it out when you see it. Oh, I do all my calculations in the methods called by the button click events, except for the *multiplication* function. That one is pretty intense, so I moved the calculations into a separate method."

Technical Requirements   Your modifications to the scientist's application must meet the following requirements:

■ Only members of the Users group can run the method linked to the Add button.

■ Only members of the Administrators group can run the methods linked to the Subtract or Multiply button.

■ Only the CPhilp user can run the method linked to the Divide button.

■ You must use the most secure techniques possible for restricting access to the methods.

■ You must hide buttons users do not have access to.

■ You must detect access attempts by underprivileged users and display a friendly message informing them that access has been denied.

Questions

Answer the following questions for your boss:

1. How will you to hide the buttons that are inaccessible to users?

2. Which techniques will you use to protect each of the *addButton_Click*, *subtractButton_Click*, *divideButton_Click*, and *multiply* methods?

3. Open the C# or Visual Basic .NET application named RBS by using Microsoft Visual Studio .NET, and make the updates requested by the IT Manager. Show your work.

Lesson Summary

- You use the *PrincipalPermission* class to specify user name, role, and authentication requirements.

- Declarative RBS demands restrict access to an entire method by throwing an exception if the current principal does not meet the specified access requirements.

- Use declarative RBS demands by setting the principal policy, creating a *try/catch* block to handle users with insufficient privileges, and declaring a *PrincipalPermission* attribute to declare the method's access requirements.

- You use imperative RBS demands to restrict access to portions of a method by throwing an exception if the current principal lacks the necessary permissions.

- Use imperative RBS demands by setting the principal policy, creating a *try/catch* block to handle users with insufficient privileges, creating a *PrincipalPermission* object to declare the method's access requirements, and then calling the *Principal-Permission.Demand* method.

- Use the *WindowsPrincipal.IsInRole* method to make decisions based on group memberships. Declarative RBS demands are perfect for situations in which your application calls a method directly, and access to the entire method must be restricted. Use imperative RBS demands when you need to protect only a portion of a method, or when you are protecting a method that can be called by a Windows event.

Lesson 4: Creating Custom Authentication Methods

In Lessons 2 and 3, you learned how to perform typical RBS tasks using standard Windows security. This is useful for applications where the only approach for identifying users is their Windows logon information. However, it won't satisfy you if you use a back-end database or other mechanism to store information about users and validate their credentials.

For developers who require a different authentication mechanism, the runtime provides the *System.Security.Principal.IIdentity* and *System.Security.Principal.IPrincipal* interfaces. You can extend these interfaces by implementing your own classes with additional properties and functionalities. For example, you could create your own *IIdentity*-based class that includes custom user attributes such as name and address, or you could create your own *IPrincipal*-based class that implements hierarchical roles.

After this lesson, you will be able to

- Describe the purpose of the *IIdentity* interface.
- Create a custom identity class by using the *IIdentity* interface.
- Explain the purpose of the *IPrincipal* interface.
- Create a custom principal class by using the *IPrincipal* interface.
- Create simple, custom user privilege models by using the *GenericIdentity* and *Generic-Principal* classes.
- Use declarative and imperative RBS demands with custom identities and principals.
- Create a custom authentication mechanism by creating a class that provides methods your application can use.

Estimated lesson time: 35 minutes

What Is the *IIdentity* Interface?

The *IIdentity* interface is a template for creating identity classes. If you completed Lesson 2, you are already familiar with the *IIdentity* interface, although you might not realize it. The *WindowsIdentity* class is an implementation of *IIdentity*, and the bulk of *WindowsIdentity*'s properties and methods are inherited directly from *IIdentity*. Similarly, *FormsIdentity* and *PassportIdentity* implement *IIdentity* for working with Web authentication, and the *GenericIdentity* class provides a very flexible implementation of *IIdentity*.

See Also   For more information about Web authentication, see Chapter 9.

If none of the existing implementations of *IIdentity* suits your needs, you can extend *IIdentity*'s functionality by creating your own class based on it. By doing this, you can add any additional properties you see fit. After creating the class, you can use the new class in the same ways you used *WindowsIdentity* in Lessons 2 and 3.

To implement *IIdentity*, you must implement the following properties:

- ***AuthenticationType***   A string used to store a description of the user's authentication mechanism. Applications can use this property to determine whether the authentication mechanism can be trusted. For example, one application might determine that Passport authentication meets the security requirements but Basic authentication does not. If you create a custom authentication mechanism, specify a unique *AuthenticationType*.

- ***IsAuthenticated***   A Boolean value that should be set to true if the user has been authenticated. If you create your own custom authentication mechanism, set this value when the user is authenticated.

- ***Name***   A string that stores the user's user name. This property must exist, even when your authentication mechanism does not use a user name. It must uniquely identify the user; only one account should have any given name.

Additionally, you will need to implement a constructor that defines each of the object's properties.

How to Create a Custom Identity Class

To create a custom identity class, implement it based on *IIdentity* and at a minimum override the *AuthenticationType*, *IsAuthenticated*, and *Name* properties. Then add any other properties or methods required by your application. Finally, add at least one constructor that allows the calling application to define the standard and custom properties.

The following class implements *IIdentity* and adds properties for the user's first and last name, address, city, state, and zip code. This class provides two constructors: one that takes no parameters and initializes all properties as null, and a second that initializes every property.

```csharp
using System;
using System.Security.Principal;

namespace CustomRBS
{
    /// <summary>
    /// Summary description for CustomIdentity.
    /// </summary>
    public class CustomIdentity : IIdentity
```

```
        {
            // Implement private variables for standard properties
            private bool isAuthenticated;
            private string name;
            private string authenticationType;

            // Implement private variables for custom properties
            private string firstName;
            private string lastName;
            private string address;
            private string city;
            private string state;
            private string zip;

            // Allow the creation of an empty object
            public CustomIdentity()
            {
                this.name = String.Empty;
                this.isAuthenticated = false;
                this.authenticationType = "None";

                this.firstName = String.Empty;
                this.lastName = String.Empty;
                this.address = String.Empty;
                this.city = String.Empty;
                this.state = String.Empty;
                this.zip = String.Empty;
            }

            // Allow caller to create the object and specify all properties
            public CustomIdentity(bool isLogin, →
    string newAuthenticationType, string newFirstName, string newLastName, →
    string newAddress, string newCity, string newState, string newZip)
            {
                // Create a unique username by concatenating first and last name
                this.name = newFirstName + newLastName;
                this.isAuthenticated = isLogin;
                this.authenticationType = newAuthenticationType;

                this.firstName = newFirstName;
                this.lastName = newLastName;
                this.address = newAddress;
                this.city = newCity;
                this.state = newState;
                this.zip = newZip;
            }

            // Implement public read-only interfaces for standard properties
            public bool IsAuthenticated
            {
                get { return this.isAuthenticated; }
            }
```

```csharp
        public string Name
        {
            get { return this.name; }
        }

        public string AuthenticationType
        {
            get { return this.authenticationType; }
        }

        // Implement public, read-only interfaces for custom properties
        public string FirstName
        {
            get { return this.firstName; }
        }

        public string LastName
        {
            get { return this.lastName; }
        }

        public string Address
        {
            get { return this.address; }
        }

        public string City
        {
            get { return this.city; }
        }

        public string State
        {
            get { return this.state; }
        }

        public string Zip
        {
            get { return this.zip; }
        }
    }
}
```

```vb
Imports System
Imports System.Security.Principal

Public Class CustomIdentity
    Implements IIdentity
    Private _isAuthenticated As Boolean
    Private _name As String
    Private _authenticationType As String
    Private _firstName As String
    Private _lastName As String
    Private _address As String
    Private _city As String
    Private _state As String
    Private _zip As String
```

```
    Public Sub New()
        Me._name = String.Empty
        Me._isAuthenticated = False
        Me._authenticationType = "None"
        Me._firstName = String.Empty
        Me._lastName = String.Empty
        Me._address = String.Empty
        Me._city = String.Empty
        Me._state = String.Empty
        Me._zip = String.Empty
    End Sub

    Public Sub New(ByVal isLogin As Boolean, ➞
ByVal newAuthenticationType As String, ByVal newFirstName As String, ➞
ByVal newLastName As String, ByVal newAddress As String, ➞
ByVal newCity As String, ByVal newState As String, ByVal newZip As String)
        Me._name = newFirstName + newLastName
        Me._isAuthenticated = isLogin
        Me._authenticationType = newAuthenticationType
        Me._firstName = newFirstName
        Me._lastName = newLastName
        Me._address = newAddress
        Me._city = newCity
        Me._state = newState
        Me._zip = newZip
    End Sub

    Public ReadOnly Property IsAuthenticated() As Boolean ➞
Implements IIdentity.IsAuthenticated
        Get
            Return Me._isAuthenticated
        End Get
    End Property

    Public ReadOnly Property Name() As String Implements IIdentity.Name
        Get
            Return Me._name
        End Get
    End Property

    Public ReadOnly Property AuthenticationType() As String ➞
Implements IIdentity.AuthenticationType
        Get
            Return Me._authenticationType
        End Get
    End Property

    Public ReadOnly Property FirstName() As String
        Get
            Return Me._firstName
        End Get
    End Property

    Public ReadOnly Property LastName() As String
        Get
            Return Me._lastName
```

```
            End Get
    End Property

    Public ReadOnly Property Address() As String
        Get
            Return Me._address
        End Get
    End Property

    Public ReadOnly Property City() As String
        Get
            Return Me._city
        End Get
    End Property

    Public ReadOnly Property State() As String
        Get
            Return Me._state
        End Get
    End Property

    Public ReadOnly Property Zip() As String
        Get
            Return Me._zip
        End Get
    End Property
End Class
```

Note This code shows how to implement a custom identity based on *IIdentity*. However, if you want to add properties to a Windows logon while still using the Windows token or other Windows security properties, base your custom identity on the *WindowsIdentity* class instead. The same applies for *IPrincipal* and *WindowsPrincipal*.

What Is the *IPrincipal* Interface?

Just as *WindowsIdentity* (covered in Lesson 2) is based on *IIdentity*, *WindowsPrincipal* and *GenericPrincipal* classes are based on the *IPrincipal* interface. Objects based on the *IPrincipal* interface represent the security context of a user, including that user's identity and any roles or groups to which they belong.

To implement *IPrincipal*, you must implement at least one constructor, one property, and one method. The constructor must accept an *IIdentity* object and an array of strings containing the identity's roles, though you can add overloaded constructors. The property that you must implement is *IPrincipal.Identity*, which should return the principal's identity object (which must be defined when the object is constructed). The method is the Boolean *IPrincipal.IsInRole*, which takes a single string and the role being queried, and returns true when the principal's identity is a member of that role. Otherwise, it returns false.

You can add some interesting functionality by overriding *IPrincipal*:

- Add a *Roles* property that returns an array of strings containing the roles the user is a member of.

- Add *IsInAllRoles* and *IsInAnyRole* methods that determine whether the user is a member of multiple roles.

- Add *IsHigherThanRole* and *IsLowerThanRole* methods to enable hierarchical group memberships. For example, a principal who is a member of the Presidents role would evaluate IPrincipal.IsHigherThanRole("Vice-Presidents") as true.

How to Create a Custom Principal Class

To create a custom principal class, implement it based on *IPrincipal*, and at a minimum override the constructor, the *Identity* property, and the *IsInRole* method. For example, the following class implements the *IPrincipal* interface without extending the functionality:

```csharp
using System;
using System.Security.Principal;

namespace CustomRBS
{
    public class CustomPrincipal : IPrincipal
    {
        // Implement private variables for standard properties
        private IIdentity _identity;
        private string [] _roles;

        // Allow caller to create the object and specify all properties
        public CustomPrincipal(IIdentity identity, string [] roles)
        {
            _identity = identity;
            _roles = new string[roles.Length];
            roles.CopyTo(_roles, 0);
            Array.Sort(_roles);
        }

        // Implement public read-only interfaces for standard properties
        public bool IsInRole(string role)
        {
            return Array.BinarySearch(_roles, role) >=0 ? true : false;
        }

        public IIdentity Identity
        {
            get
            {
                return _identity;
            }
        }
    }
}
```

```vb
Imports System
Imports System.Security.Principal

Public Class CustomPrincipal
    Implements IPrincipal
    ' Implement private variables for standard properties
    Private _identity As IIdentity
    Private _roles As String()

    ' Allow caller to create the object and specify all properties
    Public Sub New(ByVal identity As IIdentity, ByVal roles As String())
        _identity = identity
        roles.CopyTo(_roles, 0)
        Array.Sort(_roles)
    End Sub

    ' Implement public read-only interfaces for standard properties
    Public Function IsInRole(ByVal role As String) As Boolean →
Implements IPrincipal.IsInRole
        Return False
    End Function

    Public ReadOnly Property Identity() As IIdentity →
Implements IPrincipal.Identity
        Get
            Return _identity
        End Get
    End Property
End Class
```

How to Create Simple, Custom User Privilege Models

If you don't want to use any of the classes based on *IIdentity* and *IPrincipal* that are built into the runtime, and you need only the basic functionality provided by the *IIdentity* and *IPrincipal* interfaces, use *System.Security.Principal.GenericIdentity* and *System.Security.Principal.GenericPrincipal*. These classes, provided by the runtime, implement only the properties and methods required by the interfaces. They each provide constructors that your application must use to specify each class's properties.

GenericIdentity has two overloaded constructors. To create a new *GenericIdentity* object, you can use just a user name, or you can use both a user name and an authentication type. You can't later change these values; you must specify them when the object is created. The following code sample demonstrates both usages:

```csharp
using System.Security.Principal;
...
GenericIdentity myUser1 = new GenericIdentity("AHankin");
GenericIdentity myUser2 = new GenericIdentity("TAdams", "SmartCard");
```

```vb
Imports System.Security.Principal
...
Dim myUser1 As GenericIdentity =  New GenericIdentity("AHankin")
Dim myUser2 As GenericIdentity =  New GenericIdentity("TAdams", "SmartCard")
```

GenericPrincipal has only a single constructor that requires both a *GenericIdentity* object and an array of strings containing the identity's roles. The following code sample extends the previous code sample to demonstrate how to create a *GenericPrincipal* object, where *myUser1* is a *GenericIdentity* object that was previously created:

```csharp
String[] myUser1Roles = new String[]{"IT", "Users", "Administrators"};
GenericPrincipal myPrincipal1 = new GenericPrincipal(myUser1, myUser1Roles);
```

```vb
Dim myUser1Roles() As String =  New String() {"IT", "Users", "Administrators"}
Dim myPrincipal1 As GenericPrincipal =  New GenericPrincipal(myUser1,myUser1Roles)
```

After creating the principal object, the `myPrincipal1.IsInRole("Users")` method would return true.

How to Use RBS Demands with Custom Identities and Principals

Whether you define custom *IIdentity* and *IPrincipal* interfaces or use *GenericIdentity* and *GenericPrincipal*, you can take advantage of the same declarative and imperative RBS techniques used for *WindowsIdentity* and *WindowsPrincipal*. To do this, perform the following steps in your application:

1. If not using *GenericIdentity* and *GenericPrincipal*, override the *IIdentity* and *IPrincipal* interfaces.

2. Create an *IIdentity* object representing the current user.

3. Create an *IPrincipal* object based on your *IIdentity* object.

4. Use or import the *System.Threading* namespace, and set the *Thread.CurrentPrincipal* property to your *IPrincipal* object.

5. Add any declarative or imperative RBS demands required.

The following console application performs all these steps to demonstrate how to use declarative RBS demands with the *GenericIdentity* and *GenericPrincipal* classes. In this example, only members of the IT role might run the *TestSecurity* method. Two identities and principals are created. The object *myUser1*, with the user name AHankin, is a member of the IT role and should be able to run the method. The object *myUser2*, with the user name TAdams, is not a member of that role.

```csharp
using System;
using System.Security.Permissions;
using System.Security.Principal;
using System.Threading;

namespace GenericIdentityExercise
{
    class Class1
    {
        [STAThread]
        static void Main(string[] args)
        {
            GenericIdentity myUser1 = new GenericIdentity("AHankin");
            GenericIdentity myUser2 = new GenericIdentity("TAdams");

            String[] myUser1Roles = new String[]{"IT", "Users", ↴
"Administrators"};
            GenericPrincipal myPrincipal1 = ↴
new GenericPrincipal(myUser1, myUser1Roles);

            String[] myUser2Roles = new String[]{"Users"};
            GenericPrincipal myPrincipal2 = ↴
new GenericPrincipal(myUser2, myUser2Roles);

            try
            {
                Thread.CurrentPrincipal = myPrincipal1;
                TestSecurity();

                Thread.CurrentPrincipal = myPrincipal2;
                TestSecurity();
            }
            catch(Exception ex)
            {
                Console.WriteLine(ex.GetType().ToString() + ↴
" caused by " + Thread.CurrentPrincipal.Identity.Name);
            }
        }

        [PrincipalPermission(SecurityAction.Demand, Role = "IT")]
        private static void TestSecurity()
        {
            Console.WriteLine(Thread.CurrentPrincipal.Identity.Name + ↴
" must be in IT.");
        }
    }
}
```

```vbnet
Imports System
Imports System.Security.Permissions
Imports System.Security.Principal
Imports System.Threading
```

```
Module Module1
    Sub Main()
        Dim myUser1 As GenericIdentity = New GenericIdentity("AHankin")
        Dim myUser2 As GenericIdentity = New GenericIdentity("TAdams")

        Dim myUser1Roles As String() = New String() {"IT", "Users", ⟶
"Administrators"}
        Dim myPrincipal1 As GenericPrincipal = ⟶
New GenericPrincipal(myUser1, myUser1Roles)

        Dim myUser2Roles As String() = New String() {"Users"}
        Dim myPrincipal2 As GenericPrincipal = ⟶
New GenericPrincipal(myUser2, myUser2Roles)

        Try
            Thread.CurrentPrincipal = myPrincipal1
            TestSecurity()

            Thread.CurrentPrincipal = myPrincipal2
            TestSecurity()
        Catch ex As Exception
            Console.WriteLine(ex.GetType.ToString + " caused by " + ⟶
Thread.CurrentPrincipal.Identity.Name)
        End Try
    End Sub

    <PrincipalPermissionAttribute(SecurityAction.Demand, Role:="IT")> _
    Private Sub TestSecurity()
        Console.WriteLine(Thread.CurrentPrincipal.Identity.Name + ⟶
" must be in IT.")
    End Sub
End Module
```

This application produces the following output, which verifies that the declarative RBS demand does protect the *TestSecurity* method from users who are not in the IT role:

```
AHankin must be in IT.
System.Security.SecurityException caused by TAdams
```

How to Create a Custom Authentication Mechanism

This topic shows how to create a custom authentication mechanism and then provides best practices for storing user credentials and offsetting weak authentication.

To Create a Custom Authentication Mechanism

To create a custom authentication mechanism, add a class to your project that implements security and authentication functionality. At a minimum, create the following objects:

■ **A custom identity by implementing the *IIdentity* interface**   This identity should not include the user's password as a property, because the password should never be accessible to the application.

- **A custom principal by implementing the *IPrincipal* interface**   This principal should expose as little information about the user as possible. For example, do
  not allow the application to query the roles the user belongs to unless absolutely
  essential for the application's planned functionality. Instead, implement only the
  IsInRole method. Remember, custom principals must accept and store your custom
  identity object during construction.

- **A method to determine whether a user's credentials are valid**   Generally,
  the developer calling this method will use it in a conditional, so the method
  should return a Boolean value. Provide event logging for successful and unsuccessful authentication attempts.

- **A method that returns an identity given the user's user name**   After a user's
  credentials are validated, the application will need to create an identity object for
  the user by calling this method.

The practice at the end of this lesson includes a sample application that implements a
custom authentication method. The following is a shell for implementing the bare minimum authentication functionality:

```csharp
public class CustomAuthentication
{
    public static bool ValidateCredentials(string username, string password)
    {
        // TODO: implement authentication
    }

    public static CustomIdentity GetUser(string username)
    {
        // TODO: return identity
    }
}
```

```vb
Public Class CustomAuthentication
    Public Shared Function ValidateCredentials(ByVal username As String, ByVal password
As String) As Boolean
        ' TODO: implement authentication
    End Function

    Public Shared Function GetUser(ByVal username As String) As CustomIdentity
        ' TODO: return identity
    End Function
End Class
```

Best Practices for Storing User Credentials

The server that authenticates the user must be able to determine that the user's credentials are valid. To do this, the custom method performing the authentication must have
access to the information store that contains data that can be used to verify the user's
credentials. How to store this information and where to store it are important decisions
to make when designing a custom authentication mechanism.

Naturally, it is important that this information remains confidential. You can, in theory, store user credentials anywhere. You could even create static arrays of strings containing user names and passwords in your code, though it wouldn't be secure or manageable. More likely, you will want to store user credentials in a back-end database such as Microsoft SQL Server.

The way the user credentials are stored determines how difficult it is for an attacker to misuse the information and whether those user credentials can be migrated to a new authentication system in the future. Never store passwords in an unencrypted form. You can use encryption to protect your stored passwords in two ways: hashing or reversible encryption.

The trade-off between hashing and encryption is straightforward. If you store users' passwords in a hashed form, they are just as useful for validating a user's credentials, but an attacker cannot easily identify the passwords, even when the attacker gains access to the data. However, storing passwords in a hashed form prevents administrators from migrating those passwords to a different system in the future. If you store passwords in a reversibly encrypted format, your users can unencrypt those passwords to migrate them to a new system. However, an attacker who gains access to the encryption key and the encrypted passwords can easily determine the unencrypted passwords.

Off the Record   Migrating to a new system and requiring users to create new passwords is incredibly costly—but almost nobody uses reversible encryption to store passwords. The fact is, hashing is slightly more secure, few people have the foresight to plan for migration, and developers rarely make an effort to make it easier for customers to stop using applications.

See Also   For more information about using cryptography in your application, see Chapter 8, "Protecting Data by Using Cryptography."

If you choose to store passwords in a database, it is imperative that you use database ACLs to restrict access to the tables storing user information. It might seem obvious that only administrators should have access to a table containing user credentials, but it is tricky in practice because unauthenticated users must be able to query the user table to determine whether their credentials are valid.

However, they do not have to query the user table directly. Instead, create a stored procedure that handles the authentication, and grant only unauthenticated users access to the stored procedure. The stored procedure should accept the user's credentials (such as a user name and password) as parameters, compare the credentials to the protected user table, and return an access token to the application if the user's credentials are valid.

> ## Real World   Authentication Is Only as Strong as Its Weakest Link
>
> Boston winters are tough for a Texas boy like myself, so I try to take a trip every winter to a warm place. This year, my wife and I flew down to Key West, with a layover in Miami.
>
> We had to go through security in Miami. Before I could get into line, a uniformed security guard checked my ID (yes, authentication!) and then verified that the name matched my ticket (authorization!). Another guard checked my ID as I waited in line. Finally, the security guard at the scanner checked my ID. I don't mind that they checked my ID three times, because their security policies reduce the potential for abuse by requiring *collusion* (where more than one trusted insider must work together to bypass security measures). Besides, I'm willing to trade convenience for increased security.
>
> However, things were a little different when I flew back from Key West. The ticketing agent (not a security guard) checked my ID, and then I boarded the plane. When we changed planes in Miami, we didn't leave the secure area, so I boarded the plane without being re-authenticated.
>
> The second security guard in Miami didn't trust the first security guard to properly authenticate me, and the third guard didn't trust either of the first two guards. However, it seems odd to me that they all trusted the airline employee with the flowery shirt at the counter in Key West. When you're defending against sophisticated attackers, remember that authentication is only as strong as its weakest link. If you provide multiple ways to access your application's functionality and data, strive to provide equal levels of protection for each.

Best Practices for Offsetting Weak Authentication

If you choose to implement a custom authentication mechanism in your application, you might discover that your choices are limited. Although you might consider only two-factor authentication to be secure enough to determine a user's identity for the purpose of authorizing that user to access your application, your user might be willing to enter only a user name and password. Often, convenience is more important than strong authentication.

You can offset the risks of weak authentication, though. Properly logging authentication events enables administrators to track down attackers, which reduces the risks of repeat offenders. It also reduces the risk of attacks by insiders who are familiar with the security mechanisms. Similarly, systems administrators can further reduce the risk of weak authentication by frequently reviewing security logs and vigorously pursuing offenders.

Design The weaker the authentication mechanism, the more important event logging becomes.

You can see these techniques in use in the physical world. Credit cards used on the Internet require only single-factor authentication. Many, many people probably have access to credit card numbers: waitresses, cashiers, employees of e-commerce sites, employees of Web hosting providers who manage e-commerce sites, and others. Although credit card fraud is common on the Internet, it is controlled because credit card companies collect the data required to track down offenders and work with law enforcement agencies to pursue and punish attackers.

Practice: Creating Custom Authentication Methods

In this practice, you design an application around a legacy database that uses a non-Windows user database. Read the scenario and then complete the exercise that follows. If you are unable to answer a question, review the lessons and try the question again. You can find answers to the questions in the "Questions and Answers" section at the end of this chapter.

Scenario

You are a developer in the IT department of Litware, Inc., a company that manages electronic distribution for software companies. Your boss asks you to develop a Windows Forms application for the Accounting department. The application needs to work with the existing database to enable the Accounting team to keep track of accounts payable, and, for authorized users, to issue payments. You interview key personnel and review technical requirements before coming up with your solution.

Interviews Following is a list of company personnel interviewed and their statements:

- **IT Manager** "The accounting team wanted to upgrade their commercial accounting package, but it costs like a zillion dollars and I said we could write our own program to add the new functionality they needed for, like, half that cost. They just need to enter payments when a bill comes in, and then click a button to make the payment. Oh, they're concerned about security because apparently they don't trust some of their people. I'm not sure how they want to control things, but I will tell you that the user accounts and groups they use to access the application are stored in the database, not in our Active Directory."

- **Accountant** "Our needs, actually, are pretty simple. We have three different types of employees: temps, accountants, and managers. The temps do data entry, and create new accounts payable entries. The accountants pay bills, but only if these bills are less than $1,500. Any bill $1,500 or higher must be paid by a manager. I'm sure you're interested in the technical details, so you should meet with the database administrator."

■ **Database Administrator**   "This accounting database is a nightmare, but we're stuck with it. There's one big table, called Users, that has a row for each user containing the user name and password *in clear text*. Yeah, I told you it was bad, but at least you won't have to fool with encryption. There's another table named Groups that contains a row for every group membership. So, for example, John the temp has a row in the Users table containing his user name and password, and a row in the Groups table that indicates he is a member of the Temps group. Lori the IT manager happens to be in both the Accountants and Managers groups, so she has one row in the Users table and two rows in the Groups table. Make sense?"

Technical Requirements   Create a Windows Forms application that implements a customized authentication mechanism that queries the accounting database. Assume you will have two methods: *AddBill* and *PayBill*. Use each user's group memberships to determine whether the user can run a particular method.

Exercise

Your boss shows up and asks you the following questions:

1. Which classes or interfaces will you use to implement the custom authentication mechanism?

2. How will you restrict access to the *AddBill* method?

3. How will you restrict access to the *PayBill* method?

Lesson Summary

■ Use the *IIdentity* interface to build custom user types. *IIdentity* is the basis for *WindowsIdentity*, *GenericIdentity*, and other identity types built into the runtime.

■ To create a custom identity class, extend the *IIdentity* interface by overriding the existing properties and adding your custom methods and properties.

■ The *WindowsPrincipal* and *GenericPrincipal* classes are based on the *IPrincipal* interface. Use *WindowsPrincipal* to authorize users based on Windows account information and groups, and use *GenericPrincipal* when implementing simple custom authentication and authorization systems.

■ To create custom principal classes, implement a new class based on the *IPrincipal* interface; override the constructor, the *Identity* property, and the *IsInRole* method; and then add your custom functionality.

- To create simple, custom user models, use the *GenericIdentity* and *GenericPrincipal* classes instead of the *IIdentity* and *IPrincipal* interfaces.

- To create declarative and imperative RBS demands with custom identities and principals, set the *Thread.CurrentPrincipal* property to your custom principal.

- To create a custom authentication mechanism, implement your own identity and principal classes and then create methods to validate the user's credentials and return the user's identity object.

Lab: Implementing Role-Based Security

In this lab, you make recommendations for restricting access to an application's components using RBS. Read the scenario and then complete the exercise that follows. If you are unable to answer a question, review the lessons and try the question again. You can find answers to the questions in the "Questions and Answers" section at the end of this chapter.

Scenario

You are a developer for Blue Yonder Airlines. Your company's upper management recently decided to deploy new computers to the desks of every ticketing agent. Management wants to put the additional computing power to use with a new graphical application. Your boss asks you to submit a plan for implementing RBS in the new application. You start by interviewing key personnel and reviewing the technical requirements that he gave you.

Interviews

Following is a list of company personnel interviewed and their statements:

- **Development Manager**   "We've had some preliminary meetings and it sounds like we'll be deploying Windows XP Professional with the latest version of the .NET Framework to the new computers. So, it makes sense to build our new application on the .NET Framework. Well, the reason I've decided to put you on the team designing this application is that I know you're an expert on role-based security, and RBS is going to be very important in the new application. See, if we don't selectively restrict access to application functionality, we'll have the guys who throw the luggage on the plane giving themselves frequent flier miles."

- **IT Manager** "One of the challenges of any new application is backward-compatibility. Well, you're saddled with making the new application backward-compatible with our existing system. We're not going to be rolling out the new application overnight. In fact, the new and old applications will probably run alongside each other for years. So, your new application is going to have to work with the very old system we use today, which stores user credentials in a database. It's not Active Directory, but it works. The design is pretty typical in that users can be members of groups, like *TicketingAgent* and *BaggageAgent*, but there's also a ranking assigned to users that indicates how much trust we assign them within their roles. For example, a user who is a member of the *TicketingAgent* group and has a Rank of 3 is allowed to upgrade a passenger to first class, but can't grant frequent flier miles. You have to be a *TicketingAgent* with a Rank of 4 to grant frequent flier miles."

- **Director of Operations** "I'm thrilled that we're getting rid of that old system. Obviously security is important to us, because many people could benefit by abusing our internal system. We have to train every new employee on the system anyway, so I won't be broken-hearted if you change the authentication system. I know the employee identification cards have the employee number stored on the magnetic strip, and the new computers will have card readers. Maybe you can take advantage of that."

Technical Requirements

The new application must meet the following requirements:

- Implements the existing group- and hierarchy-based privilege system.

- Restricts access to application functionality based on group memberships and user rank.

Exercise

To create the plan for your boss, answer the following questions:

1. Which classes or interfaces will you recommend be used for RBS within the application?

2. How will users be authenticated? Does your recommendation fall into the category of something you have, something you know, something you are, or a combination thereof?

Chapter Summary

- Authentication verifies your identity, whereas authorization verifies that you have access. More secure authentication mechanisms, including biometrics and multi-factor authentication, are less convenient for users.

- The .NET Framework provides the *WindowsIdentity* and *WindowsPrincipal* classes to enable assemblies to analyze the current user's Windows authentication credentials.

- Role-based security (RBS) demands are a very secure technique for restricting access to methods because they throw an exception when security requirements are not met. Declarative RBS demands restrict access to an entire method, whereas imperative RBS demands restrict access to portions of a method.

- The simplest way to create a custom authentication mechanism is to use the *GenericIdentity* and *GenericPrincipal* classes, and then create your own class to handle authentication. If you must extend the classes, you can build new classes based on the *IIdentity* and *IPrincipal* interfaces.

Exam Highlights

Before taking the exam, review the key points and terms that are presented in this chapter. You need to know this information.

Key Points

- The relationship between authentication and authorization

- The classes and techniques used to examine a user's Windows security credentials

- The advantages and disadvantages of declarative and imperative RBS demands, as well as the classes and techniques used for each

- The interfaces and classes available for building custom authentication mechanisms, and the requirements for each

Key Terms

authentication   The process of identifying a user

authorization   The process of verifying that a user is allowed to access a requested resource

collusion   A method for preventing security abuses by requiring more than one trusted insider to work together to bypass security measures

declarative RBS demands   Access restrictions that are declared as an attribute to a method and that instruct the runtime to perform an access check before running the method

imperative RBS demands   Access restrictions that are declared within your code and can be used to restrict access to portions of code on a very granular basis

multifactor authentication   The process of combining two or more authentication methods to significantly reduce the likelihood that an attacker will be able to impersonate a user during the authentication process

principal policy   The scheme that the .NET Framework uses to determine which default principal will be returned when the current principal is queried by an application

role-based security (RBS)   Authenticating users and then authorizing them based on the permissions assigned to their user accounts and group memberships

something you are   An authentication technique that verifies some aspect of the user's physical person, such as his or her fingerprint or ability to create a signature

something you have   An authentication technique that verifies the user possesses an object, such as a smart card, that only he or she should possess

something you know   An authentication technique that verifies the user knows a secret, such as a PIN or a password, that only he or she should know

Questions and Answers

Page
5-7

Practice: Thinking About Authenticating and Authorizing Users

1. List every time you have been authenticated in the past week. How many of those authentications required something you have? Something you are? Something you know? How many of them required two-factor authentication?

Everyone's experiences are different, but the following are some common authentication techniques:

- Driver's license: something you have, something you are
- Passport: something you have, something you are
- Retail credit card use: something you have, something you are
- Online credit card use: something you know
- ATM cards: something you have, something you know
- Signing a contract: something you are
- Calling a bank and providing identifying information: something you know

2. List every time you have been authorized in the past week. Which of these authorizations were separate from authentication? Which did not require any authentication?

Everyone's experiences are different, but many people experience the following authorizations:

- **Using a credit card**   After you prove that you are the owner of the card, the credit card company must authorize the charge against your card. The acts of authorization and authentication are separate, because it's possible for you to be authenticated as the card-holder but be denied authorization for a particular charge.

- **Driving a car**   Cars have plates and stickers that signify they are properly inspected and registered, and are thus authorized to use public streets. In this case, there is authorization without authentication.

- **Entering your workplace**   Your office probably restricts who can enter. Most offices combine authentication and authorization into a single phase. If you have a proper ID card and can authenticate yourself, you are automatically authorized to enter the office.

- **Opening a lock with a key**   Each time you open a lock, you prove that you are authorized to access the asset protected by that lock. Though the key is something you have, possessing the key is not a form of authentication because it does not necessarily prove who you are.

- **Interacting with a pet**   Pets recognize you, which is a form of authentication. If they like you, they might let you pet or play with them, which is a form of authorization. If they recognize you but don't like you enough to let you pet them, you're authenticated but not authorized. Some pets don't require authentication or authorization for some actions, such as accepting food.

3. Biometrics are not often used for authentication. Why do you think that is the case?

Most experts agree that biometrics are not commonly used because people feel they are intrusive and the cost of the equipment is too high.

Practice: Authorizing Users with Windows Security

Page
5-17

Exercise

1. Write an application that meets the technical requirements, and show your work.

Although your answer will vary, the following code will work:

```csharp
using System;
using System.Security.Principal;

namespace CheckDeveloperRights
{
    /// <summary>
    /// Determines whether the current user has appropriate developer rights.
    /// </summary>
    class Class1
    {
        [STAThread]
        static void Main(string[] args)
        {
            // Create a WindowsIdentity object representing the current user
            WindowsIdentity currentIdentity = WindowsIdentity.GetCurrent();

            // Create a WindowsPrincipal object representing the current user
            WindowsPrincipal currentPrincipal =
new WindowsPrincipal(currentIdentity);
            bool userCanDevelop = true;

            // Store the computer name to construct local group names
            string computerName = System.Environment.MachineName;

            if (currentPrincipal.IsInRole(WindowsBuiltInRole.Administrator) ||
currentPrincipal.IsInRole(WindowsBuiltInRole.PowerUser))
            {
                Console.WriteLine
("User is a member of Administrators or Power Users.");
                Console.WriteLine
("Remove the user from these groups before beginning development.");
                userCanDevelop = false;
            }

            if (!(currentPrincipal.IsInRole(computerName + @"\VS Developers") &&
currentPrincipal.IsInRole(computerName + @"\Debugger Users") &&
currentPrincipal.IsInRole(WindowsBuiltInRole.User)))
            {
                Console.WriteLine("User lacks appropriate memberships.");
                Console.WriteLine("Users should be a member of VS Developers,
Debugger Users, and Users.");
                userCanDevelop = false;
            }
```

```
                  if (userCanDevelop)
                  {
                      Console.WriteLine→
("Group memberships verified. Proceed with development.");
                  }
              }
          }
      }
```

```
Imports System.Security.Principal

Module Module1
    Sub Main()
        ' Create a WindowsIdentity object representing the current user
        Dim currentIdentity As WindowsIdentity = WindowsIdentity.GetCurrent()

        ' Create a WindowsPrincipal object representing the current user
        Dim currentPrincipal As WindowsPrincipal = →
New WindowsPrincipal(currentIdentity)
        Dim userCanDevelop As Boolean = True
        ' Store the computer name to construct local group names
        Dim computerName As String = System.Environment.MachineName

        If (currentPrincipal.IsInRole(WindowsBuiltInRole.Administrator) Or →
currentPrincipal.IsInRole(WindowsBuiltInRole.PowerUser)) Then
            Console.WriteLine→
("User is a member of Administrators or Power Users.")
            Console.WriteLine→
("Remove the user from these groups before beginning development.")
            userCanDevelop = False
        End If

        If (Not (currentPrincipal.IsInRole(computerName +→
"\VS Developers") And currentPrincipal.IsInRole(computerName +→
"\Debugger Users") And currentPrincipal.IsInRole(WindowsBuiltInRole.User))) Then
            Console.WriteLine("User lacks appropriate memberships.")
            Console.WriteLine→
("Users should be a member of VS Developers, Debugger Users, and Users.")
            userCanDevelop = False
        End If

        If (userCanDevelop) Then
            Console.WriteLine→
("Group memberships verified. Proceed with development.")
        End If
    End Sub
End Module
```

Practice: Selecting and Implementing RBS

Page
5-27

Exercise 1: Identifying the Proper RBS Technique

1. You must restrict access to a method based on a user's group memberships. You want to use the most secure method possible. Which technique will you use? Choose the correct answer.

   a. *WindowsPrincipal.IsInRole*

   b. Imperative RBS demands

   c. Declarative RBS demands

   The answer is c. Declarative RBS demands restrict access to an entire method, while offering the highest level of resistance to security vulnerabilities.

2. You must restrict access to a method that is called by a Windows event based on a user's group memberships. If the user lacks sufficient access, you want to log an event and display a message to the user. You want to use the most secure method possible. Which technique will you use? Choose the correct answer.

   a. *WindowsPrincipal.IsInRole*

   b. Imperative RBS demands

   c. Declarative RBS demands

   The answer is b. Imperative RBS demands restrict access to code by throwing an exception. Unfortunately, declarative RBS demands are defined as an attribute to a method, and it is difficult to catch security exceptions thrown by a declarative RBS demand when the method is called by a Windows event.

3. You are writing a method for a console application that lists options available to a user based on his group memberships. Which technique should you use? Choose the correct answer.

   a. *WindowsPrincipal.IsInRole*

   b. Imperative RBS demands

   c. Declarative RBS demands

   The answer is a. *WindowsPrincipal.IsInRole* is perfect when you simply need to branch your code based on user memberships and the code is not performing security-sensitive tasks.

Page
5-28

Exercise 2: Using RBS Demands

1. How will you to hide the buttons that are inaccessible to users?

   Create a *WindowsPrincipal* object based on the current user, and then use the *WindowsPrincipal* .*IsInRole* method to check the user's group memberships when the form is initialized. Based on those memberships, set the *Visible* state of the inaccessible buttons to false. For the Divide button, create a *WindowsIdentity* object based on the current user, and verify that the *Windows-Identity.Name* value is equal to *COMPUTERNAME\CPhilp*.

2. Which techniques will you use to protect each of the *addButton_Click*, *subtractButton_Click*, *divideButton_Click*, and *multiply* methods?

You should:

- Use imperative RBS demands to protect the *addButton_Click*, *subtractButton_Click*, and *divideButton_Click* methods, since these are called directly by Windows events.

- Use declarative RBS demands to protect the *multiply* method, since this method is called directly by the assembly and not by a Windows event.

- Catch all *System.Security.SecurityException* exceptions and display an ambiguous error message to the user.

3. Open the C# or Visual Basic .NET application named RBS by using Microsoft Visual Studio .NET, and make the updates requested by the IT Manager. Show your work.

The following code will work (some code generated by Visual Studio .NET has been omitted for simplicity):

```csharp
using System;
using System.Drawing;
using System.Collections;
using System.ComponentModel;
using System.Windows.Forms;
using System.Data;

// Include Principal and Permissions namespaces for RBS functionality
using System.Security.Principal;
using System.Security.Permissions;

namespace DeclarativeRBS
{
    /// <summary>
    /// GUI app that provides access to highly confidential algorithms.
    /// </summary>

    public class Form1 : System.Windows.Forms.Form
    {
        private System.Windows.Forms.Button addButton;
        private System.Windows.Forms.Button multiplyButton;
        private System.Windows.Forms.Label answerLabel;
        private System.Windows.Forms.TextBox integer1;
        private System.Windows.Forms.TextBox integer2;
        private System.Windows.Forms.Button subtractButton;
        private System.Windows.Forms.Button divideButton;
        private System.ComponentModel.Container components = null;

        public Form1()
        {
            InitializeComponent();

            // Create a WindowsIdentity object representing the current user
            WindowsIdentity currentIdentity = WindowsIdentity.GetCurrent();
```

```
                  // Create a WindowsPrincipal object representing the current user
                  WindowsPrincipal currentPrincipal = new ↵
WindowsPrincipal(currentIdentity);

                  // Set the security policy context to Windows security
                  System.AppDomain.CurrentDomain.SetPrincipalPolicy(↵
PrincipalPolicy.WindowsPrincipal);

                  // Hide the subtract and multiply buttons
                  // if the user is not an Administrator
                  if (!currentPrincipal.IsInRole(WindowsBuiltInRole.Administrator))
                  {
                      subtractButton.Visible = false;
                      multiplyButton.Visible = false;
                  }

                  // Hide the Add button if the user is not in the Users group
                  if (!currentPrincipal.IsInRole(WindowsBuiltInRole.User))
                  {
                      addButton.Visible = false;
                  }

                  // Hide the Divide button if the user is not named CPhilp
                  if (!(currentIdentity.Name.ToLower() == ↵
System.Environment.MachineName.ToLower() + @"\cphilp"))
                  {
                      divideButton.Visible = false;
                  }
              }

          protected override void Dispose( bool disposing )
          {
              if( disposing )
              {
                  if (components != null)
                  {
                      components.Dispose();
                  }
              }
              base.Dispose( disposing );
          }

          [STAThread]
          static void Main()
          {
              Application.Run(new Form1());
          }

          private void addButton_Click(object sender, System.EventArgs e)
          {
              try
              {
                // Demand that user is member of the built-in Users group
                // Because this method is called by a Windows event,
                // protect it with a imperative RBS demand
```

```
                    PrincipalPermission userPermission = new →
PrincipalPermission(null, @"BUILTIN\Users");
                    userPermission.Demand();

                    // Perform super-secret mathematical calculations
                    int answer = (int.Parse(integer1.Text) + →
int.Parse(integer2.Text));
                    answerLabel.Text = answer.ToString();
                }
                catch(System.Security.SecurityException ex)
                {
                    // Display message box explaining access denial
                    MessageBox.Show("You have been denied access.");
                    // TODO: Log error
                }
            }

        private void multiplyButton_Click(object sender, System.EventArgs e)
        {
            try
            {
                // Perform super-secret mathematical calculations
                answerLabel.Text = multiply(int.Parse(integer1.Text), →
int.Parse(integer2.Text)).ToString();
            }
            catch (System.Security.SecurityException ex)
            {
                // Display message box explaining access denial
                MessageBox.Show("You have been denied access.");
                // TODO: Log error
            }
        }

        // Because the multiply function is not called directly from a Windows
        // event, protect it with a declarative RBS demand
        [PrincipalPermission(SecurityAction.Demand, →
Role = @"BUILTIN\Administrators")]
        private int multiply(int int1, int int2)
        {
            return int1 * int2;
        }

        private void subtractButton_Click(object sender, System.EventArgs e)
        {
            try
            {
                // Demand that user is member of the built-in Administrators
                // group. Because this method is called by a Windows event,
                // protect it with a imperative RBS demand
                PrincipalPermission administratorPermission = new →
PrincipalPermission(null, @"BUILTIN\Administrators");
                administratorPermission.Demand();

                // Perform super-secret mathematical calculations
                int answer = (int.Parse(integer1.Text) - →
int.Parse(integer2.Text));
```

```csharp
            answerLabel.Text = answer.ToString();
        }
        catch(System.Security.SecurityException ex)
        {
            // Display message box explaining access denial
            MessageBox.Show("You have been denied access.");
            // TODO: Log error
        }
    }

    private void divideButton_Click(object sender, System.EventArgs e)
    {
        // Concatenate the computer and username
        string allowUser = System.Environment.MachineName + @"\cphilp";
        try
        {
            // Demand that user has the username "cphilp" on the local
            // computer. Because this method is called by a Windows event,
            // protect it with a imperative RBS demand
            PrincipalPermission administratorPermission = new ⮑
PrincipalPermission(allowUser, null);
            administratorPermission.Demand();

            // Perform super-secret mathematical calculations
            Decimal answer = (Decimal.Parse(integer1.Text) / ⮑
Decimal.Parse(integer2.Text));
            answerLabel.Text = Decimal.Round(answer, 2).ToString();
        }
        catch(System.Security.SecurityException ex)
        {
            // Display message box explaining access denial
            MessageBox.Show("You have been denied access.");
            // TODO: Log error
        }
    }
}
}
```

```vbnet
' Include Principal and Permissions namespaces for RBS functionality
Imports System.Security.Principal
Imports System.Security.Permissions

Public Class Form1
    Inherits System.Windows.Forms.Form

    Public Sub New()
        MyBase.New()

        'This call is required by the Windows Form Designer.
        InitializeComponent()

        'Add any initialization after the InitializeComponent() call
        ' Create a WindowsIdentity object representing the current user
        Dim currentIdentity As WindowsIdentity = WindowsIdentity.GetCurrent()
```

```vb
        ' Create a WindowsPrincipal object representing the current user
        Dim currentPrincipal As WindowsPrincipal = New →
WindowsPrincipal(currentIdentity)

        ' Set the security policy context to Windows security
        System.AppDomain.CurrentDomain.SetPrincipalPolicy(→
PrincipalPolicy.WindowsPrincipal)

        ' Hide the subtract and multiply buttons if the user is not an Administrat
or
        If Not currentPrincipal.IsInRole →
(WindowsBuiltInRole.Administrator) Then
            subtractButton.Visible = False
            multiplyButton.Visible = False
        End If

        ' Hide the Add button if the user is not in the Users group
        If Not currentPrincipal.IsInRole(WindowsBuiltInRole.User) Then
            addButton.Visible = False
        End If

        ' Hide the Divide button if the user is not named CPhilp
        If Not (currentIdentity.Name.ToLower() = →
System.Environment.MachineName.ToLower() + "\cphilp") Then
            divideButton.Visible = False
        End If
    End Sub

    Private Sub multiplyButton_Click(ByVal sender As System.Object, →
ByVal e As System.EventArgs) Handles multiplyButton.Click
        Try
            ' Perform super-secret mathematical calculations
            answerLabel.Text = multiply(Integer.Parse(integer1.Text), →
Integer.Parse(integer2.Text)).ToString()
        Catch ex As System.Security.SecurityException
            ' Display message box explaining access denial
            MessageBox.Show("You have been denied access.")
            ' TODO: Log error
        End Try
    End Sub

    ' Because the multiply function is not called directly from a Windows
    ' event, protect it with a declarative RBS demand
    <PrincipalPermission(SecurityAction.Demand, Role:="BUILTIN\Administrators")> _
    Private Function multiply(ByVal int1 As Integer, →
ByVal int2 As Integer) As Integer
        Return int1 * int2
    End Function

    Private Sub addButton_Click(ByVal sender As System.Object, →
ByVal e As System.EventArgs) Handles addButton.Click
        Try
            ' Demand that user is member of the built-in Users group
            ' Because this method is called by a Windows event, protect it
            ' with a imperative RBS demand
```

```vb
                Dim userPermission As PrincipalPermission = ↴
New PrincipalPermission(Nothing, "BUILTIN\Users")
                userPermission.Demand()

                ' Perform super-secret mathematical calculations
                Dim answer As Integer = (Integer.Parse(integer1.Text) + ↴
Integer.Parse(integer2.Text))
                answerLabel.Text = answer.ToString()
            Catch ex As System.Security.SecurityException
                ' Display message box explaining access denial
                MessageBox.Show("You have been denied access.")
                ' TODO: Log error
            End Try
        End Sub

    Private Sub subtractButton_Click(ByVal sender As System.Object, ↴
ByVal e As System.EventArgs) Handles subtractButton.Click
            Try
                ' Demand that user is member of the built-in Administrators group
                ' Because this method is called by a Windows event, protect it
                ' with an imperative RBS demand
                Dim administratorPermission As PrincipalPermission = ↴
New PrincipalPermission(Nothing, "BUILTIN\Administrators")
                administratorPermission.Demand()

                ' Perform super-secret mathematical calculations
                Dim answer As Integer = (Integer.Parse(integer1.Text) - ↴
Integer.Parse(integer2.Text))
                answerLabel.Text = answer.ToString()
            Catch ex As System.Security.SecurityException
                ' Display message box explaining access denial
                MessageBox.Show("You have been denied access.")
                ' TODO: Log error
            End Try
        End Sub

    Private Sub divideButton_Click(ByVal sender As System.Object, ↴
ByVal e As System.EventArgs) Handles divideButton.Click
            ' Concatenate the computer and username
            Dim allowUser As String = System.Environment.MachineName + "\cphilp"
            Try
                ' Demand that user has the username "cphilp" on the local
                ' computer. Because this method is called by a Windows event,
                ' protect it with a imperative RBS demand
                Dim administratorPermission As PrincipalPermission = ↴
New PrincipalPermission(allowUser, Nothing)
                administratorPermission.Demand()

                ' Perform super-secret mathematical calculations
                Dim answer As Decimal = (Decimal.Parse(integer1.Text) / ↴
Decimal.Parse(integer2.Text))
                answerLabel.Text = Decimal.Round(answer, 2).ToString()
            Catch ex As System.Security.SecurityException
                ' Display message box explaining access denial
                MessageBox.Show("You have been denied access.")
```

```
            ' TODO: Log error
        End Try
    End Sub
End Class
```

Practice: Creating Custom Authentication Methods

Page
5-46

Exercise

1. Which classes or interfaces will you use to implement the custom authentication mechanism?

Use *GenericIdentity* and *GenericPrincipal*, because the simple relationship between users and groups used by the accounting application does not require you to create custom classes based on *IIdentity* and *IPrincipal*.

2. How will you restrict access to the *AddBill* method?

Use declarative RBS demands to restrict access to *AddBill*. As long as a user is authenticated and is a member of one of the Temps, Accountants, or Managers group, the user can use that method.

3. How will you restrict access to the *PayBill* method?

Use declarative RBS demands to restrict access to authenticated members of the Accountants or Managers group. Within the method, use the *GenericPrincipal.IsInRole* method to verify that the user is a member of the Managers role if the value of the bill being paid is $1,500 or higher.

Lab: Implementing Role-Based Security

Page
5-48

Exercise

1. Which classes or interfaces will you recommend be used for RBS within the application?

The legacy system does not use Windows Security, nor does it fit any of the other identity and principal classes built into the .NET Framework. Therefore, you will need to create custom classes based on *IIdentity* and *IPrincipal*.

2. How will users be authenticated? Does your recommendation fall into the category of something you have, something you know, something you are, or a combination thereof?

Employees have identification badges and card readers, which means the expense associated with distributed smart cards isn't a factor. Use the badges to identify the user, which falls into the category of something you have. Additionally, require the user to enter a password—something you know. This will prevent a lost badge from being abused.

6 Implementing Code Access Security

Why This Chapter Matters

Everyone knows you shouldn't log on to your computer as an Administrator. The reason isn't because you don't trust yourself not to delete your hard drive—it's because you don't trust the *applications* you run. When you run an unmanaged application, that code gets all the privileges your user account has. If you accidentally run a virus or a Trojan horse, the application can do anything your user account has permissions to do. So, you are forced to restrict application permissions by logging on with minimal privileges.

Doesn't make much sense, does it? You should be able to control the permissions that individual applications have. If a friend sends me a new text editor, I should be able to restrict it to opening a window and prompting me to open and save files—and nothing else. It shouldn't be able to send e-mails, upload files to a Web site, or create files without asking me.

Code access security (CAS) gives users the ability to restrict on a very granular level what managed code can do. As a developer, you must understand how to create applications that work even when some permissions are restricted. You can also use CAS to improve your application's security by restricting which callers can use your code.

Exam Objectives in this Chapter:

- Work with .NET Security policies. Tools include the .NET Framework Configuration tool and the Code Access Security Policy tool.
- Implement security for an application or shared library by using .NET code access security.
  - Demand a code access permission such as *FileIOPermission*.
  - Group code access permissions into a permission set.
  - Override code access security checks.
  - Protect a resource in a library.
  - Specify the permission requests of an application.
  - Customize code access security.

■ Analyze the code access permissions of an assembly by using the Permissions View tool.

■ Write code that addresses failures in a manner than does not compromise security.

    ❑ Write code that defaults to a permission set that is more secure than the permission set that existed before the errors or issues occurred.

■ Implement security by using application domains.

Lessons in this Chapter:

Before You Begin

To complete the practices, examples, and lab exercises in this chapter, you must have one computer running Microsoft Windows Server 2003. During the course of performing the exercises in this chapter, the computer's security can be reduced. Therefore, the computer should not be a production computer and should not be connected to any network, especially the Internet, even if a firewall is present. Install Microsoft Visual Studio .NET 2003 using the default settings.

Lesson 1: Explaining Code Access Security

Code access security (CAS) is a new type of security. Using CAS will require you to understand completely new security concepts. This lesson describes the concept behind CAS and each of the components used by the .NET Framework to implement CAS.

After this lesson, you will be able to

■ Describe the purpose of CAS.

■ List the four most important elements of CAS and the significance of each.

■ Describe how security policy defines an assembly's permission set.

■ Explain how CAS works with operating system security.

Estimated lesson time: 15 minutes

What Is Code Access Security?

Code access security (CAS) is a security system that allows administrators and developers to control application authorization similarly to the way they have always been able to authorize users. With CAS, you can allow one application to read and write to the registry while restricting access for a different application. You can control authorization for most of the same resources you've always been able to restrict using the operating system's role-based security (RBS), including:

■ The file system

■ The registry

■ Printers

■ The event logs

You can also restrict resources that you can't control using RBS. For example, you can control whether a particular application can send Web requests to the Internet, or whether an application can make DNS requests. These are the types of requests that malicious applications are likely to make to abuse a user's privacy, so it makes sense that CAS allows you to restrict those permissions.

Unfortunately, CAS can be applied only to managed applications that use the .NET Framework runtime. Unmanaged applications run without any CAS restrictions, and are limited only by the operating system's RBS. If CAS is used to restrict the permissions of an assembly, the assembly is considered *partially trusted*. Partially trusted assemblies must undergo CAS permission checks each time they access a protected resource. Some assemblies are exempt from CAS checks, and are considered *fully trusted*. Fully trusted assemblies, like unmanaged code, can access any system resource that the user has permissions to access.

The Elements of Code Access Security

Every security system needs a way to identify users and determine what a user can and can't do, and CAS is no exception. However, because CAS identifies and assigns permissions to applications rather than to people, it can't use the user names, passwords, and access control lists (ACL) that you're accustomed to.

Instead, CAS identifies assemblies using evidence. Each piece of evidence is a way that an assembly can be identified, such as the location where the assembly is stored, a hash of the assembly's code, or the assembly's signature. An assembly's evidence determines which code group it belongs to. Code groups, in turn, grant an assembly a permission set. The sections that follow describe each of these components in more detail.

What Is Evidence?

Evidence is the information that the runtime gathers about an assembly to determine which code groups the assembly belongs to. Common forms of evidence include the folder or Web site the assembly is running from and digital signatures. You can also create custom evidence types, as discussed in Lesson 5.

> **Note**   I would have preferred to use the term identification instead of evidence. To me, evidence sounds like a set of clues you would use to track down someone who didn't want to be identified. In CAS, evidence is used just like a person's passport, password, and PIN—it is information that proves identity and describes an individual as deserving a certain level of trust.

Table 6-1 shows the common types of evidence that a host can present to the runtime. Each row corresponds to a member class of the *System.Security.Policy* namespace.

Table 6-1   Evidence Types

Evidence	Description
Application directory	The directory in which the assembly resides.
Hash	The cryptographic hash of the assembly, which uniquely identifies a specific version of an assembly. Any modifications to the assembly will make the hash invalid.
Publisher	The assembly's publisher's digital signature, which uniquely identifies the software developer.
Site	The site from which the assembly was downloaded, such as *http://www.microsoft.com*.
Strong name	The cryptographic strong name of the assembly, which uniquely identifies the assembly's namespace.

Table 6-1 **Evidence Types**

Evidence	Description
URL	The URL from which the assembly has downloaded, such as *http://www.microsoft.com/assembly.exe*.
Zone	The zone in which the assembly is running, such as the Internet Zone or the Local Intranet Zone.

There are two types of evidence: host evidence and assembly evidence. *Host evidence* describes the assembly's origin, such as the application directory, URL, or site. Host evidence can also describe the assembly's identity, such as the hash, the publisher, or the strong name. *Assembly evidence* is custom user- or developer-provided evidence. Although Lesson 5 covers how to create custom evidence, the vast majority of evidence you will work with will be host evidence.

What Is a Permission?

A *permission* is a CAS access control entry. For example, the File Dialog permission determines whether an assembly can prompt the user with the Open dialog box, the Save dialog box, both, or neither. Figure 6-1 shows the File Dialog permission being configured.

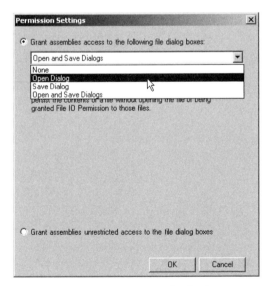

Figure 6-1 Permissions specify whether an assembly can and can't do specific actions.

By default, 19 permissions are available for configuration in the .NET Framework Configuration tool. Each corresponds to two members of the *System.Security.Permissions* namespace: one for imperative use and one for declarative use. Table 6-2 describes each of these permissions.

Table 6-2   Default Permissions

Permission	Description
Directory Services	Grants an assembly access to the Active Directory. You can specify paths, and whether Browse or Write access is available.
DNS	Enables or restricts an assembly's access to submit DNS requests.
Environment Variables	Grants assemblies access to environment variables, such as *Path*, *Username*, and *Number_Of_Processors*. You can grant an assembly access to all environment variables, or specify those that the assembly should be able to access. To view all environment variables, open a command prompt and run the command Set.
Event Log	Provides an assembly access to event logs. You can grant unlimited access, or you can limit access to browsing or auditing.
File Dialog	Controls whether an assembly can prompt the user with the Open dialog box, the Save dialog box, or both.
File IO	Restricts access to files and folders. You can grant an assembly unrestricted access, or you can specify a list of paths and whether each path should grant Read, Write, Append, or Path Discovery access.
Isolated Storage File	Grants assemblies access to isolated storage. You can configure the level of isolation and the size of the disk quota.
Message Queue	Allows an assembly to access message queues, which can be restricted by path and access type.
OLE DB	Lists the OLE DB provider that an assembly can access, and controls whether blank passwords are allowed.
Performance Counter	Controls whether an assembly can read or write performance counters.
Printing	Limits an assembly's ability to print.
Reflection	Controls whether an assembly can discover member and type information in other assemblies.
Registry	Restricts access to registry keys. You can grant an assembly unrestricted access, or you can specify a list of keys and whether each key should grant Read, Write, or Delete access.
Security	Provides granular control over the assembly's access to various CAS features. All assemblies must at least have the Enable Assembly Execution setting to run. This permission also controls whether assemblies can call unmanaged code, assert permissions, and control threads, among other settings.
Service Controller	Specifies which services, if any, an assembly can browse or control.

Table 6-2 Default Permissions

Permission	Description
Socket Access	Used to control whether an assembly can initiate TCP/IP connections. You can control the destination, port number, and protocol.
SQL Client	Controls whether an assembly can access SQL Servers, and whether blank passwords are allowed.
User Interface	Determines whether an assembly can create new windows or access the clipboard.
Web Access	Determines whether the assembly can access Web sites, and which Web sites can be accessed.

What Is a Permission Set?

A *permission set* is a CAS ACL. For example, the Internet default permission set contains the following permissions:

- File Dialog
- Isolated Storage File
- Security
- User Interface
- Printing

The LocalIntranet zone contains more permissions based on the theory that code running on your local network deserves more trust than code running from the Internet:

- Environment Variables
- File Dialog
- Isolated Storage File
- Reflection
- Security
- User Interface
- DNS
- Printing
- Event Log

The .NET Framework includes seven default permission sets, as described in Table 6-3.

Table 6-3   Default Permission Sets

Permission Set	Description
FullTrust	Exempts an assembly from CAS permission checks.
SkipVerification	Enables an assembly to bypass permission checks, which can improve performance, but sacrifices security.
Execution	Enables an assembly to run, and grants no other permissions.
Nothing	Grants no permissions to an assembly. The assembly will not even be allowed to run.
LocalIntranet	Grants a generous set of permissions to assemblies, including the ability to print and access the event log. Notably, does not allow the assembly to access the file system except through the open and save dialog boxes.
Internet	Grants a restricted set of permissions to an assembly. Generally, you can run an assembly with this permission set with very little risk. Even malicious assemblies should not be able to cause any serious damage when run with this permission set.
Everything	Grants assemblies all permissions. This is different from FullTrust, which skips all CAS security checks. Assemblies with the Everything permission set will still be subject to CAS checks.

What Are Code Groups?

Code groups are authorization devices that associate assemblies with permission sets. Code groups provide a similar service to CAS as user groups provide to RBS. For example, if an administrator wants to grant a set of users access to a folder, the administrator creates a user group, adds the users to the group, and then assigns file permissions to the group. Code groups work similarly, except that you don't have to manually add individual assemblies to a group. Instead, group membership is determined by the evidence that you specify as the code group's membership condition.

For example, any code running from the Internet should be a member of the Internet_Zone code group. As you can see from Figure 6-2, the Internet_Zone code group's default membership condition is that the host presents Zone evidence, and that piece of Zone evidence identifies the assembly as being in the Internet zone.

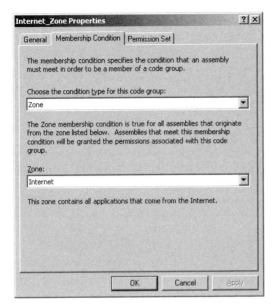

Figure 6-2   The Internet_Zone code group membership is restricted by using Zone evidence.

Whereas user groups control authorization based on distributed ACLs associated with each resource, code groups use centralized permission sets. For example, Figure 6-3 shows that the Internet_Zone code group assigns the Internet permission set. For convenience, the dialog box lists the permission set's individual permissions. However, you cannot specify individual permissions for a code group. A code group must be associated with a permission set.

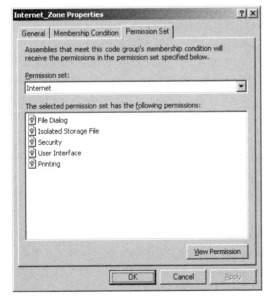

Figure 6-3   The Internet_Zone code group assigns the Internet permission set.

> ### Best Practices for Working with Files
>
> Applications running in the Internet and LocalIntranet zones do not receive the *FileIOPermission* and, as such, cannot directly access files. They do, however, have *FileDialogPermission*. Therefore, assemblies in the Internet zone can open files by prompting the user to select the file using an *OpenFileDialog* object. Assemblies in the LocalIntranet zone can also save files by using the *SaveFileDialog* object.
>
> To access files without *FileIOPermission*, call the *ShowDialog* method of either *OpenFileDialog* or *SaveFileDialog*. If the user selects a file, you can use the file handle returned by the *OpenFile* method to access the file.

It might seem limiting that you can specify only a single type of evidence and a single permission set for a code group. However, just like a user account can be a member of multiple user groups, an assembly can be a member of multiple code groups. The assembly will receive all the permissions assigned to each of the code groups (known as the *union* of the permission sets). Additionally, you can nest code groups within each other, and assign permissions only if the assembly meets all the evidence requirements of both the parent and child code groups. Nesting code groups allows you to assign permissions based on an assembly having more than one type of evidence. Figure 6-4 shows the Microsoft_Strong_Name code group nested within the My_Computer_Zone code group, which in turn is nested within the All_Code group.

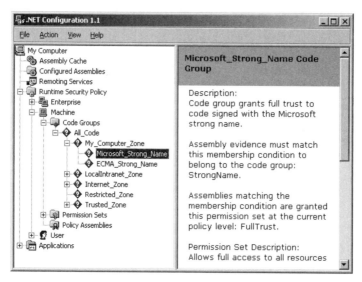

Figure 6-4   You can nest code groups to require multiple types of evidence.

Table 6-4 lists the default machine code groups residing directly within the All_Code code group. Additionally, some of these code groups contain nested code groups.

Table 6-4   Default Code Groups

Code Group	Evidence	Permission Set
My_Computer_Zone	Zone: My Computer	FullTrust
LocalIntranet_Zone	Zone: Local Intranet	LocalIntranet
Internet_Zone	Zone: Internet	Internet
Restricted_Zone	Zone: Untrusted sites	Nothing
Trusted_Zone	Zone: Trusted sites	Internet

Code groups are very customizable, as described further in Lesson 5. For example, the Internet_Same_Site_Access code group grants assemblies running in the Internet zone access to connect back to their site of origin. Naturally, administrators can create custom code groups to meet unique security requirements.

What Is Security Policy?

A *security policy* is a logical grouping of code groups and permission sets. Additionally, a security policy can contain custom assemblies that define other types of policies. Security policies provide administrators with the flexibility to configure CAS settings at multiple levels. By default, there are three configurable policy levels: Enterprise, Machine, and User.

> **Note**   There's actually a fourth policy level: the Application Domain. Lesson 5 in this chapter explains more about application domains.

The Enterprise level is the highest security policy level, describing security policy for an entire enterprise. Enterprise security policy can be configured by using the Active Directory directory service. Machine policy, the second security policy level, applies to all code run on a particular computer. User policy is the third level, and it defines permissions on a per-user basis. The runtime evaluates the Enterprise, Machine, and User levels separately, and grants an assembly the minimum set of permissions granted by any of the levels (known as the *intersection* of the permission sets). By default, the Enterprise and User security policies grant all code full trust, which causes the Machine security policy to alone restrict CAS permissions.

The Usefulness of Multiple Layers of Security Policy

To understand how security policies are used, consider an application developer who wants to play with an assembly she downloaded from the Internet. The developer has downloaded the assembly to her local computer, so it will run within the My Computer zone. The developer's computer is a member of an Active Directory domain, and a domain administrator has created a code group in the Enterprise security policy that grants assemblies on the local computer the Everything permission set. This is more restrictive than the FullTrust permission set that the Machine security policy grants assemblies in the My Computer zone, so the Everything permission set takes precedence.

The developer isn't sure that the assembly is safe to run, however, so she wants to apply the Internet permission set to prevent the assembly from writing to the disk or communicating across the network. She doesn't log on to her computer as an Administrator, but she can still launch the .NET Framework Configuration tool and modify the User security policy. (Standard users aren't allowed to modify the Machine security policy.) By modifying the User security policy, she can restrict assemblies in the My Computer zone to the Internet permission set. Assemblies she runs will be restricted without affecting other users of the same computer.

The assembly is a member of three code groups: one in the Enterprise security policy, one in the Machine security policy, and one in the User security policy. The runtime determines the assembly's permissions by comparing each code group's permission sets, and using the most restrictive set of permissions shared by all three permission sets (the intersection). Because the FullTrust and Everything permission sets contain all the Internet permission set's permissions (plus a few more permissions), the most restrictive set of permissions is exactly that defined by the Internet permission set.

How CAS Works with Operating System Security

CAS is completely independent of operating system security. In fact, you must use entirely different tools to administer CAS. Although you can control a user or group's file permissions using Microsoft Windows Explorer, you have to use the .NET Framework Configuration tool to grant or restrict an assembly's file permissions.

CAS works on top of existing operating system security. When determining whether an assembly can take a particular action, both CAS and the operating system security are evaluated. The most restrictive set of permissions is applied. For example, if CAS grants an assembly access to write to the C:\Windows\ folder, but the user running the assembly does not have that permission, then the assembly *will not* be able to write to the folder. Figure 6-5 shows how CAS relates to operating system security.

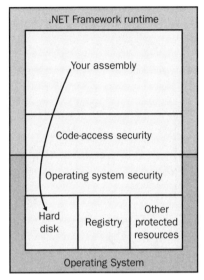

Figure 6-5   CAS complements, but does not replace, role-based security.

 Important   No assembly can have more permissions than the user running the assembly, regardless of how the assembly uses CAS.

Figure 6-6 shows the decision-making process used to determine whether an assembly can access a file.

For the sake of simplicity, Figure 6-6 does not show RBS that you might have built into the assembly. Understanding how CAS and RBS interact can be confusing, because if you build RBS into your application, you will actually have two layers of RBS. RBS that you build into your application is evaluated first, and it determines whether you want to allow the user to run your code. Next, the .NET Framework runtime determines whether your code is allowed to do what it is attempting. Finally, the operating system uses its own RBS to determine whether the user running the assembly has permissions to perform the requested action.

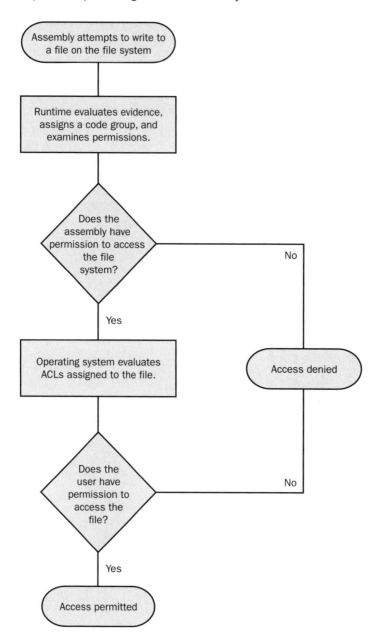

Figure 6-6 Before an assembly can access a file, both the runtime and the operating system must approve the request.

Practice: Explaining Code Access Security

Read the scenario and then complete the exercise that follows. If you are unable to answer a question, review the lessons and try the question again. You can find answers to the questions in the "Questions and Answers" section at the end of this chapter.

Scenario

You are a developer at Blue Yonder Airlines. The CEO of your company read an article that quoted a security analyst who stated that the .NET Framework can prevent viruses from spreading. You run into him in the hallway and he says, "Hey, I just read this article in the paper. What's this about the .NET Framework? It's got some kind of new security that can stop programs from doing bad things, eh? Maybe you can install it on my computer so that I don't have to worry about viruses spreading, or about other dangerous software sending my private files off to the Internet somewhere." He then asks you a series of questions.

Exercise

Answer the following questions for your CEO.

1. Can .NET Framework CAS prevent viruses from spreading? Why or why not?

2. Will installing the .NET Framework on my computer improve the security? If not, what will it accomplish?

3. Could a .NET Framework–based virus running in the Internet zone, with the default CAS permissions, effectively replicate itself across our network? Why or why not?

4. Could a malicious .NET Framework–based assembly running in the Intranet zone, with the default CAS permissions, delete files on your hard drive? Why or why not?

Lesson Summary

- CAS is a security system that authorizes managed assemblies to access system resources.

- CAS is implemented by using the following four components:

    - Evidence, which identifies an assembly

    - Permissions, which describe which resources an assembly can access

    - Permission sets, which collect multiple permissions

    - Code groups, which assign permissions to an assembly based on evidence

- A security policy is a logical grouping of code groups and permission sets. You can use multiple levels of security policy to simplify CAS administration. Assemblies receive the most restrictive set of permissions assigned by each of the policy levels.

- CAS permissions can never override a user's operating system permissions. An assembly's effective permissions are the intersection of the permissions granted to the assembly by CAS and to the user by the operating system.

Lesson 2: Configuring Code Access Security

CAS is a new type of security system, and you must use new tools to administer it. The preferred tool for manually configuring CAS is the .NET Framework Configuration tool, a graphical tool that you can use to configure security policies, code groups, and permission sets. If you need to configure CAS from a command line or a batch file, you can use the Code Access Security Policy tool, also known as Caspol. Caspol provides similar functionality to the .NET Framework Configuration tool but is easier to automate.

After this lesson, you will be able to

- Use the .NET Framework Configuration tool to configure CAS.
- Use Caspol to configure CAS.

Estimated lesson time: 35 minutes

How to Use the .NET Framework Configuration Tool

The .NET Framework Configuration Tool provides a graphical interface for managing .NET Framework security policy and applications that use remoting services. This tool also allows you to manage and configure assemblies in the global assembly cache.

Note This chapter covers using the .NET Framework Configuration tool only to manage CAS policy.

To run the .NET Framework Configuration Tool:

1. While logged on as a standard user or an administrator, open Control Panel.
2. If your operating system is Microsoft Windows XP, double-click Performance And Maintenance.
3. Click Administrative Tools.
4. Double-click Microsoft .NET Framework Configuration.

After opening the .NET Framework Configuration Tool, you can perform many different CAS-related tasks, including:

- Evaluating an assembly to determine which code groups it is a member of
- Evaluating an assembly to determine which permissions it will be assigned
- Adding a new permission set
- Adding a new code group

- Increasing an assembly's trust

- Adjusting zone security

- Resetting policy levels

The following sections provide procedures for performing these tasks.

How to Determine Which Code Groups Grant Permissions to an Assembly

When troubleshooting CAS permissions, you might need to determine which code groups grant permissions to your assembly. To do this, launch the .NET Framework Configuration tool and perform the following steps:

1. Click Runtime Security Policy.

2. Click Evaluate Assembly.

    The Evaluate An Assembly Wizard appears.

3. On the What Would You Like To Evaluate page, click the Browse button. Select your assembly, and then click Open.

4. Click the View Code Groups That Grant Permissions To The Assembly option. Click Next.

5. Expand each policy level to determine which code groups grant permissions to your assembly. Figure 6-7 shows an assembly that receives permissions from the My_Computer_Zone code group.

Figure 6-7   Use the Evaluate An Assembly Wizard to determine which code groups apply permissions to your assembly.

6. Click Finish.

How to Determine Total CAS Permissions Granted to an Assembly

When troubleshooting CAS permissions, you might need to determine which permissions the runtime will grant to your assembly. To do this, launch the .NET Framework Configuration tool and perform the following steps:

1. Click Runtime Security Policy.

2. Click Evaluate Assembly.

   The Evaluate An Assembly Wizard appears.

3. On the What Would You Like To Evaluate page, click the Browse button. Select your assembly, and then click Open.

4. Click the View Permissions Granted To The Assembly option. Click Next.

5. The wizard displays each permission assigned to your assembly, as shown in Figure 6-8. To view the detailed permission settings, select any permission and then click the View Permission button.

Figure 6-8   The Evaluate An Assembly Wizard can list all the CAS permissions that the runtime will potentially grant to your assembly.

6. Click Finish.

How to Add a Permission Set

To create a new permission set, launch the .NET Framework Configuration tool and perform the following steps:

1. Expand Runtime Security Policy.

2. Expand Enterprise, Machine, or User, depending on the policy level in which you want to define the permission set.

3. Click Permission Sets. In the right pane, click Create New Permission Set.

4. On the Identify The New Permission Set page, specify a name and description. Click Next.

5. On the Assign Individual Permissions To Permission Set page (Figure 6-9), perform the following steps:

    a. Click the permission you want to add to the permission set, and click Add.

    b. For each permission, specify the permission settings that are unique to that permission and click OK.

    c. Repeat this process for each individual permission required by your permission set.

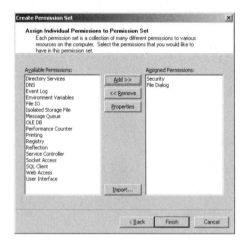

Figure 6-9   Specify the individual permissions that make up the permission set.

6. Click Finish.

How to Add a Code Group

To add a code group, launch the .NET Framework Configuration tool and perform the following steps:

1. Expand Runtime Security Policy.

2. Expand Enterprise, Machine, or User, depending on the policy level in which you want to define the code group.

3. Expand All_Code, and examine the existing child code groups. If the code group you want to create will define a subset of permissions for an existing code group, click that code group. Otherwise, click All_Code.

4. Click Add A Child Code Group.

5. On the Identify The New Code Group page, type a name and a description, as shown in Figure 6-10, and then click Next.

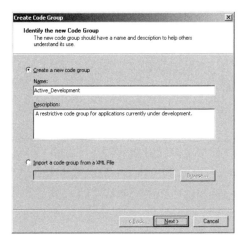

Figure 6-10   Specify a name and description for the new code group.

6. On the Choose A Condition Type page, specify the condition type for the code group by choosing the evidence the runtime will use to identify the code. Click Next.

7. On the Assign A Permission Set To The Code Group page, click the Use Existing Permission Set option if one of the current permission sets exactly meets your needs. Otherwise, click Create A New Permission Set. Click Next.

8. If you selected Create A New Permission Set, perform the following steps:

    a. On the Identify The New Permission Set page, specify a name and description. Click Next.

    b. On the Assign Individual Permissions To Permission Set page, click the permissions you want in the permission set, and click Add. For each permission, specify the permission settings that are unique to that permission and click OK. Click Next.

9. On the Completing The Wizard page, click Finish.

How to Increase an Assembly's Trust

If you restricted the default CAS permissions on your computer, you might need to grant additional trust to specific assemblies to grant them the permissions they need to run correctly. To do this, launch the .NET Framework Configuration tool and perform the following steps:

1. Click Runtime Security Policy.

2. Click Increase Assembly Trust.

The Trust An Assembly Wizard appears.

3. On the What Would You Like To Modify page, click Make Changes To This Computer to adjust the Machine policy level, or click Make Changes For The Current User Only to affect the User policy level. Click Next.

> **Note**   You must be an administrator to adjust the Machine policy level.

4. On the What Assembly Do You Want To Trust page, click Browse. Select the assembly you want to trust, and then click Open. Click Next.

5. On the Choose The Minimum Level Of Trust For The Assembly page, as shown in Figure 6-11, select the minimum trust level for the assembly. Click Next.

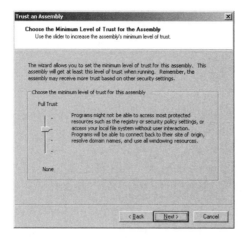

Figure 6-11   Trust specific assemblies to grant them additional access without affecting all assemblies in the same zone.

6. On the Completing The Wizard page, review your selections, and then click Finish.

How to Adjust Zone Security

By default, the .NET Framework includes five zones, each with a unique set of CAS permissions. You should make use of these default zones whenever possible, but you might need to change the permission set a zone uses. To do this, launch the .NET Framework Configuration tool and perform the following steps:

1. Expand Runtime Security Policy, expand Machine, and then expand All_Code.

2. Click the zone you want to adjust. In the right pane, click Edit Code Group Properties.

3. Click the Permission Set tab (shown in Figure 6-12), and then click an item in the Permission Set list to specify the desired permission set. Click OK.

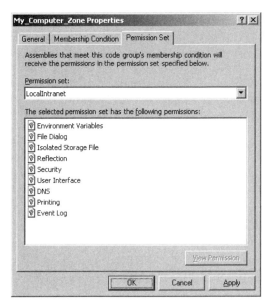

Figure 6-12   Adjust the permissions assigned to a zone by adjusting the associated code group's properties.

Configuring Runtime Security Policy for Development

As a developer, one of the first things you should do is to adjust the permission set assigned to the My_Computer_Zone code group. By default, it's set to Full Trust, which means any CAS statements in your applications will be completely ignored. Change this to the Everything permission set, which grants similar permissions, but respects CAS statements in assemblies. Alternatively, you can further restrict access to local assemblies by choosing another permission set.

How to Reset Policy Levels

You might need to restore the default policy levels after making modifications. To do this, launch the .NET Framework Configuration tool and perform the following steps:

1. Click Runtime Security Policy. In the right pane, click Reset All Policy Levels.

2. Click Yes, and then click OK.

The .NET Framework Configuration tool restores the original policy level settings, including removing all custom code groups and permission sets that you created.

How to Use the Code Access Security Policy Tool

You can use the Code Access Security Policy tool (Caspol.exe) to examine and modify Machine-, User-, and Enterprise-level code access security policies. Although the .NET Framework Configuration tool is the most convenient tool to use for manual configuration, Caspol provides similar functionality at the command line.

> **Note**   Caspol features a dizzying set of parameters, and this book will cover only a handful of the most common. For complete instructions, at the command prompt, run this command: `Caspol -?`.

Caspol Parameters

Caspol uses an extremely complicated set of options. Table 6-5 lists the most commonly used options. The –addgroup and –chggroup options take additional parameters in the form of membership conditions and flags. Membership conditions, described in Table 6-6, are the evidence that the .NET Framework will use to determine which code group to assign an assembly. Flags define the name, description, and other options and are listed in Table 6-7.

> **Note**   Most of the options have abbreviated versions that are not listed in the tables. For complete usage information, at a command prompt, run `caspol -?`.

Table 6-5   Commonly Used Caspol Options

Option	Description
-addfulltrust *assembly_file*	Adds an assembly that implements a custom security object (such as a custom permission or a custom membership condition) to the full trust assembly list for a specific policy level. The *assembly_file* argument specifies the assembly to add. This file must be signed with a strong name.
-addgroup *parent_name membership_condition permission_set_name [flags]*	Adds a new code group. The *parent_name* argument specifies the name of the code group that will be the parent of the code group being added. The *membership_condition* argument specifies the membership condition for the new code group (described in Table 6-6). The *permission_set_name* argument is the name of the permission set that will be associated with the new code group. You can also set one or more flags for the new group (described in Table 6-7).

Table 6-5   Commonly Used Caspol Options

Option	Description
-all	Indicates that all options following this one apply to the Enterprise, Machine, and current User policy.
-chggroup *name* {*membership_condition* | *permission_set_name* | *flags*}	Changes a code group's membership condition, permission set, or the settings of the exclusive, levelfinal, name, or description flags. The *name* argument specifies the name of the code group to change. The *permission_set_name* argument specifies the name of the permission set to associate with the code group. See Tables 6-6 and 6-7 for information about the *membership_condition* and *flags* arguments.
-enterprise	Indicates that all options following this one apply to the Enterprise-level policy. Users who are not enterprise administrators do not have sufficient rights to modify the Enterprise policy, although they can view it.
-execution {on | off}	Turns on or off the mechanism that checks for the permission to run before code starts to run.
-help	Displays command syntax and options for Caspol.
-list	Lists the code group hierarchy and the permission sets for the specified Machine, User, Enterprise, or all policy levels.
-listdescription	Lists all code group descriptions for the specified policy level.
-listfulltrust	Lists the contents of the full trust assembly list for the specified policy level.
-listgroups	Displays the code groups of the specified policy level or all policy levels. Caspol displays the code group's label first, followed by the name, if it is not null.
-listpset	Displays the permission sets for the specified policy level or all policy levels.
-machine	Indicates that all options following this one apply to the Machine-level policy. Users who are not administrators do not have sufficient rights to modify the Machine policy, although they can view it. For administrators, -machine is the default.
-quiet	Temporarily disables the prompt that is normally displayed for an option that causes policy changes.
-recover	Recovers policy from a backup file. Whenever a policy change is made, Caspol stores the old policy in a backup file.
-remgroup *name*	Removes the specified code group. If the specified code group has child code groups, Caspol also removes all the child code groups.

Table 6-5   Commonly Used Caspol Options

Option	Description
-rempset *permission_set_name*	Removes the specified permission set from policy. The *permission_set_name* argument indicates which permission set to remove. Caspol removes the permission set only if it is not associated with any code group. The built-in permission sets cannot be removed.
-reset	Returns policy to its default state.
-resolvegroup *assembly_file*	Shows the code groups to which a specific assembly (*assembly_file*) belongs.
-resolveperm *assembly_file*	Displays all permissions that the security policy would grant the assembly (*assembly_file*) if the assembly were allowed to run.
-security {on | off}	Turns code access security on or off. When code access security is disabled, all code access demands succeed.
-user	Indicates that all options following this one apply to the User-level policy for the user on whose behalf Caspol is running. For nonadministrative users, -user is the default.
-?	Displays command syntax and options for Caspol.exe.

Table 6-6   Caspol Membership Conditions

This Membership Condition	Specifies
-all	All code.
-appdir	The application directory. If you specify -appdir as the membership condition, the URL evidence of code is compared with the application directory evidence of that code. If both evidence values are the same, this membership condition is satisfied.
-hash *hash_algorithm* {-hex *hash_value* | -file *assembly_file* }	Code that has the given assembly hash. To use a hash as a code group membership condition, you must specify either the hash value or the assembly file.
-pub { -cert *cert_file_name* | -file *signed_file_name* | -hex *hex_string* }	Code that has the given software publisher, as denoted by a certificate file, a signature on a file, or the hexadecimal representation of an X509 certificate.
-site *website*	Code that has the given site of origin. For example: -site www.microsoft.com.

Table 6-6   Caspol Membership Conditions

This Membership Condition	Specifies
-strong -file *file_name* {name | -noname} {version | -noversion}	Code that has a specific strong name, as designated by the filename, the assembly name as a string, and the assembly version in the format major.minor.build.revision. For example: -strong -file myAssembly.exe myAssembly 1.2.3.4
-url *URL*	Code that originates from the given URL. The URL must include a protocol, such as http:// or ftp://. Additionally, a wildcard character (*) can be used to specify multiple assemblies from a particular URL. To specify a file share on a network, use the syntax "-url *<servename>**<sharename>**". The trailing * is required to properly identify the share.
-zone *zonename*	Code with the given zone of origin. The *zonename* argument can be one of the following values: MyComputer, Intranet, Trusted, Internet, or Untrusted.

Table 6-7   Caspol Flags

Flag	Description
-description "*description*"	If used with the –addgroup option, specifies the description for a code group to add. If used with the –chggroup option, specifies the description for a code group to edit. You must add double quotation marks around the description, even if it does not include spaces.
-exclusive {on|off}	When set to on, indicates that only the permission set associated with the code group you are adding or modifying is considered when some code fits the membership condition of the code group. When this option is set to off, Caspol considers the permission sets of all matching code groups in the policy level.
-levelfinal {on|off}	When set to on, indicates that no policy level below the level in which the added or modified code group occurs is considered. This option is typically used at the Machine policy level. For example, if you set this flag for a code group at the Machine level and some code matches this code group's membership condition, Caspol does not calculate or apply the user-level policy for this code.

Table 6-7   Caspol Flags

Flag	Description
-name "*name*"	If used with the -addgroup option, specifies the scripting name for a code group to add. If used with the -chggroup option, specifies the scripting name for a code group to edit. The name argument must be enclosed in double quotation marks, even though it cannot include spaces.

How to Perform Common Tasks with Caspol

The following list provides usage examples for common tasks that you might want to perform with Caspol.

- **To grant an assembly full trust** caspol -addfulltrust *assemblyname.exe*

    For example, to grant the C:\Program Files\Mine\Mine.exe assembly full trust, you would run the following command:

    ```
    caspol-addfulltrust "C:\Program Files\Mine\Mine.exe"
    ```

- **To add a code group to the Machine policy** caspol -machine -addgroup *Parent_Code_Group   Membership_Conditions Permission_Set* -name "*Group_Name*"

    For example, to add a code group named My_Code_Group to the Machine policy level's All_Code group, using a URL of *http://devserver\devshare*, which grants LocalIntranet permissions, you would run the following command with administrative privileges:

    ```
    caspol -machine -addgroup All_Code -url \\devserver\devshare\* LocalIntranet -name
    "My_Code_Group"
    ```

- **To add a code group to the User policy** caspol -user -addgroup *Parent_Code_Group Membership_Condition Permission_Set* -name "*Group_Name*"

    Similarly, to add a code group named User_Code_Group to the User policy level's All_Code group, using a site of *http://www.contoso.com*, which grants FullTrust permissions, you would run the following command:

    ```
    caspol -user -addgroup All_Code -site www.contoso.com FullTrust -name
    "User_Code_Group"
    ```

> **Tip** You must close and re-open the .NET Framework Configuration tool to see changes caused by Caspol. But then again, if you have the .NET Framework Configuration tool open, why are you using Caspol?

■ **To adjust zone security for a Machine policy**   `caspol -chggroup` *Code_Group*
Permission_Set

For example, to change the Machine My_Computer_Zone security policy to use the
Intranet permission set, run the following command with administrative privileges:

```
caspol -chggroup My_Computer_Zone LocalIntranet
```

■ **To reset policy levels for the Machine policy level**

```
caspol -recover
```

Practice: Configuring Code Access Security

In this practice, you configure CAS using both the graphical .NET Framework Configuration tool and the command-line Caspol tool. Complete Exercises 1 through 3. If you
are unable to complete a procedure or answer a question, review the lesson materials
and try again. You can find answers to the questions in the "Questions and Answers"
section at the end of this chapter.

> **Important**   The last step of Exercise 2 will restore your original settings to ensure future
> practices work correctly.

Exercise 1: Compiling and Testing the Permissions of a Sample Assembly

In this exercise, you compile and test the permissions of a sample assembly in a
restricted My_Computer zone.

1. Log on to your computer as an Administrator.

> **Note**   For other practices in this chapter, and most tasks on your computer, you should be
> logged on as a standard user. This practice is an exception, because it uses the default C$
> share, which only administrators have access to by default. You can log on as a standard user
> if you create a new share that can be accessed by standard users.

2. Use Windows Explorer to copy the ListPermissions folder from the companion CD
to your My Documents\Visual Studio Projects\ folder. You can choose either the
C# or Visual Basic .NET version.

3. In Windows Explorer, select the My Documents\Visual Studio Projects\ folder,
and then double-click ListPermissions.csproj or ListPermissions.vbproj.

Visual Studio .NET 2003 will open the ListPermissions project.

4. Click the Build menu, and then click Build Solution.

Visual Studio .NET 2003 compiles the application.

5. Copy the ListPermissions.exe file to the root of your C drive.

6. Open a command prompt, and run the command `C:\ListPermissions.exe`. List-Permissions runs and displays several common permissions, and whether the assembly currently has that permission. Notice that you have all the listed permissions. Press ENTER.

   a. Why does the assembly have all the permissions?

7. Run the command `\\127.0.0.1\c$\ListPermissions.exe`. Notice that you are now missing several permissions, in particular, IsolatedStorageFilePermission is missing. Press ENTER.

   a. Why is the assembly now missing permissions, and what code group determined the permissions?

Exercise 2: Creating a Code Group and Permission Set with the .NET Framework Configuration Tool

In this exercise, you use the .NET Framework Configuration tool to create a code group that uses a new permission set.

1. Launch the .NET Framework Configuration tool by opening Control Panel and then Administrative Tools. Right-click Microsoft .NET Framework 1.1 Configuration and then click Run As. In the Run As dialog box, click The Following User, and provide the Administrator user account credentials. Click OK.

2. Expand Runtime Security Policy, Machine, Code Groups, and then All_Code.

3. Click All_Code, and then click Add A Child Code Group in the right pane.

4. In the Name box, type **Local_Shared_Folder**. In the Description box, type **Code run from a network drive mapped to the local shared C: drive**. Click Next.

5. On the Choose A Condition Type page, select URL. In the URL box (as shown in Figure 6-13), type **file://127.0.0.1/c$/*** and then click Next.

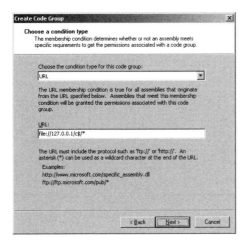

Figure 6-13   Use the URL condition to specify code groups for assemblies running from shared folders.

6. On the Assign A Permission Set To The Code Group page, click the Create A New Permission Set option. Click Next.

7. On the Identify The New Permission Set page, type **GenerousPermissions** in the Name box. In the Description box, type **Permissions for the ListPermissions assembly**. Click Next.

8. On the Assign Individual Permissions To Permission Set page, double-click Isolated Storage File. In the Permission Settings dialog box, select Grant Assemblies Unrestricted Access To File-Based Storage. Click OK, and then click Next.

9. On the Completing The Wizard page, click Finish.

10. Open a command prompt, and run the command \\127.0.0.1\c$\ListPermis-sions.exe. Notice that ListPermission now has the *IsolatedStorageFilePermission*. Press ENTER.

   a. Why does the assembly now have *IsolatedStorageFilePermission*?

Exercise 3: Modifying a Code Group with the Caspol Tool and Restore Default Settings

In this exercise, you modify the newly created code group with the Caspol tool, test the change, and then restore the default settings.

1. Open the Visual Studio .NET 2003 Command Prompt by clicking Start, All Programs, Microsoft Visual Studio .NET 2003, Visual Studio .NET Tools. Right-click Visual Studio .NET 2003 Command Prompt and then click Run As. Click The Following User, provide your administrator credentials, and then click OK.

2. Run the following command to change the Local_Shared_Folder code group permission set to Everything:

   ```
   caspol -chggroup Local_Shared_Folder Everything
   ```

3. Run \\127.0.0.1\c$\Listpermissions. Notice that the assembly now has all permissions, indicating that the Local_Shared_Folder code group now has the Everything permission set.

4. Restore the default CAS settings by running the command `caspol -recover`.

Lesson Summary

■ The .NET Framework Configuration tool is a graphical tool to configure any aspect of CAS. To use the tool, launch Microsoft .NET Framework Configuration from the Administrative Tools group.

■ The Code Access Security Policy tool, Caspol, is a command-line tool with a large number of options for controlling almost every aspect of CAS behavior. To use Caspol, call it from the directory that the .NET Framework is installed into.

Lesson 3: Using Assembly Permission Requests

Lesson 1 taught that CAS can restrict permissions granted to an application. Because of this, you must plan to have your application run in a partially trusted security context. In some situations, CAS security will be so restrictive that your application won't have the permissions required for even the most basic functionality, and the runtime should detect this problem and prevent your assembly from running. In other situations, your application will have more permissions than necessary, which violates the principle of least privilege and makes your application unnecessarily vulnerable to abuse.

You can use declarative CAS demands to ensure your assembly has all necessary permissions, but none that it does not require. As an additional benefit, administrators deploying your application can examine the assembly's declarative CAS demands to identify the minimum permissions they need to grant to take advantage of all your application's functionality.

After this lesson, you will be able to

- Describe why you should use CAS assembly declarations.
- List the classes built into the .NET Framework for CAS permissions.
- List the three types of CAS assembly declarations.
- Create CAS assembly declarations.
- Explain the guidelines for effectively implementing CAS assembly declarations.

Estimated lesson time: 40 minutes

Reasons to Use CAS Assembly Declarations

There are four main reasons to use CAS assembly declarations:

- **To enable administrators to use the Permview tool to analyze your assembly's permission requirements**   Administrators deploying your application to users will need to grant your assembly permissions to run. Although you can, and should, describe the required permissions in your application's documentation, using CAS declarations to add the requirements to your assembly's metadata allows administrators to examine permission requirements at will.

- **To ensure the runtime will never run your application without granting access to required resources**   If you have not built exception handling into your application to respond to situations where your assembly lacks the necessary CAS permissions, use *SecurityAction.RequestMinimum* to declare all CAS permissions required by your application. If a user attempts to run your application and CAS security policy does not grant a required permission, the runtime will throw an exception. Users might not be able to identify the problem based on the exception information displayed by the runtime, but an administrator should understand the problem. Either way, using *SecurityAction.RequestMinimum* is better than having unexpected exceptions while your application is running.

■ **To create a small sandbox for your application to ensure an attacker does not manipulate your application to cause it to access unintended resources** The principle of least privilege reduces the chances of an attacker abusing your assembly by causing it to take unintended actions such as revealing the contents of private files, destroying data, or propagating malicious viruses and worms. By using assembly CAS declarations to restrict your assembly's CAS permissions to the bare minimum, you eliminate the risk of an attacker manipulating your application into accessing resources that it would not normally access.

■ **To verify that your application can run with limited CAS permissions, and therefore run in partially trusted zones** There is currently no way to easily identify the permissions required by an application. However, if you develop and test your application using *SecurityAction.RequestOptional* CAS declarations, the runtime will grant your assembly only those permissions you specify. If you add code that requires additional permissions, the runtime will throw a *System.Security .Policy.PolicyException* indicating the required permission. You can then add another *SecurityAction.RequestOptional* CAS declaration, ensuring you maintain an accurate list of required permissions.

Classes for CAS Permissions

CAS can restrict access to many types of resources, from files and folders, to printers, to network access. For each type of resource that can be protected, the .NET Framework provides a class. Table 6-8 lists each class used for assembly CAS declarations, and the permissions that must be configured with the .NET Framework Configuration tool to grant an assembly access.

Note The .NET Framework also provides attribute classes for each of the classes listed in Table 6-8. The attribute classes have Attribute appended to the name. You don't need to worry about this when writing code, though, because the .NET Framework will automatically use the attribute classes when you reference these classes declaratively.

Table 6-8   Classes Used for Assembly CAS Declarations

Class	Permission
System.Data.Odbc.OdbcPermission	Requires Full Trust
System.Data.OleDb.OleDbPermission	OLE DB
System.Data.SqlClient.SqlClientPermission	SQL Client

Table 6-8 Classes Used for Assembly CAS Declarations

Class	Permission
System.Data.OracleClient.OraclePermission	Requires Full Trust
System.Diagnostics.EventLogPermission	Event Log
System.Diagnostics.PerformanceCounterPermission	Performance Counter
System.DirectoryServices.DirectoryServicesPermission	Directory Service
System.Drawing.Printing.PrintingPermission	Printing
System.Messaging.MessageQueuePermission	Message Queue
System.Net.DnsPermission	DNS
System.Net.SocketPermission	Socket Access
System.Net.WebPermission	Web Access
System.Security.Permissions.EnvironmentPermission	Environment Variables
System.Security.Permissions.FileDialogPermission	File Dialog
System.Security.Permissions.FileIOPermission	File IO
System.Security.Permissions.IsolatedStoragePermission	Isolated Storage File
System.Security.Permissions.PermissionSet	Security
System.Security.Permissions.PrincipalPermission	Security
System.Security.Permissions.PublisherIdentityPermission	Security
System.Security.Permissions.ReflectionPermission	Reflection
System.Security.Permissions.RegistryPermission	Registry
System.Security.Permissions.ResourcePermissionBase	Security
System.Security.Permissions.SecurityPermission	Security
System.Security.Permissions.SiteIdentityPermission	Security
System.Security.Permissions.StrongNameIdentityPermission	Security
System.Security.Permissions.UIPermission	User Interface
System.Security.Permissions.UrlIdentityPermission	Security
System.Security.Permissions.ZoneIdentityPermission	Security
System.ServiceProcess.ServiceControllerPermission	Service Controller
System.Web.AspNetHostingPermission	Web Access

Each class has unique members that you can use to further control permissions. For example, you can set the *OleDbPermissionAttribute.AllowBlankPassword* property to control whether your assembly will be allowed to use a blank password. Similarly, the *DirectoryServicesPermissionAttribute.Path* property can be defined to limit your assembly's access to a specific branch of Active Directory. Because of the large number of classes, this book will not describe the use of each class and property.

> **See Also**   Search for a class in MSDN to find detailed information about a permission class's unique properties.

Because the permission attribute classes are inherited from the *CodeAccessSecurity-Attribute* class, they share some common properties and methods. However, you generally need to be familiar with only two standard properties:

- **Action**   Specifies the security action to take. Set this using the *SecurityAction* enumeration.

- **Unrestricted**   A Boolean value that specifies that the permission enables access to all the class's permissions. Setting this value to true is equivalent to selecting the Grant Assemblies Unrestricted Access To The File System option when specifying permission settings with the .NET Framework Configuration tool, as shown in Figure 6-14.

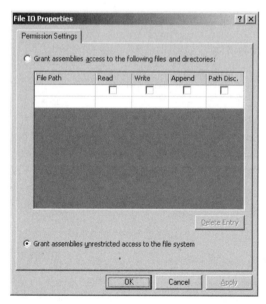

Figure 6-14   Setting the *Unrestricted* property to true for a permission is analogous to granting unrestricted access to a permission.

Types of Assembly Permission Declarations

All permission attribute classes define the *Action* property, which specifies how the runtime will interpret the permission. When creating assembly CAS declarations, you must always set the *Action* property to one of three members of the *SecurityAction* enumeration. The following list describes each of these choices:

- **SecurityAction.RequestMinimum**   Requires a permission for your assembly to run. If your assembly lacks the specified CAS permission, the runtime will throw a *System.Security.Policy.PolicyException*.

- **SecurityAction.RequestOptional**   Refuses all permissions not listed in a *SecurityAction.RequestOptional* or *SecurityAction.RequestMinimum* declaration. Defining permissions with this action ensures your application will have no more permissions than those you have declared. If your assembly lacks the requested CAS permissions, the runtime will *not* throw an exception, unlike its behavior with *SecurityAction.RequestMinimum*. Therefore, use both *SecurityAction.RequestMinimum* and *SecurityAction.RequestOptional* together when your application cannot adapt to a missing permission.

- **SecurityAction.RequestRefuse**   Reduces the permissions assigned to your application. Use this type of declaration to ensure your application does not have access to critical resources that could potentially be abused. Unlike *SecurityAction.RequestMinimum*, this declaration will never cause the runtime to throw an exception at load time.

> **Off the Record**   If these security action names are confusing, the problem is not just you. Why is a declaration called *RequestMinimum* if it's actually a requirement? The name *RequestMinimum* sounds like your code is politely asking for permissions. Given the way *RequestMinimum* behaves, it should be called *RequireMinimum*, because the runtime doesn't respond nicely to a request for permissions that it can't provide—it throws an exception and refuses to run your assembly. Also, the runtime is never going to grant your code permissions that the code wouldn't have had anyway. *RequestOptional* should actually be called *RefuseAllExcept*, because the primary purpose is to explicitly list only those CAS permissions your application should have.

How to Create Assembly Declarations

Lesson 2 of Chapter 3, "Testing Applications for Vulnerabilities," taught how to examine an assembly to determine which permissions the assembly required or requested. As a developer, you use declarative CAS demands to create these requests. For example, the following code sample shows an assembly that requires CAS read access to the

C:\boot.ini file. If security policy does not grant that permission to the assembly, the runtime will throw an exception before running the assembly.

```csharp
using System;
using System.Security.Permissions;

[assembly:FileIOPermissionAttribute(SecurityAction.RequestMinimum, →
Read=@"C:\boot.ini")]
namespace DeclarativeExample
{
    class Class1
    {
        [STAThread]
        static void Main(string[] args)
        {
            Console.WriteLine("Hello, World!");
        }
    }
}
```

```vbnet
Imports System.Security.Permissions

<Assembly: FileIOPermissionAttribute(SecurityAction.RequestMinimum, →
Read := "C:\boot.ini")>
Module Module1
    Sub Main()
        Console.WriteLine("Hello, World!")
    End Sub
End Module
```

Note The sample assembly doesn't actually access the C:\boot.ini file. CAS declarations are completely arbitrary. It's up to you to make sure they're consistent with your application's requirements.

The preceding examples used *SecurityAction.RequestMinimum* to cause the .NET Framework runtime to throw an exception if the assembly did not have CAS permissions to read the C:\boot.ini file. This ensures the assembly will not run unless the runtime provides the required permission, therefore preventing the application from experiencing problems while running. However, throwing the exception does not improve the security of the assembly, because it does nothing to restrict the assembly's permissions.

Exam Tip For the exam, remember that CAS is significant only for partially trusted assemblies. The runtime completely ignores CAS declarations for fully trusted assemblies.

To improve the assembly's security, specify the *SecurityAction.RequestOptional* or *SecurityAction.RequestRefuse* enumerations for the permission's *Action* property. Optionally, you can combine multiple declarations in a single assembly. For example, if you want the runtime to throw an exception if you don't have access to the HKEY_LOCAL_MACHINE\Software registry key, and you don't want any other CAS permissions (except, of course, the Enable Assembly Execution security permission), you would use the following declarations:

```
[assembly:RegistryPermission(SecurityAction.RequestMinimum, →
Read=@"HKEY_LOCAL_MACHINE\Software")]
[assembly:RegistryPermission(SecurityAction.RequestOptional, →
Read=@"HKEY_LOCAL_MACHINE\Software")]
```

```
<Assembly:RegistryPermission(SecurityAction.RequestMinimum, →
Read := "HKEY_LOCAL_MACHINE\Software")>
<Assembly:RegistryPermission(SecurityAction.RequestOptional, →
Read := "HKEY_LOCAL_MACHINE\Software")>
```

You can combine *RequestMinimum*, *RequestOptional*, and *RequestRefuse*, but combining *RequestOptional* and *RequestRefuse* might accomplish nothing. After all, *RequestOptional* refuses all permissions except those explicitly listed. The only case in which you would combine *RequestOptional* and *RequestRefuse* is to refuse a subset of the specified *RequestOptional* permissions.

For example, the following declarations would cause the runtime to throw an exception if the assembly did not have CAS printing permissions. The runtime would deny all CAS permissions except printing and file system access to the C drive. Access to the C:\Windows directory would also be denied.

```
[assembly:PrintingPermission(SecurityAction.RequestMinimal)]
[assembly:FileIOPermissionAttribute(SecurityAction.RequestOptional, →
Read=@"C:\")]
[assembly:FileIOPermissionAttribute(SecurityAction.RequestRefuse, →
Read=@"C:\Windows\")]
```

```
<Assembly: PrintingPermission(SecurityAction.RequestMinimal)>
<Assembly: FileIOPermissionAttribute(SecurityAction.RequestOptional, →
Read := "C:\")>
<Assembly: FileIOPermissionAttribute(SecurityAction.RequestRefuse, →
Read := "C:\Windows\")>
```

Permview Refresher

Chapter 3 discussed the Permview command-line tool, but the tool will make more sense now that you understand assembly-level security declarations. If you use the Permview command-line tool to examine the preceding code sample, you'll see the following output. Notice that the *SecurityAction.RequestMinimum* declaration is listed in the Minimal Permission Set section, the *SecurityAction.RequestOptional* declaration is listed in the Optional Permission Set section, and the *SecurityAction.RequestRefuse* declaration is listed within Refused Permission Set:

```
Microsoft (R) .NET Framework Permission Request Viewer.  Version 1.1.4322.573
Copyright (C) Microsoft Corporation 1998-2002. All rights reserved.

minimal permission set:
<PermissionSet class="System.Security.PermissionSet"
               version="1">
   <IPermission class="System.Drawing.Printing.PrintingPermission, System.Drawing,
 Version=1.0.5000.0, Culture=neutral, PublicKeyToken=b03f5f7f11d50a3a"
               version="1"
               Level="NoPrinting"/>
</PermissionSet>

optional permission set:
<PermissionSet class="System.Security.PermissionSet"
               version="1">
   <IPermission class="System.Security.Permissions.FileIOPermission, mscorlib, Ve
rsion=1.0.5000.0, Culture=neutral, PublicKeyToken=b77a5c561934e089"
               version="1"
               Read="C:\"/>
</PermissionSet>

refused permission set:
<PermissionSet class="System.Security.PermissionSet"
               version="1">
   <IPermission class="System.Security.Permissions.FileIOPermission, mscorlib, Ve
rsion=1.0.5000.0, Culture=neutral, PublicKeyToken=b77a5c561934e089"
               version="1"
               Read="C:\Windows\"/>
</PermissionSet>
```

Guidelines for Using Assembly Declarations

Follow these guidelines to choose which CAS assembly declarations to use:

- Use *SecurityAction.RequestMinimum* assembly declarations to require every permission needed by your assembly that your assembly does not imperatively check for.

- Use *SecurityAction.RequestOptional* assembly declarations to list every permission your assembly uses. Declare the most granular permissions possible, including specific files or registry keys that will be accessed.

- Use *SecurityAction.RequestRefuse* assembly declarations to further refine permissions listed with *SecurityAction.RequestOptional* assembly declarations.

Practice: **Using Assembly Permission Requests**

In this practice, you analyze example assembly declarations to predict the application's behavior. Then, you update an assembly you have written with CAS assembly declarations. Complete Exercises 1 and 2. If you are unable to answer a question, review the lesson materials and try the question again. You can find answers to the questions in the "Questions and Answers" section at the end of this chapter.

Exercise 1: Anticipating Declarative Permission Request Results

Answer the following questions.

1. An administrator runs the following console application with the Everything permission set.

```
using System;
using System.Security.Permissions;
using System.IO;
using System.IO.IsolatedStorage;
using System.Drawing.Printing;

[assembly:PrintingPermission(SecurityAction.RequestMinimum)]
[assembly:FileIOPermissionAttribute(SecurityAction.RequestOptional, ➞
Read=@"C:\")]
[assembly:FileIOPermissionAttribute(SecurityAction.RequestRefuse, ➞
Read=@"C:\Windows\")]

namespace DeclarativeExample
{
    class Class1
    {
        [STAThread]
        static void Main(string[] args)
        {
            Console.WriteLine("Reading one line of the boot.ini file:");
            StreamReader sw = new StreamReader(@"C:\boot.ini");
            Console.WriteLine("First line of boot.ini: " + sw.ReadLine());
        }
    }
}
```

```
Imports System.Security.Permissions
Imports System.IO
Imports System.IO.IsolatedStorage
Imports System.Drawing.Printing

<Assembly: PrintingPermission(SecurityAction.RequestMinimum)>
<Assembly: FileIOPermissionAttribute(SecurityAction.RequestOptional, →
Read := "C:\")>
<Assembly: FileIOPermissionAttribute(SecurityAction.RequestRefuse, →
Read := "C:\Windows\")>

Module Module1
    Sub Main(ByVal args As String())
        Console.WriteLine("Reading one line of the boot.ini file:")
        Dim sw As StreamReader = New StreamReader ("C:\boot.ini")
        Console.WriteLine("First line of boot.ini: " + sw.ReadLine)
    End Sub
End Module
```

What will the output from the application be?

2. The developer changes the assembly CAS declarations as follows:

```
[assembly:PrintingPermission(SecurityAction.RequestMinimum)]
[assembly:FileIOPermissionAttribute(SecurityAction.RequestOptional, →
Read=@"C:\Temp\")]
[assembly:FileIOPermissionAttribute(SecurityAction.RequestRefuse, →
Read=@"C:\Windows\")]
```

```
<Assembly: PrintingPermission(SecurityAction.RequestMinimum)>
<Assembly: FileIOPermissionAttribute(SecurityAction.RequestOptional, →
Read := "C:\Temp\")>
<Assembly: FileIOPermissionAttribute(SecurityAction.RequestRefuse, →
Read := "C:\Windows\")>
```

What will the output of the application now be? Why?

3. The developer makes a couple more changes to the assembly CAS declarations as follows:

```
[assembly:PrintingPermission(SecurityAction.RequestMinimum)]
[assembly:FileIOPermissionAttribute(SecurityAction.RequestMinimum, →
Read=@"C:\Temp\")]
[assembly:FileIOPermissionAttribute(SecurityAction.RequestRefuse, →
Read=@"C:\Windows\")]
```

```
<Assembly: PrintingPermission(SecurityAction.RequestMinimum)>
<Assembly: FileIOPermissionAttribute(SecurityAction.RequestMinimum, →
Read := "C:\Temp\")>
<Assembly: FileIOPermissionAttribute(SecurityAction.RequestRefuse, →
Read := "C:\Windows\")>
```

What will the output of the application now be? Why?

Exercise 2: Adding Assembly Permission Requests

Open the last assembly that you created as part of your job, and add the most granular assembly permission requests possible. Be very specific—if your assembly needs access to only a single file, limit your file system access to that file. If you use Web services, restrict the *WebPermission* object to allow your assembly access only to the server and path that the Web service uses. If your assembly does not explicitly check for the permissions, configure the assembly permission requests so that the runtime will throw an exception if the permissions are not present before the runtime runs the assembly.

Lesson Summary

- Use CAS assembly declarations because they enable administrators to view the permissions required by your application, prevent your application from running without sufficient permissions, restrict the permissions granted to your application, and enable you to isolate your application to verify compatibility with partially trusted zones.

- The .NET Framework provides more than a dozen classes for CAS permissions, describing resources such as the file system, the registry, and printers.

- There are three types of CAS assembly declarations: *RequestMinimum*, *RequestOptional*, and *RequestRefuse*.

- To create assembly declarations, add assembly attributes by using permission classes.

- Use *RequestMinimum* declarations when your application doesn't handle missing permissions appropriately, use *RequestOptional* to list every permission required by your application, and use *RequestRefuse* to further restrict your *RequestOptional* permissions.

Lesson 4: Protecting Methods with Code Access Security

Chapter 5, "Implementing Role-Based Security," taught how to add RBS demands to your application to cause the .NET Framework to throw an exception when the user did not meet your security requirements. Like RBS demands, CAS can also be used either imperatively or declaratively. However, CAS demands authorize the calling code, not the user. CAS demands are used to verify that the assembly that calls your assembly, method, or class has the necessary CAS permissions before the .NET Framework runtime runs your code.

This lesson teaches how and why to use both imperative and declarative CAS demands.

After this lesson, you will be able to

- List the types of method permission requests.
- Describe how method permission requests should be used to maximize application security.
- Use CAS to require specific permissions for individual methods.
- Restrict permissions for a method to reduce the risk of the method being misused by an attacker.
- Use the *Assert* method to relax permissions and improve performance.
- Use permission sets to demand, restrict, or assert multiple permissions simultaneously.

Estimated lesson time: 55 minutes

Types of Method Permission Requests

Although there are only three types of CAS assembly declarations, you have six options available for imperative and declarative permissions within a method. The following list describes each:

- **Assert**   Instructs the runtime to ignore the fact that callers might not have the specified permission. Assemblies must have the Assert Any Permission That Has Been Granted security permission setting.

- **Demand**   Instructs the runtime to throw an exception if the caller, and all callers higher in the stack, lack the specified permission.

- **Deny**   Causes the runtime to reduce the method's access by removing the specified permission.

- *__InheritanceDemand__*   Instructs the runtime to throw an exception if the assembly inheriting from the class lacks the specified permission.

- *__LinkDemand__*   Causes the runtime to throw an exception if the immediate caller, but not callers higher in the stack, lack the specified permission.

- *__PermitOnly__*   Instructs the runtime to reduce the method's access by removing all permissions except for the specified permission.

To understand each of these methods, consider a group of four guests who wish to enter an exclusive party. The host (your method) has hired a bouncer (the .NET Framework runtime) to make sure that only guests (calling assemblies) with an invitation (a CAS permission) are allowed to enter the party (call your method).

If the host calls *InvitedGuests.LinkDemand()*, the bouncer will check the invitation of the first guest, and then allow everyone else into the party. This is quick, but it might let people sneak into the party. If the host calls *InvitedGuests.Demand()*, the bouncer will check the invitation of every guest individually. This takes more time, but it ensures nobody can sneak in.

To speed up the process of checking invitations, the first invited guests might use *InvitedGuests.Assert()* to assure the bouncer that all the guests in the group were invited—assuming the bouncer trusted the first guest enough. This would also allow the first guest to bring guests who lacked invitations. This could be a good thing, if the host wanted to have a lot of people at the party but didn't want to hand out too many invitations (which might fall into the wrong hands). However, it could be a bad thing if a thief discovered that he could sneak into the party.

If the host wanted to ensure people danced at the party (and never did anything else), the host would use *Dancing.PermitOnly()* to instruct the bouncer to make sure guests stayed on the dance floor. If the host wanted people to do anything *but* dance, the host would use *Dancing.Deny()* to prevent anyone from dancing.

Guidelines for Using Method Permission Requests

As a developer, you have many choices for implementing CAS in your applications. Choosing how to implement CAS for a particular situation can be complicated, however. Follow these guidelines to choose which CAS methods to use:

- Use *SecurityAction.PermitOnly* declarations to limit the permissions available to each method. List every permission the method requires.

- Use *SecurityAction.Deny* declarations to further refine the permissions available to each method.

- Use *CodeAccessPermission.PermitOnly* to imperatively reduce permissions when a section of a method requires fewer permissions than the rest of the method. This is particularly important when calling objects created by third parties. Use *CodeAccessPermission.RevertPermitOnly* to restore the permission.

- Use *CodeAccessPermission.Assert* when you want to allow partially trusted code to call a method that requires permissions the caller might lack. Review your code carefully for potential security vulnerabilities; *Assert* can be abused by an attacker to gain elevated privileges. After you have performed the functions requiring elevated privileges, use *CodeAccessPermission.RevertAssert* to restore the original permissions.

- Only use *CodeAccessPermission.Demand* only when your assembly implements customized functionality that does not rely on functionality built into the .NET Framework, such as calls to unmanaged code.

> **Off the Record**   There's a school of thought that says declarative security demands are less secure than imperative security demands, because declarative demands can reveal to attackers too much about the code's design and potential vulnerabilities. It's true that declarative security demands are a bit easier for an attacker to analyze; however, a sophisticated attacker could also examine imperative demands by using a tool that analyzes your assembly's intermediate language (IL) code. It's a bit harder for the attacker to analyze IL than to analyze the declarative security demands, but it wouldn't make much of a difference to an attacker who was sophisticated enough to make use of security demand information. Also, declarative demands are faster than imperative demands.

Lesson 2 of Chapter 2, "Using Secure Coding Best Practices," taught how attackers can abuse canonicalization problems to cause your application to process files it was not intended to process. For example, if you had written an application that displayed text files but was specifically not supposed to display the C:\boot.ini file, an attacker could submit a filename containing special characters to trick your application into displaying the file. You can, and should, follow the best practices described in that chapter to prevent canonicalization problems. However, implementing defense-in-depth requires providing multiple layers of protection whenever possible. Using declarative and imperative CAS permission demands to restrict your application's access is an excellent way to add a layer of protection.

Techniques for Demanding Permissions

Two of the *SecurityAction* enumerations and two of the *CodeAccessPermission* methods cause the runtime to throw an exception if the specified CAS permission is missing: *Demand* and *LinkDemand*. The difference between the two enumerations and methods is that *Demand* causes the permission check to verify the access of all callers, whereas *LinkDemand* verifies only the immediate caller.

To understand the difference, compare the *Demand* process demonstrated in Figure 6-15 to the *LinkDemand* process demonstrated in Figure 6-16. As you can see, *Demand* will detect whether any caller lacks the demanded permission or permission set, and will throw an exception. This is more secure than using *LinkDemand*, which checks only the immediate caller. However, as with almost every security mechanism, there is a trade-off. *Demand* requires the runtime to do more checks, which requires more processing time and slows performance. Using *LinkDemand* improves performance but increases the risk of an attacker successfully bypassing the check.

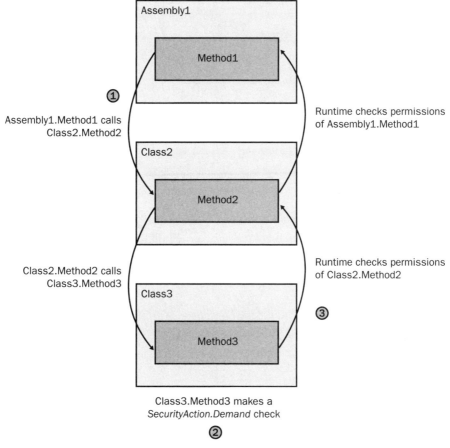

Figure 6-15   *Demand* checks all callers for a permission.

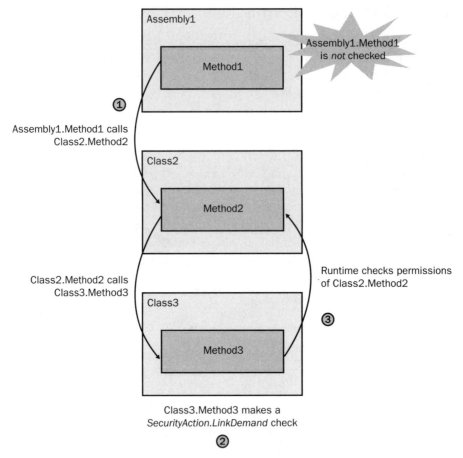

Figure 6-16   *LinkDemand* checks only the immediate caller.

Important   *Demand* and *LinkDemand* do *not* check the current method's permissions—they check the caller. However, if your assembly calls a private method that uses *Demand* or *Link-Demand*, the runtime *will* check your assembly's permission, because in this case your assembly is the caller.

How to Analyze Granted Permissions

If you need to determine whether your assembly has a particular CAS permission, don't use *Demand*. *Demand* is designed to check an assembly's *caller* for permission, not the assembly itself. Instead, use the *System.Security.SecurityManager.IsGranted* method, as demonstrated by the following code sample:

```
FileIOPermission filePermissions = new ⤳
FileIOPermission(FileIOPermissionAccess.Read, @"C:\Windows\");
if ( SecurityManager.IsGranted(filePermissions) == true )
    // Assembly can read the C:\Windows directory
else
    // Assembly cannot read the C:\Windows directory
```

```
Dim filePermissions As FileIOPermission =  New ⤳
FileIOPermission(FileIOPermissionAccess.Read, "C:\Windows\")
If SecurityManager.IsGranted(filePermissions) = True Then
    ' Assembly can read the C:\Windows directory
Else
    ' Assembly cannot read the C:\Windows directory
End If
```

The ListPermissions sample application used in the Lesson 2 practice uses this method; examine the source code on the companion CD for a working example.

Tip   Most classes in the .NET Framework use demands to ensure callers have the permissions required to use them, so also calling *Demand* is redundant. For example, if you're reading a line from a text file using a *StreamWriter* object, the object itself will demand *FileIOPermission*. Generally, use demands to protect custom resources that require custom permissions.

How to Declaratively Demand CAS Permissions

Creating CAS method declarations is very similar to creating CAS assembly declarations. However, you must create the declarations as attributes to the method instead of to the assembly, and you must use different *SecurityAction* enumerations. Just as with RBS, discussed in Chapter 5, you can specify CAS permissions either declaratively or imperatively. To create a declarative request, use one of the classes discussed in Lesson 3 of this chapter with the *SecurityAction.Demand* or *SecurityAction.LinkDemand* enumerations. The following sample is a simple class that uses the *FileIOPermissionAttribute* and *WebPermissionAttribute* classes to declaratively verify that callers of particular methods have access to specific files and the *http://www.microsoft.com* Web site.

```csharp
using System;
using System.IO;
using System.Net;
using System.Security.Permissions;

namespace CASDemands
{
    public class CASProtectedClass
    {
        [FileIOPermission(SecurityAction.Demand, ➙
Write = @"C:\Program Files\")]
        public static void createProgramFolder()
        {
            // Method logic
        }

        [WebPermission(SecurityAction.Demand, ➙
ConnectPattern = @"http://www\.microsoft\.com/.*")]
        public static void requestWebPage()
        {
            // Method logic
        }
    }
}
```

```vb
Imports System.IO
Imports System.Net
Imports System.Security.Permissions

Public Class CASProtectedClass
    <FileIOPermissionAttribute(SecurityAction.Demand, ➙
Write := "C:\Program Files\")> _
    Public Shared Sub createProgramFolder()
        ' Method logic
    End Sub

    <WebPermission(SecurityAction.Demand, ➙
ConnectPattern:="http://www\.microsoft\.com/.*")> _
    Public Shared Sub requestWebPage()
        ' Method logic
    End Sub
End Class
```

If you write classes that other developers will derive from, you can restrict which assemblies can inherit from your classes using the *SecurityAction.InheritanceDemand* enumeration. For example, only assemblies signed with the C:\Certificates\MyCertificate.cer certificate would be able to inherit from the following class:

```csharp
[PublisherIdentityPermission(SecurityAction.InheritanceDemand, ➙
CertFile = @"C:\Certificates\MyCertificate.cer")]
public class ProtectedInheritance
{
    // Class logic
}
```

```vb
<PublisherIdentityPermission(SecurityAction.InheritanceDemand, →
CertFile:="C:\Certificates\MyCertificate.cer")> _
Public Class ProtectedInheritance
    ' Class logic
End Class
```

You can use the same declarative syntax to protect individual class members from being overridden by a derived class. This is necessary only when you want to provide levels of protection for individual members that are higher than those for the base class.

How to Imperatively Demand CAS Permissions

For each of the *SecurityAction* enumerations used to specify CAS declarations, there is a *CodeAccessPermission* method with the same name and function used for imperative permissions. You will use the *SecurityAction* enumerations for declarative security, and the *CodeAccessPermission* methods for imperative security. The technique is similar to the imperative RBS demands discussed in Chapter 5, except that you must use one of the CAS permission classes. The following sample performs the same checks as the sample code that used declarative CAS demands, but it performs the check imperatively.

```csharp
using System;
using System.IO;
using System.Net;
using System.Security.Permissions;
using System.Text.RegularExpressions;

namespace CASDemands
{
    public class CASImperativeClass
    {
        public static void createProgramFolder()
        {
            try
            {
                FileIOPermission filePermissions = new →
FileIOPermission(FileIOPermissionAccess.Write, @"C:\Program Files\");
                filePermissions.Demand();
                // Method logic
            }
            catch
            {
                // Error-handling logic
            }
        }

        public static void requestWebPage()
        {
            try
            {
                Regex connectPattern = new →
Regex(@"http://www\.microsoft\.com/.*");
                WebPermission webPermissions = new →
```

```
WebPermission(NetworkAccess.Connect, connectPattern);
            webPermissions.Demand();
            // Method logic
        }
        catch
        {
            // Error-handling logic
        }
    }
  }
}
```

```vb
Imports System.IO
Imports System.Net
Imports System.Security.Permissions
Imports System.Text.RegularExpressions

Public Class CASImperativeClass
    Public Shared Sub createProgramFolder()
        Try
            Dim filePermissions As FileIOPermission = New →
FileIOPermission (FileIOPermissionAccess.Write, "C:\Program Files\")
            filePermissions.Demand()
            ' Method logic
        Catch
            ' Error handling logic
        End Try

    End Sub

    Public Shared Sub requestWebPage()
        Try
            Dim connectPattern As Regex = New →
Regex("http://www\.microsoft\.com/.*")
            Dim webPermissions As WebPermission = New →
WebPermission(NetworkAccess.Connect, connectPattern)
            webPermissions.Demand()
            ' Method logic
        Catch
            ' Error handling logic
        End Try
    End Sub
End Class
```

Tip Remember, the advantage of using imperative demands is that you can catch the security exception within your method and deal with it gracefully. If you just want to throw an exception back to the caller, use a declarative demand.

Techniques for Limiting Permissions

Always use CAS assembly declarations to restrict the CAS permissions granted to your assembly so that your assembly has only the bare minimum required for all functionality. You can control permissions on a more granular level by restricting permissions for individual methods using method declarations, or by restricting permissions within methods using imperative statements.

Two of the *SecurityAction* enumerations and permission methods cause the runtime to reduce CAS permissions: *Deny* and *PermitOnly*. The difference between the two enumerations is that *Deny* removes a single permission or permission set, whereas *PermitOnly* removes all permissions except the requested permission or permission set. Recall from Lesson 3 that *Deny* performs a similar function to *RequestRefuse*, whereas *PermitOnly* is similar to *RequestOptional*.

> **Exam Tip**   For the exam, remember to use *RequestRefuse* and *RequestOptional* for assembly declarations, and use *Deny* and *PermitOnly* for methods.

How to Declaratively Limit Permissions

The following two declarations demonstrate how to prevent a method from accessing the C:\Windows\ directory, and how to limit outgoing Web requests to only *http://www.microsoft.com*:

```
[FileIOPermission(SecurityAction.Deny, All = @"C:\Windows\")]
[WebPermission(SecurityAction.PermitOnly, ConnectPattern = →
@"http://www\.microsoft\.com/.*")]
```

```
<FileIOPermissionAttribute(SecurityAction.Deny, All := "C:\Program Files\")> _
<WebPermission(SecurityAction.PermitOnly, →
ConnectPattern:="http://www\.microsoft\.com/.*")> _
```

> **Tip**   Declarative security criteria must be static. If you need to dynamically generate file paths, Web addresses, or any other aspects of the security criteria, you must enforce the security limitations imperatively.

How to Imperatively Limit Permissions

The following sample forces the same limitations as the sample code that used declarative CAS demands, but limits the permissions imperatively.

```csharp
// Deny access to the Windows directory
FileIOPermission filePermissions = new →
FileIOPermission(FileIOPermissionAccess.AllAccess, @"C:\Windows\");
filePermissions.Deny();
// Method logic

// Permit only Web access, and limit it to www.microsoft.com
Regex connectPattern = new Regex(@"http://www\.microsoft\.com/.*");
WebPermission webPermissions = new WebPermission(NetworkAccess.Connect, →
connectPattern);
webPermissions.PermitOnly();
// Method logic
```

```vb
' Deny access to the Windows directory
Dim filePermissions As FileIOPermission = New →
FileIOPermission(FileIOPermissionAccess.AllAccess, "C:\Windows\")
filePermissions.Deny()
' Method logic

' Permit only Web access, and limit it to www.microsoft.com
Dim connectPattern As Regex = New Regex("http://www\.microsoft\.com/.*")
Dim webPermissions As WebPermission = →
New WebPermission(NetworkAccess.Connect, connectPattern)
webPermissions.PermitOnly()
' Method logic
```

If part of your code needs to use a permission that you previously blocked with *Deny* or *PermitOnly*, use the *System.Security.CodeAccessPermission.RevertDeny* or *System.Security.CodeAccessPermission.RevertPermitOnly* static methods to re-enable the permission.

Best Practice for Handling Errors

Use *PermitOnly* to limit permissions during error-handling routines. Attackers often initiate an error condition in an application and then abuse that error condition to perform tasks that would not be possible under normal circumstances. Using *PermitOnly* to limit CAS permissions to the bare minimum required to log the event and report an error to the user significantly reduces the risk that your error-handling routine can be abused. If your application will continue running after the error, be sure to revert to your original permissions—otherwise, normal application functionality will not be available.

For example, the following code catches an exception, restricts CAS permissions to those required to add events, and then reverts to the previous permission set:

```csharp
try
{
    // Assembly logic
}
catch
{
    EventLogPermission errorPerms = new →
EventLogPermission(PermissionState.Unrestricted);
    errorPerms.PermitOnly();
    // Log event
    CodeAccessPermission.RevertPermitOnly();
}
```

```vbnet
Try
    ' Assembly logic
Catch
    Dim errorPerms As EventLogPermission = New →
EventLogPermission (PermissionState.Unrestricted)
    errorPerms.PermitOnly
    ' Log event
    CodeAccessPermission.RevertPermitOnly
End Try
```

> **Tip**   Restricting permissions to those required for a specific block of code is an excellent example of following the principle of least privilege. Although it's particularly important during error-catching routines, you can use this technique to limit the permissions of any block of code.

How to Relax Permissions and Potentially Improve Performance

Using CAS demands improves the security of an assembly but can decrease performance. In particular, calling a permission's *Demand* method is costly because it forces the runtime to systematically check the permission of every caller. *LinkDemand*, discussed earlier, is one way to improve upon the performance of the *Demand* method, but it sacrifices some level of security. Another technique is the *Assert* method, which causes the runtime to bypass any security checks.

> **Important**   *CodeAccessPermission.Assert* is nothing like the *assert* function in C or C++.

Permission objects include the *Assert* method to enable a method to vouch for all callers. Figure 6-17 shows how a call to *Assert* stops the runtime from checking the CAS permissions of assemblies higher in the stack. This has two effects: improving performance by reducing the number of permission checks, and allowing underprivileged code to call methods with higher CAS permission requirements.

For example, if you create a *RegistryPermission* object and call the *Assert* method, your assembly must be granted *RegistryPermission*, but any code calling your assembly does not require the permission. If you call another method that uses *Demand* to require *RegistryPermission*, *Demand* will succeed whether or not your caller has been granted *RegistryPermission*.

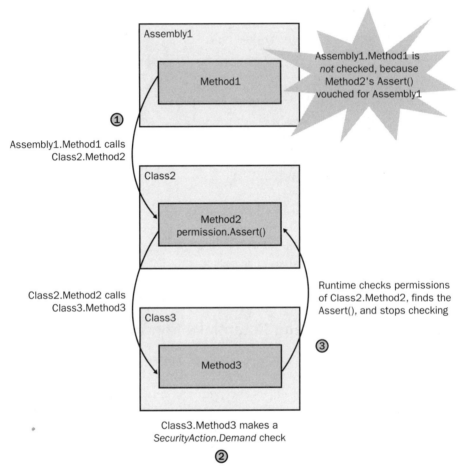

Figure 6-17 Assert blocks demand checks, increasing performance and allowing underprivileged code to call methods with CAS permission requirements.

You can use *Assert* either declaratively or imperatively, and the syntax is identical to other types of CAS declarations. The following example asserts permissions declaratively:

```
[FileIOPermission(SecurityAction.Assert, All = @"C:\Windows\")]
[WebPermission(SecurityAction.Assert, ConnectPattern = ⮑
@"http://www\.microsoft\.com/.*")]
```

```
<FileIOPermissionAttribute(SecurityAction.Assert, ⮑
All := "C:\Program Files\")> _
<WebPermission(SecurityAction.Assert, ⮑
ConnectPattern:="http://www\.microsoft\.com/.*")> _
```

Although the following example asserts permissions imperatively:

```
// Block all CAS permission checks for file access to the Windows directory
FileIOPermission filePermissions = new ⮑
FileIOPermission(FileIOPermissionAccess.AllAccess, @"C:\Windows\");
filePermissions.Assert();
// Method logic

// Block all CAS permission checks for Web access to www.microsoft.com
Regex connectPattern = new Regex(@"http://www\.microsoft\.com/.*");
WebPermission webPermissions = new WebPermission(NetworkAccess.Connect, ⮑
connectPattern);
webPermissions.Assert();
// Method logic
```

```
' Block all CAS permission checks for file access to the Windows directory
Dim filePermissions As FileIOPermission = New ⮑
FileIOPermission(FileIOPermissionAccess.AllAccess, "C:\Windows\")
filePermissions.Assert()
' Method logic

' Block all CAS permission checks for Web access to www.microsoft.com
Dim connectPattern As Regex = New Regex("http://www\.microsoft\.com/.*")
Dim webPermissions As WebPermission = ⮑
New WebPermission(NetworkAccess.Connect, connectPattern)
webPermissions.Assert()
' Method logic
```

To successfully use *Assert*, the assembly must have the *SecurityPermissionFlag.Assertion* privilege as well as the privilege being asserted. In the .NET Framework Configuration tool, *SecurityPermissionFlag.Assertion* is represented by the Assert Any Permission That Has Been Granted item in the Security permission properties dialog box. The FullTrust, LocalIntranet, and Everything permission sets have this permission. Figure 6-18 shows the granular permissions for the LocalInternet Security permission, which allows assertions.

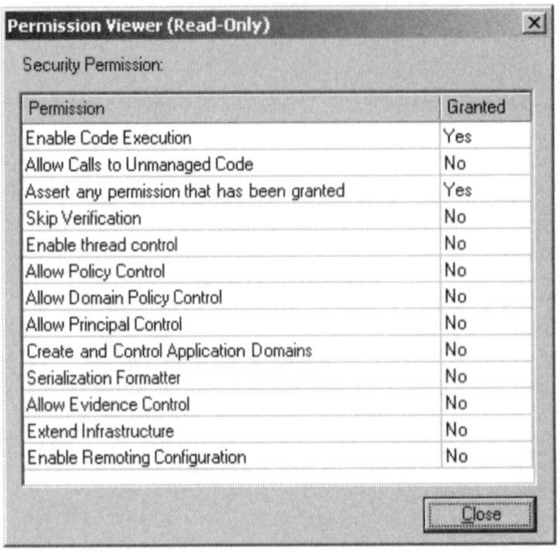

Figure 6-18   Assemblies must have the Assert Any Permission That Has Been Granted permission to successfully call Assert.

Using *Assert* allows an assembly to vouch for the security of lesser-privileged assemblies. This is an excellent way to grant additional functionality to assemblies that would normally lack CAS permissions. For example, you can use an *Assert* to allow an assembly in the Internet zone to save a file to the user's disk. Simply create an assembly with the *AllowPartiallyTrustedCallersAttribute*. Then, create a public method that writes the file, create a *FileIOPermission* object, and call the *Assert* method before writing the file. The assembly in the Internet zone can save a file to a user's disk without requiring the administrators to grant file permissions to the Internet zone.

Calling Trusted Code from Partially Trusted Code

To prevent partially trusted code from bypassing security checks, partially trusted code can't call strong-named assemblies by default. You can control this on an assembly-by-assembly basis, however, by adding the *AllowPartiallyTrustedCallers-Attribute* assembly-level custom attribute:

```
[assembly:AllowPartiallyTrustedCallers]
```

If your assembly doesn't have a strong name, partially trusted code can access your public methods even when you don't add that attribute. That's all the more reason to use strong names, which are discussed in Chapter 7, "Maximizing Security During Deployment."

To decrease the opportunity for an attacker to abuse asserted permissions, use the *CodeAccessPermission.RevertAssert* static method. As the name suggests, calling this method erases the assertion and returns CAS permission checking to the normal state. Use a *try/finally* block to ensure that you call *RevertAssert* after every *Assert*, even if a failure occurs. The following method demonstrates this and is also an excellent example of how to fail to a more secure permission set:

```csharp
FileIOPermission filePermissions = new →
FileIOPermission(FileIOPermissionAccess.Write, @"C:\Inetpub\");
filePermissions.Assert();
try
{
    StreamWriter newFile = new StreamWriter(@"C:\Inetpub\NewFile.txt");
    newFile.WriteLine("Lesser privileged applications can save a file.");
    newFile.Close();
}
finally
{
    CodeAccessPermission.RevertAssert();
}
```

```vbnet
Dim filePermissions As FileIOPermission = New FileIOPermission →
(FileIOPermissionAccess.Write, "C:\Inetpub\NewFile.txt")
filePermissions.Assert
Try
    Dim newFile As StreamWriter = New StreamWriter ("C:\Inetpub\NewFile.txt")
    newFile.WriteLine("Lesser privileged applications can save a file.")
    newFile.Close
Finally
    CodeAccessPermission.RevertAssert
End Try
```

Assert does have a few limitations. You can use *Assert* only once in a method. If you need to assert multiple permissions, you will need to create a custom permission set (described in this lesson). Also, *Assert* doesn't override the operating system's RBS, regardless of the assembly's CAS permissions. If a user lacks permission to write to the D drive and runs an assembly with full trust that asserts that file permission, the *Assert* will succeed, but the assembly still won't be able to write to the D drive. The assembly is still limited by the user's access restrictions.

How to Use Permission Sets

Permission sets are a collection of permissions that can be used imperatively in the same ways you use individual permissions. Use the *System.Security.Permissions.PermissionSet* class to create a permission set, and then use the *AddPermission* method to specify the permissions that define the permission set. Then, you can call any standard permission methods, including *Assert*, *Demand*, *Deny*, and *PermitOnly*.

For example, the following code creates a permission set consisting of read access to the C:\Windows folder, write access to the C:\Inetpub\ folder, and read access to the HKEY_LOCAL_MACHINE\Software registry key. Then, it demands access to all those resources to cause the runtime to throw an exception if any of the specified permissions are not available.

```csharp
PermissionSet myPerms = new PermissionSet(PermissionState.None);
myPerms.AddPermission(new →
FileIOPermission(FileIOPermissionAccess.Read, @"C:\Windows"));
myPerms.AddPermission(new →
FileIOPermission(FileIOPermissionAccess.Write, @"C:\Inetpub"));
myPerms.AddPermission(new →
RegistryPermission(RegistryPermissionAccess.Write, @"HKEY_LOCAL_MACHINE\Software"));
myPerms.Demand();
```

```vb
Dim myPerms As PermissionSet = New PermissionSet(PermissionState.None)
myPerms.AddPermission(New →
FileIOPermission (FileIOPermissionAccess.Read, "C:\Windows"))
myPerms.AddPermission(New →
FileIOPermission (FileIOPermissionAccess.Write, "C:\Inetpub"))
myPerms.AddPermission(New →
RegistryPermission (RegistryPermissionAccess.Write, "HKEY_LOCAL_MACHINE"))
myPerms.Demand
```

> **Tip**   You can call *Assert* only once in a method, so if you need to assert multiple permissions, you *must* use a permission set.

Practice: Protecting Methods with Code Access Security Demands

In this practice, you work with *Deny* and *Assert* methods to validate your understanding of both declarative and imperative CAS permissions. Complete Exercises 1 through 4. If you are unable to complete a procedure or answer a question, review the lesson materials and try again. You can find answers to the questions in the "Questions and Answers" section at the end of this chapter.

Exercise 1: Experimenting with the Default Permission Set

In this exercise, you experiment with declarative and imperative CAS demands and determine how each reacts when CAS is not restricted.

1. Log on to your computer as a standard user account configured as a Microsoft Visual Studio .NET developer with the user name StandardUser.

> **Tip**   For detailed instructions, see Lesson 3, Exercise 1 of Chapter 4, "Taking Advantage of Platform Security."

2. Use Windows Explorer to copy the CASDemands folder from the companion CD, in either Visual Basic.NET or C#, to your C:\Documents and Settings\StandardUser \CASDemands\ folder.

3. In Windows Explorer, double-click C:\Documents and Settings\StandardUser \CASDemands\CASDemands.sln to open the solution in Visual Studio .NET.

4. In Visual Studio .NET, click the Debug menu, and then click Start Without Debugging.

   Visual Studio .NET builds and launches the assembly.

5. In the Code Access Security application, click the Create File With No Demand button, and then answer the following questions:

   a. What zone is the assembly running in?

   b. What permission set did the .NET Framework runtime grant the assembly?

   c. What type of exception was thrown, and why was that particular type of exception thrown?

6. In the Code Access Security application, click the Create File With Declarative Demand button, and then answer the following questions.

   a. What type of exception was thrown, and why was that particular type of exception thrown?

   b. Notice that the error message reads Failed When Attempting To Create The File, and not Failed Before Attempting To Create The File. Use Visual Studio .NET to examine the *declarativeDemandButton_Click* method. This method calls the *declarativeCreateFile* method, which requires write access to a file that the user lacks permission to create. Why was the exception thrown within the *createFile* method, and not thrown when the declarative security demand was processed before the *declarativeCreateFile* method was run?

7. In the Code Access Security application, click the Create File With Imperative Demand button, and then answer the following questions:

   a. What type of exception was thrown, and why was that particular type of exception thrown?

8. Close the Code Access security application, but leave Visual Studio .NET open.

Exercise 2: Restricting Permissions to the My Computer Zone

In this exercise, you restrict permissions to the My Computer Zone.

1. Log on to your computer as a standard user account configured as a Microsoft Visual Studio .NET developer with the user name StandardUser. For detailed instructions, refer to Chapter 4, Lesson 3, Exercise 1.

2. Click Start, and then click Control Panel.

3. Double-click Administrative Tools.

4. Right-click Microsoft .NET Framework 1.1 Configuration, and then click Run As.

5. In the Run As dialog box (Figure 6-19), click The Following User. In the User Name box, type **Administrator**. In the Password box, type the Administrator password. Click OK.

Figure 6-19   Configuring machine CAS requires administrative privileges.

The .NET Framework Configuration tool appears, running with the administrative privileges that are required for reconfiguring machine CAS.

6. In the .NET Framework Configuration tool, expand Runtime Security Policy, expand Machine, expand Code Groups, and then expand All_Code.

7. Right-click My_Computer_Zone, and then click Properties.

8. Click the Permission Set tab and then set Permission Set to Internet, as shown in Figure 6-20.

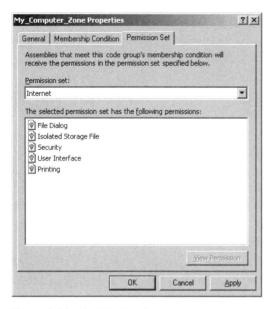

Figure 6-20   Setting My_Computer_Zone to Internet permissions restricts file IO access.

9. Click OK.

Exercise 3: Experimenting with the Default Permission Set

In this exercise, you experiment with declarative and imperative CAS demands and determine how each reacts when CAS is restricted.

> **Important**   To complete this exercise, you must have completed Exercise 1 and Exercise 2 in this practice.

1. Log on to your computer as a standard user account configured as a Microsoft Visual Studio .NET developer with the user name StandardUser.

> **Tip**   For detailed instructions, see Chapter 4, Lesson 3, Exercise 1.

2. In Visual Studio .NET, open the CASDemand solution. Click the Debug menu, and then click Start Without Debugging.

   Visual Studio .NET builds and launches the assembly. As shown in Figure 6-21, the assembly no longer has unrestricted permissions.

Figure 6-21 The .NET Framework warns you that the application is running in a partially trusted context.

3. In the CASDemand application, click the control box in the upper-left corner to remove the bubble.

4. In the CASDemand application, click the Create File With No Demand button, and then answer the following questions.

   a. What zone is the assembly running in?

   b. What permission set did the .NET Framework runtime grant the assembly?

   c. What type of exception was thrown, and why was that particular type of exception thrown?

5. In the CASDemand application, click the Create File With Declarative Demand button, and then answer the following questions:

   a. What type of exception was thrown, and why was that particular type of exception thrown?

   b. In which method was the exception caught?

6. In the CASDemand application, click the Create File With Imperative Demand button, and then answer the following questions:

   a. What type of exception was thrown, and what method caught the exception?

7. Use the .NET Framework Configuration tool with administrative privileges to reset all policy levels, as described in Lesson 2 of this chapter.

Exercise 4: Granting Access to Partially Trusted Code

In this exercise, you modify a class to enable code without *FileIOPermission* to write to the disk.

1. Log on to your computer as a standard user account configured as a Microsoft Visual Studio .NET developer with the user name StandardUser.

> **Tip**   For detailed instructions, see Chapter 4, Lesson 3, Exercise 1.

2. Use Windows Explorer to copy the TrustedClass folder from the companion CD, in either Visual Basic.NET or C#, to your C:\Documents and Settings\StandardUser \TrustedClass\ folder. Then, copy the PartiallyTrustedAssembly folder to your C:\Documents and Settings\StandardUser\PartiallyTrustedAssembly\ folder.

3. Open the Visual Studio .NET 2003 Command Prompt by clicking Start, All Programs, Microsoft Visual Studio .NET 2003, Visual Studio .NET Tools. Right-click Visual Studio .NET 2003 Command Prompt and then click Run As. Click The Following User, provide your administrator credentials, and then click OK.

4. At the administrator command prompt, run the following command to share the folder that will contain your assembly with the name Untrusted:

```
net share untrusted="C:\Documents and Settings\StandardUser\↵
My Documents\PartiallyTrustedAssembly\bin\Debug" /GRANT:Users,READ
```

```
net share untrusted="C:\Documents and Settings\StandardUser\↵
My Documents\PartiallyTrustedAssembly\bin" /GRANT:Users,READ
```

5. Next, run the following command to share the folder that will contain your class with the name Trusted:

```
net share trusted="C:\Documents and Settings\StandardUser\↵
My Documents\TrustedClass\bin\Debug" /GRANT:Users,READ
```

```
net share trusted="C:\Documents and Settings\StandardUser\↵
My Documents\TrustedClass\bin" /GRANT:Users,READ
```

6. In Windows Explorer, double-click C:\Documents and Settings\StandardUser \TrustedClass\TrustedClass.sln to open the solution in Visual Studio .NET.

7. In Visual Studio .NET, click the Build menu, and then click Build Solution.

   Visual Studio .NET creates the TrustedClass.dll assembly. While you have the solution open, examine the *Distrust* class. Note that it has one member: *WriteToFile*, which uses a *StreamWriter* class, which automatically demands *FileIOPermission*.

8. In Windows Explorer, double-click C:\Documents and Settings\StandardUser \PartiallyTrustedAssembly\PartiallyTrustedAssembly.sln to open the solution in Visual Studio .NET.

9. In Solution Explorer, right-click References, and then click Add Reference.

10. In the Add Reference dialog box, click the Browse button. In the Select Component dialog box, type **\\127.0.0.1\Trusted\TrustedClass.dll**. Click Open, and then click OK.

11. In Visual Studio .NET, click the Build menu, and then click Build Solution.

    Visual Studio .NET creates the TrustedClass.dll assembly.

12. Open a command prompt without administrative privileges. At the command prompt, issue the following command:

    ```
    \\127.0.0.1\untrusted\PartiallyTrustedAssembly
    ```

    a. PartiallyTrustedAssembly attempts to write to a file. Did it succeed?

    b. Examine the source code, and explain the behavior.

13. Add a method to *TrustedClass.Distrust* named *WriteToFileWrapper* that uses *Assert* to block the *FileIOPermission* demand, and then rebuild the assembly. Modify the PartiallyTrustedAssembly source code to call *WriteToFileWrapper* instead of *WriteToFile*.

    a. What code did you write to create the assembly?

14. At the command prompt, issue the following command:

    ```
    \\127.0.0.1\Untrusted\PartiallyTrustedAssembly
    ```

    a. PartiallyTrustedAssembly attempts to write to a file. Did it succeed? Why or why not?

15. Now, you must increase the *TrustedClass* assembly's trust to enable it to use an *Assert*. Launch the .NET Framework configuration tool using administrative privileges. Click Runtime Security Policy, and then click Increase Assembly Trust in the right pane.

16. On the What Would You Like To Modify page, click Make Changes To This Computer, and then click Next.

17. On the Which Assembly Do You Want To Trust page, type **\\127.0.0.1\trusted\trustedclass.dll** and then click Next.

18. On the Choose The Minimum Level Of Trust For The Assembly page, move the slider to Full Trust. Click Next, and then click Finish.

19. At the command prompt, issue the following command:

    ```
    \\127.0.0.1\Untrusted\PartiallyTrustedAssembly
    ```

    a. PartiallyTrustedAssembly attempts to write to a file. Did it succeed? Why or why not?

20. Remove the shares you created by running the following commands at an Administrator command prompt:

```
net share trusted /delete
net share untrusted /delete
```

21. Use the .NET Framework Configuration Tool with administrative privileges to reset all policy levels, as described in Lesson 2 of this chapter.

Lesson Summary

■ You can use six different methods to control permissions in an assembly: *Assert, Demand, Deny, InheritanceDemand, LinkDemand,* and *PermitOnly.*

■ You should use *PermitOnly* and *Deny* within an assembly to reduce the likelihood of the assembly being misused by an attacker. Use *Demand* and *LinkDemand* only when accessing custom resources or unmanaged code.

■ You can use *Demand* and *LinkDemand* to protect methods either declaratively or imperatively. You can use *InheritanceDemand* declaratively to restrict which assemblies can derive new classes from your own.

■ You can use *PermitOnly* and *Deny* both declaratively and imperatively to restrict the permissions assigned to a method.

■ To bypass CAS demands and enable underprivileged assemblies to call privileged methods, use *Assert.*

■ Permission sets have the same capabilities as individual permissions, but apply a single action to multiple permissions simultaneously. To create a permission set, use the *System.Security.Permissions.PermissionSet* class, and then use the *AddPermission* method to specify the permissions that define the permission set. Then, you can call any standard permission methods, including *Assert, Demand, Deny,* and *PermitOnly.*

Lesson 5: Customizing Code Access Security

All developers should take advantage of CAS to improve the security of their applications. However, some developers will have more specific needs and will need to create custom evidence, permissions, membership conditions, code groups, and application domains. This lesson covers the fundamentals of implementing custom code access security and is intended to start you moving in the right direction. This lesson does not, however, provide a detailed discussion of implementing custom CAS classes.

After this lesson, you will be able to

- Describe the purpose of an application domain.
- Use an application domain to launch assemblies with limited permissions.
- Create custom evidence, membership conditions, and permissions.

Estimated lesson time: 25 minutes

What Is an Application Domain?

An *application domain* is a logical container that allows multiple assemblies to run within a single process but prevents them from directly accessing other assemblies' memories. Application domains offer many of the features of a process, such as separate memory spaces and access to resources. However, application domains are more efficient than processes, enabling multiple assemblies to be run in separate application domains without the overhead of launching separate processes. Figure 6-22 shows how a single process can contain multiple application domains.

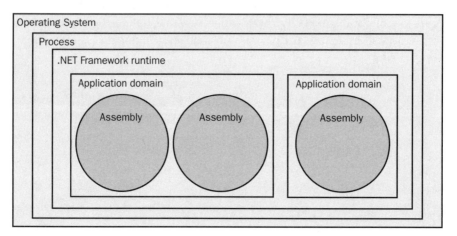

Figure 6-22   Application domains keep assemblies separate within a single process.

Important   The .NET Framework runtime manages application domains, whereas the operating system manages processes.

The best example of application domains in use is the ASP.NET worker process in Internet Information Services (IIS) 5.0, implemented by Aspnet_wp.exe. If 10 people visit an ASP.NET Web site simultaneously, ASP.NET will create a separate application domain for each user. Essentially, ASP.NET runs 10 separate instances of the assembly. Each instance of the assembly can store a property called *userName* without any concern that other instances will be able to access or overwrite the contents of the property. This same effect could be achieved by launching the same assembly in 10 separate processes, but switching between the processes would consume processor time, thus decreasing performance.

How to Use an Application Domain to Launch Assemblies with Limited Permissions

Most of the time, you will rely on the existing runtime hosts to automatically create application domains for your assemblies. Examples of runtime hosts built into Windows are ASP.NET, Internet Explorer (which creates a single application domain for all assemblies from a specific Web site), and the operating system. You can configure the behavior of these application domains by using friendly tools such as the Internet Information Services Manager and the .NET Framework Configuration tool.

However, just as Aspnet_wp.exe creates application domains to isolate multiple instances of an assembly, you can create your own application domains to call assemblies with little risk that the assembly will take any action or access any resources that you have not specifically permitted. For example, you might use an application domain to launch another assembly with a limited set of permissions. Figure 6-23 shows how an assembly can host application domains.

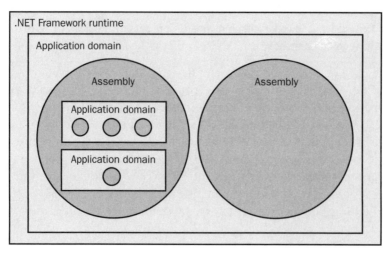

Figure 6-23   Assemblies can host child application domains.

Important   To create application domains, your assembly must have the *SecurityPermission.ControlAppDomain* permission. This permission is represented by the Create And Control Application Domains check box in the Security Properties dialog box of the .NET Framework Configuration tool.

In Lesson 1, a Note pointed out that the application domain is a fourth security policy level. Because it is a separate policy level, an application domain can be configured with the same elements that the Enterprise, Machine, and User policy levels have: code groups with membership conditions and permission sets to define the permissions assigned to newly launched assemblies. The application domain is the lowest policy level, and can grant only a subset of the permissions granted by the higher-level security policies.

When you create an application domain from within an assembly, you can configure evidence, permission sets, membership conditions, and code groups. However, you can't use the .NET Framework Configuration tool. Instead, you'll have to create and assign those objects dynamically in your assembly. The sections that follow describe the techniques and classes used to configure application domains.

How to Launch Assemblies in Private Application Domains

Creating a new application domain and launching an assembly within that domain is as simple as creating an instance of the *System.AppDomain* class with a friendly name, and then calling the *ExecuteAssembly* method, as the following code demonstrates:

```
AppDomain myDomain = AppDomain.CreateDomain("MyDomain");
myDomain.ExecuteAssembly(@"C:\SecondAssembly.exe");
```

```
Dim myDomain As AppDomain = AppDomain.CreateDomain("MyDomain")
myDomain.ExecuteAssembly("C:\SecondAssembly.exe")
```

Calling an assembly in this manner provides isolation for the assembly but does not take advantage of the huge power and flexibility built into application domains.

How to Provide Host Evidence for an Assembly

When you create an application domain and launch assemblies, you have complete control over the host evidence. As a result, you have complete control over the permissions that will be assigned to the assembly. To provide evidence for an assembly, first create a *System.Security.Policy.Evidence* object, and then pass it as a parameter to the application domain's overloaded *ExecuteAssembly* method.

When you create an *Evidence* object with the constructor that requires two object arrays, you must provide one array that represents host evidence, and a second that provides assembly evidence. Either of the arrays can be null, and unless you have specifically created an assembly evidence class, you will probably assign only the host evidence property. It might seem odd that *Evidence* takes generic object arrays instead of strongly typed *Evidence* objects. However, evidence can be *anything*: a string, an integer, or a custom class. So, even if you are using the evidence types built into the .NET Framework, you will have to add them to an object array.

The simplest way to control the permissions assigned to an assembly in an application domain is to pass Zone evidence by using a *System.Security.Policy.Zone* object and the *System.Security.SecurityZone* enumeration. The following code demonstrates using the *Evidence* constructor that requires two object arrays by creating a *Zone* object, adding it to an object array named *hostEvidence*, and then using the object array to create an *Evidence* object named *internetEvidence*. Finally, that *Evidence* object is passed to the application domain's *ExecuteAssembly* method along with the filename of the assembly:

```
Using System.Security;
Using System.Security.Policy;
…
object [] hostEvidence = {new Zone(SecurityZone.Internet)};
Evidence internetEvidence = new Evidence(hostEvidence, null);

AppDomain myDomain = AppDomain.CreateDomain("MyDomain");
myDomain.ExecuteAssembly(@"C:\SecondAssembly.exe", internetEvidence);
```

```
Imports System.Security
Imports System.Security.Policy
…
Dim hostEvidence As Object() = {New Zone (SecurityZone.Internet)}
Dim internetEvidence As Evidence = New Evidence (hostEvidence, Nothing)
Dim myDomain As AppDomain = AppDomain.CreateDomain("MyDomain")
myDomain.ExecuteAssembly("C:\SecondAssembly.exe", internetEvidence)
```

> **Note**   The *AppDomain.ExecuteAssembly* method has overloads that allow you to pass command-line arguments, too.

The result is that the specified assembly will run in an isolated application domain with only the permission set granted to the Internet_Zone code group. When the application domain launches the assembly, the runtime analyzes the evidence provided. Because the evidence matches the Internet zone, the runtime assigns it to the Internet_Zone code group, which in turn assigns the Internet permission set.

> **Important**   To provide host evidence for an assembly, your assembly must have the *Security-Permission.ControlEvidence* permission. This permission is represented by the Allow Evidence Control check box in the Security Properties dialog box of the .NET Framework Configuration tool.

You can also create more customized evidence by creating an *Evidence* object and adding built-in or custom objects. The following code sample uses the empty *Evidence* constructor to show how to specify Site, URL, and Zone evidence that simulate the assembly originating from Microsoft's Web site, at *http://www.microsoft.com/assembly.exe*:

```
Using System.Security;
Using System.Security.Policy;
...
Evidence fakeEvidence = new Evidence();
fakeEvidence.AddHost(new Site("www.microsoft.com"));
fakeEvidence.AddHost(new Url("http://www.microsoft.com/assembly.exe"));
fakeEvidence.AddHost(new Zone(SecurityZone.Internet));

AppDomain myDomain = AppDomain.CreateDomain("MyDomain");
myDomain.ExecuteAssembly(@"C:\SecondAssembly.exe", fakeEvidence);
```

```
Imports System.Security
Imports System.Security.Policy
...
Dim fakeEvidence As Evidence = New Evidence
fakeEvidence.AddHost(New Site ("www.microsoft.com"))
fakeEvidence.AddHost(New Url ("http://www.microsoft.com/assembly.exe"))
fakeEvidence.AddHost(New Zone (SecurityZone.Internet))
Dim myDomain As AppDomain = AppDomain.CreateDomain("MyDomain")
myDomain.ExecuteAssembly("C:\SecondAssembly.exe", fakeEvidence)
```

Important   Controlling evidence is useful for maximizing application security because the assembly has its permissions restricted as if it came from the Internet. But the assembly isn't coming from the Internet—it's stored on the C drive. Essentially, the sample code has provided false evidence to the runtime. Providing evidence to the runtime can also be used to grant an assembly *more* permissions than it would normally receive, which is a powerful capability. Therefore, restricting the *SecurityPermission.ControlEvidence* permission is very important.

How to Provide Host Evidence for an Application Domain

You can also provide evidence for entire application domains. The technique is similar to providing evidence for a new assembly, and it uses an overload of the *AppDomain.CreateDomain* method that accepts an *Evidence* object, as the following code sample demonstrates:

```
Using System.Security;
Using System.Security.Policy;
…
Zone safeZone = new Zone(SecurityZone.Internet);
object [] hostEvidence = {new Zone(SecurityZone.Internet)};
Evidence appDomainEvidence = new Evidence(hostEvidence, null);
AppDomain myDomain = AppDomain.CreateDomain("MyDomain", appDomainEvidence);
myDomain.ExecuteAssembly(@"C:\SecondAssembly.exe");
```

```
Imports System.Security
Imports System.Security.Policy
…
Dim safeZone As Zone = New Zone (SecurityZone.Internet)
Dim hostEvidence As Object() =  {New Zone (SecurityZone.Internet)}
Dim appDomainEvidence As Evidence = New Evidence (hostEvidence, Nothing)
Dim myDomain As AppDomain = AppDomain.CreateDomain("MyDomain", appDomainEvidence)
myDomain.ExecuteAssembly("C:\SecondAssembly.exe")
```

Membership Condition Classes

You can add custom code groups to application domains that you create. Before you can create a code group, however, you must create a membership condition and a permission set. The .NET Framework includes the following eight membership condition classes, which enable you to specify membership conditions that match all code or that match each of the seven types of evidence:

- *AllMembershipCondition*
- *ApplicationDirectoryMembershipCondition*
- *HashMembershipCondition*
- *PublisherMembershipCondition*
- *SiteMembershipCondition*

- *StrongNameMembershipCondition*

- *UrlMembershipCondition*

- *ZoneMembershipCondition*

You will need to create a membership condition object each time you create a code group class. The membership conditions are logically named, and you should specify the evidence used by the membership condition when you create the object. For example, the following code creates a *UrlMembershipCondition* object with the *http:// www.microsoft.com/assembly.exe* URL:

```
UrlMembershipCondition myCondition = new ↴
UrlMembershipCondition("http://www.microsoft.com/assembly.exe");
```

```
Dim myCondition As UrlMembershipCondition = New ↴
UrlMembershipCondition("http://www.microsoft.com/assembly.exe")
```

The *AllMembershipCondition* class does not require evidence to be specified, because it will match all code. The default *All_Code* code group uses the *AllMembershipCondition* class.

Code Group Classes

The .NET Framework includes four code group classes, all derived from *System.Security.Policy.CodeGroup*:

- **System.Security.Policy.FileCodeGroup**   A code group with a membership condition that you specify and a permission set allowing only *FileIOPermission* to the directory from which the code is run.

- **System.Security.Policy.FirstMatchCodeGroup**   A code group that must contain multiple child code groups to be unique. Assemblies are assigned the permission set of the *first* child code group with a matching membership condition, combined with the permission set assigned to the *FirstMatchCodeGroup* parent object. The differences between this and *UnionCodeGroup* is that *UnionCodeGroup* creates a permission set based on *all* child code groups with matching membership conditions. If this code group has no child code groups, it will behave exactly like *UnionCodeGroup*.

- **System.Security.Policy.NetCodeGroup**   A code group with a membership condition that you specify, and a permission set allowing only *WebPermission* to the site from which the code is run. Access is granted only for the protocol over which the code was run, with the exception of code run over the HTTP protocol, which is also granted access to HTTPS.

- ***System.Security.Policy.UnionCodeGroup***   The code group most commonly used by both the .NET Framework and developers. Assemblies are assigned the permission set of *all* child code groups with a matching membership condition, combined with the permission set assigned to the *UnionCodeGroup* parent object. If this code group has no child code groups, it will behave exactly like *FirstMatch-CodeGroup* and simply grant assemblies the permission set assigned to the *Union-CodeGroup* object if the membership condition matches.

If you simply want to create a code group that behaves like those you're familiar with from working with the .NET Framework Configuration tool and Caspol, use *UnionCode-Group*. When you create a code group, you must provide the constructor a membership condition object and a *PolicyStatement* object. The *PolicyStatement* object is a simple object that consists of a permission set and a set of attributes. You must pass to new *CodeGroup* objects a *PolicyStatement* rather than a *PermissionSet*, so you must create a *PolicyStatement* based on your permission set for just this purpose.

How to Create Application Domains with Custom Security Policies

To create an application domain with custom security policies, you must create membership conditions, code groups, policy statements, permission sets, and a policy level. To start, consider the following code sample, which shows how to create a code group that uses a membership condition matching the URL *http://www.microsoft.com/assembly.exe* and the Internet permission set:

```
UrlMembershipCondition safeMembership = new→
UrlMembershipCondition("http://www.microsoft.com/assembly".exe");
PermissionSet safePermissionSet = →
PolicyLevel.CreateAppDomainLevel().GetNamedPermissionSet("Internet");
PolicyStatement safePolicyStatement = new PolicyStatement(safePermissionSet);
CodeGroup safeCodeGroup = new UnionCodeGroup(safeMembership, →
safePolicyStatement);
```

```
Dim safeMembership As UrlMembershipCondition = →
New UrlMembershipCondition("http://www.microsoft.com/assembly.exe")
Dim safePermissionSet As PermissionSet = →
PolicyLevel.CreateAppDomainLevel.GetNamedPermissionSet("Internet")
Dim safePolicyStatement As PolicyStatement = →
New PolicyStatement(safePermissionSet)
Dim safeCodeGroup As CodeGroup = →
New UnionCodeGroup(safeMembership, safePolicyStatement)
```

After you define the custom code group, you must create a *PolicyLevel* object and add that code group to the policy level. *PolicyLevel* objects always have a root code group (defined by the *PolicyLevel.RootCodeGroup* property), although additional, nested code groups can also be used. The following code extends the previous code sample to define a policy level, create an application domain, and then specify the custom policy level as the application domain's security policy:

```csharp
PolicyLevel safePolicyLevel = PolicyLevel.CreateAppDomainLevel();
safePolicyLevel.RootCodeGroup = safeCodeGroup;

AppDomain myDomain = AppDomain.CreateDomain("MyDomain");
myDomain.SetAppDomainPolicy(safePolicyLevel);
```

```vb
Dim safePolicyLevel As PolicyLevel = PolicyLevel.CreateAppDomainLevel
safePolicyLevel.RootCodeGroup = safeCodeGroup

Dim myDomain As AppDomain = AppDomain.CreateDomain("MyDomain")
myDomain.SetAppDomainPolicy(safePolicyLevel)
```

How to Customize Code Access Security

The previous examples demonstrate fairly simple uses of application domains that leverage the security policies, code groups, membership conditions, permissions, and evidence built into the .NET Framework. Although most developers will never have the need, you can extend the .NET Framework's CAS to implement custom classes for each of these object types. Combined, you can build application domains with security policies as powerful as those the .NET Framework runtime uses.

The sections that follow discuss how to create custom classes that you can use directly from within your applications, or that can be integrated directly into the .NET Framework runtime. You can also create custom code groups by inheriting from the *System.Security.Policy.CodeGroup* class. You might do this if you weren't satisfied with the logic provided by *FirstMatchCodeGroup* and *UnionCodeGroup*, and you wanted to use a different decision-making process to determine a resulting permission set. However, the need for custom code groups is much less significant than the need for custom evidence, membership conditions, and permissions, and it will not be discussed in detail in this book.

See Also For detailed information about creating custom code groups, see the book Programming .NET Security (O'Reilly & Associates, 2003).

How to Create Custom Evidence

The .NET Framework includes a handful of evidence types, as discussed in Lesson 1. Though it is not a simple task, you can create and use custom evidence types and enable the .NET Framework to base security decisions on your evidence. This would enable you to create custom code groups that used your custom evidence as part of a membership condition. Developers would then have to use your evidence classes to present evidence to the runtime so that their assemblies would run within the custom code group.

The only requirement for implementing a custom evidence class is that the class must be serializable. As long as you meet that single requirement, you can present any managed class as evidence. The evidence classes built into the .NET Framework provide the best examples of how to implement your own evidence. The *System.Security.Policy.Site* evidence class provides the Web site from which an assembly originates as evidence for policy evaluation. The related *System.Security.Policy.SiteMembershipCondition* class is used to determine, based on the site evidence, whether an assembly belongs to a code group by comparing a *System.Security.Policy.Site* evidence object to a specified condition.

Most of the built-in evidence classes also include a related identity permission class. For example, the *Site.CreateIdentityPermission* method creates a new permission that developers can use to restrict access to a specific site. Similarly, the *Publisher.CreateIdentityPermission* method can be used to restrict access to assemblies that provide evidence of being created by a specific publisher. Only the application directory and hash evidence types do not provide a *CreateIdentityPermission* method.

If you create a custom evidence class that provides the *CreateIdentityPermission* method, inherit from the *System.Security.Policy.IIdentityPermissionFactory* interface. Otherwise, just use *System.Runtime.Serialization.ISerializable*.

> **Important**   If you do create your own assembly evidence classes, use cryptography to protect the evidence from tampering. Otherwise, a malicious attacker could easily modify your evidence. Cryptography is discussed in Chapter 8, "Protecting Data by Using Cryptography."

How to Create a Custom Membership Condition

For each type of evidence, there must be a corresponding membership condition. The requirement for this is straightforward; code groups make decisions based on membership conditions, which in turn determine whether evidence matches the conditions. Therefore, when creating custom evidence, you must create both an evidence class and a membership condition class.

Membership condition classes should be derived from *System.Security.Policy.IMembershipCondition*, *System.Security.ISecurityEncodable*, and *System.Security.ISecurityPolicyEncodable*. The most important method to override is *IMembershipCondition.Check*, which accepts an evidence object and returns a Boolean value that identifies whether the specified evidence satisfies the membership condition. You will also need to implement the *ToXml* and *FromXml* methods (from the *ISecurityEncodable* and *ISecurityPolicyEncodable* interfaces) to enable your membership condition to be imported into the .NET Framework Configuration tool. Finally, implement the obligatory *Copy* method.

To add your membership condition to a code group with the .NET Framework Configuration tool, first call your permission's *ToXml* method, and save the results to a file. Then, simply click the Import button on the Choose A Condition Type page of the Create Code Group Wizard, and import your XML file.

How to Create a Custom Permission

The .NET Framework includes a large number of permissions that will meet the needs of almost all developers. You can, however, create your own permission classes, and use those permissions to restrict access to custom resources that cannot be restricted using the standard permission classes.

For example, you could create a custom permission class to enable developers to restrict code's access to individual tables within your application's database. This custom permission could use flags to determine which tables code could access, and whether the code would be allowed to query, update, or manage the table. Developers creating solutions that use your database architecture could then use the permission to restrict access to third-party components, enabling the developer to leverage the components without worrying about the components updating or managing the data unless those permissions were specifically granted.

To create a custom permission, create a new assembly and specify the assembly attribute: [assembly:AllowPartiallyTrustedCallers]. As discussed in Lesson 4, this attribute enables code that is not fully trusted to use a strong-name class. Later, you must add your assembly to the Global Assembly Cache (GAC), which requires a strong name. You can sign an assembly with a strong name using the Strong Name tool (Sn.exe). Because you should avoid requiring code to be fully trusted to take advantage of your assembly, you should specify the *AllowPartiallyTrustedCallers* attribute unless you specifically plan to require all assemblies that use your class to be fully trusted.

See Also For more information about the *AllowPartiallyTrustedCallers* attribute, see Lesson 4 in this chapter.

Next, create a class that implements the *IPermission* interface. The simplest way to implement *IPermission* is to inherit from *CodeAccessPermission*. Additionally, you might want to implement the *IUnrestrictedPermission* interface, which allows more granular permission settings within the class and easily enables all settings.

Note Almost all permissions built into the .NET Framework implement *IUnrestrictedPermission*.

Then, override the constructor and the following members in your new class:

- **Copy**   Creates and returns an identical copy of the current permission object.

- **FromXml**   Reconstructs a security object with a specified state from an XML encoding.

- **Intersect**   Creates and returns a permission that is the intersection of the current permission and the specified permission. In other words, this method returns the most restrictive set of permissions that both the current and specified permission contain. This method is similar to a Boolean And operation.

- **IsSubsetOf**   Determines whether the current permission is a subset of the specified permission.

- **ToXml**   Creates an XML encoding of the security object and its current state.

- **Union**   Creates and returns a permission that is the union of the current permission and the specified permission. In other words, this method returns the least restrictive set of permissions that either the current or specified permission contains. This method is similar to a Boolean Or operation.

- **IsUnrestricted (if implementing *IUnrestrictedPermission*)**   Returns a value indicating whether unrestricted access to the resource is allowed.

> **Important**   You should not implement custom CAS permissions if you want to restrict what users can do. Instead, create a custom authentication method, as discussed in Lesson 4 of Chapter 5.

This is all you need to do to enable your permission to be used imperatively. However, if you want to create a permission that can be used declaratively, create a second class with *Attribute* appended to the name. Inherit this second class from *CodeAccessSecurityAttribute*, and implement the self-explanatory *CreatePermission* member. Also, add any properties required to specify your custom permissions on a more granular level.

Finally, you need to make the .NET Framework aware of your new permission. First, ensure the assembly is strong-named. Then, add your assembly to the GAC using the .NET Framework Configuration tool. Next, use the .NET Framework Configuration tool to grant the assembly full trust.

Now you can use the custom permission in any way you use the standard .NET Framework permissions. To add your permission to a permission set with the .NET Framework Configuration tool, first call your permission's *ToXml* method and save the results to a file. Then, simply click the Import button on the Assign Individual Permissions to a Permission Set page of the Create Permission Set Wizard, and import your XML file.

Practice: Customizing Code Access Security

In this practice, you write an application that creates custom application domains to launch assemblies with restricted permissions. Read the scenario and then complete the exercise that follows. If you are unable to answer a question, review the lessons and try the question again. You can find answers to the questions in the "Questions and Answers" section at the end of this chapter.

Scenario

You are a developer for Baldwin Museum of Science. Your end users run your application from a variety of different locations. Because the .NET Framework runtime assigns different permission sets based on the assembly's location, your assembly is often running in a partially trusted environment. This has caused problems for your end users. Your manager asks you to interview key company personnel and to then come to her office to answer some questions. Your manager needs you to create an application that creates an application domain and launches an assembly in the new application domain using Internet zone permissions to enable more realistic testing procedures.

Interviews Following is a list of company personnel interviewed and their statements:

- **Customer Support Manager** "We're getting a lot of calls from customers who want to deploy our app from a Web server. It seems like this doesn't work for some reason, though. Users end up getting different errors. From the way they describe the errors, it seems like the application crashes at different times depending on whether the application is launched from the public Internet or the user's local intranet. Right now we just tell them to copy it to their local computer and run it, and that seems to solve the problem. The IT guys don't like this workaround, though, and want to know why we can't make it work from a Web server."

- **Development Manager** "I talked to the Customer Support Manager, and it sounds like users are having problems because of code access security restrictions. We need to start testing our application in different zones so that we can identify problems when permissions are restricted. Do me a favor and write an application that allows our Quality Assurance team to run our application in different zones."

Exercise

Respond to the following statements from your manager.

1. At a high level, describe how you would create the application.

2. I asked you to create an application that creates an application domain and launches the CASDemands assembly in the new application domain using Internet zone permissions. Show me your work.

Lesson Summary

- Application domains are logical containers that allow multiple assemblies to run within a single process while preventing them from directly accessing another assembly's memory. They isolate assemblies within a process.

- To use an application domain to launch assemblies with limited permissions, you create application domains and specify the evidence assigned to assemblies, which in turn allows you to control the assembly's permissions.

- To customize CAS, create custom evidence, membership conditions, and permissions by implementing interfaces included with the .NET Framework.

Lab: Implementing Code Access Security

In this lab, you identify how CAS can reduce the risks of exposing internal functionality to external users. Read the scenario and then complete the exercise that follows. If you are unable to answer a question, review the lessons and try the question again. You can find answers to the questions in the "Questions and Answers" section at the end of this chapter.

Scenario

You are an application developer for City Power & Light. You and your co-workers have been creating applications for internal use using the .NET Framework since Microsoft first made it available. However, you have never made use of CAS. Now, requests from people within your organization could expose your internal application to attacks from the outside. CAS might be able to limit your risk. Your manager asks you to interview key people and then come to his office to answer his questions about CAS.

Interviews

Following is a list of company personnel interviewed and their statements:

- **Development Manager**   "The people in charge of customer and partner relations are begging us to let outsiders access your app's functionality. I know that it can be done with Web services, but I'm concerned about security. Sure, nothing should be able to happen by letting someone query for a number or submit an electronic request, but you never know. I'd like some assurance that someone submitting a request for current pricing will not be able to gain elevated privileges, or write a virus to the disk of our application server, etcetera."

- **IT Manager**   "Today, we're doing nothing with code access security. I know it's there, but it's pretty much left at the default settings. If you want us to adjust this, just let us know."

- **Director of Customer Relations**   "Several of our high-usage customers want access to functionality within our internal applications. I'm not a developer, but after meeting with the customers, I think the consensus is that they want to use Web services to query our internal applications for current pricing and availability of high-capacity power. I want them to be able to do that, but I'm more than a little scared about exposing our applications to the Internet."

- **Partner Relationship Manager**   "We work closely with other power companies to exchange capacity as needs shift. Today, that's a manual process involving a phone call, negotiations, and one of our employees clicking some buttons in your application. We could realize a great deal of efficiency if we could automate this with Web services. After talking about it with your manager, I know it can be done, but I also know he's concerned that someone could misuse our application to take over our systems or some such nonsense."

- **End User**   "Whatever you do, don't make me learn any new passwords."

Exercise

Answer the following questions for your manager.

1. How can you expose internal methods to partners and customers while virtually eliminating the possibility that they could be misused to read or write to the file system?

2. What class would you use to restrict your application's access to the file system?

3. What is the best way for the IT Manager to configure CAS permissions for all computers in your Active Directory?

4. How will end users be affected by implementing CAS security?

Chapter Summary

- CAS controls managed code's access similarly to the way that operating system security restricts a user's access to system resources.

- You can configure CAS by using either the .NET Framework Configuration tool or the Caspol command-line tool.

- Assembly permission requests enable administrators to view the permission requirements of an assembly. They can also dramatically reduce the likelihood of an assembly being abused by ensuring the assembly cannot access any system resources that it does not require.

- You can control CAS permissions within an assembly either imperatively or declaratively, allowing more granular control than can be accomplished with assembly declarations. This further increases the application's security.

- You can create application domains to carefully control the evidence and permissions assigned when launching new assemblies. Even though the .NET Framework provides a great deal of flexibility for implementing CAS, you can customize and extend each element of CAS to meet your specific needs.

Exam Highlights

Before taking the exam, review the key points and terms that are presented in this chapter. You need to know this information.

Key Points

- How security policy determines which permissions to assign to an assembly.

- How to manage security policy.

- How to control permissions both imperatively and declaratively.

- List the techniques that are available for controlling permissions, and the circumstances in which each is appropriate to use.

- How and why to create application domains.

Key Terms

application domain   A logical container that allows multiple assemblies to run within a single process while preventing them from directly accessing another assembly's memory

assembly evidence   Evidence that an assembly presents that describes the assembly's identity, such as the hash, the publisher, or the strong name

code access security (CAS)   A security system that allows administrators and developers to authorize applications, similar to the way they have always been able to authorize users

code group   Authorization device that associates assemblies with permission sets

evidence   The way an assembly is identified, such as the location where the assembly is stored, a hash of the assembly's code, or the assembly's signature

fully trusted   An assembly that is exempt from CAS permission checks

host evidence   Evidence that an assembly's host presents describing the assembly's origin, such as the application directory, URL, or site

partially trusted code   An assembly that must undergo CAS permission checks each time it accesses a protected resource

permission   A CAS access control entry

permission set   A CAS access control list consisting of multiple permissions

security policy   A logical grouping of code groups, permission sets, and custom policy assemblies

Questions and Answers

Practice: Explaining Code Access Security

Page
6-15
Exercise

1. Can .NET Framework CAS prevent viruses from spreading? Why or why not?

    No. As long as operating systems allow unmanaged code to run, viruses can bypass CAS simply by not leveraging the .NET Framework. Unmanaged code is exempt from CAS permission checks.

2. Will installing the .NET Framework on my computer improve the security? If not, what will it accomplish?

    No. It will, however, let you run applications that use the .NET Framework.

3. Could a .NET Framework–based virus running in the Internet zone, with the default CAS permissions, effectively replicate itself across our network? Why or why not?

    No, a virus based on the .NET Framework would be restricted by the Internet permission set, which restricts assemblies from communicating across the network except to contact the site from which the assembly originated.

4. Could a malicious .NET Framework–based assembly running in the Intranet zone, with the default CAS permissions, delete files on your hard drive? Why or why not?

    No. The Intranet zone does not allow assemblies to directly access the file system. The most the assembly could do is prompt you to open or save files.

Practice: Configuring Code Access Security

Page
6-29
Exercise 1: Compiling and Testing the Permissions of a Sample Assembly

6. Open a command prompt, and run the command `C:\ListPermissions.exe`. ListPermissions runs and displays several common permissions, and whether the assembly currently has that permission. Notice that you have all the listed permissions. Press ENTER.

    a. Why does the assembly have all the permissions?

        The assembly is currently running in the My_Computer_Zone because you launched it from the C drive. By default, that zone uses the FullTrust permission set.

7. Run the command \\127.0.0.1\c$\ListPermissions.exe. Notice that you are now missing several permissions, in particular, IsolatedStorageFilePermission is missing. Press ENTER.

a. Why is the assembly now missing permissions, and what code group determined the permissions?

The assembly is now being run from a shared folder. Therefore, it is running from the Internet zone. Because the IP address being used is the special loopback address, it is part of the Internet_Same_Site_Access code group.

Page 6-30

Exercise 2: Creating a Code Group and Permission Set with the .NET Framework Configuration Tool

10. Open a command prompt, and run the command \\127.0.0.1\c$\ListPermissions.exe. Notice that ListPermission now has the *IsolatedStorageFilePermission*. Press ENTER.

a. Why does the assembly now have *IsolatedStorageFilePermission*?

The assembly is currently running in both the Local_Shared_Folder code group and the Internet_Same_Site_Access code group. The permissions in the *GenerousPermissions* permission set have been added to the previously existing permissions.

Practice: Using Assembly Permission Requests

Page 6-41

Exercise 1: Anticipating Declarative Permission Request Results

1. An administrator runs the following console application with the Everything permission set.

```csharp
using System;
using System.Security.Permissions;
using System.IO;
using System.IO.IsolatedStorage;
using System.Drawing.Printing;

[assembly:PrintingPermission(SecurityAction.RequestMinimum)]
[assembly:FileIOPermissionAttribute(SecurityAction.RequestOptional, ⮑
Read=@"C:\")]
[assembly:FileIOPermissionAttribute(SecurityAction.RequestRefuse, ⮑
Read=@"C:\Windows\")]

namespace DeclarativeExample
{
    class Class1
    {
        [STAThread]
        static void Main(string[] args)
        {
            Console.WriteLine("Reading one line of the boot.ini file:");
            StreamReader sw = new StreamReader(@"C:\boot.ini");
            Console.WriteLine("First line of boot.ini: " + sw.ReadLine());
        }
    }
}
```

```
Imports System.Security.Permissions
Imports System.IO
Imports System.IO.IsolatedStorage
Imports System.Drawing.Printing

<Assembly: PrintingPermission(SecurityAction.RequestMinimum)>
<Assembly: FileIOPermissionAttribute(SecurityAction.RequestOptional, ⟶
Read := "C:\")>
<Assembly: FileIOPermissionAttribute(SecurityAction.RequestRefuse, ⟶
Read := "C:\Windows\")>

Module Module1
    Sub Main(ByVal args As String())
        Console.WriteLine("Reading one line of the boot.ini file:")
        Dim sw As StreamReader = New StreamReader ("C:\boot.ini")
        Console.WriteLine("First line of boot.ini: " + sw.ReadLine)
    End Sub
End Module
```

What will the output from the application be?

The declarative permissions will not stop the assembly from reading the first line of the C:\boot.ini file. Therefore, the output will be:

```
Reading one line of the boot.ini file:
First line of boot.ini: [boot loader]
```

2. The developer changes the assembly CAS declarations as follows:

```
[assembly:PrintingPermission(SecurityAction.RequestMinimum)]
[assembly:FileIOPermissionAttribute(SecurityAction.RequestOptional, ⟶
Read=@"C:\Temp\")]
[assembly:FileIOPermissionAttribute(SecurityAction.RequestRefuse, ⟶
Read=@"C:\Windows\")]
```

```
<Assembly: PrintingPermission(SecurityAction.RequestMinimum)>
<Assembly: FileIOPermissionAttribute(SecurityAction.RequestOptional, ⟶
Read := "C:\Temp\")>
<Assembly: FileIOPermissionAttribute(SecurityAction.RequestRefuse, ⟶
Read := "C:\Windows\")>
```

What will the output of the application now be? Why?

This time, the *Security.Action.RequestOptional* request has changed. Instead of requesting access to the entire C drive, the assembly requests access only to the C:\Temp\ folder. Because this type of request causes the runtime to deny access to every resource that was not specifically requested, the runtime will throw an exception when the assembly attempts to read the C:\boot.ini file. Therefore, the output will be the following (simplified for brevity):

```
Reading one line of the boot.ini file:

Unhandled Exception: System.Security.SecurityException: Request for the permission
 of type System.Security.Permissions.FileIOPermission, mscorlib, Version=1.0.5000.
0, Culture=neutral, PublicKeyToken=b77a5c561934e089 failed.
```

3. The developer makes a couple more changes to the assembly CAS declarations as follows:

```
[assembly:PrintingPermission(SecurityAction.RequestMinimum)]
[assembly:FileIOPermissionAttribute(SecurityAction.RequestMinimum, →
Read=@"C:\Temp\")]
[assembly:FileIOPermissionAttribute(SecurityAction.RequestRefuse, →
Read=@"C:\Windows\")]
```

```
<Assembly: PrintingPermission(SecurityAction.RequestMinimum)>
<Assembly: FileIOPermissionAttribute(SecurityAction.RequestMinimum, →
Read := "C:\Temp\")>
<Assembly: FileIOPermissionAttribute(SecurityAction.RequestRefuse, →
Read := "C:\Windows\")>
```

What will the output of the application now be? Why?

This time, there are no *SecurityAction.RequestOptional* requests. Therefore, the only permissions denied to the assembly are those listed with *SecurityAction.RequestRefuse*. The application will run to completion, and the output will be:

```
Reading one line of the boot.ini file:
First line of boot.ini: [boot loader]
```

Practice: Protecting Methods with Code Access Security Demands

Page
6-60

Exercise 1: Experimenting with the Default Permission Set

5. In the Code Access Security application, click the Create File With No Demand button, and then answer the following questions:

    a. What zone is the assembly running in?

    The assembly is using the My_Computer_Zone because it is being run from the computer's local file system.

    b. What permission set did the .NET Framework runtime grant the assembly?

    By default, the My_Computer_Zone grants assemblies the FullTrust permission set.

    c. What type of exception was thrown, and why was that particular type of exception thrown?

    The .NET Framework threw a *System.UnauthorizedAccessException* because the user, StandardUser, did not have access to create new files within the C:\Documents and Settings\Administrator\ folder.

6. In the Code Access Security application, click the Create File With Declarative Demand button, and then answer the following questions.

a. What type of exception was thrown, and why was that particular type of exception thrown?

The .NET Framework threw a *System.UnauthorizedAccessException* because the user, StandardUser, did not have access to create new files within the C:\Documents and Settings\Administrator\ folder.

b. Notice that the error message reads Failed When Attempting To Create The File, and not Failed Before Attempting To Create The File. Use Visual Studio .NET to examine the *declarativeDemandButton_Click* method. This method calls the *declarativeCreateFile* method, which requires write access to a file that the user lacks permission to create. Why was the exception thrown within the *createFile* method, and not thrown when the declarative security demand was processed before the *declarativeCreateFile* method was run?

Declarative code access security demands will cause an exception to be thrown when the *code* itself lacks the required permission. In this case, the *user* lacks the required permission, but the code does have CAS permissions to create the file. Therefore, the declarative security demand is successful, but the more restricted role-based security requirement enforced by the operating system causes the .NET Framework runtime to throw an exception when the application attempts to create the file itself in the *createFile* method.

7. In the Code Access Security application, click the Create File With Imperative Demand button, and then answer the following questions:

a. What type of exception was thrown, and why was that particular type of exception thrown?

The .NET Framework threw a *System.UnauthorizedAccessException*, just like it did for the other buttons, because CAS is not being taken into account because the assembly is running with the FullTrust permission set.

Page
6-63
Exercise 3: Experimenting with the Default Permission Set

4. In the CASDemand application, click the Create File With No Demand button, and then answer the following questions.

a. What zone is the assembly running in?

The assembly is using the My_Computer_Zone because it is being run from the computer's local file system.

b. What permission set did the .NET Framework runtime grant the assembly?

Because you used the Administrator account to modify the default configuration, the My_Computer_Zone will grant the Internet permission set to the assembly.

    c. What type of exception was thrown, and why was that particular type of exception thrown?

> The .NET Framework threw a *System.Security.SecurityException* because the application, running in the Internet zone, did not have CAS permissions to use the file system.

5. In the CASDemand application, click the Create File With Declarative Demand button, and then answer the following questions:

    a. What type of exception was thrown, and why was that particular type of exception thrown?

> The .NET Framework threw a *System.Security.SecurityException* for the same reasons it threw the exception when you clicked the Create File With No Demand button.

    b. In which method was the exception caught?

> The Failed Before Attempting To Create File error message indicates that exception was caught in the *declarativeDemandButton_Click* method, because the exception was thrown when the declarative demand associated with the *declarativeCreateFile* method was processed. The .NET Framework runtime never ran the *createFile* method, because it was prevented by the security demand.

6. In the CASDemand application, click the Create File With Imperative Demand button, and then answer the following questions:

    a. What type of exception was thrown, and what method caught the exception?

> As with the declarative security demand, the *System.Security.SecurityException* was caught before it reached the *createFile* method. In this case, the exception was caught in the *imperativeDemandButton_Click* method.

Page
6-64

Exercise 4: Granting Access to Partially Trusted Code

12. Open a command prompt without administrative privileges. At the command prompt, issue the following command:

```
\\127.0.0.1\untrusted\PartiallyTrustedAssembly
```

    a. PartiallyTrustedAssembly attempts to write to a file. Did it succeed?

> No, it failed and reported a *SecurityException* because a request for *FileIOPermission* failed.

    b. Examine the source code, and explain the behavior.

> PartiallyTrustedAssembly calls the *TrustedClass.Distrust.WriteToFile* method. This method uses the .NET Framework's *StreamWriter* object, which contains a demand for *FileIOPermission*. Once the *StreamWriter* object issues the demand, the runtime checks each caller for the CAS permission. Because PartiallyTrustedAssembly lacks the permission, the runtime throws a *SecurityException*.

13. Add a method to *TrustedClass.Distrust* named *WriteToFileWrapper* that uses *Assert* to block the *FileIOPermission* demand, and then rebuild the assembly. Modify the PartiallyTrustedAssembly source code to call *WriteToFileWrapper* instead of *WriteToFile.*

   a. What code did you write to create the assembly?

   The exact code will vary, but it should resemble the following:

```csharp
public static void WriteToFileWrapper(string fileName, string contents)
{
    // Assert permission to allow caller to bypass security check
    FileIOPermission newFilePermission = new ➔
FileIOPermission(FileIOPermissionAccess.Write, fileName);
    newFilePermission.Assert();
    try
    {
        WriteToFile(fileName, contents);
    }
    finally
    {
        // Clean up the assertion
        CodeAccessPermission.RevertAssert();
    }
}
```

```vb
Public Shared Sub WriteToFileWrapper(ByVal fileName As String, ByVal contents ➔
As String)
    'Assert permission to allow caller to bypass security check
    Dim newFilePermission As FileIOPermission = New ➔
FileIOPermission(FileIOPermissionAccess.Write, fileName)
    newFilePermission.Assert()
    Try
        WriteToFile(fileName, contents)
    Finally
        ' Clean up the assertion
        CodeAccessPermission.RevertAssert()
    End Try
End Sub
```

14. At the command prompt, issue the following command:

```
\\127.0.0.1\Untrusted\PartiallyTrustedAssembly
```

   a. PartiallyTrustedAssembly attempts to write to a file. Did it succeed? Why or why not?

   No, it failed and reported a *SecurityException* because a request for *SecurityPermission* failed. The new method attempts to use an *Assert*, which is a security permission it lacks because of the permission set assigned to *TrustedClass*.

19. At the command prompt, issue the following command:

```
\\127.0.0.1\Untrusted\PartiallyTrustedAssembly
```

a. PartiallyTrustedAssembly attempts to write to a file. Did it succeed? Why or why not?

Yes, it succeeded, because the *WriteToFileWrapper* method includes an *Assert* that blocks the *StreamWriter*'s inherent *Demand* from checking the permissions of PartiallyTrustedAssembly. Additionally, *TrustedClass* has sufficient trust to use the *Assert*.

Practice: Customizing Code Access Security

Page
6-80

Exercise

1. At a high level, describe how you would create the application.

You should create an application that prompts the user to select a zone and an assembly. Based on their selections, you should launch the assembly in an application domain with evidence that would cause it to be assigned to the code group corresponding to the selected zone.

2. I asked you to create an application that creates an application domain and launches the CASDemands assembly in the new application domain using Internet zone permissions. Show me your work.

Although several techniques would work, the simplest way to do this is to assign Internet zone evidence to the assembly, as the following code demonstrates:

```
Using System.Security;
Using System.Security.Policy;
…
object [] hostEvidence = {new Zone(SecurityZone.Internet)};
Evidence internetEvidence = new Evidence(hostEvidence, null);

AppDomain myDomain = AppDomain.CreateDomain("QADomain");
myDomain.ExecuteAssembly(@"C:\path\CASDemands.exe", internetEvidence);
```

```
Imports System.Security
Imports System.Security.Policy
…
Dim hostEvidence As Object() = {New Zone (SecurityZone.Internet)}
Dim internetEvidence As Evidence = New Evidence (hostEvidence, Nothing)
Dim myDomain As AppDomain = AppDomain.CreateDomain("QADomain")
myDomain.ExecuteAssembly("C:\path\CASDemands.exe", internetEvidence)
```

When the CASDemand application runs, the runtime should warn you that the application is running in a partially trusted context. If you do not receive this warning, you have not successfully restricted the assembly's permissions.

Lab: Implementing Code Access Security

Page
6-82

Exercise

1. How can you expose internal methods to partners and customers while virtually eliminating the possibility that they could be misused to read or write to the file system?

    You can build CAS functionality into your application to limit the permissions available and specifically restrict access to the file system. Use assembly declarations to limit the permissions your assembly receives to the bare minimum. Protect methods using method declarations. Finally, you can use imperative CAS security to control permissions within a method. If a method does need to write to the file system, you can ensure that the window of opportunity is as small as possible.

2. What class would you use to restrict your application's access to the file system?

    You would use *FileIOPermission*.

3. What is the best way for the IT Manager to configure CAS permissions for all computers in your Active Directory?

    The IT Manager can use the Enterprise security policy to configure CAS permissions.

4. How will end users be affected by implementing CAS security?

    They shouldn't be negatively affected at all.

7 Maximizing Security During Deployment

Why This Chapter Matters

One of the most overlooked application vulnerabilities is also one of the simplest for attackers with development skills to exploit: the potential replacement of legitimate application components. By default, managed assemblies identify each other by a filename and nothing more. Any attacker who can modify the name of an assembly can change your application's flow, and even force the application to run malicious code.

Fortunately, the Microsoft .NET Framework provides strong names to make it more difficult for an attacker to impersonate a legitimate assembly. Strong names identify an assembly by using several different factors, including a private key that only the original developer should have access to. If an attacker replaces or modifies a strong-named assembly, the .NET Framework runtime detects the modification and throws an exception before any malicious code is run. Lesson 1 in this chapter describes how to add strong names to your applications, and Lesson 2 teaches you how to effectively deploy strong-named assemblies in the global assembly cache.

Exam Objectives in this Chapter:

■ Release applications in a manner that minimizes security risks.

    ❑ Evaluate when to sign an assembly.

    ❑ Implement delayed signing.

    ❑ Create a strong-named assembly.

    ❑ Configure security settings by using the .NET Framework Configuration tool and the Code Access Security Policy tool at deployment.

Lessons in this Chapter:

Before You Begin

To complete the practices, examples, and lab exercises in this chapter, you must have one computer running Microsoft Windows Server 2003. During the course of performing the exercises in this chapter, the computer's security can be reduced. Therefore, the computer should not be a production computer and should not be connected to any network, especially the Internet, even if a firewall is present. Install Microsoft Visual Studio .NET 2003 using the default settings.

Lesson 1: Signing Assemblies with Strong Names

Strong names can greatly reduce the opportunity that attackers have to replace your assemblies with malicious software. However, assemblies are not signed with strong names by default. This lesson provides background about the purpose of strong names and how you can use them to add security to your applications.

After this lesson, you will be able to

- Explain the purpose of strong names.
- Explain the purpose of the Strong Name tool (Sn.exe).
- Explain the process of signing assemblies.
- Describe the purpose of delayed signing, including the security benefits of using delayed signing and how the process of delayed signing differs from the standard process used to sign assemblies.
- Use code access security to control permissions to assemblies and methods based on a caller's strong name properties.

Estimated lesson time: 30 minutes

What Is a Strong Name?

A *strong name* is a reliable assembly identifier that reduces the possibility of an attacker modifying or impersonating an assembly. The strong name consists of the assembly's simple text name, version number, and culture, plus a public key and a digital signature. The public key and digital signature components of the strong name are generated by the Strong Name tool (Sn.exe).

See Also   For more information about private/public key pairs and public key cryptography, see Chapter 8, "Protecting Data by Using Cryptography."

When you reference a strong-named assembly, you greatly reduce the risk of an attacker impersonating that assembly to change your application's behavior. An assembly's references include a token that represents the public key of any referenced assemblies that had strong names at the time the developer first referenced them. This *token* is a portion of the full public key, and to save space, the token is stored instead of the much longer public key.

When one assembly calls a strong-named assembly, the runtime compares the key stored in the referencing assembly's manifest with the key used to generate the strong name for the referenced assembly. If the .NET Framework security checks pass and the bind succeeds, the referencing assembly has a guarantee that the referenced assembly's bits have not been tampered with and that these bits actually come from the developers of the referenced assembly.

> **Important**   Assemblies can carry full Authenticode signatures in addition to a strong name. Authenticode signatures include a certificate from a certification authority, which can be used to establish trust. Strong-named assemblies, however, do not require code to be signed in this way. In fact, the keys used to generate the strong name signature do not have to be the same keys used to generate an Authenticode signature.

The Purpose of Signing an Assembly with a Strong Name

As mentioned earlier, you sign an assembly with a strong name to reduce the likelihood that an attacker will modify or impersonate your assembly to trick an application into calling malicious code. When you add a reference to a strong-named class assembly, the .NET Framework runtime checks the class's strong name at runtime. If the class assembly was modified or replaced after you added the reference, the .NET Framework throws an exception.

Similarly, you can use code access security (CAS) to ensure only strong-named assemblies can call a class that you create. You can restrict callers to assemblies signed with a particular strong name key, assemblies with specific version numbers, or assemblies with an exact name. Combined with CAS, strong names can ensure that only other officially approved assemblies generated by trusted members of your organization can call your classes.

When you use strong names, users installing updates to your assembly can rest assured that the updates were created by the same developers who created the original assembly. Although strong names do not prove the developer's identity or organization, they do prove that two versions of an assembly were signed with the same key pair. Because only you have that key pair, an attacker cannot release an update to your application.

Another reason to use strong names is that only assemblies with strong names can be loaded into the global assembly cache (GAC). The *global assembly cache* is a container that the .NET Framework uses to store class libraries that can be accessed from other managed assemblies. After an assembly is loaded into the GAC, other assemblies reference it by using the strong name rather than by referencing the file's location on the hard disk.

This is different from the typical model of storing class assemblies in the same directory that each calling assembly is stored. Storing class assemblies in the same directory as each calling assembly allows the application to be installed by simply copying the files, but each application that calls a class assembly must store a separate copy of the assembly. If the developer releases an update to the assembly, administrators must seek out and replace every copy of the assembly. Adding a shared assembly to the GAC makes it easier for systems administrators to manage shared assemblies, because the GAC stores a single copy of the shared class assembly that can be accessed by any assembly that references the class using the assembly's strong name.

Changes Caused by Strong Naming

By default, strong-named assemblies cannot call nor be called by assemblies without strong names. When you reference a strong-named assembly, you expect to get certain benefits, such as versioning and naming protection. If you reference a strong-named assembly that then references an assembly without a strong name, an attacker can simply replace the assembly without the strong name to change your application's behavior. Therefore, the runtime allows strong-named assemblies to reference only other strong-named assemblies.

Additionally, by default, strong-named assemblies can be called only by fully trusted assemblies. The runtime enforces this requirement because assemblies in the GAC are visible to potentially malicious, partially trusted assemblies, and therefore are likely to be targeted for abuse. If you plan to have a partially trusted assembly reference an assembly in the GAC, the shared assembly must have the *AllowPartiallyTrustedCallers* assembly attribute set. Before you add this attribute, however, carefully review the code to ensure there is minimal opportunity for abuse by a malicious application.

What Is the Strong Name Tool (Sn.exe)?

The Strong Name command-line tool (Sn.exe) generates keys for strong naming, manages those keys, and manually signs assemblies. You will use the Sn.exe tool to perform five common tasks:

- **Generate a key pair** Strong names are based on private/public key pairs. Though you can acquire a key in more complex ways, you can use the *-k* parameter to generate a new key pair.

- **Install a key into the CSP container** When you generate a new key pair, the key pair is stored in a file. A more secure location is the strong name cryptographic service provider (CSP). To copy a key pair from a file to a strong name CSP container, use the *-i* parameter. You can later delete the container with the *-d* parameter.

- **Extract a public key** Delayed signing, described later in this lesson, is a two-part signing process. The first part of this process requires the public key from the strong name key pair. You can use the *-e*, *-p*, *-tp*, and *-Tp* parameters to extract public keys from different sources.

- **Re-sign an assembly** The second part of the delayed signing process requires you to re-sign an assembly by using the *-R* or *-RC* parameters.

- **Verify an assembly** Use Sn with the *-v* parameter to verify that an assembly has a strong name.

> **Exam Tip** For the exam, make sure you are extremely comfortable using the Sn tool.

The complete list of parameters used by the Sn tool is shown in Table 7-1.

Table 7-1 Sn.exe Parameters

Parameter	Description
-c [csp]	Set the name of the CSP to use for strong name operations.
-d container	Delete key container named *container*.
-D assembly1 assembly2	Verify *assembly1* and *assembly2* differ only by signature.
-e assembly outfile	Extract public key from *assembly* into *outfil*.
-i infile container	Install key pair from *infile* into a key container named *container*.
-k outfile	Generate a new key pair and write it into *outfile*.
-m [y | n]	Enable *(-m y)*, disable *(-m n)*, or check *(-m)* to determine whether key containers are machine-specific rather than user-specific.
-o infile [outfile]	Convert public key in *infile* to text file *outfile* with comma-separated list of decimal byte values. If *outfile* is omitted, text is copied to Clipboard instead.
-p infile outfile	Extract public key from key pair in *infile* and export to *outfile*.
-pc container outfile	Extract public key from key pair in *container* and export to *outfile*.
-q	Quiet mode. This option must be first on the command line and will suppress any output other than error messages.
-R assembly infile	Re-sign signed or partially signed assembly with the key pair in *infile*.
-Rc assembly container	Re-sign signed or partially signed assembly with the key pair in the key container named *container*.
-t[p] infile	Display token for public key in *infile* (together with the public key itself if *-tp* is used).
-T[p] assembly	Display token for public key of *assembly* (together with the public key itself if *-Tp* is used).
-v[f] assembly	Verify *assembly* for strong name signature self-consistency. If *-vf* is specified, force verification even if disabled in the registry.
-Vl	List current settings for strong name verification on this machine.

Table 7-1   Sn.exe Parameters

Parameter	Description
-Vr assembly [userlist]	Register *assembly* for verification skipping (with an optional, comma-separated list of user names for which this will take effect). Verification skipping bypasses strong name validation. *Assembly* can be specified as *** to indicate all assemblies, or as **,publicKeyToken* to indicate all assemblies with the given public key token.
-Vu assembly	Unregister *assembly* for verification skipping. The same rules for *assembly* naming are followed as for *-Vr*.
-Vx	Remove all verification-skipping entries.
-?	Displays help text.

The remaining sections in this lesson provide detailed instructions for and examples of using Sn.

The Process of Signing Assemblies

To assign a strong name to an assembly, you perform these three steps:

1. Use the Sn tool to generate a key file, and optionally install it into a key container.

2. Add the *AssemblyCulture*, *AssemblyVersion*, and *AssemblyDelaySign* attributes and also either the *AssemblyKeyFile* or *AssemblyKeyName* attributes to the assembly.

3. Build the assembly.

The sections that follow describe each of these steps.

How to Generate a Key File

To generate a key file, open a command prompt and use the Sn tool with the *-k* option. For example, the following steps generate a key file with the name KeyFile.snk:

1. Open the Visual Studio .NET 2003 Command Prompt from the Visual Studio .NET Tools group.

2. Run the following command:

   ```
   sn -k KeyFile.snk
   ```

   The Sn tool generates a key file in the current folder.

Real World   Key Management Mistakes

If you're going to use public key security, you must *guard* the keys carefully. If an attacker gets your private key, you are in worse shape than if you hadn't used public key security in the first place, because you will assume that signed assemblies were signed by a trusted source.

Back when the Web was young, I was developing Perl CGIs for one of the first e-commerce sites. We decided we needed to implement some communications security, so we purchased and installed a key pair from a certification authority. Then, we left the key pair stored unprotected on the server's hard drive. Later, when I had a better grasp on the security implications, I was very embarrassed to learn that I had left the private key so poorly protected. If a sophisticated attacker had acquired the private key, he would have been able to impersonate our server and decrypt our communications.

You face similar risks managing strong name key pairs. If an attacker acquires your key pair, he could create assemblies and make them appear as if they had been signed by you. The attacker could then replace your assembly with his malicious assembly, and replace all or parts of your application's functionality with his own.

How to Install a Key File Into a Key Container

To install a key file into a key container, open a command prompt and use the Sn tool by using the *-i* option. For example, perform the following steps to install the key file with the name KeyFile.snk into the strong name CSP key container named CodeSigning:

1. Open the Visual Studio .NET 2003 Command Prompt from the Visual Studio .NET Tools group.

2. Run the following command:

   ```
   sn -i KeyFile.snk CodeSigning
   ```

   The Sn tool installs the key file in the CodeSigning key container. If you later need to delete the key and container, use the following command:

   ```
   sn -d CodeSigning
   ```

How to Add Strong Name Attributes to an Assembly

The Sn tool examines the assembly for several attributes that are used to generate the strong name. If you are using Microsoft Visual Studio .NET, specify the attributes in the AssemblyInfo.cs or AssemblyInfo.vb file. Visual Studio .NET automatically creates all these attributes for C# projects, but creates only *AssemblyVersion* for Visual Basic .NET projects (requiring you to add the other required attributes). These attributes are:

- **AssemblyCulture**   A value that defines which culture the assembly is intended to be used with. This is generally left blank to specify that the assembly is not culture-specific. The following example sets the value to "en-US" to specify that the assembly is US English-specific:

```
[assembly: AssemblyCulture("en-US")]
```

```
<Assembly: AssemblyCulture("en-US")>
```

- **AssemblyVersion**   The assembly version information, used to ensure strong names are version-specific. Version information consists of the following four values:

  - Major Version

  - Minor Version

  - Build Number

  - Revision

  You can, however, allow the compiler to specify the revision and build numbers by using the *. For example, you could manually specify the revision and build numbers by specifying the value "1.0.16.235", or you could automatically specify the numbers by setting the attribute to "1.0.*". The following sample illustrates the default value:

```
[assembly: AssemblyVersion("1.0.*")]
```

```
<Assembly: AssemblyVersion("1.0.*")>
```

- **AssemblyDelaySign**   Set to either true or false, this attribute determines whether delayed signing is used. The following sample illustrates setting this value to false (the default):

```
[assembly: AssemblyDelaySign(false)]
```

```
<Assembly: AssemblyDelaySign(False)>
```

- **AssemblyKeyFile**   Set to the relative path from the output directly to the key file. Set this attribute only if you are signing with a key file and not using the strong name CSP. For example, if your key file is located in your project directory and named KeyFile.snk, set this attribute to "..\..\KeyFile.snk" for projects built with the default output path of Visual Studio .NET, as the following code sample illustrates:

```
[assembly: AssemblyKeyFile(@"..\..\KeyFile.snk")]
```

```
<Assembly: AssemblyKeyFile("..\..\KeyFile.snk")>
```

You can also specify the absolute path, as the following code sample illustrates:

```
[assembly: AssemblyKeyFile(@"C:\Documents and →
Settings\StandardUser\KeyFile.snk")]
```

```
<Assembly: AssemblyKeyFile("C:\Documents and →
Settings\StandardUser\KeyFile.snk")>
```

> **Tip**   You must manage the strong name CSP with the Sn tool. You cannot use the Certificates snap-in.

- **AssemblyKeyName**   Set to the container and key name in your strong name CSP to which you have installed a key file. For example, if you installed a key file to the CodeSigning container, you would set this value to "CodeSigning", as the following sample illustrates:

```
[assembly: AssemblyKeyName("CodeSigning")]
```

```
<Assembly: AssemblyKeyName("CodeSigning")>
```

Combined, a simplified AssemblyInfo file for a strong-named assembly that used a key stored in the KeySigning CSP container, did not specify a culture, and did not use delayed signing, would resemble this:

```
using System.Reflection;
using System.Runtime.CompilerServices;

// Default attributes not related to strong naming
[assembly: AssemblyTitle("")]
[assembly: AssemblyDescription("")]
```

```
[assembly: AssemblyConfiguration("")]
[assembly: AssemblyCompany("")]
[assembly: AssemblyProduct("")]
[assembly: AssemblyCopyright("")]
[assembly: AssemblyTrademark("")]

// Attributes related to strong naming
[assembly: AssemblyVersion("1.0.*")]
[assembly: AssemblyDelaySign(false)]
[assembly: AssemblyKeyName("CodeSigning")]
[assembly: AssemblyCulture("")]
```

```
Imports System
Imports System.Reflection
Imports System.Runtime.InteropServices

' Default attributes not related to strong naming
<Assembly: AssemblyTitle("")>
<Assembly: AssemblyDescription("")>
<Assembly: AssemblyCompany("")>
<Assembly: AssemblyProduct("")>
<Assembly: AssemblyCopyright("")>
<Assembly: AssemblyTrademark("")>
<Assembly: CLSCompliant(True)>

' Attributes related to strong naming
<Assembly: AssemblyVersion("1.0.*")>
<Assembly: AssemblyDelaySign(False)>
<Assembly: AssemblyKeyName("CodeSigning")>
<Assembly: AssemblyCulture("")>
```

How to Verify that an Assembly Has a Strong Name

After you build an assembly with a strong name, use the Sn tool with the *-v* option to verify that the assembly does indeed have a strong name. The following demonstrates Sn's response when asked to verify an assembly that does not have a strong name:

```
C:\>sn -v "C:\NonSn_Assembly.dll"

Microsoft (R) .NET Framework Strong Name Utility Version 1.1.4322.573
Copyright (C) Microsoft Corporation 1998-2002. All rights reserved.

C:\NonSn_Aassembly.dll does not represent a strongly named assembly
```

And the following demonstrates an assembly with a strong name:

```
C:\>sn -v "C:\Sn_Assembly.dll"

Microsoft (R) .NET Framework Strong Name Utility  Version 1.1.4322.573
Copyright (C) Microsoft Corporation 1998-2002. All rights reserved.

Assembly 'C:\Sn_Assembly.dll' is valid
```

What Is Delayed Signing?

Delayed signing is a two-part strong name signing process that requires a central authority to sign assemblies and limits the distribution of your strong name private key. Limiting the distribution of the private key is extremely important, because the more people who can access the private key, the higher the risk of someone abusing it. The standard process for signing assemblies requires every developer to have access to the private key. In many organizations, this is an unacceptable risk.

The people most likely to abuse your private key are the people within your company. If you distribute your organization's strong name key pair to every developer, what happens when a developer becomes disgruntled and leaves the company? If that developer retained a copy of the key pair, he could create assemblies that impersonated your organization's strong-named assemblies. Combine the strong name key pair with the developer's deep knowledge of your application, and the developer is a formidable foe.

Strong name key pairs generated by the Sn tool do not rely on a robust public key infrastructure, and it is impossible to effectively revoke a strong name key pair that has been compromised. Therefore, you must make every effort to limit the number of individuals who have access to your strong name key pair. The best way to do this is to use delayed signing.

The Process of Delayed Signing

To assign a strong name to an assembly by using delayed signing, the following five steps must be performed:

1. The key manager uses the Sn tool to generate a key file, and optionally install it into a CSP key container.

2. The key manager extracts the public key and then distributes it to developers, who save the public key file to their computers or install it into a strong name CSP key container.

3. Developers add the *AssemblyCulture*, *AssemblyVersion*, and *AssemblyDelaySign* attributes, and also either the *AssemblyKeyFile* or *AssemblyKeyName* attributes to the assembly.

4. Developers build the assembly.

5. When an assembly is ready for publishing, developers send it to the key manager, who signs the assembly.

Figure 7-1 shows this process.

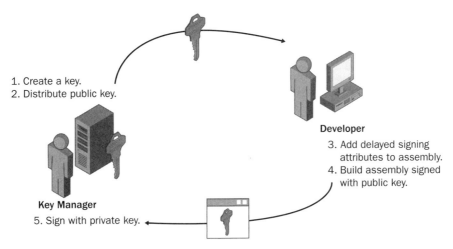

1. Create a key.
2. Distribute public key.

Developer

3. Add delayed signing attributes to assembly.
4. Build assembly signed with public key.

Key Manager
5. Sign with private key.

Figure 7-1   Delayed signing provides centralized key management.

How to Extract the Public Key from a Key Pair

Developers use a strong name public key to partially sign their code for testing purposes. To provide that public key to developers without providing the private key as well, the key manager must extract the public key from the key pair generated by the Sn tool. To extract the public key from the key pair stored in the CSP, issue the following command:

```
sn -pc Container PublicKeyFilename.snk
```

To extract the public key from the key pair file, issue the following command:

```
sn -p KeyPairFilename.snk PublicKeyFilename.snk
```

See Also   Exercise 1 in the practice at the end of this lesson includes an example of how to extract a public key.

After extracting the public key, developers should save the public key to their computers and specify the filename of the public key with the *AssemblyKeyFile* assembly attribute. When they build an assembly using only a public key, the assembly will be considered partially signed.

How to Re-Sign a Partially Signed Assembly

After a developer creates a partially signed assembly, the key manager must sign the assembly using a key pair generated by the Sn tool. This key pair must include both the private and public keys. To re-sign a partially signed assembly using a key pair file, issue the following command:

```
sn -R Assembly KeyPairFilename.snk
```

To re-sign a partially signed assembly using a key pair stored in the strong name CSP container, issue the following command:

```
sn -Rc Assembly Container
```

After re-signing, the assembly is officially strong named.

How to Use Strong Names with Code Access Security

As discussed in Chapter 6, "Implementing Code Access Security," CAS can be used to grant and restrict access to applications and methods. When you add strong names to assemblies, you can use the components of a strong name to control access and the privileges granted to code. In particular, this is useful for restricting access to assemblies published by your own organization and signed with your organization's strong name private key.

How to Restrict Access to Assemblies and Methods

One of the best ways to protect your code from misuse is to require callers to have strong names with a particular public key. You can use the *System.Security.Permissions.StrongNameIdentityPermission* class either imperatively or declaratively to require callers to have a specific name, public key, or versions. For example, the following code sample demonstrates a method that can be called only by strong-named callers signed with the private key corresponding to the specified public key:

```
using System;
using System.Security.Permissions;

[StrongNameIdentityPermission(SecurityAction.Demand, →
PublicKey="0024000004800000940000000602000000240000525341310004000001000105"+
"38a4a19382e9429cf516dcf1399facdccca092a06442efaf9ecaca33457be26ee0073c6bde5"+
"1fe0873666a62459581669b510ae1e84bef6bcb1aff7957237279d8b7e0e25b71ad39df3684"+
"5b7db60382c8eb73f289823578d33c09e48d0d2f90ed4541e1438008142ef714bfe604c41a4"+
"957a4f6e6ab36b9715ec57625904c6")]
public static void SecretAction()
{
    // Method logic
}
```

```
Imports System.Security.Permissions

<StrongNameIdentityPermission(SecurityAction.Demand, →
PublicKey:="0024000004800000940000000602000000240000525341310004000000100" +
"0100538a4a19382e9429cf516dcf1399facdccca092a06442efaf9ecaca33457be26ee0" +
"073c6bde51fe0873666a62459581669b510ae1e84bef6bcb1aff7957237279d8b7e0e25" +
"b71ad39df36845b7db60382c8eb73f289823578d33c09e48d0d2f90ed4541e143800814" +
"2ef714bfe604c41a4957a4f6e6ab36b9715ec57625904c6")>
Module Module1
    Sub Main()
        ' Method logic
    End Sub
End Module
```

Note that the public key property is passed to the *StrongNameIdentityPermission* object as a very long hexadecimal string. This is the public key itself, not the much shorter public key token. To identify this string from a strong name key pair file, run the following command:

```
sn -tp KeyPairFilename.snk
```

Alternatively, you can extract the public key from a signed assembly by running the following command:

```
sn -Tp AssemblyFilename
```

Note   Use a capital T option when extracting from an assembly.

Either way, Sn will display both the public key and the key token, as the following example demonstrates:

```
C:\>sn -tp KeyFile.snk

Microsoft (R) .NET Framework Strong Name Utility  Version 1.1.4322.573
Copyright (C) Microsoft Corporation 1998-2002. All rights reserved.

Public key is
070200000024000052534132000400000010001005f25f3c9c71de6b5d12a59794d803149f30c56
187ee199850638d1ff8996aa489660d8964a22209170aecf1efcd214c98f36b8cfc7ba61d684ca
b6a8578ef03715a519353f38e155e739019daac6cf2ed808abaad50b7f76168d01b798ce0913c0
c3dc7992486db65d272a9bae4f3f95e9f4a1a8482a8082053baa63b9d62efc41a80347e9192789
c2bd6f17674b3a5d98eb9f733ab8c2b8848aefaa699aeaaa762ee88b3b9943558e2f41751409f0
47a63377e32eff50641cdc0bb97b6bfffe9f654cca479b7777f9b2946a997e42142d3bc3cba608
057ef9b3a2ab0b5465d083432185e3424c031fe61acbe26c078d32a43656dede49d33bfbd22b30
962cfd41f963ee1d69cbe18cd2c7113334f6a2d75fc9d8520879d6a6166c4be9f57a0fdb0915f3
932737364f64326cca00903b7434e8372b731a71ccefcd4b6a1db2127dcf40535b854833264656
5251c557d449d8f289199ab0984cc5efabbd09371fbe74bbef9b19954d12d8aadc17f891679819
24247b97eb809a6ccfdaa95cc762b596c8df61709a47ddb078826fa1a5ff0f6c629b3acfe2bcb7
cd630f2b2b7505badeaec27eb91bf8457fd0548741ebc4df3585bbb9db9a75d7360a62586e2dc6
81a3d0af7d6c657413ce8ecea30254e074111c558bee8edae6c328df97b78c4c812b9d4bd36289
4300c62e13a468d6bef320333f5b4e903127bfe9a01609fe383dbe6a0c074eba80a380b23a36e8
541b23a26e22df24793224d012ac9ad2e8aa1324ff34679c43180eadff7d0befb597e7ba7db86b
7db5143ca2b9ca90f85b45

Public key token is d0cae9697a9a0030
```

See Also   For more information about code access security, see Chapter 6.

How to Create a Membership Condition for a Strong Name with the .NET Framework Configuration Tool

To use graphical tools to create a code group and membership condition that specify assemblies according to the strong name, perform the following steps:

1. Launch the .NET Framework Configuration tool as an administrator.

2. Expand Runtime Security Policy.

3. Expand Enterprise, Machine, or User, depending on the type of code group you want to add. Then, expand Code Groups.

4. Right-click All_Code, and then click New.

5. On the Identify A New Code Group page, provide a name and description, and then click Next.

6. On the Choose A Condition Type page, select Strong Name.

7. Click the Import button, and select an assembly signed with the strong name you want to use. Click Open.

   By default, the membership condition will apply to all assemblies with the same public key. Any assembly signed with the same private key will have a matching public key.

8. To restrict the membership condition to assemblies with a specific name, select the Name check box, and then type a name. To restrict the membership condition to a specific assembly version, select the Version check box and type a version number. Figure 7-2 shows a membership condition that applies to a single signed assembly of a specific version.

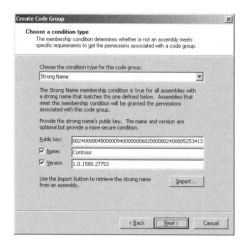

Figure 7-2 Code groups can use strong name properties as membership conditions.

How to Create a Membership Condition for a Strong Name Using Caspol

To use command-line tools to create a code group and membership condition that specify assemblies according to the strong name, use the following command:

```
caspol -addgroup Parent_Code_Group -strong -file File_Name {name | -
noname} {version | -noversion} Permission_Set -name "Group_Name"
```

For example, to add a code group named Strong_Named that matches assemblies signed with the public key of the C:\Assembly\MyApp.exe assembly and grants them Full Trust, run the following command:

```
caspol -addgroup All_Code -strong -file C:\Assembly\MyApp.exe -noname -
noversion FullTrust -name Strong_Named
```

When prompted, type **y** and press ENTER to confirm the addition.

Practice: Signing Assemblies with Strong Names

In this practice, you use delayed signing to sign an assembly, and then attempt to replace it with a malicious, unsigned assembly. Read the following scenario and then complete the exercises that follow. If you are unable to answer a question or complete a procedure, review the lesson and try the question again. You can find answers to the questions in the "Questions and Answers" section at the end of this chapter.

Scenario

You are a developer for Contoso, Inc., a firm that manages financial transactions between major banks. Recently, one of your customers raised concerns about the trustworthiness of your software. They want to be assured that one of your developers cannot act alone to change code in your internal software to redirect funds during a transfer. Your company's Chief Security Officer (CSO), Elena Velez Amezaga, has asked you to identify and demonstrate a method to require components to be approved by a central authority at your organization before they can be used in the production version of your application.

Interviews   Following is a list of company personnel interviewed and their statements:

- **Guido Pica, Customer IT Manager**   "By hiring your company, we are trusting you with our finances, and the finances of our customers. But I don't trust *you*; in fact, I don't trust any individual. I trust processes, and I trust security-in-depth. I want to know that collusion is required between multiple members of your staff before any malicious code can make it into your software. Show me that one rogue programmer can't insert code into your internal application to steal our funds, and I'll sleep better at night."

- **Elena Velez Amezaga, CSO**   "Guido has a good point. We are being irresponsible, and arguably negligent, by allowing developers to publish their own code without requiring approval. What assurance can you give that we will use only code that has been approved?"

- **Cigdem Akin, Development Manager**   "Given the requirements we're seeing from our customers and the CSO, I'd like to approve any assemblies before they get published. Do me a favor, and show me how such a system would work, and demonstrate an attempted attack by inserting an assembly that hasn't been approved."

- **Nancy Anderson, Developer**   "I don't know why they don't trust us. It's not like I have a criminal record or anything."

Technical Requirements   Identify a method to ensure that only assemblies that have been approved by the development manager can be used in your internal application. Demonstrate the use to the manager, and then demonstrate how a potential attacker could attempt to insert an unapproved assembly and then fail.

Exercise 1: Generating Keys for Delayed Signing

In this exercise, you play the role of a key manager and generate a key pair to be used for delayed key signing.

1. Follow the instructions in Lesson 3, Exercise 1 of Chapter 4, "Taking Advantage of Platform Security," to create two user accounts named StandardUser and Key-Manager. The StandardUser account will represent a developer and should have development privileges, whereas the KeyManager account will represent the administrator responsible for managing keys, and needs only standard user privileges.

2. Log on to your computer as KeyManager.

3. Open the Visual Studio .NET 2003 Command Prompt by clicking Start, All Programs, Visual Studio .NET 2003, Visual Studio .NET Tools, and then Visual Studio .NET 2003 Command Prompt.

4. At the command prompt, generate a new key pair for strong naming by issuing the following command:

   ```
   sn -k Contoso.snk
   ```

5. Install the key pair into the CSP by issuing the following command:

   ```
   sn -i Contoso.snk Contoso
   ```

6. Delete the original key pair file to ensure it cannot be abused by issuing the following command:

   ```
   del Contoso.snk
   ```

7. Extract the public key from the key pair stored in the CSP by issuing the following command:

```
sn -pc Contoso ContosoPublicKey.snk
```

8. Copy the public key file to a location on the file system that is accessible to all users by running the following commands:

```
Mkdir C:\key
copy ContosoPublicKey.snk C:\key\
```

Exercise 2: Creating a Strong-Named Assembly Using Delayed Signing

In this exercise, you create an assembly that is signed with only a public key, and then you answer some questions about what you did.

> **Important**   To complete this exercise, you must have completed Exercise 1.

To Create an Assembly Signed with Only a Public Key

1. Log on to your computer as StandardUser.

2. Use Microsoft Visual Studio .NET to create a new class in either C# or Visual Basic .NET. Name the project Contoso.

3. Rename the default *Class1* class to **Math** and remove the default constructor. Add a single static function named **Add** that accepts two integers, adds them, and returns the result.

4. Add assembly attributes to your project so that the assembly will use delayed signing based on the C:\Key\ContosoPublicKey.snk file.

5. Build your assembly.

6. Use the Sn tool to view your assembly's public key token to verify that your assembly was created with a strong name using the public key.

7. Use the Sn tool to verify that the assembly is not yet strongly named.

8. Create a folder named C:\Assembly\, and copy your assembly to the folder so that the key manager can access the file.

Questions   Answer the following questions about the preceding procedure.

1. What attributes did you add to your assembly?

2. What command did you use to view the token of the public key in your assembly?

3. What command did you use to verify that your assembly does not yet have a strong name?

Exercise 3: Completing a Delayed Signing

In this exercise, you act as a key manager to sign an assembly that has been signed with only a public key.

> **Important**   To complete this exercise, you must have completed Exercises 1 and 2.

1. Log on to your computer as KeyManager.

2. Open the Visual Studio .NET 2003 Command Prompt by clicking Start, All Programs, Visual Studio .NET 2003, Visual Studio .NET Tools, and then Visual Studio .NET 2003 Command Prompt.

3. At the command prompt, copy the assembly to the C:\Key\ folder by issuing the following command:

   ```
   copy C:\Assembly\Contoso.dll C:\Key\
   ```

4. At the command prompt, re-sign the partially signed assembly by issuing the following command:

   ```
   sn -Rc C:\Key\Contoso.dll Contoso
   ```

5. Finally, verify that the assembly has a strong name by issuing the following command:

   ```
   sn -v C:\Key\Contoso.dll
   ```

Exercise 4: Referencing the Strong-Named Assembly

In this exercise, you create a project that references the strong-named assembly and then answer some questions about what you did.

> **Important**   To complete this exercise, you must have completed Exercises 1, 2, and 3.

To Create a Project that References a Strong-Named Assembly

1. Log on to your computer as StandardUser.

2. Use Microsoft Windows Explorer to copy C:\Key\Contoso.dll to C:\Assembly \Contoso.dll, overwriting the partially signed assembly with the strong-named assembly.

3. Use Microsoft Visual Studio .NET to create a new Windows Forms project in either C# or Visual Basic .NET. Name the project **Calculator**.

4. Add a reference to the strong-named assembly C:\Key\Contoso.dll by following these steps:

   a. Click the Project menu, and then click Add Reference.

   b. In the Add Reference dialog box, click the Browse button, select C:\Assembly \Contoso.dll, and then click Open.

   c. Click OK to return to Visual Studio .NET.

5. Add two text boxes, a label, and a button to the form. Users will use the text boxes to enter two integers. When the button is clicked, the two integers will be passed to the *Contoso.Math.Add* method, and the result will be displayed in the label. Figure 7-3 shows what your form should look like.

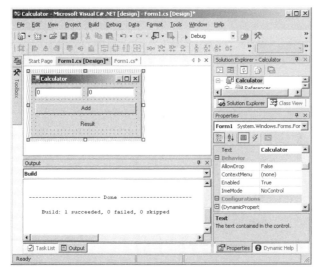

Figure 7-3   The Calculator application will reference a strong-named assembly.

6. Add a method to the button that passes the values in the two text boxes as integers to the *Contoso.Math.Add* method, and that displays the results using the label. Though the names you use for variables will vary, your code should resemble the following:

```csharp
private void addButton_Click(object sender, System.EventArgs e)
{
    int int1 = int.Parse(int1Textbox.Text);
    int int2 = int.Parse(int2Textbox.Text);
    int result = Contoso.Math.Add(int1, int2);
    resultsLabel.Text = result.ToString();
}
```

```vbnet
Private Sub addButton_Click(ByVal sender As Object, ByVal e As System.EventArgs)
    Dim int1 As Integer = Integer.Parse(int1Textbox.Text)
    Dim int2 As Integer = Integer.Parse(int2Textbox.Text)
    Dim result As Integer = Contoso.Math.Add(int1, int2)
    resultsLabel.Text = result.ToString
End Sub
```

7. Build, run, and test your application to verify that it works correctly. Afterward, close the Calculator application and Visual Studio .NET.

8. Use Visual Studio .NET to open the Contoso project you created in Exercise 2. Modify the project by performing the following steps:

   a. Comment out the *AssemblyKeyFile* attribute.

   b. Change the + operator in the *Add* method to a -, to demonstrate how an attacker could maliciously modify an assembly.

   c. Rebuild the assembly.

9. Use Windows Explorer to copy the new, unsigned Contoso.dll file to the directory you used to build the Calculator project. You should overwrite the existing Contoso.dll file, which has a strong name.

10. Re-run Calculator by double-clicking the executable file in Windows Explorer. Click the Add button.

   An unhandled exception appears, as shown in Figure 7-4.

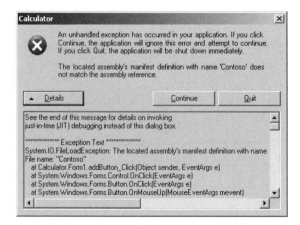

Figure 7-4 The runtime verifies the signature of strong-named assemblies against the signature that was present when the assembly was originally referenced.

Questions Answer the following questions about the preceding procedure.

1. Why did the runtime throw an exception?

2. How does throwing an exception prevent an attacker from replacing an assembly with one that contains malicious content?

3. You've protected the components that are being called by the main application. How can you ensure that the individual components can never be called by an application that hasn't been signed?

Lesson Summary

- Strong names are reliable assembly identifiers that uniquely identify an assembly. They can be used to reduce the risk of an attacker replacing your software with malicious code.

- The Strong Name tool (Sn.exe) is a command-line tool and your primary tool for creating and managing strong name keys and for signing assemblies.

- The process of signing an assembly includes three steps:

    a. Generate a key file.

    b. Add strong name attributes to the assembly's source code.

    c. Build the assembly.

- Delayed signing is a two-part strong name signing process that separates the public and private strong name keys, enabling enterprises to centralize assembly signing and restrict the distribution of private keys. The fewer people who have access to a private key, the lower the risk of the key being abused.

- To use strong name assemblies with code access security, add the *StrongNameIdentityPermission* class either declaratively or imperatively. You can use code access security to limit callers to those assemblies with strong names, specific public keys, and specific version numbers.

Lesson 2: Configuring the Global Assembly Cache

One of the benefits of building applications with the .NET Framework is that you can take advantage of simplified deployment. In fact, deployment can be so simple that it can be accomplished entirely by copying files. However, in some circumstances you will need to configure the destination runtime environment to allow your application to run in the most secure environment possible. Specifically, you might need to add assemblies to the global assembly cache to enable administrators to centrally manage your strong-named assemblies.

After this lesson, you will be able to

- Describe the global assembly cache and how it can be used to simplify the distribution of updates.
- Use several different techniques to add assemblies to the GAC.

Estimated lesson time: 25 minutes

What Is the Global Assembly Cache?

As you learned earlier in this chapter, the global assembly cache (GAC) is a centralized store for managed assemblies. If a single assembly is used by only one application, you don't need to store the assembly in the GAC. Instead, simply store the assembly file in the application directory. However, if you have multiple applications that use a single, shared assembly, you can and should install that assembly in the destination runtime environment's GAC.

Exam Tip   Understanding the GAC is important, but you probably won't see the GAC on this exam—it's not officially listed in the objectives. So dedicate your study time elsewhere if you're using this book for exam preparation.

Installing an assembly into the GAC means that multiple applications will each use the single, shared copy of the assembly. From a security perspective, the primary benefit is simplified security updates. If you release an update to an assembly to resolve a security vulnerability, administrators need to update only the single copy of the assembly that resides in the GAC. This is much simpler and more reliable than seeking out multiple copies of an assembly that are stored in the application directories of multiple applications.

Off the Record   In theory, the GAC offers better protection for assemblies because access is restricted to administrators. In reality, users probably won't have access to update the assembly files stored in an applications directory either, so the GAC doesn't add much.

How to Add Assemblies to the GAC

There are several different ways to install an assembly in the GAC, and each should be used under different circumstances. Whichever method you use, the user adding the assembly to the GAC must have administrator privileges. Therefore, if you add an assembly to the GAC as part of your application's setup procedure, you must instruct users to authenticate as an administrator.

The sections that follow describe the different ways to add assemblies to the GAC and then describe four of the techniques for doing so. However, in most cases, you should rely on the Windows Installer.

Ways to Add Assemblies to the GAC

There are five ways to add assemblies to the GAC:

- **Automatically, with Windows Installer**   The preferred way to add assemblies to the GAC during setup, this technique enables Windows Installer to track references.

- **Manually, with the .NET Framework Configuration Tool**   The preferred way to manually add assemblies to the GAC, the .NET Framework Configuration tool provides graphical GAC management functions.

- **Manually, at a command line; or automatically, in a batch file with GacUtil**   The GacUtil tool provides administrators with command-line or batch file control over the GAC. Avoid using GacUtil to add assemblies to the GAC during your setup procedure, because GacUtil is distributed only with the .NET Framework SDK, and will not be present on most target computers.

- **Manually, with Windows Explorer**   Windows Explorer includes a shell extension for managing the GAC. Use Windows Explorer to quickly add an assembly to the GAC manually by copying and pasting the DLL.

- **Automatically, by directly calling APIs**   Though not recommended because the APIs are not officially supported, you can theoretically directly access the GAC management APIs from within an application.

See Also   GAC APIs will not be further described in this book. For more information about GAC APIs, see the Microsoft Knowledge Base article "DOC: Global Assembly Cache (GAC) APIs Are Not Documented in the .NET Framework Software Development Kit (SDK) Documentation" (article 317540) on the support page of the Microsoft Web site at *http://support.microsoft.com/?kbid=317540*.

How to Add Assemblies to the GAC with Windows Installer

The best way to install assemblies in the GAC is to configure your project to use the Windows Installer. The Windows Installer automatically keeps track of the references to an assembly, and will ensure that the assemblies you add to the GAC are removed when the last application that references them is uninstalled.

To create a setup project that installs an assembly into the GAC, follow these steps:

1. Launch Microsoft Visual Studio .NET 2003, and open the project that requires an assembly to be installed in the GAC.

2. Open the File menu, click Add Project, and then click New Project.

3. In the Project Types pane, click Setup And Deployment Projects. In the Templates pane, click Setup Project. Type a name for your project, and then click OK.

   Visual Studio .NET opens the new project.

4. Right-click File System On Target Machine, click Add Special Folder, and then click Global Assembly Cache Folder.

   Visual Studio .NET creates a new folder that appears in the left pane.

5. If the assembly is not part of the current solution, right-click Global Assembly Cache Folder, click Add, and then click Assembly. Click the Browse button, select the assembly, and then click Open. Click OK to return to Visual Studio .NET.

   If the assembly is part of the current solution, right-click Global Assembly Cache Folder, click Add, and then click Project Output. In the Project list of the Add Project Output Group dialog box (Figure 7-5), select the project that generates the assembly that should be added to the GAC. Then, specify the release configuration for each of the project components, and click OK.

Important   The assembly must be strong named to be added to the GAC. If you are using delayed signing, the assembly is only partially named when built by Visual Studio .NET. Therefore, you cannot specify delayed signing project output to be added to the GAC.

Figure 7-5   Setup projects can automatically add assemblies to the GAC.

When you deploy the Setup.exe and the .MSI files generated by the project, Windows Installer handles the installation of the assembly into the GAC. If the administrator later uninstalls the project, Windows Installer verifies that there are no more references to the shared assembly and removes the assembly from the GAC.

How to Add Assemblies to the GAC with the .NET Framework Configuration Tool

To manually add an assembly to the GAC, first assign a strong name to the assembly. Then, perform the following steps:

1. Launch the .NET Framework Configuration tool as an administrator.

2. Right-click Assembly Cache, and then click Add.

3. In the Add An Assembly dialog box, select the assembly you want to add to the GAC, and then click Open.

   The .NET Framework Configuration tool adds your assembly to the GAC.

How to Add Assemblies to the GAC from the Command Line

To add assemblies to the GAC from the command line or a batch file, first assign a strong name to the assembly. Then, use the /i parameter of the GacUtil command-line tool (included with the .NET Framework) to install the assembly to the global assembly cache. For example, the following command adds the assembly C:\Assembly\Contoso.dll to the GAC without referencing a specific assembly:

```
gacutil /i C:\Assembly\Contoso.dll
```

The previous command syntax will successfully add an assembly to the GAC, but the assembly will remain even after it is no longer needed because no reference to an application was provided. When you reference an application, Windows tracks which applications are using a specific assembly and can automatically remove the assembly after all applications that use it have been removed. To add a reference to an application, use GacUtil with the following syntax:

```
gacutil /i Assembly /r FILEPATH Application "Description"
```

For example, the following command adds the assembly C:\Assembly\Contoso.dll to the GAC and references the C:\Program Files\MyApp\MyApp.exe executable:

```
gacutil /i C:\Assembly\Contoso.dll /r FILEPATH →
"C:\Program Files\MyApp\MyApp.exe" "My Application"
```

How to Add Assemblies to the GAC Using Windows Explorer

You can also add assemblies to the GAC by copying them directly to the %windir%\assemblies\ directory. As Figure 7-6 shows, Windows Explorer even provides an interface for viewing and managing the GAC when you browse to this directory. Windows Explorer provides this functionality using the Assembly Cache Viewer shell extension, implemented in SHFusion.dll.

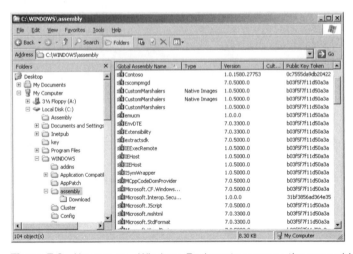

Figure 7-6   You can use Windows Explorer to manage the assembly cache.

> **Note**   You'll see the GAC referred to as Fusion occasionally because that was the internal name of the project at Microsoft dedicated to eliminating problems with shared DLLs.

Practice: Configuring Destination Runtime Environments

In this practice, you create a setup project that installs an assembly into the GAC by using the Windows Installer. Then, you run the resulting setup procedure to install and uninstall the assembly. Read the scenario and then complete the exercises that follow. If you are unable to answer a question or complete a procedure, review the lessons and try the question again. You can find answers to the questions in the "Questions and Answers" section at the end of this chapter.

Scenario

You are a developer at the Graphic Design Institute. Your job is not a glamorous one—you are responsible for creating behind-the-scenes classes that provide the business and transaction logic that are shared between multiple applications at your organization. Other developers create the front-end interfaces and use your classes to store transactions and communicate with internal databases.

There are a total of six .NET Framework applications that use your library. Some users use only one of the applications; others use three or four. Today, each developer distributes a separate copy of the latest version of your assembly and stores it in the application's installation folder. As a result, users might have several copies of your assembly, and possibly multiple versions.

After a recent security training, you added robust input validation features to your assembly. You want to ensure users receive the updated assembly immediately; however, most of the other developers will not redistribute their applications for several months. You have more security enhancements planned, including adding communications encryption and strong authentication. To simplify the distribution of these future updates, your manager wants you to identify a way to store and distribute your assembly that enables you to update a single copy of the assembly.

Interviews   Following is a list of company personnel interviewed and their statements:

- **Kari Hensien, Developer**   "I do appreciate the importance of your security updates, but I'm just not ready to release a new version. Seems like your life would be easier if you just put together your own setup project and stored your assembly in a centralized location."

- **Chris Ashton, Development Manager**   "I'm glad to see the company realizing the benefits of your security training. I don't want to disrupt other developers' release cycles each time you make an improvement, though. Come up with a way to store a centralized version of your application, and we'll have the other developers stop distributing your assembly on their next release."

■ **Brian Johnson, IT Manager** "The way these apps are installed, I can't imagine how we're going to update your assembly. I mean, there might be six copies of it on any given computer. Since users can pick their own install directories, I don't even know for sure where they'd be. Whatever happened to the good ol' days, when DLLs were all stored in the Windows directory? Oh wait, that was a mess, too. Well, we'll work with you, but please keep in mind that the easier your app is to update, the quicker and more reliably we'll be able to distribute your security updates, and the more secure our company will be."

Technical Requirements Create a setup project that installs an assembly in the GAC.

Exercise 1: Creating a Setup Project that Installs an Assembly into a GAC

In this exercise, you create a setup project to add an assembly to the GAC automatically.

> **Important** To complete this exercise, you must have completed all exercises in the Lesson 1 practice earlier in this chapter.

1. Log on to your computer as StandardUser and open the Calculator project in Visual Studio .NET.

2. Open the File menu, click Add Project, and then click New Project.

3. In the Project Types pane, click Setup And Deployment Projects. In the Templates pane, click Setup Project. In the Name field, type **CalculatorSetup**, as shown in Figure 7-7. Click OK.

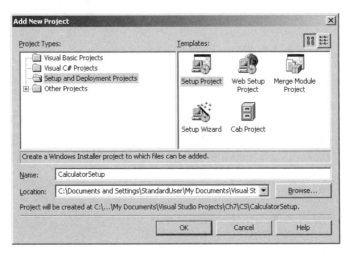

Figure 7-7 Add a setup project to automatically install the Contoso library into the GAC.

Visual Studio .NET opens the new project.

4. Right-click File System On Target Machine, click Add Special Folder, and then click Global Assembly Cache Folder.

   Visual Studio .NET creates a new folder that appears in the left pane.

5. Right-click Global Assembly Cache Folder, click Add, and then click Assembly.

6. Click the Browse button. In the Select Component dialog box, select C:\Assembly \Contoso.dll, and then click Open. Click OK to return to Visual Studio .NET.

7. Click the Build menu, and then click Build CalculatorSetup.

8. Close all instances of Visual Studio .NET.

9. Create a new folder named C:\Assembly\CalculatorSetup\, and then use Windows Explorer to copy the three files from the CalculatorSetup project's output directory to C:\Assembly\CalculatorSetup\.

Exercise 2: Installing and Uninstalling an Assembly to the GAC

In this exercise, you run the CalculatorSetup project, verify that it installs the Contoso assembly into the GAC, and then answer some questions about what you've done.

1. In the CalculatorSetup project's output folder, use Windows Explorer to double-click Setup.exe.

   The Install Program As Other User dialog box appears, as shown in Figure 7-8.

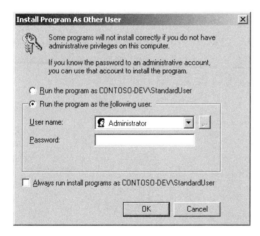

Figure 7-8 Windows Server 2003 automatically prompts for administrative credentials when installing applications.

2. Click Run The Program As The Following User. In the User Name field, select Administrator. In the Password field, type the Administrator password. Click OK.

   The CalculatorSetup Wizard appears.

3. On the Welcome To The CalculatorSetup Setup Wizard page, click Next.

4. On the Select Installation Folder page, accept the default settings and click Next.

5. On the Confirm Installation page, click Next.

6. On the Installation Complete page, click Close to exit the wizard.

7. Launch the .NET Framework Configuration tool by opening Control Panel and then Administrative Tools. Double-click Microsoft .NET Framework 1.1 Configuration.

   The .NET Framework Configuration tool appears.

8. In the left pane, click Assembly Cache. In the right pane, click View List Of Assemblies In The Assembly Cache. Scroll through the list and verify that the Contoso assembly has been added to the GAC.

   For now, leave the .NET Framework Configuration tool open. Next, you uninstall CalculatorSetup and verify that the assembly has been removed from the GAC.

9. In the CalculatorSetup project's output folder, use Windows Explorer to double-click Setup.exe. Provide the Administrator credentials when prompted, and then click OK.

   The CalculatorSetup Wizard appears.

10. On the Welcome To The CalculatorSetup Setup Wizard page, click Remove CalculatorSetup, as shown in Figure 7-9. Click Finish.

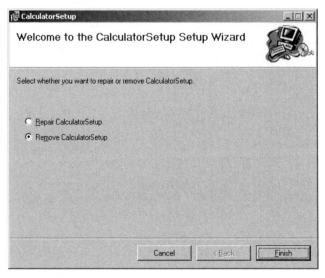

Figure 7-9 Windows installer manages assemblies in the GAC similar to unmanaged DLLs.

11. On the Installation Complete page, click Close.

12. Return to the .NET Framework Configuration tool. Click the View menu, and then click Refresh Assembly List. Scroll through the list and verify that the Contoso assembly has been removed from the GAC.

Questions

Answer the following questions.

1. You had previously been using strong names with your assembly. What changes will the other developers need to make to their applications to work with your assembly now that it is stored in the GAC?

2. After installing the assembly in the GAC, where on the file system will your assembly reside?

Lesson Summary

- The global assembly cache (GAC) is a centralized store for shared assemblies. By using the GAC to store an assembly that is referenced by multiple applications, you can update the assembly by replacing a single file.

- You can use several different tools to add an assembly to the GAC: the Windows installer, the .NET Framework Configuration tool, the GacUtil command-line tool, Windows Explorer, and APIs. Generally, however, you should use the Windows installer because it automatically tracks references to the shared assembly.

Lab: Reducing Assembly Impersonation Vulnerabilities

In this lab, you must suggest additional secure techniques for distributing components for a fictitious company. Read the scenario and then complete the exercise that follows. If you are unable to answer a question, review the lessons and try the question again. You can find answers to the questions in the "Questions and Answers" section at the end of this chapter.

Scenario

You are a developer for Margie's Travel, a travel agency that specializes in organizing vacations for customers who insist on highly customized itineraries. You and your team are responsible for developing both the graphical, internal application used by travel agents, and the Web-based ASP.NET application that customers access directly.

During an audit yesterday, the security engineer at your organization, Russell Hunter, discovered unexpected Web requests being transmitted from your intranet to a server on the public Internet. Closer investigation revealed that the Web requests contained detailed information about your customers and their itineraries, including their credit card numbers and addresses. Russell investigated further and discovered that the Web requests were being transmitted from the internal application that your team developed, named MargieAgent.exe. You were immediately called into a meeting, and you haven't slept since.

As you began to debug the code in your application line-by-line, you discovered that the problem lay in a third-party assembly. Your company uses a component created by Proseware, Inc., that exposes a set of classes that simplify recording transactions to a database. The component is implemented in an assembly named Proseware.dll.

The component itself was not creating the outgoing Web requests, however. Instead, the Web requests were created by a wrapper class that impersonated the Proseware, Inc., classes—it transmitted the data contained within the requests, and then passed the original requests on to the Proseware classes. An attacker had renamed the original Proseware.dll file to Proseware-Core.dll, and then named her class Proseware.dll. You draw a picture to help you explain to your colleagues what happened:

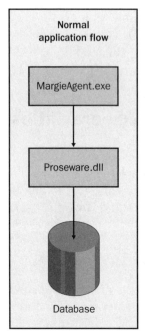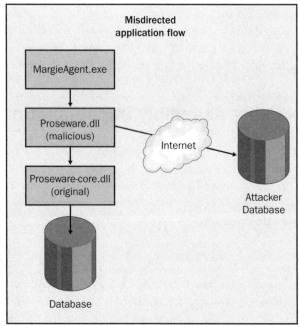

You must discuss the problem with people inside your organization and at Proseware, Inc., and then tell your boss how you can help prevent the problem in the future.

Interviews

Following is a list of company personnel interviewed and their statements:

- **Russell Hunter, Security Engineer**   "Thanks for your analysis of the application behavior. What we have here is a classic man-in-the-middle attack. Usually we see these when an attacker manipulates DNS to trick clients into sending requests to the attacker's server instead of the legitimate server, but this one is happening between components of your application. They're caused by the same vulnerability. Just like any Web server that doesn't use an SSL certificate, the third-party component you are using doesn't have any way to prove its identity. So, your application trusts any file that happens to be named Proseware.dll. Therefore, anybody who has permission to rename a file can create a man-in-the-middle exploit. Question is, how do we validate the third-party component using something other than a filename? Tell ya what. You figure out how to prevent this in the future, and I'll track down who did it. It's probably that developer that quit a few weeks ago, what's his name—Max Benson."

- **Margie Shoop, President, Margie's Travel**   "We'll probably be going out of business soon, but on the off chance that we don't lose all our customers, we should find a way to prevent this in the future. Whose fault is it, anyway: ours or Proseware's? I set up a meeting with Proseware's president and development manager. Don't pull any punches."

- **Kim Abercrombie, President, Proseware, Inc.**   "I'm really sorry to hear about your recent compromise. I understand it was caused by an attacker renaming our file, and then impersonating it with his own. We do our best to create secure components, but I don't know what we can do to fix problems you have with desktop access restrictions. You shouldn't let users modify application files. Anyway, as a sign of good faith, I'm prepared to offer you our preferred customer discount of 15 percent off additional client licenses and upgrades."

- **Jay Henningsen, Development Manager, Proseware, Inc.**   "Look, we're both developers, but I'm no security guy. I don't really know how this could have been prevented, but then again, I don't really know what a man-in-the-middle attack is. You tell me how I can make this better, and I'll do it."

Technical Requirements

Identify techniques that will prevent people from replacing critical application components with malicious code. The technique must allow you to use Proseware's classes without enabling anyone outside of Proseware to impersonate their assembly.

Exercise

Answer the following questions for your boss.

1. How can Proseware make it more difficult for an attacker to create classes that impersonate their assembly?

2. How can Margie's Travel reduce the risk of a developer injecting malicious code into an application?

3. If Proseware, Inc., uses strong names, what resource would an attacker need access to so that she could impersonate one of the libraries?

Chapter Summary

- Strong names greatly reduce the opportunity attackers have to impersonate your assemblies, which increases security for both you as a developer and your customers. The Strong Name tool (Sn.exe) is the single most important tool for using strong names.

- The global assembly cache stores a single copy of shared assemblies that can be referenced by multiple applications. The benefit of using the global assembly cache is that assemblies can be easily updated.

Exam Highlights

Before taking the exam, review the key points and terms that are presented in this chapter. You need to know this information.

Key Points

- Using the Sn tool to generate strong name keys

- Adding attributes to an assembly to generate a strong name when you build the assembly

- Implementing the delayed signing process in your organization to limit the risk of a strong name private key from falling into the hands of a potential attacker

- Using the global assembly cache to store a single copy of a shared assembly in the .NET Framework runtime environment

Key Terms

global assembly cache (GAC)   A container that the .NET Framework uses to store class libraries that can be accessed from other managed assemblies.

strong name   A reliable assembly identifier that reduces the possibility of an attacker modifying or impersonating an assembly. The strong name consists of the assembly's simple text name, version number, and culture, plus a public key and a digital signature.

Questions and Answers

Exercise 2: Creating a Strong-Named Assembly Using Delayed Signing

Page
7-19

Questions

1. What attributes did you add to your assembly?

   You should have added or updated the following attributes:

   ```
   [assembly: AssemblyDelaySign(true)]
   [assembly: AssemblyKeyFile(@"C:\Key\ContosoPublicKey.snk")]
   ```

   ```
   <Assembly: AssemblyDelaySign(True)>
   <Assembly: AssemblyKeyFile("C:\Key\ContosoPublicKey.snk")>
   <Assembly: AssemblyCulture("")>
   ```

   Note that the *AssemblyVersion* attribute (and *AssemblyCulture* attribute in C# only) already existed and did not need to be updated.

2. What command did you use to view the token of the public key in your assembly?

   You should have used the following command:

   ```
   sn -T assemblyPath
   ```

3. What command did you use to verify that your assembly does not yet have a strong name?

   You should have used the following command, which will return an error:

   ```
   sn -v assemblyPath
   ```

Exercise 4: Referencing the Strong-Named Assembly

Page
7-22

Questions

1. Why did the runtime throw an exception?

   The updated version of the Contoso assembly did not have a strong name that matched the strong name of the assembly that you referenced when you created the Calculator project.

2. How does throwing an exception prevent an attacker from replacing an assembly with one that contains malicious content?

   The .NET Framework will allow the application to call the referenced assembly only if it has a matching strong name. To generate an assembly with the same strong name, the attacker needs the developer's private key. Without the private key, the attacker cannot create an assembly that will trick the runtime into calling a malicious method.

3. You've protected the components that are being called by the main application. How can you ensure that the individual components can never be called by an application that hasn't been signed?

You can use CAS to require that callers have a strong name and are signed with your company's public key.

Exercise 2: Installing and Uninstalling an Assembly to the GAC

Page
7-33

Questions

1. You had previously been using strong names with your assembly. What changes will the other developers need to make to their applications to work with your assembly now that it is stored in the GAC?

The developers need to stop distributing the assembly; they don't need to do anything else. The runtime will find your assembly in the GAC because the existing references identify your assembly by the strong name.

2. After installing the assembly in the GAC, where on the file system will your assembly reside?

Your assembly will be stored in the %windir%\assembly\ folder.

Lab: Reducing Assembly Impersonation Vulnerabilities

Page
7-36

Exercise

1. How can Proseware make it more difficult for an attacker to create classes that impersonate their assembly?

Proseware can assign a strong name to their assembly. The .NET Framework runtime will check the strong name when linking to the assembly and will throw an exception if it has not been signed by their private key.

2. How can Margie's Travel reduce the risk of a developer injecting malicious code into an application?

Margie's Travel should use strong names and implement a process that requires assemblies to be developed and signed by different people. One way to do this is to use delayed signing.

3. If Proseware, Inc., uses strong names, what resource would an attacker need access to so that she could impersonate one of the libraries?

The attacker would need Proseware, Inc.'s private key that they use to sign assemblies.

Section 3
Protecting Data and Networked Applications

Section 3 of this book teaches how to keep confidential data private and protect networked applications from attack. The three chapters in this section provide instruction for using cryptography, designing Web applications and Web services that are resistant to attack, and using remoting while minimizing the exposure to vulnerabilities.

- Chapter 8, "Protecting Data by Using Cryptography," teaches the fundamentals of cryptography, encryption, hashing, and digital signatures. You will learn to choose the best encryption algorithm to use for various situations. When you complete this chapter, you should understand how to protect data, whether it is stored on a disk or transmitted across a network.

- Chapter 9, "Hardening ASP.NET Applications," explains how to make Web applications and Web services resistant to attack. This chapter is particularly important because Web applications are subjected to more attacks than any other type of application.

- Chapter 10, "Improving Security When Using External Components and Services," teaches how to reduce the risk of calling external methods when using remoting, Web services, and COM components.

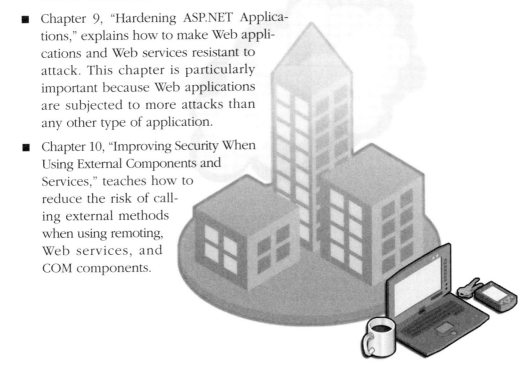

8 Protecting Data by Using Cryptography

Why This Chapter Matters

Data is most vulnerable when it is stored persistently or transferred across a network. An attacker with access to the hard disk or network infrastructure might be able to capture your application's data and either extract private information from the data or modify the data. However, you are not defenseless. You can use cryptography to protect the privacy and integrity of the data that your application stores or transfers. The .NET Framework provides classes for several different types of cryptography, including symmetric and asymmetric encryption, hashing, and digital signatures. This chapter teaches when and how to use each type of cryptography.

Exam Objectives in this Chapter:

- Sign data by using certificates.

- Implement data protection.

    - Use .NET cryptographic techniques.

        - Encrypt and decrypt data by using symmetric and asymmetric cryptographic functions.

        - Compute hashes by using cryptographic functions.

        - Write code to create cryptographically random numbers for cryptographic functions.

    - Encrypt and decrypt data by using the Data Protection API (DPAPI).

Lessons in this Chapter:

Before You Begin

To complete the practices, examples, and lab exercises in this chapter, you must have one computer running Microsoft Windows Server 2003. During the course of performing the exercises in this chapter, the computer's security can be reduced. Therefore, the computer should not be a production computer and should not be connected to any network, especially the Internet, even if a firewall is present. Install Microsoft Visual Studio .NET 2003 using the default settings.

Lesson 1: Encrypting and Decrypting Data with Symmetric Keys

Many people are introduced to encryption at an early age. Children protect even the most mundane communications from imaginary spies with a secret decoder ring—a toy with two rings that translates encrypted characters to unencrypted characters. The rings on a decoder ring rotate, and a message can be decrypted only when the two rings are lined up correctly. To exchange an encrypted message, the children must first agree on how the rings will line up. After they have exchanged this secret piece of information, they can freely pass encrypted messages without worrying that someone will be able to decrypt them. Even if an imaginary spy had a decoder ring, the spy would need to know how to position the rings to decrypt the message.

Because both the sender and the recipient of the message must know the same secret to encrypt and decrypt a message, secret decoder rings are an example of symmetric key encryption. Symmetric key encryption is a game for children, but it is also the foundation for most encrypted communications today. As children know, encryption is a fun topic. You should enjoy building it into your application, and you'll greatly reduce the chance of private communications being compromised.

After this lesson, you will be able to

- Describe what symmetric key encryption allows you to do.
- List the classes in the .NET Framework used for symmetric key encryption and their common methods and properties.
- Establish a symmetric key—both randomly and based on a password.
- Encrypt and decrypt messages by using symmetric keys.
- Describe the Data Protection API, and describe how and when it should be used.

Estimated lesson time: 45 minutes

What Is Symmetric Key Encryption?

Symmetric key encryption, also known as secret-key encryption, is a cryptography technique that uses a single secret key to both encrypt and decrypt data. Symmetric encryption algorithms (also called *ciphers*) process plain text with the secret encryption key to create encrypted data called *cipher text*. The cipher text cannot easily be decrypted into the plain text without possession of the secret key. Figure 8-1 shows symmetric key encryption and decryption.

Important   The cryptography community commonly uses the terms cipher text and plain text, but encryption isn't limited to processing text. In fact, the algorithms included with the .NET Framework cannot process text directly.

Encryption

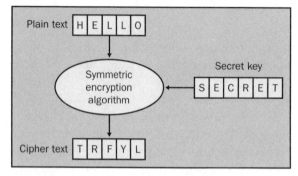

Decryption

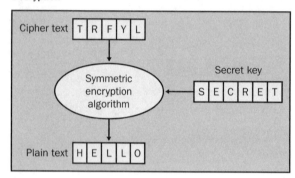

Figure 8-1 Symmetric encryption uses the same key for encryption and decryption.

Symmetric algorithms are extremely fast and are well suited for encrypting large quantities of data. Even though symmetric encryption is very secure, an attacker can identify the plain text given the cipher text and enough time. To identify the plain text, the attacker needs to use only a brute force attack to sequentially generate symmetric keys until the attacker has tried every single possibility. Typically, the time required to try all keys is hundreds of years, if not longer, because the attacker would need to try at least 2^{56} key possibilities. More secure symmetric algorithms use longer keys that would take exponentially longer to crack.

> **Note**   You won't have to design your own cryptographic algorithms; just use the ones provided by the .NET Framework. You can do this without understanding exactly how they work, which is fortunate, because they are extremely complex. To keep the lessons as concise as possible, this book focuses on the implementation of cryptography, and not the theory behind it.

The disadvantage of secret-key encryption is that it presumes two parties have already agreed on a key. Agreeing on a symmetric key is a challenge, because the key itself cannot be encrypted. If you've decided to use encryption, it must be because you don't trust your system to prevent an attacker from gaining access to your data. Therefore, users must find a secure way to exchange secret keys. After the secret keys are exchanged, encrypted data can be freely exchanged between the parties. However, keys should be changed on a regular basis for the same reasons that passwords should be changed regularly. Each time the key must be changed, users must resort to the secure communication mechanism.

Figure 8-2 shows how users must transfer both the encrypted message and the key using different communication mechanisms to enable the recipient to decrypt the message while preventing an attacker who can capture your communications across only a single network from decrypting the message. Keys are often transferred by voice across the phone network, sent physically through the mail system, or carried to the recipient. After the shared secret has been established, the two peers can use it to encrypt and decrypt any number of messages.

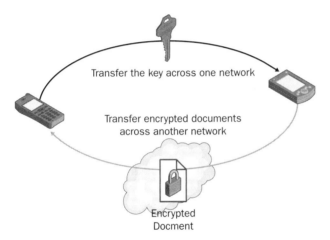

Figure 8-2   Symmetric key encryption requires separately exchanging both the key and the encrypted document.

The need to establish a shared secret key rules out symmetric encryption for encrypting spontaneous network communications. For example, symmetric key encryption is not initially used between a Web client and Web server, because users on the Internet aren't typically willing to wait several days while the Web site physically mails them a secret key. Instead, Web sessions are initially established by using asymmetric keys.

See Also   Asymmetric keys are discussed in Lesson 2 of this chapter.

Symmetric Algorithm Classes in the .NET Framework

Most of the .NET Framework's cryptography functionality is built into the *System.Security.Cryptography* namespace, including the four implementations of symmetric encryption algorithms. Table 8-1 shows symmetric encryption algorithm classes.

Table 8-1   Symmetric Cryptography Classes

Class	Key Length	Description
SymmetricAlgorithm	N/A	The base class from which all symmetric algorithms are derived.
RijndaelManaged	128 through 256 bits, in 32-bit increments	The .NET Framework implementation of the Rijndael symmetric encryption algorithm. As a government encryption standard, this algorithm is also known as Advanced Encryption Standard, or AES. *RijndaelManaged* is the only .NET Framework symmetric encryption class that is fully managed. All other encryption classes call unmanaged code. Because of this, *RijndaelManaged* is the preferred choice when your application will be running in a partially trusted environment.
DES	56 bits	The Data Encryption Standard (DES) is a symmetric encryption algorithm that uses relatively short key lengths that are vulnerable to cracking attacks. As a result, it should be avoided. However, it remains commonly used because it is compatible with a wide range of legacy platforms.
RC2	Variable	An encryption standard designed to replace DES that uses variable key sizes.
TripleDES	156 bits, of which only 112 bits are effectively used for encryption	The .NET Framework implementation of the Triple DES (3DES) symmetric encryption algorithm, it essentially applies the DES algorithm three times.

All symmetric algorithm classes are derived from the *System.Security.Cryptography. SymmetricAlgorithm* base class and share the following properties:

■ **BlockSize**   Gets or sets the block size of the cryptographic operation in bits. The block size is the number of bits that the algorithm processes at a single time, and can usually be ignored when creating applications that use encryption.

■ **FeedbackSize**   Gets or sets the feedback size of the cryptographic operation in bits. The feedback size determines one aspect of the algorithm's encryption technique; however, as a developer, you can safely ignore this property.

■ **IV**   Gets or sets the *initialization vector (IV)* for the symmetric algorithm. Like the *Key* property, both the encryptor and decryptor must specify the same value. To avoid the overhead of transferring the IV securely between the encryptor and decryptor, you might choose to statically define the IV in your application, or to derive this from the *Key* property.

- ***Key***   Gets or sets the secret key for the symmetric algorithm. Keys are automatically generated if you have not specifically defined them. After encryption, you must store this value and transfer it to the decryptor. During decryption, you must specify the same key used during encryption.

- ***KeySize***   Gets or sets the size of the secret key used by the symmetric algorithm in bits. When you create a symmetric algorithm object, the runtime will choose the largest key size supported by the platform. As a result, you can usually ignore this property. However, if the message's recipient does not support the same key sizes as the sender, you must set this property to the highest value supported by both the encryptor and the decryptor.

- ***LegalBlockSizes***   A *KeySizes* array that gets the block sizes that are supported by the symmetric algorithm. Each array member contains *MinSize* and *MaxSize* properties, which define the valid key ranges in bits, and a *SkipSize* property that specifies in bits the interval between valid key sizes.

- ***LegalKeySizes***   A *KeySizes* array that gets the key sizes that are supported by the symmetric algorithm. Each array member contains *MinSize* and *MaxSize* properties that define the valid key ranges in bits, and a *SkipSize* property that specifies the interval between valid key sizes in bits.

- ***Mode***   A property set to one of the *CipherMode* enumeration values that determines one aspect of the encryption algorithm's behavior. Usually this property is set to Cipher Block Chaining (CBC), which is the default. You should usually leave this set to CBC. If you do change this value, you must change it at both the encryptor and decryptor.

- ***Padding***   A *PaddingMode* enumeration value, this determines how the encryption algorithm fills out any difference between the algorithm's block size and the length of the plain text. You should generally not change this property.

Understanding Initialization Vectors

You don't need to understand what initialization vectors do to use encryption, as long as you know that you must synchronize the IV values for both the encryptor and decryptor. If you are interested in their purpose, remember that all the symmetric encryption algorithms included with the .NET Framework are block encryption algorithms, which divide data into separate pieces and encrypt them individually. To prevent patterns from forming in the blocks, the second block of data is encrypted with the results of the first block, the third block is encrypted with the results of the second block, and so on. The first block of data has no preceding block, however, so the encryption algorithm uses the initialization vector to obscure the first block. In other words, an initialization vector is data that symmetric encryption algorithms use to further obscure the first block of data being encrypted, which makes unauthorized decrypting more difficult.

Additionally, the symmetric algorithm classes each share the following methods (standard object methods have been omitted):

■ **CreateDecryptor** To decrypt messages, you must create a symmetric algorithm object and call this method to create an *ICryptoTransform* object that a *CryptoStream* object can use to decrypt the stream.

> **Note** As you will see from the examples later in this chapter, these methods are simpler to use than they seem.

■ **CreateEncryptor** Creates a symmetric encryptor object used by *CryptoStream* objects to encrypt a stream.

■ **GenerateIV** Generates a random initialization vector to be used for the algorithm. Generally, there is no need to call this method, because IVs are automatically randomly generated unless you specifically define them. You will call this method only when you have defined IV and later need to use a different, random IV.

■ **GenerateKey** Generates a random key to be used for the algorithm. Like *GenerateIV*, you need to call this method only when you have already defined the *Key* property and later need to use a random key.

■ **ValidKeySize** Determines whether the specified key size is valid for the current algorithm and returns a Boolean value. Use this when you are working with an unknown symmetric algorithm class to verify that your key is valid for the given algorithm.

Best Practices for Choosing a Symmetric Key Algorithm

Use the Rijndael algorithm whenever both the encryptor and decryptor are running on Microsoft Windows XP or later operating systems; otherwise, use Triple DES. Out of all symmetric-key algorithms supported by the .NET Framework, the U.S. government–approved Rijndael algorithm is considered the most secure. This algorithm supports 128-, 192-, and 256-bit keys. Another reason to choose Rijndael is that it is the only implementation that is natively supported by the .NET Framework. The other algorithms must make calls to unmanaged code. The managed implementation of the Rijndael algorithm is supported only on Windows XP or later, and on the systems with the .NET Framework installed. If your application needs to communicate with unmanaged applications running on Microsoft Windows 2000 or earlier, use Triple DES instead.

Although you should generally choose the algorithm that provides the highest level of security and is supported by all clients, you might find encryption's processing

---

overhead slowing down your application. MSDN has a very detailed article comparing the performance of these algorithms titled "Performance Comparison: Security Design Choices"; it is available on the Microsoft Web site at *http://msdn.microsoft.com/library/en-us/dnbda/html/bdadotnetarch15.asp*.

How to Establish a Symmetric Key

Before you can encrypt and decrypt messages by using symmetric encryption, both the encryptor and decryptor must have the same key. You can't use just any piece of data as a key, however. Symmetric encryption algorithms must use keys of a specific length, as listed earlier in Table 8-1. Therefore, you cannot simply set the *Key* property to a user-provided password. You can, however, generate a valid key based on a user-provided password. Alternatively, you can use the randomly generated, highly secure key automatically created by the .NET Framework. If you rely on the .NET Framework to generate an encryption key for you, you must ensure that the key is transferred to the decryptor as securely as possible.

In the sections that follow, you will first learn to visually display keys to make experimenting with encryption simpler. Then you will learn to generate a random key. Finally, you will learn the guidelines, process, and technique for generating a symmetric key based on a password.

How to Display Keys

It is difficult to visualize keys because they are simply a very long series of bits, and they can't be easily expressed as a string. You can't even easily display them as a decimal integer, because the .NET Framework includes only classes that handle up to 64-bit numbers, and the Rijndael, RC2, and TripleDES algorithms all support much longer keys. There are two common techniques for displaying keys: in hexadecimal, and using Base64 encoding.

The following code sample displays a random Rijndael key in hexadecimal:

```
SymmetricAlgorithm myAlg = new RijndaelManaged();
Console.Write("Key: 0x");
foreach (byte thisByte in myAlg.Key)
    Console.Write(thisByte.ToString("X"));
Console.WriteLine();
```

```
Dim myAlg As SymmetricAlgorithm = New RijndaelManaged
Console.Write("Key: 0x")
For Each thisByte As Byte In myAlg.Key
    Console.Write(thisByte.ToString("X2"))
Next
Console.WriteLine
```

The other common technique for displaying keys is to convert the bytes to a Base64-encoded string, which uses uppercase and lowercase letters, numbers, and special characters to represent 6 bits with each character. This creates a shorter representation of the key, since hexadecimal represents only 4 bits with each character. To display a key using Base64 encoding, use or import the *System.Text* namespace, and use the following code in a console application:

```csharp
SymmetricAlgorithm myAlg = new RijndaelManaged();
Console.WriteLine(Convert.ToBase64String(myAlg.Key));
```

```vb
Dim myAlg As SymmetricAlgorithm = New RijndaelManaged
Console.WriteLine(Convert.ToBase64String(myAlg.Key))
```

How to Create a Random Key

If you must generate a new encryption key, the simplest way is to create a random key. The reality is that nothing about a computer is truly random; however, the .NET Framework is capable of generating pseudo-random numbers that are sufficient for cryptographic purposes. To generate a random key, simply create and use a symmetric algorithm object. If you specify a value for the *Key* property and later want to use a random key, call the *GenerateKey* method.

> ### Generating Cryptographically Random Values
>
> Although the .NET Framework automatically generates random keys for you, you might find a need to manually generate your own key. For example, if you are saving a file and you want to minimize the likelihood of an attacker guessing the filename, you should generate a long, random filename. Do not use the *System.Random* class, however, because that class was not designed for creating cryptographically random numbers. Instead, use the *System.Security.Cryptography.RNGCryptoServiceProvider* class.
>
> The *RNGCryptoServiceProvider* class generates random values when you call the *GetBytes* method. This produces only arrays of random bytes, however, so you will need to convert the random bytes into the format you require. The most useful class for converting these random bytes into numbers is the *System.BitConverter* class, which includes static methods for converting random bytes into every common numeric class. The following console application code generates a random value, and then converts it to a 64-bit unsigned integer and a double floating point value:
>
>
>
> ```csharp
> RNGCryptoServiceProvider rand = new RNGCryptoServiceProvider();
> byte[] randValue = new byte[256];
> rand.GetBytes(randValue);
> Console.WriteLine(System.BitConverter.ToUInt64(randValue,0));
> Console.WriteLine(System.BitConverter.ToDouble(randValue,0));
> ```

```
Dim rand As RNGCryptoServiceProvider = New RNGCryptoServiceProvider
Dim randValue(256) As Byte
rand.GetBytes(randValue)
Console.WriteLine(System.BitConverter.ToUInt64(randValue, 0))
Console.WriteLine(System.BitConverter.ToDouble(randValue, 0))
```

Several applications have been vulnerable to having encryption keys cracked very quickly because they did not use an entirely random algorithm for generating cryptographically random numbers. If an attacker discovers that your application generates a limited set of values because of a poor random number–generating algorithm, the attacker can break through your protection much quicker. For this reason, always use *RNGCryptoServiceProvider* rather than *System.Random* or your own random number–generating algorithm.

Guidelines for Creating a Key with a Password

Generate symmetric encryption keys from a password when you rely on users to transfer the secret key. The biggest challenge of using symmetric encryption is securely transferring the shared secret between the encryptor and decryptor. Reading a 128-bit key (32 characters when expressed in hexadecimal) over the phone is time consuming and error-prone. People are, however, accustomed to exchanging passwords over the phone.

Passwords are often a single word or a phrase; however, the best passwords are random numbers, letters, and other characters. Even the most complex random password will still be easier to exchange than a 128-bit (or longer) key. Unfortunately, unless it is a very, very long password, it will also be less secure. Although an attacker would need to attempt a maximum 2^{128} encryption keys to find a 128-bit encryption password, a 10-character complex password would require only about 2^{56} combinations. Furthermore, because most passwords are not cryptographically random, the attacker could further reduce the number of guesses required by using a password dictionary.

You cannot directly use passwords as encryption keys, but you can use the *System.Security.Cryptography.PasswordDeriveBytes* class to turn a password into a key. This is particularly useful when a shared secret has already been established between an encryptor and a decryptor. For example, if you create a custom authentication mechanism and your application is privy to the user's user name and password, you could concatenate the user's own user name and password to derive the same key at both the encryptor and decryptor.

PasswordDeriveBytes requires three values in addition to the user's password: a salt value, an initialization vector, and the number of iterations used to generate the key. Ideally, all these values are randomly generated. Changing any of these values produces a different key, requiring you to use the same values at both the encryptor and decryptor. Therefore, when random values are used, the values must be exchanged in the same way the password is exchanged. For this reason, it is usually not possible to securely exchange these values in addition to the password. Instead, you can specify static values that both the encryptor and decryptor applications have stored within their source code, but it is more secure to generate the values based on other shared secret information, such as the password.

The Process of Encryption and Decryption Using a Password

Encrypting and decrypting data using a password works similarly to standard symmetric cryptography, except that the encryption and decryption keys must be determined using the password and a seed, as shown in Figure 8-3. Both the encryptor and decryptor must use the exact same password and key for the decryption to be successful.

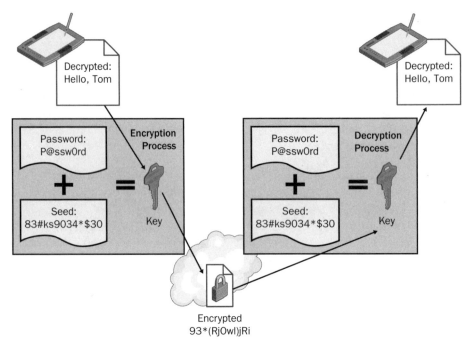

Figure 8-3   Generating a key based on a password allows for simplified exchange of the shared secret.

How to Create a Key with a Password

Creating symmetric keys based on a password requires several different values to be synchronized between the encryptor and decryptor:

- The password
- The salt value
- The number of iterations used to generate the key

The simplest way to specify these values is to pass them to the *PasswordDeriveBytes* constructor, along with the hashing algorithm to use. This version of the overloaded constructor is defined by the following code:

```
public PasswordDeriveBytes(
    string strPassword,
    byte[] rgbSalt,
    string strHashName,
    int iterations
);
```

```
Public Sub New( _
    ByVal strPassword As String, _
    ByVal rgbSalt() As Byte, _
    ByVal strHashName As String, _
    ByVal iterations As Integer _
)
```

After initialization, you can retrieve a key by calling the *PasswordDeriveBytes.GetBytes* method. *GetBytes* accepts the number of bytes to return as an integer. When deriving a key, determine the length based on the number of bits required by the algorithm object's *KeySize* and *BlockSize* properties. Note that both *KeySize* and *BlockSize* are defined as a number of bits, whereas the *PasswordDeriveBytes.GetBytes* method requires a number of bytes. You must divide the number of bits required for the key by 8 to determine the number of bytes required.

Besides the key, the encryption algorithm must also have the same initialization vector specified at both the encryptor and decryptor. For optimal security, when only a password is shared between the encryptor and decryptor, you should also generate the initialization vector based on the password. Whereas the length of the key being generated must be based on the *KeySize* property, the length of the initialization vector must be based on the encryption algorithm's *BlockSize* property.

The following sample code generates a key and initialization vector for a previously created *myAlg* SymmetricAlgorithm object using a previously created string named *password*. This code uses static values for the salt and number of iterations used by the password generation algorithm:

```
byte[] saltValueBytes  = Encoding.ASCII.GetBytes("This is my salt");
PasswordDeriveBytes passwordKey = new PasswordDeriveBytes⟶
(password, saltValueBytes, "SHA1", 3);
myAlg.Key = passwordKey.GetBytes(myAlg.KeySize/8);
myAlg.IV = passwordKey.GetBytes(myAlg.BlockSize/8);
```

```
Dim saltValueBytes As Byte() = Encoding.ASCII.GetBytes("This is my salt")
Dim passwordKey As PasswordDeriveBytes = New PasswordDeriveBytes ⟶
(password, saltValueBytes, "SHA1", 3)
myAlg.Key = passwordKey.GetBytes(myAlg.KeySize / 8)
myAlg.IV = passwordKey.GetBytes(myAlg.BlockSize / 8)
```

To see this code in use, examine the following console application that generates a key based on a password provided as a command-line argument:

```csharp
using System;
using System.Text;
using System.Security.Cryptography;


namespace DisplayKey
{
    class Class1
    {
        [STAThread]
        static void Main(string[] args)
        {
            SymmetricAlgorithm myAlg = new RijndaelManaged();
            // Define a static salt value
            byte[] saltValueBytes  = Encoding.ASCII.GetBytes("saltValue");

            // Create the PasswordDeriveBytes object with the password
            // and salt value
            PasswordDeriveBytes passwordKey = new ⮕
PasswordDeriveBytes(args[0], saltValueBytes, "SHA1", 3);

            // Generate a key. GetBytes takes a byte length,
            // rather than a bit length,
            // requiring you to divide the KeySize property by 8
            myAlg.Key = passwordKey.GetBytes(myAlg.KeySize/8);
            myAlg.IV = passwordKey.GetBytes(myAlg.BlockSize/8);

            // Display the generated key to the console in hex.
            Console.Write("Key: 0x");
            foreach (byte thisByte in myAlg.Key)
                Console.Write(thisByte.ToString("X2") + " ");
            Console.WriteLine();
        }
    }
}
```

```vbnet
Imports System.Text
Imports System.Security.Cryptography

Module Module1

    Sub Main(ByVal args As String())
        Dim myAlg As SymmetricAlgorithm = New RijndaelManaged
        ' Define a static salt value
        Dim saltValueBytes As Byte() = Encoding.ASCII.GetBytes("saltValue") ⮕

        ' Create the PasswordDeriveBytes object with the password
        ' and salt value
        Dim passwordKey As PasswordDeriveBytes = New ⮕
PasswordDeriveBytes(args(0), saltValueBytes, "SHA1", 3)
```

```
      ' Generate a key. GetBytes takes a byte length, rather than a bit
      ' length, requiring you to divide the KeySize property by 8.
      myAlg.Key = passwordKey.GetBytes(myAlg.KeySize / 8)
      myAlg.IV = passwordKey.GetBytes(myAlg.BlockSize / 8)

      ' Display the generated key to the console in hex.
      Console.Write("Key: 0x")
      For Each thisByte As Byte In myAlg.Key
          Console.Write(thisByte.ToString("X2") + " ")
      Next
      Console.WriteLine()
   End Sub

End Module
```

The sample console application simply generates and displays a key. However, because the algorithm object will always have the same key and initialization vector when a given password is supplied, this object could easily be extended to encrypt and decrypt documents.

How to Encrypt and Decrypt Messages by Using Symmetric Keys

After both the encryptor and decryptor have the same key, they can begin exchanging encrypted messages. The .NET Framework makes this very easy. In fact, using encryption is very similar to reading and writing to standard files and streams, and it requires only a few additional lines of code. To encrypt or decrypt messages in your application, perform the following tasks:

1. Create a *Stream* object to interface with the memory or file that you will be reading from or writing to.

2. Create a *SymmetricAlgorithm* object.

3. Specify the algorithm's key, the initialization vector, or both.

4. Call *SymmetricAlgorithm.CreateEncryptor()* or *SymmetricAlgorithm.CreatDecryptor()* to create an *ICryptoTransform* object.

5. Create a *CryptoStream* object using the *Stream* object and the *ICryptoTransform* object.

6. Read from or write to the *CryptoStream* object just like any other *Stream* object.

The following console application demonstrates these steps by reading an unencrypted file, encrypting it with the Rijndael algorithm, and saving the encrypted results as a new file. The console application takes two command-line arguments: the unencrypted filename, and the name of the file to create. Only the *Main* method is shown, but the application requires the *System.IO* and *System.Security.Cryptography* namespaces.

```csharp
string unencryptedFileName = args[0];
string encryptedFileName = args[1];

// Step 1: Create the Stream objects
FileStream unencryptedFile = new FileStream(unencryptedFileName,→
FileMode.Open, FileAccess.Read);
FileStream encryptedFile = new FileStream(encryptedFileName, →
FileMode.OpenOrCreate, FileAccess.Write);

// Step 2: Create the SymmetricAlgorithm object
SymmetricAlgorithm myAlg = new RijndaelManaged();

// Step 3: Specify a key (optional)
myAlg.GenerateKey();

// Read the unencrypted file into fileData
byte[] fileData = new byte[unencryptedFile.Length];
unencryptedFile.Read(fileData, 0, (int)unencryptedFile.Length);

// Step 4: Create the ICryptoTransform object
ICryptoTransform encryptor = myAlg.CreateEncryptor();

// Step 5: Create the CryptoStream object
CryptoStream encryptStream = new CryptoStream(encryptedFile, →
encryptor, CryptoStreamMode.Write);

// Step 6: Write the contents to the CryptoStream
encryptStream.Write(fileData, 0, (int)unencryptedFile.Length);

// Close the file handles
encryptStream.Close();
unencryptedFile.Close();
encryptedFile.Close();
```

```vbnet
Sub Main(ByVal args As String())
    Dim unencryptedFileName As String = args(0)
    Dim encryptedFileName As String = args(1)

    ' Step 1: Create the Stream objects
    Dim unencryptedFile As FileStream = New FileStream →
(unencryptedFileName, FileMode.Open, FileAccess.Read)
    Dim encryptedFile As FileStream = New FileStream →
(encryptedFileName, FileMode.OpenOrCreate, FileAccess.Write)

    ' Step 2: Create the SymmetricAlgorithm object
    Dim myAlg As SymmetricAlgorithm = New RijndaelManaged

    ' Step 3: Specify a key (optional)
    myAlg.GenerateKey()

    ' Read the unencrypted file into fileData
    Dim fileData(unencryptedFile.Length - 1) As Byte
    unencryptedFile.Read(fileData, 0, CType(unencryptedFile.Length, Integer))
```

```
' Step 4: Create the ICryptoTransform object
Dim encryptor As ICryptoTransform = myAlg.CreateEncryptor

' Step 5: Create the CryptoStream object
Dim encryptStream As CryptoStream = New CryptoStream↴
(encryptedFile, encryptor, CryptoStreamMode.Write)

' Step 6: Write the contents to the CryptoStream
encryptStream.Write(fileData, 0, CType(unencryptedFile.Length, Integer))

' Close the file handles
encryptStream.Close()
unencryptedFile.Close()
encryptedFile.Close()
End Sub
```

As Figure 8-4 shows, the console application successfully creates an encrypted file. Because the key is randomly generated, running the application repeatedly generates different results each time. Because the key is not stored, the file can never be decrypted. The key is simply an array of bytes and can be stored by using the *Binary-Writer* object or by transferring the key across a network.

Figure 8-4   The sample application successfully encrypts the text file.

The code for decrypting a file is almost identical to the code for encrypting a file, except that the decrypting code must read the encryption key that was used to encrypt the data rather than randomly generate it, and it must call decryption methods instead of encryption methods. To reverse the process to decrypt a file, simply make the following changes to an application:

■ Change the code for step 3 to read the key and initialization vector that was used to encrypt the data.

■ Change the code for step 4 to use the *CreateDecryptor* method instead of *CreateEncryptor*.

■ Change the code for step 5 to use the *CryptoStreamMode.Read* enumeration instead of *CryptoStreamMode.Write*.

■ Change the code for step 6 to read from the *CryptoStream* object.

What Is DPAPI?

The Data Protection API (DPAPI) is a library that encrypts and stores data for an individual user or an entire computer. DPAPI was designed to be extremely easy to use. Although it does use encryption, it does not require the application calling DPAPI to specify a key. Instead, the user's password is used to derive a key. This saves the application developer from the burden of key management. Additionally, it makes DPAPI an excellent way to store encryption keys.

Windows 2000 and later operating systems provide DPAPI. DPAPI is part of the Cryptography API and is implemented in Crypt32.dll. The API consists of two methods, *CryptProtectData* and *CryptUnprotectData*. DPAPI can work with either the machine store or the user store.

Exam Tip DPAPI is covered here because it is an exam objective. For the exam, know what it is and what it can do. If you're developing exclusively for the .NET Framework, you can safely forget about DPAPI after the exam. DPAPI is unmanaged, and there are better ways to encrypt data from managed applications.

The following sections explain how to use DPAPI and then provide best practices for using DPAPI.

How to Use DPAPI

DPAPI defaults to the user store, although you can specify that the machine store be used by passing the *CRYPTPROTECT_LOCAL_MACHINE* flag to the DPAPI functions. The user profile approach affords an additional layer of security because it limits who can access the secret. Only the user who encrypts the data can decrypt the data. The machine store approach is easier to develop because it does not require user profile management. However, unless an additional *entropy* parameter is used, this approach is less secure because any user on the computer can decrypt data. Entropy is a value designed to make deciphering the secret more difficult. Although using an entropy value can improve security, the overhead of storing the entropy value while preventing attackers from accessing it defeats the purpose of using DPAPI.

Note Use of the DPAPI user profile requires additional development when creating ASP.NET applications, because you need to take explicit steps to load and unload a user profile. ASP.NET does not automatically load a user profile.

See Also   For detailed instructions about creating a class to interface between managed applications and the unmanaged DPAPI library, see the "How To: Create a DPAPI Library" topic in the "Building Secure ASP.NET Applications: Authentication, Authorization, and Secure Communication" paper on the Microsoft Web site at *http://msdn.microsoft.com/library/en-us /dnnetsec/html/SecNetHT07.asp.*

Best Practices for Using DPAPI

Avoid using DPAPI from managed applications. Although Win32 applications *should* use DPAPI to protect persistent data, the .NET Framework does not provide a managed wrapper for DPAPI. As a result, you must create your own class for accessing DPAPI functionality. As a general rule, avoid calling unmanaged code whenever possible—it requires your application to have elevated code access security (CAS) permissions, and it creates a potential opportunity for attackers to bypass CAS restrictions.

See Also   For more information about CAS, see Chapter 6, "Implementing Code Access Security."

Instead of using DPAPI, consider creating an asymmetric key pair to encrypt your data. Then, store the keys in a cryptographic service provider (CSP). Your application can later retrieve the key pair from the CSP to decrypt the data.

See Also   For more information about asymmetric keys, see Lesson 2 in this chapter.

Practice: Encrypting and Decrypting Data with Symmetric Keys

In this practice, you will create a class library that encrypts and decrypts files by using symmetric encryption based on a password. Read the scenario and then complete the exercise that follows. If you are unable to answer a question, review the lesson and try the question again. You can find answers to the questions in the "Questions and Answers" section at the end of this chapter.

Scenario

You are a developer for Trey Research, a company that performs outsourced research tasks for enterprises. Trey is a very distributed company, with 500 employees scattered around the world, primarily working out of home offices. Your development team has five developers total and has created a document management application based on the .NET Framework to simplify the transfer of documents between employees. The application uses the employee's personal e-mail account to transfer files, which means your internal, confidential files might be transferred across and stored on untrusted mail servers.

Your management wants to reduce the risk of attackers acquiring the documents during e-mail transfers and successfully viewing them. Encryption seems like the best solution, and your management has asked for your help. You interview key personnel and review the technical requirements before coming up with a solution.

Interviews Following is a list of company personnel interviewed and their statements:

- **Deborah Poe, Development Manager** "We've never used encryption before, which is kind of stupid since we're transferring these highly confidential documents across the Internet. Actually, I'm not as concerned about the network transfer as I am about the documents being stored on random mail servers. Well, none of the other developers on our team know anything about encryption, so I'm going to ask you to put together a library that makes it easy for the others to encrypt and decrypt files. The ultimate goal is to have our researchers type a password to encrypt a file. Then, they can call the person they're sending it to, and tell them the password to decrypt it. Why don't you ask Mark what functions would be most useful?"

- **Mark Hassall, Developer** "I'm glad you're taking on this encryption thing. Encryption blows my mind. I don't have the brain cells to learn it. Well, we just need to create encrypted and unencrypted copies of files. Why don't you create an assembly with two static methods: *Encrypt* and *Decrypt*. I'll provide the old filename, the new filename, and the password that the user provided. I don't know anything about encryption, so I'll leave the rest up to you."

Technical Requirements Create a class assembly with two public, static methods:

- *Encrypt* (string *unencryptedFileName*, string *encryptedFileName*, string *password*)

- *Decrypt* (string *encryptedFileName*, string *unencryptedFileName*, string *password*)

Create the library, and create a simple console or Windows Forms application to verify that the Windows Forms application can successfully encrypt and decrypt files.

Exercise

Answer the following questions to provide your solution to the Trey management team.

Tip For a working example of the class, refer to the PasswordEncryption project on the companion CD.

1. Which encryption algorithm did you use? Why?

2. Which classes and methods did you use to generate the encryption key based on the user password? How did you generate the salt value? How did you write the code to generate the key and initialization vector?

3. Which class did you use to write to and read from the encrypted files?

Lesson Summary

- Symmetric key encryption is a cryptographic technique for protecting the privacy of data in situations where both the encryptor and decryptor have access to the same secret key. Among other uses, symmetric key encryption is used to protect some IPSec communications and to perform bulk encryption of Web communications.

- There are four symmetric algorithm classes in the .NET Framework: *RijndaelManaged*, *DES*, *TripleDES*, and *RC2*.

- To create a random symmetric key, simply create a symmetric encryption object. The .NET Framework automatically generates a random symmetric key when you create a symmetric algorithm object. If you use this random key, you must transfer it to the decryptor without compromising its privacy. Alternatively, you can generate a key based on a user password by using the *PasswordDeriveBytes* class.

- To encrypt and decrypt messages, create a symmetric algorithm class and then create a *CryptoStream* class to read or write the encrypted data.

- The Data Protection API (DPAPI) is a Win32 library for storing and retrieving encrypted data without manually generating keys. Unfortunately, there is no managed interface for the library, and you should avoid it when creating .NET Framework applications.

Lesson 2: Encrypting and Decrypting Data with Asymmetric Keys

Asymmetric encryption overcomes symmetric encryption's most significant disability: requiring both the encryptor and decryptor to know a shared secret. Asymmetric encryption relies on key pairs. In a key pair, there is one public key and one private key. The public key can be freely shared because it cannot be easily abused, even by an attacker. Messages encrypted with the public key can be decrypted only with the private key, allowing anyone to send encrypted messages that can be decrypted only by a single individual.

After this lesson, you will be able to

- Describe what asymmetric encryption allows you to do.
- Name the class used for asymmetric encryption, and list the significant methods and properties.
- Export and import asymmetric keys and key pairs.
- Store key pairs for later reuse.
- Encrypt and decrypt messages using asymmetric encryption.

Estimated lesson time: 60 minutes

What Is Asymmetric Encryption?

Asymmetric encryption, also known as public-key encryption, is a cryptography technique that uses separate private and public keys to encrypt and decrypt data. Asymmetric encryption uses a private key that must be kept secret from unauthorized users, and a public key that can be made public to anyone. The public key and the private key are mathematically linked; data encrypted with the public key can be decrypted only with the private key, and data signed with the private key can be verified only with the public key. The public key can be made available to anyone; it is used for encrypting data to be sent to the keeper of the private key.

 Note Public-key cryptographic algorithms are also known as asymmetric (meaning *different*) algorithms, because one key is required to encrypt data and another is required to decrypt data.

The asymmetric encryption process begins with a public key being exchanged. Generally, both the client and server exchange public keys. However, if only one side of the communication needs to be encrypted, only the peer receiving encrypted communications must provide a public key.

After the public keys are exchanged, communications are encrypted using the recipient's public key. Such communications can be decrypted only by the recipient, because only the recipient holds the private key that matches the public key. Figure 8-5 shows a simple asymmetric encryption arrangement in which only one side of the communications provides a public key.

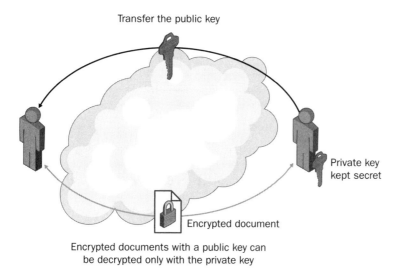

Transfer the public key

Private key
kept secret

Encrypted document

Encrypted documents with a public key can
be decrypted only with the private key

Figure 8-5   Asymmetric cryptography uses separate keys for encryption and decryption.

Asymmetric algorithms are not as fast as symmetric algorithms but are much more difficult to break. Asymmetric algorithms are not well suited to encrypting large amounts of data because of the performance overhead. One common use of asymmetric algorithms is to encrypt and transfer a symmetric key and initialization vector. The symmetric encryption algorithm is then used for all messages being sent back and forth. This is the technique used by HTTPS and SSL to encrypt Web communications—asymmetric encryption is used only during session establishment. This common combination of asymmetric and symmetric encryption is shown in Figure 8-6.

The other significant challenge of asymmetric encryption is key management. To manage keys, organizations typically implement a public key infrastructure (PKI), such as Certificate Services included with Windows Server 2003. A *PKI* is an infrastructure for distributing, managing, and revoking certificates in an organization. As a developer, you will generally not be responsible for configuring a PKI.

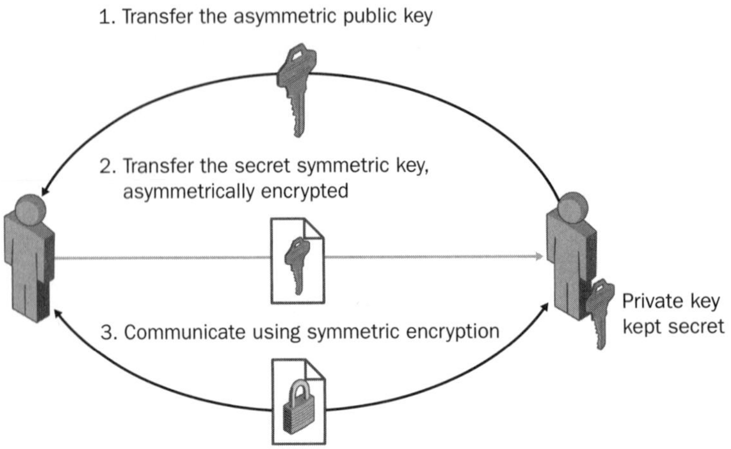

1. Transfer the asymmetric public key

2. Transfer the secret symmetric key,
   asymmetrically encrypted

Private key
kept secret

3. Communicate using symmetric encryption

Figure 8-6   Combine asymmetric and symmetric algorithms to optimize security and performance.

Asymmetric Algorithm Classes in the .NET Framework

The .NET Framework provides two classes for working with asymmetric encryption, and they are both based on the *System.Security.Cryptography.AsymmetricAlgorithm* class. This base class has the following properties, several of which are identical to the *SymmetricAlgorithm* counterparts:

- **KeyExchangeAlgorithm**   Gets the name of the key exchange algorithm. Generally, you do not need to directly access this property.

- **KeySize**   Gets or sets the size of the secret key used by the symmetric algorithm in bits.

> **Note**   Asymmetric keys are much larger than symmetric keys. For example, whereas a typical symmetric key is 182 bits, the .NET Framework implementation of the RSA algorithm supports key lengths from 384 through 16384 bits.

- **LegalKeySizes**   A *KeySizes* array that gets the key sizes that are supported by the symmetric algorithm. Each array member contains *MinSize* and *MaxSize* properties that define the valid key ranges in bits, and a *SkipSize* property that specifies the interval between valid key sizes in bits.

- **SignatureAlgorithm**   Gets the URL of an XML document describing the signature algorithm. Generally, you do not need to directly access this property.

Unlike the *SymmetricAlgorithm* base class, the *AsymmetricAlgorithm* base class has no useful methods. Instead, the encryption functionality is built into the objects that implement the *AsymmetricAlgorithm* class. The .NET Framework provides two implementations of this class:

- ***RSACryptoServiceProvider***   Used for all asymmetric encryption and decryption. *RSACryptoServiceProvider* is the .NET Framework implementation of the RSA algorithm. RSA is named for the last initial of its three creators—Ronald Rivest, Adi Shamir, and Leonard Adleman—who developed the algorithm in 1977. The *RSACryptoServiceProvider* class is a managed wrapper around the unmanaged RSA implementation provided by the Cryptography API.

- ***DSACryptoServiceProvider***   Used for digitally signing messages, this is also a managed wrapper around unmanaged code.

> **See Also**   For more information about *DSACryptoServiceProvider*, see Lesson 4 in this chapter.

In addition to the properties provided by *AsymmetricAlgorithm*, *RSACryptoServiceProvider* provides the following properties:

- ***PersistKeyInCsp***   Gets or sets a value indicating whether the key should be persisted in the cryptographic service provider (CSP). Set this to true when you want to reuse the key without exporting it.

- ***UseMachineKeyStore***   Gets or sets a value indicating whether the key should be persisted in the computer's key store instead of in the user profile store.

The default constructors always populate the algorithm parameters with the strongest defaults available to the run-time environment, giving you the strongest algorithm possible without changing any settings. The *RSACryptoServiceProvider* class also includes methods for encrypting and decrypting, as well as for importing and exporting keys. The following list describes each of these methods:

- ***Decrypt***   Decrypts data with the RSA algorithm.

- ***Encrypt***   Encrypts data with the RSA algorithm.

- ***ExportParameters***   Exports an *RSAParameters* structure, which defines the algorithm's key pair. Pass true to this method to export both the private and public key, or pass false to export only the public key.

- ***FromXmlString***   Imports a key pair from an XML string.

- ***ImportParameters***   Imports to a public key or key pair the specified *RSAParameters* object.

- ***SignData***   Computes the hash value of the specified data and stores the signature in a byte array.

- ***SignHash***   Computes the signature for the specified hash value by encrypting it with the private key and storing the signature in a byte array.

- **VerifyData** Verifies the specified signature data by comparing it to the signature computed for the specified data.

- **VerifyHash** Verifies the specified signature data by comparing it to the signature computed for the specified hash value.

How to Export and Import Asymmetric Keys and Key Pairs

RSA keys are much more complex than symmetric encryption keys. In fact, RSA keys are called parameters and are represented by an *RSAParameters* structure. Table 8-2 lists the significant members of this structure and their purpose. The structure includes several parameters that are not listed, but you will not need to directly access these: *DP*, *DQ*, *InverseQ*, *P*, and *Q*.

Table 8-2 *RSAParameters* **Structure Members**

Parameter	Description
D	The private key.
Exponent	Also known as *e*, this is the short part of the public key.
Modulus	Also known as *n*, this is the long part of the public key.

You will almost always need to export your public key, because without the public key, nobody can send encrypted messages to you. To export your public key to an instance of the *RSAParamaters* structure, use the *RSACryptoServiceProvider.ExportParameters* method, and pass it a Boolean *false* parameter. The *false* parameter causes the method to export only the public key. If it were set to true, *ExportParameters* would export both the public and private key.

Important Export your private key only if you need to reuse it later. If you do store it, your application must protect the privacy of the private key.

The following code sample demonstrates how to create a new instance of an RSA algorithm and export its automatically generated public key to an *RSAParameters* object named *publicKey*:

```
// Create an instance of the RSA algorithm object
RSACryptoServiceProvider myRSA = new RSACryptoServiceProvider();

// Create a new RSAParameters object with only the public key
RSAParameters publicKey = myRSA.ExportParameters(false);
```

```vb
' Create an instance of the RSA algorithm object
Dim myRSA As RSACryptoServiceProvider = New RSACryptoServiceProvider

' Create a new RSAParameters object with only the public key
Dim publicKey As RSAParameters = myRSA.ExportParameters(False)
```

After you create an *RSAParameters* object, you can freely access any of the byte array parameters described in Table 8-2. If you need to store or transmit the export key or keys, you should use the *RSACryptoServiceProvider.ToXmlString* method instead. Like *ExportParameters*, this method takes a Boolean value that indicates whether the private key should be exported. However, *ToXmlString* stores the data in an XML format that can be easily stored, transferred, and imported with the *FromXmlString* method. The following example shows an abbreviated version of an exported RSA key pair created by calling *RSACryptoServiceProvider.ToXmlString(true)*.

```xml
<RSAKeyValue>
    <Modulus>vilaR5C3XtmH5…IGZNTs=</Modulus>
    <Exponent>AQAB</Exponent>
    <P>699j5bpT04JlVkjz…66sYYxLG6VQ==</P>
    <Q>zmNovTJlGUamU1Vk…EMtEJqhZgzhTw==</Q>
    <DP>OWBf5p7qB6JzB7xek…tkQGoiMBK+Q==</DP>
    <DQ>NLbZUrGjduA/99K…scf2pOzQTvKw==</DQ>
    <InverseQ>BYZ3vVwb/N+…HjPcGz7Yg==</InverseQ>
    <D>Jz81qMuPbP4MdEaF/…hYZ5WmrzeRRE=</D>
</RSAKeyValue>
```

How to Store Key Pairs for Later Reuse

When you create an *RSACryptoServiceProvider* object, the object automatically creates a key pair as needed. Therefore, you can work with asymmetric encryption without manually generating a key pair. If you are not storing encrypted data, you do not need to store the key pair. For example, if you are using asymmetric encryption to protect network communications, there is generally no need to save the key pair for later use. However, if your application must decrypt files that were created by another application or an earlier instance of your application, you will need to store your key pair.

In Chapter 7, "Maximizing Security During Deployment," you worked with the Strong Name tool. One feature of the Strong Name tool is that it allows you to create key pairs and save them in a cryptographic service provider (CSP). It was important to save the keys that you used so that you could reuse them in the future. If your application needs to reuse key pairs in the future, the *RSACryptoServiceProvider* includes the ability to save keys in a CSP by using CryptoAPI key storage.

To store your private keys persistently, add the following elements to your code:

1. Create a *CspParameters* object.

2. Specify the *CspParameters.KeyContainerName* property.

3. Create an *RSACryptoServiceProvider* object using the overloaded constructor that accepts a *CspParameters* object.

4. Set the *RSACryptoServiceProvider.PersistKeyInCsp* property to true.

The .NET Framework handles creating and retrieving keys automatically. The first time you specify a *CspParameters* object and set the *PersistKeyInCsp* property to true, the .NET Framework will create the key container and store your key. If you run the same application again, the .NET Framework will detect that a key container with that name already exists, and will retrieve the stored private key. For example, if you run this console application repeatedly, it will display the same private key every time:

```csharp
// Create a CspParameters object
CspParameters persistantCsp = new CspParameters();
persistantCsp.KeyContainerName = "AsymmetricExample";

// Create an instance of the RSA algorithm object
RSACryptoServiceProvider myRSA = new RSACryptoServiceProvider(persistantCsp);

// Specify that the private key should be stored in the CSP
myRSA.PersistKeyInCsp = true;

// Create a new RSAParameters object with the private key
RSAParameters privateKey = myRSA.ExportParameters(true);

foreach (byte thisByte in privateKey.D)
{
    Console.Write(thisByte.ToString("X2") + " ");
}
```

```vbnet
' Create a CspParameters object
Dim persistantCsp As CspParameters = New CspParameters
persistantCsp.KeyContainerName = "AsymmetricExample"

' Create an instance of the RSA algorithm object
Dim myRSA As RSACryptoServiceProvider = New ⤶
RSACryptoServiceProvider (persistantCsp)

' Specify that the private key should be stored in the CSP
myRSA.PersistKeyInCsp = True

' Create a new RSAParameters object with the private key
Dim privateKey As RSAParameters = myRSA.ExportParameters(True)

For Each thisByte As Byte In privateKey.D
    Console.Write(thisByte.ToString("X2") + " ")
Next
```

However, if you change the *KeyContainerName* value and rerun the application, the application will display a new private key, because the .NET Framework will not find an existing key container.

How to Encrypt and Decrypt Messages Using Asymmetric Encryption

To encrypt and decrypt messages using asymmetric encryption, call the *RSACryptoServiceProvider.Encrypt* and *RSACryptoServiceProvider.Decrypt* methods. Both take two parameters:

- ■ **byte[] rgb**   An array of bytes containing the message to be encrypted or decrypted.

- ■ **bool fOAEP**   A Boolean value. When set to true, encryption and decryption will use OAEP data padding, which is supported only on Windows XP and later operating systems. When set to false, PKCS#1 v1.5 data padding will be used. Both the encryption and decryption methods *must* use the same data padding.

What Is Data Padding?

Data padding is a cryptographic technique used by asymmetric algorithms to protect against attacks that rely on the unencrypted text being simple. The .NET Framework supports two padding schemes for the RSA algorithm: Optimal Asymmetric Encryption Padding (OAEP) and PKCS #1 v1.5. Generally, use OAEP, because it is newer and more secure than PKCS. Use PKCS only when you are communicating with a legacy client that you know does not support OAEP. Currently, all Windows operating systems released prior to Windows XP lack support for OAEP, including Windows 2000.

The most challenging aspect of encryption is converting data into the byte array format. To convert strings to byte arrays, use the *System.Text.Encoding.Unicode.GetBytes* and *System.Text.Encoding.Unicode.GetString* methods. For example, the following console application encrypts a string using PKCS#1 v1.5 data padding, and then immediately decrypts and displays the string:

```csharp
string messageString = "Hello, World!";
RSACryptoServiceProvider myRsa = new RSACryptoServiceProvider();

byte[] messageBytes = Encoding.Unicode.GetBytes(messageString);
byte[] encryptedMessage = myRsa.Encrypt(messageBytes, false);

byte[] decryptedBytes = myRsa.Decrypt(encryptedMessage, false);
Console.WriteLine(Encoding.Unicode.GetString(decryptedBytes));
```

```vb
Dim messageString As String = "Hello, World!"
Dim myRsa As RSACryptoServiceProvider = New RSACryptoServiceProvider

Dim messageBytes As Byte() = Encoding.Unicode.GetBytes(messageString)
Dim encryptedMessage As Byte() = myRsa.Encrypt(messageBytes, False)

Dim decryptedBytes As Byte() = myRsa.Decrypt(encryptedMessage, False)
Console.WriteLine(Encoding.Unicode.GetString(decryptedBytes))
```

Whichever encoding method you use to convert the data into a byte array, be sure you use a matching decoding method after decrypting the data.

Practice: Encrypting and Decrypting Data with Asymmetric Keys

In this practice, you will create a Windows Forms application that encrypts and decrypts files by using asymmetric encryption. Read the scenario and then complete the exercise that follows. If you are unable to answer a question, review the lesson and try the question again. You can find answers to the questions in the "Questions and Answers" section at the end of this chapter.

Scenario

You are a developer for Trey Research, a company that performs outsourced research tasks for enterprises. Trey is a very distributed company, with 500 employees scattered around the world, primarily working out of home offices. Your development team has five developers total, and has created a document management application based on the .NET Framework to simplify the transfer of documents between employees. The application uses the employee's personal e-mail account to transfer files, which means your internal, confidential files might be transferred across and stored on untrusted mail servers.

Your management wants to reduce the risk of attackers acquiring the documents during e-mail transfers and being able to successfully view them. Encryption seems like the best solution, and your management has asked for your help. You interview key personnel and review technical requirements before coming up with your solution.

Interviews   Following is a list of company personnel interviewed and their statements:

■ **Deborah Poe, Development Manager**   "Thanks for creating that class library. It works great. The only problem is that our staff is still required to call each other with a password each time they want to send a document. That's kind of a pain. To make matters worse, we discovered that the staff has decided to use the same password for everything to save them some time. Clearly, the password-based encryption isn't going to work for us. I've heard about asymmetric encryption. From what I understand, if we used that to encrypt things, we would never have to worry about secretly transmitting passwords or keys, correct? People could just send their public keys around, and even if a bad guy intercepted one, they wouldn't be able to use it to decrypt anything, right? Well, I know GUIs aren't your thing, so I had Mark put together the shell of a Windows Forms application. All you need to do is to complete all of the TODO comments that Mark has added to the code."

■ **Mark Hassall, Developer**   "I put together this shell of a Windows Forms application for you. I added menu items for different things, like saving and loading key pairs, exporting and importing public keys, and encrypting and decrypting messages. Just look at the form's code, and write the code described by each of the TODO comments, and I think it should work."

Exercise

Write code for the following methods, test the application by transferring encrypted messages between two instances of the application, and then answer the questions that follow.

■ ***loadKeyMenuItem_Click***   Called when the user clicks Load Private Key on the Key menu. This should load a key pair from a file and store it in the *myRSA* object.

■ ***saveKeyMenuItem_Click***   Called when the user clicks Save Private Key on the Key menu. This should export the *myRSA* private key to a file.

■ ***importKeyMenuItem_Click***   Called when the user clicks Import Public Key on the Send Messages menu. This should read a file containing a public key and store it in the *otherRSA* object.

■ ***saveMessageMenuItem_Click***   Called when the user clicks Save Encrypted Message on the Send Messages menu. This should prompt the user to save a file, encrypt the contents of *messageTextBox* with the *otherRSA* object, and then save the encrypted data to the file the user specified.

■ ***exportKeyMenuItem_Click***   Called when the user clicks Export Public Key on the Receive Messages menu. This should create a new file containing only the public key from the *myRSA* object.

■ ***loadMessageMenuItem_Click***   Called when the user clicks Load Encrypted Message on the Receive Messages menu. This should prompt the user to open a file, decrypt the file with the *myRSA* object, and then display the unencrypted file in *messageTextBox*.

■ ***DisplayKeys***   Should display the *myRSA* public and private keys in *myPrivateKeyTextBox* and *myPublicKeyTextBox*, and display the *otherRSA* public key in *otherPublicKeyTextBox*.

The Windows Forms project named PublicKeyEncryptor is located on your companion CD and is available in both C# and Visual Basic .NET. The application has a single form that is intended to display text-encoded versions of the private key (*myPrivateKeyTextBox*), the public key (*myPublicKeyTextBox*), and the recipient's public key (*otherPublicKeyTextBox*). Additionally, *messageTextBox* allows users to enter messages for encryption and should be used to display decrypted messages. Figure 8-7 shows what the application's user interface will resemble when you complete the application.

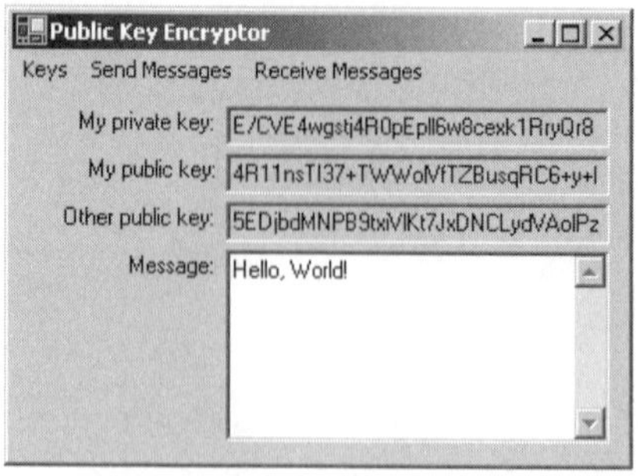

Figure 8-7   The application's user interface

As shown in Figure 8-8, both the sender and recipient will run the application. The recipient must be able to export the public key, which the sender will import. The sender will then encrypt a message with the public key. The recipient will open the encrypted message, decrypt it using the recipient's private key, and display the unencrypted message.

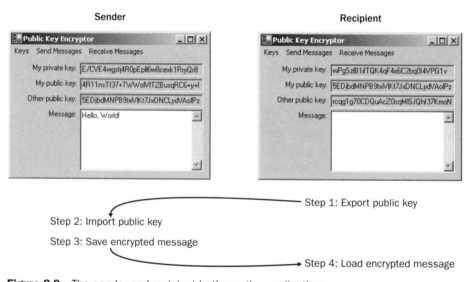

Figure 8-8   The sender and recipient both run the application.

1. What code did you write for the *loadKeyMenuItem_Click* method?

2. What code did you write for the *saveKeyMenuItem_Click* method?

3. What code did you write for the *importKeyMenuItem_Click* method?

4. What code did you write for the *saveMessageMenuItem_Click* method?

5. What code did you write for the *exportKeyMenuItem_Click* method?

6. What code did you write for the *loadMessageMenuItem_Click* method?

7. What code did you write for the *DisplayKeys* method?

Lesson Summary

- Asymmetric encryption is a cryptographic encryption method for protecting the privacy of data that uses a key pair. The key pair consists of a public key and a private key. The private key must be used to decrypt messages with the public key. Asymmetric encryption is more secure than symmetric encryption, but much slower.

- The *RSACryptoServiceProvider* is the only asymmetric encryption algorithm provided with the .NET Framework that can be used for encrypting and decrypting messages.

- To export private keys, use the *ToXmlString* or *ExportParameters* methods. To import private keys, use the *FromXmlString* or *ImportParameters* methods.

- If you need to decrypt data that was encrypted by an earlier instance of your application, you must store the key pair. Although you can store the key pair after exporting it, the simplest way to store key pairs is to set the *PersistKeyInCsp* parameter to true.

- To encrypt and decrypt messages, exchange public keys and call the *RSACryptoServiceProvider.Encrypt* and *RSACryptoServiceProvider.Decrypt* methods.

Lesson 3: Validating Data Integrity with Hashes

Another important use of cryptography is protecting data integrity by using hashes. A hash is a checksum that is unique to a specific file or piece of data. You can use a hash value to verify that a file has not been modified after the hash was generated.

After this lesson, you will be able to

- Describe a hash.
- List the hash algorithms included with the .NET Framework.
- Compute a non-keyed hash.
- Compute a keyed hash.

Estimated lesson time: 25 minutes

What Is a Hash?

A *hash* is a value that summarizes a larger piece of data and can be used to verify that the data has not been modified since the hash was generated. Hash algorithms map binary values of an arbitrary length to small binary values of a fixed length, known as hash values. A *hash value* is a unique and extremely compact numerical representation of a piece of data. If you hash a paragraph of plain text and change even one letter of the paragraph, a subsequent hash will produce a different value. It is computationally improbable to find two distinct inputs that hash to the same value.

You use hash values when you do not wish to ever recover the original value. You cannot derive the original data from the hash, even if the original data is very small. In other words, creating a hash is a one-way operation. Hashes are often used to store passwords. After the hash of the password has been stored, the application can verify the password by calculating the hash of the provided password and comparing it to the stored hash. The two hash values will match if the user has provided the same password; however, an attacker cannot determine the original password even if the attacker gains access to the password's hash value.

Off the Record   Storing the hash of a password is better than storing the actual password. However, attackers can use databases of hashed passwords to quickly identify original passwords from their hashes. So, using a common hashing algorithm to protect passwords provides very little deterrence to a sophisticated attacker.

Hash Algorithms in the .NET Framework

The .NET Framework includes five non-keyed hash algorithms and two keyed hash algorithms. Table 8-3 lists each of the non-keyed hash algorithms included with the .NET Framework. Each is a member of the *System.Security.Cryptography* class, and is derived from *System.Security.Cryptography.HashAlgorithm*.

Table 8-3   Non-Keyed Hashing Algorithms

Abstract Class	Implementation Class	Description
MD5	*MD5CryptoServiceProvider*	The Message Digest algorithm. The hash size for the MD5 algorithm is 128 bits.
SHA1	*SHA1CryptoServiceProvider*	The Secure Hash Algorithm 1. The hash size for the SHA1 algorithm is 160 bits.
SHA256	*SHA256Managed*	The Secure Hash Algorithm 256. The hash is 256 bits.
SHA384	*SHA384Managed*	The Secure Hash Algorithm 384. The hash is 384 bits.
SHA512	*SHA512Managed*	The Secure Hash Algorithm 512. The hash is 512 bits.

You have to take care to prevent attackers from modifying a hash value. If an attacker can modify a hash, he or she can effectively defeat the purpose of the hash. *Keyed hash algorithms* are algorithms that protect against modification of the hash by encrypting it by using a secret key that both the sender and receiver must have. Table 8-4 lists each of the keyed hash algorithms included with the .NET Framework. Each is a member of the *System.Security.Cryptography* class and is derived from *System.Security.Cryptography.KeyedHashAlgorithm*.

Table 8-4   Keyed Hashing Algorithms

Class	Description
HMACSHA1	Hash-based Message Authentication Code using *SHA1*. Used to determine whether a message sent over an insecure channel has been tampered with, provided that the sender and receiver share a secret key. HMACSHA1 accepts keys of any size, and produces a hash sequence of length 20 bytes.
MACTripleDES	Message Authentication Code using *TripleDES*. Like *HMACSHA1*, *MACTripleDES* is used to determine whether a message sent over an insecure channel has been tampered with, provided that the sender and receiver share a secret key. *MACTripleDES* uses a key of length 8, 16, or 24 bytes, and produces a hash sequence of length 8 bytes.

> ### Real World   Hash Algorithms Aren't Always Unique
>
> Many years ago I was a developer creating a database that indexed thousands and thousands of files for one of the first major Internet download services. A single file was often submitted using multiple filenames, so avoiding duplicate files required more than simply checking to see whether the filename already existed. Initially, I sorted through the files to verify that each was unique by examining the size and contents of the files. However, this was an extremely slow process.
>
> I decided to create an index of files by using an MD5 hash of each file. Then, my application could check whether a file already existed simply by looking up the MD5 hash. I was surprised when my application found a duplicate file. After checking into it further, I discovered that it had found two unique files that produced the same hash! This was supposed to be mathematically impossible; however, because the size of the MD5 hash was a reasonably small 128 bits and the size of the files was much larger, the possibility existed that multiple files would produce the same hash. In my case, I had stumbled across such an unlikely occurrence. Using a longer hash, such as SHA512, further reduces the likelihood of such an occurrence.

How to Compute a Non-Keyed Hash

To compute a non-keyed hash, perform the following steps in your code:

1. Create the hash algorithm object.

2. Store the data to be hashed in a byte array.

3. Call the *HashAlgorithm.ComputeHash* method.

4. Retrieve the *HashAlgorithm.Hash* byte array, which contains the hash value.

The following console application demonstrates how to create a hash by calculating the hash of the file specified in *args[0]*, and displaying the hash using Base64 text encoding.

```
// Step 1: Create the hash algorithm object
MD5 myHash = new MD5CryptoServiceProvider();

// Step 2: Store the data to be hashed in a byte array
FileStream file = new FileStream(args[0], FileMode.Open, FileAccess.Read);
BinaryReader reader = new BinaryReader(file);

// Step 3: Call the HashAlgorithm.ComputeHash method
myHash.ComputeHash(reader.ReadBytes((int)file.Length));

// Step 4: Retrieve the HashAlgorithm.Hash byte array
Console.WriteLine(Convert.ToBase64String(myHash.Hash));
```

```vb
Sub Main(ByVal args As String())
    ' Step 1: Create the hash algorithm object
    Dim myHash As MD5 = New MD5CryptoServiceProvider

    ' Step 2: Store the data to be hashed in a byte array
    Dim file As FileStream = New FileStream (args(0), →
FileMode.Open, FileAccess.Read)
    Dim reader As BinaryReader = New BinaryReader (file)

    ' Step 3: Call the HashAlgorithm.ComputeHash method
    myHash.ComputeHash(reader.ReadBytes(CType(file.Length, Integer)))

    ' Step 4: Retrieve the HashAlgorithm.Hash byte array
    Console.WriteLine(Convert.ToBase64String(myHash.Hash))
End Sub
```

Repeatedly running that console application to calculate the hash of a single file will always produce the same hash result until the file is modified. After the file is modified, the hash result also changes. Consider the following console output, which creates a new text file, computes the hash repeatedly, and then modifies the file. After the file is modified, the hash also changes:

```
C:\>echo Hello, World! > HashThis.txt

C:\>HashExample HashThis.txt
h7GTmgvuZdN0SGR0A6qdBA==

C:\>HashExample HashThis.txt
h7GTmgvuZdN0SGR0A6qdBA==

C:\>echo Hello, again. >> HashThis.txt

C:\>HashExample HashThis.txt
F1QQWOeK/Yc2EwNR2BxCuw==
```

Because all non-keyed hash algorithms are derived from a single class, you can change the hash algorithm used simply by changing the algorithm declaration. For example, you can replace the declaration in the previous code sample with any of the following declarations. Each will produce different hash results:

```csharp
SHA1 myHash = new SHA1CryptoServiceProvider();
SHA256 myHash = new SHA256Managed();
SHA384 myHash = new SHA384Managed();
SHA512 myHash = new SHA512Managed();
```

```vb
Dim myHash As SHA1 = New SHA1CryptoServiceProvider
Dim myHash As SHA256 = New SHA256Managed
Dim myHash As SHA384 = New SHA384Managed
Dim myHash As SHA512 = New SHA512Managed
```

The more bits used in the hash, the longer the hash that will be displayed. To later verify that the data has not been modified, simply recalculate the hash using the same algorithm, and compare the two values.

How to Compute a Keyed Hash

To compute a keyed hash, perform the following steps in your code:

1. Create a secret key that is shared among all parties who will compute or verify the hash.

2. Create the hash algorithm object using the secret key. If you do not provide a secret key, one will be automatically generated for you.

3. Store the data to be hashed in a byte array.

4. Call the *KeyedHashAlgorithm.ComputeHash* method.

5. Retrieve the *KeyedHashAlgorithm.Hash* byte array, which contains the hash value.

The following console application demonstrates how to create an HMACSHA1 hash by calculating the hash of the file specified in *args[1]* by using a password specified in *args[0]* to generate a secret key:

```csharp
// Step 1: Create a secret key
byte[] saltValueBytes  = Encoding.ASCII.GetBytes("This is my salt");
PasswordDeriveBytes passwordKey = new PasswordDeriveBytes→
(args[0], saltValueBytes, "SHA1", 3);
byte[] secretKey = passwordKey.GetBytes(16);

// Step 2: Create the hash algorithm object
HMACSHA1 myHash = new HMACSHA1(secretKey);

// Step 3: Store the data to be hashed in a byte array
FileStream file = new FileStream(args[1], FileMode.Open, FileAccess.Read);
BinaryReader reader = new BinaryReader(file);

// Step 4: Call the HashAlgorithm.ComputeHash method
myHash.ComputeHash(reader.ReadBytes((int)file.Length));

// Step 5: Retrieve the HashAlgorithm.Hash byte array
Console.WriteLine(Convert.ToBase64String(myHash.Hash));
```

```vb
Sub Main(ByVal args As String())
    ' Step 1: Create a secret key
    Dim saltValueBytes As Byte() = Encoding.ASCII.GetBytes("This is my salt")
    Dim passwordKey As PasswordDeriveBytes = New PasswordDeriveBytes →
(args(0), saltValueBytes, "SHA1", 3)
    Dim secretKey As Byte() = passwordKey.GetBytes(16)

    ' Step 2: Create the hash algorithm object
    Dim myHash As HMACSHA1 = New HMACSHA1 (secretKey)
```

```
    ' Step 3: Store the data to be hashed in a byte array
    Dim file As FileStream = New FileStream (args(1), FileMode.Open, ⇥
FileAccess.Read)
    Dim reader As BinaryReader = New BinaryReader (file)

    ' Step 4: Call the HashAlgorithm.ComputeHash method
    myHash.ComputeHash(reader.ReadBytes(CType(file.Length, Integer)))

    ' Step 5: Retrieve the HashAlgorithm.Hash byte array
    Console.WriteLine(Convert.ToBase64String(myHash.Hash))
End Sub
```

If either the file contents or the password changes, the computed hash will also change. This ensures both the sender and recipient used the same password to generate the hash, which prevents an attacker from modifying the hash. Consider the following console output, which creates a new text file, computes the hash repeatedly, and then modifies the file. After either the file or the password (and key) is modified, the hash also changes:

```
C:\>echo Hello, World! > HashThis.txt

C:\>KeyedHashExample SomePassword HashThis.txt
t04kYA9Z2ki+JbzUqe7llE6EjN4=

C:\>KeyedHashExample SomePassword HashThis.txt
t04kYA9Z2ki+JbzUqe7llE6EjN4=

C:\>KeyedHashExample NotSomePassword HashThis.txt
TFNPh9TspBobOvixylyJ0fX/+vo=

C:\>echo Hello, again. >> HashThis.txt

C:\>KeyedHashExample SomePassword HashThis.txt
yW6K6G7diJEV3bV2nNttgtcCM0o=
```

Either HMACSHA1 or MACTripleDES can be used for the previous example. However, whereas HMACSHA1 accepts a secret key of any length, MACTripleDES accepts only secret keys of 8, 16, or 24 bytes.

Practice: Validating Data Integrity with Hashes

In this practice, you will create two console applications that create and validate hashes for files. Read the scenario and then complete the exercise that follows. If you are unable to answer a question, review the lesson and try the question again. You can find answers to the questions in the "Questions and Answers" section at the end of this chapter.

Scenario

You are a consultant for Proseware, Inc., a small software development company whose encyclopedia software has suddenly become extremely popular. Proseware just received their Web site bandwidth bill from their Internet service provider (ISP), and it was much higher than they expected. They want to find ways to distribute their software and data files other than having users download it directly from their Web site. However, they are concerned that users will not trust that the files have not been modified, because they were generated by Proseware. They hired you to recommend a method to allow users to verify the integrity of their files. You interview key personnel and review technical requirements before making your recommendations.

Interviews   Following is a list of company personnel interviewed and their statements:

- **Dick Dievendorff, Development Manager**   "We've been looking at using a software download service, or distributing our data files using peer-to-peer networks. I'm concerned about data integrity, though. Our users rely on the accuracy of our encyclopedia data. If they download it from someone else, what prevents it from being modified? We use an SSL certificate for our Web site, so our users know that when they connect to our site, the files are genuine. I'd be satisfied if we could post some kind of checksum on the Web site, and allow users to download an application that verifies the checksum of the data file after they've downloaded it. Can you recommend a way to generate that checksum, and create a simple console application to validate the checksum? Oh, and use as many bits as possible for the checksum. That makes people feel safer."

Technical Requirements   Create two console applications:

- **ComputeHash**   This application must take a single command-line argument: a filename. It should create output to the console that is a Base64-encoded hash of the file.

- **VerifyHash**   This application must take two command-line arguments: a filename and a Base64-encoded hash of the file. It must verify the checksum and display the results to the console.

Exercise

Create the two console applications and then answer the following questions.

1. Did you choose a keyed or non-keyed hashing method?

2. Which hashing algorithm should you use? Why?

3. What code did you write the ComputeHash application to generate the hash?

4. What code did you write the VerifyHash application to verify the hash?

Lesson Summary

- A hash is a checksum that uniquely identifies a file, a password, or other piece of data. Hashes are used to verify that a file or message has not been modified since the hash was created. Passwords are hashed to allow them to be transmitted and stored with less risk of exposing the original passwords.

- The .NET Framework includes five non-keyed algorithms and two keyed algorithms. The five non-keyed algorithms are: MD5, SHA1, SHA256, SHA384, SHA512. The two keyed algorithms are HMACSHA1 and MACTripleDES.

- To compute a non-keyed hash, use the *HashAlgorithm.ComputeHash* method.

- To compute a keyed hash, use the *KeyedHashAlgorithm.ComputeHash* method.

Lesson 4: Signing Files

Digital signatures, like real signatures, serve as proof that an individual has approved a file or other piece of data. Digital signatures are resistant to forgery and protect the signed document from modification. Using digital signatures in your application is simple after you understand asymmetric encryption and hashing, because digital signatures simply combine the two technologies. The hash component of the digital signature protects the file from modification, whereas the public key offers proof that the holder of the private key generated the hash. This lesson teaches how to add digital signature capabilities to your application.

After this lesson, you will be able to

- Describe the purpose of a digital signature.
- List the classes in the .NET Framework used for digital signatures and the most important methods.
- Generate and verify a digital signature for a file.
- Create a digital signature in an XML document.

Estimated lesson time: 25 minutes

What Is a Digital Signature?

A *digital signature* is a value that can be appended to electronic data to prove that it was created by someone who possesses a specific private key. Public-key algorithms can also be used to form digital signatures. Digital signatures authenticate the identity of a sender (if you trust the sender's public key) and help protect the integrity of data. A signature can be verified by anyone because the sender's public key can be publicly accessible and is typically included in the digital signature format.

Important   Digital signatures do not protect the secrecy of the data being signed. To protect the secrecy of the file, you must encrypt it.

Digital Signature Classes in the .NET Framework

The .NET Framework provides two classes for generating and verifying digital signatures: *DSACryptoServiceProvider* and *RSACryptoServiceProvider*. These classes use different algorithms but provide similar functionality. Each implements the following four methods for use with digital signatures:

- **SignHash**   Generates a digital signature based on the hash of a file.

 See Also   For more information about creating hashes, see Lesson 3 in this chapter.

- **SignData**   Generates a digital signature by first generating the hash for a file, and then generating a signature based on the hash.
- **VerifyHash**   Verifies a digital signature based on the hash of a file.
- **VerifyData**   Verifies a digital signature given the entire file's contents.

Digital signatures provide separate methods for signing and verifying data, whereas hashes do not provide separate methods for verification. The reason that hash algorithms do not need a separate method for signing and verifying is that the recipient can easily recreate the hash, and then compare the hash she generated to the hash the sender provided. However, digital signatures use asymmetric encryption. Therefore, the recipient cannot regenerate the signature without the sender's private key, although the signature can be verified by using the sender's public key. The *VerifyData* and *VerifyHash* methods use the public sender's public key; the *SignData* and *SignHash* methods use the sender's private key.

How to Generate and Verify a Digital Signature for a File

To generate a digital signature for a file, perform the following steps in your code:

1. Create the digital signature algorithm object.
2. Store the data to be signed in a byte array.
3. Call the *SignData* method and store the signature.
4. Export the public key.

To verify the digital signature, perform the following steps:

1. Create the digital signature algorithm object.
2. Import the signature and public key.
3. Store the data to be verified in a byte array.
4. Call the *VerifyData* method.

The following code sample is the *Main* method of a console application that accepts a filename as a command-line argument and displays a Base64-encoded digital signature for the file based on a dynamically generated key pair. The public key and digital signature are stored in variables. Then, the application verifies the signature with the public key by creating new objects.

```csharp
// Signing Step 1: Create the digital signature algorithm object
DSACryptoServiceProvider signer = new DSACryptoServiceProvider();

// Signing Step 2: Store the data to be signed in a byte array.
FileStream file = new FileStream(args[0], FileMode.Open, FileAccess.Read);
BinaryReader reader = new BinaryReader(file);
byte[] data = reader.ReadBytes((int)file.Length);

// Signing Step 3: Call the SignData method and store the signature
byte[] signature = signer.SignData(data);

// Signing Step 4: Export the public key
string publicKey = signer.ToXmlString(false);

Console.WriteLine("Signature: " + Convert.ToBase64String(signature));
reader.Close();
file.Close();


// Verifying Step 1: Create the digital signature algorithm object
DSACryptoServiceProvider verifier = new DSACryptoServiceProvider();

// Verifying Step 2: Import the signature and public key.
verifier.FromXmlString(publicKey);

// Verifying Step 3: Store the data to be verified in a byte array
FileStream file2 = new FileStream(args[0], FileMode.Open, FileAccess.Read);
BinaryReader reader2 = new BinaryReader(file2);
byte[] data2 = reader2.ReadBytes((int)file2.Length);

// Verifying Step 4: Call the VerifyData method
if (verifier.VerifyData(data2, signature))
{
    Console.WriteLine("Signature verified");
}
else
{
    Console.WriteLine("Signature NOT verified");
}
reader2.Close();
file2.Close();
```

```vbnet
Shared Sub Main(ByVal args As String())
    ' Signing Step 1: Create the digital signature algorithm object
    Dim signer As DSACryptoServiceProvider = New DSACryptoServiceProvider

    ' Signing Step 2: Store the data to be signed in a byte array.
    Dim file As FileStream = New FileStream (args(0), →
FileMode.Open, FileAccess.Read)
    Dim reader As BinaryReader = New BinaryReader (file)
    Dim data As Byte() = reader.ReadBytes(CType(file.Length, Integer))

    ' Signing Step 3: Call the SignData method and store the signature
    Dim signature As Byte() = signer.SignData(data)
```

```
' Signing Step 4: Export the public key
Dim publicKey As String = signer.ToXmlString(False)
Console.WriteLine("Signature: " + Convert.ToBase64String(signature))
reader.Close
file.Close


' Verifying Step 1: Create the digital signature algorithm object
Dim verifier As DSACryptoServiceProvider = New DSACryptoServiceProvider

' Verifying Step 2: Import the signature and public key.
verifier.FromXmlString(publicKey)

' Verifying Step 3: Store the data to be verified in a byte array
Dim file2 As FileStream = New FileStream (args(0), ⤍
FileMode.Open, FileAccess.Read)
Dim reader2 As BinaryReader = New BinaryReader (file2)
Dim data2 As Byte() = reader2.ReadBytes(CType(file2.Length, Integer))

' Verifying Step 4: Call the VerifyData method
If verifier.VerifyData(data2, signature) Then
    Console.WriteLine("Signature verified")
Else
    Console.WriteLine("Signature NOT verified")
End If
reader2.Close
file2.Close
End Sub
```

The previous example uses the *DSACryptoServiceProvider* class, but you can also use *RSACryptoServiceProvider* for digital signatures. *RSACryptoServiceProvider* usage is similar but requires providing a hash algorithm object for both the *SignData* and *VerifyData* methods. The following code sample shows only the lines that would need to change from the previous example to use *RSACryptoServiceProvider* with the *SHA1CryptoServiceProvider* hash algorithm:

```csharp
// Signing Step 1: Create the digital signature algorithm object
RSACryptoServiceProvider signer = new RSACryptoServiceProvider();

// Signing Step 3: Call the SignData method and store the signature
byte[] signature = signer.SignData(data, new SHA1CryptoServiceProvider());

// Verifying Step 1: Create the digital signature algorithm object
RSACryptoServiceProvider verifier = new RSACryptoServiceProvider();

// Verifying Step 4: Call the VerifyData method
if (verifier.VerifyData(data2, new SHA1CryptoServiceProvider(), signature))
```

```vb
' Signing Step 1: Create the digital signature algorithm object
Dim signer As RSACryptoServiceProvider = New RSACryptoServiceProvider

' Signing Step 3: Call the SignData method and store the signature
Dim signature As Byte() = signer.SignData(data, New SHA1CryptoServiceProvider)

' Verifying Step 1: Create the digital signature algorithm object
Dim verifier As RSACryptoServiceProvider = New RSACryptoServiceProvider

' Verifying Step 4: Call the VerifyData method
If verifier.VerifyData(data2, New SHA1CryptoServiceProvider , signature) Then
```

Although this simplified example creates and verifies a signature within a single application, you will typically transfer the public key and digital signature across a network. The most convenient way to transfer digital signatures is to create a binary file that contains the public key, the digital signature, and the file data itself. However, you can also transmit them as separate files or separate network communications.

How to Create a Digital Signature in an XML Document

The techniques described in the chapter up to this point require you to create custom file formats to store digital signatures. You can simplify the storage and transfer of digital signatures by using the XML digital signature specification (XMLDSIG) and the .NET Framework classes designed to enable digitally signing XML documents. XMLDSIG provides standards for creating and representing digital signatures in XML documents.

Because XML documents can contain multiple data types and are easily parsed by applications, they represent an ideal way to store and transfer digital signatures. If the document you are signing can be expressed in XML, you can even store the digital signature along with the document you are signing.

> **Important**   You can create an XML signature for any kind of document, including binary documents. It's an XML signature because the signature itself is stored in an XML file, not because the file being signed is XML-based.

All .NET Framework classes related to XML signatures are contained in the *System.Security.Cryptography.Xml* namespace. To access this namespace, add to your application a reference to the *System.Security* component.

To generate a digital signature in an XML document, perform the following steps in your code:

1. Create the digital signature algorithm object.

2. Create a reference to the XML document being signed.

3. Create an instance of the *SignedXml* class, add the XML document reference, and set the *SigningKey* property to the digital signature algorithm object.

4. Call the *ComputeSignature* method to generate the signature.

5. Access the signature by calling the *GetXML* method. Optionally, convert the XML signature to a string using the *GetXMLO.OuterXml* property.

The following code sample is the *Main* method of a console application that accepts a filename as a command-line argument. The application displays an XML digital signature for the file by using the DSA algorithm with a dynamically generated key pair. Displaying XML to the console is useful only for learning purposes. In production environments, you would generally transfer the XML content across a network or store it in a file.

```csharp
// Signing Step 1: Create the digital signature algorithm object
DSACryptoServiceProvider signer = new DSACryptoServiceProvider();

// Signing Step 2: Create a reference to the XML document being signed
FileStream file = new FileStream(args[0], FileMode.Open, FileAccess.Read);
Reference XmlReference = new Reference(file);

// Signing Step 3: Create an instance of the SignedXml class,
// and set the SigningKey property to the digital signature algorithm object.
SignedXml source = new SignedXml();
source.AddReference(XmlReference);
source.SigningKey = signer;

// Signing Step 4: Call the ComputeSignature method to generate the signature
source.ComputeSignature();

// Signing Step 5: Access the signature by calling the GetXML method
Console.WriteLine(source.GetXml().OuterXml);
file.Close();
```

```vbnet
Shared Sub Main(ByVal args As String())
    ' Signing Step 1: Create the digital signature algorithm object
    Dim signer As DSACryptoServiceProvider = New DSACryptoServiceProvider

    ' Signing Step 2: Create a reference to the XML document being signed
    Dim file As FileStream = New FileStream (args(0), FileMode.Open, →
FileAccess.Read)
    Dim XmlReference As Reference = New Reference (file)

    ' Signing Step 3: Create an instance of the SignedXml class,
    ' and set the SigningKey property to the digital signature algorithm
    ' object.
    Dim source As SignedXml = New SignedXml
    source.AddReference(XmlReference)
    source.SigningKey = signer

    ' Signing Step 4: Call the ComputeSignature method to generate the
    ' signature
    source.ComputeSignature
```

```
' Signing Step 5: Access the signature by calling the GetXML method
Console.WriteLine(source.GetXml.OuterXml)
file.Close
End Sub
```

To view the XML digital signature in Internet Explorer, compile the sample application using the project name GenerateSignature, and run the following commands:

```
GenerateSignature filename > output.xml
explorer output.xml
```

Internet Explorer will format and display the XML file, as shown in Figure 8-9.

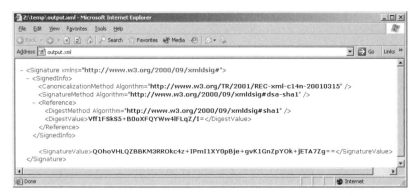

Figure 8-9   Storing digital signatures in XML enables simple storage, transfer, and verification.

The digital signature contains the following elements:

- **SignatureMethod algorithm**   In this example, this element contains the value *http://www.w3.org/2000/09/xmldsig#dsa-sha1*. This references the XML document that describes the use of the DSA algorithm for digital signatures.

- **SignatureValue**   In this example, the SignatureValue is the DSA signature of the file, Base64-encoded.

- **DigestMethod Algorithm**   In this example, the element contains the value *http://www.w3.org/2000/09/xmldsig#sha1*. This describes the SHA1 hashing algorithm, which DSA used to generate the hash for the file.

- **DigestValue**   In this example, the DigestValue element is the SHA1 hash of the file, Base64-encoded.

Practice: Validating Data with Hashes

In this practice, you will create two console applications that create and validate digital signatures to protect files from modification. Read the scenario and then complete the exercise that follows. If you are unable to answer a question, review the lesson and try the question again. You can find answers to the questions in the "Questions and Answers" section at the end of this chapter.

Scenario

You are a consultant for Proseware, Inc., a small software development company whose encyclopedia software has suddenly become extremely popular. Proseware recently received their Web site bandwidth bill from their Internet service provider, and it was much higher than they expected. They decided to distribute their data files using other techniques, and hired you to create a pair of console applications that created and validated hashes for their application and data files. Now, they've decided they want the additional security afforded by digital signatures. They hired you again to recommend a method to allow users to verify the integrity of their files, as well as to verify that the file hash originated from Proseware. You interview key personnel and review the technical requirements before you come up with your solution.

Interviews   Following is a list of company personnel interviewed and their statements:

- **Dick Dievendorff, Development Manager**   "Those two console applications you created for us work great. I should have asked you for something a little different, however. After watching our Web traffic, I think I'd like to start distributing the hashes to our users using another Web site as well. I don't trust the people who manage the Web site as well as I do my own people, so I'd like to post hashes that they can't modify. After talking to another developer, I understand you can probably update the hash console applications to create and verify digital signatures. Unless I'm mistaken, digital signatures are like hashes that are signed with a private key. Eventually, I'd like to build the signature verification into our applications, in which case we could store the public key in the application code itself. For the time being, however, go ahead and store the public key in the local computer's CSP. That'll get us through the proof-of-concept phase, anyway."

Technical Requirements   Create two console applications:

- **ComputeSignature**   This application must take two command-line arguments: the filename of the file that will be hashed, and the filename to store the digital signature file. This application should generate a random public key the first time it is used, and store it in the local CSP.

- **VerifySignature**   This application must take two command-line arguments: the filename of the file that was signed, and the filename containing the digital signature. It should retrieve the public key used to sign the file from the local CSP. It must verify the signature and display the results to the console.

Exercise

Create the applications and then answer the following questions.

1. What code did you write the ComputeSignature application to generate the hash?

2. What code did you write the VerifySignature application to generate the hash?

Lesson Summary

- A digital signature is a value that can be appended to electronic data to prove that it was created by someone who possesses a specific private key. Digital signatures can be used to verify the integrity of data because it contains a hash and are typically used to prove that a particular person or organization created a file. Digital signatures also use asymmetric encryption, enabling you to verify that the holder of a particular private key generated the hash and created the signature.

- You can use both the *DSACryptoServiceProvider* and the *RSACryptoServiceProvider* classes in the .NET Framework to generate digital signatures.

- To generate a digital signature, create a digital signature class and call the *SignData* method. To verify a digital signature, create a digital signature class, retrieve the signature, and call the *VerifyData* method.

- To create a digital signature in an XML document, create an instance of the *SignedXml* class, and then call the *ComputeSignature* method. You can access the signature by calling the *GetXML* method.

Lab: Protecting Data by Using Cryptography

In this lab, you must recommend cryptography techniques to solve various business problems for a fictitious company. Read the scenario and then complete the exercise that follows. If you are unable to answer a question, review the lessons and try the question again. You can find answers to the questions in the "Questions and Answers" section at the end of this chapter.

Scenario

You are a developer for Blue Yonder Airlines. Blue Yonder Airlines is a national airline that has been growing rapidly in the past two years and has more than quadrupled the number of flights in that time period. Blue Yonder Airlines has only a handful of developers, however. Your manager recently sent you to security training, and now plans to use your skills to provide recommendations for different security problems throughout the organization.

Exercise

Answer the following questions for your manager.

1. We keep the master records of all flights and passengers in a centralized database. An application that our team created then transfers that data to remote offices. What's the best way to encrypt this data?

2. Our application stores user names and passwords in a database. How should we protect those passwords?

3. Occasionally we distribute bonuses to employees and customers in the form of frequent flier miles and upgrades. These bonuses are always distributed from the central office. We want the application running at the remote offices to be able to verify that the bonus originated from the central office. How can we do this?

Chapter Summary

- To protect the privacy and integrity of the data that your applications store, you can use cryptography. The .NET Framework provides classes for several different types of cryptography, including symmetric and asymmetric encryption, hashing, and digital signatures.

- Use symmetric encryption for situations in which the encryptor and decryptor have access to shared, secret information, and when performance is important.

- Use asymmetric encryption for situations in which the encryptor and decryptor do not have access to shared, secret information. If transferring more than a small amount of information, use asymmetric encryption to transfer a shared secret, and then use symmetric encryption for optimal performance.

- Hashing generates a checksum that uniquely represents the piece of data being hashed. By recalculating the hash after a data transfer, a hash can be used to verify that the original data has not been modified. To create a hash, call the *HashAlgorithm.ComputeHash* method, and then retrieve the *HashAlgorithm.Hash* value.

- Digital signatures combine the data integrity features of hashing with the proof of identity offered by asymmetric encryption. Digital signatures can be used to verify that a particular user approves of a piece of data, and that the piece of data has not been modified since the signature was created. Unlike a hash, a digital signature cannot be modified or recreated by anyone who does not possess the private key used to create the signature.

Exam Highlights

Before taking the exam, review the key points and terms that are presented in this chapter. You need to know this information.

Key Points

■ Understand when to use each of the different cryptography techniques described in this chapter: symmetric encryption, asymmetric encryption, hashing, and digital signatures.

■ Be able to encrypt and decrypt data by using symmetric encryption algorithms.

■ Be able to encrypt and decrypt data by using asymmetric encryption algorithms. Understand the importance of storing asymmetric key pairs.

■ Know the purpose of hashing and how to use the classes provided by the .NET Framework to generate hashes.

■ Be able to digitally sign documents and know how to verify signatures provided by other applications.

Key Terms

Advanced Encryption Standard (AES)   A synonym for Rijndael.

asymmetric encryption   A cryptography technique that uses separate private and public keys to encrypt and decrypt data. Also known as public-key encryption.

cipher text   Encrypted text generated by an encryption algorithm that cannot be converted to plain text without a secret key.

Data Protection Application Programming Interface (DPAPI)   A library that encrypts and stores data for an individual user or for an entire computer.

digital signature   A value that can be appended to electronic data to prove that it was created by someone who possesses a specific private key.

Data Encryption Standard (DES)   A symmetric encryption algorithm that uses relatively short key lengths that are vulnerable to cracking attacks.

encryption key   A value that can be used to encrypt and decrypt data. When used with symmetric encryption, this is also known as a shared secret.

entropy   A value designed to make deciphering the secret more difficult.

hash   A value that summarizes a larger piece of data and can be used to verify that the data has not been modified since the hash was generated.

initialization vector   Data that symmetric encryption algorithms use to further obscure the first block of data being encrypted, which makes unauthorized decrypting more difficult.

keyed hash algorithms   Algorithms that protect against modification of the hash by encrypting it by using a secret key that both the sender and receiver must have.

MD5   The Message Digest hashing algorithm. The hash size for the MD5 algorithm is 128 bits.

RC2   A symmetric encryption standard designed to replace DES that uses variable key sizes.

Rijndael   A symmetric encryption algorithm that uses key sizes of 128 through 256 bits. As a government encryption standard, this algorithm is also known as AES.

SHA1   The Secure Hash Algorithm 1. The hash size for the SHA1 algorithm is 160 bits.

shared secret   A symmetric encryption key.

symmetric encryption   A cryptography technique that uses a single secret key to encrypt and decrypt data. Also known as secret-key encryption.

Triple DES   A symmetric encryption standard that uses 156-bit keys. Essentially, Triple DES repeats the DES algorithm three times.

XML digital signature specification (XMLDSIG)   A standard for creating and representing digital signatures in XML documents.

Questions and Answers

Practice: Encrypting and Decrypting Data with Symmetric Keys

Page
8-20

Exercise

> **Tip** For a working example of the class, refer to the PasswordEncryption project on the companion CD.

1. Which encryption algorithm did you use? Why?

   Answers will vary. Any of the symmetric encryption algorithms would work; however, Rijndael is the best choice because it is a fully managed library and provides an extremely high encryption level.

2. Which classes and methods did you use to generate the encryption key based on the user password? How did you generate the salt value? How did you write the code to generate the key and initialization vector?

   You should have used the *PasswordDeriveBytes* class to generate the encryption key based on the password value passed by the calling application. Although the salt value does not necessarily need to be static, it does need to be the same for the encryption and decryption functions. Therefore, a static salt value is the best choice.

   You need a key of a specific length to match the algorithm's key length requirement. The *SymmetricAlgorithm* class reports the key length in bits, whereas the *PasswordDeriveBytes.GetBytes* method accepts a number of bytes as a parameter. Therefore, you must divide the *SymmetricAlgorithm.KeySize* property by 8. Although your answer will vary, the following code would work, assuming that you created the *SymmetricAlgorithm* object with the name *myAlg*, and the *PasswordDeriveBytes* object with the name *passwordKey*:

```csharp
byte[] saltValueBytes = Encoding.ASCII.GetBytes("This is my salt");
PasswordDeriveBytes passwordKey = new PasswordDeriveBytes→
(password, saltValueBytes, "SHA1", 3);
myAlg.Key = passwordKey.GetBytes(myAlg.KeySize/8);
myAlg.IV = passwordKey.GetBytes(myAlg.BlockSize/8);
```

```vb
Dim saltValueBytes As Byte() = Encoding.ASCII.GetBytes("This is my salt")
Dim passwordKey As PasswordDeriveBytes = New PasswordDeriveBytes →
(password, saltValueBytes, "SHA1", 3)
myAlg.Key = passwordKey.GetBytes(myAlg.KeySize / 8)
myAlg.IV = passwordKey.GetBytes(myAlg.BlockSize / 8)
```

3. Which class did you use to write to and read from the encrypted files?

   You should have used the *CryptoStream* class.

Practice: Encrypting and Decrypting Data with Asymmetric Keys

Page
8-31
Exercise

1. What code did you write for the *loadKeyMenuItem_Click* method?

   Although your exact code will vary, it should resemble the following code:

```
OpenFileDialog loadKey = new OpenFileDialog();
if (loadKey.ShowDialog() == DialogResult.OK)
{
    StreamReader readKey = new StreamReader(loadKey.FileName);
    myRSA.FromXmlString(readKey.ReadToEnd());
    readKey.Close();
}

DisplayKeys();
```

```
Dim loadKey As OpenFileDialog = New OpenFileDialog
If loadKey.ShowDialog = DialogResult.OK Then
    Dim readKey As StreamReader = New StreamReader (loadKey.FileName)
    myRSA.FromXmlString(readKey.ReadToEnd)
    readKey.Close
End If
DisplayKeys
```

2. What code did you write for the *saveKeyMenuItem_Click* method?

   Although your exact code will vary, it should resemble the following code:

```
SaveFileDialog saveKey = new SaveFileDialog();
if (saveKey.ShowDialog() == DialogResult.OK)
{
    StreamWriter writeKey = new StreamWriter(saveKey.FileName, false);
    writeKey.Write(myRSA.ToXmlString(true));
    writeKey.Close();
}
```

```
Dim saveKey As SaveFileDialog = New SaveFileDialog
If saveKey.ShowDialog = DialogResult.OK Then
    Dim writeKey As StreamWriter = New StreamWriter (saveKey.FileName, False)
    writeKey.Write(myRSA.ToXmlString(True))
    writeKey.Close
End If
```

3. What code did you write for the *importKeyMenuItem_Click* method?

   Although your exact code will vary, it should resemble the following code:

```
OpenFileDialog loadKey = new OpenFileDialog();
if (loadKey.ShowDialog() == DialogResult.OK)
{
    StreamReader readKey = new StreamReader(loadKey.FileName);
    otherRSA.FromXmlString(readKey.ReadToEnd());
    readKey.Close();
}

DisplayKeys();
```

```
Dim loadKey As OpenFileDialog = New OpenFileDialog
If loadKey.ShowDialog = DialogResult.OK Then
    Dim readKey As StreamReader = New StreamReader (loadKey.FileName)
    otherRSA.FromXmlString(readKey.ReadToEnd)
    readKey.Close
End If
DisplayKeys
```

4. What code did you write for the *saveMessageMenuItem_Click* method?

Although your exact code will vary, it should resemble the following code:

```csharp
SaveFileDialog saveMessage = new SaveFileDialog();
if (saveMessage.ShowDialog() == DialogResult.OK)
{
    FileStream writeMessage = new FileStream↴
(saveMessage.FileName, FileMode.Create, FileAccess.Write);
    BinaryWriter writeBinaryMessage = new BinaryWriter(writeMessage);

    byte[] messageBytes = Encoding.Unicode.GetBytes(messageTextBox.Text);
    writeBinaryMessage.Write(otherRSA.Encrypt(messageBytes, false));
    writeBinaryMessage.Close();
    writeMessage.Close();
}
```

```vb
Dim saveMessage As SaveFileDialog = New SaveFileDialog
If saveMessage.ShowDialog = DialogResult.OK Then
    Dim writeMessage As FileStream = New FileStream →
(saveMessage.FileName, FileMode.Create, FileAccess.Write)
    Dim writeBinaryMessage As BinaryWriter = New BinaryWriter (writeMessage)

    Dim messageBytes As Byte() = Encoding.Unicode.GetBytes(messageTextBox.Text)
    writeBinaryMessage.Write(otherRSA.Encrypt(messageBytes, False))
    writeBinaryMessage.Close
    writeMessage.Close
End If
```

5. What code did you write for the *exportKeyMenuItem_Click* method?

Although your exact code will vary, it should resemble the following code:

```csharp
SaveFileDialog saveKey = new SaveFileDialog();
if (saveKey.ShowDialog() == DialogResult.OK)
{
    StreamWriter writeKey = new StreamWriter(saveKey.FileName, false);
    writeKey.Write(myRSA.ToXmlString(false));
    writeKey.Close();
}
```

```vb
Dim saveKey As SaveFileDialog = New SaveFileDialog
If saveKey.ShowDialog = DialogResult.OK Then
    Dim writeKey As StreamWriter = New StreamWriter (saveKey.FileName, False)
    writeKey.Write(myRSA.ToXmlString(False))
    writeKey.Close
End If
```

6. What code did you write for the *loadMessageMenuItem_Click* method?

Although your exact code will vary, it should resemble the following code:

```csharp
OpenFileDialog loadMessage = new OpenFileDialog();
if (loadMessage.ShowDialog() == DialogResult.OK)
{
    FileStream readMessage = new FileStream(loadMessage.FileName, ⟶
FileMode.Open, FileAccess.Read);
    BinaryReader readBinaryMessage = new BinaryReader(readMessage);

    int length = (int)readMessage.Length;
    byte[] decryptedMessage = myRSA.Decrypt(readBinaryMessage.ReadBytes(length), ⟶
false);
    readBinaryMessage.Close();
    readMessage.Close();

    messageTextBox.Text = Encoding.Unicode.GetString(decryptedMessage);
}
```

```vb
Dim loadMessage As OpenFileDialog = New OpenFileDialog
If loadMessage.ShowDialog = DialogResult.OK Then
    Dim readMessage As FileStream = New FileStream ⟶
(loadMessage.FileName, FileMode.Open, FileAccess.Read)
    Dim readBinaryMessage As BinaryReader = New BinaryReader (readMessage)

Dim length As Integer = CType(readMessage.Length, Integer)
    Dim decryptedMessage As Byte() = ⟶
myRSA.Decrypt(readBinaryMessage.ReadBytes(length), False)
    readBinaryMessage.Close
    readMessage.Close

    messageTextBox.Text = Encoding.Unicode.GetString(decryptedMessage)
End If
```

7. What code did you write for the *DisplayKeys* method?

Although your exact code will vary, it should resemble the following code:

```csharp
RSAParameters myRSAParameters = myRSA.ExportParameters(true);
myPrivateKeyTextBox.Text = Convert.ToBase64String(myRSAParameters.D);
myPublicKeyTextBox.Text = Convert.ToBase64String(myRSAParameters.Modulus);

RSAParameters otherRSAParameters = otherRSA.ExportParameters(false);
otherPublicKeyTextBox.Text = ⟶
Convert.ToBase64String(otherRSAParameters.Modulus);
```

```vb
Dim myRSAParameters As RSAParameters = myRSA.ExportParameters(True)
myPrivateKeyTextBox.Text = Convert.ToBase64String(myRSAParameters.D)
myPublicKeyTextBox.Text = Convert.ToBase64String(myRSAParameters.Modulus)

Dim otherRSAParameters As RSAParameters = otherRSA.ExportParameters(False)
otherPublicKeyTextBox.Text = ⟶
Convert.ToBase64String(otherRSAParameters.Modulus)
```

Practice: Validating Data Integrity with Hashes

Page
8-40

Exercise

1. Did you choose a keyed or non-keyed hashing method?

   Because the users do not have a secret key, you should use a non-keyed hashing method.

2. Which hashing algorithm should you use? Why?

   The SHA512 algorithm generates hashes with the largest number of bits, meeting the development manager's requirement.

3. What code did you write the ComputeHash application to generate the hash?

   Although your exact code will vary, it should resemble the following code:

```csharp
using System;
using System.Security.Cryptography;
using System.Text;
using System.IO;

namespace HashExample
{
    class Class1
    {
        [STAThread]
        static void Main(string[] args)
        {
            SHA512 myHash = new SHA512Managed();

            FileStream file = new FileStream(args[0], →
FileMode.Open, FileAccess.Read);
            BinaryReader reader = new BinaryReader(file);

            myHash.ComputeHash(reader.ReadBytes((int)file.Length));

            Console.WriteLine(Convert.ToBase64String(myHash.Hash));
        }
    }
}
```

```vbnet
Imports System
Imports System.Security.Cryptography
Imports System.Text
Imports System.IO

Module Module1

    Sub Main(ByVal args As String())
        Dim myHash As SHA512 = New SHA512Managed

        Dim file As FileStream = New FileStream(args(0), →
FileMode.Open, FileAccess.Read)
        Dim reader As BinaryReader = New BinaryReader(file)
```

```
            myHash.ComputeHash(reader.ReadBytes(CType(file.Length, Integer)))

            Console.WriteLine(Convert.ToBase64String(myHash.Hash))
        End Sub

    End Module
```

4. What code did you write the VerifyHash application to verify the hash?

Although your exact code will vary, it should resemble the following code:

```csharp
using System;
using System.Security.Cryptography;
using System.Text;
using System.IO;

namespace VerifyHash
{
    class Class1
    {
        [STAThread]
        static void Main(string[] args)
        {
            SHA512 myHash = new SHA512Managed();

            FileStream file = new FileStream(args[0], →
FileMode.Open, FileAccess.Read);
            BinaryReader reader = new BinaryReader(file);

            myHash.ComputeHash(reader.ReadBytes((int)file.Length));

            if (Convert.ToBase64String(myHash.Hash) == args[1])
            {
                Console.WriteLine("Hash verified");
            }
            else
            {
                Console.WriteLine("Hash incorrect");
            }
        }
    }
}
```

```vbnet
Imports System
Imports System.Security.Cryptography
Imports System.Text
Imports System.IO

Module Module1
    Sub Main(ByVal args As String())
        Dim myHash As SHA512 = New SHA512Managed
        Dim file As FileStream = New FileStream (args(0), →
FileMode.Open, FileAccess.Read)
        Dim reader As BinaryReader = New BinaryReader (file)
        myHash.ComputeHash(reader.ReadBytes(CType(file.Length, Integer)))
        If Convert.ToBase64String(myHash.Hash) = args(1) Then
```

```
                Console.WriteLine("Hash verified")
        Else
                Console.WriteLine("Hash incorrect")
        End If
    End Sub
End Module
```

Practice: Validating Data with Hashes

Page
8-49

Exercise

1. What code did you write the ComputeSignature application to generate the hash?

    Although your exact code will vary, it should resemble the following code:

```csharp
using System;
using System.Security.Cryptography;
using System.IO;

namespace GenerateSignature
{
    class Class1
    {
        /// </summary>
        [STAThread]
        static void Main(string[] args)
        {
            CspParameters persistantCsp = new CspParameters();
            persistantCsp.KeyContainerName = "DigitalSignature";

            RSACryptoServiceProvider signer = new
RSACryptoServiceProvider(persistantCsp);
            signer.PersistKeyInCsp = true;

            FileStream file = new FileStream(args[0], FileMode.Open,
 FileAccess.Read);
            BinaryReader reader = new BinaryReader(file);
            byte[] data = reader.ReadBytes((int)file.Length);

            FileStream sigFile = new FileStream(args[1],
FileMode.Create, FileAccess.Write);
            BinaryWriter sigWriter = new BinaryWriter(sigFile);
            sigWriter.Write(signer.SignData(data,
new SHA1CryptoServiceProvider()));

            sigWriter.Close();
            sigFile.Close();
            reader.Close();
            file.Close();

        }
    }
}
```

```vbnet
Imports System.Security.Cryptography
Imports System.IO

Module Module1

    Sub Main(ByVal args As String())
        Dim persistantCsp As CspParameters = New CspParameters
        persistantCsp.KeyContainerName = "DigitalSignature"

        Dim signer As RSACryptoServiceProvider = →
New RSACryptoServiceProvider (persistantCsp)
        signer.PersistKeyInCsp = True

        Dim file As FileStream = New FileStream (args(0), →
FileMode.Open, FileAccess.Read)
        Dim reader As BinaryReader = New BinaryReader (file)
        Dim data As Byte() = reader.ReadBytes(CType(file.Length, Integer))

        Dim sigFile As FileStream = New FileStream (args(1), →
FileMode.Create, FileAccess.Write)
        Dim sigWriter As BinaryWriter = New BinaryWriter (sigFile)
        sigWriter.Write(signer.SignData(data, New SHA1CryptoServiceProvider ))

        sigWriter.Close
        sigFile.Close
        reader.Close
        file.Close
    End Sub

End Module
```

2. What code did you write the VerifySignature application to generate the hash?

Although your exact code will vary, it should resemble the following code:

```csharp
using System;
using System.Security.Cryptography;
using System.IO;

namespace VerifySignature
{
    class Class1
    {
        [STAThread]
        static void Main(string[] args)
        {
            CspParameters persistantCsp = new CspParameters();
            persistantCsp.KeyContainerName = "DigitalSignature";

            RSACryptoServiceProvider signer = new →
RSACryptoServiceProvider(persistantCsp);
            signer.PersistKeyInCsp = true;

            FileStream file = new FileStream(args[0], FileMode.Open, →
 FileAccess.Read);
            BinaryReader reader = new BinaryReader(file);
            byte[] data = reader.ReadBytes((int)file.Length);
```

```
            FileStream sigFile = new FileStream(args[1], →
FileMode.Open, FileAccess.Read);
            BinaryReader sigReader = new BinaryReader(sigFile);
            byte[] signature = sigReader.ReadBytes((int)sigFile.Length);

            if (signer.VerifyData(data, new →
SHA1CryptoServiceProvider(), signature))
            {
                Console.WriteLine("Signature verified.");
            }
            else
            {
                Console.WriteLine("Signature NOT verified.");
            }

            sigReader.Close();
            sigFile.Close();
            reader.Close();
            file.Close();
        }
    }
}
```

```
Imports System.Security.Cryptography
Imports System.IO

Module Module1

    Sub Main(ByVal args As String())
        Dim persistantCsp As CspParameters = New CspParameters
        persistantCsp.KeyContainerName = "DigitalSignature"

        Dim signer As RSACryptoServiceProvider = New →
RSACryptoServiceProvider(persistantCsp)
        signer.PersistKeyInCsp = True

        Dim file As FileStream = New FileStream(args(0), →
FileMode.Open, FileAccess.Read)
        Dim reader As BinaryReader = New BinaryReader(file)
        Dim data As Byte() = reader.ReadBytes(CType(file.Length, Integer))

        Dim sigFile As FileStream = New FileStream(args(1), →
FileMode.Open, FileAccess.Read)
        Dim sigReader As BinaryReader = New BinaryReader(sigFile)
        Dim signature As Byte() = sigReader.ReadBytes(→
CType(sigFile.Length, Integer))

        If signer.VerifyData(data, New SHA1CryptoServiceProvider, →
signature) Then
            Console.WriteLine("Signature verified.")
        Else
            Console.WriteLine("Signature NOT verified.")
        End If
```

```
            sigReader.Close()
            sigFile.Close()
            reader.Close()
            file.Close()
        End Sub

    End Module
```

Lab: Protecting Data by Using Cryptography

Page
8-51

Exercise

1. We keep the master records of all flights and passengers in a centralized database. An application that our team created then transfers that data to remote offices. What's the best way to encrypt this data?

Both symmetric and asymmetric encryption can meet the requirements, but symmetric encryption is the best choice because it minimizes administrative overhead. You can use symmetric key encryption because the data will be transferred between relatively stable computers in remote offices, and because configuring each with a secret key would be easy. Alternatively, you can use asymmetric encryption, configure a key pair at the centralized database, and distribute the public key to each of the remote offices. The application could then use asymmetric encryption to establish session keys to enable symmetric key encryption during the data transfers.

2. Our application stores user names and passwords in a database. How should we protect those passwords?

At the very least, you should store hashes of the password. A keyed hashing algorithm would be more secure than a non-keyed algorithm. Your primary deterrence must be preventing attackers from gaining access to the password database, however.

3. Occasionally we distribute bonuses to employees and customers in the form of frequent flier miles and upgrades. These bonuses are always distributed from the central office. We want the application running at the remote offices to be able to verify that the bonus originated from the central office. How can we do this?

You should use digital signatures. Store a key pair at the central office, and distribute the public key to each of the remote offices. Sign all bonus communications with the private key, and then verify the signature at the remote offices.

9 Hardening ASP.NET Applications

Why This Chapter Matters

Most of the lessons in this book pertain to both Microsoft Windows Forms applications and Web applications, but Web applications have several unique security requirements. Specifically, authenticating and authorizing users must be done differently in Web applications. Additionally, communications between the client and server are unencrypted unless a Secure Sockets Layer (SSL) certificate is installed. Because Web applications are more likely to be attacked than any other type of application, understanding how to harden an ASP.NET application is crucial.

Exam Objectives in this Chapter:

- Configure security by using Microsoft Internet Information Services (IIS) and ASP.NET.
  - ❑ Understand the security implications of impersonation.
  - ❑ Configure ASP.NET impersonation.
  - ❑ Configure Web folder permissions.
  - ❑ Set appropriate permissions on Web application files.
  - ❑ Configure a Web page or Web service to use SSL.
- Implement authentication.
  - ❑ Implement an appropriate Web application or Web service authentication mechanism to accommodate specific application security requirements.
- Write authorization code.
  - ❑ Control access to Web applications by using URL authorization.
  - ❑ Programmatically control access to functionality and data by using identities or criteria that are independent of user identity.

Lessons in this Chapter:

Before You Begin

To complete the practices, examples, and lab exercises in this chapter, you must have one computer running Microsoft Windows Server 2003. During the course of performing the exercises in this chapter, the computer's security can be reduced. Therefore, the computer should not be a production computer and should not be connected to any network, especially the Internet, even if a firewall is present. Install Microsoft Visual Studio .NET 2003 using the default settings. Then, install Microsoft SQL Server 2000 configured to use the System account, Windows authentication, and processor licensing.

Lesson 1: Configuring Authentication in ASP.NET Applications

Web applications have special requirements for authentication because rather than using conventional authentication protocols such as Kerberos, user credentials must be passed between a Web browser and the Web server. Additionally, custom authentication mechanisms are particularly common in Web applications, because Web applications available on the public Internet must often scale to support hundreds of thousands of users. To meet these authentication requirements, ASP.NET supports four types of authentication:

- Windows authentication
- Anonymous access
- Forms authentication
- Passport authentication

Don't confuse ASP.NET authentication types with these IIS authentication types: Basic authentication, Integrated Windows authentication, Digest authentication, and Passport authentication. These types authenticate users to the Web server only, and not to the application. However, IIS does forward a user's credentials to ASP.NET, allowing your application to perform ASP.NET Windows authentication with the same credentials presented to IIS.

Each of these authentication methods requires configuring Internet Information Services (IIS) by using the Internet Information Services Manager and creating one or more Web.config files. This lesson describes how to configure both IIS and your application for each of the standard Web authentication types.

See Also   This chapter strives to provide the information that you need to maximize the security of your Web applications. The topic of improving security for Web servers is massive, and most of the burden of protection falls on the shoulders of systems administrators. For more information about protecting servers, read "Securing Your Web Server" in MSDN on the Microsoft Web site at *http://msdn.microsoft.com/library/en-us/secmod/html /secmod89.asp*. For more information about protecting ASP.NET applications, read "Building Secure ASP.NET Applications: Authentication, Authorization, and Secure Communication" at *http://msdn.microsoft.com/library/en-us/dnnetsec/html/SecNetch08.asp*.

After this lesson, you will be able to

■ Explain the purpose of Web.config files.

■ Configure Web applications to require Windows authentication.

■ Configure Web applications to not use any form of authentication.

■ Create ASP.NET forms to authenticate Web users with a custom authentication mechanism.

■ Configure Web applications to require Passport authentication.

Estimated lesson time: 35 minutes

What Are Web.config Files?

Web.config files are per-folder configuration settings for ASP.NET applications. Storing configuration settings in XML-based files instead of in the registry, isolated storage, or an IIS metabase allows administrators to copy your application to a different location or to another computer and have the application run correctly. This storage method is particularly important for environments that host Web farms, where multiple Web servers run the same ASP.NET application simultaneously and incoming requests are distributed among the servers. Web farms usually have file synchronization running between the Web servers, which allows changes to a Web.config file to be automatically replicated between all computers.

Web.config files are the most granular files in the .config file hierarchy and can inherit and override the settings of higher-level configuration files. The highest .config file is the Machine.config file, which affects all .NET applications, including ASP.NET applications. You can create a hierarchy of Web.config files within your application, too. Place a Web.config file in the root folder of your application to apply default settings to all files and folders in your application. If a particular set of pages requires different security settings, store those files in a single subfolder, and add a Web.config file to that folder.

Important   The hierarchy is determined by an application's virtual folder structure, not its physical folder structure.

Figure 9-1 shows this hierarchy. In this example, App1 has a Web.config file. Therefore, App1 inherits all security settings from the computer's Machine.config file, except those overridden in the Web.config file. The Folder1 subfolder of App1 also has a Web.config file. These settings override settings in both App1's Web.config file and the computer's Machine.config file. However, any settings that are not explicitly overridden are inherited. Folder2 does not have a Web.config file, so its effective security settings will be exactly the same as App1. App2 does not have a Web.config file and will inherit all security settings from the Machine.config file.

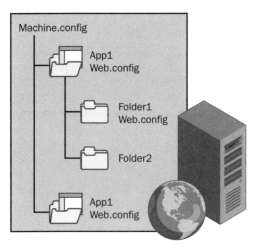

Figure 9-1   Web.config files provide hierarchical security settings.

The Machine.config file defines settings that cannot be overridden. Settings with an *allowDefinition* property set to *MachineOnly* can be defined only in the Machine.config file. Settings with an *allowDefinition* property set to *MachineToApplication* can be defined in each application, but not overridden by placing a Web.config file in an application's subfolders. For example, you can control *authentication* on an application-by-application basis because its definition sets the *allowDefinition* property set to *MachineToApplication*. You cannot, however, override *authentication* with a Web.config file in an application's subfolder unless the subfolder is configured in IIS as an independent application. The *authentication* section can be specified only at the application's root folder, as configured in IIS. The *authorization* section, which doesn't explicitly define the *allowDefinition* property, can be overridden in an application's subfolders.

See Also   This section contains only the most basic information needed to understand how to configure security for ASP.NET applications. For more detailed information, please read ".NET Framework Developer's Guide, Hierarchical Configuration Architecture" in MSDN on the Microsoft Web site at *http://msdn.microsoft.com/library/en-us/cpguide/html /cpconhierarchicalconfigurationarchitecture.asp.*

How to Configure Web Applications to Require Windows Authentication

If your application is targeted for use inside an organization, and users accessing the application will have existing user accounts within the local user database of the Web server or Active Directory, you will probably choose Windows authentication for your ASP.NET application. You can configure Windows authentication in two ways: within IIS and within your ASP.NET application. To provide defense-in-depth, use both techniques to require authentication.

When a Web application requires Windows authentication, the application rejects all requests that do not include a valid user name and password. The user's browser then prompts the user for a user name and password. Because the browser prompts the user for credentials, you do not have to create a page to request the user's user name and password. Some browsers, such as Microsoft Internet Explorer, automatically provide the user's current user name and password when the server is located on the intranet. This seamlessly authenticates the user, relieving her from retyping her password when she visits the intranet site.

Additionally, because users are authenticated against the server's local user database or Active Directory domain, using Windows authentication saves you from creating a database to store user credentials. Leveraging the Windows authentication mechanism is therefore the simplest way to authenticate users. To configure IIS to allow only anonymous access for a Web site or virtual directory on a computer running Windows Server 2003, follow these steps:

1. In the Administrative Tools program group, open the Internet Information Services (IIS) Manager.

2. In the IIS Manager console, click to expand your server name, expand Web Sites, and then click to expand the Web site.

3. Right-click the site or folder name you are configuring authentication for and click Properties.

4. Click the Directory Security tab. In the Authentication And Access Control group, click the Edit button.

5. Clear the Enable Anonymous Access check box, which is selected by default.

6. Select the Integrated Windows Authentication check box, as shown in Figure 9-2. Optionally, select Digest Windows Authentication For Windows Domain Servers to enable authentication across proxy servers.

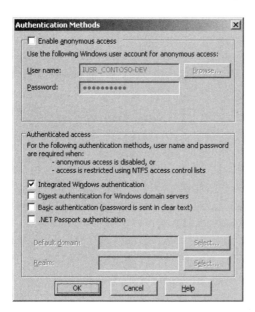

Figure 9-2 For best results, configure Windows authentication in both IIS and your application.

7. Click OK twice to return to the IIS Manager console.

At this point, all Web requests to the virtual directory will require Windows authentication—even if ASP.NET is configured for anonymous access only. Even though configuring IIS is sufficient to require users to present Windows credentials, it is good practice to edit the application's Web.config file to also require Windows authentication. To configure an ASP.NET application for Windows Authentication, edit the `<authentication>` section of the Web.config file. This section, like most sections related to ASP.NET application configuration, must be defined within the `<system.web>` section. The `<system.web>` section, in turn, must exist within the `<configuration>` section. This example shows the `<authentication>` section of the Web.config file configured to use Windows authentication, which is the default when you create a Web application project with Visual Studio .NET:

```
<configuration>
    <system.web>
        <authentication mode="Windows" />
        <authorization>
            <deny users="?" />
        </authentication>
    </system.web>
</configuration>
```

The `<authorization>` section simply requires all users to be successfully authenticated. Authorization is discussed in Lesson 2 of this chapter. For now, understand that specifying `<deny users="?" />` within `<authorization>` requires users to be authenticated, whereas specifying `<allow users="*" />` within `<authorization>` bypasses authentication entirely.

Unless your application requires no specific configuration settings, you should distribute the Web.config file with your ASP.NET application. To enable Windows authentication for an ASP.NET application, edit the Web.config file with a text editor such as Microsoft Notepad or Visual Studio .NET. Scroll through the document to find the `<authentication>` section. If this section already exists, edit it so that the `<authentication>` section includes the mode section with a setting of "Windows", as shown in the previous example. If the `<authentication>` section does not exist, the ASP.NET application will use the setting configured in the Machine.config file. To override the Machine.config setting, add the authentication section to the application's Web.config file.

How to Configure Web Applications for Only Anonymous Access

You can explicitly disable authentication for your application if you know that it will be used only by anonymous users. However, in most cases where your application does not require authentication, you should simply not provide an *authentication* configuration setting in the Web.config file, and allow the system administrator to configure authentication with IIS. This example shows a simple Web.config file that allows only anonymous access to an ASP.NET application:

```
<configuration>
    <system.web>
        <authentication mode="None" />
    </system.web>
</configuration>
```

How to Create ASP.NET Forms to Authenticate Web Users

Windows authentication presents the end user with a browser-generated dialog box. Although giving the browser the responsibility of gathering the user's user name and password enables automatic authentication in intranet sites, it gives you as a developer very little flexibility. Web applications developed for external sites commonly use form-based authentication instead. Form-based authentication presents the user with an HTML-based Web page that prompts the user for credentials. Once authenticated, a cookie with information about the user is stored within the user's browser. The browser presents this cookie with all future requests to the Web site, allowing the ASP.NET application to validate requests. This cookie can optionally be encrypted by a private key located on the Web server, enabling the Web server to detect an attacker who attempts to present a cookie that the Web server did not generate.

See Also   For general information about creating custom authentication mechanisms, see Lesson 4 in Chapter 5, "Implementing Role-Based Security."

The sections that follow teach how to configure an ASP.NET configuration file to require Forms authentication, how to add user credentials to a Web.config file, and how to create an ASP.NET Web form to authenticate users.

How to Configure a Web.config File for Forms Authentication

To configure form-based authentication (or Forms authentication), you have to create an authentication page that uses an HTML form to prompt the user for credentials. Therefore, forms-based authentication can be used on only those ASP.NET Web applications developed with this authentication method in mind. Although you can choose to rely on administrators to configure Windows or anonymous authentication, you *must* distribute a Web.config file for your application to use Forms authentication.

Administrators deploying your application should not need to modify the Web.config file, but they can control some aspects of how Forms authentication behaves, such as to configure the timeout period after which a user will need to log on again. A simple Web.config file requiring Forms authentication is shown here:

```
<configuration>
    <system.web>
        <authentication mode="Forms">
            <forms loginUrl="LoginForm.aspx" />
        </authentication>
        <authorization>
            <deny users="?" />
        </authentication>
    </system.web>
</configuration>
```

In the preceding example, all users who have not yet signed in will be redirected to the LoginForm.aspx page when they attempt to access any ASP.NET file. Typically, the form will prompt the user for a user name and password and handle authentication within the application itself. In whatever way the application handles the user's input, the user's credentials will be sent to the server as a *Hypertext Transfer Protocol (HTTP)* request—without any automatic encryption. HTTP is the protocol Web browsers and Web servers use to communicate. The best way to ensure privacy of user credentials submitted by using Forms authentication is to configure an SSL certificate within IIS, and require *Hypertext Transfer Protocol Secure (HTTPS)* for the login form. HTTPS is an encrypted form of the HTTP protocol, used by virtually every e-commerce Web site on the Internet, to protect private information about end users and to protect end users from submitting private information to a rogue server impersonating another server.

> **See Also**   For more information about using SSL certificates, see Lesson 3 in this chapter.

The user name and password can be checked against a database, a list contained in the *Web.config* file, an XML file, or any other mechanism you create. Forms authentication is tremendously flexible; however, you are entirely responsible for protecting your authentication mechanism from attackers. Because proof of authentication is stored in a cookie provided by the Web server, and that cookie generally contains only the user's user name, an attacker can potentially create a fake cookie to trick the Web server into considering the user as authenticated. ASP.NET includes the ability to encrypt and validate authentication cookies, but naturally, this protection includes some overhead for the Web server.

The type of encryption and validation used is controlled by the *protection* attribute of the <forms> section. If the *protection* attribute is not set, it defaults to *All*. If the *protection* attribute is set to *Encryption*, the cookie is encrypted with 3-DES. This encryption ensures the privacy of the data contained in the cookie but performs no validation. If the *protection* attribute is set to *Validation*, as the following example demonstrates, the server verifies the data in the cookie upon each transaction to reduce the likelihood of it being modified between the time it is sent from the browser and the time it is received by the server. If the *protection* attribute is set to *None*, neither encryption nor validation is performed. This setting reduces the overhead on the server, but it is suitable only in situations where privacy is not a concern, such as Web site personalization.

```
<authentication mode="Forms" protection="Validation" >
    <forms loginUrl="LoginForm.aspx" />
</authentication>
```

> **Important**   For optimal security (with a slight performance cost), leave protection at the default setting of *All*.

Another important attribute of the <forms> section is *timeout*, which defines, in minutes, the amount of idle time allowed between requests before the user will be forced to log on again. If the <forms> section is <forms loginUrl="YourLogin.aspx" timeout="10">, the user is forced to log on again if he does not send any requests to the ASP.NET application within 10 minutes. This number should be decreased to reduce the risk of the browser being misused while the user is away from the computer. The <forms> section has other attributes, but *loginUrl*, *protection*, and *timeout* are the most important.

How to Configure User Accounts in the Web.config File

To avoid creating a database to store user credentials, you can store the user credentials directly in the \Web.config file. The passwords can be stored in one of three formats: as clear-text; encrypted with the MD5 one-way hash algorithm; or encrypted with the SHA1 one-way hash algorithm. Using one of the two hash algorithms to mask the user credentials reduces the likelihood that a malicious user with read access to the Web.config file will gather another user's logon information. Define the hashing method used within the `<forms>` section, in the `<credentials>` section. An example is shown here:

```
<authentication mode="Forms">
    <forms loginUrl="login.aspx" protection="Encryption" timeout="30" >
        <credentials passwordFormat="SHA1" >
            <user name="Eric" ⤶
password="07B7F3EE06F278DB966BE960E7CBBD103DF30CA6"/>
            <user name="Sam" ⤶
password="5753A498F025464D72E088A9D5D6E872592D5F91"/>
        </credentials>
    </forms>
</authentication>
```

> **Real World   The Value of Password Hashing**
>
> Microsoft's official security best practice recommends you do not store user credentials in a Web.config file, even if you use a hash. I agree with that recommendation because the Web.config file is often accessible to non-administrators. However, in the real world, hashed passwords stored in a Web.config file are among the more secure custom authentication mechanisms I've seen. About two-thirds of the Web sites I've examined use a table in a database and store user names and passwords in clear-text. These sites include privately developed intranet sets, large public Web sites, and popular open source software.
>
> At least the Web.config file includes the option for hashing the passwords, which will slow an attacker down (a little bit). It's not exactly easy for an attacker to access a Web.config file, either. ASP.NET won't transfer the file to a Web browser in its default configuration. Basically, to access the Web.config file, the attacker would need a valid user logon and a method of accessing the file other than the Web server, such as a Remote Desktop session or a shared folder. If the attacker has those privileges, he could also access most of the unhashed user password databases I've seen.

To enable administrators to use hashed password information in the Web.config file, your ASP.NET application must include a page or tool to generate these passwords. The passwords are stored in hexadecimal format, and hashed with the specified hashing protocol. You can use the *System.Security.Cryptography* namespace to generate such a hash. The following console application demonstrates this by accepting a password as a command-line parameter, and displaying the hash of the password. The resulting hash can be pasted directly into the Web.config file.

```csharp
using System;
using System.Security.Cryptography;
using System.Text;

namespace HashExample
{
    class Class1
    {
        [STAThread]
        static void Main(string[] args)
        {
            SHA1CryptoServiceProvider myHash=new SHA1CryptoServiceProvider();

            byte[] password  = Encoding.ASCII.GetBytes(args[0]);
            myHash.ComputeHash(password);

            foreach (byte thisByte in myHash.Hash)
                Console.Write(thisByte.ToString("X2"));
            Console.WriteLine();
        }
    }
}
```

```vbnet
Imports System
Imports System.Security.Cryptography
Imports System.Text

Module Module1
    Sub Main(ByVal args As String())
        Dim myHash As SHA1CryptoServiceProvider =New SHA1CryptoServiceProvider
        Dim password As Byte() = Encoding.ASCII.GetBytes(args(0))
        myHash.ComputeHash(password)
        For Each thisByte As Byte In myHash.Hash
            Console.Write(thisByte.ToString("X2"))
        Next
        Console.WriteLine()
    End Sub
End Module
```

Alternatively, you can call the *FormsAuthentication.HashPasswordForStoringInConfig-File* method to generate a password hash. This method is described in the next section.

Important   You should store credentials in a .config file only during testing. Protecting passwords with a hash is little deterrent to an attacker who can read the contents of the .config file, because hashed password databases exist that can quickly identify common passwords.

The *FormsAuthentication* Class

The *FormsAuthentication* class is the basis for all forms authentication in ASP.NET. The class includes the following read-only properties:

- **FormsCookieName**   Returns the configured cookie name used for the current application.

- **FormsCookiePath**   Returns the configured cookie path used for the current application.

- **RequireSSL**   Gets a value indicating whether the cookie must be transmitted using SSL (that is, over HTTPS only).

Important   Enable *RequireSSL* for best security. This will ensure that Forms authentication is encrypted.

- **SlidingExpiration**   Gets a value indicating whether sliding expiration is enabled. Enabling sliding expiration resets the user's authentication timeout with every Web request.

Important   Disable *SlidingExpiration* for the highest level of security. This prevents a session from remaining open indefinitely.

Additionally, you can call the following methods:

- **Authenticate**   Attempts to validate the credentials against those contained in the configured credential store, given the supplied credentials.

- **Decrypt**   Returns an instance of a *FormsAuthenticationTicket* class, given a valid encrypted authentication ticket obtained from an HTTP cookie.

- **Encrypt**   Produces a string containing an encrypted authentication ticket suitable for use in an HTTP cookie, given a *FormsAuthenticationTicket* object.

- **GetAuthCookie**   Creates an authentication cookie for a given user name.

- **GetRedirectUrl**   Returns the redirect URL for the original request that caused the redirect to the logon page.

- **HashPasswordForStoringInConfigFile**   Given a password and a string identifying the hash type, this routine produces a hash password suitable for storing in a configuration file. If your application stores user credentials in the Web.config file and hashes the password, build this method into a management tool to enable administrators to add users and reset passwords.

- **RedirectFromLoginPage**   Redirects an authenticated user back to the originally requested URL. Call this method after verifying a user's credentials with the *Authenticate* method. You must pass this method a string and a Boolean value. The string uniquely identifies the user, and the method will use it to generate a cookie based on that information. The Boolean value, if true, allows the browser to use the same cookie across multiple browser sessions. Generally, this unique piece of information should be the user's user name.

- **RenewTicketIfOld**   Conditionally updates the sliding expiration on a *FormsAuthenticationTicket* object.

- **SetAuthCookie**   Creates an authentication ticket and attaches it to the cookie's collection of the outgoing response. It does not perform a redirect.

- **SignOut**   Removes the authentication ticket, essentially logging the user out.

How to Create a Custom Forms Authentication Page

When using Forms authentication, you must include two sections at a minimum:

- A Forms authentication page.

- A method for users to log out and close their current sessions.

To create a Forms authentication page, create an ASP.NET Web form to prompt the user for credentials, and call members of the *System.Web.Security.FormsAuthentication* class to authenticate the user and redirect her to a protected page. The following code sample demonstrates an overly simple authentication mechanism that just verifies that the contents of *usernameTextBox* and *passwordTextBox* are the same, and then calls the *RedirectFromLoginPage* method to redirect the user to the page she originally requested. Notice that the Boolean value passed to *RedirectFromLoginPage* is true, indicating that the browser will save the cookie after the browser is closed, enabling the user to remain authenticated if she closes and reopens her browser before her authentication cookie expires.

```csharp
if (usernameTextBox.Text == passwordTextBox.Text)
{
    FormsAuthentication.RedirectFromLoginPage(usernameTextBox.Text, true);
}
```

```vb
If usernameTextBox.Text = passwordTextBox.Text Then
    FormsAuthentication.RedirectFromLoginPage(usernameTextBox.Text, True)
End If
```

Although the authentication mechanism demonstrated in the previous code sample could never provide adequate protection for a Web application, it demonstrates the flexibility of forms authentication. You can check the user's credentials using any mechanism required by your application. Most often, the user name and a hash of the user's password will be looked up in a database.

If user credentials are stored in the Web.config file, call the *FormsAuthentication.Authenticate* method to check the credentials. Simply pass to the method the user's user name and password. The method will return true if the user's credentials match a value in the Web.config file. Otherwise, it will return false. The following code sample demonstrates the use of this method to redirect an authenticated user. Notice that the Boolean value passed to *RedirectFromLoginPage* is false, indicating that the browser will not save the cookie after the browser is closed, requiring the user to reauthenticate if she closes and reopens her browser, thus improving security:

```csharp
if (FormsAuthentication.Authenticate(usernameTextBox.Text, →
passwordTextBox.Text))
{
    // User is authenticated. Redirect them to the page they requested.
    FormsAuthentication.RedirectFromLoginPage(usernameTextBox.Text, false);
}
```

```vb
If FormsAuthentication.Authenticate(usernameTextBox.Text, →
passwordTextBox.Text) Then
    ' User is authenticated. Redirect them to the page they requested.
    FormsAuthentication.RedirectFromLoginPage(usernameTextBox.Text, False)
End If
```

In addition to creating a page to authenticate users, provide a method for users to log out of the application. Generally, this is a simple "Log out" hyperlink that calls the *FormsAuthentication.SignOut* static method to remove the user's authentication cookie.

How to Configure Web Applications to Require Passport Authentication

You can also authenticate users using a service from Microsoft called Passport. Passport is a centralized directory of user information that Web sites can use, in exchange for a fee, to authenticate users. Users can choose to allow the Web site access to personal information stored on Passport, such as the users' addresses, ages, and interests. Storing information about users worldwide within the Passport service relieves end users from maintaining separate user names and passwords on different sites. Further, it saves the user time by eliminating the need to provide personal information to multiple Web sites.

> **See Also** For more detailed information about the requirements of building a Web application that uses Passport, you can download and review the free Passport software development kit from MSDN on the Microsoft Web site at *http://msdn.microsoft.com/downloads/list /websrvpass.asp.*

Practice: Configuring Authentication in ASP.NET Applications

In this practice, you will edit the Web.config files for four applications to meet the specified authentication requirements of a fictitious organization. Read the scenario and then complete the exercise that follows. If you are unable to answer a question, review the lessons and try the question again. You can find answers to the questions in the "Questions and Answers" section at the end of this chapter.

Scenario

Northwind Traders has hired you to finish an ASP.NET application that another developer created. Although they are happy with the application, the developer did not configure the application to meet their authentication requirements. You must modify the Web.config files for the four applications so that they authenticate users according to the technical requirements.

During a meeting with the IT Manager, Eric Rothenberg, he tells you the following:

"We're happy with the Web app the other developer put together for us, except for one thing: the authentication doesn't work like we wanted. I guess we should have given him more explicit directions, and tested it out before he left on his honeymoon trip.

Right now, everyone who visits any of the four Web apps from outside our organizations gets prompted for a user name and password. If a person enters a valid Windows user name and password, the application lets them in. Otherwise, it shows them an HTTP 401.2 error, which I guess means they didn't enter valid credentials. The main Northwind app—that's our public Web presence—and anybody should be able to get to it. There are three applications contained within Northwind: Catalog, ManageCatalog, and ManageSite. Catalog should be anonymous, too, because that's how people see what we have for sale. ManageCatalog is going to be accessed by vendors and other partners, and the developer set it up for us to use user name and password pairs to the Web.config file. Apparently the passwords should be SHA1 hashed.

Can you add in some user names and passwords for us? I'll provide you with the user names and passwords we'd like to start with. Lastly, the ManageSite application should be accessed only by people with a Windows logon. Anyone with a Windows logon should be able to get in, though. Well, go ahead and make the changes, and please show me what you modified."

Technical Requirements   Configure authentication for the four applications are described in the table.

Northwind's Authentication Requirements

Application	Authentication
Northwind	Anonymous
Northwind\Catalog	Anonymous
Northwind\ManageCatalog	Forms, with the following user account and password combinations: ■ Abarr, TYiwo#33ol ■ Mhines, 83WSojfMv^ ■ Sbashary, X0$3lswWl
Northwind\ManageSite	Windows

Exercise

Configure the Web.config files and then answer the following questions to explain to your boss what you did.

1. How did you modify the Web.config file for the root Northwind application? What other changes did you make?

2. How did you modify the Web.config file for the Northwind\Catalog application?

3. How did you modify the Web.config file for the Northwind\ManageCatalog application?

4. How did you generate the password hashes for the Northwind\ManageCatalog application?

5. How did you modify the Web.config file for the Northwind\ManageSite application? What other changes did you make?

Lesson Summary

- Web.config files are per-folder configuration settings for ASP.NET applications that apply configuration settings to a Web application or a subfolder of a Web application.

- To configure Web applications to require Windows authentication, add the `<authentication mode="Windows" />` section to the application's Web.config file.

- To configure Web applications to use anonymous authentication, add the `<authentication mode="None" />` section to the application's Web.config file.

- Forms authentication enables you to build custom authentication mechanisms into ASP.NET applications. To create ASP.NET forms to authenticate Web users, add the `<authentication mode="Forms" />` section to the application's Web.config file, and create an ASP.NET form to prompt the user for logon credentials.

- To configure Web applications to require Passport authentication, add the `<authentication mode="Passport" />` section to the application's Web.config file, and use the Passport SDK to develop your application.

Lesson 2: Controlling Authorization in ASP.NET Applications

Web applications provide unique methods for restricting access. You can use Web.config files to control which users and groups can access applications, folders, and individual files. Additionally, you can expand the scope of ASP.NET's protection to files that ASP.NET does not normally process. Although most authentication and authorization techniques apply equally well to both Web applications and Web services, Web services require additional consideration because they expose the Documentation protocol, which is a potential security vulnerability.

After this lesson, you will be able to

- Restrict access to ASP.NET Web applications, files, and folders based on the user's name and group memberships.
- Limit the privileges of Web applications with code access security.
- Restrict access to users based on their IP addresses.
- Explain how IIS and ASP.NET handle file extensions.
- Reduce the attack surface of ASP.NET Web services by eliminating unnecessary protocols.

Estimated lesson time: 30 minutes

How to Restrict Access to ASP.NET Web Applications, Files, and Folders

Authentication determines a user's identity, whereas authorization defines what the user may access. Before the .NET Framework, administrators controlled Web user authorization entirely with NTFS permissions. Although NTFS permissions are still a key part of configuring security for ASP.NET applications, these permissions are now complemented by ASP.NET's authorization capabilities. Authorization is now controlled with Web.config files, just like authentication. This enables authorization to work with any type of authentication—even if the authorization doesn't use the local user database or Active Directory that NTFS permissions are based on. The use of Web.config files also makes copying file permissions between multiple Web servers as easy as copying files.

The sections that follow teach how to restrict access according to user and group names, how to restrict access to specific files and folders using either a .config file or file permissions, and how to use impersonation in an ASP.NET application.

How to Restrict Access to Users and Groups

The default Machine.config file contains the following authorization information:

```
<authorization>
    <allow users="*"/>
</authorization>
```

Unless you modified this section of the Machine.config file, or overrode the Machine.config file by adding this section to your application's Web.config file, all users permitted by your authentication configuration will be allowed to interact with all parts of your ASP.NET Web application. The `<allow users="*">` subsection of the authorization section tells ASP.NET that all users that pass the authentication requirements should be allowed access to all ASP.NET content. The * is a wildcard indicating all users, but you can also list user names or use the question mark character (?) to refer to all unauthenticated users. For example, to configure an ASP.NET application to provide access only to the users Eric and Sam, edit the Web.config file in the root of the ASP.NET application, and add the following lines within the `<system.web>` section:

```
<authorization>
    <allow users="Eric, Sam"/>
    <deny users="?"/>
</authorization>
```

The `<allow>` and `<deny>` subsections can contain *users*, *roles*, and *verbs* attributes. The *users* attribute should be set to a list of user names separated by commas; a * to indicate all authenticated or unauthenticated users; or a ? to indicate anonymous users. If Windows authentication is used, the user names should match names in the local user database or Active Directory, and might need to include a domain name (that is, "*DOMAIN\user*").

The *roles* attribute contains a comma-separated list of roles. When Windows authentication is used, roles correspond to Windows user groups. In this case, the names must exactly match group names in the local user database or Active Directory. If forms authentication is being used, these roles are defined within the application itself and cannot be defined by the systems administrator.

See Also   Don't forget that you can also use standard role-based security (RBS) to protect methods in ASP.NET applications. For more information about RBS, see Chapter 5.

The *verbs* attribute is used to restrict users and roles to specific types of HTTP requests—for example, HEAD, GET, POST, and DEBUG requests. All users should have access to the HEAD, GET, and POST verbs. Access to DEBUG can be limited to developers and administrators, if desired. Use the *verbs* attribute only when you understand how each of the different requests is used by applications. The following example demonstrates limiting access to different types of HTTP requests:

```
<authorization>
    <allow verbs="HEAD, GET, POST, DEBUG" roles="Developers"/>
    <allow verbs="HEAD, GET, POST" roles="Users"/>
    <deny users="?"/>
</authorization>
```

The Most Common HTTP Verbs

In case you haven't read the handful of Requests for Comments (RFCs) describing the HTTP protocol recently (and I hope you haven't, they're very dry), let me give you a quick description of the most common HTTP verbs. Browsers submit a *GET* request to retrieve a file. For example, the first time a user visits *http://www.microsoft.com/*, the browser submits a "GET /" request to the *www.microsoft.com* Web server.

If the user fills out a Web form—for example, to search the Microsoft.com Web site, the browser usually sends the response using an HTTP *POST* command (though forms with small amounts of input can be submitted with a *GET* command, too). *GET* and *POST* are the most commonly used commands; however, browsers will use the *HEAD* command to retrieve information about a file without actually retrieving a file. *HEAD* responses usually contain the date the file was modified, the length of the file, and the software the Web server is running.

PUT and *DELETE* commands are used by tools, such as Microsoft FrontPage or Microsoft Windows Explorer using Web folders to perform file management tasks. Applications use *DEBUG*, logically enough, for debugging, so developers need access to it but regular users do not. *TRACE* is rarely used, but can be useful for debugging and troubleshooting, and can provide some insight into how the remote server is handling the request. The *OPTIONS* command is also rarely used, but can determine what types of requests the Web server is capable of responding to.

How to Control Authorization for Folders and Files by Using .config Files

The previous techniques are useful for controlling user access to an entire ASP.NET application. To restrict access to specific files or folders, add a `<location>` section to the `<configuration>` section of the Web.config file. The `<location>` section will contain its own `<system.web>` subsection, so do not place it within an existing `<system.web>` section.

To configure access restrictions for a specific file or folder, add the `<location>` section to your Web.config with a single section: *path*. The *path* section must be set to the relative path of a file or folder; absolute paths are not allowed. Within the `<location>` section, include a `<system.web>` subsection, and any configuration information that is unique to the specified file or folder. For example, to require forms authentication for the file ListUsers.aspx and restrict access to the user named admin, add the following text to the `<configuration>` section of the Web.config file:

```
<location path="ListUsers.aspx">
    <system.web>
        <authentication mode="forms">
            <forms loginUrl="AdminLogin.aspx" protection="All"/>
        </authentication>
        <authorization>
            <allow users="admin"/>
            <deny users="*"/>
        </authorization>
    </system.web>
</location>
```

When using multiple `<location>` sections, file and subfolders automatically inherit all settings from their parent. Therefore, you do not need to repeat settings that are identical to the parent's configuration. When configuring authorization, inheritance has the potential to lead to security vulnerabilities. Consider the following Web.config file:

```
<configuration>
  <system.web>
    <authentication mode="Windows" />

    <authorization>
      <deny users="?" />

    </authorization>
  </system.web>

  <location path="Protected">
    <system.web>
      <authorization>
        <allow roles="CONTOSO\IT" />
      </authorization>
    </system.web>
  </location>
</configuration>
```

In this example, there are actually *three* layers of inheritance. The first is the Machine.config file, which specifies the default `<allow users="*"/>`. The second layer is the first `<system.web>` section in the example, which applies to the entire application. This setting, `<deny users="?"/>`, denies access to all unauthenticated users. By itself, this second layer would deny access to any user. However, combined with the

Machine.config file, this layer allows access to all authenticated users and denies access to everyone else.

The third layer is the `<location>` section, which grants access to the CONTOSO\IT group. However, this section also inherits the `<deny users="?"/>` and `<allow users="*"/>` settings. Therefore, the effective settings for the Protected subfolder are the same as for the parent folder: all authenticated users have access. To restrict access to *only* users in the CONTOSO\IT group, you must explicitly deny access to users who are not specifically granted access, as the following code demonstrates:

```
<location path="Protected">
  <system.web>
    <authorization>
      <allow roles="CONTOSO\IT" />
      <deny users="*" />
    </authorization>
  </system.web>
</location>
```

How to Control Authorization for Folders and Files by Using File Permissions

Even for publicly available content, it is good practice to tighten the NTFS file permissions on your Web server by removing the Everyone group's access. By default, the Everyone group has Read & Execute permissions to Web content, as shown in Figure 9-3. If you do remove the Everyone permission, you'll discover that ASP.NET applications cannot execute unless both the ASPNET user account (on IIS 5.0) or the Network Service account (on IIS 6.0) and the IUSR_*MachineName* user accounts have read permissions to the .aspx files.

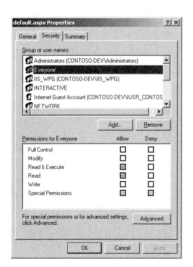

Figure 9-3   The Everyone group has permission to read ASP.NET application files by default.

The IUSR_*MachineName* account needs only Read & Execute privileges to those files that are requested directly by the browser—generally the .aspx and .asmx files. If the application was built using code-behind techniques, the .aspx files might refer to other files with extensions of .aspx.cs or .aspx.vb. If this is the case, only the ASPNET account (on IIS 5.0) or the Network Service account (on IIS 6.0) needs Read & Execute privileges to the code-behind files. Modifying permissions on a file-by-file basis can be difficult to maintain, however, because you must disable inheritable permissions for each file, and administrators must adjust the permissions for each file any time they make changes.

Table 9-1 lists the minimum permissions that an IIS IUSR_*ComputerName* Internet Guest Account and both the ASPNET account (IIS 5.0) or the Network Service account (IIS 6.0) must have. These permissions are valid only for applications where the source code is compiled in a DLL file before the application runs, such as applications created by using Microsoft Visual Studio .NET. Individual users or groups must have additional permissions to update the files. Permissions are shown for individual file types. For all file types, if the IUSR_*ComputerName* account and the ASPNET account (IIS 5.0) or Network Service account (IIS 6.0) have these permissions, you can remove the Everyone account and the Authenticated Users account from the file's ACL.

Table 9-1   Permissions Required for ASP.NET Applications

File Type	Internet Guest Account Permissions	ASPNET Account (IIS 5.0) or Network Service Account (IIS 6.0) Minimum Permissions
Folders	Read (required for access to default document)	Read
.asax	No Access	Read
.ascx	No Access	Read
.ashx	No Access	Read
.asmx	Read	Read
.aspx	No Access	Read
.config	No Access	Read
.cs	No Access	No Access
.csproj	No Access	No Access
.dll	No Access	Read
.licx	No Access	No Access
.pdb	No Access	No Access
.rem	No Access	Read
.resources	No Access	No Access
.resx	No Access	No Access

Table 9-1   Permissions Required for ASP.NET Applications

File Type	Internet Guest Account Permissions	ASPNET Account (IIS 5.0) or Network Service Account (IIS 6.0) Minimum Permissions
.soap	No Access	Read
.vb	No Access	No Access
.vbproj	No Access	No Access
.vbdisco	No Access	No Access
.webinfo	No Access	No Access
.xsd	No Access	No Access
.xsx	No Access	No Access

How to Configure Impersonation by Using .config Files

By default, ASP.NET applications make all requests for system resources from the ASP-NET account (IIS 5.0) or the Network Service account (IIS 6.0). This setting is configurable, of course, and is defined in the `<processModel>` item of the `<system.web>` section of the Machine.config file. The relevant default settings for this section are:

```
<processModel
    enable="true"
    userName="machine"
    password="AutoGenerate"
/>
```

The *userName* and *password* sections define the account ASP.NET impersonates when requesting system resources on behalf of Web users. The "machine" setting for *userName* means that ASP.NET will use the account named ASPNET (IIS 5.0) or the Network Service account (IIS 6.0). The "AutoGenerate" setting for *password* forces ASP.NET to use a random password—which is much more secure than typing the password in the Machine.config file.

These settings are sufficient for most ASP.NET implementations. However, in many cases, administrators will need to configure ASP.NET to impersonate the client's authenticated user account, IIS's anonymous user account, or a specific user account. This configuration is done by editing the impersonate section of the `<identity>` section of the Machine.config (for server-wide settings) or Web.config (for application- or directory-specific settings) files. To enable impersonation of the client's authenticated Windows account, or IIS's IUSR_*MachineName* account for anonymous access, add the following line to the `<system.web>` section of the Web.config file:

```
<identity impersonate="true" userName="" password=""/>
```

When IIS is configured for anonymous access, ASP.NET will make requests for system resources using the IUSR_*MachineName* account. When a user authenticates directly to IIS using a Windows logon, ASP.NET impersonates that user account. To enable ASP.NET to impersonate a specific user account, regardless of how IIS authentication is handled, add the following line to the `<system.web>` section of the Web.config file and replace the *DOMAIN*, *UserName*, and *Password* attributes with the account logon credentials:

```
<identity impersonate="true" userName="DOMAIN\UserName" password="Password"/>
```

How to Implement Custom Impersonation

Configuring impersonation in .config files applies to all ASP.NET code covered by the scope of the .config file. If users are authenticating with highly privileged accounts, such as accounts that have administrator privileges or accounts that are authorized to make changes to a back-end database, these permissions might be excessive. You can follow the principle of least privilege while enabling users to perform tasks that require higher privileges; however, you must do so by leaving ASP.NET impersonation disabled and impersonating the authenticated user only when the elevated permissions are required.

If you need to impersonate a user for only a section of your code, use the *System.Security.Principal.WindowsImpersonationContext* class. Simply create the object by creating a *System.Security.Principal.WindowsIdentity* object for the authenticated user and calling the *Impersonate* method. Create a *WindowsIdentity* object based on the user's Windows credentials by casting the *User.Identity* object (which is contained within the *Page* object). The following code sample demonstrates using this technique to display the current user's name in three labels:

```csharp
using System.Security.Principal;
…
// Displays "NT AUTHORITY\NETWORK SERVICE" in user1Label
user1Label.Text = WindowsIdentity.GetCurrent().Name;

// Impersonate the user with the account they used to authenticate
WindowsImpersonationContext realUser;
realUser = ((WindowsIdentity)User.Identity).Impersonate();

// Displays domain and username of authenticated user in user2Label.
// For example, "CONTOSO-DEV\Administrator"
user2Label.Text = WindowsIdentity.GetCurrent().Name;

// Perform tasks that require user permissions

// Undo the impersonation, reverting to the previous user context
realUser.Undo();

// Displays "NT AUTHORITY\NETWORK SERVICE" in user3Label
user3Label.Text = WindowsIdentity.GetCurrent().Name;
```

```vb
Imports System.Security.Principal
…
' Displays "NT AUTHORITY\NETWORK SERVICE" in user1Label
user1Label.Text = WindowsIdentity.GetCurrent.Name

'Impersonate the user with the account they used to authenticate
Dim realUser As WindowsImpersonationContext
realUser = CType(User.Identity, WindowsIdentity).Impersonate

' Displays domain and username of authenticated user in user2Label.
' For example, "CONTOSO-DEV\Administrator"
user2Label.Text = WindowsIdentity.GetCurrent.Name

' Perform tasks that require user permissions

' Undo the impersonation, reverting to the previous user context
realUser.Undo

' Displays "NT AUTHORITY\NETWORK SERVICE" in user3Label
user3Label.Text = WindowsIdentity.GetCurrent.Name
```

To use this technique effectively, leave ASP.NET impersonation disabled but require Windows authentication. Create the *WindowsImpersonationContext* object, and call the *WindowsIdentity.Impersonate* method immediately before performing a task that requires privileges that the Network Service account lacks, such as making an update to a database. After the task has been completed, call the *WindowsImpersonationContext.Undo* method to return to the Network Service security context.

How to Use Code Access Security to Limit Privileges

You can control the level of trust granted to external applications that your ASP.NET Web application might call. By default, trust is not a factor for ASP.NET applications, because the Machine.config file is preconfigured to give full trust to ASP.NET applications. This snippet from the Machine.config file shows the default settings of the `<securityPolicy>` and `<trust>` sections:

```xml
<securityPolicy>
    <trustLevel name="Full" policyFile="internal"/>
    <trustLevel name="High" policyFile="web_hightrust.config"/>
    <trustLevel name="Medium" policyFile="web_mediumtrust.config"/>
    <trustLevel name="Low" policyFile="web_lowtrust.config"/>
    <trustLevel name="Minimal" policyFile="web_minimaltrust.config"/>
</securityPolicy>

<trust level="Full" originUrl=""/>
```

The `<securityPolicy>` section defines the different levels of trust that might be specified for ASP.NET applications. Each `<trustLevel>` subsection defines a unique level of trust and has two attributes: *name* and *policyFile*. The *name* attribute gives the trust level a friendly name that will be referenced in the `<trust>` section, and the *policyFile* attribute references another configuration file (located in the same folder containing the Machine.config file) that contains the details of that level's trust settings. By default, five different levels of trust exist: Full, High, Low, None, and Minimal. The Full trust level does not have a configuration file, because it causes the runtime to simply skip all code access security (CAS) checks.

The `<trust>` section defines the level of trust that ASP.NET applications run from a remote URL will receive. The default setting in the Machine.config file grants all applications Full trust. To configure an application run from http://remoteapp/appdir/ to run with a Low level of trust, add this line to the Web.config file:

```
<trust level="Low" originUrl="http://remoteapp/appdir/" />
```

How to Restrict User Access by Using IP Addresses

A common technique for restricting authorization to Web applications is to verify a user's IP address. You can use one of two techniques to restrict authorization based on source IP address: configure restrictions in IIS or check the source IP address from within your ASP.NET application. The more efficient way to control access based on source IP address is to add IP address restrictions within IIS. Access that is restricted within IIS can be updated easily by systems administrators. Figure 9-4 shows IIS configured to allow only requests from the 192.168.1.0 subnet.

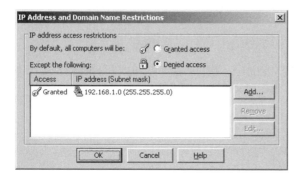

Figure 9-4   IIS can restrict access based on IP address, network ID, and domain name.

Alternatively, you can restrict access within your ASP.NET code by checking the user's source IP address. The user's IP address is contained in the *Request.UserHostAddress* property, and you can verify all or portions of the user's IP address by using regular expressions. If you choose to control authorization based on the IP address, you must enable administrators to specify the IP addresses and networks in your application's configuration. Even if your application is for internal use, administrators must be able to renumber networks without modifying your application's source code.

Tip   Source IP filtering should not be your only authorization technique, because source IP addresses can be spoofed by skilled attackers with direct access to your network. However, source IP filtering can be a useful part of a defense-in-depth approach.

How IIS and ASP.NET Handle File Extensions

IIS authentication, when enabled, authenticates all requests for a folder regardless of the type of file being retrieved. ASP.NET authentication works very differently, however, and can authenticate only those requests that IIS passes to the .NET Framework. By default, IIS 5.0 with the .NET Framework installed is configured to pass requests for files ending in the extensions .asax, .ascx, .ashx, .asmx, .aspx, .axd, .config, .cs, .csproj, .java, .jsl, .licx, .rem, .soap, .vb, .vbproj, .webinfo, .resx, .resources, .vjsproj, and .vsdisco. This means that requests for any *other* file will not be passed through ASP.NET, and therefore cannot be controlled by ASP.NET authentication.

Here is a practical example: Your company uses a public Web site to sell recipes written using Adobe Acrobat. These .PDF files are located in the /recipes/ virtual directory. Users should be able to download these recipes only after they pay a fee and the application assigns them a unique user name and password. You created an ASP.NET application that uses Forms authentication to verify users, and you configured the /recipes/ virtual directory to require Forms authentication by setting the `<authentication>` section of the virtual directory's Web.config file appropriately. However, after the first user purchases a recipe, he e-mails the URL of the .pdf file to his friends, and other people are able to download the file directly without being authenticated.

This problem occurs because files with extensions that are not associated with the aspnet_isapi.dll file are processed directly by IIS, and therefore cannot trigger an ASP.NET authentication event. The .pdf extension is not one of the extensions mapped to ASP.NET; therefore, IIS retrieves the file from the context of its anonymous user account and sends the file to the user. To overcome this, add .pdf to the IIS extension mappings as described in the next section. After this change is made, IIS will send all requests for files ending in .pdf to ASP.NET. ASP.NET will enforce authentication rules and redirect users requesting the file to the logon page. To ensure the security of a virtual directory authenticated with ASP.NET, map all file extensions of documents that should be protected to the aspnet_isapi.dll file.

The following sections show how to configure additional ASP.NET file types in IIS 6.0 and .config files.

> **Important**   Processing static files through ASP.NET increases the overhead of each request, thereby reducing scalability. Use this technique only for file types that must have access controlled by ASP.NET.

How to Configure Additional ASP.NET File Types in IIS 6.0

To configure ASP.NET to process specific non-standard file types, follow these steps:

1. Launch the Internet Information Services (IIS) Manager.

2. In the left pane, expand Web Sites. Right-click the Web site or application folder you want to configure, and then click Properties.

3. Click the Directory or Home Directory tab. In the Application Settings group, click the Configuration button.

   The Application Configuration dialog box appears, as shown in Figure 9-5.

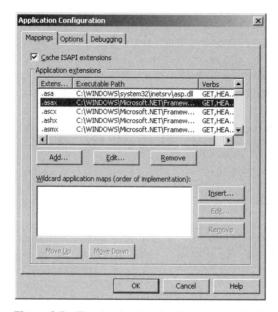

Figure 9-5   The Application Configuration dialog box enables you to configure which file extensions are processed by ASP.NET.

4. In the Application Extensions list, click .ASAX, and then click Edit. Highlight the contents of the Executable box, and press CTRL+C to copy the path to the Clipboard. Click Cancel.

5. Click the Add button.

6. In the Executable box, press CTRL+V to paste the path of the Aspnet_Isapi.dll file. In the Extension box, type the file extension you want ASP.NET to handle. Optionally, click the Limit To option button and provide a comma-delimited list of HTTP verbs, such as *GET* or *HEAD*. Finally, click OK.

   Figure 9-6 shows a new extension mapping being created to handle files ending with a .jpg extension.

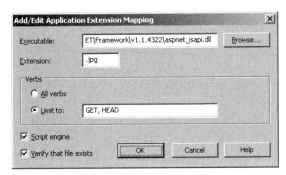

Figure 9-6   To add an extension, at a minimum, configure the Aspnet_Isapi.dll executable and the file extension.

7. Click OK twice to return to the Internet Information Services (IIS) Manager.

To ensure all file types will require ASP.NET authentication, configure a wildcard application map. To configure ASP.NET to process all file types, follow these steps:

1. Launch the Internet Information Services (IIS) Manager.

2. In the left pane, expand Web Sites. Right-click the Web site or application folder you want to configure, and then click Properties.

3. Click the Directory or Home Directory tab. In the Application Settings group, click the Configuration button.

4. In the Application Extensions list, click .ASAX, and then click Edit. Highlight the contents of the Executable box, and press CTRL+C to copy the path to the Clipboard. Click Cancel.

5. Click the Insert button.

6. In the Executable box (shown in Figure 9-7), press CTRL+V to paste the path of the Aspnet_Isapi.dll file, and then click OK.

Figure 9-7 Configuring a wildcard causes ASP.NET to handle all file types.

7. Click OK twice to return to the Internet Information Services (IIS) Manager.

How to Configure Additional ASP.NET File Types in .Config Files

Notice that many of the file extensions IIS is configured to pass to ASP.NET should never be called by users. Typically, only files ending in .aspx will be called by users. There is no *legitimate* reason for a typical user to request a file ending in .cs or .vb. However, IIS is configured to pass them to ASP.NET, and ASP.NET in turn filters these requests. If IIS were to fulfill the request by transferring the files, the attacker would gain access to your application's source code. However, by default, ASP.NET intercepts the requested file, detects that the file extension should not be part of a legitimate request, and drops the request.

> **Tip** If for some reason your application is installed on a server that has not been configured for ASP.NET applications, your source code might be vulnerable. If you create an installation project (rather than relying on XCOPY deployment), always verify that the .NET Framework is installed on the host before installation.

ASP.NET is configured by default to accept requests for some specific file extensions and to reject others. Because most applications use standard file extensions, developers rarely modify ASP.NET extension mappings in Web.config files. Therefore, extension mappings are almost always drawn from the `<httpHandlers>` subsection of the `<system.web>` section of the Machine.config file. The following code is a sample of the `<httpHandlers>` section in the Machine.config file, which the .NET Framework processes from top to bottom.

```
<add verb="*" path="*.vjsproj" type="System.Web.HttpForbiddenHandler"/>
<add verb="*" path="*.java" type="System.Web.HttpForbiddenHandler"/>
<add verb="*" path="*.jsl" type="System.Web.HttpForbiddenHandler"/>
<add verb="*" path="trace.axd" type="System.Web.Handlers.TraceHandler"/>
<add verb="*" path="*.aspx" type="System.Web.UI.PageHandlerFactory"/>
<add verb="*" path="*.ashx" type="System.Web.UI.SimpleHandlerFactory"/>
<add verb="*" path="*.asmx"
    type="System.Web.Services.Protocols.WebServiceHandlerFactory,
    System.Web.Services, Version=1.0.5000.0, Culture=neutral,
    PublicKeyToken=b03f5f7f11d50a3a" validate="false"/>
<add verb="*" path="*.rem"
    type="System.Runtime.Remoting.Channels.Http.HttpRemotingHandlerFactory,
```

```
    System.Runtime.Remoting, Version=1.0.5000.0, Culture=neutral,
    PublicKeyToken=b77a5c561934e089" validate="false"/>
<add verb="*" path="*.soap"

    type="System.Runtime.Remoting.Channels.Http.HttpRemotingHandlerFactory,
    System.Runtime.Remoting, Version=1.0.5000.0, Culture=neutral,

    PublicKeyToken=b77a5c561934e089" validate="false"/>
<add verb="*" path="*.asax" type="System.Web.HttpForbiddenHandler"/>
<add verb="*" path="*.ascx" type="System.Web.HttpForbiddenHandler"/>
<add verb="GET,HEAD" path="*.dll.config" type="System.Web.StaticFileHandler"/>
<add verb="GET,HEAD" path="*.exe.config" type="System.Web.StaticFileHandler"/>
<add verb="*" path="*.config" type="System.Web.HttpForbiddenHandler"/>
<add verb="*" path="*.cs" type="System.Web.HttpForbiddenHandler"/>
<add verb="*" path="*.csproj" type="System.Web.HttpForbiddenHandler"/>
<add verb="*" path="*.vb" type="System.Web.HttpForbiddenHandler"/>
<add verb="*" path="*.vbproj" type="System.Web.HttpForbiddenHandler"/>
<add verb="*" path="*.webinfo" type="System.Web.HttpForbiddenHandler"/>
<add verb="*" path="*.asp" type="System.Web.HttpForbiddenHandler"/>
<add verb="*" path="*.licx" type="System.Web.HttpForbiddenHandler"/>
<add verb="*" path="*.resx" type="System.Web.HttpForbiddenHandler"/>
<add verb="*" path="*.resources" type="System.Web.HttpForbiddenHandler"/>
<add verb="GET,HEAD" path="*" type="System.Web.StaticFileHandler"/>
<add verb="*" path="*" type="System.Web.HttpMethodNotAllowedHandler"/>
```

Notice that source code and project file extensions such as .vjsproj and .java are assigned to the appropriately named *System.Web.HttpForbiddenHandler*. Pages that should be processed, such as .aspx files, are handled by *System.Web.PageHandlerFactory*. Near the end of the code, the line `<add verb="GET,HEAD" path="*" type="System.Web.StaticFileHandler"/>` catches any processing requests submitted using either the HTTP *GET* or *HEAD* commands that have not yet been processed, and processes them using the *System.Web.StaticFileHandler* handler. This default handler allows you to configure IIS to send any file extensions to ASP.NET to protect the files with ASP.NET authentication, while still allowing Web browsers to retrieve the files normally. The final line of this code, `<add verb="*" path="*" type="System.Web.HttpMethodNotAllowedHandler"/>`, catches any request using HTTP verbs that has not yet been handled and throws an exception.

If you ship files that should simply be transferred by IIS without being processed but should still be protected by ASP.NET authentication, specify the *System.Web.StaticFileHandler* handler. If you ship files that have other extensions with your ASP.NET Web application, direct administrators to configure IIS to add those file extensions to ASP.NET for processing. If those files should never be processed by ASP.NET or downloaded by users, add sections to the `<httpHandlers>` section to enable those file extensions to be handled by *System.Web.HttpForbiddenHandler*, as shown in this example:

```
<add verb="*" path="*.passwords" type="System.Web.HttpForbiddenHandler"/>
```

How to Reduce the Attack Surface of ASP.NET Web Services

ASP.NET Web services enable applications to exchange XML information using standard Web protocols. This is a simple concept with significant implications—Web services enable information traditionally exchanged between a Web server and a Web browser to be consumed by different types of clients. Web services enable you to transfer easily parsed XML information using standardized Internet protocols. Instead of just running a Web site, businesses can exchange data with partners and customers programmatically, enabling incredible improvements to automation and efficiency.

ASP.NET Web services, such as those that expose application functionality using Simple Object Access Protocol (SOAP), are based on ASP.NET and as such have most of the same security issues. Even though the client is no longer a Web browser, the primary protocols are still HTTP and HTTPS. Firewalls, .config files, authorization, encryption, file permissions, extension mappings, impersonation, and trust are all virtually identical for ASP.NET Web applications and Web services. However, developers and administrators also need to understand several configuration issues that are unique to ASP.NET Web services.

One aspect of the default behavior of ASP.NET Web services that has security implications is the Documentation protocol, which automatically generates a browser-friendly interface when a user navigates to an .asmx file. As shown in Figure 9-8, this interface provides detailed information about the Web service methods available and the information these methods require as parameters, and it even allows someone to manually call these methods without writing a client application. Although Web services are designed to be simple to connect to, you might not want the details of Web services exposed to anyone with a browser.

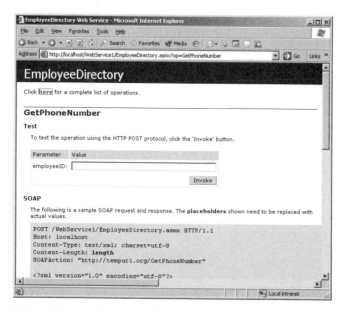

Figure 9-8   The Documentation protocol is useful for both developers writing a client-side application and attackers identifying potential entry points.

The behavior of the Documentation protocol is defined in the `<webServices>` section of the Machine.config file. By default, the Machine.config file contains:

```
<webServices>
    <protocols>
        <add name="HttpSoap"/>

        <add name="HttpPost"/>

        <add name="HttpGet"/>

        <add name="Documentation"/>

    </protocols>
</webServices>
```

Therefore, to disable the Documentation protocol, edit the Web.config file for the application, and add the following section to the `<system.web>` section:

```
<webServices>
    <protocols>
        <remove name="Documentation"/>

    </protocols>
</webServices>
```

Additionally, to reduce your application's attack surface, remove any protocols that your application does not specifically remove.

Practice: Controlling Authorization in ASP.NET Applications

In this practice, you will create an ASP.NET Web application that displays the Boot.ini text file while using the principal of least privilege. Read the scenario and then complete the exercise that follows. If you are unable to answer a question, review the lessons and try the question again. You can find answers to the questions in the "Questions and Answers" section at the end of this chapter.

Scenario

After you configured authentication to meet Northwind Traders' requirements, they asked you to create a simple ASP.NET Web application to display the contents of the C:\Boot.ini file on the Web server. Although this sounds like a simple task, a phone call with the IT Manager, Eric Rothenberg, uncovers some additional complexity:

"Thanks again for fixing that authentication problem we had. Our sysadmins have asked for a Web page that just displays the Web server's Boot.ini file. They use it because we have a complex Web site architecture with several servers, and it helps them figure out which servers double as test servers, and which are production servers. Here's the catch, though. I don't want to change the permissions on the Boot.ini file so that just anyone can read it. The Web server doesn't have the file permissions to access to the Boot.ini file by default, and I don't want the Web server to be able to directly access the Boot.ini file. Instead, I'd like to have the administrator provide Windows credentials, and have your application use those credentials to show the file. We'll probably add more pages later, so if you can avoid having the entire application run with the user's administrative credentials, I'd appreciate it. Oh—and name the project Show-BootIni. You can place it in the C:\Inetpub\Wwwroot\ShowBootIni\ folder."

You review the company's technical requirements before creating the ASP.NET Web application.

Technical Requirements   Create an ASP.NET Web application in the C:\Inetpub \Wwwroot\ShowBootIni\ folder using either C# or Visual Basic .NET. Use impersonation to take advantage of the user's Windows credentials to display the contents of the C:\Boot.ini file.

Exercise

Create the ASP.NET Web application and then answer the following questions to explain to the IT Manager how you created the application and why you did what you did.

1. What authentication method did you use? Why?

2. How did you implement impersonation? Why?

3. What XML did you add within the Web.config file?

4. What code did you write to display the C:\Boot.ini file?

Lesson Summary

- To restrict the access of specific users and groups to ASP.NET Web applications, files, and folders, configure the <authorization> section of an application's Web.config file.

- To use code access security to limit privileges for a Web application, modify the <trust> section of a Web.config file.

- To restrict user access based on users' IP addresses, examine the *Request.UserHost-Address* property.

- IIS and ASP.NET each determine how to process user requests based on the file's extension. Each much be separately configured to provide security for non-standard types of files.

- To reduce the attack surface of ASP.NET Web services, eliminate unnecessary Web services protocols by adding a <webServices> <protocols> section to your application's Web.config file using one or more <remove> subsections.

Lesson 3: Configuring SSL to Encrypt Web Communications

Most Web communications are unencrypted and can be easily interpreted by anyone with access to the network media. Many Web applications exchange confidential information, such as user credentials, and require additional communications protection. Secure Sockets Layer (SSL) is the most common way to encrypt Web communications. This lesson will teach you the purpose of SSL certificates and how to configure them to protect Web communications.

Exam Tip   Generally, systems administrators are responsible for configuring SSL certificates. However, Microsoft has provided an exam objective specifically to ensure developers are familiar with SSL certificates. As a result, this topic is important for passing the exam.

After this lesson, you will be able to

- Explain the purpose of SSL certificates.
- Configure IIS to use SSL certificates issued by Windows Server 2003 Certificate Services.
- Configure IIS to require SSL encryption for a Web site or application.

Estimated lesson time: 25 minutes

What Are SSL Certificates?

Secure Sockets Layer (SSL) certificates are documents that contain public key pairs that can be used to encrypt Web communications. SSL certificates cannot be dynamically generated, unlike the key pairs discussed in Chapter 8, "Protecting Data by Using Cryptography." Instead, SSL certificates are generated by a *certification authority (CA)*, which is a service that generates certificates. CAs can be run by a public company such as Verisign to issue certificates to paying customers, or CAs can be managed by an internal IT department by using software such as a computer running Windows Server 2003 with Certificate Services.

SSL is widely used because it provides strong authentication, message privacy, and data integrity. Unlike other proprietary techniques for improving communication security, SSL is an open standard that is widely deployed and supported by a variety of servers and clients. As a result of the wide adoption, the security community has carefully examined the SSL standards and popular SSL implementations. This close examination, combined with the relative maturity of the SSL standards, has resulted in a highly secure method for authenticating clients and servers and protecting the privacy of communications.

The most common use of SSL is to authenticate Web servers and to encrypt communications between Web browsers and Web servers. SSL, when used to protect the HTTP, is referred to as HTTPS.

> **Off the Record** Everyone always warns that HTTPS carries a performance overhead, but for most Web sites, this overhead is so insignificant that it doesn't matter.

In the sections that follow, you will learn the process of SSL encryption, how to obtain SSL certificates, how a single SSL certificate applies to only a single Web site, and how SSL certificates authenticate servers.

The Process of SSL Encryption

SSL provides encryption, authentication, and data integrity by using a public key certificate. When the SSL session is established, the server's public key certificate is used to encrypt and exchange a shared secret between the client and server. This shared secret is then used to encrypt communications for the rest of the session. The following steps describe the process of establishing an SSL session:

1. The Web client requests the public key from the Web server.
2. The server sends the public key to the client.
3. The client sends the server a session key, encrypting it with the public key.
4. The server decrypts the session key received from the client by using the server's private key.

The session key can then be used as a shared secret to encrypt and decrypt data exchanged between the client and server. This process is shown in Figure 9-9.

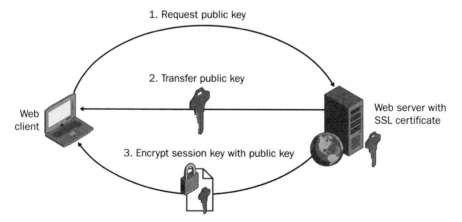

Figure 9-9 HTTPS uses public key encryption to securely exchange a symmetric session key.

> **Exam Tip**   Remember that SSL uses both public key (asymmetric) encryption and secret key (symmetric) encryption. Public keys are used for authentication and to transmit the secret key. The secret key is then used to encrypt the data, because encrypting and decrypting data with a secret key uses less processing time than public key encryption.

How SSL Certificates Are Obtained

To use SSL, the server must have a suitable public key certificate. SSL is one of the most common uses for public key certificates, and, as a result, you can obtain SSL certificates from a wide variety of places. Any organization with a computer running Windows Server 2003 can deploy Certificate Services to issue SSL certificates without any additional cost. These certificates are suitable for intranet scenarios, in which both the servers and the clients are controlled by a single organization. These certificates should not be used for communications among more than one organization, however.

As with any public key infrastructure (PKI), SSL certificates can be trusted only when the root certification authority (CA) is trusted. In intranet scenarios, administrators can use Group Policy objects (GPOs) to add an internal CA to the list of trusted root CAs on clients on the intranet, but it is much more difficult to configure clients on the public Internet. For this reason, if you do not control the client computers, obtain an SSL certificate from a public CA that is trusted by the client applications that will be establishing a connection to your server. As shown in Figure 9-10, Internet Explorer is configured by default to trust a large number of public CAs.

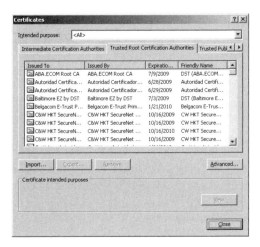

Figure 9-10   Internet Explorer trusts a large number of root CAs by default.

Exam Tip   Some CAs, including Verisign, offer free certificates for testing purposes. These certificates are generally not issued by the CA's trusted root certificate and, as a result, will not be automatically trusted by client browsers. However, these testing certificates are a perfect way to gain experience with publicly issued certificates to prepare for the exam.

If the client does not trust the CA that issued your certificate, the client will usually show a warning to the end user, as shown in Figure 9-11. This warning does not prevent the user from establishing an SSL-encrypted session with your server. However, the warning might cause the user to cancel the connection. Although establishing a connection to a server with an untrusted CA still provides encryption and message integrity, using an SSL certificate issued by an untrusted CA defeats the purpose of the authentication provided by SSL.

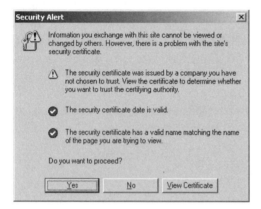

Figure 9-11   Internet Explorer issues a warning when it receives an SSL certificate issued by an untrusted CA.

Design   If you decide to use public certificates for SSL, take some time to choose your CA carefully. The prices charged for certificates vary widely, from free to several thousands of dollars. Additionally, you should be sure that the CA will continue to actively pursue being trusted by common Web browsers. If you are curious about what a CA needs to go through to become trusted, read about the WebTrust for Certification Authorities program sponsored by The American Institute for Certified Public Accountants (AICPA) on the WebTrust Web site at *http://www.webtrust.org/certauth.htm*.

The Scope of SSL Certificates

You can use SSL certificates to allow users to verify the identity of your Web site and to encrypt traffic sent between the client and the Web site. It is important to understand that an SSL certificate identifies a *Web site*, and not a *Web server*. A single Web server can host multiple Web sites. Alternatively, multiple Web servers can host a single Web site to provide redundancy and scalability. SSL certificates identify the server only by the domain name, and not by the path to a file or folder. Therefore, a single Web site cannot use different SSL certificates for different applications.

For example, an Internet service provider (ISP) that hosts Web sites for 20 customers on a single Web server needs 20 SSL certificates to allow each site to use encryption. Alternatively, if an ISP stores a copy of a Web site on 10 different servers to allow the Web site to remain online in the event of a hardware failure, the same certificate can be installed on all 10 servers.

SSL certificates use the *fully qualified domain name (FQDN)* to identify the Web site. The FQDN is the full domain name of the site, such as *www.microsoft.com*. When the client retrieves the site's SSL certificate, the client checks the FQDN of the Web site against the *subject name*, also known as the *common name*, listed in the certificate. Checking the name used to identify the site against the name listed in the certificate prevents a rogue Web site from intercepting traffic destined for a different site.

Though you assign SSL certificates to individual Web sites, you can configure SSL to help protect confidential data on a URL-by-URL basis. One part of the Web site might require encryption of data transmissions with SSL (by specifying HTTPS in the URL), and another part of the Web site might allow unencrypted data transmission (by specifying HTTP in the URL). This flexibility in security configuration allows you to provide encryption of confidential data as required while not incurring the performance penalty inherent in encryption and decryption.

> **See Also**   To better understand how SSL certificates are used, visit your favorite e-commerce Web site. While browsing the catalog, notice that the URL uses the http:// protocol. Next, attempt to purchase an item. At some point during the purchase process, you will begin to use SSL, and the URL will show that the https:// protocol is being used. E-commerce sites typically use HTTPS only when exchanging private information, because doing so reduces the burden of public key cryptography and encryption on their Web servers.

How SSL Certificates Authenticate Servers

SSL certificates help reduce the risk of attacks against the Domain Name System (DNS). For example, an attacker could compromise your DNS server and add a DNS record for the FQDN *www.microsoft.com* so that the FQDN resolved to the IP address of a rogue Web site. When you visited *http://www.microsoft.com*, your requests would actually be sent to the rogue Web site. The rogue Web site could then collect any information you intended to send to *www.microsoft.com*, which might include personal information or credit card numbers.

However, if you visited *https://www.microsoft.com*, the rogue Web site would have to return an SSL certificate to your Web browser. The rogue Web site could return a certificate with the common name *www.microsoft.com*, but no trusted CA would issue such a certificate. Therefore, your Web browser would warn you that the CA was untrusted. Alternatively, the rogue Web site could perform a true man-in-the-middle attack and forward your Web browser *www.microsoft.com*'s actual certificate. However, the rogue Web site would not be able to establish an SSL session with your browser, because it would not have the private key associated with the public key in the certificate.

How to Configure IIS to use SSL Certificates Issued by Windows Server 2003 Certificate Services

Using HTTPS on an IIS Web server requires the server to have a certificate installed and configured. The exact process you will use to configure the certificate varies depending on the source of the certificate; however, you will always use the Web Server Certificate Wizard built into IIS to create a certificate request and to assign a certificate to a Web site. Windows Server 2003 provides two interfaces for requesting and approving certificates: Web-based enrollment, and the Certificates console. The following sections show how to request a new certificate and assign an existing certificate to a Web site.

How to Request a New Certificate

To request a new certificate by using the Web Server Certificate Wizard, follow these steps:

1. Launch the Internet Information Services (IIS) Manager.

2. Expand the computer name, and then expand Web Sites. Right-click the Web site for which you want to configure an SSL certificate, and then click Properties.

3. Click the Directory Security tab, and then click the Server Certificate button.

   The Web Server Certificate Wizard appears.

4. On the first page of the Web Server Certificate Wizard, click Next.

   The Server Certificate page appears.

5. Click Create A New Certificate, and then click Next.

6. If you need to send the certificate request to an offline CA, click Prepare The Request Now, But Send It Later. If you want to enroll by using an enterprise CA and there is one present in your domain, click Send The Request Immediately To An Online Certification Authority. Click Next.

7. On the Name And Security Settings page, type a name for the new certificate that will help you remember its purpose. Leave the Bit Length setting at its default unless you have determined specifically that a greater bit length is required. Click Next.

8. On the Organization Information page, type a description in the Organization and Organizational Unit boxes. Click Next.

9. On the Your Site's Common Name page, type the common name for the computer. This should be the name that other computers will use to find the server on the intranet or Internet. Click Next.

10. On the Geographical Information page, select your Country/Region, State/Province, and City/Locality. Click Next.

11. If you chose Prepare The Request Now, But Send It Later in step 3, type a name for the file. If you chose Send The Request Immediately To An Online Certification Authority in step 3, select the CA from the Certification Authorities list.

12. Click Next twice, and then click Finish.

If you chose Prepare The Request Now, But Send It Later in step 6, submit the certificate request to a CA. You can use a public CA, in which case, they will provide a process for you to submit the certificate request. If you are submitting the request by using Web-based enrollment on a Windows Server 2003 CA, follow these steps:

1. Start Internet Explorer.

2. In the address bar of Internet Explorer, type **http://***ca-name***/certsrv**. Click Go.

3. If you are not automatically authenticated, provide your user name and password when prompted, and then click OK.

4. Click Request A Certificate.

5. Click Advanced Certificate Request.

6. Click Submit A Certificate Request By Using A Base-64-Encoded CMC Or PKCS #10 File, Or Submit A Renewal Request By Using A Base-64-Encoded PKCS #7 File.

7. Use Notepad to open the certificate request file that you saved earlier. Copy the contents of the certificate request file and paste it into the Saved Request box in Internet Explorer.

8. Click the Certificate Template list, and then click Web Server. Click Submit.

At this point your certificate request is submitted to the CA. If the CA is an enterprise root CA and you have sufficient privileges, your request might be automatically approved. Otherwise, you will need to use the Certificates console to approve the request by following these steps:

1. Launch the Certification Authority console from the Administrative Tools group.

2. In the left pane, click Pending Requests. As shown in Figure 9-12, the request you submitted is visible.

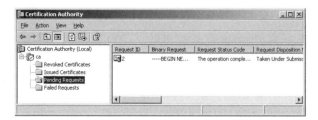

Figure 9-12 In production environments, certificates usually need to be approved by an administrator.

3. Right-click the request, click All Tasks, and then click Issue.

4. Click Issued Certificates to verify that the certificate was successfully issued.

5. In Internet Explorer, return to the URL **http://*ca-name*/certsrv** and click View The Status Of A Pending Certificate Request.

6. On the View The Status Of A Pending Certificate Request page, click the Saved-Request Certificate link.

7. On the Certificate Issued page, click Download Certificate. When prompted, click Save, and save the file to the computer. Click Close.

How to Assign an Existing Certificate to a Web Site

After you have a suitable certificate, install it in IIS by following these steps:

1. Launch the Internet Information Services (IIS) Manager.

2. Expand the computer name, and then expand Web Sites. Right-click the Web site for which you want to configure an SSL certificate, and then click Properties.

3. Click the Directory Security tab, and then click the Server Certificate button.

    The Web Server Certificate Wizard appears.

4. On the first page of the Web Server Certificate Wizard, click Next.

    The Server Certificate page appears.

5. Click Assign An Existing Certificate. Click Next.

6. On the Available Certificates page, click a certificate, and then click Next.

7. On the SSL Port page, leave the default port of 443 selected, and then click Next.

8. Click Next again, and then click Finish.

How to Configure IIS to Require SSL Encryption for a Web Site or Application

By default, IIS will accept both unencrypted HTTP and encrypted HTTPS requests after a certificate is configured. If you do not want to allow unencrypted requests, open the Web site properties dialog box, click the Directory Security tab, click the Edit button, and then select the Require Secure Channel (SSL) check box, as shown in Figure 9-13. Optionally, you can select the Require 128-Bit Encryption check box. Today, most clients will support 128-bit encryption, which is very difficult for an attacker to break. If you do not select the Require 128-Bit Encryption check box, clients that support 128-bit encryption will still use 128-bit encryption.

Figure 9-13   Requiring HTTPS for a Web server ensures all communications are encrypted.

Off the Record   Requiring HTTPS encryption isn't all that useful because browsers don't automatically try to connect by using HTTPS. So if a user types just your Web server's domain name into a browser, as most users will do, the browser will attempt to connect with unencrypted HTTP. If you don't allow unencrypted HTTP, IIS returns a fairly complicated error message. Some users will read the message and follow the instructions to connect to the Web site by using https:// in the URL, but others will simply think the Web server is down.

A better way to require HTTPS is to set up a separate Web site in IIS to redirect standard HTTP requests to HTTPS. That way, when a user types just your domain name in a Web browser, your Web server will automatically redirect that user to your Web site using HTTPS.

Practice: Configuring SSL to Encrypt Web Communications

In this practice, you will create and configure an SSL certificate. Read the scenario and then complete the exercises that follow.

Scenario

Northwind Traders has an additional task for you: adding an SSL certificate to their public Web site at *www.northwindtraders.com*. Eric Rothenberg, the IT manager, calls you and says:

"We have one more task for you. I know this is more of a sysadmin task, but we don't have anyone who can do it for us, and you seem to know what you're doing. Could you install an SSL certificate on our Web site? I can pay you, but I don't have a budget to buy a certificate. If there's a way we can get one without buying it ourselves, I would appreciate it. Use IT for the organization. Our headquarters are in Woburn, Massachusetts."

You review the technical requirements before creating and configuring the SSL certificate.

Technical Requirements Install Certificate Services on the computer, and use it to generate an SSL certificate with the following settings:

- Web site name: *www.northwindtraders.com*
- Organization: Northwind Traders
- Organizational Unit: IT
- Location: Woburn, MA

Exercise 1: Installing Certificate Services

In this exercise, you will install Certificate Services on your Windows Server 2003 test computer.

> **Important** You must have the Windows Server 2003 installation media available during this exercise.

1. Log on to your computer using the Administrator account.

> **Note** You can use RunAs to perform these tasks, but Microsoft does not recommend system administrators log on to servers using standard user accounts. After all, you should never log on to a server unless you're performing administrative tasks, and this exercise simulates managing a server.

2. Run the following command from a command prompt to trick the computer into resolving the hostname *www.northwindtraders.com* to the local computer:

   ```
   echo 127.0.0.1 www.northwindtraders.com >> %systemroot%\system32\drivers\etc\hosts
   ```

3. Launch the Add/Remove Windows Component Wizard from within the Add Or Remove Programs Control Panel applet.

4. On the Windows Components page, select the Certificate Services check box, as shown in Figure 9-14. Click Next.

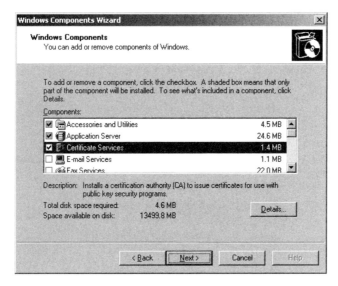

Figure 9-14   Add Certificate Services to enable issuing your own certificates.

5. On the CA Type page, select the Stand-Alone Root CA option. Click Next.

6. On the CA Identifying Information page, in the Common Name For This CA box, type **ca**. In the Distinguished Name Suffix box, type **DC=northwindtraders, DC=com**, as shown in Figure 9-15. Click Next.

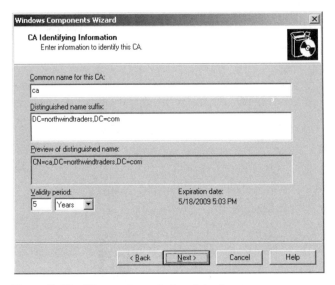

Figure 9-15 CAs require a distinguished name.

Exam Tip Don't worry too much about the details of setting up a CA. The point of this exercise is to generate an SSL certificate to fulfill an exam objective, not to understand the details of deploying and managing CAs.

7. On the Certificate Database Settings page, click Next.

8. When prompted, click Yes to restart IIS. When prompted to enable ASP, click Yes again.

Exercise 2: Generating a Certificate Request

In this exercise, you will generate an SSL certificate request.

1. Log on to your computer using the Administrator account.

2. Launch the IIS Manager console.

3. Expand the server node, and then expand Web Sites. Right-click Default Web Site, and then click Properties.

4. Click the Directory Security tab, and then click Server Certificate.

   The Web Server Certificate Wizard appears.

5. On the Welcome To The Web Server Certificate Wizard page, click Next.

6. On the Server Certificate page, click Create A New Certificate. Click Next.

7. On the Delayed Or Immediate Request page, click Next.

8. On the Name And Security Settings page, click Next.

9. On the Organizational Information page, type **Northwind Traders** in the Organization box and type **IT** in the Organizational Unit box, as shown in Figure 9-16. Click Next.

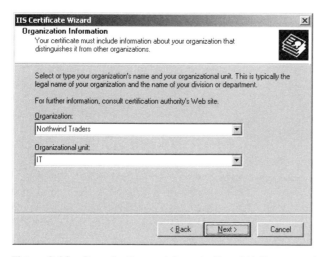

Figure 9-16   Organization and Organizational Unit are required components of an SSL certificate, though they are not generally used during server authentication.

10. On the Your Site's Common Name page, type **www.northwindtraders.com** in the Common Name box. Click Next.

11. On the Geographical Information page, type **MA** in the State/Province list. Type **Woburn** in the City/Locality list. Click Next.

12. On the Certificate Request File Name page, note the location in which the file is being created. Click Next twice, and then click Finish. Click OK to return to the IIS Manager console.

Exercise 3: Submitting and Approving a Certificate Request

In this exercise, you will submit the certificate request that you generated in Exercise 2, approve it, and then download the certificate.

Important   To complete this exercise, you must have completed both Exercise 1 and Exercise 2.

1. Log on to your computer using the Administrator account.

2. Launch Internet Explorer, and visit the URL *http://www.northwindtraders.com /certsrv/*.

   The Microsoft Certificate Services Web page appears, as shown in Figure 9-17.

Figure 9-17   Certificate Services enables certificates to be requested by using a Web browser interface.

3. Click Request A Certificate.

4. On the Request A Certificate page, click Advanced Certificate Request.

5. On the Advanced Certificate Request page, click Submit A Certificate Request By Using A Base-64-Encoded CMC Or PKCS #10 File, Or Submit A Renewal Request By Using A Base-64-Encoded PKCS #7 File.

6. On the Submit A Certificate Request Or Renewal Request page, open the file you generated in Exercise 2 (probably C:\CertReq.txt) in Notepad, copy the contents, and paste it into the Base-64-Encoded Certificate Request box. Click Submit.

7. Launch the Certification Authority console from the Administrative Tools group.

8. In the left pane, click Pending Requests. The request you submitted should be visible.

9. Right-click the request, click All Tasks, and then click Issue.

10. Click Issued Certificates to verify that the certificate was successfully issued.

11. In Internet Explorer, return to the URL *http://www.northwindtraders.com/certsrv/* and click View The Status Of A Pending Certificate Request.

12. On the View The Status Of A Pending Certificate Request page, click the Saved-Request Certificate link.

13. On the Certificate Issued page, click Download Certificate. When prompted, click Save, and save the file to the desktop. Click Close.

Exercise 4: Installing an SSL Certificate

In this exercise, you will install the SSL certificate on your Web server.

> **Important** To complete this exercise, you must have completed Exercises 1 through 3.

1. Log on to your computer using the Administrator account.

2. Launch the IIS Manager console.

3. Expand the server node, and then expand Web Sites. Right-click Default Web Site, and then click Properties.

4. Click the Directory Security tab, and then click Server Certificate.

The Web Server Certificate Wizard appears.

5. On the Welcome To The Web Server Certificate Wizard page, click Next.

6. On the Pending Certificate Request page, select Process The Pending Request And Install The Certificate, and then click Next.

7. On the Process A Pending Request page, click Browse and select the certificate file you saved in Exercise 3. Click Next.

8. On the SSL Port page, leave the port number set to the default of 443, as shown in Figure 9-18, and then click Next.

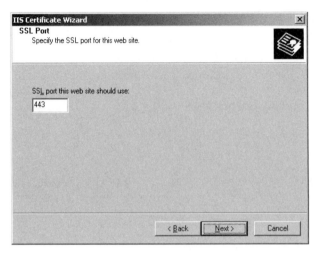

Figure 9-18   By default, HTTPS uses port 443.

9. On the Certificate Summary page, click Next, and then click Finish. Click OK to return to the IIS Manager console.

Exercise 5: Verifying the Installation of the SSL Certificate

In this exercise, you will test the installation of your SSL certificate.

> **Important**   To complete this exercise, you must have completed Exercises 1 through 4.

1. Log on to your computer using the Administrator account.

2. Use Internet Explorer to visit the URL *https://www.northwindtraders.com/certsrv/*. Note that the protocol specified is HTTPS, not HTTP. When you enter the URL, Internet Explorer will warn you that you are about to view a page over a secure connection.

3. In the lower right corner, hover your cursor over the image of the padlock. The Tip SSL Secured (128 bit) will appear.

4. Double-click the padlock. As shown in Figure 9-19, Internet Explorer displays the information contained in the certificate. Click OK.

Figure 9-19   Users can view the details of a server's SSL certificate.

5. In Internet Explorer, enter the URL *https://localhost/certsrv/* in the address bar. As shown in Figure 9-20, Internet Explorer warns you that the name on the certificate does not match the name of the site. Specifically, the name you entered in the address bar, localhost, does not match the common name on the certificate, *www.northwindtraders.com.*

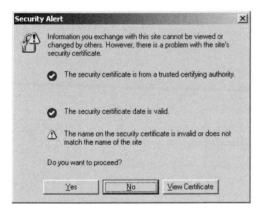

Figure 9-20   The name users enter in the address bar must match the common name listed in the SSL certificate, or the user's browser will display a warning.

6. Click No to return to Internet Explorer.

7. Remove the certificate request file, and store the SSL certificate file in a safe location. If an attacker retrieves the SSL certificate, she can use it to impersonate your server or decrypt traffic.

Lesson Summary

- SSL certificates are documents that contain public key pairs that can be used to encrypt Web communications. They validate a server's identity and encrypt communications between the Web client and server.

- To configure IIS to use SSL certificates issued by Windows Server 2003 Certificate Services, use the Web Server Certificate Wizard to generate a certificate request, use Certificate Services Web enrollment to submit the request and retrieve the approved certificate, and use the Certificates console to approve certificate requests.

- To configure IIS to require SSL encryption for a Web site or application, select the Require Secure Channel check box on the Web site's or virtual directory's Directory Security tab.

Lab: Using Windows Authentication and Authorization in an ASP.NET Application

In this lab, you will create an ASP.NET Web application that meets the authentication and authorization requirements of a fictitious organization. Read the scenario and then complete the exercise that follows. If you are unable to answer a question, review the lessons and try the question again. You can find answers to the questions in the "Questions and Answers" section at the end of this chapter.

Scenario

You are a developer for Woodgrove Bank, a financial institution offering checking and savings accounts to consumers. They are deploying a new ASP.NET intranet application and need some help configuring the security. The Web application has several subfolders, and each subfolder is managed by a different organization within Woodgrove Bank. You meet with each of the managers and review the technical requirements to determine how you should configure security for that organization's subfolder.

Interviews

Following is a list of company personnel interviewed and their statements:

- **Misty Shock, IT Manager**   "Hi. We're in the process of creating an ASP.NET application for our intranet. It's located in the /Woodgrove/ virtual folder of our Web server's default Web site. The application should be accessible only to users who have a valid account in the WOODGROVE Active Directory domain, but because we use Internet Explorer internally, I suppose they'll be automatically authenticated. Several of the internal groups will have their own subfolders in the application, including IT. Check with each of the managers to determine how they want security configured. For the IT subfolder, I just want members of the IT group in the Woodgrove domain to be able to access it. Oh—I'd rather not have Web.config files in each of the subdirectories. Can you put all the security configuration information in a single file, please?"

- **Reed Koch, Marketing Manager** "For now, I'd like our Marketing subfolder to be accessible to members of the Marketing group. Oh, also, give Eran access to it. Eran's the manager of Sales. I don't know what his user account name is."

- **Mathew Charles, Customer Service Manager** "I've got nothing to hide. You can let anybody look at our CustServ folder. I mean, provided they're an employee."

- **Eran Shtiegman, Sales Manager** "Please don't let anybody but me access the Sales folder. My salespeople will flip out if they see the changes to the incentive plan early. My user account is EShtiegman. Sometimes I have to enter it like Woodgrove-backslash-EShtiegman."

Technical Requirements

Create a single Web.config file for the application that configures permissions for each of the subfolders according to the requirements outlined in the following table. Require Windows authentication for every file in the application.

Application Authorization Requirements for Woodgrove Bank

Folder	Authorized Users
/Woodgrove/	All authenticated users
/Woodgrove/IT/	All members of the WOODGROVE\IT group
/Woodgrove/Marketing/	All members of the WOODGROVE\Marketing group, and the WOODGROVE\EShtiegman user account
/Woodgrove/CustServ/	All authenticated users
/Woodgrove/Sales/	Only the WOODGROVE\EShtiegman user account

Exercise

Configure security for Woodgrove Bank, and then answer the following questions.

1. What does the Web.config file that you created look like?

2. Besides creating a Web.config file, how can you further protect the folders?

Chapter Summary

- You can control authentication for an ASP.NET application by shipping a Web.config file with your application. In the `<authentication>` section, specify an authentication mode of *Windows*, *Forms*, *Passport*, or *None*.

- To control authorization in your ASP.NET application, add an `<authorization>` section to your application's Web.config file. If different files and folders have different authorization requirements, create separate Web.config files for each folder, or add `<location>` sections to the root application's Web.config file. You can also control authorization by using the IIS Manager console, configuring file permissions, and checking the user's source IP address.

- SSL certificates are used to enable HTTPS, a protocol that encrypts Web communications. You can generate requests for SSL certificates and install SSL certificates by using the IIS Manager console. Windows Server 2003 includes Certificate Services, which can generate SSL certificates. However, only certificates issued by trusted certification authorities will be accepted by default on common Web browsers.

Exam Highlights

Before taking the exam, review the key points and terms that are presented in this chapter. You need to know this information.

Key Points

- Creating a Web.config file to configure the authentication type for your application

- Adding `<location>` sections to a Web.config file to granularly restrict access

- Using the IIS Manager console to configure both authentication and authorization

- Setting file permissions to control authorization when using Windows authentication

- Creating and installing SSL certificates to enable encryption of Web communications

Key Terms

certification authority (CA)   A service that generates certificates. CAs can be run by a public company such as Verisign and issue certificates to paying customers, or CAs can be managed by an internal IT department by using a computer running Windows Server 2003 and Certificate Services.

Fully Qualified Domain Name (FQDN)   The full domain name of a server, such as *www.microsoft.com*.

Hypertext Transfer Protocol (HTTP)   The protocol that the Web browser and Web servers use to communicate.

Hypertext Transfer Protocol Secure (HTTPS)   HTTPS is an encrypted form of the HTTP protocol. It is used by virtually every e-commerce Web site on the Internet to protect private information about end users and to protect end users from submitting private information to a rogue server that is impersonating another server.

Secure Sockets Layer (SSL)   A protocol for secure network communications using a combination of public and secret key technology. Primarily used to encrypt Web communications.

SSL certificates   Documents that contain public key pairs that can be used to encrypt Web communications. SSL certificates cannot be dynamically generated.

Web.config files   Per-folder configuration settings for ASP.NET applications. Storing configuration settings in XML-based files instead of the registry, isolated storage, or the IIS metabase allows administrators to copy your application to a different location or to another computer and have it run correctly.

Questions and Answers

Practice: Configuring Authentication in ASP.NET Applications

Page
9-17
Exercise

1. How did you modify the Web.config file for the root Northwind application? What other changes did you make?

To enable anonymous access, the authentication and authorization sections should be configured as follows:

```
<authentication mode="None" />
<authorization>
    <allow users="*" />

</authorization>
```

Then, you should use the IIS Manager console to enable anonymous access and disable all other authentication mechanisms for the Northwind application.

2. How did you modify the Web.config file for the Northwind\Catalog application?

To enable anonymous access, the authentication and authorization sections should be configured as follows:

```
<authentication mode="None" />
<authorization>
    <allow users="*" />

</authorization>
```

If you already configured the IIS Manager console to enable anonymous access and disable all other authentication mechanisms for the Northwind application, the Northwind\Catalog application will automatically inherit those settings. Therefore, you can choose to not provide a Web.config file at all and allow the settings to be inherited from the root Northwind application.

3. How did you modify the Web.config file for the Northwind\ManageCatalog application?

To enable Forms authentication, the authentication and authorization sections should be configured as follows:

```
<authentication mode="Forms">
    <forms loginUrl="login.aspx" protection="Encryption" timeout="30" >
        <credentials passwordFormat="SHA1" >
            <user name="Abarr" ⤸
password="7EC77426BEE5D3915BC0B15AA8B8B0DA18BDA383"/>

            <user name="Mhines" ⤸
password="84D55DA66626517040B68C379CFD5B287D6EFDF2"/>
            <user name="Sbashary" ⤸
password="A0EC13FBF382A09D33D6C112E10700330D0A94BC"/>
        </credentials>
```

```
        </forms>
    </authentication>

    <authorization>
        <deny users="?" />

    </authorization>
```

4. How did you generate the password hashes for the Northwind\ManageCatalog application?

You should have created an application which generated SHA1 hashes, either using the *System.Security.Cryptography* namespace, or by calling the *FormsAuthentication.HashPasswordForStoringInConfigFile* method from an ASP.NET application.

5. How did you modify the Web.config file for the Northwind\ManageSite application? What other changes did you make?

This authentication section didn't require any modification, because it was already configured to use Windows authentication. However, the authorization section did not deny access to unauthenticated users and, as a result, needed to be modified. The authentication and authorization sections should be as follows:

```
<authentication mode="Windows" />

<authorization>
    <deny users="?" />

</authorization>
```

Additionally, you should have configured the IIS Manager console to require authentication for the Northwind\ManageSite application.

Practice: Controlling Authorization in ASP.NET Applications

Page
9-36
Exercise

1. What authentication method did you use? Why?

You should have used Windows authentication, because you need the user to provide Windows credentials that the application can use to access the file.

2. How did you implement impersonation? Why?

Although you could configure impersonation in the application's Web.config file, that would grant the application unnecessary privileges. Instead, you should leave impersonation disabled in the Web.config file, and implement impersonation only for the section of code that requires the user's elevated privileges.

3. What XML did you add within the Web.config file?

You should configure the `<authentication>` and `<authorization>` sections as follows:

```
<configuration>
    <system.web>
```

```
            <authentication mode="Windows" />
            <authorization>
                <deny users="?" />
            </authentication>
        </system.web>
</configuration>
```

4. What code did you write to display the C:\Boot.ini file?

The following code would work if added to the *Page_Load* method, assuming you created a *Text-Box* object named *bootIniTextBox*:

```
using System.Security.Principal;
using System.IO;
…
// Impersonate the user with the account they used to authenticate
WindowsImpersonationContext realUser;
realUser = ((WindowsIdentity)User.Identity).Impersonate();

// Perform tasks that require user permissions.
// Read the boot.ini file.
StreamReader bootIniReader = File.OpenText(@"C:\boot.ini");
bootIniTextBox.Text = bootIniReader.ReadToEnd();
bootIniReader.Close();

// Undo the impersonation, reverting to the normal user context
realUser.Undo();
```

```
Imports System.Security.Principal
Imports System.IO
…
' Impersonate the user with the account they used to authenticate
Dim realUser As WindowsImpersonationContext
realUser = CType(User.Identity, WindowsIdentity).Impersonate

' Perform tasks that require user permissions.
' Read the boot.ini file.

Dim bootIniReader As StreamReader = File.OpenText("C:\boot.ini")
bootIniTextBox.Text = bootIniReader.ReadToEnd
bootIniReader.Close()

' Undo the impersonation, reverting to the normal user context
realUser.Undo()
```

Lab: Using Windows Authentication and Authorization in an ASP.NET Application

Page
9-56

Exercise

1. What does the Web.config file that you created look like?

Your Web.config file should resemble the following:

```
<?xml version="1.0" encoding="utf-8" ?>
<configuration>
```

```
  <system.web>
    <authentication mode="Windows" />

    <authorization>
        <deny users="?" />

    </authorization>
  </system.web>

  <location path="IT">
   <system.web>
     <authorization>
         <allow roles="WOODGROVE\IT" />
         <deny users="*" />
     </authorization>
   </system.web>
  </location>

  <location path="Marketing">
   <system.web>
     <authorization>
         <allow roles="WOODGROVE\Marketing" />
         <allow users="WOODGROVE\EShtiegman" />
         <deny users="*" />
     </authorization>
   </system.web>
  </location>

  <location path="Sales">
   <system.web>
     <authorization>
         <allow users="WOODGROVE\EShtiegman" />
         <deny users="*" />
     </authorization>
   </system.web>
  </location>
</configuration>
```

You also could have explicitly created a `<location>` section for the CustServ folder. However, because its permissions are identical to those of the parent folder, creating the `<location>` section is unnecessary.

2. Besides creating a Web.config file, how can you further protect the folders?

You can use NTFS file permissions to further restrict access to the folders. This would provide defense-in-depth protection.

10 Improving Security When Using External Components and Services

Why This Chapter Matters

Securing an application when you can't trust the user is challenging, because you have to authenticate the user, authorize the request, and validate the input. These same tasks are necessary when calling external components and services, making a distributed application even more complex to provide security for. You must use care to minimize the risk associated with calling external components and services. This chapter provides guidelines for evaluating the risk posed by different types of components and development techniques that take advantage of security features built into the Microsoft .NET Framework.

Exam Objectives in this Chapter:

- Analyze the security implications of calling unknown code. Third-party components include .NET components, legacy COM components, ActiveX controls, Microsoft Win32 DLLs, and Web services.
    - Write code to verify that the identity of a COM component matches the identity expected.
    - Validate that data to and from third-party components conforms to the expected size, format, and type.
    - Test for the integrity of data after transmission.
    - Evaluate unmanaged code.
- Access remote functionality in a manner that minimizes security risks.
    - Use Web Services Enhancements for Microsoft .NET (WSE).
    - Configure .NET remoting for security.

Lessons in this Chapter:

Before You Begin

To complete the practices, examples, and lab exercises in this chapter, you must have one computer running Microsoft Windows Server 2003. During the course of performing the exercises in this chapter, the computer's security can be reduced. Therefore, the computer should not be a production computer and should not be connected to any network, especially the Internet, even if a firewall is present. Install Microsoft Visual Studio .NET 2003 using the default settings.

Lesson 1: Minimizing Risk When Calling External Components

The .NET Framework has a far more robust set of security features than any other development platform previously released by Microsoft. New development can and should take advantage of these security features. However, developers have invested a great deal of time into creating applications for older platforms, such as Win32, COM, and ActiveX. The .NET Framework was designed to allow you to interoperate with components built on these platforms, but you must give up the security benefits of the .NET Framework to do so.

After this lesson, you will be able to

- List the risks associated with calling different types of third-party components.
- Explain and apply the best practices for limiting the risk of calling third-party components.
- Write code that verifies that an external DLL has not been modified before calling it from your application.

Estimated lesson time: 15 minutes

The Risks of Calling Third-Party Components

The risks of calling unmanaged components are great. Unmanaged components operate outside of the common language runtime, and therefore are exempt from Code Access Security (CAS) checks. Additionally, because unmanaged components lack strong naming, there is a greater risk that an attacker will replace the components with malicious code. As a result, you should call unmanaged components only when absolutely necessary. When you do have to call them, however, you can limit the risk that they will perform malicious acts by instructing users to run your application with a limited permission user account. Role-based security enforced by the operating system *will* affect both managed and unmanaged code.

Calling managed components also carries risk. First, if the component is unsigned, an attacker could modify or replace it. Second, the developer might not be as rigorous as you are about using secure coding best practices, and thus might expose a security vulnerability. Finally, it's possible that the developer will add malicious code that performs an attack against you, such as transmitting private information, opening a backdoor, or destroying your data. The most effective way to limit these risks is to use the principle of least privilege, and configure code access security to grant minimal rights to the .NET component.

There are even risks when calling services on remote computers. The .NET Framework makes calling external Web services by using Simple Object Access Protocol (SOAP) extremely easy, and this is a powerful capability. However, Web services have no inherent security. Unless you encrypt data prior to sending it to a Web service, or you specifically configure the Web reference to use HTTPS, your confidential data will traverse the network unencrypted. Any attacker with access to the network media will be able to capture and view the information.

Table 10-1 summarizes these risks by listing external components that .NET developers often call and important risks that each carries. This table also lists techniques for mitigating those risks.

Table 10-1   Risks and Mitigators for Calling Third-Party Components

Component	Risks	Risk Mitigators
.NET components	■ Vulnerable to modification or replacement when not strongly signed. ■ Might contain security vulnerabilities. ■ Might contain malicious code.	■ Call only strongly signed .NET components. ■ Use CAS to restrict the privileges of external .NET components. ■ Use components created only by trusted developers.
COM components and Win32 Dynamic Link Libraries (DLLs)	■ Not restricted by CAS. ■ Might be vulnerable to buffer overruns. ■ Vulnerable to modification or replacement.	■ Instruct users not to run your application with administrator privileges. ■ Validate input and output. ■ Avoid using COM components.
ActiveX controls	■ Not restricted by CAS. ■ Requires access to the registry.	■ Instruct users not to run your application with administrator privileges. ■ Validate input and output. ■ Avoid using ActiveX components.
Web services	■ Vulnerable to man-in-the-middle attacks. ■ Network communications might be compromised. ■ External server might not protect the privacy of your data.	■ Communicate only with Web services that use SSL certificates to verify the server's identity. ■ When the Web service supports it, encrypt data prior to transmission. ■ Access only trusted Web services.

In addition to the drawbacks listed in Table 10-1, be aware that your assembly must have the unmanaged code permission to call anything other than a .NET component.

Best Practices for Calling Unmanaged Code

When you cannot avoid calling unmanaged code, follow these best practices to reduce the risk of security vulnerabilities:

- **Validate all input and output** Though native, managed .NET Framework libraries are essentially resistant to buffer overflows, unmanaged libraries are not. If you pass data to an unmanaged library, it is possible for an attacker to exploit a buffer overflow or similar vulnerability in the unmanaged code by passing data to your assembly. Therefore, it is critical to validate that all input passed to an unmanaged library meets the length and type requirements of the library. You should also validate all output received from an unmanaged library to reduce the risk of an attacker replacing the unmanaged library with malicious code.

See Also For more information about data validation, see Lesson 1 of Chapter 2, "Using Secure Coding Best Practices."

- **Create a wrapper class to hold unmanaged DLL functions** Wrapping a frequently used DLL function in a managed class is an effective approach to encapsulate platform functionality. Although it is not mandatory to do so in every case, providing a class wrapper is convenient because defining DLL functions can be cumbersome and error-prone. From a security perspective, add input and output validation to your wrapper class. Creating and using a wrapper class with data validation removes the possibility that you will forget to properly validate data, and therefore makes your application more secure and requires you to write less code.

- **Avoid running code with an administrator account** Unmanaged code is not affected by CAS, but it is affected by the operating system's role-based security restrictions. If a user runs your application with a standard user account, the damage the unmanaged code can do is minimized.

How to Verify External File Integrity

You always assume additional risk when calling unmanaged code, because unmanaged code such as COM objects can be maliciously modified or replaced. When your assembly calls such an object, the malicious code runs with full trust. One way to mitigate that risk is to verify the integrity of a file before calling a method that it contains. The simplest way to verify file integrity is to calculate the hash of a file, and compare it to a previously generated hash.

> **See Also**   For more information about creating hashes, see Lesson 3 of Chapter 8, "Protecting Data by Using Cryptography."

Verifying the integrity of an external file is not as straightforward as it seems. For example, most developers rely on the .NET Framework runtime to locate the path of an external DLL by providing only the relative filename. This is good practice, because it allows your application to work in environments that use non-standard directory structures. However, if you rely on the .NET Framework to determine the path of a DLL, there is no way to guarantee that the file your code is verifying matches the file the runtime actually loads.

The following console application demonstrates how to verify the SHA512 hash of an external DLL by explicitly naming the full path to the DLL in the *DllImport* attribute, computing the hash, and then throwing an exception if the newly calculated hash does not match the hash of the DLL when the assembly is created:

```csharp
using System;
using System.Security.Cryptography;
using System.Text;
using System.IO;
using System.Runtime.InteropServices;
using System.Security;

class VerifyHash
{
    [DllImport(@"C:\windows\system32\User32.dll")]
    public static extern int MessageBox(int h, string m, string c, int type);
    [STAThread]
    static void Main(string[] args)
    {
        // Statically store the Base64-encoded hash
        // created by the developer at compile time
        string correctHash = "WGrKRLJpyLo4FBSPFDl4xY+C5C9XwFZEolT00rA9➜
hXK0GnbH3+hbh6asRlblSesN4MdGX//GIkWOXYjX+kFdoQ==";

        // Generate a new hash and store it in the actualHash string
        SHA512 newHash = new SHA512Managed();
        FileStream file = new FileStream➜
(@"C:\windows\system32\User32.dll", FileMode.Open, FileAccess.Read);
        BinaryReader reader = new BinaryReader(file);
        newHash.ComputeHash(reader.ReadBytes((int)file.Length));
        string actualHash = Convert.ToBase64String(newHash.Hash);

        // Throw an exception if the original and current hash do not match
        if (correctHash != actualHash)
            throw new SecurityException("User32.dll hash not verified");

        // The hashes matched, so the DLL has not been modified.
        // Therefore, it's safer to call it.
        MessageBox(0, "User32.dll hash verified!", "Notification", 0);
    }
}
```

```
Imports System
Imports System.Security.Cryptography
Imports System.Text
Imports System.IO
Imports System.Runtime.InteropServices
Imports System.Security

Module Module1

    <DllImport("C:\windows\system32\User32.dll")> _
Public Function MessageBox(ByVal h As Integer, ByVal m As String, →
ByVal c As String, ByVal type As Integer) As Integer
    End Function

    Sub Main()
        ' Statically store the Base64-encoded hash
        ' created by the developer at compile time
        Dim correctHash As String = "WGrKRLJpyLo4FBSPFD14xY+C5C9Xw→
FZEolT00rA9hXK0GnbH3+hbh6asRlb1SesN4MdGX'GIkWOXYjX+kFdoQ=="

        ' Generate a new hash and store it in the actualHash string
        Dim newHash As SHA512 = New SHA512Managed
        Dim file As FileStream = New →
FileStream("C:\windows\system32\User32.dll", FileMode.Open, FileAccess.Read)
        Dim reader As BinaryReader = New BinaryReader(file)
        newHash.ComputeHash(reader.ReadBytes(CType(file.Length, Integer)))
        Dim actualHash As String = Convert.ToBase64String(newHash.Hash)

        ' Throw an exception if the original and current hash do not match
        If Not (correctHash = actualHash) Then
            Throw New SecurityException("User32.dll hash not verified")
        End If

        ' The hashes matched, so the DLL has not been modified.
        ' Therefore, it's safer to call it.
        MessageBox(0, "User32.dll hash verified!", "Notification", 0)
    End Sub
End Module
```

This technique works; however, it has significant drawbacks:

■ You cannot rely on Visual Studio .NET to automatically handle the reference. Instead, you must explicitly list the full path using the *DLLImport* attribute.

■ If an administrator changes the path to the DLL, your application will not be able to load the DLL.

■ Legitimate modifications to the DLL, such as security updates, will cause the hash check to fail.

■ You must sign your assembly to prevent a sophisticated attacker from modifying the hash value stored in your assembly.

> **Off the Record**   Improved security always comes with a trade-off. In this case, checking the hash of an external DLL comes with very significant trade-offs. Avoid using this technique unless your security requirements absolutely demand that you call unmanaged code and you can verify that the external object was not modified since you tested it.

Practice: Minimizing Risk When Calling External Components

In this practice, you analyze three application architectures to identify the risks caused by calling external components. Read the scenario and complete the exercise that follows. If you are unable to answer a question, review the lesson and try the question again. You can find answers to the questions in the "Questions and Answers" section at the end of this chapter.

Scenario

You are a security consultant for Woodgrove Bank. The IT Manager, Misty Shock, joined Woodgrove Bank about a month ago. Her boss has asked her to evaluate and improve the security of their applications. Misty has previous experience performing risk analysis, but little experience analyzing Windows-based applications for potential vulnerabilities. Misty has hired you to analyze the risk associated with three of Woodgrove Bank's internal applications. You meet Misty in her office, and she describes the project.

"Good to meet you. I know you have a Windows-based development background, which is something I lack. I am familiar with application security, but my background is primarily in UNIX-based data processing applications. That's a bit of a problem, because Woodgrove is a .NET house. Anyway, I asked our developers to put together architecture diagrams for our three most important internal applications. One application, named Teller, is used by tellers who deal with customers to carry out transactions on behalf of customers. Another application, named Reporting, is used by management to analyze the daily transactions. The third application is our ASP.NET-based Web site, which we call 'the Web site.' Hopefully these diagrams are self-explanatory, because I can't make sense out of them."

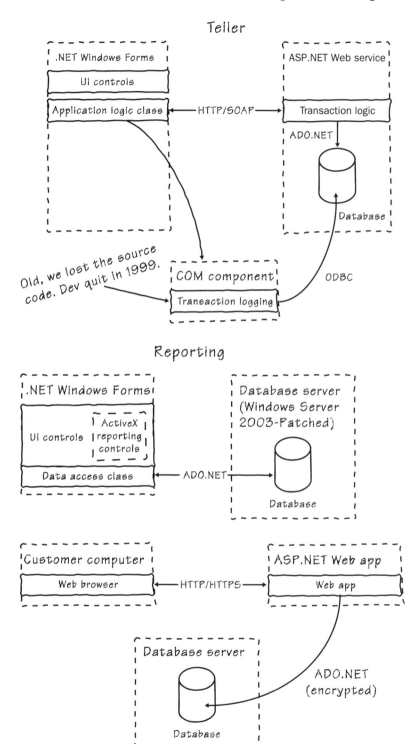

Teller

Reporting

Evaluate the risks associated with each of the applications, and then answer Misty's questions.

Exercise

Answer the following questions to provide your assessment of the risks of each application.

1. What risks are associated with the Teller application?
2. What can be done to mitigate the risks associated with the Teller application?
3. What risks are associated with the Reporting application?
4. What can be done to mitigate the risks associated with the Reporting application?
5. What risks are associated with the Web site?
6. What can be done to mitigate the risks associated with the Web site?

Lesson Summary

-   There is a security risk associated with calling third-party components, because you cannot be certain the code is secure and, depending on the type of component, the component might be exempt from CAS checks.

-   To limit the risk of calling unmanaged code, validate all input and output, create a managed wrapper class, and instruct users not to run your application with administrator privileges.

-   To verify that an external DLL called by your application has not been modified, import the DLL using the absolute path to the DLL, and compare the hash of the DLL at that location to a known good hash stored in your source code.

Lesson 2: Maximizing Security for Web Services

Web services are the preferred way for applications to communicate across a network. Web services resemble standard browser-oriented Web applications, but they make it simple for a wide variety of clients to call methods on the Web service server and retrieve data that can be easily processed by the client application. Just like any Web server, a Web service requires security. Specifically, the standard security elements of authentication, authorization, and encryption should be used to protect any Web service that is not intended to be publicly available.

This lesson teaches how to create Web service servers and clients that take advantage of the security features built into the .NET Framework and the Web Services Enhancements (WSE) extension.

 See Also   This lesson assumes that you have experience working with Web services. If you do not, visit Microsoft's Web Services Development Center at *http://msdn.microsoft.com /webservices/*.

After this lesson, you will be able to

- Build a Web services server that requires authentication based on the standard .NET Framework and a client capable of submitting credentials.
- Describe the purpose of WS-Security and the capabilities it adds to standard Web services.
- Describe Web Services Enhancements (WSE) and why you might want to use it.
- List the most important classes provided by WSE.
- Use WSE to add standards-based authentication to a Web service.

Estimated lesson time: 40 minutes

How to Authenticate a Web Service Client

You can authenticate a Web service client in two ways: using the user's current credentials from her current desktop session, or using alternate credentials. To pass to the Web service the user credentials from the user's current desktop session, set the *System.Web .Services.Protocols.SoapHttpClientProtocol.Credentials* object to *System.Net.CredentialCache .DefaultCredentials*. The following code sample creates a new *SoapHttpClientProtocol* object based on an imaginary Web service located at *http://www.northwindtraders.com /EmployeeServices*, and configures the object to use the current user's credentials:

```csharp
com.northwindtraders.www.EmployeeServices server = →
new com.northwindtraders.www.EmployeeServices();
server.Credentials = System.Net.CredentialCache.DefaultCredentials;
```

```vb
Dim server As com.northwindtraders.www.EmployeeServices = →
New com.northwindtraders.www.EmployeeServices
server.Credentials = System.Net.CredentialCache.DefaultCredentials
```

This code causes the user's user name and password to be added to the HTTP headers. Microsoft Internet Information Services (IIS) uses these headers for authentication in exactly the same way it authenticates a user who enters a user name and password when prompted by a Web browser.

Explicitly providing credentials is only slightly more complicated. The following code sample from a console application gathers the user's credentials from command-line arguments and prepares a *SoapHttpClientObject* object to present those credentials:

```csharp
// Prompt for a username and password
Console.WriteLine(@"Enter username in the format domain\username: ");
string username = Console.ReadLine();
Console.WriteLine("Enter password: ");
string password = Console.ReadLine();

// Create the Web services object
com.northwindtraders.www.EmployeeServices server = →
new com.northwindtraders.www.EmployeeServices();

// Create a credentials object and assign it the user's credentials
NetworkCredential credentials = new NetworkCredential(username, password);

// Now, assign that value to the Web service's credentials
server.Credentials = credentials;
```

```vb
' Prompt for a username and password
Console.WriteLine("Enter username in the format domain\username: ")
Dim username As String = Console.ReadLine
Console.WriteLine("Enter password: ")
Dim password As String = Console.ReadLine

' Create the Web services object
Dim server As com.northwindtraders.www.EmployeeServices = →
New com.northwindtraders.www.EmployeeServices

' Create a credentials object and assign it the user's credentials
Dim credentials As NetworkCredential = →
New NetworkCredential (username, password)

' Now, assign that value to the Web service's credentials
server.Credentials = credentials
```

Note   C# console applications, when created with Visual Studio .NET, automatically grab the command-line parameters and put them into the *args[]* array. Microsoft Visual Basic .NET doesn't do this, so you'd have to add an array of strings named *args()* as a parameter for the *Main* method.

Unfortunately, this technique has a significant drawback: it uses either Kerberos or Integrated Windows authentication provided by IIS. Many non-Microsoft Web services clients won't have libraries to provide credentials in these authentication formats. There is a standardized method for providing Web services credentials called WS-Security that provides a more flexible authentication mechanism.

What Is WS-Security?

WS-Security (Web Services Security Language) is a standard for adding authentication, signatures, and encryption to SOAP Web services communications. It defines extensions to SOAP that allow you to pass security tokens that you can use to verify the identity of clients, validate that a message has not been modified in transit, and improve the privacy of communications by encrypting a message. The *Web Services Interoperability Organization* (WS-Interoperability), an organization dedicated to improving Web services standards, published WS-Security in April of 2002, and at the time of this writing, implementations of WS-Security were still evolving.

See Also   For more information about WS-Interoperability, see the Web Services Interoperability Organization Web site at *http://www.ws-i.org/*.

WS-Security does not define the authentication, signature, or encryption algorithms, but rather provides a way for the client and server to communicate information about the authentication, signature, and encryption algorithms being used. For example, if the XML Signature standard is used to sign a Web services communication, a WS-Security SOAP header can contain the information defined by the XML Signature that conveys how the message was signed, the key that was used, and the resulting signature value. Similarly, if an element within the message is encrypted, the encryption information, such as that conveyed by XML Encryption, can be contained within the WS-Security header.

See Also   View the WS-Security schema at *http://schemas.xmlsoap.org/ws/2002/07 /secext/*.

The whole point of standards is to let different implementations interoperate. Standards don't always work, though. I was fascinated with Web services when they were new, because I completely bought into the idea that they would change the way businesses communicated. I loved the idea that two businesses could create Web services using their platform of choice and not have to struggle with getting the applications to communicate.

I was wrong on a couple of accounts. Web services didn't take off quickly, largely because businesses were cutting back on technology spending when Web services were beginning to gather momentum. I was also wrong about different platforms communicating easily. When both implementations were new, I tried developing a Web services client and server with Perl and the .NET Framework, but I couldn't get them to interoperate no matter how much energy I put into my attempt. However, when the client and server were both created with the same development platform, they communicated perfectly. If I couldn't get the two platforms to work together, what were the odds that developers at different organizations could solve the problems?

Those problems later went away, but the lesson remains true: early implementations of standards usually aren't standard. The newer the implementation, the more difficult it will be to get different platforms to work together. Remember this when using the new Web services standards released by the WS-Interoperability group. If you plan to develop clients and servers with different platforms early in a standard's lifetime, allocate some extra time for troubleshooting.

How WS-Security Changes XML Messages

WS-Security adds its own header with a unique schema to XML Web services messages. The following sample shows an XML message with just the WS-Security header:

```xml
<?xml version="1.0" encoding="utf-8"?>
<s:Envelope
  xmlns:s="http://schemas.xmlsoap.org/soap/envelope/"
  xmlns:wsse="http://schemas.xmlsoap.org/ws/2002/12/secext">
  <s:Header>
    <wsse:Security>
      ...
    </wsse:Security>
  </s:Header>
  <s:Body>
    ...
  </s:Body>
</s:Envelope>
```

Notice that the envelope defines the XML namespace *wsse* as the WS-Security schema located at *http://schemas.xmlsoap.org/ws/2002/12/secext*. WS-Security does define its own namespace; however, this namespace is a relatively simple one that heavily relies on other existing security standards.

WS-Security Elements that Simplify Authentication

WS-Security provides the following elements to simplify authentication:

- ***UsernameToken***   Used to pass the user name and password when the Web service is using custom authentication. This element can contain both a user name and a password, as the following example illustrates:

```
<wsse:Security
 xmlns:wsse="http://schemas.xmlsoap.org/ws/2002/12/secext">
 <wsse:UsernameToken>
  <wsse:Username>User</wsse:Username>
  <wsse:Password>P@ssw0rd</wsse:Password>
 </wsse:UsernameToken>
</wsse:Security>
```

- ***BinarySecurityToken***   Used to pass binary authentication tokens such as Kerberos Tickets and X.509 Certifications. Generally, using *BinarySecurityToken* will be more secure than using *UsernameToken*. *BinarySecurityToken* contains only an encoded binary value. The following example illustrates a Kerberos ticket (note the *ValueType* attribute):

```
<wsse:Security
 xmlns:wsse="http://schemas.xmlsoap.org/ws/2002/12/secext">
 <wsse:BinarySecurityToken
  ValueType="wsse:Kerberosv5ST"
  EncodingType="wsse:Base64Binary">
   RWs6we…
 </wsse:BinarySecurityToken>
</wsse:Security>
```

The following example shows an X.509 certificate. Notice that the *ValueType* attribute specifies the meaning of the token:

```
<wsse:Security
 xmlns:wsse="http://schemas.xmlsoap.org/ws/2002/12/secext">
 <wsse:BinarySecurityToken
  ValueType="wsse:X509v3"
  EncodingType="wsse:Base64Binary">
   IjWmvc93…
 </wsse:BinarySecurityToken>
</wsse:Security>
```

What Is Web Services Enhancements?

Web Services Enhancements (WSE) is a toolset for using WS-Security with ASP.NET Web services. You can use WSE to take advantage of WS-Security capabilities, such as signing and encrypting Web services communications using Kerberos tickets, X.509 certificates, user name and password credentials, and other custom binary and XML-based security tokens. WSE also supports the ability to establish a trust-issuing service for the retrieval and validation of security tokens, as well as the ability to establish more efficient long-running secure communication via secure conversations.

Exam Tip   Be familiar with WSE for the exam. Spend some time playing with it and making the examples in this chapter work. Don't try to memorize every class included with WSE, though—your time is better spent learning the difference among the various cryptography algorithms discussed in Chapter 8 (hint, hint).

WSE is not included with the .NET Framework, so you must download it separately from the MSDN Web site at *http://msdn.microsoft.com/webservices/downloads/*. After installation, documentation is available in the Microsoft WSE 2.0 program group.

Note   You'll probably see WSE wrapped into the .NET Framework standard namespaces at some point in the future. Hopefully, upgrading your code won't be any more difficult than changing the namespace.

The Most Important WSE Classes

WSE includes dozens of classes for using WS-Security as well as enhancements to the Web services classes built into the .NET Framework. This section explores the most important security-related WSE classes. Each of the following classes is in the *Microsoft.Web.Services2* namespace. These classes are discussed in more detail in the sections that follow.

- **WebServicesClientProtocol**   The basis for WSE communications. This class is derived from, and used similarly to, *WebServicesClientProtocol*. Essentially, you can use it exactly like *WebServicesClientProtocol*, but several new methods are exposed to provide additional functionality.

- **SoapContext**   Typically accessed by calling the *WebServicesClientProtocol.RequestSoapContext* or *WebServicesClientProtocol.ResponseSoapContext* methods, this class contains the bulk of WS-Security-related configuration settings.

- **Security**   This class represents the WS-Security header. Typically accessed as a member of the *SoapContext* class, the *Security* class's *Elements* and *Tokens* properties are used to specify user credentials and cryptography keys.

- **UsernameToken**   A class that relates directly to the WS-Security *UsernameToken* element, this class can be used to sign or encrypt a SOAP message. Typically added to the *Security.Tokens* collection.

■ ***X509SecurityToken***   A class typically used to add X.509 certificates to a *Security* object. When the WSE parses an incoming message and encounters an *X509SecurityToken*, the signature that is created by this token (if one exists) is verified, or a *SoapHeaderException* is thrown.

See Also   For an overview of WSE functionality, see "Programming with Web Services Enhancements 2.0"on the MSDN Web site at *http://msdn.microsoft.com/library/en-us /dnwse/html/programwse2.asp*. For complete documentation of all the WSE classes, see the WSE documentation.

The *Microsoft.Web.Services2.WebServicesClientProtocol* Class

The *Microsoft.Web.Services2.WebServicesClientProtocol* class inherits from *SoapHttpClientProtocol*, and most of the methods and properties you will work with are shared with *SoapHttpClientProtocol*. It does provide several unique public properties, as listed in Table 10-2.

Important   This class cannot be called from partially trusted code.

Table 10-2   Unique *WebServicesClientProtocol* Properties

Properties	Description
Destination	The *EndpointReference* object that specifies the SOAP message recipient. This object includes the *Address* property, which specifies a WS-Addressing type address, but basically amounts to the server URL. Typically, you do not need to directly access this property.
Pipeline	Returns the *Pipeline* object that allows custom filtering of SOAP messages. Unless you are implementing custom filtering, you do not need to work with this property.
RequestSoapContext	Returns a *SoapContext* object containing the security, routing, and other XML Web services architecture-specific information associated with a SOAP request. You will modify this object to provide user credentials and other WS-Security information.
ResponseSoapContext	Returns the *SoapContext* object containing the security, routing, and other XML Web services architecture-specific information associated with a SOAP response.
Url	Gets or sets the URL of the Web service method to communicate with. If you specified the URL when adding the Web reference, you do not need to modify this in your code.

The *Microsoft.Web.Services2.SoapContext* Class

WSE features for a Web services connection are specified by using a *SoapContext* object. Typically, you work with this class after creating a *WebServicesClientProtocol* object by calling the *WebServicesClientProtocol.RequestSoapContext* or *WebServicesClientProtocol.ResponseSoapContext* methods. Table 10-3 shows the class's two most useful public methods.

Table 10-3   *SoapContext* Methods

Method	Description
Add	Adds an element with the specified key and value to the context's property collection.
Remove	Removes the element with the specified key.

Table 10-4 shows the class's most useful public properties.

Table 10-4   *SoapContext* Properties

Property	Description
Actor	Gets the SOAP actor associated with the SOAP message.
Addressing	Represents the WS-Addressing SOAP headers for the *SoapContext* object.
Attachments	Gets a collection of DIME attachments associated with the SOAP message.
Channel	Gets or sets the channel that was used to receive the context.
ContentType	Gets the HTTP Content-Type header of the SOAP request or SOAP response.
Envelope	Gets the *SoapContext* object for the current request.
ExtendedSecurity	Gets the contents of the SOAP message.
IdentityToken	Gets the security headers that are not intended for the ultimate recipient of the SOAP message.
IsInbound	Gets or sets the identity security token for a SOAP message.
IsOneWay	Gets a value indicating whether the SOAP message was received.
Processed	Gets or sets an object in the context property bag.
Referrals	Specifies whether the *SoapContext* has been processed by the filter.
Security	Gets the *Microsoft.Web.Services2.Security.Security* object containing the referral-related information associated with the SOAP message. The *Security* object is very important, because you will use it to add user credentials, certificates, digital signatures, and other WS-Security elements to it.

The *Microsoft.Web.Services2.Security.Security* Class

You use the *Security* class to specify user credentials, certificates, digital signatures, and other WS-Security elements. This class contains the two important properties, shown in Table 10-5:

Table 10-5   *Security* Properties

Method	Description
Tokens	Use this collection to add digital signatures and encryption keys to a Web services request.
Elements	Use this collection to add user credentials and certificates to a Web services request. A token in a security header can be a UsernameToken, an X509SecurityToken, or a custom binary security token.

The *Microsoft.Web.Services2.Security.Tokens.UsernameToken* Class

The *UsernameToken* class relates directly to the WS-Security element with the same name. Generally, you will specify this class's most important properties with one of the overloaded constructors. The most useful constructor accepts a user name, a password, and a *PasswordOption* enumerator as arguments:

```
public UsernameToken(string, string, PasswordOption);
```

```
Public Sub New(String, String, PasswordOption)
```

The *PasswordOption* enumerator has three values:

- **SendHashed**   Causes an SHA-1 hash of the password to be sent in the SOAP message. Sending the SHA-1 hash is much more secure than sending a plaintext password.

- **SendNone**   Causes no password to be sent. This value prevents the password from being intercepted, but it also prevents a user from successfully authenticating. Useful only for providing identity without proof of that identity.

- **SendPlainText**   Causes the password to be transmitted in plaintext. If you use this technique, you must provide encryption at another layer to prevent an attacker from capturing the password. Either SSL or IPSec can be used to encrypt the communication.

The *Microsoft.Web.Services2.Security.Tokens.X509SecurityToken* Class

Use the *X509SecurityToken* class to sign, encrypt, and pass security credentials in a SOAP message. The most useful of the two overloaded constructors creates this class based on an existing *X509Certificate* object. Generally, you do not have to set any of the class's properties after creating the class.

How to Use WSE to Add Standards-Based Authentication to a Web Service

WSE provides a complex, flexible set of classes. The sections that follow detail common, fundamental tasks, including adding a WSE reference to a project in Visual Studio .NET and creating a WSE Web services server and client.

How to Add WSE to a Project in Visual Studio .NET

Before you can use WSE in a project, you must add a reference to the assembly. You can do this manually by following the instructions provided with the WSE documentation; however, the WSE Visual Studio add-in makes this process much simpler. You should perform this process on both the Web services server and client.

To add WSE to a project in Visual Studio .NET:

1. Close Visual Studio .NET if it is open.

2. Download and install WSE on your development computer. Be sure to select the option to install the Visual Studio .NET add-in.

3. Open or create a project in Visual Studio .NET.

4. Right-click the project in Solution Explorer, and click WSE Settings 2.0.

5. Select Enable This Project For Web Services Enhancements. If your project is an ASP.NET Web service, also select Enable Microsoft Web Services Enhancement Soap Extensions, as shown in Figure 10-1.

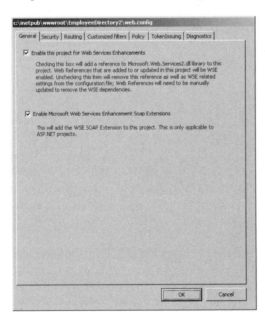

Figure 10-1   Use the WSE Visual Studio add-in to simplify adding WSE to your project.

6. Click OK.

7. You might be warned that files have been modified outside of the editor because of the updates made by the WSE add-in. If you are, click Yes.

8. At a minimum, use or import the *Microsoft.Web.Services2* namespace on any classes that use WSE.

How to Create a WSE Server

To create a WSE server, create a standard Web service, and then add a reference to WSE by following the instructions provided in the section titled "How to Add WSE to a Project in Visual Studio .NET." Then recompile your Web service.

The following is an example of an ASP.NET Web service class generated by using Visual Studio .NET. This class uses WSE and leverages WS-Security to simulate returning an employee's phone number given the employee's ID. Notice the code itself contains no references to WSE and does not inherit from a WSE class. However, when the assembly is compiled, the additional functionality will be available.

> **Note**   For simplicity, the Component Designer–generated code has been omitted from the source code sample.

```csharp
public class EmployeeServices : System.Web.Services.WebService
{

    public EmployeeServices()
    {
        InitializeComponent();
    }

    [WebMethod]
    public string GetEmployeePhoneNumber(string id)
    {
        // TODO: Fill in database query
        return "555-555-0123";
    }
}
```

```vb
Imports System.Web.Services

<System.Web.Services.WebService→
(Namespace:="http://tempuri.org/EmployeeServicesVB/Service1")> _
Public Class EmployeeServices
    Inherits System.Web.Services.WebService

    <WebMethod()> _
    Public Function GetEmployeePhoneNumber(ByVal id As String) As String
        Return "555-555-0123"
    End Function
End Class
```

How to Create a WSE Client that Uses WS-Security Authentication

To create a WSE client, perform the following steps:

1. Create a standard Web services client.

2. Add a Web reference to the Web service by using the WSE Visual Studio add-in. If the Web reference was added, you must update it.

3. Append **Wse** to the Web services class names.

4. Specify any WSE-specific information.

The following is a sample console WSE client that prompts the user for credentials and sends the user name and password to the sample WSE server (located at the imaginary *http://www.northwindtraders.com* address) described in the previous section:

```csharp
using System;
using Microsoft.Web.Services2;
using Microsoft.Web.Services2.Security.Tokens;


class Class1
{
    [STAThread]
    static void Main(string[] args)
    {
        // Prompt for a username and password
        Console.WriteLine(@"Enter username in the format domain\username: ");
        string username = Console.ReadLine();
        Console.WriteLine("Enter password: ");
        string password = Console.ReadLine();

        // Create the Web services object
        // Note that object names have "Wse" appended
        com.northwindtraders.www.EmployeeServicesWse services = ⟶
new com.northwindtraders.www.EmployeeServicesWse();

        // Specify a UsernameToken element
        UsernameToken token = new UsernameToken⟶
(username, password, PasswordOption.SendPlainText);
        services.RequestSoapContext.Security.Tokens.Add(token);

        // Call the GetEmployeePhone Number Web method
        // with the credentials the user provided.
        // Provide an explanation if the credentials were rejected.
        try
        {
            Console.WriteLine("Phone number: " + ⟶
services.GetEmployeePhoneNumber("12345"));
        }
        catch (Exception ex)
        {
            Console.WriteLine("Error: " + ex.Message);
        }
    }
}
```

```vb
Imports Microsoft.Web.Services2
Imports Microsoft.Web.Services2.Security.Tokens

Module Module1
    Sub Main()
        ' Prompt for a username and password
        Console.WriteLine("Enter username in the format domain\username: ")
        Dim username As String = Console.ReadLine
        Console.WriteLine("Enter password: ")
        Dim password As String = Console.ReadLine

        ' Create the Web services object
        ' Note that object names have "Wse" appended
        Dim services As com.northwindtraders.www.EmployeeServicesWse = ⮕
New com.northwindtraders.www.EmployeeServicesWse

        ' Specify a UsernameToken element
        Dim token As New UsernameToken⮕
(username, password, PasswordOption.SendPlainText)
        services.RequestSoapContext.Security.Tokens.Add(token)

        ' Call the GetEmployeePhone Number Web method
        ' with the credentials the user provided.
        ' Provide an explanation if the credentials were rejected.
        Try
            Console.WriteLine("Phone number: " + ⮕
services.GetEmployeePhoneNumber("12345"))
        Catch ex As Exception
            Console.WriteLine("Error: " + ex.Message)
        End Try
    End Sub
End Module
```

When run, the console application generates the following output when valid Windows credentials are provided:

```
Enter username in the format domain\username:
northwindtraders\administrator
Enter password:
V4lldU53R
Phone number: 555-555-0123
```

This would result in an XML request being generated with a WS-Security *UsernameToken* element resembling the following:

```xml
<wsse:UsernameToken>
  <wsse:Username>northwindtraders\administrator</wsse:Username>
  <wsse:Password Type="wsse:PasswordText">
    V4lldU53R
  </wsse:Password>
  <wsse:Nonce>
    LoE3fjEoNnekfjLWeXz==
  </wsse:Nonce>
  <wsu:Created>2004-05-24T13:23:42Z</wsu:Created>
</wsse:UsernameToken>
```

When invalid credentials are provided, the WSE Web service rejects the credentials, and the runtime throws a *System.Web.Services.Protocols.SoapHeaderException* exception. The console application displays the following output in this circumstance:

```
Enter username in the format domain\username:
Attacker
Enter password:
H4x0rU
Error: The security token could not be authenticated or authorized
```

How to Create a WSE Server that Uses Authorization

An earlier example demonstrated how to create a Web services server that uses WSE without writing any code. This technique enables you to easily extend existing Web services; however, it does not take advantage of WSE's capabilities.

You can examine the Web services request to check the authentication information and the user's credentials by creating a *SoapContext* object by calling the *RequestSoapContext.Current* method. The *SoapContext.Tokens* collection contains the same set of tokens the client added, including the *UsernameToken* object if that type of authentication was used.

The following method expands the previous WSE sample server, verifies the type of authentication, verifies that a hashed (rather than plaintext) password was provided, and verifies that the user name is Administrator. When these conditions are not met, an exception is thrown.

```csharp
[WebMethod]
public string GetEmployeePhoneNumber(string id)
{
    // Get the current request
    SoapContext requestContext = RequestSoapContext.Current;

    // Reject request if there is more than one security token
    if (requestContext.Security.Tokens.Count != 1)
        throw new SoapException("Request must have one security token",→
SoapException.ClientFaultCode);

    foreach (SecurityToken token in requestContext.Security.Tokens)
    {
        // Reject request if not a UsernameToken type
        if (!(token is  UsernameToken))
            throw new SoapException("UsernameToken required",→
SoapException.ClientFaultCode);

        // Reject request if not using a hashed password.
        UsernameToken userToken = (UsernameToken)token;
        if (userToken.PasswordOption != PasswordOption.SendHashed)
            throw new SoapException("Invalid password type", →
SoapException.ClientFaultCode);
```

```
        // Verify that account is named Administrator
        if (userToken.Username.ToLower() != "administrator")
            throw new SoapException("Account not authorized", ↵
SoapException.ClientFaultCode);
    }

    // TODO: Fill in database query
    return "555-555-0123";
}
```

```vb
<WebMethod()> _
Public Function GetEmployeePhoneNumber(ByVal id As String) As String
    ' Get the current request
    Dim requestContext As SoapContext = RequestSoapContext.Current

    ' Reject request if there is more than one security token
    If Not (requestContext.Security.Tokens.Count = 1) Then
        Throw New SoapException("Request must have one security token",↵
SoapException.ClientFaultCode)
    End If
    For Each token As SecurityToken In requestContext.Security.Tokens
        ' Reject request if not a UsernameToken type
        If Not (TypeOf token Is UsernameToken) Then
            Throw New SoapException ("UsernameToken required", ↵
SoapException.ClientFaultCode)
        End If

        ' Reject request if not using a hashed password.
        Dim userToken As UsernameToken = CType(token, UsernameToken)
        If Not (userToken.PasswordOption = PasswordOption.SendHashed) Then
            Throw New SoapException ("Invalid password type", ↵
SoapException.ClientFaultCode)
        End If

        ' Verify that account is named Administrator
        If Not (userToken.Username.ToLower = "administrator") Then
            Throw New SoapException ("Account not authorized", ↵
SoapException.ClientFaultCode)
        End If
    Next

    ' TODO: Fill in database query
    Return "555-555-0123"
End Function
```

Practice: Maximizing Security for Web Services

In this practice, you create a Web service server that requires authentication and a client that prompts the user for authentication. Read the scenario and then complete the exercise that follows. If you are unable to answer a question, review the lesson and try the question again. You can find answers to the questions in the "Questions and Answers" section at the end of this chapter.

Scenario

You are a developer for Blue Yonder Airlines. Your manager, Tony Krijnen, has asked you to create a proof-of-concept Web service server and client to enable ticketing agents to query the company's database to determine the number of available seats on a given flight. Tony calls you into his office.

"This should be easy. I just want to see that these Web services work okay and that they can use authentication and authorization. Write me a Web services server that returns the number of seats available on a flight when the Web services client provides a flight number. For now, just return the number 5 to the client, regardless of what flight number the client requests. It's just a proof-of-concept. Call the application 'Ticketing.' Require that the user provide the client with a user name and password, and proof that she or he is a member of the Agents group in our domain. Also, write a Web services client using Windows Forms that can talk to the application, and call the client 'Agent.'"

Exercise

Complete the task for your boss. Then answer the following questions to provide your assessment of the risks of each application.

1. What mechanism did you choose to implement authentication? Why?

2. How did you configure IIS?

3. What did you add to the server's Web.config file?

4. What code did you write to create the Web service server?

5. What code did you write to create the Web service client?

Lesson Summary

■ To authenticate to a Web service using the standard .NET Framework classes, define a value for the *SoapHttpClientProtocol.Credentials* object.

■ WS-Security is a standard released by the WS-Interoperability group to add standards-based security features to Web services. WS-Security features include authentication, encryption, and data integrity.

■ Web Services Enhancements (WSE) is a free download from Microsoft that extends the Web services capabilities included with the .NET Framework to include WS-Security.

■ The most important class included with WSE is *WebServicesClientProtocol*. After creating an instance of this class to represent a remote Web server, you can access the *SoapContext.Security* class to add user credentials and cryptography certificates.

■ To use WSE, install WSE on both the client and server and add a reference to WSE to your .NET project. Then, replace the standard *SoapHttpClientProtocol* objects with *WebServicesClientProtocol* objects by appending **Wse** to the class names.

Lesson 3: Maximizing Security for Remoting

Remoting provides similar functionality to the Web services discussed in Lesson 2, but it relies on .NET Framework technology to provide better performance than standards-based Web services can offer. Many of the security concepts are the same as for Web services, however, because remoting servers can be hosted by an ASP.NET server. This lesson discusses best practices for maximizing the security of remoting services and provides code samples for authenticating remoting clients.

After this lesson, you will be able to

- Describe what remoting is.
- Explain and apply the best practices for implementing security features into remoting servers and clients.
- Create remoting servers that require authentication and remoting clients capable of providing user credentials.
- Restrict access to a remoting service by using file authorization.

Estimated lesson time: 30 minutes

What Is Remoting?

Like Web services, *remoting* is a communication mechanism for two .NET Framework applications running in separate application domains. Unlike Web services, remoting is not standardized, and both the client and server applications must be built on the .NET Framework. Although not being standardized is a significant disadvantage for heterogeneous environments, remoting adds support for events, the allocation and deallocation of objects, and other .NET Framework-related capabilities.

Remoting can occur between two .NET Framework applications running on a single computer or on different computers. When remoting links computers running different applications, the applications communicate across a network. However, remoting has no default authentication, authorization, or encryption mechanisms. Therefore, network communications might be subject to attack and require special security considerations.

 See Also   This book will cover security best practices only for using remoting and will not cover the fundamentals of using remoting. For more information about remoting, read "An Introduction to Microsoft .NET Remoting Framework" on the MSDN Web site at *http://msdn .microsoft.com/library/en-us/dndotnet/html/introremoting.asp*.

Remoting does not have its own security model. Authentication and authorization between the client (also known as a proxy) and the server (also known as a remote object) must be performed either by the host or within your application. Remoting works with two different types of hosts:

- **A custom assembly**   Requires you to create your own custom authentication mechanism because it does not provide any built-in security features. Custom assemblies use *TcpChannel* for network communications, a specialized protocol based on Transmission Control Protocol (TCP).

> **See Also**   For more information about creating custom authentication mechanisms, see Lesson 4 of Chapter 5, "Implementing Role-Based Security."

- **ASP.NET**   Leverages ASP.NET and IIS to provide authentication and authorization. ASP.NET uses *HttpChannel*, a remoting communication channel that works on top of HTTP.

Unlike Web services clients, remoting clients are typically configured by using a .config file. This .config file typically contains the server's host name and the service's port number. By placing this information into a configuration file, administrators can easily customize the settings to meet the needs of the network deploying the application.

Best Practices for Remoting Security

When creating remoting servers that should not be publicly accessible, follow these security best practices:

- If you are hosting a remote object in ASP.NET by using *HttpChannel*, configure IIS and ASP.NET to require authentication. Use URL authorization to restrict access to specific users.

> **Important**   The Forms and Passport authentication methods are not supported by remoting.

- If you are hosting a remote object in a service or other executable by using *TcpChannel*, build a custom authentication mechanism to validate a user's identity.

- Use encryption and hashing to protect user credentials when they are transmitted between the remoting client and server.

- Recommend that administrators use HTTPS (for *HttpChannel*-hosted servers) and IPSec (for *TcpChannel*- or *HttpChannel*-hosted servers) to encrypt remoting sessions.

See Also   For more information about HTTPS, see Lesson 3 of Chapter 9, "Hardening ASP.NET Applications."

- If you are using Windows user accounts for authentication, use impersonation in your remoting server to reduce the likelihood that a user will gain elevated privileges by calling your remoting server.

- If you are not using Windows user accounts for authentication, build a custom authorization mechanism to restrict user access. Use CAS to restrict your application's privileges.

See Also   For more information about creating custom authentication mechanisms, see Chapter 5, Lesson 4. For more information about impersonation, see Chapter 9, Lesson 2.

- Validate all input from clients as if it is malicious.

See Also   For more information about validating input, see Chapter 2, Lesson 1.

How to Authenticate Remoting Clients

If your remoting object requires authentication and authorization, host it in ASP.NET. You can then leverage many ASP.NET authentication and authorization techniques by configuring the ASP.NET application's Web.config file. Specifically, you can use Windows authentication (but not Forms or Passport authentication), and all authorization techniques.

See Also   For more information about ASP.NET authentication, authorization, and impersonation, see Chapter 9, Lesson 1 and Lesson 2.

If the remoting server is hosted in ASP.NET, you can configure authentication and authorization using IIS and ASP.NET without writing any code. However, you do have to write code to enable the client to present user credentials. Your remoting client can gather user credentials in two different ways: automatically, by using the currently logged-on user's credentials; and manually, by prompting the user for credentials. The following sections discuss these two techniques.

How to Automatically Provide the Current User's Credentials

As you might recall from Chapter 9, Microsoft Internet Explorer can automatically send the current user's logon credentials to a Web server on the local intranet. Using the default credentials provides single–sign on to the user by not requiring her to manually type her user name and password. The .NET Framework remoting client provides similar functionality when the *useDefaultCredentials* property of the remoting client is set to true.

To automatically authenticate to a remoting server, configure the following settings:

- On the server, configure IIS to require authentication.

- On the server, configure the ASP.NET Web.config file to require Windows authentication.

> **See Also**   See Chapter 9 for instructions on configuring IIS and ASP.NET to require authentication.

- Configure the remoting client's .Config file to set the *useDefaultCredentials* property of the <channel> element to true.

- Write code in the remoting client to gather the current user's credentials from the current session and add them to the remoting channel.

To configure the remoting client's .config file, define the <channel> element as:

```
<channel ref="http client" useDefaultCredentials="true" />
```

Then, call *ChannelServices.GetChannelSinkProperties* to obtain the collection containing the remoting channel's properties. Update the "credentials" element of the collection with the user's credentials. Assuming the server accepts the user's credentials, you can then use the remoting channel as you normally would. The following sample console application sets the default credentials programmatically when *useDefaultCredentials* in the .config file is set to true:

```
using System;
using System.Collections;
using System.Diagnostics;
using System.Net;
using System.Reflection;
using System.Runtime.Remoting;
using System.Runtime.Remoting.Channels;
using System.Security.Principal;

class Class1
{
    [STAThread]
    static void Main(string[] args)
    {
        // Load the remote configuration file
        RemotingConfiguration.Configure("RemClient.exe.config");
```

```
        // Create the proxy class. This class must
        // have been referenced based on the remote server's assembly
        ServiceClass server = new ServiceClass();

        // Create the collection by calling GetChannelSinkProperties
        IDictionary channelProperties =   ↴
ChannelServices.GetChannelSinkProperties(server);

        // Add the credentials
        channelProperties["credentials"] = CredentialCache.DefaultCredentials;

        // Authenticated remoting channel established
    }
}
```

```vb
Imports System
Imports System.Collections
Imports System.Diagnostics
Imports System.Net
Imports System.Reflection
Imports System.Runtime.Remoting
Imports System.Runtime.Remoting.Channels
Imports System.Security.Principal

Module Module1

    Sub Main(ByVal args As String())
        ' Load the remote configuration file
        RemotingConfiguration.Configure("RemClient.exe.config")

        ' Create the proxy class. This class must
        ' have been referenced based on the remote server's assembly
        Dim server As ServiceClass = New ServiceClass

        ' Create the collection by calling GetChannelSinkProperties
        Dim channelProperties As IDictionary =   ↴
ChannelServices.GetChannelSinkProperties(server)

        ' Add the credentials
        channelProperties("credentials") = CredentialCache.DefaultCredentials

        ' Authenticated remoting channel established
    End Sub

End Module
```

How to Manually Provide Credentials

If you do not want to have your remoting client automatically send the user's current credentials, disable *useDefaultCredentials* in the client's .config file, prompt the user for credentials, and then add the credentials to the channel properties. On the server, you must first configure ASP.NET authentication by using the Web.config file. On the client, you must provide the user's credentials before making any calls to the remote object. User credentials are stored in an *IDictionary* object that can be retrieved by calling the *ChannelServices.GetChannelSinkProperties(remoteObject)* method.

To manually authenticate to a remoting server, configure the following settings:

- Configure IIS to require authentication.

- Configure the ASP.NET Web.config file to require Windows authentication.

> **See Also** See Chapter 9 for instructions on configuring IIS and ASP.NET to require authentication.

- Configure the remoting client's .config file.

- Write code in the remoting client to prompt the user for credentials and add these credentials to the remoting channel.

After configuring these settings, you first disable the use of default credentials by modifying the <channel> element in the client's .config file:

```
<channel ref="http" useDefaultCredentials="false" />
```

Then, within your assembly, call *ChannelServices.GetChannelSinkProperties* to obtain the collection containing the remoting channel's properties. Next, you build a *NetworkCredential* object containing the credentials provided by the user. Create a *CredentialCache* object by using the *NetworkCredential* object, and update the "*credentials*" element with the user's credentials. Assuming the server accepts the user's credentials, you can use the remoting channel as you normally would. Configure the client to pass the user's credentials to the remote server, as the following sample console application demonstrates:

```csharp
using System;
using System.Collections;
using System.Diagnostics;
using System.Net;
using System.Reflection;
using System.Runtime.Remoting;
using System.Runtime.Remoting.Channels;
using System.Security.Principal;

class Class1
{
    [STAThread]
    static void Main(string[] args)
    {
        // Assign credentials to variables from
        // command-line parameters for readability
        string domain = args[0];
        string username = args[1];
        string password = args[2];
```

```
        // Load the remote configuration file
        RemotingConfiguration.Configure("RemClient.exe.config");

        // Create the proxy class. This class must
        // have been referenced based on the remote server's assembly
        ServiceClass server = new ServiceClass();

        // Create the collection by calling GetChannelSinkProperties
        IDictionary channelProperties =  ⟶
ChannelServices.GetChannelSinkProperties(server);

        // Create a credentials object and assign it the user's credentials
        NetworkCredential credentials =  ⟶
new NetworkCredential(username, password, domain);

        // Grab a reference to the remote server and extract the URI.
        // The URI is needed when adding the credentials
        ObjRef objectReference = RemotingServices.Marshal(server);
        Uri objectUri = new Uri(objectReference.URI);
        CredentialCache credCache = new CredentialCache();

        // Add the credentials.
        // The second argument is the authentication type, and can be
        // "Negotiate", "Basic", "Digest", "Kerberos" or "NTLM"
        credCache.Add(objectUri, "NTLM", credentials);
        channelProperties["credentials"] = credCache;
        channelProperties["preauthenticate"] = true;

        // Authenticated remoting channel established
    }
}
```

```
Imports System
Imports System.Collections
Imports System.Diagnostics
Imports System.Net
Imports System.Reflection
Imports System.Runtime.Remoting
Imports System.Runtime.Remoting.Channels
Imports System.Security.Principal

Module Module1

    Sub Main(ByVal args As String())
        ' Assign credentials to variables from
        ' command-line parameters for readability
        Dim domain As String = args(0)
        Dim username As String = args(1)
        Dim password As String = args(2)

        ' Load the remote configuration file
        RemotingConfiguration.Configure("RemClient.exe.config")

        ' Create the proxy class. This class must
        ' have been referenced based on the remote server's assembly
```

```
        Dim server As ServiceClass = New ServiceClass

        ' Create the collection by calling GetChannelSinkProperties
        Dim channelProperties As IDictionary = ⌐
ChannelServices.GetChannelSinkProperties(server)

        ' Create a credentials object and assign it the user's credentials
        Dim credentials As NetworkCredential = ⌐
New NetworkCredential(username, password, domain)

        ' Grab a reference to the remote server and extract the URI.
        ' The URI is needed when adding the credentials
        Dim objectReference As ObjRef = RemotingServices.Marshal(server)
        Dim objectUri As Uri = New Uri(objectReference.URI)
        Dim credCache As CredentialCache = New CredentialCache

        ' Add the credentials.
        ' The second argument is the authentication type, and can be
        ' "Negotiate", "Basic", "Digest", "Kerberos" or "NTLM"
        credCache.Add(objectUri, "NTLM", credentials)
        channelProperties("credentials") = credCache
        channelProperties("preauthenticate") = True

        ' Authenticated remoting channel established
    End Sub

End Module
```

How to Restrict Access to a Remoting Service by Using File Authorization

A remoting service hosted in ASP.NET uses the Web.config file to specify a virtual file-name that maps to the remoting service. However, that file (such as Service.rem) does not actually exist. Therefore, you cannot control authorization by configuring its NTFS file permissions. You can, however, use NTFS file permissions to control authorization if you create a physical file with the .rem or .soap extension within your application's virtual directory.

To configure file authorization for remoting, follow these steps:

1. Create a file with the same name as the *objectUri* (for example, Service.rem) in the root of the application's virtual directory.

2. Add the following line to the top of the file and save the file:

    ```
    <%@ webservice class="YourNamespace.YourClass" ... %>
    ```

3. Add an appropriately configured access control list (ACL) to the file using Windows Explorer.

> **See Also**   For more information about configuring ACLs, see Lesson 1 of Chapter 4, "Taking Advantage of Platform Security."

You can obtain the *objectUri* from the Web.config file used to configure the remote object on the server. Look for the `<wellknown>` element, as shown in the following example:

```
<wellknown mode="SingleCall",
    objectUri="RemoteMath.rem",
    type="RemotingObjects.RemoteMath,
    RemotingObjects,
    Version=1.0.000.000,
    Culture=neutral,
    PublicKeyToken=4b5ae668c251b606"/>
```

Practice: Maximizing Security for Remoting

In this practice, you provide guidance for a friend who is creating a client/server application and is concerned about application security. Read the scenario and then complete the exercise that follows. If you are unable to answer a question, review the lesson and try the question again. You can find answers to the questions in the "Questions and Answers" section at the end of this chapter.

Scenario

A few years ago, you were a developer for City Power & Light. Since then, you've moved on and become an independent consultant. You still keep in touch with your ex-co-workers, though. While writing an application for a client from your home office, you receive an instant message from Dave Richards, a developer with whom you worked at City Power & Light:

Dave says:

Hey there. You around?

Dave says:

I got a question for you. We've moved on to .NET, and the boss is asking me to write this client/server app, with both the client and server in .NET.

Dave says:

I don't even know where to start. I mean, I got the client under control, but how do the client and server communicate?

Dave says:

There are gonna be like hundreds of clients, so I gotta pick something that's fast because the boss isn't gonna pay for more processors for that old server. It's gotta pass the boss' usual authentication/authorization/encryption security test, too.

Dave says:

How do I do it? Web services? Remoting? *HttpChannel* or *TcpChannel?* Do these have security built in? It boggles my mind.

Exercise

Think about Dave's situation and answer his questions. Then, answer the following questions to provide your assessment of the risks of each application.

1. Should Dave use Web services or remoting? Why?

2. If Dave uses remoting, should he use *HttpChannel* or *TcpChannel?* Why?

3. If Dave uses remoting, is security built in?

4. How can Dave provide authentication for remoting?

5. How can Dave provide authorization for remoting?

6. How can Dave provide encryption for remoting?

Lesson Summary

- Remoting is a high-performance, non-standard network communication mechanism that provides no built-in security.

- You can provide authentication, authorization, and encryption for remoting services if you follow the best practices. You should host the remoting service in ASP.NET whenever possible, and leverage the authentication, authorization, and encryption capabilities of IIS and ASP.NET. If you are not hosting the remoting service in ASP.NET, use IPSec for encryption and build a custom authentication mechanism.

- To authenticate remoting clients, host the remoting service in ASP.NET and configure ASP.NET to require authentication. Then, configure the remoting client's .config file to set the *useDefaultCredentials* property of the `<channel>` element to true. Finally, write code in the remoting client to gather the current user's credentials from the current session and add them to the remoting channel.

- To use file access control lists to restrict access to a remoting service, create a file with the same name as the *objectUri* in the root of the application's virtual directory, and then configure that file's ACL.

Lab: Designing an Architecture for a Distributed Application

In this lab, you design an architecture for a distributed application to minimize the security risks. Read the scenario and then complete the exercise that follows. If you are unable to answer a question, review the lessons and try the question again. You can find answers to the questions in the "Questions and Answers" section at the end of this chapter.

Scenario

You are a software architect for Fourth Coffee. Fourth Coffee is an importer/exporter that purchases coffee beans from growers around the world and provides the raw materials to coffee distributors in the United States. Fourth Coffee management has identified an opportunity to improve their distribution channels and their relationships with their customers by investing in technology.

Specifically, they want to create a new application that will enable customers to check inventory and prices, and to place orders. A Web site isn't sufficient—customers must be able to integrate the information into their own internal applications. You interview key personnel at Fourth Coffee before making your architecture recommendations.

Interviews

Following is a list of company personnel interviewed and their statements:

- **David So, Fourth Coffee Development Manager** "As you know, we outsource most of our development. Some of these developers are…not as skilled as you. They get the job done; it's just that I've learned they make a better product when we keep the plan as simple as possible. So, please do make every effort to meet everyone's requirements, but please don't plan to use a whole bunch of new technologies to get it done. Keep it as simple as possible. In fact, we have this COM object that we built to simplify database transactions. If you can use that instead of making the developers create a new data access class, I know my life would be easier."

- **Betsy Stadick, Fourth Coffee Chief Security Officer** "I'll be frank. We've made some enemies. There are organizations that don't like some of our suppliers. These organizations aren't above using illegal methods to deter us. These organizations are becoming more technology savvy. Any app we make publicly available is going to be attacked. Plan for it. If someone breaks into our app, they'll grab our pricing information. If people see how cheap these coffee beans really are, our customers aren't going to be able to sell $5 lattés anymore. Then, we're all out of work."

■ **Rebecca Laszlo, Customer IT Manager**   "I'm jazzed you guys are putting up this new app. I mean, come on you guys, we're still *faxing* in bean orders! This is the twenty-first century, people! It's totally dumb to have my guys use a computer to generate a fax and fax the info over to you, just to have your guys type the fax into your computer system. Let's make these computers talk to each other directly over the Internet. We're a Solaris crew—how 'bout you?"

Exercise

Answer the following questions to provide your solution to the Fourth Coffee management team.

1. How do you recommend Fourth Coffee enable the customer to communicate with your Web application? Why?

2. What technique will you recommend Fourth Coffee use to ensure an attacker does not connect to your Web service? Why?

3. How will you ensure an attacker does not capture and analyze the traffic going to and from your Web service? Why did you recommend that technique?

4. Can the new application use the COM object to communicate with the database? If so, what are the drawbacks?

Chapter Summary

■ Calling external components from an application adds risk, because you cannot trust that component, and it might perform a malicious act. That risk increases when the external component is not part of the .NET Framework, because CAS restrictions will not apply to the component. To minimize risk, carefully validate all input to and output from external components, and avoid using external components not based on the .NET Framework.

■ Web services based on ASP.NET support IIS authentication, authorization, and encryption. For interoperability with non-Microsoft clients, use the authentication and encryption features of WS-Security by using the Web Services Enhancements .NET Framework extension.

■ The best way to provide authentication, authorization, and encryption for remoting clients is to host the remoting server in IIS and take advantage of the security features of IIS.

Exam Highlights

Before taking the exam, review the key points and terms that are presented in this chapter. You need to know this information.

Key Points

- Comparing the level of risk associated with different types of external components, including Win32, COM, and ActiveX components

- Knowing how to minimize the risk of calling external components and Web services

- Configuring IIS to require authentication and authorization for Web services and remoting clients

- Writing Web services and remoting clients that provide authentication information to the server

- Understanding the advantages of using Web Services Enhancements

Key Terms

remoting   A communication mechanism for two .NET Framework applications running in separate application domains.

Web Services Enhancements (WSE)   A free Microsoft download that adds WS-Security extensions to the .NET Framework.

Web Services Interoperability Organization (WS-Interoperability)   An organization dedicated to improving Web services standards. Among other extensions to Web services standards, WS-Interoperability creates the WS-Security standards.

WS-Security   A standard for adding authentication, signatures, and encryption to SOAP Web services communications.

Questions and Answers

Practice: Minimizing Risk When Calling External Components

Page
10-10

Exercise

1. What risks are associated with the Teller application?

   The Teller application has the following risks:

   - Communications between the application logic class and the transaction logic class occur using HTTP and SOAP, which is unencrypted.
   - The application logic class makes calls to an unmanaged COM component, which is not restricted by CAS.
   - The COM component's source code is not available, and might contain security vulnerabilities or even malicious code.
   - The two database connections don't say that they're encrypted, so this should be double-checked.

2. What can be done to mitigate the risks associated with the Teller application?

   The following measures can be taken to mitigate the risk with the Teller application:

   - The HTTP connection should be upgraded to HTTPS by adding an SSL certificate.
   - Users running the Teller application should log on to their computers with standard user accounts.
   - The COM component should be rewritten using the .NET Framework.
   - The database connections should be encrypted.

3. What risks are associated with the Reporting application?

   The Reporting application has the following risks:

   - The UI controls in the Microsoft Windows Forms application call an ActiveX component, which is not restricted by CAS. Though unlikely, the ActiveX component could perform malicious acts on the computer.
   - The two database connections don't say that they're encrypted, so this should be double-checked.

4. What can be done to mitigate the risks associated with the Reporting application?

   The following measures can be taken to mitigate the risk with the Reporting application:

   - Users running the Reporting application should log on to their computers with standard user accounts.
   - The COM component should be rewritten using the .NET Framework.

5. What risks are associated with the Web site?

Although there are potentially many risks when hosting a Web application, the Web site does not have any obvious risks because it calls external components.

6. What can be done to mitigate the risks associated with the Web site?

No changes to the architecture are required.

Practice: Maximizing Security for Web Services

Page
10-26
Exercise

1. What mechanism did you choose to implement authentication? Why?

You could choose either the standard Web services libraries built into the .NET Framework or WSE. The standard libraries are sufficient, however, and a better choice because both the server and client will be built with the .NET Framework.

2. How did you configure IIS?

You should have configured the application's virtual directory to require authentication.

3. What did you add to the server's Web.config file?

You should have configured it for Windows authentication and to limit access to the Agents group, as the following sample demonstrates:

```
<system.web>
    <authentication mode="Windows" />
    <authorization>
        <allow roles="BLUEYONDER\Agents" />
        <deny users="*" />
    </authorization>
</system.web>
```

4. What code did you write to create the Web service server?

The exact code you wrote will vary, but the following server would work:

```
[WebMethod]
public int GetAvailableSeats(int flightNumber)
{
    return 5;
}
```

```
<WebMethod()> _
Public Function GetAvailableSeats(ByVal flightNumber As Integer) As Integer
    Return 5
End Function
```

Note that no authentication or authorization code was necessary, because that task is handled by IIS.

5. What code did you write to create the Web service client?

The exact code you wrote will vary. Assuming the Web server is named blueyonderairlines.com, you had text boxes named *usernameTextBox*, *passwordTextBox*, and *flightTextBox*, and a label named *seatsLabel* to display the result. The following code attached to a click button event would work:

```csharp
private void goButton_Click(object sender, System.EventArgs e)
{
    // Create the Web services object
    com.blueyonderairlines.Ticketing server = ⟶
new com.blueyonderairlines.Ticketing();

    // Create a credentials object and assign it the user's credentials
    NetworkCredential credentials = new NetworkCredential⟶
(usernameTextBox.Text, passwordTextBox.Text);

    // Now, assign that value to the Web service's credentials
    server.Credentials = credentials;

    // Issue the Web request
    seatsLabel.Text = server.GetAvailableSeats(flightTextBox.Text).ToString();
}
```

```vb
Private Sub goButton_Click(ByVal sender As System.Object, ⟶
ByVal e As System.EventArgs) Handles goButton.Click
    ' Create the Web services object
    Dim server As com.blueyonderairlines.Ticketing = ⟶
New com.blueyonderairlines.Ticketing

    ' Create a credentials object and assign it the user's credentials
    Dim credentials As NetworkCredential = ⟶
New NetworkCredential(usernameTextBox.Text, passwordTextBox.Text)

    ' Now, assign that value to the Web service's credentials
    server.Credentials = credentials

    ' Issue the Web request
    seatsLabel.Text = server.GetAvailableSeats(flightTextBox.Text).ToString
End Sub
```

Practice: Maximizing Security for Remoting

Exercise

Page
10-36

1. Should Dave use Web services or remoting? Why?

Dave should use remoting because both the client and server are based on the .NET Framework, and performance is important.

2. If Dave uses remoting, should he use *HttpChannel* or *TcpChannel?* Why?

HttpChannel is the better choice because Dave can use ASP.NET to provide security.

3. If Dave uses remoting, is security built in?

No, remoting has no built-in security.

4. How can Dave provide authentication for remoting?

Dave can require authentication in IIS and ASP.NET, and then provide the user credentials within the remoting client.

5. How can Dave provide authorization for remoting?

Dave can use ASP.NET's authorization capabilities to provide authorization, or he can add a physical file matching the remoting server's virtual name and restrict the ACL.

6. How can Dave provide encryption for remoting?

Dave should host the remoting server in ASP.NET and configure IIS with an SSL certificate. Optionally, he can configure the server and client to use IPSec.

Lab: Designing an Architecture for a Distributed Application

Page
10-38
Exercise

1. How do you recommend Fourth Coffee enable the customer to communicate with your Web application? Why?

Fourth Coffee should use Web services because Web services, unlike remoting, are standards-based and allow for communications between different platforms.

2. What technique will you recommend Fourth Coffee use to ensure an attacker does not connect to your Web service? Why?

Fourth Coffee should host the Web service in ASP.NET and use ASP.NET for authentication. This takes the burden of creating an authentication mechanism off the developers.

3. How will you ensure an attacker does not capture and analyze the traffic going to and from your Web service? Why did you recommend that technique?

Fourth Coffee should host the Web service in ASP.NET, install an SSL certificate, and require HTTPS to encrypt all traffic. This technique is simpler to create than building encryption into the Web service itself. Alternatively, IPSec would provide similar functionality without requiring the developers to write additional code.

4. Can the new application use the COM object to communicate with the database? If so, what are the drawbacks?

Yes, .NET Framework applications can call COM objects. However, COM objects are not restricted by CAS. Therefore, attackers have a greater opportunity to exploit a vulnerability in the COM object to compromise your server than if the component were rewritten using the .NET Framework.

Glossary

access control list (ACL) A term most commonly used to refer to a discretionary access control list (DACL).

Advanced Encryption Standard (AES) A synonym for Rijndael. See *Rijndael*.

application domain A logical container that allows multiple assemblies to run within a single process while preventing them from directly accessing another assembly's memory.

assembly evidence Identification that an assembly presents that describes the assembly's identity, such as the hash, the publisher, or the strong name.

AssemblyInfo A configuration file that contains security information about an assembly. Among other configuration items, the AssemblyInfo file contains an assembly's strong name information.

asymmetric encryption A cryptography technique that uses separate private and public keys to encrypt and decrypt data. Also known as public-key encryption.

authentication The process of identifying a user.

authorization The process of verifying that a user is allowed to access a requested resource.

buffer overflow An attack in which the attacker submits user input that is longer than the application was designed to process.

canonicalization The process of simplifying a path to its most simple, absolute form.

canonicalization attack An attack that takes advantage of special characters that the operating system uses to identify filenames.

certification authority (CA) A service that generates certificates. CAs can be run by a public company such as VeriSign and issue certificates to paying customers, or CAs can be managed by an internal IT department by using a computer running Microsoft Windows Server 2003 and Certificate Services.

cipher text Encrypted text generated by an encryption algorithm that cannot be converted to plain text without a secret key.

code access security (CAS)   A security system that allows administrators and developers to authorize applications, similar to the way they have always been able to authorize users.

code group   An authorization device that associates assemblies with permission sets.

collusion   A method for preventing security abuses by requiring two or more trusted insiders to work together to bypass security measures.

cross-site scripting   An attack that exploits Web server applications to cause them to display malicious content to end users.

Data Encryption Standard (DES)   A symmetric encryption algorithm that uses relatively short key lengths that are vulnerable to cracking attacks.

Data Protection Application Programming Interface (DPAPI)   A library that encrypts and stores data for an individual user or an entire computer.

declarative RBS demands   Access restrictions that are declared as an attribute to a method and that instruct the runtime to perform an access check before running the method.

defense-in-depth   A technique for reducing the risk associated with potential vulnerabilities by providing multiple, redundant layers of protection.

digital signature   A value that can be appended to electronic data to prove that the data was created by someone who possesses a specific private key.

discretionary access control list (DACL)   An authorization restriction mechanism that identifies the users and groups that are assigned or denied access permissions on an object.

encryption key   A value that can be used to encrypt and decrypt data. When used with symmetric encryption, this is also known as a shared secret.

entropy   A value designed to make deciphering the secret more difficult.

evidence   The way an assembly is identified, such as the location where the assembly is stored, a hash of the assembly's code, or the assembly's signature.

exploits   A successful attack that uses a vulnerability to expose private information, gain elevated privileges, or deny legitimate users of a service.

Fully Qualified Domain Name (FQDN)   The full domain name of a server, such as *www.microsoft.com*.

fully trusted   An assembly that is exempt from CAS permission checks.

global assembly cache (GAC)   A container that the .NET Framework uses to store class libraries that can be accessed from other managed assemblies.

hash   A value that summarizes a larger piece of data and can be used to verify that the data has not been modified since the hash was generated.

host evidence   Evidence that an assembly's host presents describing the assembly's origin, such as the application directory, URL, or site.

Hypertext Transfer Protocol (HTTP)   The communications standard that the Web browser and Web servers use to communicate.

Hypertext Transfer Protocol Secure (HTTPS)   An encrypted form of the HTTP protocol. It is used by virtually every e-commerce Web site on the Internet to protect private information about end users and to protect end users from submitting private information to a rogue server that is impersonating another server.

imperative RBS demands   Access restrictions that are declared within your code and can be used to restrict access to portions of code on a very granular basis.

inherited permission   Permissions that propagate to an object from its parent object.

initialization vector   Data that symmetric encryption algorithms use to further obscure the first block of data being encrypted, which makes unauthorized decrypting more difficult.

isolated storage   A private file system managed by the .NET Framework.

isolated storage files   Files that provide access to read and write isolated storage files (or simply files) within stores. Isolated storage files behave exactly like conventional files that are stored directly on a file system, but they exist within an isolated storage store.

isolated storage stores   Separate isolated storage systems that are implemented as a single file in the file system.

keyed hash algorithms   Mathematical procedures that protect against modification of the hash by encrypting the hash by using a secret key that both the sender and receiver must have.

MD5   The Message Digest hashing algorithm. The hash size for the MD5 algorithm is 128 bits.

multifactor authentication   The process of combining two or more authentication methods to significantly reduce the likelihood that an attacker will be able to impersonate a user during the authentication process.

parameterized SQL commands   Database instructions that use typed parameters and parameter placeholders to ensure that input data is checked for length and type.

partially trusted code   An assembly that must undergo CAS permission checks each time it accesses a protected resource.

permission   In the context of CAS, an access control entry.

permission set   A CAS access control list consisting of multiple permissions.

physical path   The location of a folder or file on a local hard drive, such as C:\Inetpub\Wwwroot\Docs\Index.htm.

principal policy   The scheme that the .NET Framework uses to determine which default principal will be returned when the current principal is queried by an application.

RC2   A symmetric encryption standard, designed to replace Data Encryption Standard (DES), that uses variable key sizes.

regular expression   A set of characters that can be compared with a string to determine whether the string meets specified format requirements.

remoting   A communication mechanism for two .NET Framework applications running in separate application domains.

Rijndael   A symmetric encryption algorithm that uses key sizes of 128 through 256 bits. As a government encryption standard, this algorithm is also known as AES.

role-based security (RBS)   An authentication and authorization system that assigns permissions to user accounts and group memberships.

Secure Sockets Layer (SSL)   Documents that contain public key pairs that can be used to encrypt Web communications.

security access control list (SACL)   A usage event logging mechanism that determines how file or folder access is audited.

security policy   A logical grouping of code groups, permission sets, and custom policy assemblies.

SHA1   The Secure Hash Algorithm 1. The hash size for the SHA1 algorithm is 160 bits.

shared secret   A symmetric encryption key.

something you are   An authentication technique that verifies some aspect of the user's physical person, such as his or her fingerprint or ability to create a signature.

something you have   An authentication technique that verifies the user possesses an object, such as a smart card, that only he or she should possess.

something you know   An authentication technique that verifies the user knows a secret, such as a PIN or a password, that only he or she should know.

SQL injection   An attack that inserts database commands into user input to modify commands sent from an application to a back-end database.

SSL certificates   Documents that contain public key pairs that can be used to encrypt Web communications. SSL certificates cannot be dynamically generated.

stored procedures   A series of SQL commands that is stored within the database and called like an application, rather than submitted like a query.

strong name   A reliable assembly identifier that reduces the possibility of an attacker modifying or impersonating an assembly. The strong name consists of the assembly's simple text name, version number, and culture, plus a public key and a digital signature.

symmetric encryption   A cryptography technique that uses a single secret key to encrypt and decrypt data. Also known as secret-key encryption.

test-first development   A methodology followed by developers that involves creating unit tests before the units themselves.

Triple DES   A symmetric encryption standard that uses 156-bit keys. Essentially, Triple DES repeats the DES algorithm three times.

unit testing   A technique that developers use to automatically test an application's components after making updates.

unit tests   Modules that exercise other modules.

virtual path   The location from which Web content is requested, such as /docs/index.htm.

vulnerability   A security weakness in an application that can be exploited by an attacker.

Web.config files   Per-folder configuration settings for ASP.NET applications. Storing configuration settings in XML-based files instead of in the registry, in isolated storage, or in the IIS metabase allows administrators to copy your application to a different location or to another computer and have it run correctly.

Web Services Enhancements (WSE)   A free Microsoft download that adds WS-Security extensions to the .NET Framework.

Web Services Interoperability Organization (WS-Interoperability)   An organization dedicated to improving Web services standards. Among other extensions to Web services standards, WS-Interoperability creates the WS-Security standards.

WS-Security   A standard for adding authentication, signatures, and encryption to SOAP Web services communications.

XML digital signature specification (XMLDSIG)   A standard for creating and representing digital signatures in XML documents.

Index

Symbols

$ character, regular expressions, 2-7
(?pattern) character, regular expressions, 2-8
(?!pattern) character, regular expressions, 2-8
(?=pattern) character, regular expressions, 2-8
(pattern) character, regular expressions, 2-8
* character, regular expressions, 2-7
+ character, regular expressions, 2-7
. character, regular expressions, 2-7
? character, regular expressions, 2-7
-? option, Caspol, 6-26
-? parameter (used by Strong Name
    command-line tool), 7-7
[^a-z] character, regular expressions, 2-8
[^xyz] character, regular expressions, 2-8
[a-z] character, regular expressions, 2-8
[xyz] character, regular expressions, 2-8
\ character, regular expressions, 2-7
^ character, regular expressions, 2-7
{n,} character, regular expressions, 2-7
{n,m} character, regular expressions, 2-7
{n} character, regular expressions, 2-7

A

access
  applications, least privileges, 1-35 to 1-45
  ASP.NET authorization
    custom impersonation, 9-26 to 9-27
    file and folder access, 9-21 to 9-23
    file permissions, 9-23 to 9-25
    impersonation, 9-25 to 9-26
    users and groups, 9-20 to 9-21
  customizing authentication
    creating identity class, 5-32 to 5-36
    credential storage, 5-42 to 5-43
    custom mechanism, 5-41 to 5-42
    custom principal class, 5-37 to 5-38
    custom privilege models, 5-38 to 5-39
    IIdentity interface, 5-31 to 5-32
    IPrincipal interface, 5-36 to 5-37
    practice exercise, 5-45 to 5-46
    RBS demands, 5-39 to 5-41
    weak authentication, 5-44 to 5-45
  Internet files, 6-10
  RBS demands
    conditions to use, 5-25 to 5-27
    declarative, 5-19 to 5-21
    imperative, 5-22 to 5-25
    practice exercise, 5-27 to 5-29
    PrincipalPermission class, 5-18 to 5-19
access control lists. *See* ACLs (access control lists)
AccountOperator member, WindowsBuiltInRole class, 5-14
ACE, 4-3
ACLs (access control lists), 4-1 to 4-3, 5-6
  configuring, 4-8
    command-line, 4-12 to 4-15
    .NET Framework applications, 4-15 to 4-17
    Windows Explorer, 4-9 to 4-12
  discretionary access control list (DACLs), 4-3
  effective permissions calculation, 4-7 to 4-8
  permissions, 4-4 to 4-7
  practice exercises, 4-17 to 4-18
    batch file ACL modification, 4-18 to 4-19
    setup ACLs modification, 4-20
  security access control lists (SACLs), 4-3 to 4-4
  user privileges, 1-38 to 1-39
ActiveX controls, risks of calling, 10-4
Actor property, SoapContext class, 10-18
Add Class command (Project menu), 3-4
Add method, SoapContext class, 10-18
Add Reference command (Project menu), 3-4
Add Reference dialog box, 3-4
-addfulltrust option, Caspol, 6-25
Addressing property, SoapContext class, 10-18
Administrator member, WindowsBuiltInRole class, 5-14
administrators
  error message handling, 2-46, 2-47
  non-Administrator user accounts, 4-31
    Windows Server 2003, 4-32 to 4-33
    Windows XP, 4-33 to 4-34
  running code, 10-5
Advanced Encryption Standard (AES), 8-52
Advanced Security Settings dialog box, 4-10 to 4-12
AES (Advanced Encryption Standard), 8-52
algorithms
  asymmetric key encryption, 8-23 to 8-26
  hashes, 8-35 to 8-36
  symmetric key encryption, 8-3 to 8-9
    methods, 8-8 to 8-9
    properties, 8-6 to 8-7
    selection, 8-8
-all membership condition, Caspol, 6-26
-all option, Caspol, 6-25
AllMembershipCondition membership condition class,
    6-73

X–Y–Z

What do you think of this book?
We want to hear from you!

Do you have a few minutes to participate in a brief online survey? Microsoft is interested in hearing your feedback about this publication so that we can continually improve our books and learning resources for you.

To participate in our survey, please visit:

www.microsoft.com/learning/booksurvey

And enter this book's ISBN, 0-7356-2121-7. As a thank-you to survey participants in the United States and Canada, each month we'll randomly select five respondents to win one of five $100 gift certificates from a leading online merchant.* At the conclusion of the survey, you can enter the drawing by providing your e-mail address, which will be used for prize notification *only*.

Thanks in advance for your input. Your opinion counts!

Sincerely,

Microsoft® Learning

Learn More. Go Further.

To see special offers on Microsoft Learning products for developers, IT professionals, and home and office users, visit: *www.microsoft.com/learning/booksurvey*

* No purchase necessary. Void where prohibited. Open only to residents of the 50 United States (includes District of Columbia) and Canada (void in Quebec). Sweepstakes ends 6/30/2005. For official rules, see: *www.microsoft.com/learning/booksurvey*

Microsoft® Windows® Server 2003 Standard Edition 180-Day Evaluation

The software included in this kit is intended for evaluation and deployment planning purposes only. If you plan to install the software on your primary machine, it is recommended that you back up your existing data prior to installation.

System requirements

To use Microsoft Windows Server 2003 Standard Edition, you need:
- Computer with 550 MHz or higher processor clock speed recommended; 133 MHz minimum required; Intel Pentium/Celeron family, or AMD K6/Athlon/Duron family, or compatible processor (Windows Server 2003 Standard Edition supports up to four CPUs on one server)
- 256 MB of RAM or higher recommended; 128 MB minimum required (maximum 4 GB of RAM)
- 1.25 to 2 GB of available hard-disk space*
- CD-ROM or DVD-ROM drive
- Super VGA (800 × 600) or higher-resolution monitor recommended; VGA or hardware that supports console redirection required
- Keyboard and Microsoft Mouse or compatible pointing device, or hardware that supports console redirection

Additional items or services required to use certain Windows Server 2003 Standard Edition features:
- For Internet access:
  - Some Internet functionality may require Internet access, a Microsoft Passport account, and payment of a separate fee to a service provider; local and/or long-distance telephone toll charges may apply
  - High-speed modem or broadband Internet connection
- For networking:
  - Network adapter appropriate for the type of local-area, wide-area, wireless, or home network to which you wish to connect, and access to an appropriate network infrastructure; access to third-party networks may require additional charges

Note: To ensure that your applications and hardware are Windows Server 2003–ready, be sure to visit **www.microsoft.com/windowsserver2003**.

* Actual requirements will vary based on your system configuration and the applications and features you choose to install. Additional available hard-disk space may be required if you are installing over a network. For more information, please see **www.microsoft.com/windowsserver2003**.

Uninstall instructions

This time-limited release of Microsoft Windows Server 2003 Standard Edition will expire 180 days after installation. If you decide to discontinue the use of this software, you will need to reinstall your original operating system. You may need to reformat your drive.

System Requirements

The practices and labs in this training kit emphasize security design and not implementation; however, the book does contain a few hands-on practices to help you learn about designing security for a Microsoft Windows-based network. To complete the hands-on practices, your system must meet the following minimum requirements:

- **Microsoft Windows Server 2003, Enterprise Edition or Standard Edition**   A 180-day evaluation edition of Microsoft Windows Server 2003, Standard Edition, is included on the CD-ROM.

- **Microsoft Visual Studio .NET 2003**   A 60-day evaluation edition of Microsoft Visual Studio .NET 2003 is included on the DVD-ROM.

- **Computer and processor**   450 megahertz (MHz) minimum is required. Use the Intel Pentium/Celeron family, the AMD K6/Athlon/Duron family, or a compatible processor. (Windows Server 2003, Enterprise Edition supports up to eight CPUs on one server.) 733 MHz recommended.

- **Memory**   160 megabytes (MB) of memory is the minimum required; maximum 32 gigabytes (GB) of RAM. 256 MB or more is recommended.

- **Hard disk**   6 GB of available hard-disk space is required to install Windows Server 2003, Visual Studio .NET 2003 with the Microsoft Developer Network (MSDN), and Microsoft SQL Server 2000. (More room will be required to install additional operating system features.)

- **Drive**   A CD-ROM or DVD-ROM drive is required.

- **Display**   Super VGA or hardware that supports console redirection is required.

- **Peripherals**   A keyboard and Microsoft Mouse, or a compatible pointing device, or hardware that supports console redirection is required.

- **Miscellaneous**   Internet access and networking requirements:
    - Some Internet functionality might require Internet access, a Microsoft Passport account, and payment of a separate fee to a service provider. Local and/or long-distance telephone toll charges might apply. A high-speed modem or broadband Internet connection is recommended.
    - For networking, you must have a network adapter appropriate for the type of local-area, wide-area, wireless, or home network to which you want to connect and access to an appropriate network infrastructure. Access to third-party networks might require additional charges.

Uninstall Instructions

The time-limited release of Microsoft Windows Server 2003, Standard Edition, will expire 180 days after installation. If you decide to discontinue using this software, you will need to reinstall your original operating system. You might need to reformat your drive. Additionally, the time-limited release of Microsoft Visual Studio .NET 2003 will expire 60 days after installation. If you decide to discontinue using this software, you will need to uninstall it from Add or Remove Programs in the Control Panel.